HISTORIA RELIGIONUM

VOLUME I
RELIGIONS OF THE PAST

HISTORIA RELIGIONUM

HANDBOOK FOR THE HISTORY OF RELIGIONS

EDITED BY

C. JOUCO BLEEKER

Professor of the History
and the Phenomenology of Religions
in the University of Amsterdam

AND

GEO WIDENGREN

Professor of the History and Psychology of Religions
in the University of Uppsala

VOLUME I

RELIGIONS OF THE PAST

SECOND IMPRESSION

E. J. BRILL

LEIDEN · NEW YORK · KØBENHAVN · KÖLN
1988

First Impression 1969

Library of Congress Cataloging
lc number 76-503128

ISBN   90 04 08928 4

TABLE OF CONTENTS

GEO WIDENGREN, Professor of the History and Psychology of Religions, University of Uppsala, Sweden

E. O. JAMES, Professor Emeritus of the History of Religions, University of London, Oxford, England

C. J. BLEEKER, Professor of the History and Phenomenology of Religions, University of Amsterdam, Holland

W. H. PH. RÖMER, Ph. D., Senior Lecturer, Department of Oriental Studies, University of Groningen, Holland

H. RINGGREN, Professor of Old Testament Exegesis, University of Uppsala, Sweden

GEO WIDENGREN, Professor of the History and Psychology of Religions, University of Uppsala, Sweden

H. OTTEN, Professor of Ancient Oriental Studies, Philipps University, Marburg, Germany

JACQUES DUCHESNE-GUILLEMIN, Professor of Indo-Iranian Studies, University of Liege, Belgium

A. W. H. ADKINS, Professor of Classics, University of Reading, England

PREFACE

The undersigned herewith present a new handbook of the history of religions. The handbook will appear in two volumes, the first of which deals with the religions of the past and the second with the religions of the present.

The editors of the handbook fully realize that they have entered upon a hazardous undertaking. There already exist so many handbooks of the history of religions that the legitimate question arises whether an increase in their number is justified. This reasonable objection can be countered by drawing critical attention to the character of the existing handbooks. However high their scholarly standard may be, none of them presents the history of religions as an organic entity. Actually these handbooks are series of unconnected monographs, planned by each author according to his personal viewpoint and therefore more or less arbitrarily composed. One never gets a survey of the history of religions presented as an unity and thus revealing not only the individual peculiarities of the religions of the world, but also, and more particularly, the similarities in their structure, the formal parallels in their development and their most hidden interrelation and interdependence.

The present authors are convinced that the time has come to publish a handbook which presents the religions of the world in such a way that their structural similarities become visible.

Thus they have asked their authors to follow the same scheme in writing their articles, whilst granting them the liberty to adapt it to their subject.

The basic scheme is:

§ 1 Short Description of the Essence of the Religion
§ 2 Historical Development
§ 3 Conception of the Deity
§ 4 Worship (Cult, Ethics, Myth or Doctrine)
§ 5 Conception of Man (Creation, Nature, Destiny: Path of Salvation, Personal and General Eschatology)
§ 6 Religions of the Past: Subsequent Influence
 Religions of the Present: Present Religious Situation
§ 7 Short History of the Study of the Religion
§ 8 Selected Bibliography

It is evident that even so the design of the handbook had to be limited. There was no room for general considerations, except some concluding remarks in the closing article. Nor does either volume allow the writer to tackle the interesting but difficult problem of the manifold influences which religions have exerted upon each other. The theme of the handbook must needs be restricted to a description of the religions of the world in such a manner that their ideological parallelism is made manifest.

We hope to have succeeded in publishing a handbook which will stimulate further the systematic study of the history of religions.

C. Jouco Bleeker
Geo Widengren

PROLEGOMENA

BY

GEO WIDENGREN

*The value of source-criticism as illustrated by the biographical
dates of the great founders*

INTRODUCTION

The History of Religion as a historical discipline is dependent on
the methods elaborated since generations in other historical disciplines, above all in political history. These methods imply source-
criticism which means that we have to answer *inter alia* such questions
as: How do we constitute from the manuscripts the text of the source
in question? How do we ascertain whether the source in question
partly or in its totality is authentic or not? How do we from secondary
sources work our way back to primary sources? How do we distinguish
real history from legend and myth?

The principles of *text-criticism* are accessible in all philological and
historical textbooks of an introductory character where many examples are given.

The principles for passing a judgement on the *value* of the best
available text are to be read in the introductions to political history.
Here we have to answer such questions as: How did the author in
question acquire his knowledge? Where does he use or reproduce
otherwise lost sources? Where is he dependent on oral tradition?
Where does he speak out of his own experience? Where is he dependent on legendary or mythical patterns? Such questions mean
analysis of the sources.

It is a regrettable fact that in the History of Religion these principles
of source-criticism to a considerable extent have been neglected. This
holds good for especially certain religions as we will see in the following. In our days with the marked anti-historical bias of our generation
there is a trend to mix the historical and unhistorical elements in the
available traditions by declaring a clear separation impossible. This
is a tendency observable e.g. in the treatment of the history of the
oldest period of Christianity where a pretext has been that the gospel
narratives are so-called "kerygmatic" texts. But we will find the same
tendency also in the field of other religions.

The problems connected with source-criticism will be illustrated in the following by examples chose from the biographical dates attached to the figures of the great founders, for much the same problems are always recurring in this connection.

I. We may start by taking up for examination Buddha's life as history and legend. In his case the texts are concerned above all with his birth, his so-called renunciation, the following enlightenment, his activity of teaching, i.e. his public career, and finally his death. The episodes from his life as a teacher, however, are not related in any special chronological order, they are narrated chiefly in order to serve as the framework of some moral or religious doctrine taught by him.

Source-criticism has shown that we possess two major groups of traditions about Buddha's life: one in the Mahāyāna sūtras, and the other in the Hinayāna texts, the former represented by a "collection of legends preserved in the Tibetan Scriptures, chiefly in the Vinaya" (THOMAS). "Later Sanskrit works are the Mahāvastu and the Lalitavistara, both of them showing traces of being based on originals in a popular dialect" (THOMAS).

These Mahayāna sources often correspond verbally with the texts of the Pali canon of the Theravāda-school, and there above all with the legendary material found with the contributors of commentaries, of whom Buddhaghoṣa is especially well known. We accordingly find in the Pali canon both in the Dhamma and the Vinaya accretions of legendary matter. It is very interesting to see that in such a work of monastic discipline as the Vinaya we find the oldest legendary material.

There once existed also another biography, the Abhiniskramana-sūtra, now extant only in a Chinese translation, where the legend— much in the same form as in Mahāvastu—is arranged as a continuous story. "These three works (i.e. Mahavāstu, Lalitavistara and Abhiniskramana-sūtra) represent a later stage of the legend than we find in the Pali and Tibetan Vinaya" (THOMAS).

The texts containing the legends about Buddha do not provide a basis for a credible chronology. This has to be sought for elsewhere— in the chronicles and puranas. The problem is now: do these documents on the whole provide a sufficient basis for a reliable history of Buddha's life? This question has been answered in different ways. We may illustrate the various methods by singling out in the following the names of SENART, OLDENBERG and THOMAS.

SENART represents the radical mythological interpretation of the Buddha legend, though he doesn't in any way deny that Buddha was a historical personality, the founder of Buddhism. The interesting principle underlying the interpretation as proposed by SENART is the fact that he doesn't consider the mythological elements as disconnected attachments to a historical material but as making up a totality. According to him they are integrated into a mythical complex which centres around two figures: the Cakravartin and the Mahāpuruṣa. The first term is generally translated "Universal King" and this is at any rate the meaning of it (even if its exact sense may be disputed). The Sun is the Universal King, but also an earthly ruler may be a *cakravartin*. The second term is exclusively mythological, being mentioned already in the Rigveda. Characteristic of this "Great Man" are the special marks, *lakṣaṇa*, 32 in number, by means of which a Mahāpuruṣa is recognized. The sage Asita according to the Buddha legend, when shown the newborn child Siddharta on his body found these lakṣaṇas, and was filled with joy. SENART was of the opinion that the mythical complexes of the Cakravartin and the Mahāpuruṣa had clustered around the historical Buddha and in this way had shaped his legend. He saw in Buddha's contest with Māra, the Evil One, an original myth, the fight for the Cosmic Tree, this tree itself in the legend being impersonated in the Boddhi-tree under which Buddha received the Enlightenment.

SENART's ideas were carried to the extreme by KERN whose position is too absurd to need any critical examination in our days.

OLDENBERG didn't deny the existence of mythical elements in the biography of Buddha- which would be impossible—but he emphatically denied that they had influenced the description of the life of Buddha to the extent SENART had vindicated. A typical case is the role played by the Boddhi-tree where Buddha was attacked by Māra. Here OLDENBERG cannot find behind the story of the great Temptation any traces of the cosmic mythical perspective suggested by SENART. His own method is to subtract from the legend the clearly miraculous mythical elements and declare the rest established historical facts or at least quite plausible historical records. OLDENBERG bases his analysis on the Palis texts the value of which as reliable records he values rather high. He tries to show that the Enlightenment according to the sources agrees with what we know of corresponding psychological experiences. On the other hand he consciously or unconsciously neglects the analysis of the northern tradition with its Sanskrit, East-

Iranian, Tibetan and Chinese texts. Also in the case of Buddha's life
he has not been able to liberate himself from the outdated thesis that
the Pali canon is the only authentic representative of the oldest form
of Buddhist tradition.

THOMAS has taken an altogether different position. He has carefully
investigated the age of the legendary traditions in order to ascertain
the shape and structure of the oldest traditions. Thanks to this method
he was able to criticize both the mythological interpretations of KERN
—whose theories he seems more fond of discussing than those of
SENART—and the according to Thomas "rationalistic" interpretations of OLDENBERG. In this way his source-criticism in places can
be more severe and logical than OLDENBERG's, e.g. as far as Buddha's
family relations are concerned. Thomas would seem to be rather
sceptical about the historicity of Buddha's wife and son, to take but
one example. "The chroniclers did not need to start from the historic
fact that Buddha had a wife and son. This may be true, and may rest on
unwritten tradition, but it is certain that the tradition has preserved no
information about them." On the whole we may say that source-
criticism has led THOMAS to a highly sceptical attitude to the possible
historical facts found in the legend. This scepticism, mainly going
farther than e.g. that of OLDENBERG and PISCHEL, doesn't imply that
SENARTS views are accepted. It appears that actually too little attention has been paid by THOMAS to them.

The real weakness, however, with THOMAS' important work is that
he actually never tells us what he considers possible to state as historical facts about Buddha's life (though by implication we could extract these facts from his analysis). He seems to be reluctant to state
in plain words what he thinks possible to say about the historical life
of Buddha.

A few words must finally be said about the attitude taken by two
modern scholars, LAMOTTE and BAREAU. Both of them of course admit
that the Buddha biography is full of legendary elements. When, however, they relate the circumstances of Buddha's life both of them are
content with repeating the chief narratives of this legendary biography
without making the slightest effort to distinguish between real and
fictitious matter in this biography. In this regard they go so far as to
repeat the most obvious legendary traits, e.g. the famous story of
Buddha's meeting an old man, a sick man, and a corpse. But some
passages, *inter alia* Majjhima-Nikāya I 163, describe Buddha's awareness of the problem of old age, sickness, and death as due to his own

reflections on these questions. As THOMAS puts it: "In these accounts we have no definite historical circumstances mentioned, nor any traces of the events of the legend as we find it in the commentaries and later works." Both OLDENBERG and PISCHEL had for this reason previously pointed out the real base of the legend. The more misleading it is to find the legend repeated by LAMOTTE and BAREAU without any indication of the true historical background of it.

Space forbids any more comments. Enough has presumably been said to show that modern analysis makes it possible to distinguish fairly well between facts and fiction in the relations of the life of Buddha but that historians of religion even in our own time sometimes leave their readers in ignorance about what can be said about Buddha's life with some historical correctness. That history in this case can provide only a skeleton of a biography would seem to be clear, as also the fact that the miraculous element plays a considerable role in the Buddha-biography. Nevertheless it is an urgent task to have stated by the experts in Buddhism what part of the biography may be considered historical and what under no circumstances could be classified as history in the full meaning of the word.

II. A very interesting case is the biography of Zoroaster. As the situation now is we have several texts at our disposal giving the *vita* of the founder of Zoroastrianism. The most important of them is the famous biography in Book VII of the Pahlavi compendium Dēnkart. For various reasons—above all the fact that we have only one manuscript preserved—already the establishment of a correct text causes considerable difficulties and still more the translation and understanding of the Pahlavi text. After the text-critical work and translation have been carried out provisionally it is time to tackle the real source-criticism. Research has established the fact that the Pahlavi text is based on an Avestic original text of a poetic character. I pointed out this fact several years ago and it has now been recognized in NYBERG's edition of the Pahlavi text, where several original poetic passages are marked as such. However, into MOLÉ's posthumous edition and translation of Dēnkart VII this necessary insight has, unfortunately, not found its way, perhaps owing to this gifted scholar's most remarkable lack of historical sense and tact. On the other hand MOLÉ in his commentary on the text of Dēnkart VII in a meritorious way pointed out—whenever he thought it possible—the Avestic background of those passages that are nothing but quotations from now lost Avestic texts. That the greater part of Book VII is made up of scriptural quotations was seen by SALEMANN more than 50 years ago and this great scholar also understood that the only possible method of bringing out the exact meaning of the Pahlavi text is to try to reconstruct its Avestic background. When this is done our next task will be to investigate the problem whether all Avestic quotations are poetic or not. If it turns out—as I think will be the case—that not all Avestic quotations are poetical, the further step will be to reconstruct as far as possible the once existing poetic passages in the Avesta language, which constituted the epic poem on Zoroaster's life, his *vita*. Here a comparison with e.g. Aśvaghoṣa's Buddhacarita invites itself. Then the real task of source-criticism sets in, for we have before us a highly legendary biography, in which the legendary and mythical elements dominate and where the miracles abound. We therefore must analyze the biography very closely in order to ascertain what real historical facts eventually may be hidden in it, not to be extracted from the Gathas, the Prophet's own songs.

Several methods are open to us and all of them must be used. First of all we may investigate what allusions in the Gathas of Zoroaster to his personal circumstances may have been taken up in his *vita* and expanded and further developed. Second we may get a *terminus ante quem* for some of the intrusive legendary traits by comparing this eastern *vita* with the biographical notices found in Classical authors about Zoroaster and evidently based on an existing western biography —of course influenced from the east and likewise of a highly legendary character, but remodelled by the Median Magians to suit their special purposes. The third task will be a comparison with the way in which the Buddha biography has been enlarged and developed, from the allusions in the commentaries, into a legendary *vita*. Such a comparison, paying due attention to the manner in which the miraculous element is ever increasing may prove highly instructive.

The task sketched here remains to be carried out. The attitude to the historical value of the *vita* of Zoroaster in Dēnkart VII has been rather varying, but can be said to be very negative in modern western scholarship. At the turn of this century, however, A. V. W. JACKSON wrote a biography on Zoroaster, characterized by a complete lack of source-criticism, total absense of historical sense, and a blind faith in the notices given in Book VII of Dēnkart, which were reproduced more or less integrally. This method or rather lack of method was severely criticized by SOEDERBLOM in a remarkable review of Jackson's book.

As the situation is for the present scholars in general find it the safest course to reject *in toto* the facts recorded in Dēnkart VII, even when not possessed of a legendary or mythic character. May be that this attitude is too negative. Only a thorough analysis of Zoroaster's legendary biography in this case can bring us forward to eventual new insights.

III. Turning to the West and ascending in time we find in the biographical elements in the relation of the life of Moses, the founder of Jewish religion, a remarkable blend of a few historical facts and a mass of legendary matter. The criticism of the sources in this case was much advanced by the great historian EDUARD MEYER, and after him by the O.T. exegete and historian of religions HUGO GRESSMANN who, however, in spite of many a fine analysis in some places was carried away by his own lively imagination and brilliant gift of combination.

The source-criticism of MEYER—very radical in itself—and GRESSMANN was brought to its extreme by MARTIN NOTH, leading O.T. exegete and outstanding historian of our own generation. Of all the notices extant in the O.T. he would hardly allow as a historical fact more than the notice Deut. 34, 5-6 about the tomb of Moses, where he found the point around which all later traditions had gradually clustered. Following in the steps of EDUARD MEYER he didn't accept the Moses of our sources as a real historical figure.

However, this radical scepticism cannot be defended, for it is not based upon quite sound methods but on a hyper-criticism, which is too credulous over against its own somewhat hypothetical critical observations. These criticisms have not been subjected to the necessary criticism, and the excellent scholar that was MARTIN NOTH sometimes would seem to have forgotten the Cartesian maxim: *de dubito est dubitandum*.

NOTH starts from a very apt and quite correct observation: it is a surprising fact that Moses is hardly mentioned by name by the great prophets or alluded to (except by Hoshea), until we reach the time of Jeremiah and Micah.

In the Psalms the situation is that Moses is mentioned as a mediator between God and Israel only in two passages: Ps. 103, 7 and 106, 23. In both psalms there is a clear reference to Pentateuchal traditions, which are accordingly presupposed. There is no independent tradition about Moses to be found in the Psalms.

In the historical books we find a number of references to Moses, but

in all pre-exilic literature, except when due to Deuteronomic influence, we lack the expression "the Law of Moses". This expression
is not found in prophetical literature and the Psalms either. Outside
the Pentateuchal tradition there is accordingly not to be found in pre-
exilic literature, except as far as Pentateuchal tradition is concerned,
any reference whatsoever to Moses as the great bringer of the Law to
Israel. This fact needs an explanation and this is near at hand: traditions about Moses were spread by the Levites among the northern
tribes. It is chiefly in northern Israel that we meet in pre-exilic literature traditions about Moses. Deuteronomy being of northern origin
transmitted these traditions about the great founder to the southern
kingdom after the fall of Israel, the northern kingdom.

Pentateuchal notices about Moses, regarded with such scepticism
by MEYER and NOTH, relate several concrete dates about Moses. Sub-
jecting these traditions to a critical test I have arrived at the following
conclusions.

Moses was a Levite, his name, however, being Egyptian, a hypocoristicon composed with the verb *mśï*, bear, give birth to. Tradition
also mentions other Egyptian names among his descendants. This
circumstance points to an association with Egypt.

About Aaron and Miriam, the brother and sister of Moses, it is
possible to state with certainty that while Miriam probably is a historical figure, though originally not at all the sister of Moses, Aaron
on the other hand is nothing but the legendary ancestor of a later
priesthood, the Aaronites.

The origin of Moses' wife is given differently in different traditions.
The only certain thing would seem to be that already the oldest layer
of tradition relates that he had a foreign, i.e. non-israelite wife. Equally
uncertain is the name of his father-in-law, though the extra-Pentateuchal tradition in Judges 4, 11, when compared with two passages
in the Pentateuch, viz. Ex. 2, 18 and Num. 10, 29, demonstrates that
his name was Hobab ben Reguel, probably a Qenite. Another tradition, preserved only in the Pentateuch, as is well known gives his
name as Jethro, a priest of Midian, and this tradition obviously got
the upper hand. Both traditions, however, this circumstance calls for
notice, associate Moses with some region to the east of the Sinai
peninsula.

To the same region tradition locates the vocation of Moses to his
commission as the saviour of his people from the serfdom in Egypt. The
experience itself is difficult to declare either historical or nonhistorical.

As to the Exodus from Egypt my analysis of the material available has been concentrated on Judges 1, 20, an extra-Pentateuchal tradition, agreeing with the notices given Num. 14, 24 and 30. The fact that Moses is mentioned as the leader of his people in this passage in Judges would seem to vindicate the historicity of this position of his. But then there can be no objections to the unanimous tradition in the Pentateuch itself that Moses actually conducted the people out of Egypt.

That Moses furthermore was the giver of the will of God in the form of the *tōrāh* is evident from his being a Levite. The *tōrōt* were communicated by the Levites by means of the Urim and Tummin as Deut. 33, 8-10 explicitly makes clear. In spite of the fact that it has been demonstrated that the Ten Commandments cannot be of Mosaic origin in their present form it can be contended that some of the commandments possess a Mosaic inspiration.

That much at least can be stated as the historical truth behind the figure of Moses as he appears in Pentateuchal sources. The rest is on the whole nothing but legend and saga. Quite especially the story of his birth is a result of the influence of the royal birth-legend of the Ancient Near East, as it is found above all in the legend of the birth of Sargon of Agade, CT XIII Pl. 42 f. There are later traditions about Moses in Josephus and Samaritan literature which show him still more as a legendary or even mythical hero. The miraculous element, however, occupies an important place already in the older layers of tradition.

We find accordingly that legends have clustered above all around the birth of Moses, whereas his death didn't receive the same attention. About his vocation it is difficult to say whether it is history or legend. His receiving of the Law is modelled after the pattern of the king as the bringer of revelation, as has been demonstrated in modern research. The Tablets of Law correspond to the mythic Tablets of Destiny in Mesopotamia. But Moses is altogether a historical figure.

IV. In the case of Jesus exegetes and historians are generally agreed both that there are to be found in the biographical matter of the gospels many legendary and mythic elements and that even after subtraction of this material there remains a great uncertainty about the chronology and most of the single events in the public career of Jesus as told by the four canonical gospels. What is found outside the canonical gospel tradition cannot be said to add anything to our historical knowledge about Jesus.

Already the reconstruction of the most reliable text involves many difficult problems, e.g. the position of the so-called "Western text", and the question how far we have to suppose an Aramaic oral tradition underlying the present Greek text, which should accordingly be corrected in the light of this presupposed original Aramaic form of the tradition. This problem, however, would seem to be more important for the words of Jesus than for his deeds and may therefore be left aside here.

The basis of all source-criticism must be the literary analysis of the gospel tradition in accordance with the principles formulated by the so-called form-criticism as represented above all by BULTMANN, DIBELIUS and K. L. SCHMIDT. This method may be criticized in its concrete achievements, but its principles are sound.

First of all it calls for notice that the primary aim of the gospels is kerygmatic and cultic, not historic. But providing the historical basis for the reconstruction of the life of Jesus the gospels must be subjected to the same kind of source-criticism as other texts which furnish the material for the reconstruction of the life of a historic personality.

Let us start by considering the mythical and legendary elements. That such elements are found in the gospels is above discussion and was emphasized already by D. F. STRAUSS. Such elements are found above all in the relations given of the birth and childhood of Jesus. In another connection I have analyzed the Annunciation and shown that it has its pattern in the sacral kingship of Israel and that the myth and ritual pattern in this case can be traced behind the oldest Hebrew texts back to both Egypt and Ugarit.

The story of the three Magians, the star, and the birth of Jesus on the other hand has its model in the likewise mythic-ritual pattern of the birth of the Iranian Saviour-King and his adoration by the Magians in a cave on the "Mount of Victory", as I have demonstrated some years ago. Above all significant is the fact that there existed in ancient Armenian art an independent tradition, showing the three Magians as presenting to the new-born child as their gifts golden crowns, and not at all gold, incense and myrrh, mentioned in gospel tradition because of its scriptural basis in the O.T. (Is. 60, 6). In all artistic representations of Iranian origin, where a tribute to a king is depicted, it is a characteristic trait that golden crowns are handed over to him. This was shown by CUMONT many years ago, but because he missed

the Armenian artistic tradition he was not able to follow up this line
of research. Accordingly the Iranian tradition in this case has been
stronger than the scriptural basis of the gospel legend. Likewise the
star finds its proper context only in the Iranian myth of the birth of
the Saviour-King, as also the fact that the Saviour is born in a cave-
for in some ancient Christian variants of the birth-legend the stable
actually is conceived of as a cave. This is demonstrated by the oldest
Armenian translation of the gospels, where in Matth. 2, 9 the word
gom, meaning both cave and stable, is used.

Because Jesus in tradition appears as the new Moses it is but natural
that as a new-born child he is exposed to evil plots from the reigning
king Herodes. The legendary character of these plots and the alleged
murder of all small children in Betlehem and all its surroundings is so
obvious that not many words need to be sacrificed on this theme.
Josephus who records all the mis-deeds of Herodes has nothing to
tell us on this point, and all other sources are absolutely silent.

Joseph had been warned, however, by an angel—a typical trait—
and taken his family to Egypt. For the birth in Betlehem, the flight
to Egypt, the murder of the children, and the return from Egypt
quotations from the O.T. are given as prophecies now fulfilled. This
kind of exegesis, whereby O.T. passages are interpreted in the light
of later events, in our days has been amply illustrated from the collection of commentaries on O.T. texts from Qumran. It is typical that
the infancy legends are completely lacking in our oldest gospel tradition found in the gospel of Marc. These legends are accordingly
accretions of a rather late date. The oft repeated endeavours to save
the historicity of these legends or at least part of them exhibits no
knowledge of the methods of source-criticism but an astonishing lack
of historical sense.

For the story of the temptation an O.T. background may partly be
found, as demonstrated by K. H. RENGSTORF, and this background
again belongs to the royal ritual. At the same time the fact of a temptation on the side of the Evil Power at the beginning of the public
career of the founder reminds us of the temptation of both Buddha
and Zoroaster. This story is possessed of a very marked legendary
character, which makes it difficult to discover some historical reality
behind it.

That the chronological and topographical framework of the life of
Jesus as related in the gospels has been created in an artificial way by
the authors of the gospels was demonstrated 50 years ago by K. L.

SCHMIDT in a remarkable work. Already WELLHAUSEN, however, had distinguished between sayings and actions of Jesus as transmitted by tradition, and redactional additions by the gospel-writers in order to create more comprehensive passages in the form of a running story. The necessary distinction was carried out by SCHMIDT in a very systematic way, clearly demonstrating that nearly all notices concerning places and dates are later additions.

Against these conclusions as to the lack of historical reliability in the gospel narratives it has been contended that the manner in which these narratives were handed down by means of oral tradition on the side of the traditionists would be a guarantee of their historical truth. The facts were recorded so early in this way that there was not much room for change. Of course it was not at all contended that the clearly legendary and mythic elements were anything but legends and myths. This idea of the reliability of oral tradition was expressed already in 1942 by ANTON FRIDRICHSEN, but only as far as the *sayings* of Jesus are concerned. And FRIDRICHSEN was anxious to point out that the tradition about the words and deeds of Jesus in its early stages not at all was fixed, but floating and exposed to changes. After FRIDRICHSEN, who referred to the way in which the sayings of the prophets and the great Jewish rabbis were preserved by their disciples by means of oral tradition, this idea was further developed by RIESENFELD and carried to its extremes by GERHARDSSON. The last-mentioned scholar referring to the carefully transmitted oral tradition in the Jewish law-schools defended the essential correctness of gospel tradition, which according to him was transmitted exclusively in oral form and written down by the authors of the gospels. The oral transmission would guarantee the reliability of the gospel tradition.

This position, beside showing a remarkable lack of critical spirit, has been criticized by me and other scholars because the analogy of the disciples of the Jewish teachers is not applicable here, except perhaps in such cases where the halāḵāh of Jesus has been handed down by means of oral transmission and hence carefully preserved.

The reference to the reliability of oral transmission is moreover highly misleading as far as narratives are concerned, as has been repeatedly demonstrated. And moreover, comparison between the Synoptic gospels irrefutably shows that the traditions about Jesus have been growing and developing more and more in the direction of legend and myth.

Among the most difficult parts of the gospel narratives to analyze is the story of the passion, death and resurrection of Jesus. Already STRAUSS mocked at the endeavour of the "harmonizing" exegetes of his days to reconcile the conflicting statements of the four gospels when we come to these events in the life of Jesus—actually the point of culmination in the gospels, so that they have been characterized as passion-stories with long introductions. The difference of method between the "harmonizing" exegetes and the analyzing historians may be illustrated by a reference to two well-known books, both treating of the trial of Jesus, that of BLINZLER and that of WINTER. The first book is a very clever attempt at harmonizing the narratives as they are found in the gospels, whereas the book of WINTER in a true historical way gives an analysis of the conflicting statements and tries to reconstruct the historical event as it really happened.

Equally discussed, but actually not so difficult to analyze are the resurrection narratives. Here the form-critical treatment by LYDER BRUN must, however, be supplemented by an assessment of the historical value of the various traditions. One such investigation is the well-known booklet written by H. VON CAMPENHAUSEN.

From the existing investigations it would seem possible to establish some facts. 1. The oldest tradition is represented by Paul I Cor. 15. 2. This tradition speaks only of visions. 3. The visions as related by Paul were seen a) by one Apostle (either Peter or Jacob) b) by a group of Apostles (disciples). 4. Accordingly tradition seems to waver between Peter and Jacob as the first to receive a vision of Jesus (and we may surmise that this fact reflects a rivalship between them as to the first place in the community of Jerusalem). 5. Paul has nothing to say of an empty tomb. 6. We must therefore ask ourselves whether this tradition was developed at his time or not. 7. Marc, the oldest of the gospels, has only the tradition of the empty tomb, but no visions. On the other hand we find there the exhortation from the angel to walk to Galilee where Jesus will reveal himself to his disciples (16, 1-8, vv. 9-20 being recognized as a later addition). 8. The visions recorded by the oldest tradition took place in Galilee. 9. Younger tradition spoke of visions in Jerusalem and its neighbourhood. 10. It is especially remarkable that the oldest tradition states that the women for fear didn't tell anybody of the empty tomb and the exhortation of the angel. Nevertheless younger tradition says that they *did* tell the Apostles. 11. The names of the female witnesses are variously given, their business to anoint a body after it had already been enveloped in linen clothes and put into the tomb looks rather queer as WELLHAUSEN ob-

served. 12. If the empty tomb was a proof of the resurrection as the
Marcan tradition asserts why didn't Paul mention this fact? but only
the visions. On the other hand there is nothing legendary or mythical
in the motif of the empty tomb *per se*.

As the situation is we presumably have no possibility to proceed
further. It is not possible to state what actually happened, but in this
case as in others it is quite possible to state at least what did *not* happen.
Historical research doesn't count with anything contrary to analogies
of human experience. For that reason the dominant miraculous element doesn't cause many difficulties. Some of the miracles undoubtedly possess a real background in the psychic healing powers of Jesus—
like other charismatic personalities.

We may conclude this section by emphasizing a special problem
alluded to already when speaking of the birth legends. Also in the
passion narratives we come across the references to O.T. passages.
On the whole the career of Jesus is seen as that of a royal Davidic
scion. All the life of Jesus is described in words alluding to the O.T.
sayings about the coming ruler of David's dynasty. Everything is
calculated to show that Jesus is the promised Messiah, the Davidic
king, everything in his life being in agreement with the O.T. prophecies. It stands to reason that this circumstance confronts historical
research with terribly difficult problems. What did actually happen?
What in the gospel narratives is myth and legend? And what is
history?

ANTON FRIDRICHSEN has rightly observed that an ordinary historian
occupied with general political history who eventually turns to the
study of the gospels in most cases would arrive at the conclusion that
we find in them a historical reality rendered in legendary and mythical
colours. How the short public career of Jesus actually was enacted we
are not in a position to ascertain, except as far as the milieu, the general
traits of it, and certain single dates are concerned. This conclusion presumably holds good to-day as well as in 1942 when FRIDRICHSEN
wrote his booklet about the historical value of the gospels.

V. In the case of Mani, the founder of Manichaeism, there certainly
once existed a biographical work relating his life. In his community
this *vita* ultimately was widely disseminated in many languages. This
biography, however, is lost, but a number of fragments are preserved,
scattered in various contexts. These fragmentary traditions do not
enable us to reconstruct the whole course of Mani's life, but they give

us a clear picture of what to his community were the essential points of his life: his birth, his vocation and the beginning of his public career, the end of his life and his death in prison as a martyr. For the reconstruction of this *vita* there are available above all the Arabic tradition, extant in Fihrist, three Turfan fragments in Middle Iranian laguage, and various Coptic passages in the so-called "Homilies" and "Cephalaia".

This "Life of Mani" appears to have been characterized by a strongly legendary element, a circumstance not apt to create any astonishment. Mani's biography would seem to have belonged to the category of hagiography first met with in the days of Hellenistic civilization, and then adopted by Christians and Manichees alike. The Manichaean *vita* of Mani, the founder, exhibits the literary traits characteristic of Hellenistic and Christian biographies of personalities of the same type as Mani. We find there "the same mixture of auto-biography and eye-witness stories, the same emphasis on the wonderful circumstances of birth and edifying, positively miraculous death", as I once stated it. We also meet with "the same descriptions of missionary journeys to far lands, the same meetings with mighty rulers, the same marvellous reports, the same pious speeches, the same loose agglomeration of various episodes, the so-called *praxeis*" (WIDENGREN).

When subjected to source-criticism this biography of Mani accordingly shows the well-known predilection for mythical and miraculous elements as other such legendary biographies. Quite especially Mani's birth, vocation, and first public activity in his home-land Iran, and his death are depicted in the colours of the pious legend.

On the other hand we have some texts, both in the form of auto-biographical notices and the reports of eye-witnesses, which are characterized by a very sober and exact style, in no wise sacrifying to myth and legend. Therefore it would seem to be a comparatively easy task to single out the historical biographical facts upon which we have to rely, when writing the life of Mani. Even if we have to subtract much legendary matter there is nevertheless left enough material to enable us to reconstruct Mani's life, at least in its great lines, with much more details than was the case with Buddha, Zoroaster, Moses, and Jesus. This task has in the main been carried out by H. CH. PUECH and myself in our books on Mani and Manichaeism.

VI. Among the founders of a great religion Muhammad is that one of whose life the details are best known. We have at our disposal on the one hand the Qur'ān with all its allusions to decisive events in his career and on the other hand a collection of traditions, contained in the *sīrah*, the Prophet's biography, the *ḥadīṭ*, the traditions, and the *tafsīr*, the exegetical commentaries on the Qur'ān. In these two types of sources the real historical material is found. To this we may add as a third category all the popular tracts, describing special events in the life of the Prophet such as his birth, or his ascension to heaven. We shall turn to these three categories of sources for the biography of Muhammad, in order to clarify the problem of history and legend in the biography of the Apostle of God.

That the Qur'ān is the only in all respects reliable source as far as his life is concerned is generally'admitted among historians of Islam. It was shown long ago by TOR ANDRAE that e.g. the narratives about the vocation of Muhammad must be analysed and criticized in the light of what the Qur'ān has to tell us, Sūrah 53, 6-10. In this case tradition has mixed the real historical happening with a legendary description, adapted to what the oldest exegesis thought *must* have been the Prophet's experience of his calling to be the Apostle of God. Traditionists and exegetes imagined that Muhammad's vocation must have taken place in the same manner as the call of a *kāhin* to his profession. Hence a hadit was invented, describing Muhammad's unpleasant experience in the cave where the angel gave him the command: "Recite", *iqra'*. In that way they thought that a Qur'ān, "Recitation", had been introduced by Sūrah 96, 1-4: *iqra' bismi rabbika*, corresponding to the angel Gabriel's exhortation: *iqra'*. The Sūrah 96, according to the *sīrah* composed by Ibn Hišām after the older biography written by Ibn Isḥāq, therefore was the first revelation communicated to Muhammad.

In this case a careful analysis of the traditions coupled with a comparison with the sayings of the Qur'ān enabled TOR ANDRAE to demonstrate that the real experience of Muhammad at the occasion of his vocation was the vision of a heavenly being, "in the highest horizon", descending to Muhammad.

About the birth and childhood of the Prophet the Qur'ān has very little to tell us, actually nothing at all concerning the circumstances of his birth. The prophetical legend, however, has enveloped this event in a garment of mythical traits. Special light-phenomena were seen. When his mother Āminah had born him a light went forth from her body that illuminated the castles of Syria, Ibn Sa'd I 1, p. 63. The French scholar BASSET referred to similar phenomena in the Buddha legend, in the Life of Apollonios of Tyana, and in the *Evangelium Infantiae*, to which references TOR ANDRAE added the very adequate reference to the legend of Zoroaster, Dēnkart VII, II 3. At the time when he wrote his brilliant thesis "Die Person Muhammeds in Lehre und Glauben seiner Gemeinde" (1917) he was not aware of the literary structure of the Zarathustra legend in Dēnkart. Above all he didn't know that the Pahlavi text in Dēnkart was based on Avestic sources (cf. above section II). In our days it would be impossible to admit—as TOR ANDRAE actually did—that part of the Dēnkart traditions might have been influenced by Islamic conceptions instead of *vice versa*.

It is not necessary to point out all other legendary traits in the life of Muhammad as found in the sources outside the Qur'ān. They are carefully enumerated in TOR ANDRAE's famous book just referred to. Let us instead look at the well-known description of Muhammad's so-called "Night Journey" to Jerusalem, alluded to in Sūrah 17, 1. This verse actually gives a very brief allusion to this enigmatic event, saying only:

> Glory be to Him, who carried His servant by night
> from the holy mosque to the farthest mosque,
> the precincts of which we have blessed,
> that we might show him some of Our signs.
> He is the all-hearing, the all-seeing.
>
> ARBERRY's transl. p. 274 (with a minor change)

While there is some uncertainty about the exact meaning of the expression *al-masǧid al-'aqṣā* there was a unanimous opinion among exegetes and traditionists that it meant that the Apostle of God had undertaken a journey to Jerusalem, and from there an ascension, *mi'rāǧ*, to heaven. As I have devoted a comprehensive analysis to the *mi'rāǧ*-legend I can confine myself to pointing out—as I did already in the Proceedings of the Amsterdam Congress 1950—that in this case myth has overcome history. Muhammad himself did *not* claim to have received the whole revelation, the Qur'ān, at his ascension. He did not descend from heaven bringing with him the Holy Book, as he ought to have done according to the myth and ritual pattern of the Ancient Near East. Thus Muhammad himself emfatically denied that he had followed the pattern and this fact caused him attacks from his opponents at Mecca. But in the 13th century book *Liber Scale* (extant only in a Latin translation) Muhammad is made to relate how he ac-

tually was given the Qur'ān in heaven by Allah himself. And this
against the clear words of the Qur'ān in Sūrah 17, 95. All this has been
developed at some length in my monograph "Muhammad, the Apostle
of God, and his Ascension".

The subtraction of mythical and legendary traits from the biography
of Muhammad doesn't cause the historians any difficulties in the cases
mentioned here, and in similar cases.

The situation is much more complicated when we proceed to the
analysis of such parts of the *sīrah* where there is no immediate impression of legendary influences, but where a trenchant source-criticism wouldn't admit any true historical reality of the biographical
details. Here the most radical attitude was taken by HENRY LAMMENS,
who, however, cannot be said to have been quite unbiased. By all
means he tried to demonstrate that Muhammad and his intimate
friends and helpers such as Abu Bakr and 'Umar didn't belong to the
upper classes of Meccan society but to its poorest layers— absolutely
contrary to what tradition has to tell us. He further contends that
Muhammad never had any son—his qunyah Abū Qāsim being void
of any such significance—and that his daughter Fāṭimah because of her
ugliness had to be given to the unimportant "fatty" 'Alī etc. In short:
all unfavourable things ever said about Muhammad, his family, and
his friends are accepted as historical truth. The positive traits, however, are declared the result of conscious propaganda.

As shown by BECKER, however, LAMMENS actually has drawn his
"historical" picture of Muhammad and his inner circle by using typical
tendentious traditions. This, says BECKER, is the same method as used
by Islamic historians, only that they are eager to draw an ideal picture
of the Apostle of God, whereas LAMMENS seems to take a special
pleasure in presenting Muhammad as unworthy as possible.

LAMMENS finds in the *sīrah* nothing but the product of the *tafsīr*
and the *ḥadīt* and this position is generally accepted among western
scholars. Everything therefore turns around the historical value of the
ḥadīt and the *tafsīr*. BECKER has rightly emphasized that in the *tafsīr*
we have to distinguish between two different parts: 1. such parts
where a dogmatic tendency is easily discernible. These parts lack all
historical value. 2. such parts that are purely exegetical. They reveal
the fact that there existed a historical tradition, e.g. about the battles
of Badr, Uhud etc., being a parallel of the wording of the Qur'ān
(though much more circumstantial). This tradition is generally free
from tendency and hence possessed of a certain historical value, though

it must be analyzed in the light of available evidence. I should like to add here that in the tradition also of this kind there may be a certain tendency for or against ʿAlī and his family. We have found that LAMMENS e.g. used the anti-ʿAlī traditions nearly exclusively.

The situation in the case of the *ḥadīṯ* is of a similar character. GOLDZIHER has demonstrated in his masterly analysis of the *ḥadīṯ*-literature that the great majority of the *ḥadīṯ*-s were nothing but freely invented traditions. But we posses also very old traditions which *may* contain historical facts. BECKER seems rather pessimistic about the objective criteria at our disposal for sorting out this true tradition. "Hier zu scheiden vermag nur der historische Instinkt, und deshalb wird man immer nur zu subjektiven Resultaten kommen." For my own part I am slightly more optimistic. The great NOELDEKE, who also criticized LAMMENS' positions, pointed out that beside the Qurʾān we have embedded in the mass of traditions some authentic documents, as shown by WELLHAUSEN in his analysis of them, viz. Muhammad's letters to the various tribes and also the so-called "Constitution of Medinah." From the Qurʾān and these documents we are able to reconstruct a picture of Muhammad's life in its main lines. The material contained in *tafsīr*, and *sīrah* serves to supplement many historical details—in such cases of course where no tendency can be discovered.

Such a critical scholar as RÉGIS BLACHÈRE in his book "Le probleme de Mahomet" (1952), though accepting on principle the fact that the Qurʾān is the only reliable source of Muhammad—leaving aside the authentic documents, accepted as authentic also by BLACHÈRE—when it comes to writing the life of Muhammad relates the well-known incidents found in the *sīrah*. It would seem then, that there is a *communis opinio* among most scholars concerning the historical facts found in tradition.

About the popular tracts I can of course be very brief. Beside relating well-established historical facts they are chiefly interested in the miraculous element, especially in the Prophet's *miʿrāǧ*, and cultivate the legendary and mythical traits. For the major part they accordingly lack all historical value but testify to the immense historical influence exercized by Muhammad.

NOELDEKE has rightly observed that we possess infinitely much more historical information about Muhammad than about Jesus, not to speak of Buddha and Zoroaster. He might have added also Moses as I have tried to show above. Mani and Muhammad are the two founders about whom we possess most of reliable historical information, but above all this is true of Muhammad.

VII. The atmosphere in the circle of disciples surrounding the founder being highly "charismatic" it is obvious that the narratives about his deeds and words are full of legendary and mythic elements. We have seen that the stories relating the decisive moments in his life, above all his birth and his call to his office, are apt to elevate the founder above the human sphere. As a mediator between God and men he himself occupies an intermediate position. In some cases also his parting with life marks not only the end of his human career, but also his return to the celestial world, from which he at his birth descended on earth.

That the miraculous element plays an important role during his whole earthly life we have had occasion to emphasize. The miracles are the proof of his legitimacy as the bringer of revelation, this idea comes out clearly in some lives of the founders, such as that of Jesus, Mani and Muhammad—who, however, refused to work the miracles expected from him.

All these circumstances make it imperative to subject the sources of a founder's biography to a thorough critical test. In most cases— the exceptions being Mani and Muhammad—it is not possible to reconstruct more than a bare skeleton of biographical facts.

The observations concerning source-criticism made in the case of the founder with some profit may be extended to other leading religious personalities, in the life of whom the "charismatic" element dominates, e.g. the prophetical leader in Israel, the great rabbi in Judaism, the *théios anér* in Hellenistic religion, the great ascetic in early Christianity, the outstanding mystic and leader of fraternities in Islam etc. In all these cases the criticism of the biographical sources is an urgent task—not always fully realized in our days, as our short survey has demonstrated.

SELECTED BIBLIOGRAPHY

General Introduction

BERNHEIM, E., *Lehrbuch der historischen Methode*, 6th ed. 1914.
KIRN, P., *Einführung in die Geschichtswissenschaft*, 2nd ed. Berlin 1952.
LANDBERG, G., *Historia*, Stockholm 1954.
TORSTENDAHL, R., *Historia som vetenskap*, Stockholm 1966.

SMITH, M., "Historical Method in the Study of Religion," in: "On Method in the History of Religions," *History and Theory* 1968.

Buddha

BAREAU, A., "Der indische Buddhismus," *Die Religionen Indiens*, III Stuttgart 1964.
KERN, H., *Der Buddhismus und seine Geschichte in Indien*, 1-2, Leipzig 1882-84.
LAMOTTE, E., *Histoire du bouddhisme indien*, Louvain 1958.
OLDENBERG, H., *Buddha, sein Leben, seine Lehre, seine Gemeinde*, 13th ed. Stuttgart 1959.
PISCHEL, R., Leben und Lehre des Buddha, 4th ed. Leipzig 1926.
SENART, E., *Essai sur la légende du Bouddha*, 2nd ed. Paris 1882.
THOMAS, E. J., *The Life of Buddha as Legend and History*, London 1931.

Zoroaster

JACKSON, A. V. W., *Zoroaster, the Prophet of Ancient Iran*, New York 1899.
MOLÉ, M., *La légende de Zoroastre selon les textes pahlevis*, Paris 1967.
NYBERG, H. H., *Manual of Pahlavi*, I, Wiesbaden 1964, pp. 36-61.
——, "Zarathustrabiografien i Denkart," *Religion och Bible* XIV/1955, pp. 3-19.
SALEMANN, C., *Manichaeische Studien*, I, St. Petersburg 1908.
SOEDERBLOM, N., Review of Jackson, "Zoroaster, the Prophet of Ancient Iran," *Revue de l'histoire des religions* 40/1899, pp. 427-437.
WIDENGREN, G., *Stand und Aufgaben der iranischen Religionsgeschichte*, Leiden 1955. (Reprint from NUMEN 1-2/ 1954-1955).
——, *Die Religionen Irans*, Stuttgart 1965.

Moses

GRESSMANN, H., *Moses und seine Zeit. Ein Kommentar zu den Mosesagen*, Goettingen 1913.
MEYER, E., *Die Israeliten und ihre Nachbarstämme*, Halle 1906.
NIELSEN, E., *Die Zehn Gebote*, Copenhagen 1965.
NOTH, M., *Geschichte Israels*, 3rd ed. Goettingen 1956.
PEDERSEN, J., *Israel*, III-IV, Copenhagen-London 1940.
WIDENGREN, G., *What do we know about Moses?* Volume dedicated to G. H. Davies (to be published 1969).

Jesus

BLINZLER, J., *Der Prozess Jesu*, 3rd ed. Regensburg 1960.
BRUN, L., *Die Auferstehung Christi in der urchristlichen Überlieferung*, Oslo 1925.
BULTMANN, R., *Geschichte der synoptischen Tradition*, 4th ed. Goettingen 1958.
CAMPENHAUSEN, H. v., *Der Ablauf der Osterereignisse und das leere Grab*, 2nd ed. Heidelberg 1958.
DIBELIUS, M., *Formgeschichte des Evangeliums*, 2nd ed. Tübingen 1933.
FRIDRICHSEN, A., *Våra evangeliers historiska värde*, Stockholm 1942.
GERHARDSSON, B., *Memory and Manuscript*, Upsala 1961.
RENGSTORF, K. H., "Nachwirkungen einer Formel aus dem altorientalischen Königsritual," *Atti dell'VIII congresso internazionale di storia delle religioni* Florence 1956, p. 260 f.
SCHMIDT, K. L., *Der Rahmen der Geschichte Jesu*, Berlin 1919.
STRAUSS, D. FR., *Das Leben Jesu kritisch bearbeitet*, 1-2, 4th ed. Tübingen 1840.
WELLHAUSEN, J., *Das Evangelium Marci*, 2nd ed. Berlin 1909.
——, *Das Evangelium Matthaei*, 2nd ed. Berlin 1914.
——, *Das Evangelium Lucae*, Berlin 1904.

WIDENGREN, G., *Kungar, profeter, harlekiner*, Stockholm 1961.
——, *Tradition and Literature in Early Judaism and in the Early Church*, Leyden 1963
    (Reprint from *NUMEN* 10/1963).
WINTER, P., *On the Trial of Jesus*, Berlin 1961.

Mani

KLIMA, O., *Manis Zeit und Leben*, Prag 1962.
PUECH, H. CH., *Le manichéisme. Son fondateur—sa doctrine*, Paris 1949.
WIDENGREN, G., *Mani and Manichaeism*, London 1965.

Muhammad

ANDRAE, T., "Die Legenden von der Berufung Muhammeds," *Le monde oriental*
    6/1912, pp. 5-18.
BECKER, C. H., "Prinzipielles zu Lammens' Sirastudien," *Der Islam* 4/1913, pp.
    263-269.
BLACHÈRE, R., *Le problème de Mahomet*, Paris 1952.
GUILLAUME, A., "New Light on the Life of Muhammad," Manchester, *Journal of
    Semitic Studies*, Monogr. No. 1 (no year).
LAMMENS, H., "Qoran et Tradition, comment fut composée la vie de Mahomet,"
    Recherches de science religieuse 1/1910.
——, *Fatima et les Filles de Mahomet*, Rome 1912.
NÖLDEKE, TH., "Die Tradition über das Leben Muhammeds," *Der Islam* 5/1914,
    pp. 160-170.
WATT, W. M., *Muhammad at Mecca*, Oxford 1953.
——, *Muhammad at Medina*, Oxford 1956.
WIDENGREN, G., "The Myth and Ritual Pattern in Ancient Civilization," *Pro-
    ceedings of the 7th Congress for the History of Religions*, Amsterdam 1951, pp. 102-
    105.
——, *Muhammad, the Apostle of God, and His Ascension*, Upsala 1955.

PREHISTORIC RELIGION

BY

E. O. JAMES
Oxford, England

I. The Essence of Prehistoric Religion

It now appears in the light of the available evidence that in the broadest sense of the discipline religion in all probability, in one or other of its aspects, is virtually as old as humanity itself. Moreover, many of the beliefs and practices of the higher religions, both ancient and modern, are rooted in their prehistoric prototypes, going back to the Old Stone Age. Therefore, this initial Palaeolithic phase has its allotted place in a handbook of the history of the religions of the world both past and present. The difficulty confronting such an inquiry, however, lies in the fact that the data for the most part are confined to those elements that have escaped the ravages of time and other destructive forces by becoming embodied in concrete material forms, such as the graves of the dead, sanctuaries and sacred places, cult objects, sculptures, bas-reliefs, engravings and paintings. It is true that the anthropological study of beliefs and practices current among peoples surviving to the present day in a preliterate state of culture on the fringes of civilization provide useful clues for the guidance of the archaeologist. But, as will be considered later, these have to be used with caution to avoid unverifiable and discredited theoretical conjectures about origins and developments, all too frequently made in the latter part of the last century.

So far as Early Man is concerned, the three most arresting situations with which he was confronted were those of birth, propagation, subsistence and death. These, in fact, have been the fundamental events and experiences in the structure of preliterate society at all times, creating a tension for the relief of which ways and means have had to be found. In the Palaeolithic period, when life depended largely on the hazards of the chase and of the supply of roots, berries and fish, the vagaries of the seasons, and so many unpredictable and uncontrollable circumstances by the available human means, the emotion-able strain and stress was endemic. To sublimate this a ritual technique was devised and developed to meet these requirements and to maintain equilibrium in an expanding social and religious organization.

Prior to the transition from food-collection to food-production attention was concentrated it would seem chiefly on the chase as the principal sources of the food supply, and on nutrition and propagation. As J. G. FRAZER affirmed, "to live and to cause to live, to eat food and to beget children, these were the primary wants of man in the past, and they will be the primary wants of man in the future so long as the world lasts. Other things may be added to enrich and beautify human life, but unless these wants are first satisfied, human life itself must cease to exist."[1] Therefore, around an adequate supply of food and children the institutions of religion have found expression. These together with the extension of the life-giving process to the dead, have constituted the essence of prehistoric religion, being the principal centres of emotional interest and concern.

II. HISTORICAL DEVELOPMENT

Exactly when, where and how religion first emerged remains conjectural though unmistakable indications of a conception of the continuance of life after death have now been revealed in the Dragonbone hill caves in China near Peking in Lower Pleistocene deposits which on Professor ZEUNER's calculations are dated "in the neighbourhood of 500,000 years."[2] In western Europe we know that ceremonial interment was practised perhaps 200,000 years ago, in the middle of the Palaeolithic age, as, for instance, at Le Moustier and La Ferrasie in the Dordogne and at La Chapelle-aux-Saints in the department of Corrèze in France. But it was not until the Upper Palaeolithic after the arrival of *Homo sapiens*, estimated by ZEUNER at 70,000 years ago, that attempts were made to revivify the body with lifegiving agents like red ochre, as in the burials in the Grimaldi caves on the Italian riviera, in the Paviland cave in south Wales, and at the typestation at Crô-Magnon at Les Eyzies in the Dordogne. It was then in the Upper Palaeolithic, from the Aurignacian-Gravettian to the Magdalenian periods, which terminated between 20,000 and 10,000 B.C., that the fertility and hunting cultus was firmly established to control fecundity and the food supply in addition to the cult of the dead and its mortuary rites.

The profound changes in the climatic and environment conditions that took place in northern Europe when the ice retreated at the close of Fourth Glacial period, had reciprocal cultural effects in the transitional epoch between the Palaeolithic and the Neolithic, known as the Mesolithic or Middle Stone Age. Hunting and food-gathering still persisted as the way of life, supplemented by fishing where possible. But it was a period of adaption to the post-glacial environment with its succession of Boreal and Atlantic phases between 600 and 200 B.C., characterized by physical changes in the landscape and in the fauna and flora. These had corresponding effects on the stone industries, which became predominantly microlithic with composite implements, and in all probability on the religious situation. About this, however, very little evidence is available. The dead continued to be buried in caves and covered with red ochre in the opening Azilian phase, and enigmatic smooth pebbles painted in red ochre, and other conventionalized designs at several sites occurred, probably as the last relics of Palaeolithic art. But whether or not they retained a magico-religious significance is conjectural, being the final stage of symbolical and artistic degradation. Even the more developed Maglemosian culture of the fisher and forest folk of the western Baltic with its better artistic productions has practically nothing to contribute to this sterile interlude in the development of prehistoric religion. The same applies to the Ertebølle Shell-mounds along the coast of Denmark at the close of the Mesolithic period.

Very different was the course of events after the transition from food-gathering to food-production in the fifth millennium in the Fertile Crescent from the Nile valley in the west to the valleys of the Tigris and Euphrates in the east through Palestine, Syria and the Iranian highlands. The discovery and adoption of agriculture and herding in this region in the Ancient Near East, and its diffusion throughout the greater part of the world during the succeeding millennia, introduced profound changes in the development of civilization and in the history of religion. The ritual control of fertility and the food supply now became concentrated upon the cultivation of crops, the sequence of the seasons and the rearing of flocks and herds rather than on the precarious conditions of the chase and the collection of wild edible plants. To meet the needs of these new economies religious beliefs, institutions and social structures arose adapted to the requirements of agricultural and pastoral modes of living. This occupied some five thousand years over a wide area before, at varying intervals and dates, copper and bronze came into general use as the Neolithic was replaced by the Chalcolithic and Bronze Ages for the next two thousand years. Then at different times and places iron was introduced sporadically by intrusive movements of peoples spreading especially in Asia, the Mediterranean and Europe.

It was in this series of cultural transitions that prehistoric religion pursued its course, the preliterate stage being of course by far the longest, extending from the emergence of man half a million years ago to the dawn of civilization in the Near East, in the fifth millennium, and finally reaching northern Europe in the second millennium B.C. The chronological sequence, however, is difficult to determine and define as the transition from food-gathering to food-production and their respective economies, beliefs and practices, were by no means uniformly adopted. Similarly, the use of metals was firmly established in the Near East at least two thousand years before it was introduced in northern Europe and other outlying regions far removed from the centre of prehistoric civilization. This applies equally to the closely allied development of religion which coincided with the uneven progress of post-Neolithic culture.

III. THE CONCEPTION OF DEITY

So far as prehistoric religion is concerned the most conspicuous contrast in faith and practice was in the idea and worship of Deity. Before the Neolithic transition the religious consciousness, as we have seen, was projected primarily into symbolic objects and emblems connected with the principle of fecundity, and in hunting magic and the cult of the dead. To what extent, if at all, this included an awareness of transcendence external to the world, controlling its processes and the cosmic order in general, and interpreted in terms of a primeval monotheism, so strenuously affirmed by the late WILHELM SCHMIDT, is still in debate.[1] So far from animism and polytheism becoming monotheism as a result of a long process of development, abstraction and generalization, simplification and unification, as formerly maintained by TYLOR, FRAZER and the evolutionary school of social anthropologists, it now seems that the notion of divine Providence is more fundamental than any gradual development from plurality to unity. In Palaeolithic conditions the idea of God appears to have been conceived in terms of a providential universal bounty as the Summum Bonum. This was more within the capacity of the prehistoric and preliterate mentality than speculation about the animation of nature in relation to spiritual beings and departmental divinities organized on a hierarchical basis, such as occurred in Neolithic and Bronze Age pantheons. These conceptual ideas almost certainly were a later phase of theistic development not its beginning, and, in fact, they tended to obscure the concept of a transcendent Supreme Being. But as the High God usually was less intimately concerned with everyday mundane affairs than the lesser divinities, not infrequently he was left vaguely in the background unless and until he was given a functional rôle in an organized pantheon. The Supreme Being beyond celestial phenomena, as PETTAZZONI has said, "is a less definite figure with less distinct outlines in comparison with others which represent objects of a more individualized nature, having the advantage of those characters of loftiness, supreme power and uniqueness which the sky could bestow upon him."[1]

Whether or not the Mother-goddess was the earliest manifestation of the concept of Deity, as has been contended,[2] het symbolism unquestionably has been the most prominent and persistent feature in the archaeological record from the sculptured "Venuses" of the Gravettian culture in the Upper Palaeolithic, and the images of the decorated caves, to the emblems, inscriptions and figurines of the cult when it was established in the Fertile Crescent, Western Asia, the Indus valley, the Aegean and Crete, between the fifth and the third millennia B.C., after its dispersal from its cradleland on the southern steppe in Russia and Western Asia. With the rise of agriculture and stock-rearing the Goddess became more clearly defined, and with the recognition of the duality of male and female in the generative process, her cultus was given its full weight and significance. From being the Unmarried Mother-goddess personifying the divine principle in maternity she became associated with the Young god as her son and consort.

Under Indo-European influences the concept of the cosmic Sky-god as the Creator was combined with that of the Goddess in the divine control of procreation, the weather and the creative process in general, though sometimes he became obscured by solarization and his celestial transcendence. As the all-encompassing sky, the air and "the wind blowing where it listeth," with which he became frequently associated, in prehistoric times it was usually as the Weather-god that he guaranteed the cosmic order, the continuation of life in the world and the rhythm of nature. Nevertheless, the Goddess remained the dominant figure in the seasonal drama, in which both female and male divine partners played their respective rôles in the maintenance of the sequence in nature, the fertility of the soil, and the generative process in all its varied aspects, with the shadowy cosmic figure of the Sky-father in the background controlling all things. Around them were gathered in due course a retinue of divinities engaged in their respective functions, but the God and Goddess retained their earlier status, attributes and avocations centred in the conception of Providence, propagation and nutrition, and the procuring and maintenance of the food supply and the seasonal sequence. This involved the determination of the forces of destiny, and dependence upon the divine ordering of all things. Therefore, around these basic concepts the ordinances of religion found their modes of cultic expression.

IV. WORSHIP

These consisted in magico-religious techniques and devices, prayer and spell, sacrifice and sacrament, and the manipulation of sacred power by ritual experts, or holy persons, in their several capacities. In fact, almost all that is known from the available archaeological evidence about the earliest phases of prehistoric religion is of a cultic character connected with fecundity, the chase and the disposal of the dead.

(1) *Cult.*—Thus, it was the so-called sculptured 'Venuses' that were employed as magical fertility charms, having been brought into Europe at the beginning of the Upper Palaeolithic from the Don, the middle of Russia and Malta in Siberia, where the goddess cult arose before eventually it was diffused through the Near East, the Indus valley, the Aegean and the rest of Europe. Outstanding examples are the figurines with the maternal organs strongly emphasized at Brassempouy in the Landes, and the highly conventionalized female statuettes from Willendorf in Austria, Lespugne in the Haute-Garonne, and from Malta near Lake Baikal. In the rock-shelter at Laussel in the Dordogne a realistic bas-relief of a nude obese woman, apparently in an advanced stage of pregnancy, holding in het hand the horn of a bison was carved on a block of stone. The face is featureless and the whole relief seems to have been covered with red ochre to increase its life-bestowing potency. Another sculpture depicts a copulation, or perhaps an accouchement.[1]

Women being the mothers of the human race their generative organs and maternal functions were regarded as endowed with procreative power and so became cult-objects for this purpose, like the masked dancing figures engraved on the walls of the cave of Les Combarelles between Laussel and Les Eyzies. Early man being prone to "dance out his religion" and to regard things which resemble each other as having identical properties and powers, realistic symbols and magico-religious sacred dances were regarded as the most efficacious means of bringing about urgently desired results. This is evident from the figures, engravings and frescoes often having been concealed in obscure nooks, crannies and positions in the deep recesses of inaccessible caves far from the light of day, reached only with difficulty and sometimes considerable peril. Thus, in the vast cavern of Niaux near Tarascon-sur-Ariège in the pyrenees, the paintings are from six to seven hundred metres from the entrance, separated from it by a lake often full of water and artifically deepened. Among them three small cup-like hollows under an overhanging wall have been skilfully utilized to represent wounds by drawing round them the outline of a bison with its legs drawn up, marking the cups with arrows in red ochre. In front of the expiring bison are representations of missiles. Here it would seem esoteric rites were performed in the seclusion and silence of the great "rotunda" and its "side chapels" in the heart of the limestone mountain to control by magical methods the fortunes of the chase, depicted by the wounded animals.

This is demonstrated even more clearly in the cave of Montespan near the château of the celebrated Marquise in the Haute Garonne. When it was entered by M. CASTERET in 1923 after swimming for nearly a mile in icy water through the neck of syphon, in addition to animal engravings on the walls, a number of clay models of felines were found riddled with javelin wounds, and broken in pieces, probably in a magical ceremony. On the floor the design of a horse had similar marks of thrusts on the neck, like those on the neck and chest of a small figure of a bear on a platform in the centre, and on the breast of the design of a lioness attached to the wall. Here clearly the rites had been for the purpose of killing animals in the chase by casting spells on them. Near by in a small cavity at Marsoulas, two kilometres from Salies-du-Salat, spear-markings were painted on the flank of bisons one above the other in a series of very fine superimposed polychromes, apparently indicating that they had been employed in the Magdalenian period as magical designs for a considerable time by successive generations. Indeed, the recently discovered notorious cavern-sanctuary of Lascaux near Montignac in the Dordogne must have been a cult-centre for thousands of years with its succession of techniques, described by the ABBÉ BREUIL as "the Versailles of Palaeolithic art," exhibiting almost every example of Perigordian cave decoration from the Early

Aurignacian to the end of the Magdalenian. Throughout the Upper Palaeolithic, within its sacred walls a great variety of rites must have been performed, ranging from hunting magic and the control of the food supply to mysterious commemorative symbolism depicting the hazards and tragedies of the chase.[1]

The most illuminating evidence, however, comes from the very inaccessible cave on the estate of the Count Bégouën near St. Girons in Ariège, found with very great ingenuity and skill by his three sons in 1914, and so appropriately designated Les Trois Frères. At the end of a zigzag course and crawling through a vertical shaft not much bigger than a rabbit-hole, engravings and paintings began to appear in a series of corridors and halls. In one, called "the chapel of the lioness," the head of a lion had been engraved on stalactite which had been redrawn three times in different positions. Judging from the numerous arrows it must have been frequently used as an effigy in hunting magic. The sanctuary itself is composed of an apse with recesses and converging walls covered with Perigordian and Magdalenian designs. At the end of a winding passage is an alcove with an aperture or window overlooking it. Beside it to the right is the masked figure of a man in the attitude of a hunter creeping along with bent knees seeking his prey. The legs are human but the face is enclosed in the mask of a stag with antlers; the eyes are of an owl; the ears of a wolf; the claws of a lion, and the tail of a horse.[1] If this figure, partly engraved and partly painted, outlined in black pigments, represents a sorcerer or shaman engaged in a ritual dance, as BÉGOUËN has suggested,[3] he may have stood at the window to perform his rites in the presence of the sacred design, and of the votaries assembled below, to facilitate hunting. The ABBÉ BREUIL regards it as the figure of an embryonic god of the sanctuary controlling the multiplication of the animals depicted and hunted.[4] But it seems more likely that it represented a ritual expert engaged in a sacred dance to promote success in the chase, standing in the aperture before it. Thus, at Cogul near Lérida in Catalonia a group of nine women narrow-waisted wearing skirts reaching to the knees, devoid of facial features, are portrayed on a very faded fresco dancing round a small dark-brown male figure which may have been a later edition as the scene seems to have been the work of a succession of ritual artists. Nevertheless, in its final form it represents a fertility dance of some kind.

Adjacent to Les Trois Frères in the Duc D'Audoubert on the Bégouën estate, hollowed out by the river Volp, at the end of a long

narrow passage blocked by stalactites when it was first discovered in
1912, two bisons modelled in clay were found leaning against a block
of rock seven hundred metres from the entrance. The female was
awaiting the male in a manner suggestive of copulation, while in front
of them the interlacing imprints of heels of human feet had been made
on the soft clay doubtless by those engaged in a dance to promote the
propagation of the bison.[1]

It is clear from this evidence that the ritual experts penetrated to the
depths of these awe-inspiring cavern sanctuaries, which incidentally
were never used as dwellings, to control the fortunes of the chase by
casting spells on the prey, and to maintain their supply by magico-religious ceremonies in an established cultus. These included masked
dances, representations of processions (shown in an engraving on a
pendant from the shelter of Raymonden at Chancelade near Perigueux),
and holy persons engaged in the performance of the prescribed rites
with the aid of magical cult objects in the form of charms, amulets,
life-giving agents or destructive spells. Sometimes it seems that a cult
was practised in which human beings and animals were brought together in some ritual action to establish a mystic communion with the
providential source of bounty and beneficence in a joint endeavour to
conserve and promote the food supply.

While it is most unlikely that the Palaeolithic ritual had a totemic
connotation, the conditions and purposes of the seasonal ceremonies
may have been similar to those known as Intichiuma among the native
tribes of Central Australia, designed to increase the animals on which
the community depends for its subsistence. The species depicted
certainly were not treated as totems since they were not tabu as food,
and the rites included casting a spell on the quarry in the chase to
secure its capture. About four-fifths of the representations are, in fact,
edible animals so that the cultus was primarily directed towards the
maintenance of the food supply in one or other of its aspects, and to
the giving of life through fertility symbols, dances and magical devices. It also included establishing a sacramental relationship with the
divine source of beneficence when, as apparently at Les Trois Frères,
a cult obtained in which men and animals were brought together in a
mystic communion with the providential forces of reproduction and
fecundity in such a hybrid figure as that of the so-called "Sorcerer".
To this end the ritual expert became *en rapport* with the sacred species
so venerated, believing and probably feeling himself as the human
agent for the time being to be the actual creatures he represented in

his official capacity. He did what he set out to do in the performance of the cultus. He caught and killed his prey; he made the copulation of male and female to be reproductive of offspring; he controlled the fortunes of the chase by depicting wounded animals; he uttered incantations over his designs to secure and kill the quarry; and he established a sacramental relationship between the human group and the transcendental powers responsible for its sustenance and well being.

The will to life as the primary urge was discharged by anticipatory rites giving visible and dramatic expression in response to concrete situations and current needs, supplying a vent to pent up longings and emotions. It was these ritual techniques that lay at the base of sacramental communion and sacrifice, the sacred actions being sacramentally and sacrifically efficacious not because "like produces like" but because a ritual based upon urgent practical requirements established an *ex post facto* idea of "sympathetic causation" in the production of food and propagation, the urge to act discharging itself on the symbol made effective by the ritual technique employed. As the prototype of the sacramental sign, or of the sacrificial victim, the symbol was regarded and treated in the same way as the entity it symbolized by virtue of the supernatural quality it acquired. Hence the efficacy of the designs, disguises, masks, mimetic dances and other adjuncts of the cultus executed by the ritual experts for the common good.

Inherent in this *communio*, fundamental in the sacramental principle and in the institution of sacrifice, is the giving and exchange of gifts; the pouring out of blood, or whatever may be the vital essence constituting the essential gift, because it was regarded as the symbol of life consecrated and liberated to effect union with the divine. The death or destruction of the victim is only incidental to the process of the liberation of its life. "To die is but to live again," as LOISY says, "life issues from death, and death is the condition and means of life. To destroy in order to create, to liberate through death, the power that lies latent in a living being."[1] The ritual shedding of blood to establish beneficial relations with a source of spiritual strength played a prominent part in the Palaeolithic cultus, though it was not until Neolithic times that a victim was actually employed in this capacity in agricultural society, when the chief often himself became the victim as the incarnation of the vegetation god. This custom was largely responsible for the development of human sacrifice, and from it the substitution of an animal was an easy transition, no sharp distinction being drawn between the two species, the same life principle permeating both.[2]

Similarly, the eating of sacred food, like the ritual shedding of blood, was the means whereby life, strength and its other inherent qualities were bestowed sacramentally, establishing a bond of union with the sacred order. Even in the Lower Pleistocene a cult of skulls has been detected in the Dragonbone Hill caves at Choukoutien in China in which the brain had been extracted from the crania perhaps for sacramental consumption before the heads were preserved as trophies.[1] This ritual cannibalism was also practised in a grotto at Monte Circeo on the Tyrrhenian Pomptine marshes in Italy where the brain had been removed from a Neanderthal skull which subsequently was placed within a circle of stones surrounded by animal bones. That in the Upper Palaeolithic skulls were used for sacramental purposes is suggested by their occurrence as drinking cups at Placard, Charente, in the Grotte de Trou at Montardit, and at Krapina near Zagreb in Croatia. The head being the centre of the soul-substance, the skull became an important source of spiritual power, just as blood was regarded as the vehicle of life and consciousness, both effecting a bond of union, or *sacramentum*, when consumed sacramentally to promote and preserve life. From the primary conception, going back to the threshold of prehistory, an elaborate ritual and belief emerged having for its purpose the bestowal of spiritual grace and power through efficacious signs, often intimately associated with the institution of sacrifice.

(2) While in the higher religions the approach to God through sacrifice and *communio* is usually accompanied by vocal prayer, in prehistoric times, as in modern preliterate society, essential needs and desires, and emotional impulses, found expression in gestures and ceremonial actions rather than in words. Thus, to liberate the forces that make for providential abundance rites were performed and spells, or "words of power," were uttered and invoked to bring about the required results. Early man being essentially a "ritualist" he engaged primarily in sacred actions to maintain a right relationship with the spiritual forces that controlled and regulated human affairs for the good of the community. Though the acquisition of speech was a criterion of humanity making possible the communication of ideas, at first it must have been much more restricted than muscular movement, and confined mainly to simple exclamations, incoherent cries and monosyllabic invocations, especially during dances and mimetic gestures for magical purposes. It was doubtless in such utterances directed to the transcendental source of potency that the origin of

prayer has to be sought. It is, therefore, often difficult to distinguish prayer from spell in which the efficacy resides in the words spoken and the accompanying actions performed rather than in the divine being addressed, as the supernatural power seems to lie *ex opere operato* in the magical formulae, gestures, utterances, invocations and enchantments. When desires were dramatized in mimetic rites the things done were more explicit than the words spoken. Moreover, the ethical outlook being almost exclusively that of ritual holiness, the conception of right and wrong was determined in relation to the accurate performance of the prescribed ordinances, any defects negativing the beneficial results, or making them ineffective. While a sense of gratitude for benefits received may have been latent arising out of a sense of dependence on the higher powers for daily eeds, the immediate purpose of the uttered rite or prayer was to ensure the bestowal of present and future favours.

(3) Thus, seasonal rituals and harvest "thanksgivings" were primarily utilitarian to promote the fertility of the crops during the forthcoming year under Neolithic conditions in the vegetation cultus. But here, again, the myth and ritual like the prayer and spell were integral elements in the cult-drama, and before they were given literary form and permanence after the invention of writing in the third millennium B.C., in preliterate times it would seem that themes and motifs were beginning to collect round recurrent perplexing situations requiring perpetual satisfaction. While the notion of a primeval "mythopoeic mind" or a "mythopoeic age," as some theorists have contended, cannot be sustained, prior to the rise of reflective philosophic and scientific thought and empirical knowledge, natural phenomena, causation and behaviour were conceived in terms of the imagery of myth and ritual rather than of abstract concepts, and subordinated to this type of experience. In association with crucial events causing emotional stress and tensions, stories were told and repeated at regular intervals on specific occasions explaining what happened in the primeval past to afford a reason for things being as they are. These included in due course mythological accounts of the creation of the world, the loss of immortality and the salvation and destiny of man.

V. Conception of Man

(1) The problem of the beginning and end of the universe is hardly likely to have been within the compass of Palaeolithic Man anymore than it is of modern preliterate people, except in a few cases. Man,

however, is essentially a creative being and this found expression in divers forms of technical and artistic ability long before it was conceived in terms of cosmic events, origins and destinies. The first requirements for survival were tool-making and the acquisition of speech, together with propagation and sustenance. All of these involved creative ability producing an equipment which differentiated the human species from its mammalian ancestors, and enabled it to gain the mastery over its environment by the application of its ever-increasing knowledge and skill. This, however, concentrated attention of the existing order leaving little opportunity or inclination for reflection on and speculation about the past, except in so far as former events were thought to have a definite bearing on present affairs.

As Professor BRANDON has suggested, it is not improbable that the phenomena of biological birth may have supplied the human mind with its initial conception of "Beginning."[1] This coupled with the creative urge which found expression in tool-making, the discovery of fire, sculpture, art and the first attempts at pottery-making, may have prepared the way for the mythological cosmogonies which became such a prominent feature in the Ancient Near East after the dawn of civilization. If what happened in the primeval past was of practical importance because of its permanent effects on the social structure and its laws, religious organization, beliefs, customs and prescribed rites and institutions, it inevitably became an integral element in tribal tradition, as is demonstrated in modern preliterate society. The myth lives on in its ritual and the creative period of long ago becomes an ever-present reality, re-enacted in the traditional manner on the great ceremonial occasions. In this way the sacred lore and its rites have become a consolidating force in society grounded in the ancient past and its heroes, and giving an abiding significance to the cosmological myths when it was embodied in creation stories describing the origin and transformation of the earth into its present form with its equipment of laws, customs, beliefs and rites bestowed upon mankind by its ancestral and culture heroes and handed down throughout the ages.

(2) As a creative being man by his nature readily was assigned a supernatural origin, especially if and when the physiological process of conception, paternity and partruition was not clearly understood.[1] The function of the male in procreation often being regarded as only very indirectly concerned with the birth of a particular child, the entrance of the embryo into the mother not infrequently has been

assigned to a transcendental source, as, for example, in Melanesia and among the Australian aborigines. This belief in rebirth and reincarnation carried with it the notion of an independent and separable soul, and an afterlife which, as we have seen, in some form goes back to a very early stage in the Lower Pleistocene period; the cult of the dead being closely associated with birth, generation and human destiny.

(3) Viewed in the light of the archaeological and anthropological evidence the mystery of death and the hope of immortality constituted a fundamental element in prehistoric religion and in the nature and destiny of man. The dissolution was a critical juncture requiring *rites de passage* to secure a safe passage through the gateway to the next phase of life, and liberation from terrestrial existence and its contacts. These transitional rites, comparable to those held at birth, adolescence and the cycle of the seasons, to obtain fresh outpourings of life and power, and to determine the destiny of the deceased, go back certainly to Neolithic times, and in all probability potentially to the Palaeolithic in which the situation was endemic.[1] Indeed, the idea of an immortal human destiny seems to have arisen not from speculations about a separable soul and phantoms of the living, as has been commonly supposed, but, from the ritual organization centred in a state of flux; a perpetual dying to be born again. This cyclic conception of the nature and destiny of man eventually acquired a redemptive character when the cult of the saviour-god arose in the ritual technique of salvation, though this does not appear to have emerged in the dawn of prehistoric religion.

(4) It was, however, this cyclic interpretation of the perennial sequence in the human and the natural orders that in due course led to the eschatological hope of a consummation at the end of time which would never require renewal. With the projection of the cosmological problem of creation into an indeterminate future, the ritual interpretation of birth and death was transformed into a mythology of *Urzeit* and *Endzeit*—the way of salvation culminating in the catastrophic end of the present order and the establishment of a new cosmos. Such an eschatology is not at all likely to have been within the compass of early man anymore than it is a characteristic feature in modern preliterate cultus and belief. Nevertheless, the prominence of death, disaster and destruction as everyday experiences and observations could hardly fail to have had abiding effects in Palaeolithic times. Thus, not infrequently life must have been brought to an end summa-

rily through accidents and catastrophes of various kinds, and when the cult of the dead and the hope of immortality became established, like the seasonal sequence in nature, when the allotted span of human beings was terminated they too would undergo rebirth, renewal and rejuvenation. The extension of the life-giving process to the dead, in combination with its counterpart in the natural order, doubtless paved the way for its cosmological application in relation to the beginning and ending of the universe. Then all things came to be regarded as destined to return to their origin in a grand consummation, involving the idea of judgment, restitution and renewal in accord with that of rebirth beyond the grave, and with the primeval perennial struggle between the opposed forces of cosmos and chaos enacted in the cult drama.

VI. The Study of Prehistoric Religion

The main purpose of the study of prehistoric religion has been the examination and determination of the discipline in its various aspects and manifestation prior to the appearance of written documents, from the emergence of the first hominids to the dawn of civilization, so far as this is possible from the available evidence. The discoveries of archaeology as the principal source of the data have stimulated the study of analogies drawn from surviving beliefs and practices among peoples more or less living in parallel conditions and states of culture, some of whom may go back historically to a very remote period in antiquity. Caution, however, is needed in employing these sources of information because it has proved to be all too easy to draw general conclusions about orgina and developments from disparate phenomena, brought together on grounds of superficial resemblance regardless of their diversities, comparability and provenance, in an attempt to establish an evolutionary sequence from savagery to civilization, successive in time and progressive in development. Nevertheless, it cannot be denied that the past is contained in the present, and that the fundamental tenets of prehistoric religion have been maintained in and have influenced to a considerable degree the later beliefs in respect of the conception of Deity, the cults and their worship, institutions, ritual and myth, and the conception and destiny of man, together with the idea of creation and its eschatological sequel.

Thus, the roots of the ancient civilizations, notably in the Fertile Crescent, were very deeply laid in the prehistoric past, and it was from them in this vital cradleland that most of the higher religions emerged.

Therefore, relics of these early developments are very much more
than obsolescent institutions and beliefs handed down from a remote
state of savagery. On the contrary, they are expressions of fundamental realities and values operative in prehistoric times concerning
the meaning, function and facts of existence and human destinies.
Studied phenomenologically and scientifically with the aid of the
archaeological data now available, and viewed in the light of the rest
of the contents of this handbook, that which was applicable only to
the cultural conditions of the initial stage of the discipline can be
distinguished from the elements that have retained throughout the
ages a permanent value and significance in the history of religion.

SELECTED BIBLIOGRAPHY

BLACK, D., *Fossil Man in China*. Peiping, 1933.
BOULE, H., *Les Hommes Fossiles*, Paris. 1946. 3rd. ed.
BRANDON, S. G. F., *Creation legends of the Ancient Near East*, 1963
——, *Man and His Destiny in the Great Religions*, Manchester, 1962
BRODERICK, A. H., *Early Man*, 1946
BROWN, G. BALDWIN, *The Art of the Cave-Dweller*, 1928
BUREN, E. DOUGLAS, van. *Clay Figurines of Babylonia and Assyria*, Cambridge, 1926
BURKITT. M. C., *Prehistory*, Cambridge. 1925
——, *The Old Stone Age*, Cambridge, 1955. 3rd. ed.
——, *Our Early Ancestors*, Cambridge, 1926
CHILDE, V. G., *The Dawn of European Civilization*, 5th. ed 1950
——, *Man Makes Himself*, 1941
CLARK, J. G. D., *The Mesolithic Settlements of Northern Europe*, Cambridge. 1936
COATES, A., *Prelude to History*, 1951
DÉCHELETTE, J., *Manuel d'archéologie préhistorique*, Paris, 1908
ELIADE, M., *Patterns in Comparative Religion*, 1958
HAWKES, C. F. C., *The Prehistoric Foundations of Europe*, 1940
JACKSON, J. W., *Shells as evidence of the Migrations of Early Culture*, Manchester, 1917
JAMES, E. O., *Prehistoric Religion*, 1957
——, *The Cult of the Mother Goddess*, 1959
——, *Sacrament and Sacrifice*, 1962
——, *The Worship of the Sky-god*, 1963
KEITH, A., *The Antiquity of Man*, 2 vols. 2nd. ed. 1929
KENYON, K. M., *Archaeology of the Holy Land*, 1965
LEVY, G. R., *The Gate of Horn*, 1948
LUQUET, G. H., *The Art and Religion of Fossil Man*, Oxford, 1930
MACALISTER, R. A. S., *Textbook of European Archaeology*, Cambridge, 1921
MARETT, R. R., *The Threshold of Religion*, 1914
MARINGER, J., *Vorgeschichtliche Religion*, Zurich, 1956, (E.T. 1960)
MOORE, R., *Man, Time and Fossils*, 1954
OBERMAIER, H., *Fossil Man in Spain*, Yale Press, 1925
OSBORN, H., *Men of the Old Stone Age*, 1918

PARKYNE, E. A., *Prehistoric Art.* 1915
SOLLAS, W. J., *Ancient Hunters,* 3rd. ed. 1924
VERNEAU, R., *Les Grottes de Grimaldi,* Monaco, vol. i. 1906
WERNERT, P., *Histoire génerale des religions,* vol i, Paris, 1948
WINDELS, *The Lascaux Cave Paintings,* 1948
ZEUNER, F. E., *Dating the Past,* 1953

THE RELIGION OF ANCIENT EGYPT

C. J. BLEEKER
Amsterdam, Holland

I. Characterization

The religion of ancient Egypt belongs to the category of the ancient religions.

In the first place this means that it is a dead religion. The study of such religions is beset with particular difficulties. Data are scarce and very uncommunicative, especially those from the earliest period. The people of ancient times did not take the trouble to pass on an explanation of ideas and customs the meaning of which was self evident to them but incomprehensible to us. This type of religion is known primarily as a state cult. Testimonies of personal piety are rare and generally are not significant for the character of these religions, since they are expressions of a general human religiousness. The followers of the ancient religions cannot be interviewed in order to check their own opinions against their statements. The ancients carried the secret of their faith with them to the grave. The only feasible method of fathoming the essence of the ancient religions is to gather information from all sources available. By consulting only the texts, many Egyptologists have sinned against this rule. In addition to the texts, the finds of archeology and the significance of the religious symbols must also be taken into account.

In the second place the ancient character of the old Egyptian religion contains characteristic differences from the religion of the analphabetic peoples on the one hand and from the so-called founded religions and modern religious consciousness on the other. A short description of these differences provides the best means of understanding the typological peculiarities of the religion of ancient Egypt. Modern religiousness bears an individualistic signature and is purified by critical thinking. The ancient belief is of a collectivistic, mythical and magical nature. Religions that have been founded bear the spiritual stamp imposed on them by their founder and form religious communities to which members of different peoples and races can belong. Ancient religion is the product of a nation and is a typical people's religion. Among primitive peoples who have not yet discovered writing and who seldom have formed an ordered cultural community, we find a number of interesting religious concepts which cannot readily be arranged in a system. The ancient religions which had an agrarian state as background, where writing was practised, possessed their own particular and distinctive traits. Their common characteristic is a belief in the existence of a cosmic order.

The scholar who studies the ancient Egyptian way of thought enters a world in which there are no sacred writings in the strict sense of the word, that is documents of God's revelation. Here the knowledge of God is derived from cosmic events. H. FRANKFORT has aptly remarked that "there are three spheres which the Egyptians recognized as manifestations of the divine: the power in the sun, the power in the earth, and the power in that class of animals which formed early man's most precious possession—cattle, with their connotation of creation, resurrection and procreation."[13] For the ancient Egyptians the radiant ascent of the sun from the underworld and the annual reemergence of vegetation were, in particular, demonstrations of triumphant divine life.

Thus evolved the image of a god who dies and is reborn and who proved his divinity by resurrection from the death. At the same time, therefore, there was created the dualism of death and life, or rather death was considered to have two aspects, that of enemy and that of friend, as W. B. KRISTENSEN has formulated it. In other words, death could be held to be the seat of true life.[21]

The cosmic events which revealed the nature of divine life were connected with Ma-a-t, the order which the sun-god, as creator, called into existence once and for all at the beginning of time.[1] Ma-a-t held good unconditionally. The consequence of this truth was that the ancient Egyptians entertained a static image of the world. Unlike modern man, they did not feel themselves borne by a dynamic stream of involvements which carried them to an uncertain future. They had scarcely any eschatology. They firmly believed that, in spite of periods of social disruption and moral deterioration, Ma-a-t would prevail. They believed in a sacred order which was normative in all spheres of life. They looked back to the mythical past, when the structure of the world was definitely determined, to find their religious orientation. From this faith in the unshakable cosmic order derived the optimism and joy in living which was so characteristic of them.

Related to this is the fact that, in sharp contrast to the Semitic peoples, they did not consider god and man to be separated by a deep gulf, but laid the emphasis on their interrelationship, though they were aware that man never becomes the equal of god. Not even the pharaoh, who as son of the gods was called "the good god," never "the great god."

The ancient Egyptian religion was the ferment of a homogeneous culture, that is a type of community in which religion, art, science, public life and ethical standards of behaviour do not form autonomous spheres, as in the modern age, but are closely interwoven. The structure of this cultural community was determined by what rightly has been designated a mythical-ritual pattern. This means that the life of the community was based on certain mythical truths, which were actualised by diverse rites. The dramatisation of these mythical ideas guaranteed the welfare of the state and of the individual.

It is characteristic of the ancient Egyptian that he did not attain that degree of reflection in his religious life possessed by believers of our century. This appears from the fact that his language contained no words for religion, piety, belief. It appears, too, from the remarkable circumstance that the texts never reproduce a myth in detail, only contain allusions to it, and that very many gods show an a-mythical character. The Egyptians did attempt to incorporate their many gods in systems, but they never formulated a doctrine. They possessed a profound mythical vision, which was expressed mainly in the cult. It is the cult which strongly prevails in the religion of ancient Egypt.

II. Historical Development

Every religion has its history, during which considerable changes can take place in its structure. Often the old gods lose their authority, and new gods become popular. Doctrines become out-of-date. New religious insights manifest themselves.

The religion of ancient Egypt has its history, too, and indeed a particularly long one. For more than thirty centuries, this ancient belief was the spiritual nourishment of the dwellers of the Nile valley. The question whether any evolution took place during that time is one which might justifiably be posed. Or, to express it more circumspectly, it would be difficult to avoid investigating whether any changes took place in religious thought. Especially since certain scholars have given a positive and clear answer to this question.

Already in 1912 J. H. BREASTED took his stand on this question in a book entitled *Development of Religion and Thought in Ancient Egypt*, which has won deserved fame. The main line of his argument can best be gauged by ennumerating the titles of the chapters. These are: "I. Nature and the State Make Their Impression on Religion—Earliest Systems. II. Life after Death—The Sojourn in the Tomb—Death Makes Its Impression on Religion. III. Realms of the Dead—The Pyramid Texts—The Ascent to the Sky. IV. Realms of the Dead—The Earliest Celestial Hereafter. V. The Osirianization of the Hereafter. VI. Emergence of the Moral Sense—Moral Worthiness and the Hereafter—Scepticism and the Problem of Suffering. VII. The Social Forces Make Their Impression on Religion—The Earliest Social Regeneration. VIII. Popularization of the Old Royal Hereafter—Triumph of Osiris—Conscience and the Book of the Dead—Magic and Morals. IX. The Imperial Age—The World-State Makes Its Impression on Religion—Earliest Monotheism—Ikhnaton. X. The Age of Personal Piety—Sacerdotalism and Final Decadence." Even a layman cannot help but discern in this summary list of contents the powerful grasp which BREASTED had of the course of the history of ancient Egyptian religion. His comprehensive learning and keen perception have enabled him to track down a number of factors which acted on the faith of the ancient Egyptians in the course of centuries. Nevertheless his presentation of the "Development" is not completely convincing. Various objections spring to mind, of which the main ones might be said to be: (1) Osiris is a very ancient god, and hence it is incorrect to speak of the "Osirianization of the Hereafter" and of a "Triumph of Osiris" as phases of a later development; (2) moral consciousness was not born later, but was present from the beginning; (3) the so-called monotheism, especially of Akhenaton, is not the product of mature piety, but goes back to tendencies which can be discerned even in the days of the Old Kingdom, namely in the worship of the sun-god; (4) personal piety occurred in all centuries in Egypt, and not merely in the New Kingdom; (5) the chronological scheme which Breasted links to this "Development"—omitted here for the sake of brevity—is of doubtful value. The scope of this section does not admit of any argumentation of these points of criticism. Moreover it is not essential, since, in spite of high appreciation of BREASTED's broad vision, it is easy to see that his book is strongly influenced by certain religious ideas, namely a certain belief in a spiritual evolution and an overestimation of personal religious consciousness.

Forty years later J. SPIEGEL approached the subject more circumspectly in his sketch of the "Phasen der ägyptischen Geistesgeschichte." Spiegel's choice of the concept "Geistesgeschichte" was undoubtedly deliberate: it covers a wider field than the term "history of
religion." The phases of the spiritual history described by the author
correspond closely to the usual classification of the history of Egypt.
Consider: "I. Der Kampf um den Stil (bis 2500). II. Das Reich der
Sonne (2500-2300). III. Das Zeitalter der Revolution (2300-2000). IV.
Der Ständestaat (2000-1800). V. Die Zeit der Usurpatoren (1800-1500).
VI. Das Aufklärungszeitalter (1500-1300). VII. Die Grossmacht der
Zivilisation (1300-1100). VIII. Die Zeit der Militärführer (1100-700).
IX. Die Renaissance (700-300). X. Die Konservierung (ab 300)."

Meanwhile, in *Urgeschichte und älteste Religion der Ägypter*, K. SETHE
had developed his famous theses about the evolution of religion and
public life in ancient times. This is not the place to summarise this
conception nor to offer detailed criticism of it. Briefly Sethe's vision
amounts to this, that in the mythology he sees reflected the various
phases of the complex social process which preceded the foundation
of a united Egyptian state by Menes (or Narmer), i.e. the foundation
of the towns with their local gods, the forming of the shires with their
gods, the creation of the two parts, Upper and Lower Egypt, with
Seth and Horus as patrons, and the conflicts between these two
kingdoms. It cannot be denied that in all times political and social
forces influenced religious belief and thought, certainly in ancient
Egypt. It is quite incorrect, however, to couple religious and political
processes as closely together as Sethe does. In principle the religion
is autonomous and can only be understood from its own principles.
Sethe's theory is an ingenious construction which still casts its spell
over many an Egyptologist. Gradually, however, criticism has been
voiced by scholars who are beginning to realize the artificiality of
this outline of the earliest phase of the history of Egyptian religion.

The objections which can be made to SETHE's view of the earliest,
decisive phase in the history of Egyptian religion also apply, to a
lesser degree, to the picture of religious-historical evolution created
by BREASTED and SPIEGEL. In a sense, both believe that the progress
of religious thought can be traced in the course of social and political
events. It is doubtful whether this line is a feasible one. Naturally
there is no denying that over a period of more than 3000 years the
social and cultural life underwent repeated changes. Obviously the
style of living of a contemporary of the heretic king Amenophis IV

was more sophisticated than that of his forefather of the long-past age of the pyramids. Repeated and radical changes took place in the style of clothing and of building houses, in the customs and morals, tastes and ideas in the course of the centuries. Important changes must have taken place in the lives and thoughts of the people especially during the New Kingdom, when the pharaoh's adopted an imperialistic policy, penetrated to the Euphrates in Asia Minor, and thus greatly extended the spiritual horizon of the Egyptians. How foreign patterns of behaviour were imitated and alien gods found adherents is clearly manifest. Furthermore it is obvious that the position of the individual —and therefore of his religious belief—must have differed greatly under the autocratic pharaohs of the Old Kingdom and the golden age of the New Kingdom. This need not necessarily imply that religious conception underwent radical changes, for, on the whole, there is no proof whatsoever that the social, political and cultural development radically changed the structure of the religion. Although religion is subject to the influences of its spiritual and social milieu, it develops principally according to its own concepts. This also obtains for ancient Egypt.

These considerations lead to the following conclusions: the social-cultural development in ancient Egypt provides no reliable indications of the existence of a certain development in religious thought. Moreover it should be remembered that one of the most difficult problems of the science of history is whether a meaningful line of development can be traced in the course of history, especially in that of the history of religions. This applies with particular force to the ancient world to which Egypt belonged, since the data available are scarce on the whole. With regard to Egypt, the more profound the study, the more the scholar is forced to the surprising realisation that in the course of centuries the basic pattern of Egyptian religion maintained its form with remarkable constancy. In the early dynastic period traces can still be found of alien influence, particularly from Mesopotamia, but at the beginning of the historical age was born the typically Egyptian style of life which prevailed until the latest times. This style can easily be recognised in products of art, which no matter the period to which they belong clearly manifest interrelated features and which all bear the typical Egyptian cachet. For the present this basic religious pattern will not be described. Its nature and structure will gradually emerge in the following sections. Hence the idea of a "development" can, in fact, be abandoned. Hence, too, it is permissible and possible to use data from different periods of Egyptian history to create a picture of certain conceptions of god, or forms of cult.

Additional considerations are that we are acquainted with the ancient Egyptian belief particularly in the form of state religion and that there are cogent grounds for assuming that, in it, the ancient religion of Egypt appears in its characteristic form. Naturally there was no lack of personal piety in ancient Egypt, but not only is little known about it, it is moreover of no significance for the true religion of this country. The latter thesis requires further explanation.

In his thought and evaluations, modern man is an individualist, and therefore he looks upon individual faith as the nucleus of religion. In doing so he ignores the fact that man lives in different dimensions, and that as a result his spiritual life is compounded of different strata. Firstly man is a being who can, in all truth, say: *homo sum, et nil humani a me alienum puto*. This means that in spite of differences in race, colour and culture, people in all corners of the earth and at all times can understand each other's feelings, wants and needs.

Secondly, since man is the same throughout the entire world, and in all centuries, there exists a general human piety, a sort of *religio perennis*, in which occur religious feelings of guilt, love, gratitude and faith in the Deity that can be shared by all. Nor were they wanting in ancient Egypt, even though they were rare. For example remarkable prayers of labourers from the 19th dynasty have come to light in the necropolis near Thebes, which were first studied by A. ERMAN and later by B. GUN. The latter Egyptologist calls them testimonies of "the religion of the poor." Here speak ordinary people, who confess their sins and guilt and praise the goodness and mercy of various gods who saved them in time of need. Further, an admirable work of E. DRIOTON opened up a new source for the knowledge of this personal faith, namely the study of spells found on scarabs. Many theophorous names also provide proof of the existence of personal piety.[8] These testimonies are interesting, but of no significance from the point of view of the history of religions.

The typical characteristics of a religion, however must be sought elsewhere. To spot these it must be remembered, thirdly, that religion is in fact a component of culture, even though its adherents sense that it has a metaphysical background. This is especially applicable to ancient Egypt, where religion and culture were intimately interwoven. Now every culture, particularly the homogeneous cultures of antiquity, reveals it own pattern, which is superpersonal. This pattern

rests on a choice once made by the community. From the very beginning this cultural pattern, i.e. certain habits of thought and evaluation, influences the individual and determines the structure of his
spiritual life. This applies doubly to the religious pattern of life. The
characteristic peculiarities of a given religion will therefore have to be
sought in given superpersonal religious truths. With regard to ancient
Egypt, this means that the typical Egyptian belief is contained in the
expressions of the official religion. These are often difficult to comprehend. The real task of the scholar of the history of religions is, therefore, to make religiously comprehensible that which is sometimes,
humanly spoken, hardly approachable. Now, as noted above, the
official religion reveals a pattern which has retained its form for a
period of more than thirty centuries. For this reason it would be of
little avail to search for a supposed religio-historical development.
For the main theme remains the same.

In the course of centuries, however, occur interesting variations on
this main theme. Instead of looking for an historical development
which cannot be demonstrated, it is more profitable to contemplate
three categories of phenomena, namely: (1) certain remarkable trends;
(2) a number of important episodes, and (3) four fascinating aspects
of religious life.

It is possible to distinguish three important trends which have
manifested themselves in the course of time in ancient Egyptian religious life. Firstly there was a certain "democratisation" as regards
religion. Gradually the ordinary layman officially received his share
in the religious salvation, both in life hereafter and on earth. Particularly striking is the "democratisation" of the expectation of immortality. In the Old Kingdom the pharaoh alone claimed the right
to a life after death. At most he shared this privilege with his courtiers,
who were enterred in the mastabahs grouped around the pyramid, the
grave of the king. The texts of the pyramids were funerary texts which
had only one purpose, to ensure the royal dead of a blessed fate in the
life hereafter. The assurance that the deceased pharaoh will live on in
a glorified existence is given again and again, each time in different
terms, using varying mythical symbols. We read, for instance: "This
King Pepi flies away from you, ye mortals. He is not of the earth, he
is of the sky," (5, p. 109); "O Osiris King Teti, arise!... Isis and
Nephthys have healed thee... Horus has opened for thee the eye that
thou mayest see with it..." (5, p. 147); "O this Pepi! Thou hast
departed. Thou art a glorious one, thou art mighty as a god, like the

successor of Osiris" (5, p. 163). On the one hand these spells express the belief that the pharaoh has ascended to heavenly blessedness and, on the other, that he, like Osiris, has been restored to a new life with the help of Isis, Nephthys and Horus.

It appears from the Book of the Dead, which contains a collection of spells and which was placed with the deceased in his grave as a sort of *vademecum* for the after-life, that in the New Kingdom everyone could claim the privilege which, in the Age of the Pyramids, was reserved exclusively for the pharaoh. That is why the deceased can say: "I am Atum, when he was alone in Nun, I am Re in his ascent, when he began to rule over what he had made" (Book of the Dead 113), "My hair is like Nut, my face like Re, my eyes like Hathor, my ears like Upuat, my lips like Anubis, my neck like Isis, my arms like Khnum, my back like Seth, my phallus like Osiris" (Book of the Dead 42:5 et seq.), "O Osiris, I am the son Horus, I have killed the one who did thee evil, I have removed all that was wrong with thee; I have brought thee cool water, for which thy heart yearned" (Book of the Dead 173:1 et seq.). These spells require little explanation. In them the dead expressed his firm belief that he shared the creative power of Re; he identified himself with a number of gods and declares that he played a part in the deeds which resulted in Osiris being restored to his right and in his resurrection. It is noteworthy that all these *homines ignoti* could pride themselves on enjoying in the life hereafter the privileges which were only attributed to specific monarchs in former times.

The same line of development can be discerned in the participation in salvation bestowed by the cult. In former times only the pharaoh, as sacred monarch and high priest accompanied by a few attendant priests, met the deity in the temple and honoured it with sacrifices. That is why each sacrificial formula is introduced by the stereotype phrase that it is an offer made by the king. Similarly, in later representations of festivals celebrated in honour of the gods, the pharaoh predominates to such an extent that one immediately recognises the continuation of the original concept that the pharaoh alone may consort with the gods. This cultic intercourse took place within the seclusion of the temple and was a secret act. Apparently these secret matters were gradually made accessible to more people, probably at first to members of the court and later even to commoners. In a later text the author states: "I am therein iniated (i.e. certain cultic ceremonies)... but I do not tell it to anybody." We also read the admonition: "Do not reveal what you have seen in the mysteries of the temples." These statements presuppose that in later times several people witnessed the cultic rites which were originally celebrated only by the pharaoh and a select few.

The second trend can be traced in the "theological" field. As has been pointed out above, the ancient Egyptians never recorded their myths in detail, with the single exception of the doctrine about Ptah. Apparently they had no talent for scriptural learning and theological-philosophical reflections. They did make several attemps, however, to systematise their numerous gods. In this, sacred numbers played a role, especially the numbers three and nine: they symbolise divine completion and totality. Hence it was customary to bring together a god, a goddess and a younger god in a sort of family relationship. Well-known examples of this are the triad of Memphis composed of Ptah, Sekhmet and Nefertem, and the triad of Thebes: Amon, Mut and Khonsu. Famous, too, is what is known as the Ennead of Heliopolis, composed of Atum, the sun-god, Shu and Tefnut, gods of the atmosphere, Geb, god of the earth, Nut, goddess of the sky, Osiris, Isis, Seth and Nephthys. In later texts the gods are arranged according to the new systems.

The third trend is the steadily growing worship of animals, which assumed grotesque forms in the later days of Egyptian civilisation, when large numbers of sacred animals were mummified. The relationship between the gods and the sacred animals is a strange one. Some gods often appear in the shape of an animal; for instance Horus, god of the sky, is often portrayed as a falcon. Some gods are accompanied by certain animals; for instance, Ptah has the bull Apis beside him. Many gods can be recognised by their animal heads. It would be wrong to look upon these hybrid representations of gods as a transition between an archaic animal worship and an anthropomorphical portrayal of the god, for there are primeval gods, such as Min, who are always portrayed in human form. H. FRANKFORT rightly comments that the hybrid god-figure is an ideogram for the notion: this god can appear in the animal indicated.[13] In its non-human form, the animal was looked upon as a manifestation of the divine. Apparently in later times the emphasis was placed on this notion, and this gave rise to an excess of animal worship which, from a religious viewpoint, is scarcely comprehensible.

Now the attention should be directed to three interesting episodes in the religious history of ancient Egypt, which can only be touched on briefly here. The first of these is the reformation of Amenophis IV-Akhenaton (1367-1350)[31]. This remarkable monarch completely neglected his foreign policy for the sake of his theological activities, erected a residence at El Amarna to mark his break with Amon, the powerful god of the capital Thebes and with his priesthood, and purified the cult in a "monotheistic" sense. This encompassed an endeavour to establish unity, simplicity and truth in religious life of which the sole object of worship was to be Aton the sun-god represented by the sun-disk. The other gods, in particular Amon and Mut, were stripped of their glory and were even fanatically persecuted. In that connexion, this pharaoh changed his name to Akhenaton. The natural piety which this creed engendered is best illustrated by the magnificent sun-hymn written by Akhenaton. After his premature death, the work of Akhenaton met an inglorious end because of various reasons, though primarily because its tenor was too rationalistic. Although Akhenaton was undoubtedly an original thinker, presages to his theology can be found in the primeval tradition of sun-worship. His conception, however, was too un-Egyptian to prevail.

The second episode worthy of attention is the invasion of alien gods which took place during the New Kingdom. The best known are the Canaanite Ba'al, the Hittite Sutech who is identified with Seth, Astarte and Anath who are identified with Hathor and Respu, a god of war and thunder who, together with Qadesht, the patroness of Qadesh on the Orontes, appears on monuments of the 18th and 19th dynasties in the company of Min of Coptos, a typical god of vegetation. For a while these gods were very popular, but their popularity brought no essential change in the character of the Egyptian religion, for, as noted above, the fundamental pattern of this religion continued to prevail.

This is why, thirdly, emphasis should be placed on a couple of attempts at religious restoration which were made in the later periods of Egyptian history. The first was introduced by the kings of the 26th dynasty (603-525), who wanted to eradicate all traces of foreign influence after the period of Persian dominion and who took as their norm for the restoration of religious life the style of the Old Kingdom. It was a similar aim which gave birth to the mighty temples at Denderah, Edfu, Philae and Esna in the age of the Ptolemies (322-30). The remarkable texts in these temples breathe the spirit of an endeavour at a restoration that not only copies old religious phrasing because of loyalty to the traditional pattern of creed, but also reveals the strength to endow the old motives with a new terminology.

Finally we should like to draw attention to four fascinating aspects of ancient Egyptian piety. Firstly mention should be made of the piety of the people, precisely because it is so often forgotten. Obviously data about it are not abundant. Nevertheless a number of lesser gods are known who were popular and to whom the ordinary man confided his cares and needs, for example, Thoueris (the great), a combination of a hippopotamus and a crocodile, with lion's paws and human hands which hold the sign of magic protection; Bes, a satyr, which later even became an all-god, and the seven Hathors, who protected love and prophesied the fate of the new-born.[11] Secondly mention might be made of the works on wisdom—for example the doctrine of Ptahhotep and of Kagemni, the book of wisdom of Amenemope. These writings offer maxims for the exercise of a practical wordly wisdom which, though not profound, possesses a religious background. For the wise man lives in harmony with Ma-a-t and is therefore assured of both his virtue and his happiness.[10] Connected with the books of wisdom are, thirdly, the expressions of pseudo-prophetism. This can be found, for example, in the prophesies of Neferrohu and in the spells of Ipuwer, in which the approaching disruption of the country is drastically depicted, but the hope of renewed prosperity under rule of a true monarch is also discussed. These are not the expressions of true prophetism. These books contain a *vaticinium ex eventu* intended to praise a certain monarch, or exhortations of a sage whose aim was to strengthen faith in the victory of truth and justice.[10] Fourthly, certain expressions of scepticism and doubt about the meaning of life demand attention. They are contained, *inter alia*, in the song of a harpist who exhorts the celebration of a joyful day and in the dialogue between a man weary of life and his soul, which exudes a disgust of life that sounds ultra-modern.[10] As contra-trend to the general one in a firm belief in the eternal validity of Ma-a-t, such a voice must not be ignored.

III. Conception of God

A. *Introductory remarks*

The ancient Egyptian word for God, i.e. *ntr*, is written by a hieroglyph (𓊹), which in all probability represents a pole with a flag. It resembles the flagmasts which in later times stood before the entrances of the temples. From ancient pictures it appears that this pole marked holy places. It surely was a sacral object. Therefore it obviously could serve to indicate the deity. Several attempts have been made to give an explanation of the original significance of the word *nṯr*. It is noteworthy that W. VON BISSING drew the attention to the resemblance to a word *nṯr*, which means natron—used as a means of purification—and also to be pure, to purify. It is a well known fact that purity played a great part in the ancient Egyptian cult. Above the entrance of temples one could many times read the warning: "Everybody who enters the temple, must be pure." *Nṯr* thus could have been the name of the divine being, residing in the pure cult-places. Moreover there are a few pyramid texts (697, 2096) in which *nṯr* alternates with 'life' (*'nḫ*), the soul (in the form of a bird—*b3*) and 'power' (*sḫm*). This means that *nṯr* was conceived of as a being, possessing the spontaneously creating force, which to Egyptian conception is characteristic of the deity.

The gods are often said to possess *nfrw* = 'beauty', or that they are 'fair' (*nfr*) of face. *Nfr* means 'good, beautiful'. *Nfr* is a remarkable word, because it signifies not only ethical 'good', but cosmic 'good' as well. Often *nfr* means that which is ethically correct. The explanation: "I have spoken the good, repeated the good" varies with the assurance: "I have spoken the truth, aspired to justice." But also the youth, the marriageable maiden, the colt are *nfr*, because they are young and possess unbroken vitality. Nefer-Tem is the young, newly arisen sun-god. As lord of the realm of the dead, where absolute life is seated, Osiris is called 'Unnefer', which means: the good being, i.e. the godhead who possesses the 'goodness' of spontaneously emerging life.

In chapter I it was observed that the Egyptian felt akin to the gods. This in no way diminished his respect for the mighty gods. To use the words of RUD. OTTO, he not only had a feeling for the *mysterium fascinans*, but also for the *mysterium trememdum* of the godhead. A tangible expression of the majesty of the godhead is to be found, *inter alia*, in the colonnaded chamber of Karnak, where 134 columns are ranged in 16 rows within a space measuring 103 by 52 metres. Amidst this forest of columns, the Egyptian must have felt humble in the presence of Amon. In hymns to Amon, both the deep respect and the love felt for this god are beautifully phrased: "I prostrate myself in fear of thee, I look up to thee in love," "Mighty in power, wrathful, angry of heart, mild, lord of grace, who hears the pleas."

The Ancient Egyptians worshipped many gods, some of whom were strong personalities, some vague figures. The essence of polytheism is, to use the words of M. ELIADE, that the polytheist experiences *hierophanies* in various parts of the cosmos, without either feeling the need or possessing the power to bundle these numinous impressions to form a unity. Hence there is nothing amazing in the Egyptian's belief that certain animals and plants were sacred or that certain objects possessed sacral value. Sacred is the sycomore, often connected with Nut and Hathor. Sacred is the lotus, the symbol of the rising sunlight, and the lettuce plant, token of fertility and therefore associated with Min. Mention has already been made of the sacred animals. As examples of sacred objects might be cited the royal throne and the royal sceptre, which resembles a flail. The goddess Isis bears the sign of the throne on her head: she is the personified throne which 'makes' the crown prince a king once he ascends it. The aforesaid sceptre appears to consist of a staff with the sign of 'childbirth, being born' (*msj*). It is therefore a symbol of fertility.

There are Egyptologists, in particular H. JUNKER, who aver that a sort of primeval monotheism once existed in Egypt in the form of the worship of a god who was known as 'the great one', or 'the great god'.[16] This thesis, however, is based on very shaky grounds. The ancient Egyptian religion always had a polytheistic character. True, there is some question of a certain pantheism which was linked up with Atum, whose name can be said to mean 'the all-god'. The 'monotheism' of Akhenaton was more like that sort of monotheism in which sun-worship more than once resulted in ancient times. In the literature on wisdom, 'god' or 'the god', is often discussed. Here, again, monotheism must not be sought. The reference is probably to the godhead to whom the wise man turned as his patron deity. The important thing is that a number of gods laid claim to primacy, e.g. Geb, Shu, Min, Sekhmet, Osiris, Thoth, and, above all, the sun-god.

Finally attention is merited by two characteristic features of the ancient Egyptian way of religious thinking, termed 'multiplicity of approaches' and 'multiplicity of answers' by H. FRANKFORT.[13] The first principle is the basis of polytheism: the believer approaches the divine in a number of ways. On the other hand he employs manifold symbols to express a religious truth, and in doing so is in no way averse to logical contradiction. The texts, for instance, relate that the deceased lives in the grave, sojourns in heavenly regions, resides in the underworld, accompanies the sun-god on his boat-trip, has to give account of himself before Osiris and his judges in the judgment of the dead. This is a set of mutually exclusive statements. The Egyptian was not aware of the contradictions. For him they were evidently just so many equivalent symbols for expressing a mysterious truth.

B. *Primeval gods*

Hermopolis in Central Egypt is called *Ḥmnw* in Egyptian, which means the eight-town. This town, which later became the focus of the worship of Thoth the moon-god, derived its name from an old cosmogony in which an ogdoad played a leading role. [12] These were eight primeval gods who represented chaos. Together they were believed to have created light on the so-called island of flames, and they were held to be the parents of the sun-god. The ogdoad is composed of four pairs of gods, of whom the males bear the head of a frog and the females that of a snake. These are pregnant symbols. The frog, who passes through strange metamorphoses before becoming adult, inspires the thought that he possesses the power of self-renewal. Therefore it is understandable that Heket, the goddess who promotes birth, bears the head of a frog. All ancient peoples looked upon the snake as a mysterious animal, living as it does in caves, the entrances to the underworld, and periodically casting off its skin. The Egyptians likewise held the snake to be a demonic creature—on the one hand the enemy of the sun-god, who as Apap endeavours to impede his journey through the underworld, and on the other hand the symbol of the earth which periodically causes new life to emerge, especially by the rising of the sun. And so the frog and snake heads of the primeval gods announce that inherent within them is potential life. The fact that they form pairs could mean that these gods were originally thought to be androgynous. To be specific, the character of the female partners is not clearly delineated. They could have been the 'power' of the respective gods which later became detached.

The oldest pair is Nun and Naunet. Nun is called 'the old one', 'the oldest', 'he who first existed'. He represents the primeval water which, according to various Egyptian myths about the creation, was present in the beginning. The second pair is called Huh and Hauhet. The name Huh is said to be a play on the words *ḥḥj* being 'to seek' and *ḥḥ* = 'million, great multitude'. The name is supposed to express a characteristic of the primeval water, namely its ability to spread in all directions. The third pair is called Kuk and Kauket. Their names clearly state that they represent the darkness that prevailed in the

primeval beginning. Amon and Amaunet form the fourth pair. This
Amon was later linked up with Re in Thebes, where he acted as the
powerful sun-god. In the cosmogony of Hermopolis he is the god of
the wind. He does honour to his name, which is said to be derived
from *imn*, 'to conceal'. He is the concealed, the mysterious one. It is
the invisible wind which moves the primeval water and so creates life.
K. SETHE has pointed out that a remarkable parallel can be discerned
here with the story of creation in the Bible. For we read in Genesis
1:2: "And the earth was without form, and void; and darkness was
upon the face of the deep. And the Spirit (ruach = breath, wind,
spirit) of God moved upon the face of the waters." Howsoever this
may be, among these primeval powers Amon is evidently the god
who called forth the first life from the chaos. He is therefore called
"the air which remains in all things; the breath of life in the nose of
all things, when he departs, then death comes."

C. *The sun-god*

The sun-god is known by various names. The most common one is
Re, with the sun-disk as determinative in hieroglyphic writing. He is
also called Harakhte, which means: 'Horus of the horizon'. The sun-
god is conceived of as a falcon. The bird is the determinative of
Horus, god of the sky. The name Harakhte accentuates his brilliant
emergence, which was a daily miracle to the Egyptians, a repetition
of the mythical emergence in primeval times. The horizon (*3ḫt*) is
actually the mountain of light in the East, where this world and the
underworld meet. A series of symbolic representations, of which the
door was an important one, were employed by the Egyptians in their
endeavour to elucidate the significance of the *3ḫt*. Another name of
the sun-god is Khepri or Kheprer, and hence he is often represented
by the scarab who pushes the sun-disk before him. Khepri was associated with the word *ḫprr* = beetle, and also with the verb *ḫpr* =
'to come into being', i.e. to be self-created. Popular Egyptian belief
had it that the beetle came into being spontaneously. So the sun-god
is like Khepri, the god who automatically comes into being. In
Heliopolis the sun-god was called Atum. His name is said to be connected with the verb *tm* = 'to be complete', 'to be at an end'. Hence
Atum is the evening sun which sinks. In the mythology of later times,
three of these names are linked together, for the sun-god says: "I am
Khepri in the morning, Re in the afternoon and Atum, who is in the
evening."

The sun-god is represented in various ways. In the first place by the sun-disk. This is held to be the right eye of Horus, god of the sky, whilst the moon is conceived of as his left eye.[11] Connected with both eyes are certain myths, which, for three reasons, are difficult to reconstruct. Firstly these myths are nowhere related *in extenso*. Secondly the myth of the sun-eye is intertwined with that of the moon-eye. Thirdly the myth of the sun-eye is linked up with a story about the goddess Tefnet, who lives as a savage lioness in the Nubian desert and is induced to return to Egypt by the persuasive powers of Shu and Thoth. The main idea of the myth of the sun-eye is evidently that this eye can detach itself from the deity, become an independent *numen*, leave him and return again. This representation could have had its inception in the temporary disappearance of the sun behind the clouds. Since the Egyptian sky is seldom clouded over, the influence of the moon-eye myth would perhaps be more plausible. The moon with its periodical waxing and waning very likely gave rise to the idea of departure and return. Hence the role played by Thoth the moon-god in the myth. Whatever the truth may be, this main theme apparently recurs in a number of variations. Firstly the eye is sent forth to chastise the enemies of Re, rebellious people. Secondly we read that the eye departs because it is angry with the sun-god, whereafter it allows Thoth to effect a reconciliation. These two motifs can be fused. Then there is created the story that the eye is angry, because another eye has usurped its place during its absence. The wrathful eye receives satisfaction by being allowed to adorn the forehead of the sun-god as uraeus.

This myth provides ready occasion for mentioning a second representation: the sun-disk with the uraeus, borne by wings—the uraeus being the snake which also ornaments the pharaoh's crown and which is believed to repel enemies—a symbol regularly encountered above the doors of Egyptian temples. Furthermore the sun-god is conceived of as a falcon with shining feathers, flying across the sky. The sun-god as scarab has already been discussed. Re is repeatedly portrayed as a man with a falcon-head ornamented with a sun-disk. [29]

With regard to religion, the ancient Egyptian set his compass by the mythical past. For this reason the creation myth was of eminent value. Each of the principal towns had its own conception about this process. In the myth of Heliopolis, the sun-god performed the role of creator, or rather of the one who created a cosmos out of chaos. According to this myth, there existed nothing in the beginning except

Nun, the primeval water. From Nun emerged the sun-god. Since he found nowhere to stand, he made a mound or he climbed the primordiall hill which arose from the water. In the doctrine of Heliopolis the sun-god is known as Atum. Reference to his act of creation is found in the following pyramid texts: "O Atum Kheprer, thou hast raised thyself upon thy (primordial) hill" (1652); "Hail to thee Atum, hail to thee Kheprer, who hast been self-generated, thou art high in thy name of hill, thou art created in thy name of scarabaeus." (1597). The sun-god's ascent of the primordial hill had a threefold significance: the sun-god conquered the powers of chaos, he assumed the domination of the world and he instituted Ma-a-t as the order that eternally prevails. Allusion to these events is made in pyramid text 265, which states that King Unas is coming from the island of flames —birthplace of the sun-god—and that he has set Ma-a-t in the place of the lie. Book of the Dead 17:3-5 also refers back to primeval times, when Re defeated his antagonists and appeared as first king. The primordial hill, which is also represented as a flight of stairs, fulfils a preeminent function in religious symbolism. It is the sign of divine life which rises spontaneously from death. As A. DE BUCK has demonstrated in his study on the Egyptian conceptions of the primordial hill, the hieroglyph of the verb $ḫ'j$ is a variant of it. It represents the primordial hill above which the rays of the rising sun can be seen. $Ḫ'j$ means 'to rise', with reference to the sun, 'to appear' with reference to the gods and also to the king who ascends the throne. The last-mentioned meaning links up the mythical action of the sun-god with the ascension of the throne. The pharaoh, who was looked upon as the son of the sun-god, repeated in his assumption of government the mythical ascent of the primordial hill by the sun-god. That is why the new pharaoh's ascent to the throne took place the morning after the day on which his predecessor died.

In this connexion, it is desirable that Ma-a-t, the world order, should be discussed in greater detail.[1] Ma-a-t occurs as concept and as goddess. As concept it can be interpreted as truth, justice, order in society. Thus the deceased states: "I have spoken the truth, as desired by the godhead, day after day." 'A man of Ma-a-t' is one who practises justice in every respect. All government officials, and above all the pharaoh, are called on to put Ma-a-t in practice. Particularly the pharaoh as son of the gods and sacral monarch. His task is "to make Egypt prosper, as in primeval times through the plans of Ma-a-t." On closer investigation it appears that the ethical ideals of truth, justice and social order are anchored in the cosmos. For Ma-a-t is primarily a goddess who represents cosmic order. Ma-a-t is an institution of Re and as such his daughter. But Ma-a-t is also known as his mother, for the sun-god is bound to Ma-a-t in his course. She stands as pilot in the prow of the sun-boat. It is said in an immeasurably varied image in the hymns that Re lives through Ma-a-t. Ma-a-t is also connected with Osiris. The judgment of the dead over which Osiris presides is held in the chamber of the double Ma-a-t, namely in that of life and death. The deceased's conduct in life and his spiritual quality are evaluated by Ma-a-t.

During the creation, the sun-god was assisted by Hu and Sia. [12, 21] These are two highly interesting figures. They are the personification of the creative word and of insight, divine wisdom. To comprehend the significance of Hu, it should be known that according to the ancient notion the word, and especially the solemnly pronounced word, is not an empty sound, but a potent utterance with a creative effect. And Sia embodies the typical ancient Egyptian ideal, insight into the mystery of life and death. A strange myth relates that Isis manages to trick Re into revealing his secret name: she shapes a snake which bites Re. He suffers such unbearable pain that in a desperate attempt to obtain a cure he tells Isis his secret name, i.e. his true being, his creative power—the ancient notion was that the name contains the essence of its bearer—and Isis grants him the cure. Since the nature of the godhead is inscrutable, the reader is not told what this secret name is. From that time Isis has possessed wisdom. This being so, it is not surprising that Hu and Sia belong to the crew of the sun-boat. They safeguard the passage of the sun-god, especially in the underworld.

Re continued his work of creation by calling Shu and Tefnet into existence. This he did in a remarkable way—by spitting and coughing them out. This mythical conception is based on paronomasia of the names of these two gods. Shu is the god of air; Tefnet, a wan figure, presumably represents moisture. Shu is associated with theological speculations which render him a god of some importance. Moreover he separated Geb, god of the earth, and Nut, god of the sky, the children of Shu and Tefnet. This separation is likewise a creation, for as a result life became possible. Geb and Nut are primeval gods, and Nut is the more important one. She is conceived of as spanning the earth, and as the nocturnal sky she is identical with the realm of the dead. On the inner side of the lid of the sarcophagus, she forms a protective arch over the deceased.

Naturally enough, the sun's course attracted attention at an early age. The usual supposition was that the sun-god traversed the sky in a barque. He even used two vessels, the morning-boat and the evening-boat, or rather one boat for the daytime voyage and another one for the voyage through Duat, the underworld. The sunrise and sunset were the features of this journey which attracted most attention, and they are described in numerous hymns.[29] Especially the sunrise, for this is not a mere matter of course. Every day it is a miracle, proof that the sun-god has the power to overcome death. Hence the East and the West are the two most important points in the cosmography. They correspond to left and right. The south was the point of orientation. Since the sun dies in the West, this is the typical land of the dead. The dead were called the Westerners, and on the western bank of the Nile were located the necropolises. Nevertheless this was the land of life. A hymn says: "Worship of Re, when he sinks in life...."

The symbolism which derives from the myth of creation has given shape to three famous constructions, namely the pyramids, in particular those of Gizeh, the obelisks and the sphinx. The pyramids imitate the primordial hill: the pharaohs were interred in these gigantic tombs to enable them to participate in divine life. The graceful obelisks owe their significance to the fact that they are pyramids on high, square columns. The sphinx is a lion with a human head which can represent both the sun-god and the king. The lion, the typically strong animal, symbolises the power of victory which is inherent in Re. Accordingly, the sphinx of Gizeh was called 'Harmachis (a variant of Harakhte), Kheprer, Re, Atum', in other words, he symbolises the sun-god in his different phases.[21]

Certain animals are also associated with the sun-god. The beetle has already been discussed, and so has the falcon. Others which might be mentioned are the goose and the cat. According to a myth, there emerged from an egg on the primordial hill a goose which flew off honking and so created the first light and the first sound.[11] As for the cat, or rather the tom-cat, there is the well-known conception of the tom-cat who cuts in pieces the snake, the typical enemy of the sun-god. This is the sun-god combatting darkness.

Finally, Amon-Re, patron of Thebes, should not be forgotten. As we have seen above, Amon was originally a god of the wind. Thanks to the protection of the rulers of the 12th dynasty—for the most part known as Amenemhet = 'Amon takes the lead'—and to his associ-

ation with Re, he became a powerful god whose possessions in the
New Kingdom formed an *imperium in imperio*. A famous hymn praises
both his mysterious greatness and his beneficence. His holy animal
was the ram.

The cult of the sun-god is dealt with below in the chapter on
religious worship.

D. *Sokaris-Duat*

During the night, the sun travels through the underworld for 12
hours.[2] This journey is described in a text which has been entitled
Am Duat = 'that which is in Duat'. On the walls of the royal tombs
in a valley west of Luxor are engraved this text and the accompanying
pictorial representations. The 12 hours of the night are represented as
a like number of regions, separated from each other by gateways. The
text describes how the sun-god in his boat passes through the one
hour after the other and also the subterranean creatures he encounters
on his way. The designs are placed in three horizontal rows: The
middle row shows how the sun-boat passes along the underground
river, sometimes surrounded by a flotilla of smaller boats. The sun-
god bears a ram's head to signify that he is dead but still in possession
of the power of resurrection. The rows above and below represent
both river banks, populated by diverse mysterious creatures from the
realm of the dead and by the deceased. The sun-god is enthusiastically
welcomed by all the inhabitants of the underworld, for his arrival
brings new life to them.

There is no water in the fourth and fifth hours, and the sun-boat
has to be dragged over the sand. These two hours constitute the realm
of Sokaris. The actual realm of Sokaris is so hermetically sealed off
that the sun-god catches no glimp of him, though Sokaris does hear
his voice. Sokaris, however, can be seen in the picture, standing in a
cartouche supported by two lions, who represent the earth-god Aker.
Spanning the ellipse is a pyramid crowned with the head of Isis. Above
this drawing is a bell-shaped design which represents the nocturnal
sky, from which the scarab emerges. The symbolism is evident: in the
middle of the night—from Death—comes the sunrise.

Usually Sokaris appears in human form and falcon-headed. Apparently his principal sanctuary was Ra-setau (*r3 št3w* = 'mouth of
the caves', i.e. entrance to the realm of the dead) located near Gizeh
in Sakkarah. He was the god of the portals of the underworld, of the
necropolis, of the realm of the dead, and more particularly of the 4th

and the 5th hours of Duat. Very early on he was associated with Ptah, the lord of Memphis, and with Osiris, with whom he is closely akin. Nonetheless he retained his independence.

Sokaris is a most mysterious figure. The first trait to catch the attention is what might be called his a-mythical character. This means that there is not a single myth relating his deeds or vicissitudes that has grown up around his person. And yet he was the principal in very ancient and remarkable rites and colourful festivals, which are described in the following chapter. In them his sacred barque, the *ḥnw*, plays an important part. From the rite of 'breaking open the earth' he appears to be a chthonic god: from him derives the fertile life of the earth. But its source lies deep down in the underworld. This is what is referred to by his most usual epithet: 'he who is on his sand'. This designation characterises Sokaris as god of the desert, of the region where death reigns. Hence the 4th and 5th hours of Duat, his place of residence, are portrayed as a desert. Sokaris is the god of death rather than the dead, as is Osiris, whose death and resurrection bestowed on the deceased the hope of eternal life. He is the god of the arid soil which can become fertile, of death which encompasses potential life. A proof of this is to be found in the above-mentioned representation, contained in the fifth hour, of the scarab who crawls out of the nocturnal sky: the symbol of the appearance of light in the dark of night.

E. *Osiris and his retinue*

Osiris enjoyed great popularity.[2] He was the object of worship, affection and the religious expectations of thousands of mortals in the course of many centuries. He and the divine figures about him have captured the imagination, to some extent because they were the paragons of exalted human virtues. Osiris, the wise monarch; Isis, the loving wife, utterly dismayed by the murder of her husband; Nephthys, the faithful sister; Horus, the upright son who avenges the injustice done to his father; Seth the jealous brother, the villain; Anubis and Thoth, the friends who support Osiris in his need; they are inspired by feelings familiar to every man. Besides, from the cultic dramatisation of the suffering and resurrection of Osiris the people derived their hope of blessedness in the after-life. Just as the myth of the sun-god, especially the story of the creation, profoundly influenced the state religion and specifically the ideology of the kings,—as will appear in the following chapter—so is the Osiris myth the warp and woof of the funerary cult. Reiterated endlessly is the wish that Thoth

will justify the deceased, just as he did for Osiris and Horus. Here
again the function of the mythic-ritual pattern is clearly manifest.

Nevertheless the remarkable thing is that the Egyptian texts never
relate the Osiris myth in detail. PLUTARCH was the first to record it
as a continuous story in his book 'peri Isidos kai Osiridos'. A hymn
from the 18th dynasty which contains a panegyric on Osiris mentions
a number of details, though not in any logical sequence. For the rest
the texts contain only allusions to the fate of Osiris. They are scattered
throughout diverging types of material: funerary texts such as the
pyramids and the Book of the Dead, hymns and rituals. Often the
communications contained in them are scarcely consentaneous. This
is manifest proof that the ancient Egyptians had no doctrine about
Osiris, though they did have a mythic conception of his nature and
import, which was capable of varying interpretation according to
circumstances.

By applying the necessary harmonisation the following picture of
the vicissitudes of Osiris can be drawn: Geb and Nut had four
children, two sons called Osiris and Seth and two daughters called
Isis and Nephthys. Isis was the wife of Osiris; Seth was attended by
Nephthys. Osiris ruled the world as a good regent. Seth adopted a
hostile attitude towards him and, as PLUTARCH relates, managed to
kill him by means of guile, in spite of the protection of Isis. He is said
to have tricked him into being shut up in a sarcophagus, made to fit
him exactly. He and his assistants put it in the Nile, which carried it
down to Byblos. The Egyptian texts never specifically discuss the
horrible deed of Seth. Sometimes Seth is said to have struck down
Osiris, sometimes an allusion is made to Osiris being drowned.
Though overcome by sorrow, Isis did not rest until she had recovered
the corpse of her stricken husband. Together with Nephthys she
uttered a dirge which inspired the composition of litanies for the
Osiris worship. But this song of lamentation also possessed magic
powers. Because of this and the solicitude of Anubis and the two
sisters for the maimed body, Osiris awoke to new life. Meanwhile Isis
had conceived her son Horus by the dead Osiris. Seth once more
gained possession of the body of Osiris and rent it asunder into
fourteen pieces. Isis found the pieces and buried them on the spot, in
consequence of which there are many Osiris sanctuaries in Egypt. To
protect Horus from the assaults of Seth, she secretly brought him up
in the marshy region of the Delta. When he reached manhood, she led
him before the court of the gods. There a trial was held in which

Thoth acted as counsel for father and son. Seth was condemned and Horus was recognised as his father's heir. Osiris did not return to earth, but accepted the function of lord of the underworld and supreme judge of the dead.

Osiris is such a many-sided divine personnage that it is difficult to compress his essence into a short formula. Since he reveals pronounced human traits and particularly by PLUTARCH is presented as an earthly ruler, some Egyptologists assume him to be a deified king of primeval times. This assumption is incorrect, for they entirely overlook the unmistakably cosmic traits revealed by the image of Osiris. There is nothing remarkable about the ancient Egyptians having conceived of Osiris as ruler. They had no other symbol to define his royal figure. Re, too, was held to be king. No one would think of taking him for a deified mortal king. Osiris is undoubtedly a god of vegetation, but only in a special sense which requires further definition. That Osiris represents the growing power of vegetable matter can be inferred from the drawings of his tomb, which is ornamented with shrubs or grain. In the pyramid texts Osiris is addressed thus: "O, thou whose tree is green; who stands on his field...." Elsewhere he is called Neper, 'corn'. "I live, I die, I am Osiris... I live as corn, I grow as corn". Since fertility without water is inconceivable, the text naturally declares: "Thou art indeed the Nile, which is big on the fields at the beginning of the seasons; gods and humans live from the water which is in thee". Osiris is also an earth-god; all buildings and all work on the soil takes place on the back of Osiris, who lies down as earth, states a hymn. Furthermore a relationship exists between Osiris and the moon: Osiris is supposed to have reigned for 28 years, the number of a lunar month. Finally Osiris is god of the dead. In this quality he probably assimilated in himself an ancient god known as 'the lord of the westerners' (i.e. the dead). Yet he too is by nature a god who belongs in the realm of the dead. For he personifies the mysterious divine life which is seated in the underworld and which periodically is regenerated spontaneously from death.

In Egyptian Isis is called $\mathit{S.t}$, which means 'seat, throne'. As mentioned above, there are grounds for assuming that she represents the throne, the sacred seat of the king. The king assumes his dignity by seating himself on the throne. The throne 'makes' the king. Isis is, as it were, his 'mother'. The Egyptians took this concept realistically. On a relief in the temple of Abydos, the pharaoh is seated in the lap of Isis, who in turn is seated on the typical royal throne. This conception is also based on the mythic idea that it was to Isis that Horus owned his recognition as heir to Osiris. Isis succeeded in this plan because she had wisdom at her disposal. She is called 'great in magic', which amounts to the same thing, for the ancient notion of true wisdom was insight into the mystery of life and death. Armed with this 'wisdom', Isis succeeded in bringing her stricken husband back to life. Compared with the sympathetic but rather passive Osiris, Isis is a resolute and active female personnage. Little wonder that in later times she acquired universal significance and in the Hellenistic era was patroness of mysteries called after her. Her sister Nephthys is a pale figure, although her name—the mistress of the house—suggests she once was more important.

Horus is the model of the son who stands by his father. At least in the traditional myth. Actually Horus is a complicated figure; in other words a number of gods could easily be mentioned who are called Horus and who usually had a falcon's head.[3] S. A. B. MERCER has even listed 15 gods having the name Horus. Two figurations of this godhead are undoubtedly the most important: the so-called older Horus and Horus son of Osiris. Practically they are inextricably interwoven with each other. Typologically, however, a sharp distinction must be drawn between them. The older Horus is a god of the sky. The myth says that he became involved in a violent struggle with Seth, with whom he forms a pair, and during its course Seth deprived Horus of his eye, and Horus deprived Seth of his testicles. Thoth managed to bring about a reconciliation between them. The myth expresses the conception that life and death, the antithesis of each other, can nevertheless be reconciled. The Horus in the Osiris myth, however, is a different one, the upright son who defends his father's rights and therefore deserves to be his successor.

Seth plays the role of the villain in the Osiris myth. Books dating from later periods contain the most terrible curses against Seth. Still this god is not purely and simply a horrifying figure. This is demonstrated by the fact that he was worshipped from ancient times in Ombos, in Upper Egypt—whilst Horus was the patron of the Delta—and by the circumstance that the pharaoh's named Seti were called after him. Nevertheless he is a demonic, inscrutable god. He often appears in the shape of an unknown animal which presumably belongs to the desert. Whereas Horus belongs in heaven, Seth's domain is the arid earth.

Finally attention should be paid to Anubis. He is often portrayed as a recumbent dog. This is presumably the wild dog between whom and the wolf and the jackal the Egyptian did not distinguish clearly. Probably this animal inspired the thought that it knew the road to the realm of the dead. So Anubis became the god of the dead. He is in charge of the embalming of the mummy, a function he first fulfilled for Osiris according to the myth. Closely related to him is Upuat, who is depicted as a black, standing wolf or jackal. His name means 'the opener of the ways'. He leads the way to victory, he leads the festive processions and he is also a god of the dead, who precedes the deceased along the path to the life hereafter.

F. *Thoth - Khonsu*

Thoth often appears in the shape of a baboon or an ibis. His hieroglyphic determinative is the ibis. When he appears in human form he can be recognised by his ibis-head. Presumably he belonged to the delta originally. In historical times the centre of his cult was Hermopolis magna, located halfway between Cairo and Koptos. The Greek name of this town, which was called *Ḥmnw* in Egyptian, indicates that the Greeks identified Thoth with Hermes. Like the latter he was a god of the dead and psychopompos.

Originally Thoth was a moon-god. On the one hand he is the moon itself, and on the other the lord of the moon-eye. In the latter quality he performs an important function in the myth of the moon-eye, which has already been mentioned: he searches for the lost eye, finds and returns it. He also exercises his salutary effect on the eye of Horus, which is seriously injured in the struggle with Seth. He heals it, restores it to fullness and health. In the fourth hour of the Am-Duat text on the tomb of Seti I, we see Thoth handing over this eye to Horus. This healthy eye, known as *wḏȝt*, is a special form of the divine eye, the token of life. The *wḏȝt*-eye symbolises the light that was born out of darkness, the life that emerges from death. Little wonder that it has become a popular, well-known symbol.

Because of his relationship with the moon, Thoth became 'the lord of time and the calculation of the years'. Among many peoples, and apparently those of Egypt as well, the lunar is older than the solar calendar. As regulator of time, his attribute is the palm branch, in which notches indicate the years of a man's life. On it Thoth notes the regnal years and the jubilees of the king on his coronation, or he writes these together with the name of the king on the sacred tree at Heliopolis. Thoth also keeps the annals. He records the years of men and on their birth determines their time of dying. Fate rests in his hands: "He announces the day of tomorrow and beholds what is to be".

Another of Thoth's functions is patron of writers. Libraries and archives are in his care. He is the lord of the books. He lives in 'the house of life' where wisdom is preserved. The writers offer him a libation from the bowl belonging to their writing material before commencing their work. He is highly praised by the members of this important caste in Egyptian society. "Thoth is a refuge in life and in death", as the expression has it. For it was Thoth who bestowed writing on man and, indeed, gave him his power of speech: "He is the discoverer of the words of the language." Hence he acts as 'persuader of justice'. He lays down the laws. In particular, the 'divine words' which regulate the cult derive from him. His word possesses magic power. He is 'great in magic'. As such he protects the physicians. It is characteristic of his mythic significance that Ma-a-t, cosmic order, and Seshat, goddess of writing, are mentioned as his consorts.

His true character appears most clearly in his relationship to the sun-god, to Horus and to Osiris. Thoth is one of the permanent crew of the sun-boat. His task is 'to protect the ship'. Indeed, his activities go even further. He sees to it that Re travels along a fixed route each day: "Thoth daily writes Ma-a-t for thee" is what the sun-hymn says. It was said above that Thoth healed the injured eye of Horus. Mention was also made of his functions in the Osiris myth: he acts as counsel in the legal proceedings which Seth institutes against Osiris and Horus and manages to win the case for the latter two. Hence it is Thoth who reconciles Horus and Seth and clears up the business about Osiris. This means that, as god of wisdom, he restores the equilibrium of the world that had been disturbed. Understandably enough then that the dead appeal to him, for when the dead are judged he records the outcome of weighing the heart against the feather which represents Ma-a-t. The deceased hopes that in doing so, Thoth will put in a good word for him.

In this connexion, mention might be made of another moon-god, known as Khonsu. His name is related to a verb which means 'to pass through'. A fitting denomination for a moon-god. He is depicted as a sort of mummy with two ruler's crooks in his hand, a lock of child's hair at his ear and the crescent moon on his head with in it the full moon. He is called 'the lord of time'. As such he is closely akin to Thoth. His principal temple was located in Thebes. Here he was regarded as the son of Amon and Mut. This goddess, whose name is written with the hieroglyph of a vulture which can also mean 'mother', is a sort of mother-goddess. A certain representation of Khonsu known as 'the counsellor' was held to be a healer. Popular belief ascribes the moon an influence on the body which can prove beneficial or malignant. The healing power of Khonsu is related in the legend about Bentresh, a daughter of the ruler of Bechten, the younger sister of an Egyptian queen. In order to cure her illness, Khonsu sent his double, Khonsu the counsellor, who succeeded in freeing the princess of the evil spirit which made her ill. The ruler of Bechen persuaded Khonsu the counsellor to remain. After staying there for more than three years the god succumbed to a longing for Egypt. He returned laden with gifts, which he presented to the great Khonsu.

G. *Ptah*

Ever since the first dynasty Ptah is represented as standing in an open chapel, bald of head and without the traditional beard which often ornamented gods and kings, and clad in a robe which makes him resemble a mummy, with a stand-up collar to which a tassel is attached. His hands, which project from his garment, hold a sceptre in the form of the hieroglyph $w3s$ = 'prosperity, fortune'. Later he has a beard and stands or sits in a closed chapel.[28]

Ptah is the lord of Memphis, the capital of the Old Kingdom. He was also worshipped in a number of other towns. In Memphis, Sekhmet was his wife and Nefertem his son. His standing epithet in this town was: "he who is south of the wall'. This designation is reminiscent of the 'white wall', which was built by Menes, the first king, to render the capital an impregnable fortress. One passage, indeed, calls Ptah 'he who is south of the white wall'. Evidently his temple was located on the southern side of the city. What could be the significance of this localisation? Is the South the side of life and the North the side of death? According to the Egyptian notion, the sun traverses the southern sky in day time and the northern, nocturnal sky at night, i.e. Duat, the underworld. It should be borne in mind here that Duat can mean both the realm of the dead and the nocturnal sky.

In any case Ptah has chthonic features: he is connected with the fertile soil. This is demonstrated in his relationship with the god Tatenen, whose name is said to mean: 'the risen land'. A. DE BUCK in his aforesaid study takes Tatenen to be a variant of the primordial hill which rose up from the waters of chaos. A text dealing with Ptah, which is discussed later, says of this god: "Tatenen... from whom have proceeded all things in the shape of food and viands, divine offers, all good things". In this quotation Tatenen is represented as the earth which yields its fruits. Tatenen is therefore the personification of the fertile soil which once emerged from the primeval Ocean and which yearly emerges from the inundating floods. Tatenen is depicted as a seated god with divine beard, wearing on his head two feathers on ram's horns and holding in his hand the symbol of rulership which resembles a flail. This portrayal manifestly shows that Ptah and Tatenen were originally separate gods and that they remained so despite their essential kinship. The pedestal on which Ptah stands together with Min also indicates his chthonic nature. The pedestal has a slanted front plane and is a symbol of the primordial hill, as will be explained in greater detail in the following chapter.

Ptah is characterised by a special sort of creative work in which he employs his hands. He is the divine artisan, the smith or sculptor who works with the chisel. So he shaped the gods, men, and animals. And in this capacity he is the patron of artisans and craftsmen.

It was presumably in this quality that he was called on to assist in a ceremony which served to restore the power of speech to the deceased. This ritual was the opening of the mouth. During the ritual, which was performed on the mummy after its embalmment, the priest pronounced the prescribed formulas while touching the mouth of the deceased with a peculiarly shaped metal object in order to open it. The formulas can be found in a book specially devoted to this ceremony.

Ptah owes his renown mainly to the text of Shabaka.[33] This king, who came from Ethiopia, had an ancient text engraved on stone in 720 B.C. to rescue it from oblivion. The tenor of this text is the glorification of Ptah by having diverse well-known gods act as the shape in which he appears. The real significance of the text lies in its presentation of an extremely interesting version of the creation myth, a Ptah theology which might be called a *logos* doctrine. It teaches, namely, that all things came into being because a thought entered the heart of Ptah, which his mouth voiced. Here the heart and the tongue are hypostatic properties which are personified in the gods Horus and Thoth. We read: "there arose in the heart, there arose on the tongue a thought... in which Horus is become, in which Thoth is become as Ptah". The text then goes on to argue that Ptah works as immanent *logos* in the cosmos and in culture, so that both the natural and ethical orders are based on it. "The heart is that which calls forth all knowledge; the tongue is that which repeats what has been thought by the heart". A truly profound doctrine. A unique example of theological reflection which, as we have seen, was for the rest lacking among the ancient Egyptians.

H. *Min*

Min is a characteristic, though secretive godhead, whose origins and being cannot easily be fathomed.[3] Since the earliest of times he appears in human form. On his head he wears a cap ornamented with two long feathers and a long ribbon that hangs down his back. Floating free above the raised right arm is the token of royal dignity which resembles a flail. The left arm is invisible. The body is shaped like that of a mummy and has a penis in erection. Min usually stands on a pedestal with sloping front plane. In front of him is an offertory urn decorated with flowers. Behind him we see sprouting plants or a cultic object with stylised plants or a remarkable miniature sanctuary.

Min was worshipped mainly in Achmin, the Greek Panopolis and in Koptos. In the last town his cult goes back to the prehistoric era. This was established by the discovery of three archaic statues of immense proportions on which highly interesting drawings occur, including the mysterious hieroglyphic sign which often was used to designate Min. The significance of this symbol has not yet been discovered. Its shapes on the aforesaid prehistoric statues could suggest it was a sort of fetish, a pole hung with flowers and shells and adorned with a flower, altogether a symbol of divine power and fertility.

At Koptos the Nile approaches most closely the Red Sea. Koptos was the terminus of a road leading to this sea. So Min became the protector of all who hazarded the dangers of this passage through the desert-like mountains: merchants, soldiers and labourers who worked in the quarries. This connexion with the region outside Egypt could support the hypothesis that Min is of foreign origin. There is good reason for such assumption, for the statue of Min has diverse traits which point to southerly regions, especially the land of Punt which is supposed to have been located on the Somali coast and was famous for its incense. Lack of reliable data prevent any definitive answer being given to the question whether Min as an immigrant from the South. In the historical era, Min was a typical Egyptian god. He is related to three principal gods, Horus, Isis and Amon, though does not hereby lose his identity. Perhaps it was from the older Horus that he took his martial gesture of the raised hand. Isis is held to be his mother or his wife. In Thebes he is identified with Amon. Min remains himself, however, which means he is a typically a-mythical figure whose essence has to be deduced from his attributes—and from the course of the splendid festival celebrated in his honour, which is dealt with in the following chapter.

In the first place attention must be paid to the said pedestal. In a drawing of it dating from the Old Kingdom, this pedestal has lines crossing at right angles, which characterise it as a mound of fertile earth. This fact alone demonstrates that Min is a god of fertility. This idea is confirmed by the tall plants growing behind his back. Botanists identify them as a type of lettuce that is very juicy, which was accounted a sign of fertility. During his festival Min is placed on a pedestal shaped like a flight of stairs. And then he is addressed in song: "Thou standest on the stairway of Ma-a-t". This stairway, which alternates with the pedestal with sloping front, is thus a symbol of Ma-a-t. Here it should be remembered that the conventional sign of Ma-a-t is the pedestal with sloping side which represents the primordial hill, the symbol of resurrection. Hence Min is the god who promotes fertile life. And in a paradoxical way. Reference to this is to be found in a feature of his statue which makes him repulsive to modern mind, namely the *phallus erectus* protruding from the mummified body. The Egyptians did not hesitate to use sexual images, since for them the divine creative power was manifested in sexuality. So too in the case of Min: this sexual symbol expresses his power of the *creatio ex nihilo*.

I. *Hathor*

In Egyptian Hathor's name is *Ḥt Ḥr* = 'the house of Horus' or 'my house is the sky'. In the first interpretation 'house' is supposed to be a figure of speech for womb. Hence Hathor is the mother of Horus. Howsoever this may be, she has been linked up with the sky since the pyramid texts. The form in which she appears, that of a cow, manifests her being better than this etymological explanation. In order to comprehend the significance of this divine representation, it should be borne in mind that the ancient Egyptian set great store by his cattle, not only because of the economic value they represented, the prestige ensuing from their possession and his emotional attachment to his herd, but especially because cattle were a manifestation of divine life. It is from this viewpoint that the worship of the sacred bulls should be judged. The cow is the mother-animal par excellence. Hence the divine mother is conceived of as a cow. The primeval water from which the sun-god was born is called *Mḥjt wrt* and is represented as a cow. Likewise Nut, goddess of the sky, often appears as a cow standing above the earth. Little wonder then that Hathor, who is likewise a typical mother-goddess, also appears as a cow.

However, she is not the domesticated cow, but the wild cow that dwells in the marshy regions. Vignettes from the Book of the Dead show how she emerges from a clump of papyrus. Because of the association with this habitat, the gathering of papyrus was a ceremony held in her honour. As human figure Hathor has horns with a sun-disk on her head. Hathor as cow symbolises procreative life. Hence it is not surprising that Hathor was associated with Min from times immemorial. On a relief from the pre-dynastic period the typical Hathor head appears flanked by the enigmatical emblem of Min.

Hathor is also connected with the trees. She manifests herself as a tree-goddess who proffers a beverage and refreshment to the deceased. Indeed she is a goddess of the dead. As such she is called: 'the mistress of the necropolis'. A number of interesting texts on sarcophagi relate what was expected of her by the deceased: he hopes to become writer of Hathor, to be permitted to button her breast pendant, to have her assistance in ascending to heaven. She is also one of the party on the sun-boat of Re and forms a pair with Ma-a-t. Her relationship with the sun-god is also manifested by her function as sun-eye. Then she reveals her martial aspect: for according to a well-known myth she set out to destroy the people who revolted against Re.

Still, she has also milder features. As mother-goddess she protects love and grants the blessing of children. She determines fate at childbirth. She must be honoured in song and dance, for she is the patroness of extatic, festive joy ensuing from inebriety. Throughout entire Egypt she was worshipped. In later days in Denderah especially. There she was the wife of Horus of Edfu, whom she visited annually on a journey replete with colourful ceremonial, when she evidently celebrated a divine marriage with him. In the festival rites of the Ptolemaic temples of Denderah, Edfu, Philae and Esna, she plays a dominating role.

J. *Bastet, Sekhmet, Neith, Seshat*

The scope of this concise article does not admit of a treatment of the *dei minores*. Besides this is superfluous, for few new viewpoints would emerge as regards the Egyptian conception of the gods. An exception must be made for the goddesses named in the title of this section, since they are characteristic personalities.[1]

Bastet belongs to Bubastis in the Delta. She is a very ancient goddess. It is difficult to define her original nature, because early on she was linked up with two other goddesses, Tefnet and Sekhmet, both conceived of as lionesses. Her divine animal is the cat. Often she is represented with a cat's head. Her nature is that of a cat. On the one hand she is friendly and cheerful. Exciting festivals were celebrated in her honour to the accompaniment of dance and the music of the flute and sistrum. Then again she can prove savage and wrathful. Her character is elucidated to some extent by the legend about Tefnet as sun-eye. Its motif is that, because of a dispute with Re, the sun-eye departs for Nubia, whence it is induced to return by the persuasive art of Thoth. In this story Tefnet is alternately a raging and a mildly inclined cat.

Sekhmet is portrayed as a female figure with a lion's head. At Memphis, the centre of her cult, she is the wife of Ptah. Her name signifies: 'the powerful'. She is a warlike goddess. She combats the enemies of Re and also of the king, among whose opponents she sows terror. In her warlike capacity she is connected with the uraeus of the royal diadem. She is called 'great in magic'. Magic medical knowledge was ascribed to her priests. That the annual epidemics were attributed to her is only ostensibly a contradiction, for she was a demonic goddess who could bless and heal, but also corrupt.[4]

Neith is the patroness of Sais in the Delta. Her headdress is the red crown, the headdress worn by the king as monarch of lower Egypt. Originally Neith was a goddess of war. This appears from her emblem: a pair of crossed arrows, often accompanied by a shield. She aims her arrows at the powers of evil. Hence magic and the art of healing are under her protection. She also cares for the dead. Furthermore she is the patroness of the art of weaving. Since this is a meaningful art, she was accounted a wise goddess. The Greeks identified her with Athene. According to PLUTARCH, her statue at Sais bore the following inscription: "I am all that was, and is, and shall be, and no mortal has lifted my veil."[4]

Seshat is the goddess of the arts of writing and arithmetic. Her pseudonyms are: 'she who stands at the head of the house of life (the library)', 'she who first wrote'. For the ancient Egyptians, writing was a divine art. Seshat practised this art together with Thoth, whose sister or daughter she is. She is present at the recording of the booty; she stretches the measuring line at the foundation of new buildings; she records the annals. The last-mentioned activity has little in common with historiography in the modern sense of this conception. Further, Seshat may be compared with the Moira. She is part of the group of gods and goddesses who know the cosmic order and determine fate. Like these gods, she possesses wisdom.[4]

IV. WORSHIP

There are three important themes to each religion, the concept of god, the conception of man and worship. This also applies to the ancient Egyptian religion. The last chapter was devoted to a description and phenomenological explanation of the Egyptian concept of god in its aspect of multiplicity of form. In the following chapter the conception of man is discussed. Here we direct the reader's attention to the nature of worship, which occupied such a preponderant place in ancient Egypt. If the last-mentioned concept is taken in a broad sense, it comprises three types of sacred acts: (1) the cult, i.e. the worship of the deity; (2) the religious conduct of life; (3) the myth as the distillation of reflection on the meaning of the world and culture. To these three subjects this section is devoted.

A. Cult

Since the Egyptian notion of faith was expressed to a large degree in the cult, there is abundance of material at the disposal of one who undertakes the treatment of this theme. Needless to say, the writer must limit himself to the main features. As such, the following subjects warrant consideration: the sanctuary, sacred persons, the worship of the gods in both daily service and the festivals, and the funerary cult.

a) The sanctuary

The sanctuary in itself could give rise to lengthy commentaries. However interesting in itself, information of an archeological and architectonic nature must be set aside. The point at issue is the religio-historical significance of the sanctuary. This means in practice a scrutiny of the main types of sanctuary.

The Egyptian word for temple is *ḥt nṯr* = 'the house of the godhead'. This term tells us that the original temple was a primitive construction

which differed from the huts of the people only in its location on a
sacral, fenced-off site or in a sacred wood, and its ornamentation with
divine emblems. In later times, miniature, highly stylised forms of
such archaic sanctuaries occurred as the attributes of certain gods, for
example Min. In this category of ancient temples, the *itr.tj* possess
special significance.[12]

These are the two state sanctuaries, the temples of Upper and
Lower Egypt. Both were built of reeds and rushes in a characteristic
form: the little temple of northern Egypt is kept in shape by four
corner poles which project above the vaulted roof; the sanctuary of
southern Egypt has a wooden palissade and two masts in front of the
entrance and a projecting edge to the front of the roof. In prehistoric
times the *itr.tj* were probably both royal palace and chapel. Apparently in the *itr.tj* were stored the emblems of the divine predecessors, 'the souls of Nekhen' (the old capital of Upper Egypt) and
'the souls of Pe' (the former capital of Lower Egypt). The gods of
Southern and Northern Egypt were likewise connected with the *itr.tj*.
Furthermore these chapels had an important function in the royal *śd*
festival. *Itr.tj* is a dualis. The two temples represent the dualism
typical of Egypt. This is also depicted by the red crown of Northern
Egypt and the white crown of Southern Egypt, which the pharaoh
wears alternately or simultaneously, and by the snake-goddess Wadjet
and the vulture-goddess Nekhbet, the goddesses of the Delta and of
the Nile Valley respectively, who are likewise associated with the
itr.tj. This dualism presumably owes its origin to the fact that there
were two kingdoms in prehistoric times, fused into one by Menes or
Narmer. And it always retained its administrative function. Its ideological significance, however, is that it expresses the conception that
life and death form a duality which fundamentally is a unity.[34]

The temples of the sun-god were of a special shape, at least in
ancient times. The structure of these sanctuaries gives expression to
the idea of the creation myth. In the Old Kingdom, Heliopolis was
the centre of the sun-worship. There are indications that in this town
there were a mound and a temple pond beside the sun temple, which
were imitations of the primordial hill and the primeval water respectively. This can be inferred from the statement about the visit of
the Ethiopian king Pianchi to Heliopolis. In it is said: "His Majesty
went to the army camp, which was on the west side of... (an unde-
finable location). Completed was his purification. He cleansed himself
in the *ḳbḥ* pond and his face was washed in the stream of Nun, in

which Re washes his face. He proceeded to the High Sand in Heliopolis and offered a large hecatomb on the High Sand in Heliopolis to
Re when he rose, consisting of cows etc...". An interesting communication. It informs us there was a temple pond in Heliopolis called
Nun, i.e. an imitation of the primeval water. Further there was the
'High Sand', which was an imitation of the primordial hill. Pianchi
performed a number of rites, including that of purification and the
ascent of the High Sand, following the example of Re. And moreover
at sunrise, for these rites were meant to be a repetition of the mythical
primeval events.

The sun-temple at Heliopolis has not been preserved. Fortunately
the excavations at Abu Gurab, on the western bank of the Nile to the
N.W. of Memphis, enable us to form a picture of a sun sanctuary.[24]
This temple was founded by Niuserre, a king of the fifth dynasty, who
energetically patronised the sun worship. This building has a structure
which differs vastly from the later, traditional Egyptian temple. An
impressive gatehouse gives on to an ascending path which leads to the
actual sanctuary. The latter consists of an open courtyard in which is
a short, stunted obelisk placed on a truncated, quadrilateral pedestal.
As appears shortly, the obelisk is a typical solar symbol. The plateau
on which the temple stands is elevated 16 metres above its surroundings. The pedestal of the obelisk is 20 metres high and the obelisk
itself 36 metres. From the vestibule of the temple, a narrow dark
passage runs along the encircling wall to the pedestal of the obelisk.
He who completes this journey suddenly finds himself in the blinding
sunlight, a contrast effect which the architect used to accentuate the
exceptional character of the cult of the sun-god. Consequently the
atmosphere in this temple is vastly different from that in the temples
of the later centuries, which expressed the mysterious essence of the
godhead in their dim or completely darkened chambers. The passages
of this sanctuary, for example those leading to the offer chambers, are
decorated with cheerful scenes from everyday life. They breathe the
spirit of religious joy with which many sun-hymns are permeated.
Alongside of this temple, the remains were found of a sun-boat which
represents one of the two vessels used by the sun-god in his journey
across the diurnal sky and through the underworld.[24]

The traditional Egyptian temple is a walled construction with
colonnaded galeries and one or more forecourts. In the course of the
centuries, many pharaohs had building done on the imposing complexes such as those of Luxor and Karnak. In particular the rather

well-preserved Ptolemaic temples, at Edfu and Denderah especially, clearly reveal what the function of these sanctuaries was. The Egyptian temple cannot be compared with a Greek temple or a Christian church, where the believers congregate. It is the house of the godhead, or rather the reproduction of his cosmic dwelling, and this can be traced in both the ornamentation and in the plan of the construction. With regard to the latter, it is striking that most of the temples have the appearance of a stairway, composed of a succession of building units ascending from front to back. This indicates they represent the primordial hill—the symbol of divine resurrection—conventionalised as a stairway.[21] The temple was not accessible to the ordinary man. The worship was performed by the pharaoh, assisted by a restricted number of priests and court officers. When the temple was closed, no one knew what was happening inside; in other words the cult, of which the acts were nevertheless known, was celebrated as a mystery. The temple's plan of construction added to this element of mystery. The further one was removed from the entrance, the dimmer the light, until one approached the abaton where no profane foot was permitted to tread and where the idol or the sacred ship of the godhead stood, swathed in the darkness of the mysterium tremendum.

b. Sacred persons

The paramount sacred person was the pharaoh.[12,15] He was looked upon as the son of the gods. The last of his five titles calls him outright the son of Re. The other four titles, in the case of each pharaoh furnished with laudatory appendages in poetic style and larded with mythological allusions, likewise elevate him above the level of the ordinary mortal. For they are: Horus (god of the sky), the two rulers (the snake-goddess and the vulture-goddess, patronesses of the two parts of Egypt), the golden Horus (gold is the flesh of the gods according to the texts), the king of Upper and Lower Egypt.

One of the miraculous tales which as Papyrus Westcar relates was told at the court of the King Cheops (4th dynasty), contains the legendary dramatisation of the idea that the pharaoh is the physical son of the sun-god, at least as far as three monarchs of the 5th dynasty are concerned, namely, Userref, Sahure and Keku. According to this story Reddedet, wife of the priest of Re, conceived three children by the sun-god. At their birth she received divine assistance; for Isis and Nephthys, Meshkent and Heket (two goddesses of birth) went to her house in the guise of music girls, accompanied by Khnum. They expedited the delivery. Isis gave each child her name and explained it by a salutation which contained an allusion. Meskhent each time pronounced: "a king who shall assume kingship in this entire country". They were true children of the gods, described as follows: "a child of one ell, which already had sturdy limbs; the covering of his body was of gold and his head cloth of genuine lapis lazuli".

This ideology of the kings has found its classical formulation in the texts and reliefs in the temple of queen Hatshepsut at Deir el Bahri, which describe the sacral marriage between the queen and Amon-Re. In an extremely chaste manner is narrated and depicted how the god Amon approaches the queen and unites with her in love. We see how the god and the queen are seated opposite each other on a state-bank with Neith and Selkit supporting their feet. The god is handing the queen the emblems of life and prosperity. The text gives the following poetic explanation: "Utterance of Amon-Re, lord of Thebes, who presides over Karnak. He made his form like the majesty of this husband, the King Okheparkere (Thutmosis I). He found her as she slept in the beauty of the palace. She waked at the fragrance of the god, which she smelled in the presence of his majesty. He went to her immediately, *coivit cum ea*, he imposed his desire upon her, he caused that she should see him in his form as a god. When he came before her, she rejoiced at the sight of his beauty, his love passed into her limbs, which the fragrance of the god flooded; all his odours were from Punt. Utterance by the king's-wife and king's-mother Ahmose, in the presence of the majesty of this august god, Amon, Lord of Thebes: 'How great is thy form! It is splendid to see thy front; thou hast united my majesty with thy favours; thy dew is in all my limbs'".[6] Thereafter the god Khnum shapes the royal child together with its *k3*, which is animated by Heket. Then Khnum and Heket apparently conduct the queen to the lying-in room, for now the designs show the course of the delivery. The queen is seated on a throne placed on a royal bench. Isis and Nephthys support her arms. The newly-born baby—in this event Hatshepsut—is shown to the father who takes it in his arms and blesses it. Divine beings attend to bestow vitality on the newly-born. Hathor presents the child to Amon, who takes it in his arms and blesses it. The newly-born is put to the breast and presented to the gods of Northern and Southern Egypt. Since Hatshepsut probably had to overwin opposition to her ascent as a woman to the throne, some Egyptologists have supposed that the myth of her divine parentage was intended to guarantee the legitimacy of her royal office.

Nevertheless the presentation of the divine parentage of Hatshepsut was in no way an exclusively political and constitutional fiction. In the temple at Luxor, for example, is preserved a duplicate of it pertaining to Amenhotep III, whose ascent to the throne gave rise to no difficulties as far as we know. Later kings similarly claimed to be the offspring of Re. In the Ptolemaic temples are several reproductions of this divine birth. And when Alexander the Great had himself recognised as son of the gods by the oracle of Amon of the Siwa oasis, he acted in perfect accordance with an aged Egyptian tradition which went back to at least the fifth dynasty.[25]

To avoid misunderstanding, it is perhaps expedient to define in greater detail the sacral dignity of the pharaoh. Although he was descended from the sun-god, this did not make him the equal of the gods. The pharaoh is always designated 'the good god' and never 'the great god', the predicate of the true gods. It was from his divine parentage that the pharaoh derived his great power, which must have been unlimited especially in the Old Kingdom. He dominates to such an extent in the texts and reliefs of martial scenes and religious ceremonies that he seems to be the only one to take action, while courtiers, priests and soldiers simply attend as supernumeraries. There is no sign at all of the ordinary people. The real state of affairs was certainly otherwise, especially in later centuries: skilled counsellors, ambitious court officials and powerful nobles profoundly influenced government policy, especially when the pharaohs were weak. Some pharaohs were not of royal blood, but were self-appointed rulers. Others, despite their sacral dignity, proved to be realistic politicians and ambitious strategists.

Nonetheless they were and remained sacral monarchs. That meant that they not only possessed great powers, but also had to bear a heavy responsibility. Often they are represented as despots who arbitrarily manipulated with the life and happiness of their subjects. The pyramid builders especially have called down on themselves this judgment. Nothing could be less true. From the official instructions handed over to high dignitaries on their assumption of office, we know that the Egyptians required high standards of justice, love of truth and humanity of all government officials. The same obtained doubly for the pharaoh. As son of Re he was the stadtholder of the godhead on earth and, as such, responsible for the welfare of his people, and not merely in the sense that by wise policy he had to maintain order in his kingdom and increase material welfare, but also in the sense that, as divine offspring, he was expected to propitiate the cosmic powers. It is highly dubious if Egypt ever knew the custom of regicide, that is the custom followed in some parts of Africa of violently removing kings who were too weak or ignorant to take care of their people, so that illness, famine or other catastrophes overcame them. It is certain, however, that the sacral dignity of the pharaohs had to be renewed periodically, as will appear in the treatment of the festivals. It is also an established fact that the principal duty of the pharaoh was to maintain Ma-a-t in his kingdom. Various pronouncements make mention of this responsibility. Amenemhet I, for example, declared the boundaries of the shires to be as inalterably fixed 'as the heavens'. He performed this work of organisation 'because he set such store by Ma-a-t". Amenophis III was called on 'to make Egypt flourish, as in primeval times, by means of the plans of Ma-a-t'. Ramses IV declared: "I have brought order (ma-a-t) into this land which did not exist (previously)". These quotations demonstrate the pharaohs' appreciation of the responsibility ensuing from their sacral dignity. Hence it is not mere flattery, but also admiration and gratitude, which moved the courtiers to say to the pharaos: "Thou art Re in physical guise, Khepri in his true shape, thou art the living example of thy father Atum in Heliopolis".[1]

For many years now, the sacral king of the ancient peoples has attracted the full attention of students of the history of religions. Remarkably enough, they have overlooked the significance of the queen. This is exceptionally great, at least as far as Egypt is concerned, Diverse circumstances contributed to making the queen an influential personnage. In the first place the good position of the wife in general, as appears from the loving attitude of the husbands to their wives manifested in the texts and reproductions of deceased couples. Accordingly the youth were taught respect for their mothers. Furthermore Egyptian history has produced a number of queens who shared the governmental cares of their husbands or sons in a tactful and active way and were able to offer wise counsel. From no segment of ancient history are we so well acquainted with the royal consort as from ancient Egypt. Ahmose, founder of the 18th dynasty, for example, was supported in his work by three outstanding women: his grandmother, his mother and his wife. Though not of royal blood, Teje, wife of Amenophis III was an energetic woman who exercised great influence on the affairs of state, even after the demise of her husband, during the reign of Amenophis IV who neglected foreign policy for the sake of his reformation campaign. The image of his

charming wife, Nefretete, is clearly imprinted on the minds of all who
have seen her magnificent bust. The texts suggest that the queen had
a limited fortune of her own and a staff of servants which usually
included a few favourites. From the human and social viewpoint
therefore the queen was a highly respected person. Little wonder that
Hatshepsut, who was apparently not lacking in energy and talent,
succeeded in ascending to the throne.

Ideologically, the significance of the queen is founded on her
function as mother of the sacral monarch. In this respect she is even
more indispensable than the pharaoh himself. In the myth of the
divine parentage of the pharaoh, his earthly father plays no part
whatsoever, and the divine father is a supermundane, intangible figure.
The queen dominates the stage in this event. She is the medium
through which her son is injected with his divine nature. She provides
the legitimacy of his claim to the throne. That is why general Harem-
heb, who founded the 19th dynasty after a period of disturbance,
married a princess of royal blood to guarantee royal power for his
successor. These data are testimonials of the sacral dignity of the
queen. Her titles are in accordance with this. In the New Kingdom
she is called: 'the consort of the god, the mother of the god, the great
wife of the king, the mistress of both countries'. Hence it is not surprising that some pharaohs mention their mother, but not their father,
in their titles. The prototypes of the queen were held to be Mut and
Tefnet, two goddesses who played in the world of gods the role of
queen, albeit a weaker one.

The cultic function of the queen was in harmony with her sacral
role. In the period from the 18th to the 20th dynasties she bore the
title: 'consort of the god' (i.e. Amon-Re). In this quality one of her
duties was to play the sistrum, for she often accompanied the king
during the celebration of the daily service, at least in theory. In any
case she attended the big festivals, for example when the $ḏd$ pillar was
erected—a ceremony discussed below—and when the king celebrated
the $ḥb$ $śd$, a ritual dealt with presently. A striking fact is that she is the
only woman in the procession at the festival of the procession ($pr.t$)
of Min. She is even the only one, in addition to the king, to perform
an important ritual: at a certain moment she makes a ceremonial
circumambulation of the king while reciting seven times appropriate
formulas. This ritual action marks her influential position and sacral
function.[3]

The sacral function of the pharaoh is most clearly manifested during the festivals he celebrates. Apart from the triumphal festivals, there were three important royal festivals: the ascent of the throne, the coronation and the *šd* festival. A more detailed description of these festivals is given below. At present we direct the reader's attention to an aspect of the pharaoh's sacral function which is made evident especially during the festivals, but which is often, remarkable enough, ignored. The pharaoh performed all the cultic ceremonies in his capacity as high priest. Properly speaking, his sacral dignity was based on his priestly office. As divine son he formed the link between the realm of the gods and the world of man. He was the intermediary, the true priest. As such in particular he participated in the festivals of the gods. And in theory it was he who made all the offers dedicated in ancient Egypt, as stated in the stereotype opening words of the offer incantations.

In practice the king was usually replaced by a priest. Since purity was the main requisite for participation in the cult, the priests who were especially required to fulfill this condition can definitely be accounted sacral persons.[4] For the rest the priestly office was not sharply segregated from profane duties, so that some officials could combine it with a governmental post, as appears from their titles. Further it is difficult to form a clear picture of the degrees and organisation of the body of priests. In addition to the lay priests, divided into groups, who alternately had service, there were at least three classes of professional priests: the *w'b* ('the pure'), the *ḫrj ḥb* (the priest who reads aloud the holy texts) and the *ḥm nṯr* ('the servant of the godhead). Women also held priestly office. In some cases the priestly office was hereditary. This fact suggests that originally the priestly duties were performed by the hereditary heads of a clan or shire, so that the cultic function was passed on from father to son at the same time as the rulership over a principality. Gradually a certain class of priests was evolved, the members of which were united in colleges. Synods of priests were even held in the Ptolemaic era. At the head of the priests attached to an important temple such as that of Amon-Re at Thebes, there was a high priest. These priests undoubtedly possessed not only high authority and great influence, but also a comprehensive cultic knowledge and a profound insight into the meaning of religious symbols. Nevertheless they must not be mistaken for scholars and speculative theologians. Scholarship and theology in the modern sense were not known in ancient Egypt. Learning was an admixture of certain techniques based on acute and accurate observation and on magic practices. This is in no way meant as a derogation of magic, of which the religious significance is discussed in a following section. The main thing in this connexion is to note that in ancient Egypt there did not prevail that intellectual climate of reflection in which a scientific theology can develop. The priests were wise men who disposed of a certain amount of sacral and profane knowledge, but they were neither scholars nor holders of esoteric knowledge, as is averred by some.[4]

c. Sacred objects

This category comprises, in the first place, the elements of the cultic equipment such as altars, incense burners, libatory vessels and all other things used in the worship of the gods. As sacred objects may also be counted the crowns and sceptres of the pharaoh and the priestly *regalia*. They possessed a symbolic meaning and were sometimes considered divine beings, which is sufficiently witnessed by the fact that there are hymns dedicated to the royal crowns.

The statues of the gods and the divine ships merit special attention. The magnificent statues of the gods which once adorned the temples have been lost. Fortunately a large number of smaller statues have been preserved which, supplemented with the portrayals of the gods on temple walls and in papyri, give us some idea of how the Egyptian pictured his gods. One striking feature of them catches the eye, which was noted above in chapter II: many divine figures have an animal head. This semi-theriomorphic representation of a god is the expression of the concept that the divine can be portrayed by an animal, for certain animals are sacred because of their mysterious nature. The last remark also throws light on the religious import of the statue of the god as such: in so far as it indicates the essential and inscrutable being of the godhead it depicts, it has a symbolic function.

This rule is applicable in a special sense to the sacred boats, which play a prominent role in the cult of certain gods, such as Osiris and Amon. Osiris had a boat called *nšm.t*. The sacred vessel of Amon, which the reliefs show with a ramshead decoration at the prow and stern, bears the name *wsr ḥ3t* ('strong, as regards the front, the prow'). An important function was also fulfilled by the boat in the funerary cult, because the deceased was transported to his last resting place in one. That the sacred boats possessed an independent religious significance is adequately manifested by the fact that they were used not only to transport gods and the dead across the Nile, but, as evidenced by

can be made by man. Thereafter the idol was clad and anointed. At the end of the day the priest once more solemnly closed the naos.[34]

A second interesting cultic text pertains to the hour service in the cult of Osiris.[17] These rites were celebrated every hour, both during the day-time and at night, a proof of how strong a grip the worship of Osiris had on the minds of the people. In this text is continuously heard the lamentation about the terrible fate of Osiris, who was defeated by Seth. Two litanies are devoted to this theme which were recited in the Osiris service by women who represented Isis and Nephthys. According to the myth, the two sisters knelt by the corpse of Osiris to voice their lamentations. This dirge not only expressed the acute sorrow of both goddesses, but also possessed adjuratory power and awakened Osiris. The same effect was expected of the aforesaid litanies. The remarkable thing is that in the litanies the tone of dismay and sorrow is so real that one might easily imagine one hears the sorrowing wails of a woman who has just lost her husband. Thus speaks the mourning woman Isis: "My heart is distressed for thee; I invoke thee, so that my voice will penetrate to the high heaven; my heart is hot; humidity is in my eyes". There is indeed a close connexion between the funerary cult and the worship of Osiris: in later times every deceased was called Osiris and at his funeral two women mourned. The exorcising power of the litanies is expressed in the words: "Raise, thou hast risen from the dead; thou must not die, thy *k3* will live".

The last remark gives occasion to discuss the magic tenor of many rites. This article does not permit of a digression on the role played by magic in ancient Egypt, nor of an investigation into the complicated question of the essence of magic. Suffice it to note that in an ancient religion like that of ancient Egypt, magic and religion were inextricably fused. Moreover cultic magic is incontrovertably the purest form of this remarkable phenomenon. Setting aside all sorts of dubious forms of magic, attention should be concentrated on this fact. Now there can be no doubt that the Egyptian expected certain cultic acts to have a magic effect. Properly considered, indeed, the rite is nothing but the dramatisation of a mythic truth. From the solemn word which accompanied the rite emanated a creative power and magic effect, for the word and deed realised the divine truth, to the salvation of the individual and the community. It is not surprising then that the cult was of a dramatic character. Nevertheless E. DRIOTON[18] and TH. H. GASTER go too far when they argue that dramatic texts existed in ancient Egypt. This is unlikely, since Egyptian literature has produced no drama. All that were known were rituals with a dramatic tenor. Linked up with the aforesaid characteristics of the cult is the fact that this often contains an element of mystery. Evidently the ancient Egyptians realised that the central religious truth is an *arcanum*. They interpreted this conception in various ways in the construction of the temple and in the worship. As we have seen, the temple was not the gathering place of the believers, but the dwelling of the godhead, which could only be entered by those selected for this purpose. Repeatedly the texts mention cultic *arcana* to which living or dead are initiated. Hence the warning: "Do not reveal what you have seen in the mysteries of the temples," and someone declares: "I am therein initiated (i.e. certain cultic ceremonies)...but I do not tell it to anybody." The reliefs of the festival procession of Min manifestly omit the central ritual, namely the raising of Min on his stairway. Apparently because it was a mystery.[3]

It is in the light of these considerations that the three acts must be viewed which, everywhere in the world, constitute the service of worship, namely the prayer, the offer and the sacrament. There is no lack of texts of prayers and of offer formulas, of representations of offers. By prayer and offering the Egyptian paid homage to the gods. The offering consisted of presenting all sorts of gifts or libations. Burnt offerings also occurred. These rituals also possessed magic import, as is witnessed by the fact that the same effect as that from the actual offering was expected from the portrayal of the offer and the recitation of the offertory spell performed on behalf of the dead. A clear example of a sacrament is found in the text at Denderah about the celebration of the Osiric festival in the month of Khoiak, in which instructions are given for the making of two images from a dough of sand and corn, which represent the broken and restored body of Osiris. These images possessed sacramental significance.

The Egyptians devoted as much care to the cult of the dead as to the worship of the gods. It is certainly no mere coincidence that the majority of the rudiments of the grandiose civilisation which once flourished in the Nile Valley pertain to the funerary cult: the pyramids, the graves of the nobles, numerous temples, the mummies, many papyri, the utensils placed in the graves for the use of the deceased, etc. The motive for this extensive cult of the dead was the conviction that man continues to exist after death and that his blessedness in the hereafter depends on the conservation of his body in the form of a mummy, on the possession of diverse utensils placed with him in his grave and on a regular mortuary cult maintained by a body of priests appointed to this end. In this light should also be viewed the plan of construction and the ornamentation of the graves. The construction of the grave, specifically the significance of the pyramid, was discussed in another context. With respect to the ornamentation of the grave, there was a reason for illustrating the passages of the royal graves to the west of Thebes, for example, with the texts and representations of the book *Am Duat* which describe the journey of the sun-god through the underworld. This ornamentation expresses the hope that the pharaoh might participate in the sun-god's power of resurrection. As for the burial ritual, this likewise was performed to guarantee the deceased a life hereafter. After the embalmment, for example, there took place the ritual of opening the mouth, by which the deceased had his mouth restored to him. The funeral procession included official female mourners who lamented the deceased and wished him a blessed fate in the hereafter. As aforesaid, symbolic significance was attached to the ship on which the sarcophagus was carried to the necropolis: on the other side of the Nile the ship was placed on a sledge and drawn to the grave. Here the boat has no practical function, only a religious significance. The funeral was followed by the regular mortuary cult. To ensure the continuance of the mortuary offerings, eminent Egyptians had created a foundation to meet the costs involved. The ten contracts concluded by the local prince Hepzefi of Siut of the Middle Kingdom with the priests of the necropolis to maintain his mortuary cult are famous.[4]

e. Festivals

The festivals constituted the highlights of cultic life and therefore merit a separate treatment. There is all the more reason for this, because since time immemorial the Egyptians celebrated characteristic festivals, as is witnessed by the stone of Palermo which contains the annals of the earliest dynasties, and because in later times the number of festival days took up almost half of the year, according to the information in the festival calendar of Medinet Habu.

Nothing is known of a great many festivals except their names, and so no picture can be formed of their celebration. The significance of certain categories of festivals can be understood without any difficulty. These are the festivals connected with the rising of the Nile and the seasonal work in the fields, or the ones which celebrated certain events

in the calendars. It is understandable that the beginning of the Nile
flood was celebrated with a festival. The agrarian background of certain festivals of the gods is clearly manifest: they are festivals of sowing
or reaping. Special attention was paid to the last day of the year. And
New Year's Day was likewise a special occasion. Nor it it surprising
that since ages long past lunar festivals were celebrated, especially
when there was a new moon. More recent studies by M. Alliot,
L. Christophe, H. W. Fairman and S. Sauneron have made us
better acquainted with the festivals celebrated in the Ptolemaic age
at Denderah Edfu, Esna and Philae. These festivals are partially of
ancient origin and partially new and of local significance. Since the
relevant texts are more communicative than the older documents, they
provide a more lucid picture of the solemnities than the older sources.
A survey of this material, leaving aside the duller data, results conveniently in a division into three categories: (a) festivals of the gods;
(b) festivals of the king; (c) festivals of the dead. Often these three
types cannot easily be segregated in practice, though they can be
clearly distinguished ideologically.

Obviously the principal gods, such as Amon-Re, Osiris, Sokaris,
Horus, Hathor and Min, were venerated by magnificent festivals. It
is equally obvious that the scope of this article precludes a description
of all of them. A few examples will have to suffice. In the second
month of the season of inundation the festival of Opet was celebrated
in honour of Amon-Re, and for it the god came from Karnak to the
temple at Luxor. The god's passage over the Nile in his divine boat
was a spectacular pageant which the people joyfully watched from the
banks of the river. The texts mention several Osiris festivals, which
were possibly celebrated according to local tradition. One of renown
was the festival at Abydos, of which an account has been recorded by
Ichernofret, a courtier of Sesostris III. According to this concise
communication, the course of these 'mysteries' was as follows: Osiris
held his 'great exodus', his manifestation, with his divine boat; he was
slain by his enemies at Nedit and buried in Peker; the enemies of
Osiris were defeated and Osiris, resurrected, returned in triumph in
Abydos.[30] Min of Koptos likewise celebrated several festivals. A
famous portrayal of his 'exodus', his appearance, is in the forecourt of
the temple at Medinet Habu. This festivals has three essential phases:
(1) a harvest ritual; (2) the renewal of the pharaoh's dignity; (3) the
elevation of Min on his stairway as the manifestation of his 'birth'.[31]
In later times Hathor was the principal of a number of magnificent

festivals held, *inter alia*, on the occasion of her visit to Horus of Edfu. During this journey the goddess visited several sanctuaries. Horus went forth to meet her, and the two apparently consumated their divine marriage at Edfu.

Since the king possessed sacral dignity, he naturally formed the leading personality at a number of festivals. Firstly he celebrated triumphal festivals. Some of these dated from ages long past, such as the festival designated 'the destruction of the cave-dwellers.' In addition he celebrated the triumphs of a succesful military campaign, as is known of Thutmosis III. These festivals were not purely military occasions, but had also a religious tenor, since the pharaoh upheld the divine order in the fight with his enemies. Secondly he was in charge of the festive foundation and dedication of temples. These two ceremonies had to be performed according to a prescribed, complicated ritual. The true festivals of the kings are three in number: the ascension to the throne, the coronation and the *śd*-festival.[12, 34] The ascension to the throne took place on the morrow after the day on which the old king had died. This moment was not chosen simply because it was dynastically expedient; it was of mythical significance, because the king had to reenact the ascension to the throne of Re, the first king. The coronation took place on a date of mythical import, a day which could be accounted a New Year's Day, for example 1 Tybi which was the first day of the first month of the season of emerging vegetation. The coronation marked the beginning of a new period: the new pharaoh restored Ma-a-t and brought prosperity. The coronation ceremony is generally assumed to have consisted of three rituals, namely (1) the 'appearance' of the king before the people, wearing alternately the red and the white crowns; (2) the 'union of the two countries', a ceremony performed by two priests representing Horus and Seth or Thoth, which recalled the historical deed of Menes or Narmer and symbolised the idea that ultimately life and death must be reconciled; (3) the circumambulation of the wall (of Memphis), a re-enactment of the ritual instituted by Menes, by which he took possession of the capital and at the same time renewed life by means of a magical circuit. Apparently there were variants of this basic pattern. From a papyrus from the Ramesseum is known the rambling ceremonial by which Sesostris I assumed kingship, a sacral play containing at least 17 easily distinguishable acts.[33] A strange ritual was enacted during the *śd*-festival. This festival has wrongly been classified as a regnal jubilee that is supposed to have been celebrated after 30 years' rule. Some have incorrectly presumed that it originated in a ritual regicide. Since the earliest of times, a great number of pharaohs celebrated the *śd* festival, some even several times. Reliefs and more detailed texts have provided considerable knowledge about the *śd* festivals of Niusserre (5th dynasty), Amenophis III (18th dynasty) and Osorkon II (22th dynasty). It appears from these sources that this festival had two sets of rites, one for Upper and one for Lower Egypt, that a climax was formed by the draping of the archaic *śd* robe about the king and that an important act was performed by the king when he seated himself succesively in two chapels, wearing the red crown in one and the white crown in the other. These constant elements were accompanied by varying rituals, such as a ritual battle depicting the one between Horus and Seth and the erection of the *dd*-pillar to symbolise the resurrection of Osiris. It is my opinion that the culmination of the festival was the king's donning of the *śd* robe, which is an ancient priestly garment. The current opinion that the *śd* festival is a repetition of the coronation rites in order to renew the royal dignity is untenable, because the said coronation rites are not clearly discernable in the *śd* festival and because the royal authority was renewed annually during the Min festival. The purport of the *śd* festival is the reinvestiture of the pharaoh with the dignity of high priest.

The festivals of the dead can be dealt with briefly. Usually they can not be separated from the festivals of the gods, although they do have their own particular atmosphere and significance. Good examples are to be found in the texts and reliefs in two graves at Meir, the contracts of the district ruler Hepzefi, both of the Middle Kingdom, and the funerary customs connected with 'the beautiful festival of the desert valley' from the 18th dynasty. The tenor of these festivals is evidently the transformation of the deceased into a *3ḫu*, a glorified being of light.[32]

B. *Ethics*

In view of the predominant function fulfilled by Ma-a-t in ancient Egypt it can readily be inferred that the Egyptian expected man's behaviour as private individual and as citizen of the state to answer to high ethical standards. This does not mean there was no injustice or corruption. On the contrary, complaints about the corruption of the people are very loud, especially in times of anarchy and social disruption. It is precisely this cultural criticism which proves that the ideals of justice, love of truth and charity were taken seriously. Some of the best sources for gaining an insight into the ethics of the ancient Egyptians are the following documents: the biographies deposited by prominent people in their graves, the instruction given by Thutmosis III to his vizier Rekhmere on his installation, the books of wisdom and the protestations of innocence spoken by the deceased before the court which judged the dead, as contained in spell 125 of the Book of the Dead.

The social ethics can be inferred from what the high dignitaries say about the execution of their duties in their biographies. They aver that they have done no injustice, deprived no one of his property, oppressed no slaves—indeed they have cared for their subjects as a father and taken measures to alleviate lack of food and clothing. They claim to be 'a man of Ma-a-t', i.e. "a protector for the hardly pressed, a saviour for those who had no saviour, who let two people go home satisfied with his judgment." From the last pronouncement it appears that they acted in the spirit of the instruction received by the vizier Rekhmere. For there it is said, among other things: "...verily, to be vizier, that is not sweet, but bitter. For it is a matter of having no consideration for monarchs and government authorities, of making no person whatever his slave. What he must do is adhere to the law...treat the one thou knowest in the same way as the one thou knowest not... be wrathful only about which one ought to be wrathful...for the vizier is the one who must exercise justice for all people."

The directions for personal ethics are contained in the books of wisdom, which are so abundant in Egyptian literature, e.g. the teaching of Ptahhotep, of Kagemmi, of king Amenemhet and the book of the wisdom of Amenemope.[10] These writings do not offer profound thoughts, but specimens of typically oriental wisdom about life. They exhort charity, circumspection in speech; they caution against dishonesty, slander, cadging and the pursuit of wealth. All the virtues praised are embodied in 'the calm person', who contrasts sharply to to 'the irascible person.' The former is also called 'the truly silent one.' He is the self-controlled, modest, patient man. In the texts he is equated with 'the man of Ma-a-t,' the one who conforms to world order. Hence this wordly wisdom appears to have a religious background: the truly wise man lives according to Ma-a-t. On it are based both his virtue and his happiness.

The last-mentioned truth is confirmed in a special sense by the judgment of the dead, for immortality is the lot of only those whose conduct in life accords with Ma-a-t. Hence the deceased protests his innocence and his purity. From this so-called negative confession we can deduce these standards of ancient Egyptian ethics. Now it appears, as will be explained in greater detail in the chapter on the conception of man, that the deceased exculpates himself of three categoriss of crimes, namely ethical crimes, cultic offences and contraventions of the cosmic order. The last of these clearly reveals the religious motivation of the ethics.[1]

C. *Myth*

The ancient Egyptians cannot be denied the possession of creative ingenuity, technical insight and organisational talent. These qualities are sufficiently manifested in their orderly body politic, their books on wisdom and their magnificent and imposing works of construction. The ancient Egyptians were undoubtedly a people who had a good capacity for observation, a keen intellect and a profound insight. Nevertheless they never attained that degree of reflection and independent thinking by which experiment or logical reasoning can lead to new insights. Their learning was an admixture of practical counsel and magic practice. Moreover, as remarked in the first chapter, they lacked the speculative faculty and also the imaginative power which experiences and dramatises the event. They did not produce a systematically constructed theology. Accordingly the myths they created are of a simple structure, although they testify to a profound wisdom.

Like all true myths, the ancient Egyptian ones contain the significance of the cosmos and culture. As we have already seen, in conjunction with the rites they form the pattern of the culture and of the religion. Now the faith of the ancient Egyptians is most clearly expressed in the cult. Hence this sector of their religion is the best means of learning their way of thinking about religion. Especially since many gods are a-mythical, in other words they did not give rise to the creation of myths.

The principal myths have already been related. A few additional comments on their religious value. Primary significance was attached to the myth of creation, in which the sun-god appears as creator or rather as planner of the world. He instituted Ma-a-t, the world order which obtains eternally. From this conception emanated a static and also optimistic world image. The ancient Egyptians were not apprehensive of an uncertain future, but accepted life with faith in the knowledge that the virtue and happiness of man is guaranteed if he lives in harmony with Ma-a-t. Very closely connected with the myth of creation is the ideology of the king. The archetype of the pharaoh is Re, the first king, who is moreover his mythical father.

In addition to the sun myth, the vegetation myth with Osiris as principal actor played an important part. Thousands derived their hopes of a blessed life in the hereafter from this myth, which was dramatised in a form resembling that of mystery plays.

This character sketch of the mythic vision of the ancient Egyptians must suffice here. Two more peculiarities might be added. Interesting is the mythic cosmology, in which the West represented the land of the dead and the East the place of resurrection. Secondly there were diverse myths about holy places, as we learn from the remarkable papyrus JUMILHAC.

V. CONCEPTION OF MAN

Under this heading four points must be dealt with which touch upon the quintessence of the religious conception of man, namely, the origin of man, his being, his destiny and his expectation of life after death.

A. *Origin of Man*

It is highly remarkable that the Egyptians, who have produced numerous myths about the creation of the world, apparently were little concerned about how man came into being. Only incidental remarks about this subject are contained in the texts. A number of sun-hymns make it clear that the Egyptians considered it a matter of course that Re was accounted the creator of mankind.[29] The opening words of one of these hymns runs: "Salute, Re, who created mankind". Such eulogies do not reveal how Re created man. Nevertheless there was a strange conception about this which is supported by one of the paronomasia to which the Egyptians were so addicted. In another sun-hymn is said, namely: "Thou art the only one who created all that exists, the only one who was alone when he created all that is, from whose eyes man originated". The closing phrase alludes to the conception that mankind derived from the tears of Re, or rather of the sun-eye. This idea occurs in a certain version of the myth of the sun-eye. In it is told how the sun-eye was sent forth by Re to fight his enemies. When it returned and found another eye in its place, it became angry and shed tears from which mankind originated. This story is based on the word-play between 'tear' (*rmjt*) and 'man (*rmṯ*).

The famous hymn of Akhenaton gives most details about this subject. In it Re's activity encompasses more than just the creation of man. Difference in stature and colour of skin, the various languages and the fact that each race has its habitat where it can find its food are all attributed to the creative activity of the sun-god. The passage in question runs thus:

> "Thou hast created the earth according to thy desire,
>   Thou quite alone,
> with people, cattle and all the other animals,
>   which walk on their feet over the earth,
>   or fly with their wings across the sky.
> In the lands of Syria, Nubia and Egypt,
>   thou showest every man his own place,
>   and carest for his needs.
> Everyone has his food,
>   his span of life is calculated.
> Diverse are the languages which they speak,
>   likewise their stature:
>   the colour of their skin is different—
> So hast thou distinguished the nations".

Other gods apart from Re were looked upon as the creator of the world and hence of mankind. In this respect Ptah and Khnum especially merit attention. As for Ptah, reference might be made to the so-called Memphitic theology, which is recorded on the famous stone of king Shabaka. This theology has correctly been characterised as a *logos* doctrine, for briefly its maxim is that all came into being because a thought arose in the heart (of Ptah) and the tongue voiced it. So, too, was mankind created, indeed it might be added that this *logos* pervades the being of man. This can be inferred from the following passage: "...it happened that heart and tongue gained power over (all) limbs, because they learned that he (Ptah) was (as heart) in every body, (as tongue) in every mouth of all the gods, of all the people, of all the cattle, of all crawling animals, (and) of that which (further) lives, because (as heart) he thinks and because (as tongue) he commands all things that he wishes".[33]

Khnum can be accounted creator in only a certain respect. It is not clear whether he was really considered the creator of the human race as such. But he is the creator of the individual person who is born. He fashions the child—in the first place the royal child—in the womb of the mother. This he does in a strange way, namely on the potter's wheel. He is often depicted modelling man. Together with Heket, the goddess of birth, he promotes the delivery of the woman who gives birth to child. Later his care extends to the animals as well. All that is created sexually enters the world because of his work. Hence he is also the lord of fate. His other functions are irrelevant to the matter in hand.[4]

B. *Being of Man*

It is really only to be expected that the Egyptians, who were little inclined to be doctrinal by nature, had no anthropology in the sense of an exhaustive doctrine on the being of man which they recorded. Conclusions must be drawn from incidental remarks and disparate mythic conceptions about their way of thinking about man, that is about the relationship of body and soul, the properties of man and his ethical-religious qualities.[2]

Actually it is incorrect to query how the ancient Egyptian thought about the relationship of body and soul. The concept of an invisible soul was alien to the Egyptian. He possessed no psychology in the modern sense of the word, only a religious anthropology. In it he made no sharp distinction between the material and the spiritual part of man. Nor did he know the notion of personality as the spiritual centre of man's being, as his invariant ego. However, he was convinced that various spiritual potencies were present in man. It was to these powers that man owed his continued existence after death. Provided no misunderstanding is occasioned by this conception, the term 'plurality of souls' might be used. Or in other, more adequate words: the Egyptian discovered various aspects of the being of man. He tolerated the co-existence of these different formulations without bothering himself about logical contradictions, probably because the being of man seemed so mysterious to him, that he considered a multiplicity of images applicable to it.

In the first place, man has a body, or to use a better term: he is a body. For his person and his life are highly dependent on the condition of his body, especially after death. This implies that the deceased was thought to exist in the hereafter in a sort of physical condition. Hence the careful embalmment of the body in order to guarantee the deceased's continued existence. The deceased is therefore repeatedly assured that his body is completely intact, in other words that he can perform all functions of life. We read: "Thou art given thy eyes to

see, thy ears to hear, thy mouth to speak, thy legs to walk, thy flesh is
sound, there is nothing amiss with thee". In Egyptian the word for
body is *d̲.t*. Now it appears that *d̲.t* can be conceived of as a power
indispensable to its owner. The *d̲.t* is mentioned as the analogue to
the *k̲ȝ*, one of the so-called souls. This teaches us that the soul was
not conceived of as being purely spiritual and the body purely
material.

Of extreme importance to man is his heart (*ib*), for this is the organ
of physical life. This can be deduced from the famous tale of the two
brothers, Anubis and Bata, in which the motif of the relationship
between Joseph and the wife of Potiphar occurs. When Anubis
wrongly accuses his brother of adultery, Bata emasculates himself and
goes to the underworld. He places his heart on the blossom of a cedar
with the message that he will live again if this heart is placed in cool
water when the tree is felled. And indeed this happens. The Book of
the Dead contains several spells intended to prevent that a dead man
is deprived of his heart: for then his life is at an end. But the heart is
also the seat of consciousness and moral perception. In spell 30A of
the Book of the Dead, the deceased addresses his heart and admonishes it not to testify against him in the judgment of the dead. True,
in this judgment the heart is held to be the representative of the
ethical-religious worth of the man. The vignettes accompanying the
famous spell 125 of the Book of the Dead show how the heart is
weighed in balance against a feather, the emblem of Ma-a-t, during
the judgment of the dead.

H. C. ANDERSEN wrote an amusing and profound fairy-tale about
the man who lost his shadow. It is based on the widespread and ancient
idea that the shadow is the wraith (Doppelgänger) of man and consequently a part of his life. The Egyptians also knew of the significance
of the shadow. The determinative of the Egyptian word is a sort of
parasol, the object that casts a shadow. Here a spiritual power is
intended, as appears from the fact that the shadow is often used in
analogy to other concepts for 'soul'. And so we see this sunshade being
held by the sign of life (*'nḫ*) behind the pharaohs who combat their
enemies. Here the 'shadow' protects the king, in the same way that
the sign of the *k̲ȝ* can often be found placed behind the monarch to
afford him magical protection.

The principal 'soul' of man is his *k̲ȝ*. Not only man, but also gods
and even buildings possess a *k̲ȝ*. Moreover man can dispose over
more than one *k̲ȝ*. Re has even seven or fourteen *k̲ȝ*'s. The *k̲ȝ* helps

and protects man and makes him powerful. Various theories have been formulated about the essence of the *k3*. The fact that the *k3* often stands behind a person has induced the idea that it is a 'Doppelgänger.' Another conception is that it is a genius. This notion is capable of two interpretations. Either as guardian angel or in the original sense of the word *genius*, which is connected with *gignere* = 'to produce'. This idea arose because the *k3* is sometimes determined by the phallus or by the bull, the fertile animal. It has even been suggested that the *k3* is a totem sign, because in the early ages it was used as a sign of a collectivity and was placed upon divine standards, just like the names of shires. No traces of totemism can be discerned, however, in prehistoric Egypt. There may be some element of truth in all these explanations. This much is clear, the *k3* was a divine being. When Khnum fashions the royal child, he also models the *k3* in the image of a little child. The *k3* does not grow simultaneously with the pharaoh, though it does wear the headdress and hairstyle of the godhead, together with the curled divine beard. Sometimes the body of the *k3* is narrowed down to the proportions of a staff with arms and head crowned with the *k3* sign. The *k3* occurs several times behind the king as the hieroglyphic sign which encloses and elevates the names of the king, written in a rectangle—the so-called *k3* name. The *k3* sign represents two raised arms. A man with raised arms is the determinative of 'to be highly placed' and of 'to exult'. Apparently this sign can also express the gesture of magic protection when it is performed while standing behind the one who is protected. This must be the purport of the pyramid text 1653: "Thou (Atum) hast placed both thy arms behind them (Shu and Tefnet) because of the *k3*, for indeed thy *k3* is in them". By this gesture Atum bestows his vitality on the said gods. The same is done for man by the *k3*. Furthermore it should be known that the plural of *k3* can mean nourishment or food, which is charged with divine vitality according to ancient notion and that the *k3*'s of Re have names which can be reproduced by the conceptions 'magic power, to be green or fresh, power, to be strong, lustre, to be delightful'. Hence one receives the impression that the *k3* represents the personified vitality, the creative energy of man. The significance of the *k3* becomes manifest especially in death. To die is to go with (or: to) his *k3*. Apparently the conception varies: the deceased goes to the hereafter in the company of his *k3*; he recovers his *k3* in death. In any case he is finished with if his *k3* is taken away from him. Pyramid text 635, for example, relates that Horus deprived the enemies of the pharaoh of their *k3*'s which meant their destruction. On the other hand, man has no need to fear death if he has his *k3*. Therefore the deceased triumphantly declares: "Even if I die, my *k3* is mighty".

The conception of the *b3* places a different accent on the spiritual being of man. In short, the *b3* expresses man's desire for liberty, his will-power and also the indestructibility of his spirit, which cannot be subdued by death. The *b3* is represented as a bird with human head, which holds in its claws the hieroglyphic sign of life or of the (life-giving) wind, whilst a pot with fire, sign of life, sometimes stands before this figure. It is a widespread thought that the soul can assume the shape of a bird, during life and also, especially, after death. Spells 74 to 88 of the Book of the Dead digress on the variety of shapes the deceased can assume to demonstrate that he still lives. These include diverse animals, and especially birds. We read in the pyramid texts that the deceased flies to heaven as a bird. Certain vignettes accompanying the spells in the Book of the Dead show how the *b3* sits on the breast of the deceased, or flies up through the shaft connecting the underground mortuary chamber with the world outside. The last conception is particularly characteristic: the deceased is 'as free as a bird', in other words the power of his spirit renders him indestructible. Two circumstances demonstrate that *b3* can be described as spiritual strength or vital energy. Firstly man can possess more or less *b3*. "Horus is more *b3* than he (his enemy)". *B3* also occurs in the plural, *b3w*: a person is 'great in *b3w*". Secondly, the *b3* is often linked up with Re, especially with the rise of the sun-god. In vignettes of the Book of the Dead the *b3* is present at sunrise. Manifestly alluding to this matinal event, the deceased says: "shining I ascend, I am Re, I am strong, I am healthy" (Book of the Dead, 105:9 et seq.), and "I am *b3*, I am Re, who rises from the primeval ocean, the divine soul... I am Hu (the divine word or food), for whom no destruction exists in his name of *b3*" (Book of the Dead 83:1 et seq.).

The last conception which must be discussed in this connexion is the *3ḫw*. The verb *3ḫ* means: to be beautiful, to be glorious, to be useful. The substantive *3ḫw* can be interpreted as: Splendour, spiritual power, capacity. With regard to man, the *3ḫw* only manifests itself after death. The *3ḫw* is the glorified deceased. It is not purely and simply by virtue of his own character that man becomes *3ḫw*; he has to be elevated to *3ḫw* by the funerary ceremonial, in particular by the recitation of certain magic spells. Spell 1 of the Book of the Dead, which in a sense can be taken as the title of the book as a whole, opens with the statement that these spells serve to glorify, i.e. to render *ȝḫw* (*sȝḫw*) the deceased. The abode of the *ȝḫw* is thought to be in heaven: "the *ȝḫw* to heaven, the body to earth" (pyr. 472). Hence the *ȝḫw* is the deceased as glorified spirit.

Generally speaking, the conception 'anthropology' has a double meaning. In the first place it indicates the view of the structure of the physical-spiritual being of man which has been formed either by virtue of human experience of life or on scientific grounds. In addition to this conception of man there is also an evaluation of man which expresses the conception of his ethical-religious worth. In the case of the ancient Egyptians, these two types of anthropology cannot be segregated and scarcely distinguished. In the preceding observations, certain elements of anthropology in the first meaning of the term have already emerged, insofar as the relationship of the 'soul' to the body and the living man is concerned.

There is every reason to posit another question: what was the Egyptians' evaluation of man? Before seeking an answer to this question, it might be remarked by way of elucidation that there are two types of religious anthropology, in which the accent falls alternately on man's relationship to God and on the complete inequality of their two beings. Striking examples of the latter are to be found among the Semitic races, to be specific in the Old Testament and in Babylonian literature. According to the Babylonian myth of creation, man was created to serve the Gods. He is the slave of the sovereign gods. A leading concept of the Gilgamesh epic is expressed in the words spoken by the cup-bearer Siduri to the hero, who seeks the herb of life:

> "Gilgamesh, whither doest thou wander?
> The life that thou seekest thou shalt not find!
> When the gods created mankind,
> thy destined man for death;
> they kept life firmly in their hands".

The ancient Egyptian idea of man's relationship with the godhead contrasts vividly with this Semitic view. The Egyptian was convinced that man is akin to the godhead. In the earliest period only the pharaoh possessed the prerogative of being a son of the gods. In later times it was tacitly assumed that every man had a divine vein in his nature. To this conception the deceased owed his conviction that he was identical in essence to certain gods, striking testimonials of which have been repeatedly quoted in the course of this article. These triumphant declarations could easily give rise to a misunderstanding, namely that the Egyptian imagined himself the equal of the gods. Nothing could be less true. It was fully appreciated that gods and men were of different races. But an optimistic view was entertained of the being of man, in the sense that he trusted that by virtue of his nature he would be able to share in the indestructible divine life after his death.

This optimism did not imply, however, that man was viewed as an almost perfect being in the ethical-religious sense. The Egyptian was a realist and consequently had a keen perception of man's disposition. Bitter experience had taught him that man is capable of all sorts of misdeeds, especially during periods of social upheaval. The writings which describe these periods paint a gloomy picture of the nature of man. Thus laments the 'weary-of-life': "To whom do I speak today? Brothers are evil. Friends of today do not love... Hearts are thieves. Everyone seizes the property of his fellows... The gentle perishes. The insolent face goes everywhere... There are no just. The earth is left to those who sin... Evil strikes the country, there is no end to it". In the doctrine of king Amenemhet I we find the cynical advice: "trust not the brother; know no friend; procure no confidant—that leads to nothing". The exhortations of Ipuwer contain the following specimens of injustice of which the people are guilty in times when the government has lost all its authority: "...behold, the poor of the land have become the wealthy; he who possessed something is now one who has nothing...behold, those who possessed clothes now go about in rags; he who did not weave for himself now possesses fine linen".[10]

The Egyptian was therefore acquainted with what the philosopher KANT termed 'das radikal Böse im Menschen". Did he also have feelings of sin and guilt? This question is interesting, because the Egyptian language has a number of words for sin and guilt, and more especially because expressions of an awareness of sin do occur in Egyptian literature. However, the content of this awareness of sin should be analysed more closely. There are ten words in Egyptian which can be used to designate 'sin' and six to express the concept of 'guilt'. Closer study reveals, however, that both groups of words have more than one meaning and that they do not express the notions of 'sin' and 'guilt' exclusively. The words for sin indicate all that is bad, either what man does or what befalls him. In certain circumstances, therefore, they can be translated as: crime, injustice, calamity, suffering, damage, foolishness. The words for guilt also cover the following conceptions: mistake, failing, offence, damage. Such varying shades of meaning for the words 'sin' and 'guilt' also occur in other languages. Nevertheless it is evident that in Egyptian the word 'sin' is closely associated with the unpleasant, with foolishness, and that the word 'guilt' suggests mistake, financial or juridical shortcomings. It is therefore questionable whether the Egyptian used these words in their purely ethical and religious sense. And so this question gives rise to another one: did he really possess a clear-cut awareness of sin and guilt?

This question is complicated, because remarkable testimonials of sin and guilt have been preserved, to which reference has already been made. These date from the period of the 19th dynasty and derive from the labourers in the Theban necropolis. A. ERMAN and B. GUN have edited these texts. The latter Egyptologist gives a very fitting characterisation of these inscriptions when he calls them testimonials of 'the religion of the poor' and elucidates their significance by remarking that, in general, "the Egyptian was little disposed to humble himself before the deity and that the attitude of the 'miserable sinner', so characteristic of the Christian and other semitic religions is unknown to the official writings". That is quite true. Hence these protestations of sin and guilt are all the more interesting. The simple common folk who speak here acknowledge that they have acted wrongly towards certain gods—Amon, Ptah, Meretseger, a serpent goddess who was supposed to have her home in a mountain-top at the Westside of the Nile—that they were punished as a result, but that the godhead has proved merciful by diverting catastrophe. The following confession might serve as example:

> "(I was) an ignorant man and foolish
> who knew neither good nor evil
> I wrought transgressions against the Peak (Meretseger)
> And she chastised me".

But Meretseger pitied the punished man:

> "She turned again to me in mercy
> She caused me to forget the sickness that has been (upon me)".

In these texts the point at issue is usually an illness—often blindness —which is believed to be the punishment for sin and which is cured

by the goodness of the godhead. This cautions reflection. It is an
inducement to evaluate the quality of this awareness of sin. There are,
indeed, a few cases in which a man is aware of the sinfulness of his
heart. Usually, however, the awareness of sin and guilt does not
proceed from a feeling of unholiness, but is roused by the fact that
the persons in question were afflicted by calamity, more especially by
illness and blindness, which they believe to be the godhead's punishment for an offence. This means that the ancient Egyptian regrets that
he has been foolish and that he therefore behaved badly. This conclusion reinforces the linguistic analysis of the words for 'sin' and
'guilt', which demonstrated that the meaning of these words always
shifts in the direction of non-ethical conceptions, such as mistake,
calamity, failing.

Accordingly H. FRANKFORT has spoken of the 'absence of the
concept of sin' in ancient Egypt.[13] In his opinion "the Egyptian
viewed his misdeeds not as sins, but as aberrations. They would bring
him unhappiness because they disturbed his harmonious integration
with the existing world... He who errs is not a sinner but a fool, and
his conversion to a better way of life does not require repentance but
a better understanding... Lack of insight and lack of self-restraint
were at the root of man's misfortunes, but not a basic corruption".
This quotation from FRANKFORT's *Ancient Egyptian Religion* may give
the impression that the ancient Egyptian was motivated by a spirit of
shallow utilism. It therefore needs further explanation, which the
author partly gives, though not with the required stress. One should
clearly understand that according to the ancient Egyptian belief man
can escape from sin by living in harmony with Ma-a-t, the world
order. Both man's happiness and his virtues are guaranteed if he acts
and lives in harmony with Ma-a-t. This harmony requires insight,
wisdom. It is endangered by foolishness. Nevertheless man is considered capable of garnering the requisite wisdom and therefore of
leading a virtuous and happy life.

C. *Destiny of Man*

Since the ancient Egyptian entertained no doctrine of faith, it is
futile to investigate his conception of man's way to salvation. But he
did know how man had to behave in order to be assured of his virtue
and his happiness. He drew up certain criteria for the conduct of man.
Therefore there is every reason to ask what the Egyptian thought to
be the true destination of man. The answer to this question can be

found in what has been said above. What is needed now is an explicit formula. This is as follows: The Egyptian was convinced that the integrity of the human character and the pureness of his happiness could only be guaranteed if man lived in harmony with Ma-a-t. Numerous pronouncements testify to this view. In the book of wisdom of Amenemope, for instance, the contrast between the irascible man and the calm man, or the 'truly silent one' as he is called, is delineated. The latter practises Ma-a-t and he prospers like a tree which bears leaves and fruit. The former is like a wild tree which loses its branches and ends its existence in a shipyard or in the fire. Furthermore it was a mere matter of course to the ancient Egyptian that man had the capacity to live according to Ma-a-t and that he had the faculty to learn to know Ma-a-t. For Ma-a-t can be learned by those who possess insight. Here, therefore, there is question of an attitude towards the recognisability of the religious truth which might be termed 'gnosis'.

Now there are forces which can throw man off his course. Destiny plays tricks with man. Some gods influence his career. Did the ancient Egyptians believe in fate? To obtain clarity on this question, three types of data must be studied. In the first place information can be obtained by studying the Egyptian calendar, and then it appears that the Egyptians took account of favourable and unfavourable days, and even in five variations of them. In their calendar these days are marked with five different signs or combinations of signs, whilst the explicatory text describes the character of such days in further detail. The presupposition of this calendary learning is based on the assumption that man can avoid disaster if he knows the ill-omened days and conducts himself accordingly. In the second place, a better insight into the Egyptian conception of fate can be gained from a famous story which H. A. GARDINER has entitled: "The Tale of the Doomed Prince". The story is about a prince on whose birth the Hathors, goddesses of destiny, had prophesied: "his death will be caused by the crocodile, or the snake, or the dog". The king hoped to protect his son by shutting him up in a lonely castle. But the prince set out with his favourite dog to seek adventure in Syria and won the daughter of a king as bride. On his return, it appears that a snake and a crocodile menaced his life. He escaped both dangers, however, on the first occasion through the vigilance of his loving wife, who killed the snake and said: "Behold, your god (apparently Re) has placed one of your destinies in your hands; he will also give you the other ones".

The papyrus is badly damaged at the end, however, so the issue is not known for certain, nor if the prince's own dog caused his ruin. There is divergence of opinion among scholars about this, but the general impression one receives is that it is not a question of the prince's fate, but of three evil changes, which the prince manages to circumvent through his own fearlessness and the devotion of his wife. In the third place, attention should be paid to the three mythological representations *Š3jt*, *Rnn.t* and *Mshn.t*. *Š3jt* is destiny in both the favourable and unfavourable sense. *Rnn.t* is the midwife, the educator and also the weaver. *Mshn.t* is the goddess of birth who, as we have seen in the story in the papyrus Westcar, pronounced a salutary wish on the birth of three divine royal children. These three powers determine the course of a man's life. They appear at two decisive moments: birth and death. It is significant that they attend the judgment of the dead, in which the ethical-religious quality of a man is weighed against Ma-a-t. This means that the Egyptians did not entertain a fatalistic conception of life. They tended to be optimistic by nature and thought that the activity of fate was interwoven with the rythm of world order, Ma-a-t, with the meaningful, creative activity of divine life.

D. *Future of Man*

Many religions contain, in addition to ideas about the future of man, conceptions about the destiny of the world, in other words a general eschatology as well as an individual one. What were their relationships in the ancient Egyptian religion?

In the preceding chapter, reference was made to a sort of pseudo-prophetic literature, to writings which seem to contain prophecies, whereas in actual fact they contain admonitions, authoritative because presented as prophecies, which are really *vaticinia ex eventu*. It may safely be concluded that Egypt has no speculation about the fate of the world in the form of an eschatology. G. LANCZKOWSKI traced certain passages in spell 175 of the Book of the Dead which could possibly contain an eschatological import. The clearest pronouncements about such are made by Atum in a discourse with Osiris. In answer to Osiris' question as to how long he will exist, Atum replies: "Thou shalt exist longer than millions of millions of years. I, however, shall destroy all I created. The earth shall once again resemble the primeval ocean, the flood in the beginning. I am that which will remain—together with Osiris—after I have transformed myself once more into a serpent whom no man knows and no god sees". This obscure pronouncement alludes to a way in which the world will end that is a repetition of the deluge—which is indeed mentioned in the texts. However, this is an isolated passage, and on such an Egyptian eschatology cannot be constructed. There is nothing strange and incomprehensible about the fact that the Egyptians never created a picture of the ultimate state of the world. In religious matters their point of orientation was the past, the mythic deed of the sun-god who created the world, or rather reduced it to order and instituted Ma-a-t. They believed in Ma-a-t as the unshakable world order. Within this order took place the everlasting cyclic process of the death and resurrection of divine life.

A paucity of delineations of the end of the world there may be, the representations of man's fate after death are extant in abundance. Here we are once again confronted by the peculiar logic, or rather, to our way of thinking, singular lack of logic that is typical of the Egyptian way of thinking. In other words there are numerous representations of life after death which we experience as mutually exclusive, but which the Egyptian easily tolerated side by side. Evidently the mystery of life in the hereafter was so inexhaustible in his view that he felt diverse representations were needed to do it justice. With a little effort, six conceptions of life after death can be distinguished.[2, 19, 27]

The first conception, that the deceased lives in the grave, can be met with among numerous peoples. It was also known in ancient Egypt. Two indications of the existence of this age-old belief among the Egyptians are the offerings to the deceased at his graveside and the so-called 'serdab' of the mortuary edifice. Another is the false door in the wall of the grave, through which the deceased can make his exit. For that matter, an eminent Egyptian of the Old Kingdom announced that he had himself interred with his father so that he could see him daily.

The second conception is that the deceased sojourns in the underworld. The realm of the dead has two names, _ḫrt nṯr_, which also means necropolis, and _Duat_. Since the nocturnal sky can also be accounted the abode of the dead, _Duat_ is sometimes located in the sky. In the heart of _Duat_, Sokaris reigns. The sun-god passes through _Duat_ during the night. Many dangers beset the deceased in the underworld, as is suggested by the captions to the spells in the Book of the Dead. For they are meant to furnish the deceased with air, to see to it that his body does not perish, that he does not die a second time, etc. These spells interpret man's apprehension of death and the horrifying character of _Duat_.

In contrast to the cheerless existence which seems to await the deceased in certain parts of the underworld is the felicitous hereafter in those regions which might be called the 'islands of the blessed', to use a term from Greek mythology. These are the Jaru and Hetep fields, of which the vignette accompanying spell 110 of the Book of the Dead gives some idea: it is an agrarian countryside intersected by the arms of a river where agriculture pursues its course under highly favourable conditions. There the corn grows seven cubits high. Earthy life is continued here in an ideal manner. Especially since the deceased took with him to his grave *wšbtj* statuettes to work for him or to answer in his name when he is called upon to do any work.

It is not surprising that the starry nocturnal sky gave rise to the idea that the deceased are in the firmament. The deceased shines there as a star. Particularly the circumpolar stars which never set—known as 'the imperishable ones', 'the indefatigable ones'—were held to be the abode of the deceased. The ascent of the deceased to heaven is depicted already in the pyramid texts. Sometimes he climbs up a ladder, often he flies aloft as a bird: "he rises to heaven as a falcon; he travels up to heaven as a crane."

The belief in the revival of the deceased is primarily associated with the sun-god. Each day the sun-god dies in the West and rises again in the East in the morning. The fervent wish of the deceased is to participate in this triumphant sun-life. This privilege is guaranteed him if he is permitted to travel with the sun-boat. Re therefore takes along the deceased as oarsman in his barque. Fortunate the deceased to whom can be said: "Thou mountest this ship of Re, which the gods preferably mount and leave, in which Re journeys to the horizon."

The hope of revival after death was nourished mainly by the Osiris myth. The deceased gladly bound his fate to that of Osiris. With respect to the deceased the pyramid texts assure: "...verily as Osiris lives, so shall he live; verily, as Osiris is not dead, so shall he not die." In a grave from the 18th dynasty was found a remarkable object which symbolises the resurrection of Osiris, an object on which the deceased could fasten his hope of revival: a wooden frame on legs spread with linen and bearing a basketwork of cane; the silhouette of Osiris has been drawn in black ink in the middle of it and then covered with earth in which barley was sown, the stalks are cut off at eight centimetres. The result is a green figure symbolising the resurrection in which the deceased hopes to share.

The Osiris myth probably also influenced the conception of the judgment of the dead. Spell 125 of the Book of the Dead deals with it. The judgment of the dead is based on the idea of retribution in the hereafter. There are indications that Re originally had a major share in the judgment of the dead. In the traditional conception, Osiris is the judge of the dead. The procedure of the trial is as follows: Anubis leads the deceased into the courtroom, which is often called the chamber of the double Ma-a-t, the Ma-a-t of life and of death. The deceased's heart is weighed in balance against the feather that represents Ma-a-t. Thoth records the result. Beside the scales sits a monster who devours the condemned. If the verdict is favourable, Horus then leads the deceased to Osiris who, together with a bench of 42 judges, pronounces final judgment.

Spell 125 consists of three speeches which the dead must make at his trial. The second one is a sort of 'negative confession,' in which the deceased endeavours to demonstrate his purity and righteousness. He protests his innocence of three categories of crime. Firstly of ethical offences: "I have not caused hunger", "I have not killed," "I have not decreased the corn measure." Secondly of cultic misdemeanours: "I have not decreased the loaves of the gods; I have not stolen the food of the blessed dead." Thirdly of crimes which violate the cosmic order: "I have not impeded the (flood) water at its time; I have not destroyed budding life." By these testimonies of righteousness and purity the deceased endeavours to achieve his proclamation as *ma-a-kheru* by Thoth, just after the example of the way in which Thoth rendered Osiris *ma-a-kheru*, in other words justified him.

Ma-a-kheru is a remarkable term. When used in the profane sense, it means that a person is acquitted by a process or settling of an account. Here the term has a religious-funerary meaning. From the myth it appears that the 'justification' of Osiris took place on his resurrection. Similarly, the deceased can only prevail in the judgment of the dead if he disposes of spontaneous vitality, just like Osiris. This he does if his voice (*kheru*) is *ma-a-*, that is, in harmony with Ma-a-t, so that he is *ma-a-kheru*. Here it should be remembered that according to the Egyptian conception, the voice and the word can possess a magic-creative power. This capacity can only be tested in death. Hence in the underworld, the seat of true life, and in the presence of Ma-a-t which reigns there, judgment is passed not only on man's ethical-religious property, but also on his cosmic worth.

VI. Subsequent Influences of the Egyptian Religion

In his magnum opus *A Study of History*, A. J. Toynbee ventured the statement: "The Egyptian Society has no predecessor and no successor." This pregnant proposition testifies to the correct view which the great historian had of the intrinsic nature of Egyptian culture and religion. 'Ancient Egypt' is indeed a spiritual quantity so original in style, so completely rounded-off as entity, that no other historical example of it can be found and no imitation was possible. The first term of Toynbee's description is certainly irrefutable. In the fourth millenium B.C., an amazing process took place in the Nile Valley: spontaneously there came into being the typical Egyptian way of life which is immediately recognisable in all the products of this civilisation and which prevailed for more then three millenia. Conceivably, however, the accuracy of the second part of Toynbee's conclusion could be disputed. Admittedly, the so very homogeneous Egyptian civilisation and religion, which had already lost their inner choesion because of Hellenistic influences, came to an inglorious end when Christianity started its conquest of the Delta in the second century. But is there no trace at all of any repercussions of the typical Egyptian conceptions? This question definitely ought to be put, and it can even be answered in the affirmative.

In the first place it is a commonplace that Egypt greatly fascinated the minds of the Hellenistic age. The Greeks were always convinced that all true wisdom derived from the land of the Nile. In the Roman imperial age, many Romans looked to Egypt in wonder and envy. A certain rivalry existed between Rome and Alexandria. The favour of the Caesars oscillated. Those with dictatorial tendencies gladly took as their example the Egyptian pharaoh as son of the gods and favoured the import of Egyptian ethics and ideas; those emperors who wanted to uphold the ancient Roman democracy turned away from Egypt. The mysteries of Isis experienced forcibly the changing tides of imperial favour: they were alternately protected and reviled. These mysteries, which are known through the *Metamorphoses* of the Latin writer Apuleius—a significant fact in itself—constitute the clearest symptom of the influence which for centuries long was exercised by Egyptian religion over both the Greek-speaking and the western part of the Roman empire. For the Isis mysteries had such a hold on the minds of the people, especially of the women, that they constituted a dangerous rival to young Christianity. In 394 A.D. Isis processions still passed through the streets of Rome.

Especially interesting is the repercussion of Egyptian religion on Christianity. Understandably enough, the most obvious traces of this can be found in Egypt itself, especially dating from the first centuries of the Christian era. To find these traces, attention must first be directed to the gnosticism that had become established in Egypt before orthodox Christianity became the principal faith there. Egyptian gnosticism is a singular matter. It is not autochthonous in Egypt, though it flourished exceptionally well for a period in the Nile Valley. No doubts about this can be entertained by anyone who knows that Basilides, Carpocrates and the brilliant Valentinus lived and worked here nor by anyone who appreciates the significance of the discovery of the Coptic gnostical manuscripts at Nag Hammadi. The mental outlook in Egypt apparently favoured gnosticism. Not surprising really, in view of the fact that one of the most highly esteemed properties of ancient Egypt was wisdom, insight into the enigma of life and death personified in the goddess Sia. Naturally there was a difference in sentiment: the ancient Egyptian was optimistic by nature; the gnostic had a pessimistic outlook on life and the world. In a certain sense, however, they both endeavoured to attain *gnosis*. This yearning for *gnosis* permeates the *Corpus Hermeticum*, that remarkable literary work which evidently presents a Greek version of ancient Egyptian conceptions and which is ascribed to Hermes Trismegistos, who was really the ancient Egyptian Thoth in disguise. In these writings and those of Nag Hammadi, therefore, reminescences can easily be discerned of the ancient Egyptian religion. Sia, for example, recurs as the gnostic Ennoia, and the role played by the 'heart' and 'tongue' in the theology of Ptah is repeated in that of Nous and Logos in Poimandres. Further there is a noticeable similarity between the gnostic geography of the underworld and the ancient Egyptian description of the realm of the dead: the same twelve sections occur in it. The fearful heavenly characters created by gnostic phantasy likewise have their counterparts in the Book of the Dead.

The same can be said of the world of thought of the indigenous Coptic Christianity. A few proofs of this might be cited. Perpetuated in the personal names of Coptic Christians are the names of famous Egyptian gods, for example Osiris, Isis, Horus, Amon and Anubis. Like the ancient Egyptians, the Copts considered certain trees to be sacred, especially the tree in the neighbourhood of Cairo in whose shade the holy family is said to have rested in the flight to Egypt. In imitation of an ancient Egyptian usage, lamps were lit on the graves. Coptic monks were mummified. Like the ancient Egyptians, the Coptic Christians celebrated the festivals connected with the seasons, with the rising of the Nile water, with the phases of the moon. Ancient Egyptian dances and hymns persisted tenaciously in folklore. Particularly in the conception of the life hereafter can this lingering influence be discerned: the deceased has to pass 40 "toll-houses' of the demons, his soul is weighed by the archangel Michael, just as was done by Thoth in the ancient Egyptian judgment of the dead; the paradise that is reached by the pious closely resembles the ancient Egyptian Jaru and Hetep fields. The most convincing proof of Egyptian influence on Coptic Christendom is the identification of the hieroglyph for life ('nḫ) with the cross: the outward similarity between the two signs has given rise to the meaningful symbolism of the cross as a sign of eternal life.

Orthodox Christianity, too, contains traces of being influenced by the religion of ancient Egypt. Quite conceivably the earliest Christian hermits and monks borrowed certain features of their behaviour pattern from the ascetics who lived near the temples in the later period of Egyptian history. Furthermore it is assumed that the Christian doctrine about God's word was influenced by the 'logos' doctrine of Memphis. The portrait of Isis with her little son Horus presumably contributed to the well-known representation of the Madonna with the child Jesus. The sign of the scarab was used to indicate Christ as μονογενής and αὐτογενής. And the Phoenix who periodically re-emerges from his ashes according to legend, became the symbol of resurrection.

VII. Short History of the Study of Egyptian Religion

It is not the intention to conclude with a summary of the history of Egyptology. That subject could never be encompassed within the scope of this final chapter. Besides, this article only deals with a segment of Egyptology, the Egyptian religion. Hence the only purposeful sketch which can be given is that of the course of investigation in this special field. And even these limits can only admit of a few remarks, especially about certain ideas which have alternately predominated in this study and about the direction taken by investigation during the past decades. More than emphasising these two points is hardly feasible, for a chronological summary of all the works on Egyptian religion is not particularly elucidative and would only result in a much too comprehensive account. And besides no clear line of development can be discerned here.

To begin with, something about the event which gave rise to the science of Egyptology, namely the deciphering of the hieroglyphic script by JEAN-FRANÇOIS CHAMPOLLION in 1822 with the aid of the famous Rosetta stone. With this brilliant discovery CHAMPOLLION made the sources available. Ever since ages long past Egypt had captured the imagination; especially because of its enigmatical hieroglyphic script and its mysterious godly figures. For centuries the scholars derived their knowledge of Egyptian religion from the *Hieroglyphica* of the Egyptian HORAPOLLO. ATHANASIUS KIRCHER, a learned Jesuit of the 17th century, even endeavoured to decipher the hieroglyphs. His translation of Egyptian inscriptions, however, were mere products of his imagination, characterised by A. ERMAN as "freie Phantasie und nicht einmal geistvolle" and branded as "utter nonsense" by E. A. W. BUDGE. It is not until CHAMPOLLION made his discovery that scholars were able to form a somewhat reliable picture of the Egyptian religion.

This does not mean that immediately an open-minded view of the faith of the ancient Egyptians was formed. It is interesting to trace how eminent Egyptologists studied this material through the coloured spectacles of their own view of the world and of religion. This was especially the case with H. BRUGSCH, a renowned scholar of a former generation. His learned manual entitled *Religion und Mythology der alten Aegypter* (1891) is exclusively concerned with the mythologic systems. BRUGSCH evidently considered mythology to be the nucleus of the ancient Egyptian religion. He completely ignored such subjects as cult, magic, belief in immortality, popular religion. Moreover he interpreted the Egyptian conception of god in a pantheistic sense. Another famous pioneer of Egyptological studies, R. LEPSIUS, believed he could demonstrate that the Egyptian religion was founded on sun worship. His solar theory is as one-sided as all the efforts formerly undertaken to reduce various religions to this one principle. An important question was and still is the relationship between polytheism and monotheism in ancient Egypt. E. DE ROUGÉ and P. PIERRET were convinced that the Egyptian religion originally had a monotheistic character. Their thesis proved untenable in view of the multiplicity of gods which prevailed in Egypt since the very earliest of times. This monotheistic view recurs once more in a new guise in H. JUNKER, *Pyramidenzeit, das Wesen der altägyptischen Religion* (1949). JUNKER, an able Egyptologist, tries to demonstrate the plausibility of the theory that already in the age of the pyramids there was worshipped a god-head with the character of the so-called 'supreme being' and called 'the Great One'. A theory founded on shaky grounds.

A second weighty matter on which opinions can differ is the question whether any development can be discerned in the history of Egyptian religion. Some time ago J. LIEBLEIN drew up an historical outline with the following stages: henotheistic worship of nature, polytheism, monotheism, animal cult and emanation doctrine. Later J. H. BREASTED wrote his famous book *Development of Religion and Thought in Ancient Egypt*, a work of which the merits and weak points are discussed in the second chapter. It is not surprising that fetishism and totemism, which were in vogue for a period in the study of religions, were introduced into Egyptology to explain certain phenomena. It is no less surprising that Egyptologists could not avoid being fascinated by J. G. FRAZER's powerful work, *The Golden Bough*. R. PIETSCHMANN introduced fetishism. A. MORET sought after totemism in ancient Egypt, *inter alia* in an article called "Pharaon et totem" in his stimulating book *Mystères égyptiens* (1922). The same author also manifested himself as a faithful Frazerian, e.g. in his *La mise à mort du dieu en Egypte* (1927). All such fine and alluring theories were resolutely and skilfully eliminated from the picture of Egyptian religion when A. ERMAN wrote his well-known book *Die Religion der Ägypter* (1934). His description is based on completely reliable data, but is slightly too business-like to be fascinating. Nonetheless it is to his credit that in it adequate attention is paid to the faith of the common people, which was often neglected for the sake of the theology. Only W. M. FLINDERS PETRIE and H. O. LANGE had illuminated this facet of the Egyptian religion. Exactitude also characterises the studie devoted by K. SETHE to Egyptian religion. SETHE attributes great, indeed exaggerated value to the influence of political, social factors on the forming of the conceptions of god, as explained in the second chapter.

ERMAN and SETHE laid the foundations for a sound treatment of Egyptian religion. Nevertheless they lacked sufficient understanding of the intrinsic nature of the ancient religion to be able to fathom the ancient Egyptian faith. More congeniality with his subject is shown by J. VANDIER in his *La Religion égyptienne* (1949), although he does not succeed in sketching an integral picture. Hence it is not coincidental that he appends an "état des questions" to each chapter. A genuine comprehension of the human value of the Egyptian religion is manifested by S. MORENZ in his *Ägyptische Religion* (1960) even though he interprets the faith of the Egyptians all too personalistically. The grand master of the art of solving the mysteries of Egyptian religion is irrefutably W. BREDE KRISTENSEN. He wrote only monographs, of which his study on *Het leven uit de dood, studien over Egyptische en oud-Griekse godsdienst* (Life from death, Studies on Egyptian and ancient Greek religion) (1949) most clearly demonstrates his talent for understanding ancient religion. His pupils followed his footsteps. G. VAN DER LEEUW with *Godsvoorstellingen in de oud-aegyptische pyramidenteksten* (Conceptions of God in the Ancient Egyptian Pyramid Texts) (1916), A. DE BUCK with a study on *De Egyptische voorstellingen betreffende de oerheuvel* (The Egyptian Conception of the Primordial Hill) (1922), the present writer with a study on *Die Geburt eines Gottes, eine Studie über den ägyptischen Gott Min und sein Fest* (1956), and *"Egyptian Festivals, Enactments of Religious Renewal* (1967). One gets the impression that the Egyptologists of today think the time has passed for writing synthetising works on Egyptian religion. Only monographs appear, and these include excellent studies. For example, H. FRANKFORT compiled a study on sacral kingship in Egypt and Mesopotamia *Kingship and the Gods* (1948); MAJ. SANDMAN HOLMBERG dealt with *The God Ptah* (1946) and J. ZANDEE wrote a sound treatise on *Death as an Enemy, according to Ancient Egyptian Conception* (1960).

SELECTED BIBLIOGRAPHY

[1] C. J. BLEEKER, *De beteekenis van de Egyptische godin Ma-a-t*, 1929
[2] ———, *De overwinning op den dood, naar oud-Egyptisch geloof*, 1942
[3] ———, *Die Geburt eines Gottes, eine Studie über den ägyptischen Gott Min und sein Fest*, 1956
[4] H. BONNET, *Reallexikon der ägyptischen Religionsgeschichte*, 1952
[5] J. H. BREASTED, *Development of Religion and Thought in Ancient Egypt*, 1912
[6] ———, *Ancient Records of Egypt*, I-V, 1927
[7] J. ČERNY, *Ancient Egyptian Religion*, 1952
[8] E. DRIOTON, *Pages d'Egyptologie*, 1952
[9] A. ERMAN-H. RANKE, *Aegypten und aegyptisches Leben im Altertum*, 1922
[10] ———, *Die Literatur der Aegypter*, 1923
[11] ———, *Die Religion der Ägypter*, 1934
[12] H. FRANKFORT, *Kingship and the Gods, A Study of Ancient Near Eastern Religions as an Integration of Society and Nature*, 1948
[13] ———, *Ancient Egyptian Religion*, 1948
[14] A. GARDINER, *Egypt of the Pharaos*, 1964
[15] H. JACOBSOHN, *Die dogmatische Stellung des Königs in der Theologie der alten Aegypter*, 1939

[16] H. JUNKER, *Pyramidenzeit, das Wesen der altägyptischen Religion*, 1949
[17] ——, *Die Stundenwachen in den Osirismysterien nach den Inschriften von Dendera, Edfu und Philae* (*DWAW* 54, 1910)
[18] H. KEES, *Der Götterglaube im alten Aegypten*, 1955
[19] ——, *Totenglauben und Jenseitsvorstellungen der alten Aegypter*, 1956
[20] ——, Ägypten, (*Religionsgeschichtliches Lesebuch*, 1928)
[21] W. K. KRISTENSEN, *Het leven uit de dood*, 1949
[22] S. A. B. MERCER, *The Religion of ancient Egypt*, 1949
[23] S. MORENZ, *Ägyptische Religion*, 1960
[24] A. MORET, *Mystères égyptiens*, 1922
[25] ——, *Rois et Dieux d'Egypte*, 1922
[26] G. ROEDER, *Die ägyptische Religion in Texten und Bildern*, I-IV, 1959 ff.
[27] C. E. SANDER-HANSEN, *Der Begriff des Todes bei den Ägyptern*, 1942
[28] H. SANDMAN HOLMBERG, *The God Ptah*, 1946
[29] A. SCHARFF, *Ägyptische Sonnenlieder*, 1922
[30] H. SCHÄFER, *Die Mysterien des Osiris in Abydos*, 1904
[31] ——, *Die Religion und Kunst von El Amarna*, 1923
[32] S. SCHOTT, *Das schöne Fest vom Wüstentale, Festbräuche einer Totenstadt*, 1952
[33] K. SETHE, *Dramatische Texte zu altägyptischen Mysterienspielen*, 1928
[34] J. VANDIER, *La Religion égyptienne*, 1949
[35] J. ZANDEE, *Death as an Enemy, according to Ancient Egyptian Conceptions*, 1960

RELIGION OF ANCIENT MESOPOTAMIA

BY

W. H. PH. RÖMER*)

Groningen, Netherlands

I. The Essence of the Mesopotamian Religion

Today, more than ever before, it is practically impossible to write the history of the Ancient Mesopotamian religion and it is not surprising that such an expert on this subject as A. L. Oppenheim opined that a "Mesopotamian religion" neither can nor should be written (*Anc. Mes.* 172ff.). His reasons for this very pessimistic judgment are the paucity and the uncommunicativeness of the philological and archeological sources available at present, which greatly hinder any insight into the real essence of the religion and religious phenomena, and the difficulty of understanding "across the borders of conceptual conditioning." For example, the prayers are almost always bound to an accompanying ritual, can only be interpreted in relation to it and hence reveal almost nothing about the relationship of the individual to the divine, whilst the myths from Mesopotamia often possess greater value for the history of literature than of religion. Furthermore, although the rituals, of which the various local and chronological versions often contain unexplained divergencies, reveal the practice of the sympathetic and analogous magic frequently exercised in Mesopotamia, this is not specifically Mesopotamian. In its speculations about the mutual relationship of the various deities regarding power, function, achievement, and affiliation, which are often excessively emphasised, the theology gives a better picture of Mesopotamian scholarship than of religiousness. According to A. L. Oppenheim, diverse religious actions, such as prayers, fasting, avoidance of taboos, etc., appear to have been mainly or exclusively the task of the king. And actually in the Mesopotamian land proper only he traditionally received divine messages. The part played by the individual in the celebration of cyclic festivals, for example, was more of a ceremonial nature; at least his connexions with divinity are, on the whole, known

* Acknowledgment: the author expresses his sincere thanks to his teacher Prof. Dr. F. M. Th. de Liagre Böhl for putting at his disposal the material of his articles in: C. J. Bleeker, *De Godsdiensten der Wereld*² 2, 51ff.; in: F. König, *Christus und die Religionen der Erde* 2, 441ff., and a shorter survey in: RGG³ 1, 812ff.

to us as being rather superficial and impersonal, just as the demands made on the individual by the deities do not seem to have been great (A. L. Oppenheim).

Another serious difficulty encountered in discussing the Mesopotamian religion lies in the composite character of the religious phenomena handed down to us. Specifically, this religion can in no way be described as an absolute unity, for account must be taken of the religious representations of entirely different peoples and groups of people, namely the Sumerians and Akkadians on the one hand, and the Babylonians and Assyrians on the other. The task of determining which religious elements were contributed by which groups to the common picture of Mesopotamian religion as evolved in the course of time is one which so far has not proceeded beyond the initial stage and which probably never will be completed owing to lack of sufficiently positive indications. The Hurrians, on the contrary, who must have been in the country at least since the Akkad period (s. H. Schmökel, *HOr.* 2/3, 155 f.; I. J. Gelb, *Festschrift J. Friedrich*, 183ff.) apparently contributed nothing worthy of note to the Mesopotamian religion. Radiating northwestward, their influence appears to have been powerful in forming the pantheon and myths of the Hittites of Asia Minor. However, they do seem to have influenced the development of temple construction in Northern Mesopotamia (H. Lenzen, *ZA* 51, 34).

As can be noted today, the knowledge of the immanence of a 'divine power' (s. J. van Dijk, *OLZ* 1967, 229ff.; I.R. 384ff.; K. Oberhuber, *Der numinose Begriff* me *im Sumerischen*, Innsbruck 1963)—called 'me' in Sumerian, and conceived of not as a sort of fluidum but as something subsistent, individualised, differentiated, and impersonal in all beings and things—constituted one of the most important components of the religion of the Sumerian-speaking Mesopotamians (a). This conception never succeeded in replacing the anthropomorphic representations of deity in either the old 'Sumerian' form of religion or in that of the later Semitic-speaking Babylonians, but from time immemorial existed alongside of it. In the Akkadian text sources it is admittedly less obvious than in the Sumerian ones, nevertheless the representation of a divine immanence is not alien to the Akkadian religion, as is shown by B. Landsberger's study of the Akkadian partial equivalent *parṣum* of the Sumerian me (*AK* 2, 66ff.). It is peculiar to gods and temples; because of the related verbs, the *parṣu*'s were apparently visualized by emblems.

Furthermore it can be said in this connexion that the Akkadian texts several times speak of a vital and activating force (*lamassu*) inherent in man and probably conceived of as divine (s. W. von Soden, *BagM* 3, 148ff.), while reference might also be made here to the conception of the measure of good and bad fortune (*šīmtum*) probably awarded to everyone on his birth (A. L. Oppenheim). A. L. Oppenheim interprets the *ilu* of man (often translated as "personal (patron) god") as "some kind of spiritual endowment which is difficult to define but may well allude to the divine element in man"; *ištaru* as "his fate"; *lamassu* as "his individual characteristics" and *šēdu* as "his élan vital". In conclusion he mentions the conception *melemmu* also to be found in Sumerian texts (me-lám), roughly the "supernatural radiance" of gods and kings (s. A. L. Oppenheim, *JAOS* 63, 31ff.; J. van Dijk, *I.R.* 389; 426; *AHw.* 643), which according to the Aramaic version *gadia* of the Ancient Persian equivalent *hvarena* could pertain to personal fortune (*Anc. Mes.* 200ff.). Finally reference might be made to the important conception giš-ḫur, according to J. van Dijk, (*I.R.* 386) "(divine) fundamental plan" as the essence of things and to mum (Akkadian *mummu*, s. *AHw.* 672), which originated in the Eridu circle and which J. van Dijk, *I.R.* 387f.; *SGL* 2, 115; 115[4] interprets roughly as "forma intelligibilis of matter" (s. also below Ch. V.C.a).

Other characteristics of the Mesopotamian religion are:

(b) Polytheism and concomitantly a far-reaching tolerance. Corresponding to the mortal kings and princes with their dynasties and retinues is the hierarchy of higher and lower deities in various pantheons probably possessed by every town of any importance in the early Sumerian period. As for tolerance, Marduk's rise to eminence never led to the suppression of the other deities. In the prologue to his code Ḫammurapi claims the honour of having restored the old sanctuaries; he apparently entertained no thought of one-sided preference for his state god Marduk. Several times the influence of political developments led to the inclusion of foreign deities in the Babylonian pantheon; for example already in the Ur III period the gods Martu (s. D. O. Edzard, *WM* 1/1, 97f.) and Dagān (s. D. O. Edzard, o.c. 49f.), both of western origin, and in a later period a couple of Cassite deities (s. D. O. Edzard, o.c., 91; 92; 54f.). Sometimes the incorporation was facilitated by theological constructions, such as identification with Babylonian gods.

The collection of names of Mesopotamian gods made by A. Deimel

(1914) (PB; see also A. DEIMEL, ŠL 4/1) contains 3300 entries. There were so many cult sites in the city of Aššur that a sort of 'directory of the gods' was needed to find the way (s. R. FRANKENA, Tākultu 122ff.). A discernible tendency would seem to be that gods which were identified with constellations or parts of the universe were merely personified parts of the great cosmic entity. For example, individual gods in the Enūma eliš were identified with the great god Marduk as his attributes, a process connected with the reduction by the Babylonians of the pantheon handed down to them. Also, within the framework of theological speculation, individual gods were identified with parts of the body of Ninurta (s. SAHG akkad. 10). One wonders to what extent monotheistic (monolatrous?) tendencies can be discerned here (cf. below Ch. V.B.a).

(c) Furthermore, strong cosmic and astral features can be traced in the Mesopotamian religion. The sun, moon and planets are worshipped as representatives of the divine, they are great gods themselves, the rulers of cosmic harmony, and what happens on earth is reflected in the "celestial writing" of the stars.

(d) The vegetative and chthonic elements of life in nature, which formed a focus of religious interest in the time of the 'Sumerian religion', later on fall partially into the background, though the Marduk cult adopted certain elements (this god becomes the son of Enki through identification with Asariluḫi (cf. J. VAN DIJK, I.R. 412)), and in the circles of sun-worship they are even contested as being immoral (cf. below, the Epic of Gilgameš). On the one hand this is manifest in the nomenclature, in which names compounded with Dumuzi or other vegetation figures, none too numerous even in the earlier Sumerian period, gradually disappear, and on the other, in the fact that the sexual aspects of the goddess Ištar, which were not the only original ones of the 'Sumerian' figure of Inanna (s. J. VAN DIJK, I.R. 417ff.), are progressively superseded by the martial aspects.

(e) Another essential figure of the Mesopotamian religion, present since the earliest periods—cf. the oldest temples (J. VAN DIJK, OLZ 1967, 238ff.)!—is the striking anthropomorphism of the divine figures who, however, differ from humans on an essential point: on the whole they are immortal whereas the latter are not granted immortality apart from the hero of the Deluge, Utnapištim and his consort (see below, the Epic of Gilgameš). The human figure of many gods is known to us from cylinder seals, sculptures and from a Young Babylonian text, which describes the outward appearance of a number of gods or half-gods, including Damu, Ninurta, and Ninazu (s. F. KÖCHER, *MIO* 1,57ff.) and perhaps, too, from the texts which contain references to the clothing and ornamentation of divine images (s. W. F. LEEMANS, *SLB* 1/1; A. L. OPPENHEIM, *JNES* 8, 172ff.). The fragments of love songs, recently published by W. G. LAMBERT (*JSS* 4, 1ff.), which apparently refer to Marduk and Ištar, are likewise very anthropomorphic.

(f) If a religion possesses a great number of anthropomorphic conceptions, a rich mythology can be expected a priori, and in this respect the Mesopotamian religion comes up to expectation. Changing religious or cultic developments could be explained by, or reflected in, myths. For example, the Babylonian 'epic of creation' Enūma eliš (see below) reveals how the generations of the gods (cf. D. O. EDZARD, *WM* 1/1, 74f. and for another succession of generations of gods s. W. G. LAMBERT and P. WALCOT, *Kadmos* 4, 64ff.; J. VAN DIJK, *I.R.* 393f.) succeeded each other: Apsû-Tiāmat; Laḫmu-Laḫamu; Anšar-Kišar; Anu and his brothers; Ea (s. J. VAN DIJK, *I.R.* 394). In the Sumerian sources the cosmogony is accompanied by natural catastrophes (J. VAN DIJK, Act.Or. 28, 21ff.), but in Enūma eliš the act of creation is preceded by a theomachy. Thereupon, after peaceful consultation, the younger gods pass by Enlil and hand over the suzerainty to Marduk, their youngest member, who gains the victory over the water demons. Later it appears that Marduk is superseded in his turn by Nabû, his son. The other gods, however, continue to hold their positions of power. This process probably reflects the increasing power of the city of Babylon under the dynasty of Ḫammurapi, though sometimes the religious significance of a god did not automatically keep pace with the political significance of his city, as in the case of Eridu and Nippur. Similarily, through his identification with another powerful god (syncretism), a god can himself attain a high position of power: in Assyria there was a trend towards preference for the national god Aššur and not for the Babylonian god Marduk, whose worship had begun to take root there since the 14th century B.C. (s. D. O. EDZARD, *WM* 1/1, 96). Aššur's identification with Anšar gave him, in the eyes of his worshippers, the right of primogeniture in the family of gods. The Assyrian king Sennacherib who, showing no tolerance on this occasion, violently opposed the worship of Marduk in his blind hatred of all that was Babylonian (cf. also B. LANDSBERGER, *BBEA* 20 ft.),

apparently wanted to justify the Assyrian devastation of Babylon and
the temple of Marduk by means of the composition of the so-called
text of the verdict on Marduk (s. W. VON SODEN, *ZA* 51, 130ff.; 52,
224ff.). In it judicial sentence is evidently passed on Marduk during
an assembly of the gods, because he refused to recognise the god
Aššur's claim to power.

(g) Eschatological conceptions appear to have been entirely absent
or scarcely known in ancient Mesopotamia (s. J. VAN DIJK, *Sumer* 18,
29; W. VON SODEN, *MDOG* 96, 58).

II. HISTORICAL DEVELOPMENT

In particular the syncretisms referred to briefly above will be discussed in further detail here.

A. *Older Syncretism*

Long ago it was realised that the ancient culture of Mesopotamia
comprises not only a period of more than five thousand years, but in
addition at least two circles of entirely different peoples and languages.
Later the spiritual legacy of the Sumero-Akkadians passed to the closely affiliated peoples of Babylonia and Assyria. The latter, however,
looked upon the Sumerians, who were not akin to them, as their predecessors and adopted their literature and language for their own cult
and science.

Excavations carried out in the last decades have provided insight
into the earliest periods of the Babylonian lowlands and the more
elevated surrounding areas. Nowadays we also know something of the
predecessors of the Sumerians, traces of whom are to be found in the
toponymy (B. LANDSBERGER; s. W. NAGEL, *BJV* 4, 1ff.), and alongside of whom, as may be conjectured, the Sumerians lived in the
period immediately following on their arrival. We also know something of the beginning and the decline of the so-called Eridu, 'Obēd
and Uruk periods (circa 5000-3100 B.C.) and that these cultural strata
are of a later date than the chalcolithic cultures of the northern areas,
let alone the much older village cultures (e.g. Ǧarmō) (s. A. FALKEN-
STEIN, *FW* 2, 13ff.; W. NAGEL, *BBV* 8; H. FRANKFORT†, *CAH²* 1
XII). The reason why the alluvial areas of the south were populated
by farmers at a relatively late date is probably to be found in the geographical and climatological features of the country. Even in the

period dealt with here, the coastline and the course of the rivers were subject to great changes. Extremes of climate, moreover, rendered the plain unhealthy: during the winter inundations there were dangerous marshes (the southern areas where the Ma'dān Arabs live today were covered all the year round with reed marshes) and in the unbearably hot summers this land was an arid steppe which, even in ancient times, could only be farmed by laying down irrigation canals to compensate the lack of rain. What made the land attractive was its rich clay soil —prerequisite for fertility and....for the necessary writing materials!

In its earliest form the writing was pictographic. It is known definitely to have been a Sumerian invention (but s. now B. MEISSNER † and K. OBERHUBER, *Die Keilschrift*[3], Berlin 1967, § 57), and its presence is attested as from the Uruk IVa stratum. An interesting research project is to investigate the degree of developments and the religious way of thought of the inventors of writing, using as medium the objects selected in the script for the expression of words and thoughts (s. now K. JARITZ, *Schriftarchäologie der altmesopotamischen Kultur*, Graz 1967).

About the second half of the fourth millenium the Sumerians entered southern Mesopotamia; whence they came is a question which as yet cannot be answered with certainty. Nor can be determined with absolute certainty just how old the Sumero-Akkadian syncretism and culture-fusion are, though they are clearly manifest at the end of the third dynasty of Ur. We now know that Sargon and his daughter Enḫedu'anna were great promotors of a Sumero-Akkadian syncretism (s. J. VAN DIJK, *I.R.* 382f.).

The unified state with centres in Isin (present day Išān-Baḥriyāt), and thereafter in Larsa (now Senkereh), signifies the late flowering of the first period of creative Sumerian literary work and perhaps, too, the hey-day of early Akkadian literature from the pre-Ḫammurapi period. At the beginning the state language must still have been Sumerian, although with few exceptions the kings had Semitic names, as did already the last two monarchs of the Ur III dynasty. The ethnic and linguistic contrast between North and South is revealed for example in the legislations which came to light several years ago. The earliest legal codes, those of Urnammu of Ur and of Lipiteštar of Isin, which predate the code of Ḫammurapi by about 300 and 150 years respectively, are written in Sumerian, while the code of King Daduša(?) of Eš-nunna (now Tell-Asmar) in the North is written in Akkadian. Apart from the composition 'Enki and the world order' and the hymns per-

taining to kings of the Isin, Larsa and Ḫammurapi dynasties, the voluminous body of Sumerian literature recorded or copied during the
Ancient Babylonian period is based on older originals, mainly from the
Akkad and Ur III periods (cf. A. FALKENSTEIN, *CRRA* 2, 12ff.; W. W.
HALLO, *JAOS* 83, 167ff.). Some time ago J. VAN DIJK discovered traces
of literary turnings in very early Sumerian documents from Uruk
(*UVB* 16, 58f.). Sumerian literary compositions are already to be found
among the later texts from Fāra and Abū-Ṣalābīḫ (s. R. D. BIGGS, *JCS*
20, 78ff.; M. CIVIL and R. D. BIGGS, *RA* 60, 1ff.). The majority of the
great epic poems, the longest of which contains more than 600 lines,
deal with the figure of B/Gilgameš, whilst a few others deal with the
heroes Enmerkar and Lugalbanda (s. D. O. EDZARD, *WM* 1/1, 95),
ancient kings of Uruk. A comparison between the Sumerian legends of
Bilgameš and the Akkadian Gilgameš texts of the ancient Babylonian
period, of which as yet only a rather small number are known, further
reveals something of the difference between the spiritual attitude of the
two components of the population. The Akkadian texts, parts of which
have a very different content, not only are written in another language,
but resemble true heroic epics, being stripped of much of their magical
and mythological character and resembling in this respect the independent epic of Bilgameš and Agga of Sumerian tradition, whilst Sumerian poetry, with its principle of regular and literal repetition, betrays
something of the tendency towards order also discernible in Sumerian lists (s. W. VON SODEN, *Leistung und Grenze sumerischer und
babylonischer Wissenschaft*[2], Darmstadt 1965). The Semitic-speaking Akkadians on the contrary, preferred forcefulness and variety even in the
parallelismus membrorum of their poetry. If we consider the cosmological and cosmogonic conceptions in the Sumerian literary texts, as
dealt with in recent years by J. VAN DIJK in particular, we can discern
at least a clear difference between conceptions from sedentary (chthonic) and non-sedentary (cosmic) strata of the population (s. below).
The world was created in analogy of the way the fertile land was made
from silt, for which the goddess Nammu was perhaps responsible,
being the personification of subterranean water (s. D. O. EDZARD,
WM 1/1, 107f.). According to J. VAN DIJK her place in the Eridu cosmogony seems to be that of Tiāmat in the Enūma eliš, while later she
became Mother-Earth in the Eridu theology (s. J. VAN DIJK, *I.R.* 408).
The part she played in the creation of man according to the Enki and
Ninmaḫ myth is well-known (s. J. VAN DIJK, *ActOr.* 28, 24ff.). One
of the compositions of the Sumerian Bilgameš cycle has it that heaven

and earth were separated (or were separated by Enlil, according to the beginning of the Sumerian didactic poem on the creation of the Pickax, s. A. FALKENSTEIN, *ZA* 47, 221f.), the heaven being allotted to An, the earth to Enlil and the underworld to the goddess Ereškigala (s. J. VAN DIJK, *ActOr.* 28, 17ff.). According to a well-known myth, the interaction of the godheads Enlil and Ninlil resulted in the creation of the Moon-god, the chthonic gods Ninazu and Meslamta'ea and, according to a text handed down in late-Babylonian only, a series of function-gods and man is created by Ea (*Racc.* 46, 24ff.) and (s. above) the Pickax, the implement so important for agriculture, by Enlil. According to one tradition man was made from clay by the goddess Nammu above the Abzu (chthonic), according to other texts he emerged from the earth (cosmic: rain!) with the help of Enlil who made a hole in the ground, or merely "as grass". All this, and also the conception of Enki as the one who allots the various deities their functions in the composition 'Enki and the world order', which probably first came into being in the early Isin period (s. A. FALKENSTEIN, *ZA* 56, 44ff.), leaves a sober, almost realistic impression, quite different from the tradition in the Enūma eliš, at least as it is handed down in Akkadian, where the conflict of the gods is depicted with verve and animation. As noted by J. VAN DIJK, *ActOr.* 28, 10, the latter epic probably contains an old (chthonic) theogony which only assumes cosmic traits when Marduk slays Tiāmat and cleaves her swollen body into heaven and earth (cf. Enlil). Furthermore the conceptions relating to the figure of Dumuzi (Tammūz) appear to belong to the religious 'contribution' of the Sumerians; Ama'ušumgal (later A.-anna), later identified with him, appears early in the early dynastic period (s. A. FALKENSTEIN, *CRRA* 3, 42ff.; J. VAN DIJK, *I.R.* 425). The conception that suffering and illness are the punishment of sin appears in the Akkadian, but not in the Sumerian tradition (s. J. VAN DIJK, *SSA* 133f.).

B. *More recent Syncretism and Secularisation*

(a) The heirs of the Sumerians were the Semitic-speaking Akkadians. Lack of food drove groups of inhabitants of the Syrian-Arabian steppe and desert regions into the Mesopotamian plain. The conquering raids and invasions of the successive groups, such as Akkadians, (early) Canaanites, Aramaeans and Arabs, took place in the historical period (s. W. VON SODEN, *WZKM* 56, 177ff.).

Because of their extraction and original living conditions, the relationship to the divine powers of these steppe dwellers differed from

that of the sedentary inhabitants of the alluvial agrarian land with
their efforts at order, regularity and security. Desert gods, such as
those of Syria and Palestine where fertility depends on rainfall and not
on inundation, are characterised more by power and arbitrariness than
by a desire for order. True, rain and storm are limited to certain
seasons, but they can less readily be forecast. The concept of god entertained by the aforesaid groups is therefore characterised by two
features in particular: personal will-power and might. Related to this
is also their endeavour to give a personized representation of the
divine, by which the feeling of dependence is given a personal aspect.
One no longer feels caught up in an inexorable and unvarying cycle,
but is as a servant before one's lord, a son before one's father (cf. the
organisation of the Bedouin tribes under their Šēḫ's!).

Moreover there was the trend towards assimilation and synthesis of
the Semitic-speaking tribes, which on the whole were of a lower cultural level than the inhabitants of the agrarian region. These tribes did
not behave as despisers or destroyers of the older cultures; on the
contrary, they made their own important artistic contributions. The
Old Akkadian sculpture and glyptic testify to this. As regards religion
and culture they adapted themselves to a large degree to their predecessors, adopted their religious views and customs and fused them
with their own(Enḫedu'anna!). Even after the Sumerians were ethnic-
ally completely absorbed in the melting-pot of the peoples of Mesopotamia, their language, like Latin in the Middle Ages and later, remained the language of cult and religion, a permanent basis for the
later development.

The inhabitants of Sumer and Akkad are called Babylonians as from
the promotion of Babylon to capital of the state. Connected with this
changed status of Babylon is also the promotion of their urban god
Marduk. This phenomenon, which is of importance from the viewpoint of the history of religion, must have begun in the period of the
first dynasty of Babylon and reached its climax in the so-called "dark
age" (early Cassite period) (s. H. SCHMÖKEL, *RA* 53, 183ff.). This
same period is characterised by a clearly perceptible process of secu-
larisation during the reign of Ḫammurapi (s. below Ch. III. D). The
term "Babylonians" marks a distinction from the Assyrians, who were
related linguistically to the former. In the period of their first hey-day
and before their subjection by Ḫammurapi, the Assyrians ventured
out from the central Tigris on their conquering raids, and from the
cultural and religious aspect their relationship to the Babylonians was

roughly comparable to that of the latter to the Sumerians. As entity, then, the Babylonian-Assyrian religion was the product of a great synthesis, focus being the gods Marduk and Aššur, the latter being the city god of the city of the same name. The term 'syncretism' is therefore applicable here, since it pertains to an admixture of divergent popular religions to form a polytheistic system with a Sumerian foundation.

(b) With respect to the period after Alexander the Great, there appear to be traces of recoining the names of gods from Mesopotamian into Greek; for example from Anu and Antu at Uruk into Zeus and Hera (F. M. TH. DE LIAGRE BÖHL (s. D. O. EDZARD, *WM* 1/1, 41)), whilst Strabo's description of Borsippa as "city of Artemis and Apollo" probably refers to Nanāja-Tašmētu and Nabû (s. D. O. EDZARD, *WM* 1/1, 108). Here it is probably incorrect to speak of syncretism: an Anu-hymn from Uruk (s. C. FRANK, *ZA* 41, 193ff.) dating from the Seleucid age still manifestly bears a Mesopotamian stamp, whilst a bilingual elegy of the mother-goddess from Uruk (s. C. FRANK, *ZA* 40, 81ff.), which evidently alludes to ancient Tammuz conceptions, was recorded in the same period.

III. WORLD OF THE GODS

A. *(Ir)rational notions* (s. J. VAN DIJK, *I.R.* 384ff.; *OLZ* 1967, 229ff.).

With respect to the concept of god and the notions of immanent divine powers, reference can be made to what has been discussed above in Ch. I; s. also Ch. V, C.a.

B. *Systematization of the gods*

From early times onwards attempts were made to systematize the gods into a hierarchy of divine families. Such lists of gods (s. D. O. EDZARD, *WM* 1/1, 75), the earliest of which date from about 2600 B.C. and were recovered in Fāra (Šuruppak) and Abū Ṣalābīḫ, may be looked upon as the earliest products of theological learning. The great list of gods, which acquired canonical significance in later centuries (An: *Anum*), could also be older than Ḫammurapi and perhaps the rise of Assyria as regards basis and classification, since Marduk still plays a subordinate role and the Assyrian god Aššur is not included. This list contains after the couples of primordial deities the following main groups of gods: Anu, Enlil, Bēletilī (s. below H.g), Ea, Sîn, Ištar,

Ninurta, Nergal. The second column contains explanations of the divine names in the first column by means of Akkadian equivalents, identifications, etc. Together with each god are listed his consorts, children and retinue as well as his various names and manifestations.

The Sumerians brought together the deities of local panthea (e.g. of Eridu and Lagaš, cf. A. FALKENSTEIN, *AnOr.* 30/1, 55ff.) into groups which they called Anunna (-gods); later on, after the so-called 'Reichs-pantheon' had been developed, Anunna became the designation of the Sumerian 'great gods'. In Old Babylonian Akkadian texts the gods are divided into Igigu and Anunnaku. These terms later on often served as designations for the gods of heaven (I.) and of the earth and the netherworld (A.) respectively (s. A. FALKENSTEIN, *AS* 16, 127ff.; B. KIENAST, ibid. 141ff.; W. VON SODEN, *CRRA* 11, 102ff.; *Iraq* 28, 140ff.).

Finally it might be pointed out that the Sumerian religious conceptions, as they have gradually become known to us from Sumerian literature, reflect the views of the various strata of the population. Those of the farmers (sedentaries), who depended on springs (irrigation) for the fertility of the land, were chthonic notions and evolved especially in the Eridu theology. Those of the hunters and shepherds, who lived on the arid steppes bordering on the agrarian regions and depended on rainfall for their game and their herds, were cosmic notions, especially in the theology of Uruk (the god of heaven, An) and Nippur (Enlil) (s. J. VAN DIJK, *ActOr.* 28, 1ff.; *I.R.* 380f.). It is to the latter conceptions in particular that the thoughts of the Semitic speaking peoples, who entered the country in the course of the centuries from the desert regions, must have turned. These different thoughts emerge, inter alia, in the various myths of creation, such as the chthonic creation myths from Eridu, a creation by *formatio* (water), best known to us from the myth of Enki and Ninmaḫ, and the Enūma eliš with its generations of gods. They also emerge from the cosmic conceptions of creation from Uruk and Nippur, in which the god of heaven and Enlil play a greater role (creation myths in which heaven and earth are separated from each other, after which heaven fecundates the earth and consequently vegetation comes out by *emersio*: cf. the introduction of the myth of Bilgameš, Enkidu, and the netherworld). Several Sumerian texts mention a number of "father and mother deities" (already known in a Fāra list, connected later with the cosmic system and represented as ancestors of An and Enlil, s. J. VAN DIJK, *ActOr.* 28, 7f.; 12f.), who lived in a "primordial town" (Sumerian: uru-ul-la) and who later, as can be reconstructed from various data, were banned to the netherworld because of ὕβρις. In the Sumerian composition "Curse upon Akkade" the weeping of the people of Akkade is compared to the weeping of the 'parents of Enlil' (s. J. VAN DIJK, *I.R.* 395f.: A. FALKENSTEIN, *ZA* 57, 61, 209). According to the myth of Nergal and Ereškigala, they then acted as gate-keepers of Hades; cf. also the myth of Gilgameš in the netherworld. They personify the primeval forms of the material and spiritual culture of the Sumerian city-state. Cf. finally the part played by the body of Enmešarra in the New Year's procession (s. J. VAN DIJK, *I.R.* 394ff.).

C. Cosmic gods

The first god of the cosmic triad is the ancient Sumerian god An (Akkadian: *Anum*), whose name simply means "heaven". As ancient "Hochgott" (s. J. VAN DIJK, *I.R.* 396) he is frequently mentioned before Enlil and Ea in lists and enumerations, apart from the "father and mother deities" sometimes preceding these gods (s. J. VAN DIJK, *ActOr.* 28, 7f.; 12f.). However, his significance for religious life and especially the cult (s. J. VAN DIJK, *I.R.* 404) was only relatively small in Mesopotamia. Later he seems to be more a sort of abstraction, and apparently he is far-removed from the people, even though his role in theology is important. Out of the entire body of literature, only three short prayers have been published which are directed personally to him (s. E. EBELING, *RlA* 1, 116). According to the epic of the creation of the world (Enūma eliš), he, Enlil, and Ea presented Marduk with gifts after the latter's victory over the forces of chaos and the underworld (Tiāmat, Apsū and Kingu). According to another myth, Inanna (Ištar), who as the star Venus was originally An's daughter, was endowed by him with the rank of queen of the heavens instead of his consort Antum (s. D. O. EDZARD, *WM* 1/1, 87; W. G. LAMBERT, *JCS* 16, 71; B. LANDSBERGER, *WZKM* 56, 126[54]; J. VAN DIJK, *UVB* 18, 50; *I.R.* 418; also *ActOr* 28, 15[28]). Indeed, his worship in the famous sanctuary of Eanna at Uruk was replaced by that of this goddess. Anu was also worshipped in Dēr. It is remarkable that he was not only considered to have turned away from man, but also to be hostile to him. The deluge was attributed by preference to him and to Enlil. The seven evil spirits (Sebettu) and the dreaded female demon Lamaštum are the offspring of the celestial god Anum (s. D. O. EDZARD, *WM* 1/1, 48; 124f.; J. VAN DIJK, *I.R.* 403f.). It was not until the Persian and Hellenistic period (from the third century B.C. on) that gigantic temples were once again built in his honour in Uruk. At that time the Marduk temple Esagila in Babylon

had been in ruins ever since the Babylonians had risen against the
Persian king Xerxes, and then the ancient god of heaven was once
more brought to the foreground and was worshipped in the same way
as Marduk formerly with processions of the gods at the New Years
Festival (s. *Racc.* 61ff.). In the Assyrian capital Aššur ever since the
twelfth century, Anu had been allotted part of the ancient temple of
Adad, god of storm and thunder. There are no representations of him.
His emblem was the horned tiara, and his divine number was sixty, the
highest among the numbers of the Babylonian gods.

With Anu as lord of heaven, Enlil (Ellil) was allotted the second
and in fact most important part of the cosmos: the atmosphere and
the earth. His name is Sumerian and means: "lord, gust of wind." As
"lord of the lands," Enlil was principal god of Nibru (Nippur), religious centre of Sumer and hence of the ancient Sumerians (cf. W. W.
HALLO, *JCS* 14, 88ff. "A Sumerian Amphiktyony"). Like Anu he later
occupied a less exalted position under the Babylonians. From the lists
of gods and the composition entitled "Bilgameš in the netherworld"
we know which primeval gods preceded Enlil. According to the introduction to the Code of Ḫammurapi, Anu handed over to Marduk
"the dignity of Enlil", i.e. the rulership. His temple at Nibru was called
the Ekur ("mountain house"), a term also used for temples in general.

Enlil was not always kindly disposed towards man, as is testified by
his part in the deluge, though, on the other hand, he was held to be
the prerequisite for life in the land (s. *SGL* 1, 16f., 108ff.); for example
it was the habit of various gods to travel each year to Nibru to ask
Enlil's blessing for the rulers of their cities and for vegetation (s. D.
O. EDZARD, *WM* 1/1, 75ff.; Å. SJÖBERG, *RlA* 3, 480ff.).

The emblem of Enlil was the same as that of Anu, a horned tiara.
He was considered lower in rank than Anu, his number being accordingly fifty. The priests of Enlil in Nibru were very powerful, and so,
they were able to bring about an alliance between the Sumerian cities
in the South and the Guteans so that the empire of Akkade came to
an end (s. J. VAN DIJK, *I.R.* 406). Even in the Neo-Assyrian period the
priests of Nibru joined with Assyria against Babylon. This is highly
remarkable, since Nibru was not one of the oldest cultural centres of
Mesopotamia (s. J. VAN DIJK, *I.R.* 407).

Enlil was a universal god who also protected the hostile foreign
regions and punished Sumer if it sinned against these countries, and
of course vice versa (See J. VAN DIJK, *I.R.* 406f.).

Enlils consort was Ninlil (s. D. O. EDZARD, *WM* 1/1, 62; 113), or, according to a later myth which has been discovered recently, the goddess Sud of Ereš (s. M. CIVIL, *JNES* 26, 200ff.).

The third of the cosmic triad was the god Enki, "lord of what is below," that is the realm of the waters; Ea in Akkadian (the origin and meaning of this name are uncertain). He lived in the Apsû palace at Eridu and ruled over the waters around and under the earth and over the sources. Enki was the beneficent god, god of the sedentary Mesopotamians, lord of (practical) wisdom, of artistic ability and of incantations (water possesses magical powers, s. J. VAN DIJK, *I.R.* 408f.), who gave advice and assistance to both men and gods, more than any other god apart from his son Asariluḫi (and Marduk, with whom the latter was equated). Both play a significant role in Sumerian incantations (see below, Ch. IV. A.f). However, he could also play a dangerous role, when his wisdom was liable to imperil his protégé's, as is manifested in the Adapa myth (see below, Ch. IV. C.d). At these times he was the "divine deceiver", as the late Prof. W. B. KRISTENSEN, *Verzamelde bijdragen tot kennis der antieke godsdiensten*, Amsterdam 1947, 103ff.) characterised him.

His animal emblem was the ilex, depicted with the body of a fish because of his connexion with the realm of waters. The god is portrayed seated on his throne in his temple surrounded by running waters, with streams of water pouring from his shoulders (s. D. O. EDZARD, *WM* 1/1, 57). His number was fourty.

Typical of the figure of Enki is his role as planner of the world in the comparatively recent myth of 'Enki and the world order' (s. above Ch. II. A); in it he creates the fertility of the known world of that day, originates culture, lays down the functions of the temples and gods and instructs the gods to guard over the forms of culture (J. VAN DIJK, *I.R.* 409f.).

D. *Astral gods*

The second triad follows on the above with the numbers 30, 20 and 15. It comprised the three important heavenly bodies, the moon, the sun and Venus, star of morning and evening. The moon, friendly guide of the stars, preceded, whilst the sun, likewise masculine in this culture circle, was conceived of as judge, contester of injustice and helper of the helpless and the lonely. The moon-god was called Sîn (Sumerian Nanna, which the popular etymology of the Semites perhaps

associated with *nannāru*, "celestial luminary"). He was the first-born
son of Enlil and the father of the sun-god Šamaš. His sacred city was
Ur, located in the south in the vicinity of Eridu, the famous city with
the Ekišnugal temple and the temple tower made known by the excavations of Sir L. WOOLLEY. His second sanctuary was Ḥarrān in
western Mesopotamia. These are the two cities associated with the
traditions about the patriarch Abraham before he entered Canaan. In
numerous hymns and prayers Sîn is praised as the monarch and lord
of the gods, the "fruit which renews itself," the friendly god who,
next to Ea, Marduk and Nabû, was the most beloved one even in
ancient Babylonian times, as is evidenced by his frequent occurence
in theophorous personal names(cf. H. SCHMÖKEL, *JEOL* 19, 488f.; 491).

Sîn was portrayed as a bull with a beard of lapis lazuli; his emblem
was the supine crescent moon. Nabonidus, the last king of Babylon
before its capture by the Persians, held the god Sîn of Ḥarrān in particularly great esteem (s. W. RÖLLIG, *ZA* 56, 254f.). His consort was
called Ningal ("great queen") or Nikkal; later she was worshipped
especially in Ḥarrān, and she also is to be found in the texts from
Ugarit. His sacred number was thirty, corresponding to the number
of days in the month. According to J. VAN DIJK, *I.R.* 415 (: *MNS* 1,
13ff.), two conceptions are determinative of the Sumerian Nanna: he
was the god who assembled the astral gods in his "court" (shepherd),
and he was the god who cast a faint light in the underworld after the
last quarter of the moon, at which time offerings were made to him.

Šamaš the sun-god (Sumerian: Utu) was anything but an enemy of
man. He was the judge who maintained law and justice and punished
sin, including social misdemeanour. To use the words of A. VAN
SELMS (*MVEOL* 1, 21ff.), the Šamaš religion upheld the unity of
religious and social life, which threatened to become less coherent because of the separation between "temple" and "palace" (secularization)
ever since the reign of Ḥammurapi (cf. R. HARRIS, *JCS* 15, 117ff.).
Šamaš, the name for the sun and the sun-god is universal Semitic
(Hebr.: *Šemeš*, Arab.: *Šams*). Šamaš was greatly worshipped and
evoked in his sacred cities Larsa and, later especially, Sippar (cf.
now E. SOLLBERGER, *JEOL* 20, 50). Among the hymns composed in
his honour are some of the most beautiful and profound, from the
religious viewpoint, which have been discovered in Babylonia. Šamaš
was the god who saw and learned about everything during his diurnal
journey across the sky. He was the god who uttered oracles, the patron

god of the soothsayers. But he was also the god who each evening descended in the west into the realm of the dead and then in the morning arose again between the eastern mountains, bearing in his hand an instrument. This has been interpreted as a saw on the ground of representations on the cylinder seals which, since the Akkad period, depict the rise of Šamaš (vgl. R. M. BOEHMER, *Die Entwicklung der Glyptik während der Akkad-Zeit* 71ff.).

His symbol was the sun-disc; Aja was held to be his consort; his number was twenty.

In the early dynastic period Utu was held in high esteem in Uruk; the kings called themselves "sons of Utu" (s. D. O. EDZARD, *WM* 1/1, 126f.). There is extant a striking Sumerian prayer of King Lugalbanda of Uruk to Utu for help when left behind alone and ill in the mountains (s. A. FALKENSTEIN, *RlA* 3, 159; J. VAN DIJK, *I.R.* 416f.).

According to the Sumerian texts, the role played by this god appears to have been comparatively subordinate, but ever since the dynasty which ruled in Larsa, his sacred city, in the nineteenth and eighteenth centuries B.C., his role appears to have gained steadily in importance. The influence of the Western Semites, whose gods must have been primarily solar and other astral gods, was probably responsible for this. One of the salient features of the period of Ḫammurapi was an intensive sun-cult, as evidenced by the representations on the seal-cylinders (s. A. MOORTGAT, *VR* 39).

After Larsa was devastated by Ḫammurapi (about 1763 B.C.) the ancient North Babylonian city of Sippar became the centre of the Šamaš worship. He was the god of justice and the administration of law, who discerns and punishes all injustice, and also the guardian of social equilibrium in whom widows and orphans sought and found their refuge. In a hymn he is invoked as king of heaven and earth, without whom no justice is done nor judgment passed for the oppressed (s. *BWL* 126ff.). On this basis the Šamaš religion acquired, in addition to a judicial, a didactic, moralising character, in contradistinction to Sumerian conceptions concerning vegetation. This contradistinction is perhaps most evident in the Epic of Gilgameš (see below). In it Šamaš appears as the great guide, whilst the older Sumerian goddess Inanna (Ištar) and her unchaste worship at Uruk are censured and deprecated (s. F. M. TH. DE LIAGRE BÖHL, *Het Gilgamesjepos* [3], 16f.; W. VON SODEN, *RA* 52, 134; D. O. EDZARD, *WM* 1/1, 85). In an Uruk ritual from the Seleucid period Utu/Šamaš appears as the one who cares for the deceased (s. A. FALKENSTEIN, *UVB* 15, 36).

Thus, in the course of time, the second and third deities of the astral triad became involved in a mutual contrast. Ištar, fused with the Sumerian Inanna, acquired a particularly pre-eminent position among the Akkadians as well as the Assyrians and the western Semites, and she overshadowed the other goddesses; in her astral aspect she was the third deity of the astral group. Her name, which in its earliest form of Eštar corresponds to the Astarte of the western and the ʿAṭṭar of the southern Semites (cf. M. H. POPE, *WM* 1/2, 249f.; M. HÖFNER, *WM* 1/4, 497ff. and (G)išdarrat in Māri, s. G. DOSSIN *apud* A. PARROT, *Mission arch. de Mari* 3, 307; 330), became the generic name of "goddess" in general. She was the daughter of the Moon-god Sîn, though she was likewise considered the daughter of An, god of heaven, who raised her to the position of consort and queen of heaven (s. Ch. III. C) and the daughter of Enlil. In Assyria it was especially her (Semitic) aspect of great goddess of war and strife that was stressed, and as such she was worshipped in the cities of Aššur, Nineveh and Arbela. The dual character of this later goddess is remarkable: love and sensuality alongside of battle and victory. On the one hand, therefore, Ištar was depicted as hierodule (naked goddess) and on the other as heroine and queen. In Babylon the famous portal at the beginning of the procession street was dedicated to Ištar. For obvious reasons she was equated to Aphrodite in the Hellenistic period, though the latter did not possess Ištar's hermaphroditical aspect (cf. J. BOTTÉRO, *St.Sem.* 1, 40ff.) Representations of an Ištar barbata (s. *CAD Z* 126) are also to be found. Her sacred animal was the lion, her number fifteen, and her constellation the planet Venus. Already in the earliest texts from Uruk, Inanna has an astral aspect, and it is from it that her rosette symbol (eightpointed star, cf. E. D. VAN BUREN, *ZA* 45, 99ff.) is probably derived. Her symbol of a bundle of rushes is perhaps connected with her name Ninni, which also occurs in the earliest texts. Hence, according to J. VAN DIJK, the early Inanna of Uruk possibly had two figures: that of the celestial Inanna, daughter of Nanna and that of the terrestrial Ninni, daughter of Enki(?) (*I.R.* 417f.). Later, under Akkadian influence, she became Mother-goddess (the Sumerians held her to be a hierodule), a consort of the heaven-god An. Their son was the god Lulal of Badtibira (s. *CT* 42, 3 VI 31-32; S. N. KRAMER, *JCS* 18, 38[13]; J. VAN DIJK, o.c. 418). Inanna is further known as mother of the god Šara of Umma (s. J. VAN DIJK. l.c.). It was perhaps owing to the syncretism of the Akkad period that she became a cruel warrior-goddess (see J. VAN DIJK, *I.R.* 419; M. TH. BARRELET, *Syr.* 32, 222ff.). The greatest number of myths is woven about her figure, including the well-known history which relates how she collects the me's from Enki in Eridu (s. S. N. KRAMER, *SM*² 64ff.; *TS* 91ff.). These are listed and present an almost complete picture of the religious and material culture of the Sumerians (s. J. VAN DIJK, *I.R.* 419ff.). [s. now W. W. HALLO; J. VAN DYK, *Yner* 3].

E. *Gods of Nature*

A more comprehensive study on a broad scale of the fire-gods has yet to be made. In the first place there was Nusku, son and vizier of Enlil, so very important for the burning of the offerings to the gods and later worshipped especially in Ḥarrān. G. DOSSIN has devoted a short monograph to Gibil (Akkadian: Girra/u) as the originator of smut of vegetation (*RHR* 55, 28ff.). But Gibil (s. R. FRANKENA, *RIA* 3, 383ff.) was also held to be the one who burnt evil wizards (in the Maqlû incantations, see below).

Something must also be said of Ninurta, a god of fertility, vegetation, war, and also of hunting, and his consort Gula. Ningirsu, lord of Girsu (city-state of Lagaš), similarily a vegetation and war god, has perhaps been equated from time immemorial with the figure of Ninurta. Ninurta plays an important role in the didactic poem Lugal-e ud me-lám-bi nir-gál (s. D. O. EDZARD, *WM* 1/1, 115; J. VAN DIJK, *Sumer* 18, 19ff.), in which he allots the stones and plants a favourable or unfavourable fate according to whether they helped him or not against his mythical enemies in the mountains, particularly against the demon Asakku, in the didactic poem an-gim dím-ma and in the Anzû-myth (see below, Ch. IV. C. f). In militaristic Assyria he was worshipped as god of war and hunting. As son of Enlil he was venerated especially in Nippur, and furthermore in Kalaḫ (Assyria).

Gula was goddess of healing (see below, Ch. III. H.f) and her sacred animal was the dog (s. W. G. LAMBERT, *Or.* 36, 105ff.).

Another important godhead was Adad (cf. W. H. PH. RÖMER, *HS AO* 185ff.), god of storm and thunder. He was also called W/Mer, and corresponds to Hadad of the Aramaeans and other western Semites. He was a great god from Syria and Asia Minor, and, like the god Martu (Amurrum), he was probably a god of the Martu Bedouins (s. J. VAN DIJK, *JCS* 19, 11f.). The ancient Sumerian Iškur, whose place he assumed, was apparently of less importance. It appears that Iškur manifested himself primarily in devastating thunder storms, unlike

Adad, who brought the fructifying rains further north. Both aspects find expression in this god's symbolic animal, the bull. His emblem was the two or three-pronged lightning and his number was six. Like Šamaš, Adad was also an oracle-god. His sanctuaries in the south were at Enegi (near Ur) and Murum and in the north at Aleppo and especially at Aššur (together with Anu.)

F. *"Popular gods"*

It is remarkable but historically understandable that Marduk and Aššur, the national gods of the Babylonians and the Assyrians respectively, were not listed in this official pantheon. Marduk acquired his position in the family of the gods by virtue of his equation with the god Asariluḫi, son of Enki, who was worshipped in Eridu. As a result of the power position acquired by the first dynasty of Babylon, culminating in the reign of Ḥammurapi, Marduk was elevated to Upper Lord of the pantheon (s. Ch. II. B.a).

Aššur, national god of the Assyrians, however, continued to be an outsider not mentioned at all in the canonical list of gods, An:*Anum*. During the reign of King Sennacherib (about 700 B.C.) Assyrian priestly theologians endeavoured in vain to set him in Marduk's stead, or, by identifying him with the older god Anšar (cf. also W. VON SODEN, *SAHG* akkad. 8), even above Marduk, whose name was replaced by that of Anšar-Aššur in the Aššur version of Enūma eliš (see below, Ch. IV. C.c). The importance attached by the Assyrians to Aššur is evidenced by the fact that the god bore the same name as the oldest capital city; the name Assyria is derived from Aššur. His famous temple-tower in this oldest capital was proudly called Eḫursagkurkurra, "House of the mountain of the lands"; the younger nation, the Assyrians, claimed for their principal god Aššur sovereignty over the cosmic world-mountain. First under Šamšiadad I of Assyria and later from Šalmanassar I on (13th century B.C.) there can clearly be discerned an "Aššur-Enlil syncretism", by which Aššur became the Assyrian Enlil (s. B. LANDSBERGER and K. BALKAN, *Bell.* 14, 251f.).

The importance of this god, however, remained confined to the Assyrian kingdom. The god Aššur was not able either to equal or to replace the glory of his Babylonian rival Marduk. On the contrary, as from the 14th century B.C. Marduk had numerous worshippers in Assyria as well (s. Ch. I. f). Also during and after the political decline of Babylonia in the more than thousand years between the end of the

Ḥammurapi dynasty and that of the late-Babylonian Chaldees, the temple of Marduk in Babylon, with its renowned ziqqurrat and influential priesthood continued to be thought of as the great religious centre par excellence, even far beyond the frontiers of Babylonia.

Because of his identification with Asariluḫi, son of Enki of Eridu, Marduk became the god of exorcism. As son of Enki/Ea, Marduk was "Lord of Wisdom", which probably also implied that he could bestow the magic power of healing and higher life. His victory over the forces of chaos was commemorated and re-enacted each year at the New Year's Festival (s. W. G. LAMBERT, *JSS* 13, 106; 106[2]). After the gods conferred sovereignty on Marduk, he ranked equal with the great gods of the cosmic group. Originally his number was ten, but as appears from the song of praise in the seventh chant of the Enūma eliš, Marduk received 50 names after the number of Enlil and as epitome of all heavenly and earthly forces (s. F. M. TH. DE LIAGRE BÖHL, *Op. min.* 282ff.). His symbol was the hoe (later taken over by Nabû) and his constellation was the planet Jupiter. His emblematic animal was the serpent-dragon Mušḫuššu. Marduk's consort was Ṣarpanītum "the silver-gleaming", also called Erūa (analogous to the Assyrian Šerūja, i.e. Ištar as consort of Aššur? (s. D. O. EDZARD, *WM* 1/1, 119). In its centre in the great temple in Babylon, the Marduk cult therefore encompassed very heterogeneous features, and this resulted in a certain measure of inconsequence. Ever since the religious developments during the Ḥammurapi dynasty, Marduk was looked upon as principal god of the kingdom and was also worshipped as god of the incantations for the magical healing of the sick. Originally, however, he is thought to have possessed certain solar features, as appears from his Sumerian name Amar-Utu, "calf of Utu". This dual character of Marduk is perhaps expressed in the Enūma eliš (I 95), in which Marduk is described as a sort of Janus figure. An indication that his elevation to supreme god met with initial resistance may perhaps be found in the later Akkadian version of the Epic of Gilgameš, in which no mention is made of his name, though this is understandable as far as the Assyrian versions are concerned. In any case the Epic of Gilgameš is not included in the canonised (cf. W. VON SODEN, *MDOG* 85, 22f.; W. G. LAMBERT, *JCS* 11, 1ff.) Babylonian literature. The author of the Enūma eliš took a different view of his task, with the result that this work was recited every year in the Marduk temple in Babylonia during the New Year's Festival.

Marduk's son was Nabû, god of the neighbouring town Borsippa with its temple Ezida. His planet was Mercury, who was in close contact with the appearance and disappearance of the moon (s. E. F. WEIDNER, *HBA* 41f.). As scribe of the gods who guarded and recorded the "heavenly writing" and the "tablets of destiny", he was the god of writing and a growing threat to the eminence of his father. He also had a vegetation aspect (s. *LSS* 3/4, 25, 9-14). The religious trend which centered on Nabû was probably strongest in Assyria, and if the Assyrian kingdom had not fallen in 612 B.C. and subsequently Babylon been conquered by the Persians in 539 B.C., then a second "reformation" might have resulted in this youngest member of the pantheon acquiring the status of supreme god.

A peculiarity which Nabû shared with Marduk was that as "late" gods their part in the formation of the myths was practically negligible (s. D. O. EDZARD, *WM* 1/1, 97; 107).

G. *Gods of the netherworld. Realm of the Dead* (cf. Ch. V. C.c)

Finally mention must be made of Nergal—another manifestation of this god was Meslamta'ea, s. J. VAN DIJK, *SGL* 2, 21ff.—god of the netherworld, who was worshipped in the city of Cutha together with his consort Ereškigala, "ruler of the great place", i.e. the realm of the dead. His role was not merely that of the bringer of death and devastation, but also that of a vegetation-god (cf. K. TALLQVIST, *StOr.* 7, 394f.; the Greek Pluton). He was the god of the scorching summer sun, of fever and contagious diseases such as the plague, and in this capacity was thought to be the god of the realm of the dead. In a hymn of the DE LIAGRE-BÖHL-collection (Leyden) (s. F. M. TH. DE LIAGRE BÖHL, *Op. min.* 207ff.), Nergal is praised as archer and swordsman, mounted on a horse and invincible.

According to the Babylonian conception of the world, the realm of the dead belonged to the cosmos and not the chaos. It was the undermost half of the universe and was conceived of as a palace with seven gates and walls. The great ruler of the realm of the dead reigned over the "land of no-return" (cf. below Ch. V. C.c). In one of the best-known Babylonian myths concerning the journey of Inanna (Ištar) to the netherworld (see also below, Ch. IV. C. b), a lively and colourful description is given of the goddess's descent from the upper to the nether world and of how she is impelled to submit to the laws of the realm of the dead by being deprived of one of her jewels or garments at each gate, of how Ereškigal brings about her death, resulting in the cessation of procreation on earth according to the Akkadian version, and of how finally the goddess is revived to new life by a trick of Enki/ Ea and then released, though on condition that she sacrifices her lover Dumuzi (Tammūz), offered as ransom to the Galla-demons who accompany her (Cf. also *Gilg.*, Ninev. version, VI 46f.). For Ereškigala's association with Nergal, see below Ch. III. H.i; IV. C.h.

H. *In conclusion mention is now made of a few deities which cannot be classified in any of the abovementioned categories*

(a) The god Zababa of Kiš (an old important Semitic centre in northern Mesopotamia), who occurs already about 2500 B.C., was a war-god. The martial Inanna/Ištar was his consort. Little is said of him in the Sumerian literary texts, since Kiš did not fall within the field of vision of the older Sumerian literature (A. FALKENSTEIN, *SGL* 1, 113; Å. SJÖBERG, *ZA* 54, 63f.). In an old list of the gods from Nippur, Zababa's name follows those of the great gods; in the An: *Anum* list of the gods he is described as "Marduk of the battle". In an inscription of Waradsîn he is mentioned already as son of Enlil (s. Å. SJÖBERG, l.c.). His cultic worship is first encountered in the Larsa period. In his code, Ḥammurapi calls himself "the favourite brother(?) of Zababa". A singular esoteric text dating from the late period gives several etymological interpretations of the god's name and mentions certain rites of a festival associated with Zababa (cf. R. LABAT, *BiOr.* 10, 184f.).

(b) The goddess Nisaba belongs to the ancient gods; she occurs as early as the Fāra period, like the enigmatical figure of "Great Nisaba", of whose relationship to Nisaba nothing is known. She has various family relationships: in Nippur she was held to be the sister of Enlil, in Lagaš the sister of Ningirsu and thus daughter of Enlil, while a late tradition says she was the daughter of An. In the Ur III period and the ancient Babylonian period her consort was Ḥaja (probably a god of the livestock, s. A. FALKENSTEIN, *AnOr.* 30/1, 143[5]), but later Nabû, the god of writing, was thus entitled. She was worshipped in Umma and in Nippur, where there was a temple dedicated to her in the time of Gudea, while she is the goddess of Ereš in a collection of temple hymns attributed to Enḫedu'anna (s. A. FALKENSTEIN, *RA* 52, 129). Originally this goddess was probably a corn-goddess, judging by the basic form of the sign used to designate her name: corn-ears with blades. In addition to vegetation-goddess, she was known primarily as the goddess of the art of writing, of numbers and of learning. She appears in a dream of Gudea as maiden placing a tablet of the stars of heaven on (her) knees (s. A. FALKENSTEIN, *Divination* 65[3]; *AnOr*.30/1, 110f.). She bestows wisdom on mankind.

(c) The god Šulpa'e, mentioned already in the Fāra list of the gods and then not again until the Neo-Sumerian period (apart from the late ancient Sumerian personal name Uršulpa'e), occurs in the economic texts of the Ur III period, in which he is frequently mentioned as member of a local cycle of gods (Nippur; Keši; Adab; Umma; Lagaš; Ur), as consort of the "ancient" goddess Ninḫursaĝa, and also in the literary tradition of Nippur. Therefore, in spite of his name "youth who appears radiantly", he was perhaps not looked upon as a god of the younger generation (D. O. EDZARD, *WM* 1/1, 128). It is singular that, in the rest of Sumerian literary tradition Enki, and Enlil too on a few occasions, is called the consort of the Mother-goddess Ninḫursaĝa. According to a Sumerian hymn to Šulpa'e edited by A. FALKENSTEIN (*ZA* 55, 41ff.), the character of this god, whose importance was inferior to that of his consort Ninḫursaĝa, was extremely complicated. He manifested traits of a war-god, but also elements of a fertility-god and of one who protected wild animals. Furthermore he was delineated as a demonic figure and also as one with astral features associated with the planet Jupiter.

(d) The god Išum (s. W. H. PH. RÖMER, *JAOS* 86, 146), who seems to have first occurred in Old Akkadian personal names, is called the son of Šamaš and Ninlil in a fragment of an Old Babylonian epic. As herald of Erra, the plague-god, he plays a humane role (see below Ch. IV. C.i), similarily in the composition entitled "Vision of the netherworld of an Assyrian crown prince" (see below Ch. V. C.c). His nocturnal going about through the streets was probably made to protect the people. Up till now it has not proved possible to determine his essential character from the scanty data known of him. On one occasion he seems to be associated with fertility (s. W. G. LAMBERT, *BWL* 331). The contention that he was a fire-god cannot be proven on the ground of his name only.

(e) Erra. The cult of this god, whose name first occurs in the onomasticon of the Old Akkadian age, seems to have reached its climax at the end of the Ur III and the beginning of the ancient Babylonian period (s. J. VAN DIJK, *UVB* 18, 51; W. W. HALLO,

JAOS 83, 175; 175⁶⁶). Since in the beginning (e.g. in the Code of Ḫammurapi, KH II 69) his name was several times written without divine determinative, he was probably of foreign origin. In a Sumerian hymn Erra appears to play the role of servant of Nergal, with whom, however, he is later identified in theological speculations, for example in the myth "Nergal and Ereškigala" dating from about 1400 B.C. (see below Ch. IV. C.h). His character only manifests itself in texts from the post-ancient Babylonian period; he was a warlike god who also, like Nergal, could cause pestilential epidemics (cf. below Ch. IV. C.i). Further he was a god of the netherworld, and as such he showed ambivalent traits. A personal name from the Ur III period is Errabāštī, meaning "Erra is my life-force." His consort was called Mami, and he shared the Emešlam temple at Cutha with Nergal.

(f)   Gods of the night (s. A. L. OPPENHEIM, *AnBi.* 12, 282ff.; 295¹; cf. also *STT* 231 rev. 31-35).

There are extant several prayers addressed to these gods: one from the ancient Babylonian period in both an earlier and later version, one from Boğazköy, and several from the later period, including those which occur in the Maqlû collection of incantations. It would seem that these deities, who were used to indicate various constellations, and also the gods Gibil and Erra, were invoked when the worlds of the gods and of men were sound asleep at night in order to obtain a favourable hieromancy or to render harmless unfavourable omina.

(g)   Mother-goddesses (s. D. O. EDZARD, *WM* 1/1, 103ff.; J. VAN DIJK, *I.R.* 413ff.).

This collective name can be used, as did D. O. EDZARD, to designate those goddesses who played an important part in the creation of the gods and, in particular, of mankind. In the god-lists from the ancient Babylonian period and later (hence not in the big list from Fāra) the Mother-goddess ranks third or fourth, with as remarkable peculiarity the separate mention in each case of Inanna/Ištar, thus indicating that the latter was not thought to belong to the category of mother-goddesses. The oldest names for mother-goddesses are Ninḫursaǧa; Ninmaḫ; Damgalnunna, consort of Enki (in the Fāra and Mešalim periods). Nintu occurs in the introduction to the Sumerian account of the Deluge, and she is also creator of man in the Epic of Atramḫasīs (similarily Mami, see below Ch. V. A). Aruru was concerned in the creation of mankind (see ibid.) and, according to the Akkadian Epic of Gilgameš, created Enkidu. In Akkadian the Mother-goddess was called Bēletilī, and in the An : *Anum* list of the gods the identification Ninmaḫ = Bēletilī is followed by many other names of the Mother-goddess.

According to the Sumerian composition "Creation of the Pickaxe", Ninmena was the creator of both the royal priestess(?) and the king (D. O. EDZARD, *WM* 1/1, 105; A. FALKENSTEIN, *ZA* 55, 22f.[71]). In a broader sense, Mother-goddesses could also be conceived of as protectresses of people and towns (city-goddesses) (s. D. O. EDZARD, ibid. 105f.). The name of the goddess Ṣarpanītum was interpreted on popular etymological grounds as Zērbanītum "creator of seed", which means that her aspect of Mother-goddess is to be considered secondary (D. O. EDZARD, ibid. 106). This accords with the reconciliation and intermingling of originally distinct aspects of goddesses perceptible in the post-Ancient Babylonian period (s.W. VON SODEN, *RA* 52, 133ff.). A sharp distinction must, after the manner of J. VAN DIJK, be made between the Mother-goddesses and the vegetation-goddesses. In the cosmic conception the latter were female (e.g. Baba, Nininsina), but not in the chthonic conception (cf. Ab-ú; s. J. VAN DIJK, *I.R.* 401; 413).

Usually the consort of the Mother-goddesses is Šulpa'e (see above c).

(h) Gods of healing (s. D. O. EDZARD, *WM* 1/1, 77ff.).

The gods specially associated with healing were Damu, son of Nininsina of Isin, who assisted his mother in her work, and Sataran of Dēr. Well-known goddesses of healing were Nintinugga, Ninkarrak and Nininsina. There is extant a Sumerian letter addressed to Nintinugga: a woman called Inannakam is begging that she be healed of her illness (s. J. VAN DIJK, *SSA* 14ff.). Ninkarrak has a role, for example, in an Ancient Babylonian Lamaštum-incantation (s. W. VON SODEN, *BiOr.* 18, 72) and is also mentioned in the Code of Ḫammurapi (XXVIII r 50ff.) as the one who may bring sickness to those who do not obey the law. Nininsina was the city-goddess of Isin, "the great doctor of the Black-headed", and up to the present the earliest mention of her is to be found in the texts dating from the Neo-Sumerian period. After the first dynasty of Isin had become the leading power in Babylonia, Nininsina assumed certain aspects of the goddess Inanna, even the warlike ones (s. W. H. PH. RÖMER in: *Festschr. W. von Soden* 279ff.). Her consort was Pabilsag; her temple in Ur was called Etilmuna and in Isin Egalmaḫ. Already in the early Babylonian period she was equated with the well-known goddess Gula (cf. F. R. KRAUS, *JCS* 3, 64f.), with whom Baba was also later equated.

(i)   In conclusion a few remarks about Dumuzi (s. D. O. EDZARD, *WM* 1/1, 51ff.), called Tammūz in the Old Testament, who, according to the myth of Inanna's descent to the netherworld, was the one yielded by her as ransom to the Galla-demons who accompanied her on her way back from the netherworld. More information about his death, caused by the Galla-demons, has been revealed by another Sumerian myth (cf. A. FALKENSTEIN, *BiOr*. 22, 282; 282[22]). According to an important discovery made by A. FALKENSTEIN, this myth relates how his faithful sister Geštinanna sacrificed herself for his sake, so that alternately they spent half the year on earth and half in the netherworld (s. A. FALKENSTEIN, *ibid.*, 281). Although, as J. VAN DIJK points out in *I.R.* 423, nothing is further known of Dumuzi's return to earth, we do know that two heavenly constellations represented an apotheosis of Dumuzi and Geštinanna (s. A. FALKENSTEIN, *Festschr. W. Caskel* 108).

Apart from these myths there are a number of other Sumerian texts concerning Inanna and Dumuzi recently edited provisionally by S. N. KRAMER (*PAPS* 107, 485ff.) and also many litanies containing lamentations about the disappearance of Dumuzi and the subsequent disruption of life in nature (cf. e.g. *SAHG* sum. 34; 35). S. also TH. JACOBSEN and S. N. KRAMER, *JNES* 12, 160ff.

An early predecessor of Dumuzi was called Ama'ušumgal(anna.) Various kings of the Ur III dynasty and of Isin were identified with the latter/Dumuzi, apparently in connexion with the ἱερὸς γάμος. A. FALKENSTEIN is of the opinion that Dumuzi was not originally a god, but a human being. It would seem that certain authors tend to exaggerate the significance of the "Dumuzi-faith" in Sumer (s. J. VAN DIJK, *BiOr*. 16, 142f.). The relationship of the various Dumuzi figures known to us (including Dumuzi-abzu?) to the like-named kings mentioned in the Babylonian list of kings still presents us with difficult problems (see on this subject the recent remarks by J. VAN DIJK, *I.R.* 423ff.; s. further A. FALKENSTEIN, *CRRA* 3, 41ff.; A. MOORTGAT, ibid. 18ff.; *Tammuz* (Berlin 1949); F. R. KRAUS, *CRRA* 3, 69ff.; O. R. GURNEY, *JSS* 7, 147ff.; E. M. YAMAUCHI, *JSS* 11, 10ff.).

I. *Tutelary spirits and demons* (s. D. O. EDZARD, *WM* 1/1, 46ff.)

The Babylonians believed that the entire world was filled with gods and spirits, both good and evil. Every person had his tutelary spirit.

He was, in the words of the Babylonians, "the child of his god". His personal tutelary god (see above, Ch. I) came to his assistance, was wrathful if he sinned, but also interceded on his behalf, cf. the numerous introduction scenes in Mesopotamian glyptic art (s. e.g. A. MOORTGAT, *VR* 22f.).

But there were also evil spirits. All sickness on earth was thought to be the work of these demons or devils. There was both a scientific and a magic element in the art of healing; the sickness demons had to be expelled by material means, by rituals and exorcisms, even deceiving them if needs be, so that they would leave the body of the patient. Most dreaded were the "evil seven" (Sebettu, s. D. O. EDZARD, *WM* 1/1, 124f.; E. F. WEIDNER, *AfO* 18, 458f.) who swarmed about as children and messengers of Anu and who menaced the heavenly gods, especially the Moon-god. Women in childbirth feared especially Lamaštu (Sumerian: Dimme), the female demon. Exorcisms against her have been preserved from both the ancient Babylonian period and later times, and even an old Assyrian exorcism from Kültepe (Asia Minor) has been handed down to us (s. below Ch. IV. A.f). The demon Pazuzu, on the contrary, seems to have been looked upon as adversary of evil demons (s. P. R. S. MOOREY, *Iraq* 27, 35[20]; E. KLENGEL-BRANDT, *Or.* 37, 81ff.). The role played by these demons in everyday life was disproportionally large, and so too was the number of magic texts devoted to combating them.

IV. WORSHIP

A. *The Cult*

a. Sacred places

The site of the cult was the temple, the place where the gods received their due veneration. A distinction is to be drawn between "high temples" and "low temples". In the earliest sanctuaries the former were usually built in the shape of an artificially raised terrace surmounted by a little temple (Eridu temples). Later, when these sanctuaries developed into tower-like constructions, they were called *ziqqurratum*. The first to build the wellknown staged temple-towers which have become so characteristic of Babylonia and Syria—cf. also the temple-tower in Tshogha-Sambil (Iran) (s. W. HINZ, *Das Reich Elam*, Stuttgart 1964, 138ff.)—were the kings of the third dynasty of Ur, Urnammu and Šulgi and their successors. The top was reached by means of stairways and ramps, so that even wagons could be drawn up on high during processions. According to TH. A. BUSINK it is from this time the terraces and the top temple of the ziqqurrat gradually began to form an architectural unit. Previously this had not been so, although the ziqqurrats at Uruk and at ʿUqēr had a number of terraces even in early times. It is more than once assumed that at the New Year's Festival the ἱερὸς γάμος took place in the temple on the summit (cf. TH. A. BUSINK, *De Babylonische tempeltoren* 83ff.), which seems also to have been looked upon as a sort of gateway (*šaḫūrum*), leading perhaps to heaven. The terrace with the "high temple" was called g i - g u n₄ - n a in Sumerian and *gegunnûm* in Akkadian, and so, too, was the later staged tower or ziqqurrat (less frequently Sumerian (é) u₆-n i r, s. *AHw*. 284; A. FALKENSTEIN, *AnOr*. 30/1, 134f.). A secondary interpretation given to these sanctuaries was probably that of mountain, and furthermore they were used for astronomical observations. The temple on the summit, usually dedicated to the city-god, was possibly built so high in order to safeguard it against the continual threat of plundering and desecration by enemies; it may also be that this elevated site was thought to express the power of the principal god (TH. A. BUSINK, o.c. 82) or to effect a link between the celestial and terrestrial worlds (cf. ibid. 85). The exact measurements of the enormous temple-tower of the god Marduk in Babylon were recorded in texts after Nebuchadnezzar II had the building repaired about 600 B.C. These reveal that the length and breadth of the lowest stage and the total height of the building were all the same, not less than $91^{1}/_{2}$ metres.

Around the base of such towers the temples proper were placed as separate buildings. Excavations have made it possible to reconstruct the ground plan of a number of temples from different architectural periods and thus to reconstruct the different basic patterns and their development. The orientation of the longitudinal axis seems to have been important. Characteristic differences can be discerned between the structure of the temples of the Sumerians, the Babylonians and the Assyrians. According to H. LENZEN, *ZA* 51, 35 the Sumerian temple developed from the single-room sanctuary in the south.

The distinctive feature of the Sumerian temple is the bent axis of the cella, so that when the cella was entered the cult-image could not be seen until the turn of direction had been effected (Cf. TH. A. BUSINK, *Sumerische en babylonische tempelbouw* 20ff.; H. LENZEN, *ZA* 51, 11). In the north there evolved from the single-room sanctuary the East Tigris temple which transformed the Sumerian temple in the Diyāla region. When the court disappeared from the Sumerian temple, a court became necessary at the side, usually at the long side. Soon this court was enclosed on several sides by chambers, and so came into being the prototype of the Babylonian court-temple. In the Akkadian period the building scheme became more austere, as can be seen particularly in the Ur III period. As yet it is not certain whether the Babylonian "broad-chamber" temple, first encountered in the Egipar of Ningal in Ur, was a creation of that period or whether it already existed in the Akkad period, when the cult-chamber was already divided into an ante-cella and a main cella. This type of temple takes then, in southern Babylonia, the place of the Sumerian type.

The Babylonian court-house-temple also became more popular in Assyria, at the expense of the house-hearth-temple (i.e. the temple containing a cella with a bent axis), ever since the middle of the second millenium B.C. The difference between these temples and the Babylonian "broad-chamber" temple is that, although the ante-cella became a "broad-chamber", the main cella remained rectangular in shape. From this time onwards the cult-statue was visible from the courtyard, as in the southern Babylonian temples (s. to all this H. LENZEN, *ZA* 51, 35f.).

In a description of the capital Babylon recorded on several clay tablets (s. E. UNGER, *Babylon die heilige Stadt* 229ff.; W. W. HALLO, *JNES* 18, 56; F. M. TH. DE LIAGRE BÖHL, *Op. min.* 430ff.), the city is said to have had no less than 53 different temples during the reign of Nebuchadnezzar II, apart from the 1300 smaller chapels and offering-sites. The principal temple of the supreme god Marduk, Esagila (s. E. UNGER, o.c. 165ff.) "the house that lifts up (its) head", situated in the immediate vicinity of the ziqqurrat Etemenanki (s. TH. A. BUSINK, *JEOL* 10, 526ff.), was composed of two adjoining complexes of which the western one alone, with its sanctuary of Marduk, of his father Ea and of his son Nabû, covered an area measuring 80 by 86 metres. The complex enclosed a central square measuring 31 by 38 metres.

The great temples were not merely places where the gods were worshipped, but also centres of public life. A very large number of recovered records, particularly those from the time of Ur III, consist of lists and receipts pertaining to the administration of the temples (s. e.g. A. L. OPPENHEIM, *Wilb.*).

In conclusion it may be noted that the Sumerian names of temples and of certain of their elements hark back to the pre-historic times which determined the entire attitude to life and subsequent development of the Sumerians (s. J. VAN DIJK, *I.R.* 401ff.). J. VAN DIJK conjectures that the raised earthen terrace of the ancient "high temples", sometimes ovalshaped, and hence also of the ziqqurrat, could have been a reproduction of the primordial island (Sumerian: ki-šár), which formed part of the Sumerian cosmogonic conceptions (*I.R.* 403).

b. Sacred times

A close connexion existed between the sanctuaries and the festivals. As theological reflection led to an increased systematisation of the gods and their sanctuaries, the questions as to which days were dedicated to certain gods, and for this or some other reason were favourable or not for certain enterprises, and what one should or should not do on certain days became a science in itself. From a large group of texts known as menologies, hemerologies (s. R. LABAT, *HMA*; *MIO* 5, 299 ff.; *Iraq* 23, 88ff.; *RA* 56, 1ff.), and calendars (cf. R. LABAT, *CBSM*; *Sumer* 8, 17ff.) can be inferred the extent to which the daily life of the Mesopotamians was circumscribed by stringent ritual prescriptions and prohibitions. Such regulations were especially numerous and severe during the great festal days (cf. B. LANDSBERGER, *LSS* 6/1-2; É. DHORME, '*Religions*' 234ff.; 254) of the year; then the demons apparently played a prominent role, and the commandments and interdictions were often magical in character. For the rest it is more than once difficult to determine who were subject to these regulations; some applied perhaps to the king alone.

The most important festival of the great gods was the New Year's Festival, which lasted as long as 12 days in the month Nisan (spring) in Babylon. At that time the divine images from other cities and sanctuaries were assembled in a festal procession in Babylon. We know what the ritual was for the second to the fifth days of the New Year's Festival in Babylon. The rest has been deduced from the ritual of Uruk, where in the Hellenistic period this festival was related to the heavenly gods Anu and Antum (*Racc.* 86ff.). The sheep, of which the head was taken to the steppe and the trunk cast in the river on the morning of the fifth day, is somewhat reminiscent of the scapegoat of the Hebrew Day of Atonement. Then followed the humiliation of the king as representative of the sinful people. The priest removed all his symbols of dignity, struck him in his face, pulled his ears and made him kneel and utter a penitential prayer. The king then professed his innocence and received absolution. After the divine images from the sanctuaries in the surrounding country were collected together at the temple of Mar-

duk, the king grasped the hands of the Marduk statue on the eight day
and led it in solemn progression along the processional street to a sanctuary outside the city called the *bīt akītu*. What took place there afterwards has not yet been entirely established; Marduk was placed
there, various offerings were made by the king to Marduk, Nabû
and Nergal. Attention is to be called to an important dissertation
of A. FALKENSTEIN, *Festschrift J. Friedrich* 147ff., who demonstrated
that it was only in the first millenium that the *akītu* festival was closely
connected with the New Year's Festival in Babylon; in the Ur III
period two *akītu* festivals were celebrated annually in Ur and Nibru.
Part of the procession to the *akītu* festival house was made by ship.

On the morning of the eleventh day a banquet of the gods was held
to which were invited the heavenly and earthly powers, represented
by the statues of the gods and the priests. In conclusion the statues of
Marduk and his consort Ṣarpanītum were taken to the temple sur-
mounting the ziqqurrat, where the ἱερὸς γάμος and the determination
of destiny for the coming year appear to have taken place (s. above, a).
We know of the celebration of a New Year's Festival in Assur too
(cf. R. FRANKENA, *Tākultu* 67ff.; F. KÖCHER, *ZA* 50, 192ff.). S. shortly
an article by W. G. LAMBERT.

c. Sacred persons

Deification of the king (cf. W. H. PH. RÖMER, *SKIZ* 55ff.; Å. SJÖ-
BERG, *Or.* 35, 287ff.; J. VAN DIJK, *I.R.* 426f.; W. VON SODEN, *RGG³*
3, 1712ff.) in the sense of a divine worship of the ruling sovereign and
his predecessors only took place in actual fact during the relatively short
period of the Sumerian "renaissance" under the third dynasty of Ur.
This worship appears to have been conducted almost entirely outside
the capital city Ur itself; inside the city the king was generally considered the servant of the city-god Nanna (s. H. FRANKFORT, *Kingship and the
Gods*302, but also shortly G. PETTINATO, *ZA* 60). Before that time the
powerful rulers of the Akkade dynasty had already been considered
divine by their subjects. This is probably the origin of the later epithet
"god of the city/land (of Sumer)" applied to kings and rulers, which
occurs in royal hymns and other texts (s. A. FALKENSTEIN, *SAHG* 35;
ZA 50, 73; J. VAN DIJK, *MIO* 12, 61⁹). There was never any question
of deification of the king in Assyria.

The Danish-American scholar TH. JACOBSEN (*JNES* 2, 159ff.; *ZA*
52, 99/¹⁰) has conjectured that the Sumerian urban government and
conception of the world in the early dynastic period rested originally

on a primitive democracy. It has been established that in these early times the city-ruler administered the property of the community as representative of the gods—a system that has been described as a sort of theocratic state-socialism. If, however, account is taken of the text of the Composition of Bilgameš and Agga, one is forced to conclude that in those ancient days the ruler was indeed an autocrat, but that he was advised by assemblies of wise, old and young warriors, at least in Uruk (s. A. FALKENSTEIN, *AfO* 21, 47).

At first the exercise of the secular and the spiritual functions does not seem to have been as logically segregated as was later the case in Babylon, specifically as from the reign of Ḫammurapi. Known titles (cf. W. W. HALLO, *AOS* 43) were the Sumerian l u g a l, "king", the older e n, "(priest)lord" (cf. J. RENGER, *ZA* 58, 114ff.), which was practically limited to Uruk as royal title and became a priestly title in Ur since the Akkad period, and finally the lowest raking title e n s í, "city monarch", which signified something like "governor" in the centralised administration of the kingdom of Ur III (s. D. O. EDZARD, *FW* 2, 73ff.; A. FALKENSTEIN, *RlA* 3, 358). In Assyria the king also bore the title of "governor of Enlil" and "*šangû* (priest) of (the god) Aššur" (s. K. TALLQVIST, *StOr.* 4/3, 11f.[4]).

Dating from the period shortly after 2000 B.C. we have our first testimony of a usage that later is mentioned several times in the texts, namely the temporary appointment of a "substitute king" in times when the king himself was subject to special danger. This proxy was expected to meet the dreaded danger, for example pursuant to an eclipse of the moon, and was then put to death (s. W. VON SODEN, *Festschrift für V. Christian* 100ff.; W. G. LAMBERT, *AfO* 18, 109ff.; 109[1]; B. LANDSBERGER, *BBEA* 45[71]; H. M. KÜMMEL, *StBoT* 3, 169ff.).

The body of priests who were employed in the sanctuaries formed a sacral order, segregated from the laymen. This is not the place to discourse on the many different kinds of priests and priestesses, or even to list them. They performed certain functions in the temples during the cult (offerings, ablutions, anointings), in liturgies, and as exorcists and seers. Sometimes they exercised considerable influence, for instance the priests of Enlil in Nibru (Nippur) (cf. J. VAN DIJK, *I.R.* 405ff.) and the high priest of the Marduk temple in Babylon who possessed great political power. Suffice it to refer to the handbooks and to J. RENGER, *ZA* 58, 110ff.; 59 104ff. for further details on this subject (see also J. VAN DIJK, *I.R.* 430f.).

According to the Babylonian conception known to us from various

texts, the people were created to relieve the gods of their allotted
tasks, and the priests in particular were called on to do this. The office
of priest appears to have been hereditary on certain families. To
perform it were required a good knowledge of the Sumero-Akkadian
literature, in particular the cultic, the ability to write and to understand
the sacred language, a body free of physical handicaps and, finally,
solemn consecration as priest (cf. B. MEISSNER, *BuA* 2, 52ff.).

Most remarkable are the great divergencies between the various
cults as regards the priestesses and the temple women. We know the
names of many princesses of the Sumerian period and thereafter
who held the high rank of en-priestess *(entum)* p. ex. in the Moon
temple in Ur (s. J. RENGER, *ZA* 58, 114ff.). Some of the *nadītum*
priestesses (s. most recently J. RENGER, *ZA* 58, 149ff.; *CT* 47) who
had dedicated their lives to the service of Šamaš lived partly in a sort
of convent *(gagûm)* belonging to the temple in Sippar (cf. J. RENGER,
ZA 58, 156ff.); others however were married, though obliged to remain childless. On the other hand the service of various priestesses of
the Inanna/Ištar temple in Uruk, who engaged in sacred prostitution,
was of a very licentious nature (cf. also *Gilg.*, Ninev. version I; II).

d. The prayers

Our information on the prayers of the Babylonians and Assyrians
is none too detailed. We know most about the prayers uttered during
the cult in the temple, magic rituals and during the observation of the
behaviour and the entrails of sacrificial animals (sheep). In general it
can be said that the prayers could be said standing, kneeling or in
proskynesis. Different ways of raising the hands are known partly from
archeological findings, but as yet we do not know exactly which attitudes belong to the different prayers.

The Akkadian prayers were apparently aimed especially at lauding
the godhead in hymns, at lamenting, uttering supplications and promising gratitude. To pray was man's duty, to neglect doing so a sin;
to pray energetically and joyfully was held to be meritorious.

Only a few hymns and prayers connected with haruspicy are known
from the ancient Babylonian period. Entirely new types developped
in the Cassite age. It is remarkable that so few sacrificial prayers have
been preserved for posterity, in view of the fact that the interpretation
of sacrifices was the usual means employed by the rulers of ancient
Mesopotamia to become acquainted with the will of the gods. Possibly prayers without a prescribed text were usually uttered when

offerings were made, particularly when they were addressed to the gods of divination, Šamaš and Adad, or to the gods of the night. Such a "nocturnal prayer", a lyrical poem about the silence of the night, has been handed down to us (*SAHG* akkad. 20). A haruspical prayer addressed to Ninurta as Sirius is the only longer prayer of this type dating from the later age (s. *SAHG* akkad. 22); the majority from this period are short. The address and the closing phrases are usually the same, but the rest of the prayer varies according to purpose and circumstances.

As yet, unfortunately, we know nothing of the structure of the prayers which the chanter-priest *(zammeru)* (cf. *CAD* Z 40) sang during the Assyrian rituals. The *kalû*-priests generally continued to use Sumerian prayers until the late period (s. *AHw*. 427f.; J. KRECHER, *SKLy*. 35f.; *Racc*. 1ff.). Furthermore another type of prayer called *naqbītu* (s. *AHw*. 743f.) is known from the late Babylonian temple rituals and the New Year's ritual, and it could also be pronounced by laymen. The three *naqbītu*'s which occur in the aforesaid New Year's ritual begin in late Sumerian and are primarily proclamations of praise for the godhead. They conclude with a short entreaty for the bestowal of favours.

Royal prayers are to be found as part of dedicatory and building inscriptions of certain Neoassyrian Sargonid kings and also in the building inscriptions of the Chaldean kings of Babylon (cf. *SAHG* akkad. 24ff.). These are mainly prayers for assistance in the fight against the enemy and for long life and offspring. In addition we also find prayers for power, for a just reign, for auspicious omens and for the good preservation of the buildings in question; often, too, they entreat intercession with a higher deity. Even buildings or parts of them were expected to act as intercessors. More will be said below of personal prayers, including those of the kings, and of elegiac and penitential psalms and prayers of exorcism. (For these and further details about prayers see A. FALKENSTEIN, *RlA* 3, 156ff. for Sumerian and W. VON SODEN, ibid. 160ff. for Akkadian material; s. also W. G. LAMBERT, *AfO* 19, 47ff.).

e. The sacrificial cult (s. É. DHORME, '*Religions*' 223ff.; 253ff.)

Just as ritual goes with exorcism and healing, so does offer with prayer and hymn. Prayers of private individuals likewise only became sufficiently emphatic when accompanied by an offer. Originally an offering was, naively enough in our eyes, conceived of as food for the gods or as a tribute to which they were entitled. With regard to rituals of exorcism and atonement, the propitiatory and substitutionary character of certain offerings is more evident. In a bilingual text from the library of Aššurbānipal (*CT* 17, 37b, 14ff.) the lamb is called the substitute of the man who offers it (to the deity) instead of his own life; the lamb's neck for his neck, the lamb's breast for his breast. Just as in Israel, the sound animals of the herd were sacrificed (cf. *SAHG* akkad. 21). It is also known that sacrifices were made to the spirits of the deceased (s. *AHw.* 487 *kispu(m)*; 483 *kipsu* I). There seems to be practically no question of human sacrifices, in the true sense of the word, having been made (cf. F. M. TH. DE LIAGRE BÖHL, *Op. min.* 163ff.; A. MOORTGAT, *Tammuz* 53ff.; below Ch. V. C.c).

In addition to the sacrifice of animals, libations also constituted an important type of offering, in the form of wine, beer and oil (s. J. DANMANVILLE, *RA* 49, 57ff.).

The original purpose of offering incense could have been to envelope the sacred being in smoke so that the offerer did not come into direct contact with him. Offerings of food were also common, for example dates, figs, milk, syrup and especially loaves, which were presumably consumed by the priests after they had been offered to the godhead.

The gods had need of offerings. A humorous description in the Babylonian account of the Deluge says that, like flies, they swarm about the offering made by Utnapištim (*Gilg.* XI 161). According to another poem, the dialogue between a master and his slave (*BWL* 148, 60), an offerer can teach a god to follow him like a dog. But explicit reference should also be made to a well-known collection of wise counsels (*BWL* 104, 135ff.): "Worship your God daily; sacrifice and prayer are in keeping with incense. Keep the inclination of your heart in readiness for your God, for that is what is due to the godhead... In your education look to the tablets; piety engenders happiness, sacrifice enhances life and prayer absolves sin." Man cannot make do with sacrifice alone, he also must act in accordance with the prescriptions of the gods. He must humiliate himself before the gods even though he does not know of his own crimes, and supplications and penetential psalms are necessary as well as sacrifice. Thus we find, for example, the following pronouncement in the middle of a *namburbû* text (s. below) pertaining to certain festal days: "(All) evil and malicious practices may not approach the Sanctuary; he who brings his offering must shine like daylight; shortcomings and rebelliousness may not exist in this house of god" (*RA* 48, 134, 15-18; see further below Ch. IV. B).

f. Magic material (rituals and incantations)

Mention has already been made above of various demons who menaced the life of the Mesopotamian. A brief summary follows of the different magic means employed by the people in an endeavour to avert the dangers which threatened life in its various aspects. To some extent these means were strengthened by the assistance of the good demons already mentioned, or, as in the Šurpu collection of incantations, by a number of great gods. This summary is based on that of B. MEISSNER (*BuA* 2, 198ff.), which can be supplemented with material published later and dealing mainly with the earlier period.

The gods Enki and Asariluḫi played an important role in the Sumerian incantations (s. A. FALKENSTEIN, *LSSNF* 1; *ZA* 56, 113ff.; J. VAN DIJK, *I.R.* 412f.; *OLZ* 1967, 236[1]; J. NOUGAYROL, *ArOr.* 17/3-4, 213ff.). In one type (Marduk-Ea-type) Asariluḫi asks advice of his father Enki about the process of exorcism, which Enki then gives him after posing to his son the rhetorical question, what it is that he does not know, so that he, Enki, can add it to his knowledge (s. also above, Ch. III. C). The other types of Sumerian incantation, likewise discovered by A. FALKENSTEIN, the legitimation type, in which the exorcising priest refers for legitimation to the gods of the "white magic", at whose orders he is about to perform the exorcising acts; the "prophylactic" type, of which the main theme is an appeal to the demons and other injurious beings not to approach the person, and the "consecration" type used to consecrate the various objects needed in the ritual of exorcism prior to their use. In the Maqlû collection of incantations the fire-god plays a significant role in the burning of the effigies of the wizards and witches. Furthermore Nininsina and Gula, goddesses of healing, combat disease by means of the power of exorcism (s. above Ch. III H.h). [s. shortly *VS* 17 for non-canonical Sum. incantations].

An incantation could contain an historical-mythological introduction concerning the salutary intervention of a god in primeval times (cf. also J. VAN DIJK, *I.R.* 412f.; W. G. LAMBERT, *JSS* 13, 108; 112), which was then followed by the pronouncement of a wish that in the case in question a similar action on the part of the god might prove conducive to the health of the sufferer (s. B. MEISSNER, *BuA* 2, 208). In conclusion there followed instructions, usually medicinal or magical, dictating actions which had to follow upon the incantation. For amulets s. B. L. GOFF, *Symbols of prehistoric Mesopotamia* (New Haven-London 1963) 162ff.; E. REINER, *JNES* 19, 148ff.

All sorts of visible means of conjuration, either medicinal or exorcistic, were known: mentioned are e.g. water, diverse medicaments and unguents, gypsum and bitumen, flour-water, a circle of flour around the bed of a sick person (s. G. MEIER, *AfO* 11, 365ff.), tamarisk branches, sheep offered in atonement and various amulets (s. also R. LABAT, *RA* 54, 169ff.). Such things could also be identified with certain deities. Prophylactic tutelary figures were sometimes placed around the house of a sick person in order to drive out the demons from it. The name of the *bit mēseri* collection of incantations derives from this custom (s. G. MEIER, *AfO* 14, 139ff.; *AHw.* 134). These means were usually used in conjunction with exorcisms.

Frequently resort was had to the system of substitution, when a goat was offered to a demon in the place of the sick person. *Mutatis mutandis* the same thought underlay the making of images of people, for example in clay, the aforementioned burning of effigies of wizards and witches and, perhaps, also the removal of the brick-god from a newly built home by letting him sail away, presumably in the form of a terracotta, in a little boat filled with victuals (s. *BuA* 2, 235f.).

The magic ceremonies, of which the extant representations derive mainly from the Lamaštu rituals on the exorcism reliefs (s. C. FRANK, *LSS* 3/3; B. MEISSNER, *MAOG* 8/1-2), were usually performed in the house of the patient, in the sick room, on the roof, in a reed hut by the river, or on the steppe. Strict adherence to the ritual precepts was essential to the success of the act of exorcism. Numerous incantations have been preserved, apart from those texts containing hitherto unintelligible magic spells. For the earlier periods, reference might be made to various incantations directed against the female demon Lamaštum, which came from both Babylonia itself (s. W. VON SODEN, *Or.* 23, 337ff.; *BiOr.* 18, 71ff.) and from the Assyrian trading colony Kaniš (Kültepe) in Asia Minor (in Old Assyrian, s. W. VON SODEN, *Or.* 25, 141ff.; above Ch. III. I). As appears from the lengthy incantation against Lamaštu contained on three tablets, of which we have several recensions of the text (s. D. W. MYHRMAN, *ZA* 16, 141ff.; A. FALKENSTEIN, *LKU*, p. 8ff.; cf. also F. THUREAU-DANGIN, *RA* 18, 161ff.), she remained a dreaded figure even in later times, evidently because she constituted a danger to the new-born. Mention might also be made of an incantation against ergot in the eye (s. B. LANDSBERGER and TH. JACOBSEN, *JNES* 14, 14ff.; cf. 17, 56ff.), wind in the body (s. TH. FISH, *Iraq* 6, 184), jaundice (s. *JNES* 14, 14; 14[7]) and against a mixture of various diseases (s. A. GOETZE, *JCS* 9, 8ff.), all from the Oldbabylonian period.

For the later period, a large number of titles and purposes are mentioned in a guide to the art of exorcism which was drawn up for the temple Esagila in Babylon and in fragments of a catalogue from the library of Aššurbānipal. This king was, according to a letter, keenly interested in the collection of magic writings (s. B. MEISSNER, *BuA* 2, 212ff.).

Older, unilingual Sumerian and bilingual post-ancient Babylonian (Sumerian-Akkadian) examples of texts have been handed down to us of the collection of incantations entitled Udughulameš "evil Utukku's"; cf. also Saggiggameš "headache-demons" and Azaggigameš "bitter Asakku-demons" (s. B. MEISSNER, *BuA* 2, 216ff.; 232f.; 221f.).

The Maqlû collection preserved on nine tablets and so-called after the burning of the images of evil-doers against whom it is directed, is almost entirely devoted to the combating of human wizards and witches. The Šurpu collection, on nine tablets, partly bilingual and similarily named after the burning ceremonies accompanying it is devoted to the curing of the sick. Another related series is that of the Lipšur litanies (s. E. REINER, *JNES* 15, 129ff.).

In addition to all these texts, there have also been preserved incantations against diseases of the heart and the eyes (the latter being combated with both medicinal and magic means (s. B. MEISSNER, *BuA* 2, 234), against toothache (s. F. THUREAU-DANGIN, *RA* 36, 3f.), the sting of scorpions and against slander (s. O. R. GURNEY, *Iraq* 22, 221ff.). There were other spells which were expected to expel many diseases and other dreadful things simultaneously. Incantations were also recited in rituals against the spirits of the dead (s. W. VON SODEN, *ZA* 43, 257ff.; G. CASTELLINO, *Or.* 24, 240ff.). A special place is occupied by the many incantations in the form of prayers addressed to diverse gods, for example Ištar (s. W. G. KUNSTMANN, *LSSNF* 2; E. EBELING, *AGH*).

Magic means were also employed to achieve certain ends, for example to gain a girl's love (s. A. FALKENSTEIN, *ZA* 56, 113ff.; H. ZIMMERN, *ZA* 32, 164ff.; E. EBELING, *MAOG* 1/1), to regain lost potency (s. R. D. BIGGS, *TCS* 2), to receive favourable dreams, to succeed in business transactions, to obtain a good harvest or to get back a runaway slave (s. E. EBELING, *Or.* 23, 52ff.). S. also below Ch. V. C.b.

Besides the texts combining both incantations and ritual actions, there are also purely ritual texts which collect nothing other than the ritual prescriptions. There were cultic rituals for people as well as for divine images and the "mouth-opening" and "mouth-washing" series

(s. E. EBELING, *TuL* 100ff.; G. MEIER, *AfO* 12, 40ff.; *AHw.* 659) were used to this end. Sometimes, too, weapons underwent cultic cleaning after use (s. *AfO* 20, 40, 30ff.; 42, 36ff.; B. MEISSNER, *BuA* 2, 238).

A special type was the "atonement ritual", which was enacted to atone for matters concerning persons and affairs. These rituals show us what the penitent had to do for atonement. The most important collection of this type of ritual was the "washhouse" series (s. B. MEISSNER, *BuA* 2, 238ff.), dedicated to the complicated propitiatory rituals for the king. The king, too, had to confess his sins and to perform rituals directed against the injurious influence of lunar eclipses. Rituals relating to the king which i.a. have reference to his coronation are known from Aššur (s. K. F. MÜLLER, *MVAeG* 41/3) and from older periods (s. J. VAN DIJK, *HSAO* 233ff.). In the Assyrian *tākultu* ritual (s. R. FRANKENA, *Tākultu*) the king likewise played a part. The *Bīt rimki* series of rituals deal with the ritual bathing of the king. Letters from the Sargonid period contain frequent mention of rituals and their meticulous enactment.

B. *Ethics*

a. Sin and guilt

The religious works were written by the scholars and their pupils in the schools (cf. A. FALKENSTEIN, *Saec.* 4/2, 125ff., *WO* 1, 172ff.; C. J. GADD, *Teachers and Students in the Oldest Schools*, London 1956; J. VAN DIJK, *SSA*; E. I. GORDON, *BiOr.* 17, 122ff.). The royal libraries, collected by Tiglatpileser I in Aššur about 1100 B.C. (s. E. F. WEIDNER, *AfO* 16, 197ff.), and, in particular, by Aššurbānipal in Nineveh about 650 B.C., were mainly composed of copies of and extracts from these writings and the conceptions of priestly theology are reflected in the myths, hymns and prayers.

The impression received from the material available so far is that the cult and the rite occupied a pre-eminent position. Mankind was created to serve the gods. The Babylonian was confronted with his gods in the cult. Hence it is understandable that sin, especially unintentional and unwitting sin, was thought to be a cultic and ritual rather than an ethical and moral transgression, though a clear distinction cannot readily be drawn. The gods were entitled to the prescribed rites, which the people had to observe. The sufferer, who looked upon his sickness as punishment, often did not know exactly which god he had unwittingly offended by contravening one of the innumerable regulations. Then he would voice his complaint thus:

"What is an abomination for my god, have I unwittingly eaten... O unknown or known god, my crimes are many and great are my sins... The crime I have perpetrated, I know not; the sin I have committed is unknown to me; the abomination I have eaten, I know not; the taboo I have trodden upon is unknown to me... O my god, forgive me my sins, though they be seven times seven..." (*OECT* 6, 39ff.).

The fact that, apart from such ritual transgressions, the purely moral ones increased in importance can be discerned in the long list of sins in the so-called "mirror of confession" (Šurpu II), of which the ethic standard is high, even according to our notions. Examples of the many sins listed in it are subjugation of the weak, refusal to release the imprisoned, unchaste behaviour towards a neighbour's wife, disrespect of parents, perpetration of deceitful deeds.

b.   The moral standards upheld by the worshippers of the sun-god Šamaš likewise were very high. The wise proverbs which have been handed down to us from these circles are of a highly moral character. Emphasis was placed on self-control and on charity towards the poor and the needy in a wellknown collection of Akkadian counsels of wisdom: Your mouth shall be controlled in speaking, your speaking cautious / ... give food to eat and wine to drink / give that which is asked, provide for and honour! / his god rejoices over him who so acts / it pleases Šamaš, he rewards with his blessing!" (*BWL* 100, 26; 102, 61-64). Here, as in the great Šamaš hymn, we hear again and again the warning that licentiousness, pride and deceit are displeasing to Šamaš and are punished by him with evil, whilst the pious, and especially the judge who incorruptibly takes the side of the weak, pleases Šamaš and is rewarded with a long life. Indeed, contravention of the law was looked upon as a sin against the sun-god Šamaš, upholder of law and equity and guarantor of the state laws.

Certain temples were centres of sexual licentiousness under a sacral guise, but protest against them was also recorded. In the Epic of Gilgameš, the goddess Ištar appears with her priestesses as the great seducer, the representative of all that is frivolous and wordly, whilst friendship between men, as in the relationship between the heroes Gilgameš and Enkidu, is glorified. In the abovecited precepts and admonitions emphatic warning is voiced against the intercourse and marriage with hierodules and temple maidens and a analogy with the Book of Proverbs in the Bible, Chapters 6 and 7, is striking (*BWL* 102, 66ff.).

C. *Mythology* (s. D. O. EDZARD, *WM* 1/1)

a. The Epic of Gilgameš (s. A. FALKENSTEIN, *RlA* 3, 357ff.; F. M. TH. DE LIAGRE BÖHL, ibid. 364ff.; W. VON SODEN, *ZA* 53, 209ff.; 58, 189ff.; L. MATOUŠ, *ArOr.* 35, 16ff.).

Rightly has the epic with its twelve chants been characterised as the greatest and most beautiful poem we have from the pre-Homeric period, and rightly, too, has reference been made to the universal human traits which move us in spite of the difference in time. It is more than just an heroic epic in which are sung the adventures of two mythic heroes. It chants the tragedy of human life over which hangs the shadow of death and which, notwithstanding all efforts, is checked in its pace by inevitable death. Moreover it is the only one of the great poems whose different literary stages can be traced over a period of about fifteen centuries (cf. B. LANDSBERGER, *CahTD* 1, 31ff.).

The earlier texts, on which the Akkadian versions are partly based, are still in the Sumerian language. It is a cycle of songs distinguished from the younger Akkadian versions by the partially different contents, the language, the more monotonous form, and the much stronger mythological tint. So far we have the following Sumerian Bilgameš compositions (as the name should be read originally in Sumerian, after A. FALKENSTEIN, *RlA* 3, 357), of which no further details about the contents will be given (for this we refer to A. FALKENSTEIN, *RlA* 3, 360ff.): 1. "Bilgameš and Ḫuwawa"; 2. "Bilgameš and the heavenly bull"; 3. "Bilgameš, Enkidu, and the netherworld"; 4. "Bilgameš in the netherworld"; 5. An incompletely preserved and not yet intelligible Bilgameš myth contained in a text from Ur (*UET* 6/1, 60). The text entitled "Bilgameš and Agga" should not be classified as mythology, since it has an historical background.

The ancient Akkadian poet, who might have been a contemporary of the kings Rīmsîn and Ḫammurapi about 1775 B.C., used elements from this Sumerian tradition to form a free, poetic version and synthetis of it in his own language. To a large extent he managed to disengage himself from the sphere of the gods, and he viewed the problem of eternal life from a universal, human standpoint. As an entity—in spite of a few lacunae—our knowledge of the epic derives from the version of a younger revisor or poet, called Sînleqe'unnînî in a later tradition (approximately 12th century B.C.? Cf. W. G. LAMBERT, *JCS* 16, 66 VI 10; 76f.; J. VAN DIJK, *UVB* 18, 50; 50[128]) contained in copies from the library of King Aššurbānipal (about 650 B.

C.). At this stage the poem had, in many respects, already acquired the character of a romantic epic of chivalry, in which all emphasis is placed on heroic courage and adventure, though also on the struggle and the contrast between the state of nature and urban civilisation and the gradual, inner purification of the hero. This version is of importance for Old Testament scholars because of its vivid description of the Deluge given in the eleventh chant.

In the first half, chants I-VI, the poet sings his praise of friendship. Gilgameš, monarch of the city of Uruk, is first of all described as a voluptuary and a tyrant. Enkidu, who later becomes his friend, is however a half-animal child of nature who becomes a member of the civilised urban society, with all its advantages and moral snares, only after having associated with one of the temple maidens and thereafter with Gilgameš. These two are complementary in nature and character (cf. E. A. D. E. CARP, De dubbelganger (Utrecht-Antwerp 1964) 13ff.). Discontented with the licentious life in the city of the goddess of love, Ištar, they set out together in quest of adventure. After their victory over the evil giant Ḫuwawa (younger Ḫumbaba) near the Cedar Mountain, they return in pride and covered with glory. Then Ištar, goddess of voluptuousness, offers her love accompanied by tempting promises to Gilgameš. The contempt with which the hero rejects her (Chant VI) turns the heroic epic into a tragedy. True, in a glorious combat the heroes slay the bull of heaven sent to earth by Anu at the request of the goddess to revenge her. But then Enkidu arrogantly offends the mighty goddess. The punishment follows upon the evil deed: Enkidu falls ill and must die (chants VII and VIII). At first Gilgameš resists the realisation of this fatal loss. Then the hero is filled with the fear of death. Chants IX-XI describe his restless wanderings to the end of the world to learn from his ancestor Utnapištim how he acquired immortality. With unparalleled skill the poet describes how his goal eludes him each time it is almost within his grasp. After facing endless dangers he crosses the waters of death and, although his ancestor describes in detail his rescue from the Deluge, he gives him but meagre consolation. For even Gilgameš cannot succeed in overcoming sleep, the prerequisite for overcoming death. And the magic herb of life which he finally manages to fetch from the bottom of the sea after great exertions and disappointments is stolen from him by a serpent. Filled with sorrow but quietly resigned he returns to Uruk and finds consolation in the hope that through his heroic deeds and buildings his glory will live on in the memory of mankind. The version preserved for us of the last chant is merely an appendage in the form of a translation of a part of the Sumerian song of "Bilgameš, Enkidu and the netherworld" from the Sumerian cycle (cf. V. SCHNEIDER, *Gilgamesch*, Zürich 1967, 171ff.). Here Gilgameš calls upon the spirit of his departed friend Enkidu, who at Gilgameš's request informs him of the "law of the realm of the dead." Once again, however, he is given no hope of eternal life on earth. In the after-life, however, Gilgameš becomes one of the judges of the realm of the dead and one of the rulers over the spirits of the deceased.

b.   The myth of Inanna's/Ištar's Descent to the netherworld (s. R. BORGER, *BAL* 2, 86ff.; W. VON SODEN, *ZA* 58, 192ff.; A. FALKEN-STEIN, *Festschr. W. Caskel* (Leyden 1968) 96ff.).

This myth has been preserved in a Sumerian and an Akkadian version—the last mentioned being in recensions from Nineveh and from Aššur. The Akkadian version is broadly concordant with the Sumerian one. Ištar goes to the "Land of no return" and requests admittance of the guardian of the gate, Namtar, threatening on refusal to break open the gates of the netherworld and to raise up (to earth) the dead, so that they may eat the living. Since Ereškigala, ruler of the netherworld, fears that Ištar will rob her of her power, she orders the guardian of the gate to treat the goddess according to "the ancient rules of the netherworld." Ištar is thus compelled to appear before Ereškigala as a mortal deprived of clothing and ornaments, and she is then placed in the hands of Namtar to be killed.

Ištar's absence has its consequences on earth: all human and animal procreation ceases. Papsukkal, messenger of the gods, then seeks help for Ištar from the god Sîn, who refuses him however, and from Ea who creates the eunuch (?) Aṣûšunamir. The latter is charged to charm and enchant Ereškigala to make her give him the leather bag with the water of life. Although Ereškigala puts a curse on Aṣûšunamir, she nevertheless orders Namtar to sprinkle Ištar with the water of life, apparently in the presence of the Anunnaku, and to conduct her out of the netherworld on condition that she appoints a substitute. As she passes through the various gateways she is given back the diverse articles of clothing and jewelry taken from her on the way in. It appears that Dumuzi, "the consort of her youth," is offered up as substitute by the goddess, and Dumuzi is then lamented by his sister Bēlili.

This version of the myth closely resembles the older Sumerian versions, in which the consequences on earth of Inanna's disappearance are not mentioned and Inanna's messenger Ninšubura appeals for help for the goddess first of all to Enlil and only thereafter to Nanna. Here, too, the god Enki is the one who saves her by creating two creatures, who are sexless and therefore not subject to the laws of the nether-world (D. O. Edzard, *WM* 1/1, 88). They are to request the body of Inanna and to sprinkle it with the herb and the water of life sent along with them by Enki. Inanna is thus restored to life (cf. Ch. III. H.i).

c.   The epic of the first generations of the gods and the creation of the world by Marduk (s. D. O. Edzard, *WM* 1/1, 121ff.)

This poem, called after the opening words Enūma eliš ("When above..."), is really a panegyric in honour of the god Marduk with a lengthy mythological introduction. It was recited at the New Year's Festival and begins with the theogony, the creation of the gods in their generations. The oldest pair of gods consists of Apsû, the mass of sweet-water under the earth (cf. ground water and marshes, s. D. O. Edzard, *WM* 1/1, 38), and Tiāmat, goddess of salt water and the ocean. Of the next pairs, Laḫmu and Laḫamu were sea-demons, whilst Anšar and Kišar were abstractions of the upper and the lower world (for their exact meaning s. J. van Dijk, *I.R.* 394; 398), thus forming the transition to the heavenly gods, Anu and his descendants. Nammu, An's consort, is not mentioned in the text (cf. J. van Dijk, *ActOr.* 28, 10[16]).

Now these young gods disturb the peace of the old ones by troubling the primeval waters in their urge to create. At first Tiāmat, the prime-val ocean, remains impertubable. Apsû on the other hand becomes more concerned and seeks the advice of his chamberlain Mummu. Mummu is depicted here as the evil and satanical principle, whereas this notion, which was evolved in the chthonic world of conception of Eridu, originally signified "the from time eternal in ratione seminali existing forma intelligibilis of matter" (J. van Dijk, *I.R.* 387f.). He succeeds in stirring Apsû to resist and proposes to him an evil plan. This plan is betrayed to the heavenly gods; by means of a spell Ea succeeds in drugging and defeating Apsû, and takes Mummu captive. He establishes his sanctuary on Apsû (in Eridu, formerly situated in a Euphrates lagoon of the Persian Gulf). In the innermost chamber of this sanctuary he now begets Marduk, who fills the role of saviour in the epic. Marduk is portrayed as a giant, fully grown from the beginning,

and moreover, as it seems, as a dual godhead or Janus-figure (s. above
Ch. III. F). The explanation is perhaps that in fact two gods, those of
Eridu and Babylon, are fused in his person. However, supported by
her vizier and consort, the satanical Kingu, Tiāmat brings into being
eleven pairs of dreadful sea-monsters as her helpers and bestows on
Kingu world sovereignty with the right of fixing the destinies.

Once more the heavenly gods are desperate. In vain Ea and Anu
put their might to the test; the only saviour and avenger proves to be
the young god Marduk. In a solemn assembly of the gods, Marduk
after the banquet of the gods, is granted supreme power over all the
gods. With the aid of his storm-winds he conquers Tiāmat, splits
het body in two parts and imprisons Kingu and all her helpers. In
the fifth chant, of which an important part has now been made
known through an article by B. LANDSBERGER and V. KINNIER
WILSON (*JNES* 20, 154ff.) an account is given of how Marduk, assuming the role of Enlil in the older cosmic Sumerian tradition,
creates the cosmos and the constellations, the atmospheric phenomena
and sources out of Tiāmat's body, allots sanctuaries to Ea and the
tablets of destiny, taken from Kingu, as trophies to Anu. They then
repeatedly pay hommage to him and he is enthroned. He announces
the building of Babylon and at their request assigns the gods their
future positions. In the sixth chant follows the creation of man (Lullu)
by Ea, according to Marduk's plan, from the blood of the decapitated
Kingu, the foundation of Babylon and of Marduk's temple Esagila by
the gods. At the conclusion the gods praise their saviour and supreme
lord Marduk with his ten names, which are later increased to fifty in
the seventh chant (s. W. VON SODEN, *ZA* 47, 1ff.; F. M. TH. DE LIAGRE
BÖHL, *Op.min.* 282ff.; 504ff.).

d.   The myth of Adapa

The tenor of this myth is in fact the same as that of the great Epic
of Gilgameš: the opportunity of attaining immortality is missed by the
hero. In the form in which it has been recovered, the poem is perhaps of a more anecdotal character. The largest fragment, found at
El-Amarna in Egypt, can be supplemented at the beginning and the
end with records from King Aššurbānipal's library. As superscription
a possible choice could be: The struggle between the god of the ocean
(Ea) and the supreme god of heaven (Anu) over the person and service
of man (Adapa) (s. F. M. TH. DE LIAGRE BÖHL, *De Godsdiensten der
Wereld*[2] 2, 102).

The dramatic intrigue is simple. Ea, god of the waters and of wisdom, created the wise Adapa as his helper and servant. To this end he endowed him with intelligence but not immortality. Now at all costs he wishes to retain his attendant and helper in his service. Here the tragic moment is when Adapa, tormented by the south wind, represented apparently as a winged demon, arrogantly breaks his wings. This is a violation of the cosmic order, the sin par excellence. He must appear before the throne of the heavenly god Anu to account for his deed. Anu, who evidently would like to have this handy assistant in his service, is readily agreeable to pardon him and to open the gateway to the heavenly world for him by offering him the bread and the water of life. Now the cunning Ea had anticipated this danger. Hence he advises Adapa, it is true, how to obtain the favour and intercession of two heavenly figures, Dumuzi and Gizzida, but has resort to a warning in direct contradiction to the intent of the heavenly god: Adapa must not accept the bread and water offered, but instead a mantle and anointing-oil.

Now when Adapa takes heed of this warning and refuses the bread and water of life, Anu laughs at him and sends him back. In accordance with the poet's intent, the purport of this corresponds to the loss of the magic herb at the end of the eleventh chant of the Epic of Gilgameš. However, the motive for missing the chance is not so convincingly presented here, since the explanation would have to be either that the god Ea deliberately lied, or that the god Anu suddenly and unaccountably changed his mind. The poet evidently intended that the gods fight with different weapons. Ea's weapons are cunning and deception, Anu's careless laughter and heavenly mercy (F. M. TH. DE LIAGRE BÖHL). Anu is, and continues to be, the mightiest, and he finds a solution to the impasse into which Adapa has fallen because of his refusal.

According to F. M. TH. DE LIAGRE BÖHL (l.c.; WO 2, 427), the Assyrian fragment offers the solution:
"...Then Anu laughed aloud
    at Ea's intention.
Who among the gods of heaven and earth,
    As many as they are, has ever commanded such?
Who would have his own command
    Surpass that of Anu?"
And now Anu, with his higher power, takes action, though merely within the limits of the world order to which he is bound. He exerts

his supreme power over the entire realm of Ea, so that the latter's domain belongs to his cosmos, where Adapa, as it seems, shall rule as king of Eridu (cf. D.O. EDZARD, *WM* 1/1, 39).

e.   The Epic of Atra(m)ḫasīs (s. J. LAESSØE, *BiOr.* 13, 90ff.; *CT* 46, 1-15; L. MATOUŠ, *ArOr.* 35, 1ff.; G. PETTINATO, *Or.* 37, 165ff.).

This epic is known to some extent from an ancient Babylonian and a young Babylonian version. The Anunnaku wish to delegate their arduous work in the palaces of the gods to the seven Igigu. Apparently the latter must work hard day and night for forty years, and so they decide to dethrone the monarch of the gods, Enlil. They refuse to work and burn their tools. Enlil is shut up in the Ekur and orders Nusku to bolt the door. Anu then apparently intercedes to bring about negotiations between the parties. As a result it is decided to create mankind to relieve the gods of their work (s. W. VON SODEN, *Iraq* 28, 142f.). This task is carried out by the goddess Mami and the god Enki. Later Enlil is hindered by the noise of the mortals and endeavours to wipe them out by means of the plague and a seven-years drought. But in both cases Ea succeeds in averting the danger to the world, until Enlil causes a Deluge, from which only Atramḫasīs escapes in an ark built at the advice of Ea and called "Preserver of lives". The close similarity between the story of the flood and the eleventh tablet of the Epic of Gilgameš is remarkable (s. D. O. EDZARD, *WM* 1/1, 44f. and below Ch. V. A. and now W. G. LAMBERT; A. R. MILLARD, *Atr.*)

f.   The myth of the storm-bird Anzû (s. B. LANDSBERGER, *WZKM* 57, 1ff.)

With respect to the storm-bird Anzû, we have an Akkadian myth which has been handed down in an ancient Babylonian version and in a recension from the Neo-Assyrian period. Following on a prologue in which Ninurta is praised as the victor over Anzû, an account is given of how Anzû steals Enlil's tablets of destiny, which he had set aside with his regnal insignia when bathing. Anzû escapes to the mountains with his loot, intending to use it to obtain supreme ruler-ship over the gods. Since the divine order has been abolished by the theft of the tablets of destiny, Anum tries to find a god who will pursue Anzû. But neither Adad, nor Gibil, nor Šara of Umma is willing and able to do so. Ea counsels the mother-goddess to send her son Ningirsu (Ninurta in the Neo-Assyrian version) to combat Anzû. He must overpower and slay him with the aid of the seven winds and then bring the royal emblems of power back to the Ekur of Enlil. Ningirsu overtakes him, but now that Anzû is in possession of the tablets of destiny, he is able to divert the arrow Ningirsu shoots at him by reciting an incantation formula. Ningirsu then orders Adad to bring news of the failure to Ea. Then Ea's advice is that Ningirsu is to render the storm-bird speechless after the south wind has attacked Anzû, so that the latter cannot utter any more incantations against the arrows (D. O. EDZARD). The end of the myth is unknown as yet, though Ninurta probably succeeds in the end (s. D. O. EDZARD, *WM* 1/1, 138ff.). The bird Anzu(d) also appears in a Sumerian literary composition about an early Uruk king called Lugalbanda. This king is also the leading figure in another Sumerian text (see D. O. EDZARD, o.c. 80f.; 95 and shortly a book by C. WILCKE).

g.   The Myth of Etana (s. W. VON SODEN, *WZKM* 55, 59ff.)

We possess an ancient Babylonian, a Middle Assyrian and a Young-Babylonian version of this myth. Etana, who was a king of Kiš after the Deluge according to the Sumerian king-list, was childless. In order to acquire a son, Šamaš advises him to seek the plant of birth, and for this purpose he is to enlist the help of an eagle. In fable-form is narrated how the latter was faithless to a friendly serpent, who, on Šamaš's advice, cunningly imprisoned the eagle in a pit. This bird would tell him how he could attain his goal. After Etana liberated the eagle, he is borne heavenwards on his back, for there the plant of life can be found. When Etana can no longer see the earth beneath him, this Babylonian Icarus is seized with fear and temporarily(?) gives up his plan. Since Baliḫ is mentioned as Etana's son in the Sumerian king-list (*AS* 11, 80, 20-21), a reasonable conjecture would seem to be that Etana finally succeeded in finding the plant of birth (s. D. O. EDZARD, *WM* 1/1, 64).

h.   The Myth of Nergal and Ereškigala

This myth has been preserved in a Middle-Babylonian version found at El-Amarna in Egypt and in a more detailed recension from Sultān-tepe (s.-e. Turkey) dating from the Neo-Assyrian period. The heavenly gods make preparations for a banquet and they despatch their messenger Gaga to Ereškigala in the netherworld. The goddess is not allowed to come herself and therefore must have her portion fetched. She instructs her messenger Namtar to do this, but when Namtar appears among the gods, Nergal neglects to show him the respect due to him as an envoy of Ereškigala. The goddess then becomes enraged and orders Namtar to seek out the culprit to that he can be sent to her. But the gods do not deliver up Nergal, even though Ereškigala expresses her wish to take him as her consort. Finally Nergal, counselled by Ea, descends to the netherworld, since Ereškigala threatens otherwise to allow the dead to return to earth (cf. above, b). Nergal finally overcomes the goddess and becomes her consort (s. D. O. EDZARD, *WM* 1/1, 110). According to the Neo-Assyrian version Nergal descends to the nether-world at Ea's command, falls under the spell of Ereškigala and co-habits with her. Then, fearful of the displeasure of the gods, he returns to heaven. Ereškigala has Namtar request permission of the gods for Nergal to remain forever in the netherworld as her consort. The gods consider this undesirable and change Nergal into a misformed creature. Namtar fails to recognise him, but Ereškigala orders him to bring back forcibly the disguised god to the netherworld. Namtar first tells Nergal what he must do in order to enter the netherworld safely. On his arrival there he overcomes the goddess and once more cohabits with her. Then it appears that Anu sends a message saying that Nergal may remain forever in the netherworld (s. O. R. GURNEY, *AnSt.* 10, 105ff.).

i.   The Epic of Erra (s. B. KIENAST, *ZA* 54, 244ff.; W. G. LAMBERT, *Iraq* 24, 119ff.; A. FALKENSTEIN, *ZA* 53, 200ff.; R. FRANKENA, *JEOL* 16, 40ff.).

This epic, of which the period of origin seems to be uncertain (cf. W. VON SODEN, *MDOG* 85, 23; J. VAN DIJK, *UVB* 18, 51; 51[130-31]) relates how the "Seven godhead" (s. above Ch. III. I) stimulates the plague-god Erra to renewed activity after a period in retirement. The god Išum, herald and counsellor of Erra, tries to calm down his master and to prevent him from sinning against the gods by destroying the people. Erra, however, is determined to carry out his plan con-cerning the people, because they neglected his cult. Now it appears that Marduk has to have his insignia of sovereignty cleansed by the fire-god Gibil in the netherworld and so temporarily must leave his throne. Pending his return he hands his rulership over to Erra, who has persuaded him to agree to this temporary relinquishment of power. Marduk first extracts a promise that Erra will not misuse his power, but once Marduk descends to the netherworld, Erra breaks his word. He spreads plague, chaos and civil war over Babylonia, and in the process Babylon, city of Marduk, is also affected. In the end Išum succeeds in calming Erra, who admits the guilt he has brought down on himself.

V. The Concept of Man

A. The creation of man (s. A. HEIDEL *BG²* 61ff.; W. G. LAMBERT, *CRRA* 11, 101f.; D. O. EDZARD, *WM* 1/1, 121ff.; J. van DIJK, *I.R.* 428f.)

Different traditions are known of the creation of man. On the basis of the Sumerian literary texts already a distinction can be made between a tradition from Nippur and one from Eridu. The Nippur tradition (cosmic conception, s. J. van DIJK, *ActOr.* 28, 1ff.) in the myth of the "creation of the Pickax", has it that Enlil strikes the earth with a self-made pickax, and through the hole thus made the people rise up to the surface of the earth, comparable to the introduction to the Eridu hymn(s. J. van DIJK, *ActOr.* 28, 23f.; *I.R.* 428). Then the gods had the people take the pick-axe. The Eridu tradition (chthonic tradition, s. J. van DIJK, *ActOr.* 28, 9ff.) relates how man was created out of clay above the Abzu by the goddess Nammu, assisted by other goddesses and instructed by Enki. Nammu, mother of Enki, for that purpose had called her son up from sleep, for the gods wished to have mortals to take over their tiresome duties and so had approached her (s. J. van DIJK, *ActOr.* 28, 24ff.; *I.R.* 428f.). Later the goddess Ninmaḫ, chief assistent of Nammu, and Enki become drunken, and Ninmaḫ shapes seven defective human figures who, however, are granted subsistence by Enki. Now, however, Ninmaḫ is unable to fix the destiny for a creature fashioned by Enki, and she reproaches the latter that his creature does not react to her well-meant efforts. Enki, amused at her expense, replies that he has managed to make something out of her creations (s. A. FALKENSTEIN, *BiOr.* 5, 124f.). The Sumerian story of the Deluge, in which mention is made of the creation of man by the gods An, Enlil and Ninḫursaǧa (s. M. CIVIL, *Atr.* 138ff.; S. N. KRAMER, *SM²* 97f.; *TS* 176ff.), perhaps also derives from Eridu (*formatio*; syncretized, cf. J. van DIJK, *ActOr.* 28, 31).

Several traditions of the creation of man are preserved in Akkadian. According to the concept of the Ancient Babylonian myth of Atramḫasīs, the first man was created by the Mother-goddess Mami/Nintu in cooperation with 14 birth-goddesses. He was perhaps called Widimmu and was fashioned of clay she had requested of Enki and of the blood of a god slain at Enki's command (s. W. von SODEN, *Or.* 26, 306ff.). It is said that the gods wanted the goddess to create people to bear the yoke for the gods. The idea that man was created to serve the gods is also to be found in the introduction to a ritual from the Late-Babylonian period for the restoration of a temple, in which the king is also mentioned (s. *BG²* 65f.); in a text from Aššur, according to which the Anunnaku gods inform Enlil that they wish to slay two Lamga gods and from their blood create people, called An'ullegarra and Annegarra, to serve the gods for all times (s. *BG²* 68ff.); in the epic of the creation of the world, in which, according to Marduk's plan, Ea creates Lullu, man, from the blood of Kingu in order to serve the gods (s. above Ch. IV. C.c); and in the introduction to a bilingual incantation recited to purify the Nabû temple in Borsippa, where mankind is likewise created by Marduk and Aruru to serve the gods (*BG²* 61ff.).

B.   *The Nature of Man*

a.   Personal piety

Little information about the personal faith of the Mesopotamians is to be found in the texts. Perhaps, in this context, mention might be made of the "Message of Ludingirra to his mother", edited by M. CIVIL in *JNES* 23, 1ff., since Ludingirra must be qualified as esoteric (see J. VAN DIJK, *I.R.* 433f.). Certain testimonials are to be found in proper names, personal prayers and certain monotheistic tendencies (cf. B. HARTMANN, *NTT* 20, 328ff.), in so far as they appear to favour a given deity. A systematic study of the Mesopotamian letters from various periods would perhaps produce important data.

Akkadian nomenclature (s. J. J. STAMM, *MVAeG* 44) contains many personal names in prayer form (s. W. VON SODEN, *RlA* 3, 162f.), usually as thanks to a god for the gift of a child. Hence we find such names as "Ea is god", "Aššur is great" or the expression of joy "I swear God (exists)"; probably comparable to these is also "If it were not Marduk (,who then)!". The grateful feeling of the reliability of the divine word is expressed in such names as "He has promised and not changed," "The word of Aššur has been confirmed," or "For the second time her word has come true!". Confidence in divine aid and omnipotence is revealed in such personal names as "In God is my counsel" and "All is in the hands of God." Frequently one comes across such names as "Ea is my protection," "My support is Marduk," "Šamaš is my provider," "Šamaš is his strength," "Adad is full of mercy." Faith in the deity is also recorded in such names as "I have faith in Šamaš," I await the beckoning of my god," "I sought refuge

in the shadow of Sîn," "Nabû can do everything," "Sîn is the companion of the forsaken." Concrete expressions of gratitude were often
made; for example there were such personal names as "Šamaš has
made the dead(ly sick) healthy," "From nearby she has heard me,"
"My god has had mercy on me," "Nabû, I called on thee and was not
shamed." Faith led automatically to prayers for the fulfilment of all
sorts of wishes; these are reflected in such names as "Ea, let there be
an heir!", or "Enlil, preserve the heir unharmed." Others which occur
are "Nabû, stand by the forsaken," "May it go well with me, o Šamaš,"
"Sîn, thou hast created, protect (now also)." A prayer for the forgiveness of sins is contained in the name "Nabû, deem my sin slight."
Another name admonishes pious behaviour: "Tell it to him (i.e. the
god) and then have faith." The greatness and incomparability of the
divine helper finds witness in such names as "Who is (so) great as
Adad?" and "Who is as my god?" Dependence on the gods is expressed
in the name "Sheep of the gods"; divine love of man is expressed in
a name like "Favourite of the god."

Only a few examples of free, personal prayer are to be found in the
literature. Particular attention might be directed to a plaintive prayer
addressed by King Aššurnāṣirpal I of Assyria to Ištar, in which, on
the one hand, he reveals his self-justification through good works, but
on the other sincere feelings of guilt because of neglect of religious
duties towards the goddess in his youth (*SAHG* akkad. 14). In the
texts of Aššurbānipal have been handed down certain shorter or
longer prayers of the king, and in the inscriptions of Nabonidus can
also be found several free prayers, some spoken by his mother (s. W.
VON SODEN, *RlA* 3, 163). Free prayers occur, too, in diverse rituals
of the first millenium B.C., for example in the New Year's ritual of
Babylon. Reference might also be made in this context to the dialogue
between Aššurbānipal and Nabû (s. W. VON SODEN, ibid.).

Although we must classify the religion of Mesopotamia as polytheistic, it has long been known that, in certain hymns to the gods, the
latter are assigned epithets which by virtue of their content, can only
be applied to one deity, for example those which express omnipotence,
though there is the possibility of hyperbole. Well-known, too, is the
pronouncement on a statue from Nimrud, "In Nabû confide, trust not
in another god!" (*LSS* 3/4, 27, 12). These and like expressions could
possibly indicate a personal preference for a certain god arising out of
personal religious experience.

Theological reflection in the monotheistic trend was also concerned with this personal attitude towards the world of the gods. In a Ninurta hymn the other gods are identified with different parts of Ninurta's body (*SAHG* akkad. 10), and the goddess Baba has been equated syncretistically with various other goddesses by postulating, for example, that in the Ebarra temple in Sippar she is the goddess Ajja (cf. D. O. EDZARD, *WM* 1/1, 45). Such identifications of gods are also known from the god-list An:*Anum* dating from the Cassite period. In a spiritualised form the identification theory is to be found in a hymn to Marduk and the Pleiades, in which other gods are equated with attributes and characteristics of Marduk (*SAHG* akkad. 45). In a hymn to Marduk Aššurbānipal assigns the qualities of Anu, Enlil and Ea to him (*SAHG* akkad. 6, 3). But in Mesopotamia these trends were not consistently carried through and completely elaborated (cf. W. VON SODEN, *MDOG* 96, 45f. who prefers B. LANDSBERGER's term "monotheotetism").

On the other hand, certain tendencies towards repudiating gods in the Neo-Assyrian age may be found (s. W. VON SODEN, *AnBi.* 12, 356 ff.).

b.   The awareness of the tragic element in life and its conquest (s. F. M. TH. DE LIAGRE BÖHL, *Numen Spl.* 2, 32ff.; F. R. KRAUS, *JNES* 19, 117ff.)

In the cycles of Bilgameš, Lugalbanda and Enmerkar the mortal heroes are still too much bound up with the world of the gods and with mythology to admit of any considerable scope for reflexion on such problems as the meaning of life, death and suffering. Such figures as B/Gilgameš and Adapa first attained their full significance when individual religiosity gained ground in the Ancient Babylonian period.

The compositions pertaining to the primeval heroes Gilgameš and Adapa are centred on the questions of the avoidability of death and the unattainability of immortality for the weak humans, whom fate has placed in the power of the eternal gods, and this is something which each individual can appreciate paradigmatically. However, the Sumerian period proper was already acquainted with the conception of Utu, the sun-god, as judge (e.g. in a PN from Fāra, s. D. O. EDZARD, *WM* 1/1, 126) and guardian of the law, who sees and punishes all injustice. This suggests that even in this period a certain amount of thought was given to the individual (cf. above Ch. III.D).

The ὕβρις was held to be an essential transgression against the gods in both the Epic of Gilgameš (against Ištar) and in the myth of Adapa (against the South wind). Similarily in the myth of Inanna's descent to the netherworld and Dumuzi's fate, the latter's sinful arrogance towards Inanna appears to be the cause of his undoing in one version.

As we have seen above, both the Sumerian and the Akkadian sources relate that the purpose of man's creation was to provide offerings for the gods in order to remove all care from their existence. In the epic when Gilgameš's last effort to attain eternal youth fails, the only possible alternative is resignation, in the knowledge that through his fame at least he will continue to live in the memory of succeeding generations. And although Adapa also fails to acquire immortaility, Anu appoints him probably king of Eridu.

Sickness and death were not the only threats to man's existence. Uncertainty was also felt concerning the basis of morality, for was it not so that the rules of human ethics did not obtain in the realm of the watergod Ea of Eridu, according to the myth of Adapa, nor among the heavenly gods? Is man nothing more than a plaything in the hands or diverse contradictory powers of the upper and nether worlds? His assailments are revealed to us especially by the author of the poem *Ludlul bēl nēmeqi*, the undeservedly suffering one, who, unlike Job however, does not curse the day he was born, but begins and ends his poem with a doxology to Marduk. Another tragic figure is Etana, who gives up his effort just as he is about to reach the highest heaven, though he possibly does attain his goal in the end (s. Ch. IV. C.g).

Eschatology could have provided the solution to the tragedy, but this was scarcely or not at all known in Mesopotamia. Hence there was apparently no universal salvation from something like a world catastrophe, so that only the individual could be redeemed. This could be effected in several ways: by using magical means to strengthen his vitality and so delaying death, ignoring it as much as possible; by the intervention of certain healing-gods; as in the case of Ludlul by receiving in a divine vision the promise of healing and salvation, so that the sufferer might enter the Esagila to praise Marduk; by mysteries, of which, however, we possess no definite testimonials from Mesopotamia, even for the late period (cf. H. ZIMMERN, *ZDMG* 76, 36ff.).

Hence among the Babylonians there existed a tragic and pessimistic undertone, with not far away a certain cynicism: in the dialogue between the master and his servant this mentality is perhaps discernible (s. below Ch. V. B.c). And the touch of humour to compensate for the tragic element is likewise part of the Babylonian concept of man (s. F. R. KRAUS, *JNES* 19, 117).

c.   Theodicy (s. J. van Dijk, *SSA* 118ff.; E. I. Gordon, *BiOr*. 17, 149f.; 152; W. von Soden, *MDOG* 96, 41ff.; *ZDMG* 89, 143ff.)

Ethics in Mesopotamia were always eudemonistic. The Babylonian had to grapple with the problem of theodicy when virtue was not rewarded and specifically the pious was stricken with sickness and misery. In the dialogue known as "The Babylonian Theodicy" (*BWL* 63ff.) one of the two friends is a thorough sceptic, whilst the other endeavours again and again to rebut him by pointing out the unfathomable will of the gods. Here, for example, the doubting Thomas complains despairingly that those who neglect their gods have good fortune in everything while the devote languish and fall into destitution. All his pious friend can say in reply is that the intent of the gods, like the innermost part of heaven, cannot be fathomed. Here, too, the final conclusion is, as in Job, that man must give up trying to find a logical solution to the problem and must humbly submit himself to the inscrutable decree of God.

Another dialogue with perhaps a cynical trend is the one between the master and his slave (*BWL* 139ff.), which F. M. Th. de Liagre Böhl, (in: *Christus und die Religionen der Erde* 2, 493f.) surmises to be a sort of farce connected with the reversal of the social order on the fifth day of the Babylonian New Year's Festival (s. also E. A. Speiser *JCS* 8, 98ff.). Ever and again the slave manages to make the contrary wishes of his master appear ridiculous by all-too-ready agreement and parodied quotations (but see W. G. Lambert, *BWL* 140f.). For instance when the master wishes to do good deeds for his land, he encourages him to do so on the ground that Marduk records every good deed. As soon as the master changes his mind about this, he declares every good deed superfluous, since after death no difference can be discerned between good and evil men (*BWL* 148, 70ff.).

On a higher level in this respect is the great hymn which begins with the words "I will praise the Lord of wisdom" (*BWL* 21ff.). The poet complains that in spite of his piety and good works he has met with nothing but poverty and persecution in his long life. Wherever he looks, he sees suffering and misery. His body is ravaged by disease, though like Job of the Bible he is aware of no sin. His lament is impressive: "If I but knew that these things can be reconciled with the gods! What is good in one's own eyes is sin in the god's, what one feels to be badly made, is good in the eyes of his god. Who knows the decree of the gods in the heaven, who comprehends the counsel of the gods in the netherworld?" (*BWL* 40, 33ff.). In this instance redemption is brought by visions which proclaim recovery. Then, when Marduk's wrath has abated, the evil demons are expelled and the healed invalid starts out for Babylon to worship Marduk in his temple there. A "happy end" is also found in the Sumerian "Righteous Sufferer" composition "Man and his God" (s. S. N. KRAMER, *VTSpl.* 3, 170ff.; E. I. GORDON, *BiOr.* 17, 149f.).

C. *Man's Destiny*

a. Fixing of destiny by the gods

In an interesting dissertation A. L. OPPENHEIM, *Anc. Mes.* 201ff. recently pointed out the great significance of the concept *šīmtu* for human existence. Certain of his thoughts are reproduced below. It is related in diverse religious texts how man has received from the gods an individual and definite share of good and bad fortune which determines the entire course of his life, even the length and the nature and the sequence of the events that take place in his life, all of which are determined by an act of power on the part of one or more gods, probably at man's birth. The inevitability on the whole of the realisation of this individual share in the destiny of life which man has received appears from the following quotation from an inscription of Aššurnaṣirpal II. In it the king summarises his military feats and goes on to say: "These are the *šīmtu*'s pronounced (for me) by the great gods, who have realized them as my own *šīmtu*," even though it is possible that man may die on a day not determined for him (B. MEISSNER, *BuA* 1, 424; 424[13] (cf. [12]).

Apparently *šīmtu* comprises approximately the two Greek elements μοῖρα and φύσις both μοῖρα and *šīmtu* can express the special, divine function of the gods, their power and authority, whilst φύσις in the case of the plant μῶλυ (Homer, Odyssey) and the *šīmtu* (Sumerian: nam) of the stones, determined by Ninurta in the didactic poem Lugal (s. above Ch. III. E), indicates their "nature". Death is also included in the *šīmtu* as the closing of human destiny. The herald of death is called Namtar, "allotted destiny", and man's last experience on earth is mythologised as the demonic messenger of Ereškigala. One of the Akkadian expressions for "to die" is "to go to one's *šīmtu*(s)".

The Mesopotamian texts contain other concepts more or less related to *šīmtu*, such as *isqu* "share", "destiny" (s. *AHw.* 388f.) referring to the casting of lots to determine destiny, *uṣurtu* (Sumerian: giš-ḫur), evidently a sort of divinely predestinated course of events which determines all that happens (A. L. OPPENHEIM). According to J. VAN

DIJK (*I.R.*386) g. is the basic plan of the universe, the "state form" of the Sumerian society, the organisation of the cultic rules, the "essence" of things. Further, the term *ištaru* appears to have been used to indicate a sort of royal destiny (cf. Greek τύχη).

b. Divination (s. W. VON SODEN, *Leistung und Grenze sumerischer und babylonischer Wissenschaft*[2] 102ff.; *Divination*).

Here, as in the discussion of incantations and rituals, the relevant chapter in the work of B. MEISSNER (*BuA* 2, 242ff.) is taken as starting point, with the addition of certain more recent data in what is of necessity a very brief survey of this subject.

The basic conception of the art of divination is the notion that there exists a causal relationship between all that happens in the world and certain events in nature, which occur by chance or are artificially induced, so that future events can be foreseen by observing the said natural events. Practically no important private or public action was undertaken without first ascertaining a succesful result by means of augury.

This art was held to be of divine origin, and the gods Šamaš and Adad in particular were known as the "Lords of divination". According to a late ritual text they bestowed this art, especially the art of divination with a goblet, on Enmeduranki (cf. J. VAN DIJK, *UVB* 18, 46), a king who reigned in Sippar in the dim past, and he passed it on to others (*BBR* 24, 1ff.). It was called a secret art, *niṣirti bārûti*, "secret of the art of divination" (s. R. BORGER, *RlA* 3, 188ff.), and was the privilege of different categories of priests and sometimes, too, of women. Their task was to observe the omens from which the oracles could be inferred, and their equipment included a cedar wand and a sort of dish. As early as the Ancient Babylonian period the seers were organised in a sort of guild, headed by an "High Seer" at least in the Neo-Assyrian age, and their knowledge was passed on from father to son. Many names of these scholars are known from the numerous letters which they wrote to different authorities.

Testimonials pertaining to divination in Mesopotamia are already to be found in Sumerian records. The term máš-šu-gíd-gíd "haruspex", first occurs in texts from the third dynasty of Ur, but the term ensi (=Akkad. *ša'ilu*) has been found in Old Sumerian records. Gudea uses this title in connexion with the goddess Nanse, who explains the city-king's dream. Geštinanna explains the dreams of her brother Dumuzi. Other Sumerian terms for oracle (givers) need not be mentioned here, except perhaps the i_5-*gara*$_x$ = *egerrû* oracles (cf.

A. L. OPPENHEIM, *AfO* 17, 49ff.) mentioned now and again ever since the time of Gudea (s. A. FALKENSTEIN, *Divination* 45ff.).

A collection of liver omens, preserved in late versions, purports to derive from the time of the Akkade kings Sargon and Narāmsîn. Reference to certain past historical events, for instance to the kings Ibbisîn and Išbi'erra of Isin are often encountered in the omen texts, s. A. GOETZE, *JCS* 1, 253ff.).

Royal inscriptions from earlier and later times frequently relate how the rulers tried to learn what the outcome of a military operation would be and to obtain an answer to their question whether their building enterprises began on a favourable day, or whether their relations would remain in good health.

For the Ancient Babylonian period we have an abundance of original documents concerning hepatoscopy, lecanomancy, oneiromancy and astrology (cf. A. GOETZE, *YOS* 10, p. 1ff.), and from this time onwards reference to these things in royal inscriptions became more and more frequent. The Late Babylonian kings Nebuchadnezzar II and Nabonidus and the Neo-Assyrian monarchs Asarhaddon and Aššurbānipal often consulted the will of the gods by means of oracles, the former especially with regard to their many sacral building enterprises, the latter with regard to military operations. Some of these oracles were given in dreams, a well-known example being the promise made in a dream by Ištar to Aššurbānipal and to the king's soldiers, that she would go in front of him (s. B. MEISSNER *BuA* 2, 245f.). At first the collections of omen-texts plus interpretations were relatively small in compass; the later series *šumma ālu ina mēlê šakin* "if a city lies on a hill", comprised much more than 100 tablets dealing with the observation of the town, its wall and houses, all sorts of animals there, domestic animals, fields, gardens, birds, and sexuality (s. F. NÖTSCHER, *Or.Nr.* 31; 39-42; 51-54; *Or.* 3, 177ff.).

Two large groups of omens can be distinguished: on the one hand those which accidentally happen, such as astronomical and atmospherical occurences, motions of animals, forms at childbirth and dreams; on the other hand those caused intentionally, such as in case of the observation of the liver and divination with the goblet.

Originally the omens were interpreted in such a way that when an extraordinary phenomenon preceded an extraordinary event, it was assumed that the renewed appearance of the same phenomenon would be followed by the same event. In addition laws were drawn up determining the relationship between phenomenon and event, for ex-

ample a thought-association, or else a certain direction was considered
favourable or unfavourable. In the case of accidental omens, some
brought unconditionally good or bad fortune, but also outward appearance and place of occurence, behaviour and number played a role,
whilst in the case of induced omens an association of ideas was assumed between the phenomena and their consequence. For example,
abnormally large things were usually propitious, short and defect ones
unfavourable; omens occurring to the right concerned the observer
himself and those to the left his enemy, etc. A text-book for interpreting omens has been preserved from the later period. It provides
interesting indications about the reasoning applied (s. B. MEISSNER,
BuA 2, 269f.). We also have comments on omens by the Babylonians
themselves (s. R. LABAT, *Comm.*).

Accidental omens were of various types. A highly significant series
was that of the astrological omens entitled *Enūma Anu Enlil*, "When Anu
(and) Enlil..." (s. E. F. WEIDNER, *AfO* 14, 172ff.; 308ff.; 17,71ff.; 22,
65ff.). The most important giver of omens was the moon, in particular its
eclipses, which are frequently mentioned in the texts and generally as
being inauspicious. From the time of the Sargonids we have large
numbers of messages sent by Babylonian and Assyrian astrologers to
the king, which contain observations made from different posts
throughout the country. The observations are accompanied by interpretations. In one of these texts, an astrologer called Akullānu sends
his message to Asarhaddon accompanied by a quotation from the
relevant passages in the great work on omens mentioned above.
Sometimes, as in a letter from the astrologer Nabûmušēṣi to Asarhaddon, a detailed commentary was added to the messages. The observation of the sun as giver of omens was evidently less important, though
we have information about inauspicious eclipses of the sun. In this
same period the king received reports on the sun and its eclipses, for
example about the colour of the sun. Also important for astrono-
my were the observations made of the other planets, such as the
disappearance and appearance of Venus (cf. already for the Old
Babylonian period S. LANGDON and J. K. FOTHERINGHAM, *The Venus
tablets of Ammiẓaduga...*, Oxford 1928). The planets Jupiter, Saturnus
and Mercury were favourable on the whole, while Mars, on the contrary, was unfavourable.

Other important portents were various fixed stars, meteors, me-
teoric showers and comets, according to their relationship to the
planets and each other. Their different influences had to be assessed

against each other, and for this purpose the astrologers used special lists which enumerated the quality of each star. We have also a long list from the Late-Babylonian age, based on earlier lists, which relates diverse occurences of every-day life to certain stars. Obviously a normal conception was that the constellation of the planets at the birth of a child had a decisive influence on that child's life, but so far only horoscope texts from the late Babylonian period have been recovered (s. A. SACHS, *JCS* 6, 49ff.).

In addition to astrological omens, atmospheric omens were also considered significant by the Babylonians, and these are also summarised in the *Enūma Anu Enlil* mentioned above. The rare thunderstorms and seldom-occurring summer rains were held to be particularly ominous. The number and tone of the thunderclaps were observed and sometimes these were compared with musical instruments and animal voices, and the effect of lightning was similarily observed. The scholars also devoted their attenton to the rain, to the day of the month on which it fell. Earthquakes were naturally thought to be extremely unpropitious, and on them we have i.a. a text from Nūzi dating from the Middle Babylonian period (s. E. R. LACHEMAN, *RA* 34, 1ff.; E. F. WEIDNER, *AfO* 13, 231f.). Weather reports were sent to the Sargonid court, and even a weather forecast from the Neo-Assyrian period has been preserved (s. B. MEISSNER, *BuA* 2, 259). Use was also made of the changes in water level for the purpose of divination.

Important omens were held to be the movements of various animals, for example the flight of birds and especially hawks, the behaviour of diverse animals such as domestic animals and reptiles, especially snakes, and also of cameleons, scorpions and ants. Animal behaviour was observed for omens and reported to the king, or else the latter consulted the scholars about the purport of bird omens. A special series of omens dealt with the abnormal birth of animals and man, which is called *šumma izbu*, "when a foetus..." (s. W. VON SODEN, *ZA* 50, 182ff. and shortly a study by E. LEICHTY), after the opening words. Physiognomical and physiological things of man (s. F. KÖCHER and A. L. OPPENHEIM, *AfO* 18, 62ff.; F. R. KRAUS, *TBP*; *MVAeG* 40/2; *Or.* 16, 172ff.; *AfO* 11, 219ff.) and symptoms of illness (s. R. LABAT, *TDP*) were used already in the Ancient Babylonian age as material for omens as was the appearance of spirits of the dead. Reference should also be made to a 'Sittenkanon' in the form of omens edited by F. R. KRAUS, *ZA* 43, 77ff.

An important role in determining the future was played by dreams
as early as the time of Gudea and also later, as for example in the Old
Babylonian Māri texts (s. below). Right up to the Neo-Assyrian age,
the cuneiform libraries contained books on dreams and their interpretation. These inform us about the significance of things eaten and of
journeys apparently made in dreams (s. A. L. OPPENHEIM, *Dreams*
256ff.).

Of all the artificially produced omens, the observation of the liver
was most important, being thought to be the gift of the sun-god
Šamaš. It appears that already Sargon and Narāmsîn applied this art
(see above). Nowadays we have a rather large number of texts from
the Ancient Babylonian period containing observations on the state of
different parts of sheep livers (s. J. NOUGAYROL, *RA* 38, 67ff.; 40, 56
ff.; 44, 1ff.; A. GOETZE, *YOS* 10) and of their gall (s. K. RIEMSCHNEI-
DER, *ZA* 57, 125ff.), though the majority of the liver omens known to
us derive from the library of Aššurbānipal. Since it must have been
rather difficult for beginners to become acquainted with the anatomy
of the various parts of the liver and their anomalies, clay models of
livers were made with short inscriptions about the parts of the liver
and their ominous interpretation. Examples of these have been preserved from the early Old Babylonian period from Māri (s. M. RUT-
TEN, *RA* 35, 36ff.), from Hazor in Palestine (s. B. LANDSBERGER
and H. TADMOR, *IEJ* 14, 201ff.) and from the later period even from
Boğazköy. Models were also made of other entrails of the sheep sacrified.
From the ancient Babylonian period and the Cassite period we possess
certain reports on the observations of the entrails of the sheep (cf. M.
I. HUSSEY, *JCS* 2, 21ff.; A. GOETZE, o.c. 5ff.) sacrified which follow
a somewhat stereotype pattern of the report proper, an introductory
and a closing statement (s. A. GOETZE, *JCS* 11, 89ff.). The observer
had to weigh the favourable and unfavourable signs of the entrails
against each other; when doubt arose the observation had to be made
with two or more animals. There are extant a great many questions
put by the kings Asarhaddon and Aššurbānipal to Šamaš for information by means of haruspicy about important political matters. They
follow a stereotype pattern: first the question, thereafter the request
made to the god to ignore minor faults in the offering, then the request for information briefly summarized, and finally the statement on
what was found in the entrails. A first unfavourable result could be
followed by a repeated investigation. In some of Aššurbānipal's
questions the animal sacrified is not mentioned, but can perhaps be

inferred. In the earlier texts the result of the investigation was not always accompanied by an interpretation, but in the omen texts from Aššurbānipal's library this was done. Usually these refer to matters concerning the ordinary life of the king, sometimes also to historical events. The hepatoscopic texts were arranged according to the various sections of the liver to facilitate the orientation of the observer.

In the kidney omens, again the right side was associated with the person in question, the left with the enemy.

Of the various means used by the king of Babylon to seek an oracle recorded in Ez. 21,26 no mention has been found thus far in the Mesopotamian sources of consulting the Terāfīm and the shaking of arrows. It appears that the casting of the lot was applied in the division of inheritance and the choice of eponyms.

As already mentioned above, divination by means of a goblet (oil on water) was known already in ancient times in Mesopotamia. According to research recently carried out by G. Pettinato (ÖB) different texts from Babylon, from Aššur and from Boğazköy have been recorded so far.

Finally, another means of reading the future used in the Ancient Babylonian period was that of incense (s. G. Pettinato, RSO 41, 303 ff.), whereby the form and direction of the smoke and the flame and parts of the incense were observed and interpreted with regard to their ominous signification.

In addition to the collections of omens arranged in categories belonging together collections were also made of inauspicious omens, somewhat comparable to the Roman books of prodigies. These were, for example, those which accompanied the fall of the land of Akkad, the invasion of the city by wild animals, or matters pertaining to the cult. There were also incantations and rituals against misfortunes which were to be expected from inauspicious omens, viz. the series *namburbû* (from Sumerian nam-búr-bi "loosening there-from", s. AHw. 726) "loosening there from" (s. E. Ebeling, RA 48,1).

Then the science of oracles also included the symbolism of numbers, a record of which is to be found concerning Sargon II of Assyria's speculations on the numerical value of his own name, and the science of choosing favourable days for undertaking certain ventures. The Babylonian and Assyrian kings were in the habit of mentioning in their building reports that the foundation stone was laid on an auspicious day. When swearing oaths, obtaining audience or making offers, it was a matter of concern to select the right day, and certain seers were consulted by the king with regard to such affairs. Apparently the seers used oracles to find the answer. Later there were set collections of all the favourable and unfavourable days of the year for all possible actions, which simply stated whether they were favourable or not, or added a short statement or even detailed instructions about all sorts of matters concerning human life (s. above Ch. IV. A.b.).

Mention in this context must also be made of divine judgment, which e.g. is recorded in the code of Ḫammurapi and the Middle Assyrian laws in the form of an ordeal by water (cf. G. R. DRIVER and J. MILES, *BabLaws* 1, 61ff.; 2, 147; R. BORGER, *BAL* 3, 102) and in the Neo-Sumerian deeds, and later, as being effected by the swearing of an oath also before divine symbols (s. A. FALKENSTEIN, *NG* 1, 63ff.; H. HIRSCH, *AfOBeih.* 13, 64ff.; W. VON SODEN, *GAG* §185).

Finally there is the phenomenon of prophecy, known both in Babylonia and the adjoining regions. For the Ancient Babylonian period, special reference might be made to the important material from Māri, in which repeated mention is made of extatics in the service of the gods Dagān, Bēletekallim, and Addu (Adad). These extatics were ordered by the gods to inform those in power of their divine will concerning all sorts of practical matters. In Māri this could also be communicated through dreams (s. G. DOSSIN, *Divination* 77ff.; A. FINET, ibid. 87ff.). From later periods, too, we have data on the activities of extatics in Mesopotamia. It was in this way, for example, that Asarhaddon received a message from Ištar of Arbela promising him a long reign. We have a collection of prophecies in literary form dealing with the future of Babylonia and referring to historical events which, however, are too vaguely formulated for precise determination (s. A. K. GRAYSON and W. G. LAMBERT, *JCS* 18,7ff.; R. D. BIGGS, *Iraq* 29,117ff.; W. W. HALLO, *IEJ* 16,231ff.).

c.   Funerals and funerary customs; conceptions of the netherworld

Little is as yet known of the funerary customs in the ancient land of the two rivers (cf. B. MEISSNER, *BuA* 1,424ff.), especially with regard to the earlier periods. For the early dynastic period, the royal graves of Ur have yielded information about a form of funeral in which a number of servants accompanied members of the royal house to their grave (cf. also finds in the cemetery Y at Kiš, s. A. MOORTGAT, *Tammuz* 53;53⁶) and perhaps S. N. KRAMER, *BASOR* 94,4ff. is right in discerning a similar funerary practice in the Sumerian text of "Bilgameš in the Netherworld". "Urnammu in the Netherworld", likewise a

Sumerian text, mentions lamentations about the death of this king (Ur III period) and about a feast and gifts to seven gods of the netherworld (s. G. CASTELLINO, *ZA* 52,9ff.; S. N. KRAMER, *TMHNF* 4, p. 17f.; *JCS* 21, 104ff.).

Several references to offerings to the dead (*kispum*, s. above Ch. IV A.e) are made in Ancient Babylonian records, and from the Middle Babylonian period there is a conical tombstone with an inscription expressing the wish that the spirits(!) of the one who treats the grave in question with piety may drink pure water in the netherworld (*VS* 1,54, s. R. BORGER, *HKL* 1,351; B. MEISSNER, *BuA* 1,428; 428²); the curse that a ghost may suffer thirst is to be found in the Code of Ḫammurapi and later records. The provision of water for the ghosts of the dead was the task of the *nāq mê* (s. *AHw*. 744), the offerer of water. Dating from a later period is a ritual text containing prescriptions for a banquet of the gods, which states that a mortuary repast must be prepared to the left of the table for the ghosts of the deceased members of the family; moreover the latter were to receive handsome gifts (É. DHORME, *"Religions"* 231; 253:*BBR* 52). The care for the ghosts of the dead was important, not only for reasons of piety, but also for fear that they might otherwise wander about on earth and cause disaster.

Among the mourning customs was the utterance of lamentations as early as the Ancient Babylonian period by special priests and priestesses, who were known as *lallārum* and *lallārtum* respectively (s. *AHw*. 530), or by private individuals present. The mourner sometimes also rent his garments, or put on sackcloth, tore out the hair of his beard and beat his thighs. The body appears to have been buried usually within three days, sometimes seven days after death. Traces of cremation seem to have been found for various periods. Already in ancient times it happened that bodies were buried in dwellings in different parts of Mesopotamia and Iran. In Babylon the dead were normally buried in the houses, though the dating of the graves found there is still difficult (s. E. STROMMENGER, *BagM* 3,157ff.). Some years ago A. HALLER published a comprehensive study on the graves in Aššur, from which certain data are reproduced below, especially from B. HROUDA's summary (*WVDOG* 65,182ff.). From the Akkad period onwards in Aššur the dead were buried, seldom cremated. Underground tombs in Aššur date from roughly the Ancient Assyrian period; urn and sarcophagus graves usually date from the Middle Assyrian period. The dead were interred in a contracted or supine position. If the grave had already been used, the bones of the previously interred were pushed aside. If the deceased was not buried in a sarcophagus or pithos, rushes were spread under or wrapped about him; sometimes funeral wraps were placed on the body. In the grave were placed those things which the deceased possessed in life, and which he was apparently still thought to possess, as well as others he might need in the netherworld. Dishes were placed on his breast, goblets and bottles near his head, and all around the body little pots of make-up, perhaps to conserve the body as long as possible. It is difficult to explain the contents of grave 45 in Aššur, in which two people were buried and surrounded by inconceivably precious gifts. W. ANDRAE (o.c. 147f.) conjectured that this pair might have been a substitute king and an Ištar priestess, put to death after the ἱερὸς γάμος and buried with the royal jewelry. Lamaštu pictures on exorcism tablets were also sometimes placed in the grave. The fact that interment often took place in inhabited dwellings suggest a close connexion between the living and the dead. A small fragment of a text tells us a little about the funeral of a king from Aššur in the Neo-Assyrian period, how the stone sarcophagus was sealed with a heavy bronze lock and safeguarded against grave-despoilers and demons by means of an anathema. Furthermore mention is made of rich mortuary gifts first displayed before Šamaš and of gifts for the gods of the netherworld (s. W. VON SODEN, ZA 43,254ff.).

A few concluding words about the Ancient Mesopotamian conceptions of the netherworld might not be amiss here (s. above Ch. III. G; S.N. KRAMER, Iraq 22,59ff.; B. MEISSNER, BuA 2,143ff.). The best-known terms for the netherworld (s. K. TALLQVIST, StOr. 5/4) were perhaps Arali and "Land of no return". The location was thought to be under the earth: one descended to it and from it ascended to the earth (see above, Ch. III. G). In B/Gilgameš texts we read how the ghost of Enkidu was permitted to ascend to the earth, where he was interrogated about life in Hades. The frontier of the netherworld was formed by the river Ilurugu (Sumerian), usually called Ḫubur in Akkadian. There were seven gateways, through which gods and mortals could pass only if all their clothes and ornaments were taken from them one by one (see above, Ch. IV. Cb). The prevailing notion of life in the netherworld, a place filled with dust and briny water, was that it was not particularly pleasant, although a person who had sons had diverse privileges, and one who had someone to see to mortuary offerings on earth was in a favourable position. There are several references to judges of the netherworld, though there is no evidence of any conception of a sort of judgment of the dead based on moral behaviour during life; apparently they merely pronounced the definitive sentence of death (s. D. O. EDZARD, *WM* 1/1, 131). An important testimonial about the netherworld conception in the Neo-Assyrian period is the text "Vision of the netherworld of an Assyrian crown prince", called Kummâ. In a nocturnal panorama he sees the netherworld with fifteen deities and demons. By wishing to see the netherworld Kummâ has offended Ereškigala and is therefore threatened by Nergal. The intercession of Išum secures his freedom (s. W. VON SODEN, *ZA* 43,1ff.).

VI. THE SPHERE OF INFLUENCE OF THE RELIGION OF MESOPOTAMIA

It is practically impossible to summarize this subject. Inevitably a selection must be made of the almost immeasurable amount of material, and the necessary subjectivity cannot but produce an incomplete picture. Moreover, much remains unknown or uncertain through lack of preliminary research work.

Although the principle differences between the religions of Mesopotamia and Israel must never be forgotten, various motifs are to be found in the Old and perhaps also the New Testament, which appear to derive in one way or another from the land of the two rivers. In poetic sections of the Old Testament (cf. F. M. TH. DE LIAGRE BÖHL, *RGG*[3] 1,822ff.) reminiscenses are to be found of the splitting of a sea monster (cf. Tiāmat and the derivative Hebrew tehōm) at the time of the creation in the O.T., also thematically related to the passage of the Red Sea and the Jordan. Comparable to some extent are the installation of sun and moon in Enūma eliš V and that in Genesis I, while the Hebrew conception of the world is probably of Mesopotamian (cf. B. MEISSNER, *BuA* 2,107ff.) extraction (cf. I. BENZINGER, *Hebr. Arch.*[3] 163). The long-lived Biblical patriarchs are perhaps reflections of the long-reigning primeval kings known to us from the Babylonian king-list (cf. C. WESTERMANN, *BK* 1/1,12). The literary dependence of the Hebrew story of the Deluge on the Mesopotamian traditions can be surmised from the strikingly analogous points in the Sumerian and Akkadian stories of the Deluge and in Gen. 6-8 (warning sent to one who must survive the deluge, and the building of a ship; the bringing on board of pairs of animals; the running aground on a mountain after the flood; the despatch of birds; offering and blessing, s. D. O. EDZARD, *WM* 1/1,66). The tower of Babel is evidently the remembrance of a Babylonian ziqqurrat, while the story of building the temple in I Chr. has perhaps a theme analogous to the description of Gudea's restoration of the Eninnu (s. M. LAMBERT, *RHPhR* 1,4ff.). The Hebrew word for temple, hēkāl, derives from Sumerian via Akkadian. The title "friend of the king" also seems to be of Mesopotamian derivation (s. A. VAN SELMS, *JNES* 16,118ff.). As yet no study has been made of the question whether certain prophecies are, as literature, comparable with the few prophecies known from the Māri correspondence (cf. F. M. TH. DE LIAGRE BÖHL, *Op. min.* 63ff.), though the latter show signs of Canaanite influence. Certain themes from the Erra epic, however, have been traced in the prophecies of Ezekiel (s. R. FRANKENA, *Kanttekeningen van een assyrioloog bij Ezechiël*, Leyden 1965). Striking thematic similarities have been established between the Book Qohelet and the Epic of Gilgameš and the Akkadian works of wisdom (cf. O. LORETZ, *Qohelet und der Alte Orient*, Freiburg i.B. 1964, 132ff.; J. FICHTNER, "Die altorientalische Weisheit in ihrer israelitisch-jüdischen Ausprägung," *BZAW* 62, Giessen 1933). Certain Tammuz motifs are believed to be discernible in the Song of Songs (cf. O. EISSFELDT, *Einl. in das Alte Testament* [3]656ff.).

The later Jewish Midrāš exegesis could have been influenced by Babylonian sources (s. W. G. LAMBERT, *AfO* 17,311), and the female demon Lilit, known from non-Biblical Jewish writings, is definitely of Mesopotamian extraction (s. D. O. EDZARD, *WM* 1/1,48), as is the Jewish oil magic (s. S. DAICHES, *Babylonian Oil Magic in the Talmud and in the later Jewish Literature*, London 1913). The Greek demon-name Gello perhaps is a derivative of the Mesopotamian *gallû*-demon (s. C. FRANK, *ZA* 24,161ff.; 333f.). Elements handed down from Ancient Mesopotamian iconography have been traced in Medieval Christian art (cf. A. PARROT, *StMar.* 111ff.; G. CONTENAU, *RA* 37, 154ff.).

Regarding the New Testament, Babylonian influence might reasonably be assumed in connexion with some notions in the Apocalypse of John (cf. E. LOHMEYER, *Handb. z. N.T.* 16[2], Tübingen 1953, 48; 113).

The eastern Aramaic magic bowls found in Babylonia bear clear traces of how Jewish-Hellenistic representations were superimposed on the remains of ancient Babylonian patterns (F. ROSENTHAL, *Die aramaistische Forschung seit Th. Nöldeke's Veröffentlichungen*, Leyden 1939, 219; 219f.[4]). There is also an Aramaic anathema formula on one of the stelae from Sfire-Sugĭn, which can be traced back to a Sumero-Akkadian prototype (s. K. R. VEENHOF, *BiOr.* 20, 142ff.). The Melek Ta'uz of the Yezidi's could derive from Tammuz at least regarding the name.

It is not clear whether the conception of the generations of the gods known in ancient Syria in earlier ages underwent Mesopotamian influence (cf W. RÖLLIG, *WM* 1/2, 285f.).

Babylonian influence has been surmised in various Ethiopian incantations (s. M. LAMBERT, *RA* 50, 50) and apparently too in Manichaeism (cf. G. WIDENGREN, *Mesopotamian Elements in Manichaeism*, Uppsala 1946).

The prototype of the classical representation of Ahuramazda and the image on two of the four Achaemenid monetary types is the god Aššur in the winged sun-disc, bearing weapons and sometimes in the attitude of an archer (s. P. NASTER, *CRRA* 11, 10f.).

The Islamic representations of heavenly tablets inscribed with the divine volition appear to have been influenced by the Babylonian notion of the tablets of destiny (cf. A. J. WENSINCK, *Handwörtb. d. Islam*, Leyden 1941, 364 s.v. Lawḥ). The passion plays held in the Šiʿite world to commemorate the death of Ḥussein (Taʿzīya) perhaps perpetuate ancient Tammuz customs in their accompanying actions (cf. R. PARET, *Symbolik des Islam*, Stuttgart 1958, 72ff.).

Mesopotamian influence can often be discerned in the classical world (cf. F. DORNSEIFF, *Antike und Alter Orient*, Leipzig 1959). Astrology—important up to now—and astrological geography, horoscopy and hepatoscopy, also known to Graeco-Roman cultural circles, probably originated in Mesopotamia, while the Etruscan models of the liver must have been based on the Babylonian models (s. R. BORGER, *JEOL* 18, 317ff.). It has been conjectured that labyrinths derive from the well-known Babylonian, or Hittite, clay models of entrails used in haruspicy (cf. F. M. TH. DE LIAGRE BÖHL, *Op. min.* 324ff.). The echo of an omen-text concerning Sargon of Akkade has been traced down to Roman poets (cf. W. G. SCHILEICO, *AfO* 5, 214ff.). Greek conceptions about theogony and the generations of the gods (Hesiod) can perhaps also be traced back to a Mesopotamian example (cf. W. G. LAMBERT and P. WALCOT, *Kadmos* 4, 64ff.). No definitive answer has been found to the question whether certain elements of Greek philosophy were derived from Mesopotamia; this has been doubted in the case of Plato (s. W. J. W. KOSTER, *Le mythe de Platon, de Zarathoustra et des Chaldéens*, Leyden 1951, 82, but also TH. HOPFNER, *"Orient und griechische Philosophie"*, *AO* 4, Leipzig 1925; C. W. VOLLGRAFF, *JEOL* 7, 347ff.), but it is possible that the doctrines of Thales of Milete, of the young Aristoteles and of Zeno of Kition underwent such influence (cf. C. W. VOLLGRAFF, l.c.).

VII. Brief Sketch of the History of the Study
of Mesopotamian Religion

Only a few main points in the development of the study can be indicated in this section.

The last quarter of the 19th and the first quarter of this century were the periods of what is nowadays called Pan-Babylonism. Since F. Delitzsch Jr. *(Babel und Bibel)* began in 1902 to refute the independence of the Old Testament regarding the Babylonian world of thought, H. Winckler and A. Jeremias in particular made much, though one-sided, progress with their theory of the "analogy doctrine" (s. A. Jeremias, *Handbuch der altorientalischen Geisteskultur*[2] (Berlin-Leipzig 1929). The main issue was not merely the analogies between Mesopotamia and Israel, but more particularly the foundations of the entire ancient-Eastern image of the world, including Israel. The conception was concerned with the mutual analogy between the earthly world and the starry heavens, the microcosmos and the macrocosmos (hence in space), and the calendar and the cosmic cycle on a large scale and a small scale in the category of time. According to these scholars, the origins of this conception were to be found among the ancient Babylonians or Sumerians, whence it was widely disseminated. This viewpoint was therefore called "Pan-Babylonism". Since then research on the earliest cultures of Mesopotamia has revealed that the Babylonian lowland at the outset had been a gathering place for the most divergent races and cultures and that only later it became a centre of emanation itself. Furthermore it appeared that the observation and the worship of the constellations, on which this "astral mythology" was based, did not play such an important role in the ancient Sumerian period. This meant that "Babel" was rejected as the true land of origin of the Biblical world of thought (not of the literary forms). But probably the most serious objection was directed against the historical validity of the theory as such, and it came from the field of comparative psychology, whose spiritual father was W. Wundt even in the heyday of Pan-Babylonism. Of principle significance in this respect was the discovery of the mainly auditive, mental orientation of the Easterners (also of the Babylonians and Hebrews) as compared with the more visual orientation of the Greeks. The aforesaid conception was too static, was not dynamic enough. There could be no question of reflexions or counterparts of the heavenly and the earthly world among the peoples of the Near East such as those seen by the visual imagination, at least not as predominating principle. They were more concerned with the conflict and events at the beginning and the end of time, about which priests and prophets sang and spoke for their audiences and which they imitated in the cultic actions, hence in the ritual (s. F. M. TH. DE LIAGRE BÖHL, *JEOL* 16, 103f., whose opinion is here briefly reproduced).

The famous Assyriologist P. JENSEN postulated a remarkable combination of the then literary-critical method and Pan-Babylonism. He limited his observations on this point to the Babylonian Epic of Gilgameš, endeavouring to demonstrate its themes and series of motifs not only in the Bible and even the Gospels, but everywhere in ancient literature. Diverse analogies, such as with Homer, can hardly be denied. Here Gilgameš is only one given instance, since one of the most notorious problems is the wandering of themes in myths, sagas, and fairy tales (cf. e.g. U. EWIG, *Deutsche Volksmärchen*, Frankfurt a. M. 1960, 315ff.). On the whole the human imagination seems to be limited to a certain number of themes, hence the question of these repetitions and "Anklänge" is as much concerned with this limitation, which tends to block new ways, as with distribution by wandering singers and narrators (s. F. M. TH. DE LIAGRE BÖHL, ibid. 104f.).

The English and Scandinavian scholars in particular supported the theory of "patternism", which met with opposition from the archaeologist H. FRANKFORT and others. The term "patternism", perhaps better expressed as "schematism", is derived from the word "pattern" in its meaning of spiritual norms or stencils which allegedly always found their expression in a like manner among the most diverse cultural circles (s. F. M. TH. DE LIAGRE BÖHL, ibid. 105; 105[2]).

Only a few important phases of the further development of the study of Mesopotamian religion can be traced here.

Of the general works published in the course of time reference might be made to the book by É. DHORME (1949) which as standard work and as imposing collection of material long shall remain indispensable, to the comprehensive collections of Mesopotamian divine names by A. DEIMEL (1914; 1950), to the work of CH. F. JEAN on the Sumerian religion up to and including the Ur III period (1931) and to the collection of material on the gods mentioned in the Ur III texts made by N. SCHNEIDER (1939). Of importance, too, are the short monograph by TH. JACOBSEN on the central concerns of the Mesopotamian religion (1963) and the pessimistic and very important chapter on the

practical impossibility of writing a history of the religion of Mesopotamia in A. L. OPPENHEIM's book entitled *Ancient Mesopotamia* (1961).
Very useful anthologies of Sumerian and Akkadian hymns, prayers and
other texts in modern and readable translations are to be found, inter
alia, in the works of A. FALKENSTEIN and W. von SODEN (*SAHG*, 1953)
and the work edited by J. B. PRITCHARD (1955). Important monographs are, further, the works of B. GEMSER (1924) and J. J. STAMM
(1939) on Akkadian personal names, in which the religious significance
and background are discussed at length. H. SCHMÖKEL has published (1967) a discourse on the preference for certain divine names as
components of personal names in the various periods(*JEOL* 19, 468ff.).
J. BOTTÉRO has written about the old 'Semitic' gods of Mesopotamia
(*StSem*. 1,17ff.), H. HIRSCH about the religious data to be found in the
Old Assyrian texts from Kültepe in Asia Minor (1961), and H. FINE
on certain aspects of Middle-Assyrian religion (Cincinnati, 1955). As
early as 1923, B. LANDSBERGER pointed out the urgent necessity of distinguishing clearly between the various local cults (*OLZ* 1923, 74). In
later years F. R. KRAUS dealt with the principal deities of Isin in the
Neo-Sumerian and Old Babylonian periods (*JCS* 3, 1951) and A. FAL-
KENSTEIN with the pantheon of Lagaš at the time of Gudea (1966). In
recent years a question repeatedly dealt with has been the grouping together of the Mesopotamian gods as Anunna (Sumerian)/Anunnaku
and Igigu (Akkadian). W. von SODEN, for example, demonstrated that
these concepts underwent a change in meaning in the course of time
(1964) and pointed out the remarkable role played by these gods in the
Old Babylonian Atramḫasīs material recently published (1966). The
Sumerian material has been dealt with by A. FALKENSTEIN (1965), while
an important collection of Akkadian passages for the said groups of
gods was published by B. KIENAST (1965). Of the very important research work done by J. van DIJK on the cosmic and chtonic motifs in
Sumerian thought, only the first part has been published (1964); a short
discourse on the Sumerian religion by the same author has opened up
important new lines of thought (1968). Other fields of Sumerian religious phenomena have been investigated in the past decades. First there
is the pioneer work of S. N. KRAMER on Sumerian mythology (1944;
²1961) and the contribution made by the same author to a collection of
studies on mythologies of the ancient world (1961). D. O. EDZARD was
then in a position to publish a work in encyclopedic form on Mesopotamian mythology which deservedly may be qualified as a most important
milestone on the road to a more comprehensive knowledge of these

matters (1959). A. FALKENSTEIN and F. M. TH. DE LIAGRE BÖHL (1968) have very recently published articles on B/Gilgameš in the Sumerian and Akkadian traditions respectively. The great significance of such essential concepts as me, *parṣu*, which B. LANDSBERGER treated in a profound article in 1924, has been emphasized of late in important contributions made by J. VAN DIJK (1967), A. L. OPPENHEIM (1961) and K. OBERHUBER (1963). Repeatedly in the course of time diverse gods and texts relevant to them have been discussed in monographs; of these reference might be made to the studies of K. TALLQVIST on Aššur (1932), of F. NÖTSCHER on Ellil (1927; 1938); of H. SCHMÖKEL on Dagān (1928; 1938); of H. SCHLOBIES (1925) and E. EBELING (1932) on Adad; of A. FALKENSTEIN on Šulpa'e (1963) and of J. R. KUPPER on the iconography of Amurru (1961). The archaeologist E. D. VAN BUREN dealt with many topics concerning the Mesopotamian religion from the archaeologic view-point i.a., the god Ningizzida (1934).

What might be qualified true pioneer works are the discourse of H. ZIMMERN (1909) and of A. FALKENSTEIN (1954) on the figure of Dumuzi, still so difficult to fathom and in this context reference might also be made to a recent article by S. N. KRAMER, in which he edited a number of texts pertaining to Dumuzi (1963). Already at the beginning of this century J. HEHN devoted a study to the Babylonian concept of god as compared with the Hebrew (1913), a work which could be considered a sort of counterweight to the Pan-Babylonistic ideas which became so popular at that time (*Die biblische und die babylonische Gottesidee...*, Leipzig 1913). Two years previously C. FRANK, who afterwards also produced an important book on cultic hymns from the Ištar-Tammuz-circle (1939), dealt with the Babylonian priesthood (1911). Further there are the articles of J. RENGER on priestly officials in the Ancient Babylonian period (1967; 1969). Various dissertations on the religious aspects of kingship in Mesopotamia have been written by H. FRANKFORT (1948); C. J. GADD (*Ideas of Divine Rule in the Ancient East*, London 1948); A. FALKENSTEIN (1949) and W. H. PH. RÖMER (1965), whilst the divine parentage of the kings was dealt with by Å. SJÖBERG (1967). Recently H. M. KÜMMEL summarized the rite of the "substitute king" (1967). Highly important summaries dealing with prayer and based on Sumerian and Akkadian material have been published in recent years by A. FALKENSTEIN (1959) and W. VON SODEN (1959; 1964). Several collections of incantations have been edited in the course of time, for example those against the female demon Lamaštum by D. MYHRMAN

(1902) and W. von Soden (1954; 1956; 1961), against different diseases by A. Goetze (1955), against ergot in the eye by B. Landsberger and Th. Jacobsen (1955) and the Maqlû collection by G. Meier (1937), Šurpu by E. Reiner (1958) and the Namburbi texts by E. Ebeling (1954-1956). The last mentioned author also published a book containing texts and commentaries entitled *Tod und Leben nach den Vorstellungen der Babylonier* (1931) and wrote a new treatment of the prayers of the "lifting of the hand" (*AGH*, 1953). Conceptions of the netherworld expressed in Sumerian literary material were dealt with i.a. by S. N. Kramer (1960). Of the works on rituals, mention is made only of the book by J. Laessøe of the *bît rimki* series (1955).

The last decades have witnessed a great deal of research in the field of the Mesopotamian sapiental texts in the broadest sense of the term. Important recensions and summaries of texts, mainly of the Sumerian sources, have been published by J. van Dijk (1953) and E. I. Gordon (1960). W. G. Lambert systematically edited the Akkadian material in a detailed work of 1960. Recently (1965) W. von Soden dealt with the Mesopotamian theodicies. Publications and recensions of various groups of omen-texts have been published, for which we also refer to a summary from 1966; A. Goetze wrote on Ancient Babylonian omen texts (1947); F. Nötscher wrote on the *šumma ālu ina mêlê šakin* series (1928-1930) and R. Labat on the *enūma ana bît marṣi āšipu illiku* series. A. L. Oppenheim has published a work on dreams and the Assyrian dream-book (1956), J. Nougayrol has written studies on liver-omens (1941; 1945; 1946; 1950), K. Riemschneider on gall-omens (1965), F. R. Kraus (1935; 1939), F. Köcher and A. L. Oppenheim (1958) on physiognomical omens, G. Pettinato on divination by oil and incense (1966) and R. D. Biggs on ancient Mesopotamian potency incantations (1967), while R. Labat commented on hemerologies and menologies from Aššur (1939) and edited the series *iqqur îpuš* (1965). J. Krecher wrote a book on Sumerian cult lyrics (1966).

An infinite amount of research has still to be done on the Mesopotamian religion. In our opinion, special attention should be paid to the following fields of study:

(a) further study of the various local and greater (state) pantheons;

(b) more detailed investigations into the points of difference between the 'Sumerian' and the 'Akkadian' religious conceptions, in which subject only preliminary, though important, work has as yet been done (see above);

(c) research on such fundamental concepts, especially of the Sumerian religion, as me; giš-ḫur; garza, to which end the Akkadian sources should also be thoroughly studied;

(d) continuation of the classification and study of the Dumuzi material;
(e) monographs on Mesopotamian deities;
(f) further treatment of as wide and numerous a variety as possible of Mesopotamian religious texts.

These projects can only be successfully carried out if a working method is applied that makes full use of the most recent philological —i.e. grammatical and lexicographic—knowledge of Akkadian and Sumerian and takes into account all the material available for both languages. Furthermore this material must be interpreted as meticulously as possible, no trouble being spared, and the fullest possible reference must be made to the discoveries and problems of modern archaeology and to the sciences of religion and (para)psychology. Unfortunately, the present state of affairs regarding these branches of study makes it increasingly more difficult to realise these ideals, or even to approximate them. In any case, cooperation between the philologist and practitioners of the other branches of study mentioned above, acting as counsellors, will prove to be ever more indispensable.

SELECTED BIBLIOGRAPHY

Ch. I

R. Borger, *Handbuch der Keilschriftliteratur* 1 (Berlin 1967). Indispensable for bibliographic references.

Th. Jacobsen, "Ancient Mesopotamian Religion: The Central Concerns" (*PAPS* 107, 473ff.).

Ch. F. Jean, *La religion sumérienne d'après les documents sumériens antérieurs à la dynastie d'Isin* (-2186) (Paris 1931).

J. van Dijk, "Sumerisk religion", in: *Illustreret Religionshistorie²*, redigeret af J. P. Asmussen og J. Laessøe, G.E.C. Gads Forlag (Copenhagen 1968).

J. van Dijk, "Le motif cosmique dans la pensée sumérienne" (*ActOr*. 28,1ff.).

B. Meissner, *Babylonien und Assyrien* 2 (Heidelberg 1925).

É. Dhorme, "Les religions de Babylonie et d'Assyrie" (*Mana*, Paris 1949).

A. L. Oppenheim, *Ancient Mesopotamia. Portrait of a dead Civilization* (Chicago-London 1964) 171ff.

A. Deimel, *Pantheon Babylonicum¹* (Rome 1914).

A. Deimel, "Pantheon Babylonicum"² (*ŠL* 4/1, Rome 1950).

N. Schneider, "Die Götternamen von Ur III" (*AnOr*. 19, Rome 1939).

H. Hirsch, "Untersuchungen zur altassyrischen Religion" (*AfOBeih*. 13/14, Graz 1961).

Th. Paffrath, *Zur Götterlehre in den altbabylonischen Königsinschriften* (Paderborn 1913).

Ch. III

For the Mesopotamian deities s. D. O. Edzard, *Wörterbuch der Mythologie* 1/1 (Stuttgart 1965); many articles in *Reallexikon der Assyriologie* 1ff. (Berlin-

Leipzig 1932ff.); J. BOTTÉRO, *StSem.* 1, 17ff. S. further A. FALKENSTEIN-J. VAN DIJK, *Sumerische Götterlieder* 1/2 (Heidelberg 1959-60).

Ch. III.D

Å. SJÖBERG, *Der Mondgott Nanna-Suen in der sumerischen Überlieferung* (Stockholm 1960).

W. W. HALLO; J. VAN DIJK, "The Exaltation of Inanna" (*UNER* 3, New Haven-London 1968).

Ch. III.F

K. TALLQVIST, "Der assyrische Gott" (*StOr.* 4/3, Helsinki 1932).

Ch. III.H.i

C. FRANK, *Kultlieder aus dem Ischtar-Tamūz-Kreis* (Leipzig 1939).

Ch. IV.A.a

H. LENZEN, *Die Entwicklung der Zikurrat von ihren Anfängen bis zur Zeit der III. Dynastie von Ur* (*Ausgrabungen der Deutschen Forschungsgemeinschaft in Uruk-Warka*, Bd. 4, Leipzig 1941).

A. PARROT, *Ziggurrats et "Tour de Babel"* (Paris 1949).

Ch. IV.A.b

B. LANDSBERGER, "Der kultische Kalender der Babylonier und Assyrer" 1 (*LSS* 6/1-2, Leipzig 1915).

S. LANGDON, "Babylonian Menologies and the Semitic calendars" (*The Schweich Lectures of the British Academy* 1933, London 1935).

R. LABAT, *Hémérologies et Ménologies d'Assur* (Paris 1939).

R. LABAT, *Un calendrier babylonien des travaux, des signes et des mois* (séries *iqqur ipuš*) (Paris 1965).

S. A. PALLIS, "The Babylonian Akîtu Festival" (*Det Kgl. Danske Videnskabernes Selskab*, hist.-fil. Meddelelser 12/1, Copenhagen 1926).

J. KRECHER, *Sumerische Kultlyrik* (Wiesbaden 1966).

Ch. IV. A.c

H. FRANKFORT, *Kingship and the Gods. A Study of Ancient Near Eastern Religion as the Integration of Society & Nature* (Chicago 1948) 215ff.

C. FRANK, *Studien zur babylonischen Religion* 1 (Strassburg 1911).

Ch. IV. A.e

F. BLOME, *Die Opfermaterie in Babylonien und Israel* 1 (Rome 1934).

Ch. IV. A.f

A. FALKENSTEIN, "Die Haupttypen der sumerischen Beschwörung" (*LSSNF* 1, Leipzig 1931).

W. G. KUNSTMANN, "Die babylonische Gebetsbeschwörung" (*LSSNF* 2, Leipzig 1932).

G. MEIER, "Die assyrische Beschwörungssammlung *Maqlû*" (*AfOBeih.* 2, Berlin 1937).

E. REINER, "*Šurpu*. A Collection of Sumerian and Akkadian Incantations" (*AfO Beih.* 11, Graz 1958).

E. EBELING, *Die akkadische Gebetsserie "Handerhebung"* (Berlin 1953).

H. ZIMMERN, *Beiträge zur Kenntnis der babylonischen Religion* (*Assyriologische Bibliothek* 12, Leipzig 1901).

F. THUREAU-DANGIN, *Rituels Accadiens* (Paris 1921).

K. F. MÜLLER, "Das assyrische Ritual 1. Texte zum assyrischen Königsritual" *MVAeG* 41/3, Leipzig 1937).

R. Frankena, *Tākultu. De sacrale maaltijd in het assyrische ritueel. Met een overzicht over de in Assur vereerde goden* (Leyden 1953).

J. Laessøe, *Studies on the Assyrian Ritual and Series bît rimki* (Copenhagen 1955).

Ch. IV. B

S. Langdon, "Babylonian penitential Psalms..." (*OECT* 6, Paris 1927).

Ch. IV. C

D. O. Edzard, *WM* 1/1 (s. above Ch. III).

S. N. Kramer, *Sumerian Mythology*[2] (New York 1961).

S. N. Kramer, *Mythologies of the Ancient World* (Garden City, New York 1961) 93ff.

S. N. Kramer in: *Ancient Near Eastern Texts relating to the Old Testament*[2] (ed. by J. B. Pritchard, Princeton 1955) 37ff. Sumerian Myths and Epic Tales.

E. A. Speiser, o.c. 60ff. *Akkadian Myths and Epics.*

W. G. Lambert, *Enuma Eliš. The Babylonian Epic of Creation. The Cuneiform Text* (Oxford 1966).

F. Gössmann, *Das Era-Epos* (Würzburg 1955).

W. G. Lambert; A. R. Millard, *Astra-Ḫasis. The Babylonian story of the Flood* (Oxford 1969).

Ch. V. A

A. Heidel, *The Babylonian Genesis. The Story of Creation*[2] (Chicago 1954).

E. Sollberger, *The Babylonian legend of the Flood* (London 1962).

Ch. V. C.b

A number of authors in: *La divination en Mésopotamie ancienne et dans les régions voisines* (Paris, Presses Universitaires de France, 1966).

R. Labat, *Commentaires Assyro-Babyloniens sur les Présages* (Bordeaux 1933).

A. Goetze, "Old Babylonian Omen Texts" (*YOS* 10, New Haven 1947).

A. L. Oppenheim, *The Interpretation of Dreams in the Ancient Near East* (Philadelphia 1956).

G. Pettinato, "Die Ölwahrsagung bei den Babyloniern" 1;2 (*StSem.* 21;22, Rome 1966).

Ch. V. C.c

K. Tallqvist, "Sumerisch-akkadische Namen der Totenwelt" (*StOr.* 5/4, Helsinki 1934).

A. Haller, "Die Gräber und Grüfte von Assur" (*WVDOG* 65, Berlin 1954).

LIST OF ABBREVIATIONS

ActOr.	*Acta Orientalia* (Copenhagen).
AfO (Beih.)	*Archiv für Orientforschung* (*Beiheft*) (Berlin-Graz 1926/1933ff.).
AGH	E. Ebeling, *Die akkadische Gebetsserie "Handerhebung"* (Berlin 1954).
AHw.	W. von Soden, *Akkadisches Handwörterbuch* (Wiesbaden 1959ff.).
AK	*Archiv für Keilschriftforschung* (Berlin 1923ff.).
AnBi.	*Analecta Biblica* (Rome).
Anc. Mes.	A. L. Oppenheim *Ancient Mesopotamia. Portrait of a dead Civilization* (Chicago-London 1964).
AnOr.	*Analecta Orientalia* (Rome).
AnSt.	*Anatolian Studies* (Ankara).
AO	*Der Alte Orient* (Leipzig 1900ff.).
AOS	*American Oriental Series* (New Haven).
ArOr.	*Archiv Orientální* (Prague 1929ff.).

AS	*Assyriological Studies* (Chicago).
Atr.	W. G. LAMBERT; A. R. MILLARD, *Atra-Ḫasīs.* (Oxford 1969).
BabLaws	G. DRIVER-J. MILES, *The Babylonian Laws* 1;2 (Oxford 1952-55).
BagM	*Baghdader Mitteilungen* (Berlin).
BAL	R. BORGER, *Babylonisch-assyrische Lesestücke* (Rome 1963).
BASOR	*Bulletin of the American Schools of Oriental Research* (Jerusalem-Baghdad).
BBEA	B. LANDSBERGER, *Brief des Bischofs von Esagila an König Asarhaddon* (Amsterdam, Akademie 1965).
BBR	H. ZIMMERN, *Beiträge zur Kenntnis der babylonischen Religion* (Leipzig 1901), p. 81ff. (cited according to text numbers).
BBV	*Berliner Beiträge zur Vor- und Frühgeschichte* (Berlin).
Bell.	*Türk Tarih Kurumu-Belleten* (Ankara).
BG²	A. HEIDEL, *The Babylonian Genesis. The Story of the Creation²* (Chicago 1954).
BiOr.	*Bibliotheca Orientalis* (Leyden 1943ff.).
BJV	*Berliner Jahrbuch für Vor- und Frühgeschichte* (Berlin 1961ff.).
BK	*Biblischer Kommentar, Altes Testament* (Neukirchen 1956ff.).
BuA	B. MEISSNER, *Babylonien und Assyrien* 1;2 (Heidelberg 1920-25).
BWL	W. G. LAMBERT, *Babylonian Wisdom Literature* (Oxford 1960).
BZAW	*Beihefte zur Zeitschrift für die Alttestamentliche Wissenschaft* (Giessen-Berlin).
CAD	*The Assyrian Dictionary of the University of Chicago* (Chicago-Glückstadt 1956ff.).
CAH²	*The Cambridge Ancient History²* I;II (Cambridge).
CahTD	*Cahiers du Groupe François-Thureau-Dangin* (Paris 1960ff.).
CBSM	R. LABAT, *Un calendrier babylonien des travaux, des signes et des mois* (séries *iqqur īpuš*) (Paris 1965).
Comm.	R. LABAT, *Commentaires Assyro-Babyloniens sur les Présages* (Bordeaux 1933).
CRRA	*Compte Rendu de la... Rencontre Assyriologique Internationale.*
CT	*Cuneiform Texts from Babylonian Tablets in the British Museum* (London 1896ff.).
Divination	*La divination en Mésopotamie ancienne et dans les régions voisines* (Paris 1966).
Dreams	A. L. OPPENHEIM, *The Interpretation of Dreams in the Ancient Near East* (Philadelphia 1956).
FW	*Fischer Weltgeschichte* (Frankfurt a.M. 1965ff.).
GAG	W. VON SODEN, *Grundriss der akkadischen Grammatik* (=*AnOr.* 33, Rome 1952).
Gilg.	*Epic of Gilgameš* (ed. R. C. THOMPSON, *The Epic of Gilgamish* (Oxford 1930).
HBA	E. F. WEIDNER, *Handbuch der babylonischen Astronomie* (Leipzig 1915).
Hebr. Arch.³	I. BENZINGER, *Hebräische Archäologie³* (Leipzig 1927).
HKL 1	R. BORGER, *Handbuch der Keilschriftliteratur* 1 (Berlin 1967).
HMA	R. LABAT, *Hémérologies et ménologies d' Assur* (Paris 1939).
HOr.	*Handbuch der Orientalistik* (Leyden 1952ff.).
HSAO	*Heidelberger Studien zum Alten Orient* (Festschrift A. FALKENSTEIN, Wiesbaden 1967).
IEJ	*Israel Exploration Journal* (Jerusalem).
I.R.	*Illustreret Religionshistorie²* (redigeret af J. P. ASMUSSEN og J. LAESSØE, G.E.C. Gads Forlag, Copenhagen 1968).
Iraq	periodical *Iraq* (London 1934ff.).

JAOS	*Journal of the American Oriental Society* (Boston-New Haven 1849ff.).
JCS	*Journal of Cuneiform Studies* (New Haven 1947ff.).
JEOL	*Jaarbericht van het Vooraziatisch-Egyptisch Genootschap Ex Oriente Lux* (Leyden 1933ff.).
JNES	*Journal of Near Eastern Studies* (Chicago 1942ff.).
JSS	*Journal of Semitic Studies* (Manchester).
Kadmos	periodical *Kadmos. Zeitschrift für vor- und frühgriechische Epigraphik* (Berlin).
KH	*Code of Ḫammurapi* (s. R. BORGER, *BAL*).
LKU	A. FALKENSTEIN, *Literarische Keilschrifttexte aus Uruk* (Berlin 1931).
LSS(NF)	*Leipziger Semitistische Studien (Neue Folge)* (Leipzig 1903/31ff.).
MAOG	*Mitteilungen der Altorientalischen Gesellschaft* (Leipzig 1925ff.).
MDOG	*Mitteilungen der Deutschen Orient-Gesellschaft* (Berlin 1898ff.).
MIO	*Mitteilungen des Instituts für Orientforschung* (Berlin 1953ff.).
MNS 1	Å. SJÖBERG, *Der Mondgott Nanna-Suen in der sumerischen Überlieferung* 1 (Stockholm 1960).
MVA(e)G	*Mitteilungen der Vorderasiatisch (-Ägyptischen) Gesellschaft* (Berlin-Leipzig 1896/1922ff.).
MVEOL	*Mededeelingen en Verhandelingen van het Vooraziatisch-Egyptisch Gezelschap Ex Oriente Lux* (Leyden 1934ff.).
NG	A. FALKENSTEIN, *Die neusumerischen Gerichtsurkunden* 1-3 (Munich 1956 -57).
NTT	*Nederlands Theologisch Tijdschrift* (Wageningen).
Numen Spl.	periodical *Numen, Supplements* (Leyden).
ÖB	G. PETTINATO, *Die Ölwahrsagung bei den Babyloniern* 1;2 (*StSem*. 21; 22, Rome 1966).
OECT	*Oxford Editions of Cuneiform Texts (/Inscriptions)*.
OLZ	*Orientalistische Literaturzeitung* (Leipzig 1898ff.).
Op.min.	F. M. TH. DE LIAGRE BÖHL, *Opera minora* (Groningen-Djakarta 1953).
Or.(Nr.)	*Orientalia, Nova Series (Nr.*: of the Series prior) (Rome 1931/20ff.).
PAPS	*Proceedings of the American Philosophical Society* (Philadelphia).
PB	A. DEIMEL, *Pantheon babylonicum*[1] (Rome 1914).
PN	personal name.
RA	*Revue d'Assyriologie et d'Archéologie Orientale* (Paris 1886ff.).
Racc.	F. THUREAU-DANGIN, *Rituels Accadiens* (Paris 1921).
'Religions'	É. DHORME, *Les religions de Babylonie et d'Assyrie* (Paris 1949).
RGG³	*Die Religion in Geschichte und Gegenwart*³ (Tübingen 1957ff.).
RHPhR	*Revue d'Histoire et de Philosophie Religieuses* (Strassburg-Paris).
RHR	*Revue de l'histoire des religions. Annales du Musée Guimet* (Paris 1880ff.)
RlA	*Reallexikon der Assyriologie* (Berlin-Leipzig 1932ff.).
RSO	*Rivista degli Studi Orientali* (Rome).
Saec.	*Saeculum. Jahrbuch für Universalgeschichte* (Freiburg i.Br. 1950ff.).
SAHG	A. FALKENSTEIN-W. VON SODEN, *Sumerische und Akkadische Hymnen und Gebete* (Zürich 1953).
SGL	A. FALKENSTEIN-J. VAN DIJK, *Sumerische Götterlieder* 1;2 (Heidelberg 1959;60).
SKIZ	W. H. PH. RÖMER, *Sumerische 'Königshymnen' der Isin-Zeit* (Leyden 1965).
SKLy.	J. KRECHER, *Sumerische Kultlyrik* (Wiesbaden 1966).
ŠL	A. DEIMEL, *Šumerisches Lexikon* (Rome 1928ff.).
SLB	*Studia ad Tabulas Cuneiformes collectas a F. M. Th. de Liagre Böhl pertinentia* (Leyden 1952ff.).

*SM*²   S. N. KRAMER, *Sumerian Mythology*² (New York 1961).
SSA   J. J. A. VAN DIJK, *La Sagesse Suméro-Accadienne* (Leyden 1953).
StBoT   *Studien zu den Boğazköy-Texten* (Wiesbaden 1965ff.).
StMar.   *Studia Mariana* (Leyden 1950).
StOr.   *Studia Orientalia* (Helsinki).
StSem.   *Università di Roma. Centro di Studi Semitici, Studi Semitici* (Rome 1958ff.).
STT   O. R. GURNEY; J. J. FINKELSTEIN; P. HULIN, *The Sultantepe Tablets* 1;2 (London 1957-64).
Sumer   periodical *Sumer* (Baghdad).
Syr.   *Syria. Revue d'Art Oriental et d'Archéologie, publiée par l'Institut Français d'archéologie de Beyrouth* (Paris).
Tākultu   R. FRANKENA, *Tākultu...* (Leyden 1954).
TBP   F. R. KRAUS, *Texte zur babylonischen Physiognomatik* ($=AfOBeih$. 3, Berlin 1939).
TCS   *Texts from Cuneiform Sources* (ed. A. L. OPPENHEIM; Locust Valley-New York 1966ff.).
TDP   R. LABAT, *Traité Akkadien de Diagnostics et Pronostics Médicaux* (Paris-Leyden 1951).
TMHNF   *Texte und Materialien der Frau Professor Hilprecht Sammlung Jena, Neue Folge* (Leipzig-Berlin 1937ff.).
TS   S. N. KRAMER, *From the Tablets of Sumer* (Indian Hills 1956).
TuL   E. EBELING, *Tod und Leben nach den Vorstellungen der Babylonier* (Berlin-Leipzig 1931).
UET   *Ur Excavations, Texts* (London 1928ff.).
UM   *The University of Pennsylvania. The University Museum, Publications of the Babylonian Section* (Philadelphia 1911ff.).
UVB   *Vorläufige Berichte über die...Ausgrabungen in Uruk-Warka* (Berlin 1930ff.).
VR   A. MOORTGAT, *Vorderasiatische Rollsiegel*² (Berlin 1966).
VS   *Vorderasiatische Schriftdenkmäler der Königlichen Museen zu Berlin* (Leipzig 1907ff.).
VTSpl.   periodical *Vetus Testamentum, Supplements* (Leyden).
Wilb.   A. L. OPPENHEIM, *Catalogue of the Cuneiform Tablets of the Wilberforce Eames Babylonian Collection in the New York Public Library* ($=$ *AOS* 32, New Haven 1948).
WM   *Wörterbuch der Mythologie* (Stuttgart 1965ff.).
WO   *Die Welt des Orients* (Wuppertal-Göttingen 1947ff.).
WVDOG   *Wissenschaftliche Veröffentlichungen der Deutschen Orient-Gesellschaft* (Leipzig-Berlin).
WZKM   *Wiener Zeitschrift für die Kunde des Morgenlandes* (Vienna 1887ff.).
YNER   *Yale Near Eastern Researches* (New Haven-London).
YOS   *Yale Oriental Series, Babylonian Texts* (New Haven 1915ff.).
ZA   *Zeitschrift für Assyriologie und verwandte Gebiete/Vorderasiatische Archäologie* (Berlin-Leipzig 1887ff.).
ZDMG   *Zeitschrift der Deutschen Morgenländischen Gesellschaft* (Leipzig-Wiesbaden 1847ff.).

THE RELIGION OF ANCIENT SYRIA

BY

H. RINGGREN
Uppsala, Sweden

I. Introduction

The area here roughly defined as Syria was never by any means an ethnic unity. In the period with which we are dealing, i.e. from the earliest time down to the christianization of the area, it was the scene of a complicated historical development. Its religious history is not in any sense uniform. It is impossible, therefore, to describe the religion of Syria as a well defined and homogeneous phenomenon. There is rather a variety of different religions having, it is true, certain basic features in common but each exhibiting its own characteristics.

In addition, the documentation available is scanty and unevenly distributed, so that it is impossible to draw a coherent picture of the religious development. Much of the evidence consists of archaeological finds without any written interpretation. Even if it can be said with some degree of certainty that an object has had religious significance, it is difficult to tell exactly what that significance was.

Common to the various forms of religions of the Syrian area—as to all Semitic religions—is the great importance of the gods in the totality of religious belief. The presence of the god El in the religion of most Semitic peoples has been taken by some to indicate a primitive monotheism. Be that as it may, El is an important deity all over the area and, when a mythology can be traced, clearly the first and highest of the gods.

Canaanite religion is often, especially by Biblical scholars, characterized as a "nature religion" with a very strong emphasis on fertility. If the term is taken to mean a religion, the gods of which are nothing but personifications of natural phenomena, the statement is at best a half-truth. But the latter part of it is true: fertility is an extremely important element in most of the various modifications of West-Semitic religion that we know of. Following Biblical sources Canaanite religion is also very often judged as immoral and licentious, but this would be true only if the predominant interest in fertility is considered to be immoral.

II. Historical Development

We shall have to omit here the purely prehistorical period, from which there are only archaeological remains. From the great number of figurines of a naked goddess with her breasts and buttocks emphasized that have been found all over the area, we can conclude that there has been worship of a mother goddess which must have been the expression of a quest for fertility. This is almost all that can be said of prehistoric religion in this area.

When history dawns upon the area that is now Syria and Palestine, it is inhabited by tribes and peoples of the West Semitic stock, and it has so remained all through the period with which we have to deal.

In the Hammurabi period Western Semites founded a kingdom around Mari on the upper Euphrates. Documents from their court archives give us some glimpses also from their religious life, which can be described as a syncretism with Mesopotamian and West-Semitic elements. In the early fourteenth century B.C. there are two groups of written sources: the Amarna letters and the Ugaritic texts. The former are letters written by the princes of the Canaanite city-states to the Egyptian Pharaoh Akhenaton. They provide an instructive picture of the political life of Palestine in the fourteenth century with many sidelights on religious beliefs and practices. The Ugaritic texts come from the northern coastland of Syria. They are documents of various kinds, first discovered in 1929 at the village of Ras Shamra and therefore also known as the Ras Shamra texts. There are letters and business documents but above all a collection of mythological texts which provided us for the first time with authentic documents of Canaanite religion and mythology.

From the 10th century on there are, in the coastal area, several Phoenician inscriptions which throw some light also on religious beliefs and institutions. Such inscriptions are also spread over a wide area in the Mediterranean world where the Phoenicians had their trade centers and colonies. The most important colony was Carthage in North Africa. Here a special form of the Phoenician language developed, generally known as Punic. Here again, a number of inscriptions as well as archaeological remains throw some light on religious questions. There are also Roman authors who give casual evidence concerning the culture and religion of Carthage.

South of Phoenicia, in Palestine, the Canaanites developed a culture of high level, witnessed to by archeological evidence from, e.g., Megiddo, Hazor and Beth-Sean (Beisān). At the last-mentioned place the Egyptian influence is very strong. Inscriptions are almost absent, if we do not count the Moabite inscription of King Mesha' (ca 870 B.C.) and some Egyptian stelae from Beisān. But the Old Testament bears witness to Israel's spiritual struggle with the Canaanite religion, which threatened the purity of their own Yahwistic faith and at times led to various forms of syncretism. These scattered references in the Old Testament, however, are marked by a polemic tone, caused by the situation of struggle, and therefore can only be utilized with some reserve as sources for Canaanite religion.

Further east, in the region around Damascus and the upper course of the Euphrates, there developed from the 12th century a number of small states of Aramaeans, who spoke a language differing from the Phoenician, Canaanite and Hebrew languages in several respects. Inscriptions provide some evidence of their religion, which shows some specifically Aramaean peculiarities and more Assyro-Babylonian influence than those of the Western area. The syncretistic character of this religion increases with the time, and is very marked in the inscriptions of the city of Palmyra (1st cent. B.C.-3rd cent. A.D.) or in the Nabataean inscriptions from the region east of the Dead Sea around the beginning of our era. Here, as in Hatra (also Graeco-Roman period), the Arab element is very prominent.

Sources for our knowledge of West-Semitic religion are also some Greek authors who in various contexts report on the conditions of this area. PHILO of Byblus (ca 100 B.C.) gives an account of the Phoenician cosmogony and mythology, based on the report of a certain Phoenician priest by the name of Sanchuniaton. LUCIAN of Samosata wrote a book On The Syrian Goddess, in which he gave an account of the religious cult of his native city Hierapolis in Syria. Other Greek authors tell about the cult of Adonis, of the Hercules of Tyre, and so forth. Unfortunately, most of these accounts are either secondhand reports or contain adaptations in order to appeal to the Greek mind, so that they can be used only with caution. Held together with other sources of information, however, they supplement our knowledge on several points.

It is obvious that it is not possible to draw a coherent picture of the history of West-Semitic religion on the basis of such evidence. It is also obvious that the religious conditions of the area were not uniform

at any period. What can be offered here, therefore, is nothing but a
rough sketch, trying to collect the scattered evidence and bring it
together into some kind of a meaningful whole.

III. CONCEPTION OF THE DEITY

The common Semitic word for "God," *'ēl*, occurs more or less
frequently all over the area. The original meaning of the word is
under debate, but etymologically either 'powerful' (Heb. *'ēl*, 'power')
or 'first' (Ar. *'awwal*, 'first') is a possible derivation. Maybe both shades
of meaning are in some way related and do not exclude one another.

Though the word *'ēl* is predominantly used as a proper noun and
no regard is paid to the origin of the word, it is obvious that the idea
of strength and power is inseparately bound up with the West-Semitic
idea of god. This is also expressed through the way in which various
gods are symbolized by, or identified with, a bull, indicating their
strength and their male sexual potency as well. The fact that gods are
often referred to with epithets such as *'ādōn*, lord, *ba'al*, master, or
melek, king, points in the same direction.

In Ugaritic and Phoenician texts there are references to the gods as
being 'holy' (*qdš*). It is probable that the word carries approximately
the same meaning as in the Old Testament, i.e., divine, elevated and
"wholly other." Theophorous personal names refer to the deity as
"mighty", "elevated" and "righteous," but also as the one who "gives,"
"helps," "delivers," "protects", "supports", "blesses", "is gracious"
etc. This gives a picture of the general idea of god.

To what extent the gods were organized as a real pantheon is not
known. But the Ugaritic texts show that there has been a technical
term for the 'assembly of the gods', *pḫr 'ilm*, sometimes also *mpḫrt bn 'il*,
'the assembly of the sons of god' (i.e. of the divine beings) or *dr 'il*, 'the
generation of God (or El)'. A similar phrase is found in an inscription
from Byblus (10th cent. B.C.). Lists of offerings enumerate a number
of deities, which might also be taken as an indication that the idea of
a pantheon was not entirely absent.

First among the gods comes El. In Phoenician inscriptions the element *'ēl* occurs only in theophorous names and as the generic term
for 'god'. Possibly also the god of Byblus bore that name. El is also
mentioned in the Aramaic inscriptions from Zencirli. In the Ugaritic
texts El is clearly the head of the pantheon or the assembly of gods. He
is enthroned "at the source of the rivers", which may be a place from

which water is thought to fertilize the world like the four rivers of Paradise in the Old Testament, or the place where the waters of the sky and those of the earth meet. He is 'the father of the sons of god' and 'father of mankind', while it is doubtful if *'ab šnm* means 'father of the years' (*šnm* may be a name). In any case, one passage refers to him as great and wise and having grey hairs.

El is often referred to as 'the Bull El', and it is probable that a statue of a seated god with a horned headgear and beard is meant to represent El. Another of his epithets, *ltpn il dp'id*, refers to him as 'the benevolent and merciful god'. He is also called 'creator of the creatures'. There is an atmosphere of majesty and serenity about him, and he often gives the impression of a distant and inactive god of the type often referred to as *deus otiosus*. But this statement should not be exaggerated, for El is often mentioned in ritual texts as the object of cult and receiver of offerings. In the mythological texts, the decision of important matters is always deferred to El. A recently found text describes him participating in an exuberant banquet and exhibiting some all too human weakness.

PHILO of Byblus mentions a Phoenician god called Elos, who is said to be identical with the Greek Kronos. In the bilingual inscription from Karatepe there is a reference to *'l qn 'rṣ*, "El, the maker of the earth". The same epithet is found in a late Punic inscription and possibly in the Hittite translation of a Canaanite myth. Interestingly enough a similar epithet is found in Gen. 14:19, 22 where Melchizedek refers to El 'Elyon as "the maker (*qōneh*) of heaven and earth."

Melchizedek was "priest of El 'Elyon ('God Most High')" and king of Salem, i.e., Jerusalem, and it is obvious that he represents Canaanite religion. 'Elyon is known as a divine name also from other sources. PHILO lists "Elioun, who was called the most high" among the gods of Phoenicia, and an Aramaic inscription from ca. 750 B.C. refers to a treaty concluded "before El and 'Elyān and before heaven and earth and the deep and the sources and before day and night" as witnesses. This seems to imply that El and 'Elyon were two different gods, while the Old Testament combines the two names as referring to one god. The evidence is inconclusive. The claims that El 'Elyon was a solar god cannot be definitely proved; that he was a celestial god of some kind is certain.

The Old Testament, esp. the patriarchal narratives, mentions other gods with names containing the element El, such as *El Shaddai*, (usually translated "God Almighty", possibly 'the god of the mountain'),

El ʿōlām, the god of eternity (or, time?), *El-Beth-el*, 'the god of Bethel'. It is probable that these were originally Canaanite divine epithets. In the case of the latter deity there is also extra-biblical evidence, in so far as PHILO mentions Baitylos (i.e. Bethel) as the brother of El and Bethel occurs in a cuneiform document from ca. 675 B.C. and a god Bethel was worshipped as a separate deity by the Jewish colony at Elephantine in the 5th cent. B.C. It is probable that these represent local variations of the god El.

The most important and most active god of the Ugaritic texts is Baʿal. The name means 'master' or 'owner' and it is often used in this general sense. In the Old Testament it has always the definite article when it refers to the god and it is sometimes used in the plural, the *beʿālim*. It also occurs as the first part of the names of several local deities, the second part being most often a place-name, e.g. Baʿal-Hazor, Baʿal-Peor, Baʿal-Sidon, Baʿal-Lebanon, Baʿal-Harran (cf also the feminine Baʿalat-Gebal, 'the Lady of Byblus'), a few times another word e.g. Baʿal-Berit,' the Lord of the Covenant' (Judges 9:4) or Baʿal-Marqod, 'the Lord of Dancing'. A theory is that every place and every natural phenomenon had its *baʿal* or master and that out of these ideas the belief in one Master or Lord developed, Baʿal with a capital B. The source material at our disposal is not sufficient to allow an exact definition of the relation between the god Baʿal mentioned in the Old Testament on one hand and in the Ugaritic texts on the other, but it is clear from these texts and from the Amarna letters that Baʿal was a proper noun as early as the 15th century. The *beʿālim* may have been local forms of this god in his capacity of the patron of a city etc.

In the Ugaritic myths Baʿal is often given the epithet *Alʾiyan* which probably means 'strong' or 'mighty'. He is also called *ẓbl*, probably 'the prince', once in the more eleborate form 'the prince, lord of the earth'. The Hebrew Baʿal-Zebub (2 Ki. 1:2) may be a distortion of this name, while the N. T. Beelzebul preserves the correct form. Another epithet is *rkb ʿrpt*, 'the Rider of the clouds', which characterizes Baʿal as the god of storm and rain (a similar epithet is used of Yahweh in Ps. 68:15, cf. Ps 18:11). Baʿal's connection with rain and fertility is also shown in a passage saying that when his temple is completed "he will give abundance of rain, abundance of moisture and snow, he will utter his voice in the clouds, his flashings and lightnings on the earth." This quotation associates Baʿal with thunder and lightning, which is confirmed by other passages some of which also call him

Hadd, i.e. Hadad. A poetic description of Baʿal-Hadd shows him seated on his throne on the mountain of Ṣapān, also called 'the mountain of victory', surrounded by lightnings and with dew on his forehead and having two horns. Reliefs and statues reflect the same idea. Baʿal is depicted with a pointed beard, a helmet with horns, in one hand a club, in the other a lance, obviously symbolizing lightning. The horns seem to indicate that Baʿal was regarded as a bull, but this is never expressly stated in the texts, though in one myth he is told to have had sexual intercourse with a heifer and in another the birth of a bull-calf is announced to him. It may be that the horns are primarily a symbol of divine strength.

The nature of the identification of Hadad and Baʿal is not quite clear. Hadad is the Aramaic name of the stormgod, known also in Accadian texts as Adad. It may be that Baʿal is simply a generic term used by the Canaanites to denote the god that was otherwise called Hadad, much as Marduk was called Bel ("lord") in Babylon. Hadad is mentioned several times in Aramaic inscriptions. He is the national god who gives the king his throne and his authority. He answers prayers and grants all good things but he can also be angry and punish those who break agreements.

As the god of thunderstorm Hadad has the epithet Rammān, 'the thunderer', known in the Bible in the form Rimmon (2 Ki. 5:18) and Hadad-Rimmon (Zech. 12:11). The latter passage seams to indicate some celebration of the death of the god, which is otherwise not attested for Hadad but may reflect ideas like those connected with the Ugaritic Baʿal. LUCIAN identifies Hadad with Zeus, which again emphasizes the thunder-god aspect. He says that he is "the first and greatest god of the Syrians" and identifies him with the sun, obviously a result of the Hellenistic tendency toward solar monotheism. In Graeco-Roman times Hadad was worshipped as a solar deity e.g. in Heliopolis (Baalbek), while the identification with Zeus and Jupiter indicates the storm-god and skygod aspect.

To return to the Alʾiyan Baʿal of Ugarit, he is often referred to as the great fighter. The myths tell of his defeat of Yam, the Sea, which reminds us of Marduk's victory over Tiamat and is probably reflected in the Old Testament ideas of a struggle between Yahweh and the deep (*tehōm*). Another time the enemy of Baʿal is referred to as the dragon or Lotan; exactly the same terms occur in the Old Testament in passages representing the mythological tradition about creation. Strangely enough, this struggle with Yam is not expressly connected with creation in the Ras Shamra texts. Rather the result of Ba'al's victory seems to be that he assumes kingship.

Ba'al's archenemy, however, is Mot, or Death. According to the myth he manages to throw Baal down into the netherworld with the result that vegetation withers and dies. However, through the intervention of his sister 'Anat, Ba'al is finally restored to life so that "the heavens rain fat and the wadis run with honey". Obviously, Mot symbolizes the hot and dry season that brings death to vegetation, and the myth as a whole reflects the alternation of the seasons.

A special problem is connected with Ba'al-shamēm (Aram. Be'elshemīn) "the Lord of the Sky". Is he a special sky-god or is he only an aspect of the storm-god Ba'al with special relationship to celestial phenomena? PHILO of Byblus says that the first living beings on earth in times of drought raised their hands to the sun, whom they regarded as the only god, the lord of the sky, calling him Beelsamem, who is the same as the Zeus of the Greeks. It would seem that this statement reflects later Hellenistic syncretism, in which Zeus and the sun were identified and regarded as the highest deity.

Ba'alshamem is mentioned in Phoenician inscriptions, in Assarhaddon's treaty with the king of Tyre, at Carthage and by PLAUTUS, at Karatepe and in several Aramaic inscriptions, but none of these add substantially to his characterization. In Karatepe he seems to be identified with the Hittite stormgod. In the Zakir stela he is mentioned together with 'el-wer (probably = Hadad) and in Aramaic letters he occurs together with another skygod whose name is unfortunately missing. There is ample evidence for the worship of Be'elshemīn in the Hellenistic period, from Hauran, Palmyra, and Dura-Europos, and as late as the 5th century Isaak of Antioch reports that he was worshipped at Edessa. In Palmyra he is especially known as the gracious and benevolent god. A certain Atarsamain, i.e. 'Athtar of the sky, is known from Assyrian sources, but it cannot be made out whether the analogy with Be'elshemīn goes beyond the second element of the name.

At Carthage a god called Ba'al Ḥammōn ("the lord of the incense altar"?) was worshipped. He occurs in a great number of votive inscriptions, first alone, but later together with the goddess Tinnit and always mentioned *after* her. There are a few instances of the god in Phoenicia and at Palmyra. In Latin inscriptions he is called *frugifer* and *deus frugum*, which indicates his connection with the fruits and probably with vegetation in general. He was later indentified with the Egyptian god Amon of Siva, with the Greek Kronos and the Roman Saturnus, sometimes also with Jupiter. Some scholars have identified him with El, whose name does not occur in Africa, but there is no definite proof for this identification.

Aliyan Ba'al is often called the son of Dagan in the Ugaritic texts. But Dagan (or Dagon) himself does not occur at all in mythology. His name, too, is found rather infrequently, except for a few theophorous names, some lists of offerings, and two votive inscriptions. We know that he had a temple in the vicinity of Ba'al's temple in Ugarit, and there is a Beth-Dagon ("Dagon's house") on the coastal plain of Southern Palestine. In 1 Sam. 5 : 1-2 there is a reference to the worship of Dagon in the Philistine city of Ashdod. These instances give little or no information about the functions of the god. Etymology seems to favour some connection with the grain (Heb. *dāgān*), while association with Arabic *dağn*, 'rain', or Heb. *dāg*, 'fish' is less probable. The fact that a god with a fish-tail is depicted on coins from Aradus can probably not be used to support the latter interpretation.

Adonis is the Greek name of a god who according to Greek writers was worshipped in Syria and Phoenicia and was even adopted by the Greeks, at least from the 7th cent. B.C. The name is identical with Phoenician (and Hebrew) *'ādōn* 'Lord', but this word is not attested in the inscriptions as a proper noun but only as a divine epithet. It is probable, therefore, that Adonis is the Greek term for some local form of Ba'al.

According to the Greek sources the young Adonis was loved by Aphrodite and Persephone, the goddess of the netherworld. When the latter would not let him go, Aphrodite descended to the netherworld to set him free. Then Zeus decreed that Adonis was to spend half of the year with Aphrodite in this world and the other half with Persephone. Finally Adonis is said to have been killed by a boar, bitterly mourned by Aphrodite. It is easy to recognize elements from the Tammuz and Ba'al mythology in this narrative, and it must be a coincidence that no inscriptions give evidence for the god Adonis.

As the most important centers of Adonis worship are mentioned Byblus on the Syrian coast and Paphos in Cyprus. According to LUCIAN the former place had a temple of Aphrodite (i.e. Astarte) in which secret rites were performed in the honour of Adonis. These included wailing over Adonis "as one who has died", sacrifices and finally the god's return to life. The river which flows into the Mediterranean at Byblus bore the name of Adonis and near its source there was a sanctuary of Astarte at Aphaca. There was a picture of Adonis being killed by a bear (!) and of the goddess bemourning his death. In Is. 17:10f. there is an allusion to the so-called Adonis gardens, mentioned already by Plato, i.e. bowls with earth in which plants were forced to grow up and then withered as quickly as they had grown—a symbol of the god's flourishing and death.

Eshmun probably also belongs to the category of fertility gods. He is often mentioned in Phoenician inscriptions, especially at Sidon, and he also gained importance in Carthage. A trilingual inscription from Sardinia identifies him with Aesculapius, which shows that he was regarded as a healing god. This, however, may be a secondary feature. It has even been suggested that Eshmun might have been identical with Adonis. In any case he is sometimes given the epithet 'ādōn. DAMASCIUS reports that in his youth the god was once pursued by Astronoë (= Astarte?) and, fleeing from her, castrated himself. He died but was resuscitated by the goddess and was called Eshmun because of the warmth or fire ('esh) of the goddess that restored him to life. The etymology is false, but the rest of the story may reflect, in distorted form, real mythology.

Resheph (Heb.; other forms of the name are Rashap, Rashpān or Rasphōn) is known from the Mari and Ras Shamra texts to Punic inscriptions and Egyptian monuments. The word means either 'fire' or 'pestilence', and the god is obviously connected with fire, lightning, and plague (cf. Deut. 32:24, Hab. 3:5). In the Keret epic we are told that he, i.e. the plague, took away the sons of Keret. When one of the Amarna letters says that Nergal has killed the people of the country, even the son of the writer, it is probably Resheph that is meant. The fact that he is called b'l ḥṣ 'the lord of the arrow' calls to mind Apollo's arrows that were believed to cause illness; as a matter of fact Resheph is sometimes identified with that god. On the other hand he is also invoked for healing. Texts from Ras Shamra associate Resheph with the sun-goddess, once as the gatekeeper of the setting sun (i.e. of the netherworld?), another time as one of eleven gods who are invoked as her assistants in an incantation.

Pictures of Resheph are known only from Egypt. They show him as a fighter with shield, lance and battle-axe and a crown with an emblem in the shape of the head of a gazelle. A similar picture from Beisān has the inscription "Mekal, the god of Beisān". On the other hand, a god Mekal is mentioned in an inscription from Cyprus together with Resheph. The two gods, therefore, seem not to be identical but very similar in nature.

Melqart (orig. Melk-qart, 'the king of the city') was the city-god of Tyre, but was worshipped also in Carthage. The earliest reference to him is found in Assarhaddon's treaty with the king of Tyre. Scholars have regarded him as a sungod, but it would seem that his solar features are relatively late. As is natural for the god of a seafaring city, he is also associated with the sea and with navigation. Frazer included Melqart among the dying and rising gods, but his evidence is not always convincing. It is known that Melqart was identified with Hercules, and the myth of his being burned at the stake on Mount Oeta has also been connected with Tyre. There is evidence for a festival called the "rising (*égersis*) of Hercules" celebrated in the month of January. A Greek writer reports that the Phoenicians sacrificed quails to Hercules because he had been killed by Typhon but restored to life by Iolaos who held a quail under his nose so that the smell of the bird revived the god. It is obviously not easy to reconstruct, on the basis of these scattered facts, a myth of Melqart's death through fire, acted out in the cult through the burning of a doll—the evidence for this act is obscure and equivocal—and his final resurrection. Elements from Greek mythology have been combined with data from Phoenician religion in such a way that it is impossible to draw any definite conclusions from the material.—There are coins with an eagle or a lion as symbols of Melqart. His temple is said to have had no image of the god, but a fire was constantly burning on his altar.

Ḥōrōn is a Canaanite deity known from personal names and place-names from ca. 1900 down to ca. 600 B.C. The Book of Joshua mentions two places called Beth-Horon (Ḥōrōn's house, or temple), a prince by the name of Ḥaurān-abum, 'Ḥōrōn is father' is cursed in an Egyptian text from the 12th cent. B.C. Egyptian texts mention Ḥōrōn together with Reshef and the goddess 'Anat. He is invoked in a curse by Keret in a Ugaritic text and in a Phoenician incantation from Arslantash (7th cent. B.C.). He is also known as the patron of the city of Jabne, and an ostracon found just north of Tel Aviv mentions "gold for Ḥōrōn's temple". He is supposed to have been a chthonic deity, but there is no certain evidence for this.

Kemosh (or perhaps rather Kamosh) was the national god of the Moabites. He is mentioned a few times in the Old Testament and in King Mesha's inscriptions on the so-called Moabite stone, mostly, and for natural reasons, in connection with war. A couple of theophorous names add little to our knowledge; a list of gods equates him with Nergal. Moabite coins show a warlike figure between two torches—he *may* be Kemosh.

Milkom of the Ammonites is mentioned some times in the Old
Testament. His name is an extension of *milk*, 'king'. Additional details are not known.

An obscure Ugaritic text relates the birth of two gods, Shaḥar and
Shalim, by "the two consorts of El". The text gives no information
concerning their functions, so that only guesses can be made on the
basis of etymology, Shaḥar means 'dawn' and occurs also in the Old
Testament in passages with a mythological ring, e.g. Is. 14:12 where
a certain Helal (moon) Son of Shaḥar is mentioned. Consequently,
there is reason to assume that Shaḥar is the god of the dawn. Shalim
might then be supposed to have been the god of the evening, or dusk,
which is perhaps supported by the fact that sunset in Accadian is
shalām shamshi. The name seems to form the latter part of the name
Jerusalem which probably means "the foundation, or fortress, of
Shalim". A god Shulmān is known from Assyrian sources.

Turning now to the female deities, there are above all three variations of the great goddess, the mother and love goddess, with only
few individual differences, namely Athirat, 'Athtart and 'Anat. All
three of them occur in the Ugaritic texts but are also known in other
contexts.

It is impossible to define exactly the relationship between these
three goddesses and the anonymous mother goddess, represented by
the figurines found in this area since time immemorial. The goddess
is obviously pre-Semitic, but the three Semitic goddesses might represent variations of the same idea, namely that of the female power of
procreation as something divine and essential for the existence of life
and society.

Athirat (Asherah) is El's consort and the highest goddess in the
Ugaritic texts; in lists of offerings the two are usually mentioned
together. She is sometimes simply called *'ilt*, 'the goddess', suggesting
her perhaps as the female counterpart of El. Her commonest epithet
is *rbt 'atrt ym*, "Lady Asherah of the Sea", other interpretations as, e.g.,
"she who treads on the Sea" being uncertain. The exact nature of her
relationship with the sea is not revealed in the texts. She is also called
qnyt 'ilm, "she who creates, or bears, the gods", and "the sons of
Athirat" are the gods. In the Keret epic she and 'Anat are said to be
the two divine wet-nurses suckling the royal child.

Outside of Ugarit Asherah is known from the Amorites of the first
dynasty of Babylon, among whom she is the consort of the national
god Amurru, called "the daughter-in-law of the king of the heavens"

and "the mistress of luxuriance and voluptiousness". An Amorite king is called Abdi-Ashirta, 'the servant of Athirat', and another compound with Ashirta is found in a cuneiform letter from Taʿannek in Palestine. In the Old Testament mention is often made of the ashera or asheras, usually referring to the wooden poles that were regarded as the symbols of the goddess. At a few places, however, it seems that the goddess herself is meant, e.g. in 1 Ki. 18:19 where her prophets are mentioned, and 1 Ki. 21:6, 23:6 about her image in the temple of Jerusalem.

ʿAthtart, or Astarte as she is called in Greek texts (the Old Testament has the form Ashtoreth), is mentioned in Ugarit only in some stereotyped formulae and in cultic-liturgical texts, while the Greek authors refer to her very frequently, often identifying her with Aphrodite. She is both benevolent and terrible, the goddess of love and fertility and the goddess of war.

In the Keret epic we learn that ʿAthtart and ʿAnat are beautiful. Her epithet *šm bʿl*, 'the name of Baʿal' suggests some connection with Baʿal, the god of fertility. As goddess of war she appears in 1 Sam. 31:10, according to which the spoil is dedicated to her in her temple, and frequently in the Egyptian sources. An Egyptian papyrus from the 19th dynasty tells the story of her marriage with the tyrannical god of the sea, an otherwise unknown motif.

In the Old Testament Ashtoreth is mentioned a few times as the goddess of the Sidonians (1 Ki. 11:5, 33, 2 Ki. 23:13), but it is probable that she is meant also by the epithet 'Queen of Heaven' in Jer. 7:18, 44:17 ff., now found also in an Aramaic letter from Hermopolis.

According to PHILO of Byblus, Astarte once put on bull's horns as a symbol of authority. This may have some connection with the place-name Ashteroth-qarnayim (Gen. 14:5), "the Astarte of the two horns". A goddess from Beisān is depicted with horns, but her identification with Astarte is not entirely certain. On another occasion she wears a crown with plum-like ornaments, obviously a fertility symbol. The dove was her sacred bird; the serpent seems also to be an ancient symbol of the goddess. Serpents occur together with doves on cult objects.

Greek sources refer to the main goddess of the Aramaeans as Atargatis, which corresponds to Aramaic ʿAttar-ʿatteh. The first part is the regular Aramaic counterpart of ʿAthtar(t), while the second part is either a variant form of ʿAnat or the special name of a local deity. LUCIAN identifies her with Hera, "though she has something of the attributes of Athena, Aphrodite, Selene, Rhea, Artemis, Nemesis, and the *moiraï*". One could just as well say that she is the sum and substance of female divine power.

No myths are told about Atargatis, but Lucian describes her temple at Hierapolis in great detail. He says that she is depicted there seated on a throne carried by lions, holding in one hand a scepter, in the other a distaff, and crowned with rays and a turret. Pictures on coins confirm this description; other coins show her sitting on a lion. Fish were kept sacred for her sake.

Classical authors also mention a goddess Derketo, who seems to be a variant form of Atargatis. She was depicted with a fish-tail and at her temple there was a lake with sacred fish. In part, this reminds us of Athirat with her association with the sea, but Atargatis, too, had sacred fish. Obviously the fish in some way symbolized life and fertility.

Diodorus Siculus reports that Derketo with the young and beautiful Simios bore a daughter, Semiramis. Ashamed of her sinful love she then drowned the young man who is also called Ichthys ('fish') and expelled the girl into the desert, where she was fed by doves. Finally the goddess threw herself into the sea near Ashkelon. Obviously one object of this myth is to explain the sacred animals of the goddess. Another is to express certain ideas concerning life and fertility. But the rest is obscure. We are told that Semiramis is represented by a symbol or sign (*sēmeion*) which was standing between the statues of Hadad and Atargatis and twice a year was carried in a procession to a lake near by. An inscription from Delos, mentions the Hierapolitan triad Hadad, Atargatis and Asclepius, the latter being obviously the young god. Is there any connection between Simios-Semiramis and Eshmun, who is also identified with Asclepius? There is at least a certain similarity in sound.

'Anat is the most active of the goddesses in the Ugaritic texts. She also played an important part among the Hyksos in Egypt. On a stela from Beisān she is called "the queen of heaven, the lady of the gods". At other places she is rather infrequently attested. In a bilingual inscription from Cyprus she is identified with Athena, a goddess called 'Anath-Bethel is known from Tyre and from the Jewish colony at Elephantine. At the latter place there is also one 'Anath-Yahu, i.e. Anath the consort(?) of Yahweh. Finally her name occurs in Shamgar ben 'Anath, Jud. 5:6, and in placenames such as Beth-Anath (Josh. 9:32, Jud. 1:33) and Anathoth (the birthplace of Jeremiah).

At Ugarit ʿAnat bears the epithet *btlt*, the virgin, emphasizing her youth and female procreativeness. The epithet *rḥm*, seems to carry a similar meaning ("girl"). She is often referred to as Baʿal's sister, which at the same time, as in the Song of Songs, may mean beloved and bride. At times she is also called "the *ybmt* of the nations", the transliterated word having obviously something to do with marriage ("sister-in-law", "maitresse", "widow"?). Some rather fragmentary texts show her in sexual functions. In one text she "sings her love for Baʿal", but unfortunately the words of her song are not given.

In the epics, however, her warlike functions are by far predominant. In the Aqhat text she desires the bow of Aqhat. In the Baʿal cycle she bewails and buries her dead brother but then she attacks Mot and kills him. Another scene shows her fighting some enemies and wading in blood. She is depicted with a helmet, a battle-axe, and a spear. In Egypt she sometimes adopts the symbols of Hathor.

At Carthage the great goddess is called Tinnit (formerly read Tanit). She is foremost of rank and is usually mentioned first of all deities, even before Baʿal Ḥammōn. It would seem that Tinnit is the specific Carthaginian form of Astarte, but strangely enough there are no theophorous names containing the element Tinnit, while there are a few with Astarte. The name seems to have originated in Carthage, but there is no satisfactory explanation of it.

Tinnit is regularly called *pn Bʿl*, "the face of Baʿal", an epithet of obscure meaning, possibly referring to her image standing ʿbefore the face of Baʿal' or to the goddess as the ʿmanifestation' of Baʿal.

To judge from identifications with Greek and Roman deities, Tinnit seems to have been worshipped as the queen of heaven. There are indications that she was regarded as virgin, but she is also called ʿmother' and *nutrix*. Her symbols are those of a fertility goddess: pomegranate, ear, dove, but there are also a protecting hand and a geometrical symbol of obscure meaning: a triangle with a horizontal arm on its top crowned by a crescent.

Specific astral deities are not too common. The Ugaritic texts know a sun-goddess, Shapsh, "the lamp of the gods", but she holds no prominent place and is hardly mentioned in the lists of offerings. On the coastal plain of Palestine there is a city called Beth-Shemesh, "the temple of the sun", and the name Shimshon seems to contain traces of sun-worship. The Old Testament rejects the worship of astral deities, and refers once to horses dedicated to the sun (2 Ki. 23:11). Sun and moon symbols occur in the Canaanite temple of Hazor. A moon-god Yariḫ is mentioned in a Ugaritic text dealing with his wedding with Nikkal (Sumerian Nin-gal). Placenames indicating moon-worship are Beth-Yeraḥ and Jericho (*yerīḫō*).

IV. WORSHIP

1. *Cult, sacrifices*

The public worship of the gods was carried out either out of doors on hills and in groves or in temples.

The cult places are usually referred to by the term *bāmāh*, rendered in the English of the Bible as 'high place'. On these hills, natural or artificial, there was an altar, on which sacrifices were performed, a *maṣṣēbāh*, or stone pillar, symbolizing the male deity, and an *'ašērāh*, a wooden pole representing the goddess. Stone pillars have been found in excavations, but no wooden poles have remained. When temples were built, an artificial *bāmāh* was sometimes erected outside the building.

In Gen. 28 Jacob is told to have erected a *maṣṣēbāh* at Bethel, saying "This stone shall be God's house (*bēt-'ēl*)". PHILO of Byblus refers to stone pillars called *baitylos* or *baitylion* which are *lithoi empsychoi*, i.e. stones with a soul in them, or living stones. This shows that the pillars were regarded as the abodes of deities, but it is not clear whether the Greek word is derived from *bēt-'ēl*, or both reflect some more ancient word of unknown meaning. It is clear, however, that the word *maṣṣēbāh* is related to Arabic *nuṣb*, which denotes stones erected at the sacred place (*ḥaram*) from time to time smeared with sacrificial blood. As a matter of fact Jacob is said to have poured oil on the pillar at Bethel. Thus the data vacillate between the idea of an altar and a veritable symbol or abode of the deity itself.

Temples are known through archaeological discoveries and through pictures on coins. There is also a detailed description of Atargatis' temple at Hierapolis by LUCIAN. The temple was surrounded by an enclosed court with an altar and a pillar. In the temple there was an inner room containing the image of the deity and one or more other rooms. Some of the Canaanite and Syrian temples had a ground-plan reminiscent of Solomon's temple. In many cases there were two pillars standing at the gate of the temple, just as Yachin and Boaz in the temple of Solomon. The symbolism of these pillars is unknown. The ornaments of the Solomonic specimens seem to indicate some connection with fertility, while their names, meaning something like 'he will establish' and 'in power' may have some association with the royal dynasty.

The significance of the temple emerges from the Baʿal epic of Ras Shamra. It suggests that Baʿal needs a "house", i.e. a temple, in order to exercise full authority. The fact that the temple is usually called *bait* or *bēt*, 'house', proves that it was regarded as the residence of the deity. An Aramaic inscription reports that a king built a temple and "made the gods dwell in it".

On the high places and in the temples sacrifices were performed regularly. The Ugaritic texts describe sacrifices on special occasions. There are also several lists of offerings, enumerating sacrifices to various gods and goddesses. Punic "sacrificial tariffs" from Carthage and Marseille define the share of the priests in various offerings.

The Ugaritic texts seem to indicate that sacrifices were regarded as food for the gods. The sacrificial terminology shows interesting affinities with Old Testament vocabulary. In the Ugaritic texts there are, in addition to the general term *dbḥ* corresponding to Hebrew *zebaḥ*, (animal) sacrifice, several specific terms as e.g. *shlm*, *kll* and *shrp*, of which the first two correspond—linguistically at least—to Hebrew *shelāmîm*, "peace-offering" and *kālîl*, "whole offering", and the last must correspond to the Old Testament burnt offering. "To sacrifice" is *shqrb* or *shʿly*, literally 'to bring near' and 'to make to ascend', both of which have counterparts in the Old Testament.

The Punic texts refer to three main categories of sacrifices: *kalil*, *ṣewaʿat* and *shelem kalil*. Two of these terms have linguistic counterparts in Hebrew, but it seems that their meaning does not coincide with the Hebrew terms. *Kalil* should be a 'whole offering', *ṣewaʿat* seems to be a kind of propitiatory offering, while *shelem kalil* is possibly a 'concluding' or 'substitute offering'. The Punic texts also mention *ʿolat* corresponding to the Hebrew word for 'burnt offering', and *minḥat* which, as in Hebrew, obviously denotes a vegetable offering.

These data go to show that there is linguistic correspondence between the sacrificial terminology of the ancient Hebrews and that of the other Western Semites, while the meanings of the words do not coincide. The explanation is probably that there is a common stock of words that have been applied differently in different areas.

As we have seen there were both animal and vegetable offerings. Human sacrifice has been practiced at least in some areas. The Old Testament tells repeatedly of apostate Israelites who sacrificed their children by "letting them pass through fire to, or as, *molek*". The word *molek* was commonly taken as the name of a god, Moloch, the name being a distortion of the divine epithet *melek*, 'king'. However, it has been shown that in Punic, *molk* is a sacrificial term meaning 'offering' in general, which would indicate that the Old Testament statements, at least partly, are wrong or wrongly interpreted. Child sacrifices at Carthage are described by DIODORUS SICULUS, who says that the children were thrown on the arms of the statue of the god so that they fell into a fire burning beneath or behind the image. At least two inscriptions refer to such sacrifices, while other indications suggest that the child could be replaced by an animal. According to 2 Ki. 3:27 King Mesha' of Moab sacrificed his son in a critical situation. The Ugaritic texts, on the other hand, contain no allusions to child sacrifices.

It is obvious, that there have been special religious festivals at certain, occasions but there is no evidence of their dates or the ceremonies performed. Certain conclusions can be drawn from the mythological texts and from the reports of Greek authors.

There can be little doubt that the myth of Ba'al's death and resurrection has formed part of a cultic celebration at a seasonal festival. For everything points to a close connection between the myth and the withering and renewal of vegetation, and in addition, classical authors witness to rites of mourning at the death of Adonis, who can hardly be but a special form of Ba'al. Several details in the myth are most easily explained as reflexions of ritual actions. This is especially clear in the passage describing Anat's struggle with Mot:

> She seizes Mot, the son of El;
> with a sword she cleaves him;
> with a shovel she winnows him;
> with fire she burns him;
> with a hand-mill she grinds him;
> in the field she sows him;
> his remains the birds eat.

This makes sense if it refers to a ceremony performed with a sheaf, but hardly as the description of a struggle with a personal being. Similar harvest rites are known from other religions. There is also a description of El's mourning for Ba'al, which may also reflect real rites of wailing for the dead god.

Other parts of the myth are not as easily interpreted in terms of cultic performances. It is quite possible that certain passages describing Ba'al fighting with Prince Sea or with Mot were represented in cultic sham-fights. When a god called 'Athtar 'Ariz is made king during the absence of Ba'al, it is possible that this reflects the setting up of a substitute king during part of the festival; a similar custom is known from Babylon, but there is no definite proof that it did occur at Ugarit.

Myths referring to sexual intercourse between deities and the birth of divine children may be taken as texts belonging to the celebration of a sacred marriage. This is true of "The birth of the gracious and good gods" (Shaḥar and Shalim), in which there seem to be stage directions for the performance of a dramatic ritual, probably connected with viticulture. It may also apply to a part of the myth of Ba'al in which the birth of a calf is announced to Baal as "good tidings" (bšr).

A recently found fragment seems to allude to 'Anat eating "the flesh of her brother" (Ba'al?). The meaning of this statement is obscure, but it seems rather improbable that it reflects a rite comparable to the *sparagmos* of the Dionysus cult.

According to another text El invites the gods to a banquet with much eating and drinking and we are told that El himself becomes intoxicated. One term used for this gathering is *mrzḥ*, a word known also from other parts of the area and even in the Old Testament. It denotes a kind of cultic society or guild which came together for certain religious celebrations. The text probably provides the mythical motivation for the banquets of such guilds. A Phoenician inscription tells of a man who was "crowned" on the fourth day of such a feast, and a Punic inscription reports that the members of such a guild have presented gifts to a temple. The guilds of Palmyra are particularly well known and their banquets were regarded as meals together with the deity. Similar sacral meals are known from the Nabataeans at Petra.

Lucian gives some glimpses of the cult at Hierapolis in his book on the Syrian goddess. He says that twice a year water was fetched from "the sea" (Euphrates or a lake) and carried into the temple. He explains that the temple had been built on the crevice into which the waters of the flood disappeared and that the water was poured out into this crevice. It seems more likely, however, that the rite aimed at producing rain and should be compared with the water libation in the Jewish Feast of Tabernacles. There may be an allusion to a similar rite in one of the Ras Shamra texts.

LUCIAN also reports that the statues of Hadad and Atargatis were annually carried down to "the sea", in order to "see the sacred fish", though it is very probable that the statues were also washed and purified for the sacred marriage. He also asserts that the principal sacrificial festival of the year was called "the Pyre" or "the Lamp"; on that occasion sacrifices were hung on trees set up in the temple court and then put on fire.

There are a few allusions to rites of divination. The Ugaritic texts refer to revelations through dreams, and according to the Aqhat text Dan'el spends a night in the temple in order to receive a dream oracle. Finds of clay models of livers and lungs prove the existence of extispicy.

Several incantations give evidence of magical practices. A spell against serpents was recently discovered at Ras Shamra; it is rich in mythological allusions mentioning esp. a certain goddess Pahlat and the sun goddess Shapsh and her eleven helpers. A Phoenician incantation is found on an amulet from Arslan Tash (9th cent. B.C.); it was thought to ward off the activity of a female demon.

Magical practices are alluded to in the Aramaic treaty from Sefire, where the princes who break the agreement are threatened with fire "just as this wax is burnt in fire".

At Ugarit the priests were called *khnm*, i.e. exactly the same term as in Hebrew *kōhēn*. On one occassion there is reference to a high priest who is also chief of the *nqdm*, a term which is used also of King Mesha' of Moab (2 Ki. 3:4) and of Amos, the prophet. The corresponding Accadian word is used of the shepherds of the temple herds. The Ugaritic term may have some similar significance. Priestesses (*khnt*) are also mentioned. Aramaic inscriptions use *kmr* (*komer*, *kumrā*) as the title of the priests.

Other cultic functionaries are the *qdshm*, or holy ones, who to judge from the Old Testament took part in the sacred prostitution to promote fertility. The female counterpart is called in the Old Testament *qedēshōt*, at Ugarit they seem to have been called *'inšht*, "women". The Israelite prophets often denounce these practices as detestable (e.g. Amos 2:7, Hos. 4:14, Jer. 2:20).

Oracle priests or prophets are mentioned from time to time. Such are the *muḫḫū* of the Mari texts, who received messages from the gods in a state of ecstasy and proclaimed them to their clients, even to the rulers. The same texts mention *āpilu* or 'answering' priests. The Aramaic Zakir inscription refers to 'seers' (*ḥzyn*) and 'prophets' (*'ddn*) who proclaimed the message of Beelshemin. There is also the account of the Egyptian Wen Amon who visited Phoenicia in the 12th cent. B.C. and saw the appearance of an ecstatic prophet.

There is reason to believe that the king of the various city-states has played a considerable religious role, but the evidence available is rather scanty. The Amarna letters offer some evidence of sacral kingship, the king being regarded as a divine being, the giver of light and life. But the reference is to the Egyptian Pharaoh and the ideas are obviously influenced by Egyptian ideology. We learn little of the princes of the Canaanite city-states.

From later inscriptions we gather that the king was thought to receive his office and authority from the gods. There is also reference to his being responsible for the building and support of temples. Inscriptions from Byblus show that the king was expected to be "righteous", and that the fortune of the king and the country is dependent on his righteousness.

Our richest source of information however is the Ras Shamra material. But the utilization of these texts is controversial. Whether or not the king has played the part of Ba'al in the sacred drama reflected in the Ba'al myth is open to discussion. The character of the Keret and Aqhat epics (see below) is not entirely clear: are they mythological or (semi-)historical? However some conclusions can be drawn from these texts whatever answer is given to this question. It is obvious that King Keret is regarded as the son of El and that his son is nursed by the goddesses Athirat and 'Anat. (An ivory relief from the royal bedstead in the palace of Ugarit shows such a scene.) It is also obvious that Keret's illness causes the whole community to suffer: the rain does not fall, the crops do not grow and the supply of grain, oil, and wine runs out in the country.

The Keret epic also shows that the king was expected to care for the poor, the widows and the orphans—a royal duty known all over the ancient Near East. The Dan'el of the Aqhat text is a righteous judge according to the same general pattern. The death of his son causes drought and famine in the country. This seems to imply that the king is in some way responsible for rain and fertility, but just what his role in the fertility cult was is not expressly stated in any text.

A fragmentary tablet suggests that the king officiates at certain ceremonies of atonement in the month of Tishri. Another text seems to imply that a defeat was understood as the punishment of the gods and had to be met by sacrificial ceremonies for the expiation of the people's sin. It is probable that the king has acted on behalf of the people on such occasions.

2. *Ethics*

Little is known about the ethical ideals of the Western Semites. The existence of sexual elements in the fertility cult should obviously not be taken as lack of morals, as is sometimes done by Biblical scholars. A strong sense of social justice is implied in the royal ideology with its emphasis of the rights of the poor and weak. Filial piety is emphasized as a duty in the Keret epic.

Several inscriptions refer to the happy results of a righteous conduct: long life, good reputation, success, while sin is punished with misfortune. Obviously there was belief in some kind of divine retribution. Exactly what the term "righteousness" (*ṣdq*) implies is not clear. The terms for 'sin' in Ugaritic are *pshʿ* and *ḥtʾ*, "rebellion" and "missing the mark", exactly as in Hebrew; the latter word is attested also in Aramaic. In one case *pshʿ* is parellelled by *gʾn*, pride, suggesting something like the Greek *hybris* at the bottom of the idea of sin.

3. *Myths*

The two main sources for West-Semitic mythology are the Ugaritic texts and the account of PHILO BYBLIUS.

PHILO recounts a Phoenician myth of creation according to which there was in the beginning dark, windy air and a dark, miry chaos. The wind "fell in love with its own beginning" and as Pothos ("desire") it produced a being called Mot (prob. 'mire', *not* identical with the Mot of the Baʿal myth). From this being the rest of creation came into being in the shape of an egg, which "shone forth" together with the sun, moon, and stars. Simultaneously rational beings called Zofesamin, or 'watchers of the sky', arose—who they were is not told. When the air had grown light and warm, there came into being, "through the heat of the sea and the earth", clouds and rain, thunder and lightning, so that the rational beings got scared and began to move as male and female on the earth and in the sea. To this PHILO adds a detailed genealogy of the gods.

Two other versions of the creation story are given by the philosopher DAMASCIUS. According to one there was first Kronos, Pothos (desire) and Omichle (mist), from these arose Aër (air), "the unmixed spiritual" and Aura, "the prototype that moved the spiritual". These two bore Otos, which is the spiritual foundation of everything. According to the other there were in the beginning Ether and Air, from which arose Ulomus ('ōlām, eternity) and Chusor (an artisan god mentioned also in the Ugaritic texts and by Philo) and an egg out of which heaven and earth originated.

These reports are obviously adopted to suit Greek thinking. But certain names are authentic and the basic features are probably also genuine. The waters of chaos are known also in the Old Testament, and the air, or wind, might correspond to the rūaḥ of Gen. 1:2. The primordial egg is not otherwise known in the Semitic area but is well attested in Egypt and in the Orphic cosmogony. The nature of the texts does not allow for any discussion of the details.

The Ugaritic texts do not contain any real cosmogony, but there are two allusions to a struggle which is otherwise connected with creation. One is found in the story of Baʿal's victory over Yam, the Sea, who is defeated by means of weapons made by the artisan god Kothar-and-Ḥasis (Chusoros); the victory results in Baʿal's dominion of the world. The other allusion refers to the defeat of Lotan (the Leviathan of the Old Testament), ascribed either to Baʿal or to ʿAnat.

The Baʿal myth is preserved on a number of tablets, the connection of which is not entirely clear. Apart from the struggle with Yam, it centers around two motifs: the building of the house (i.e. temple) of Baʿal and his death and resurrection. The former exhibits the idea that the temple is essential to Baʿal's power to exercise authority and culminates in his manifestation in thunder and rain. The latter has been dealt with sufficiently above.

Two other epic cycles are prominent among the mythological texts from Ras Shamra. The Aqhat cycle tells the story of Danʾel, the righteous ruler, whose prayers and sacrifices move El to grant him a son, Aqhat. The latter refuses to give ʿAnat his wonderful bow and is punished by death. As a result of this vegetation withers away and the rain ceases to fall. His sister sets out to retrieve her brother—here the text breaks off, but it is probable that he was ultimately restored to life. This myth offers and obvious parallel to the Baʿal myth.

The Keret cycle deals with king Keret, who has lost his wife and his children but is told by El to undertake a military expedition to the country of Udum to win a new wife and so begets a son who finally threatens to overthrow his father when he falls ill and is unable to exercise kingship. No consensus has been reached as to the character of this text. It is certainly not history, but it does not seem to be a real myth either. In all probability it is a cult legend dealing with certain features of kingship.

V. Conception of Man

No account of the creation of man has come down to us. About the nature and destiny of man only a few conclusions can be drawn from the scanty evidence at hand. The Aqhat epic shows that there was emphasis on man's being mortal, while immortality was the privilege of the gods. Life was the gift of the gods and they were able to make it long or short according to their will. Personal names indicate that man was considered the servant (*'abd*) of the gods. According to his conduct man is the object of the benevolence or the wrath of the gods.

The instances of the words *npsh*, soul, and *rūḥ*, spirit, are not sufficiently numerous to warrant a clear picture of religious anthropology. It seems probable that both words were used much in the same manner as in the Old Testament. Ugaritic has a synonym of 'soul', namely *brlt*, which means either 'soul', or 'desire'.

The conception of death seems to have been very similar to that of ancient Israelite religion. Rites of mourning are described in the Ugaritic texts; they are almost identical with the Israelite custom. There is evidence for a funeral meal, but it is not clear whether it was regarded as a sacrifice to or for the deceased person. We know that sacrifices were performed at the graves of Ugarit. One Phoenician inscription expresses the wish that the dead person shall eat and drink with Hadad, i.e. share the funeral sacrifices with him. One inscription calls the tomb "house of eternity."

Obviously the realm of the dead was thought of as a subterranean place where the dead led a shadowy existence. Some fragmentary texts from Ras Shamra mention a class of beings called *rp'm*, the word being linguistically identical with Hebrew *rephā'îm*, the shadows, i.e. the dead in the netherworld. They are also called *'ilnym* which perhaps means "divine beings" or "spirits". They have something to do with threshing-floors and with plantations, and they are said to receive offerings. These facts might also apply to chthonic gods, but it is obvious that no strict borderline can be drawn between such gods and the souls of the dead; they often have much in common. There is at least one case, when 'being buried in a tomb' and 'receiving an abode among' the *rp'm* are synonymous expressions.

VI. Subsequent Influence

In a direct manner, Canaanite-Syrian religion has had no lasting influence. Certain identifications of Syrian gods with Greek deities in the Hellenistic period lost their significance when the pagan era was over. It does not seem that ancient Syrian religion influenced the early Christian church in these areas, though certain traits in Syrian Christianity might show traces of Hellenistic syncretism, but rather in so far as Gnostic and other Iranian elements are concerned.

All the greater is the indirect influence of Canaanite religion. Early Israel, at the entrance into the promised land, found before them Canaanites worshipping El, Ba'al and Astarte and practising various kinds of fertility rites. There was a process of syncretism, the details of which we cannot follow, during which a considerable number of Canaanite elements crept into the Yahwistic religion. As a matter of fact, the amalgamation was so complete, that the reaction of the prophets was unable to distinguish what was historically speaking originally Canaanite and what was Israelite. Even the institution of ecstatic prophecy itself was probably of Canaanite origin, and the institution of kingship which became decisive for the growth of prophetic messianism, had been adopted by Israel from her neighbours. This influence continues down into Christianity with its insistence that Jesus was the promised Messiah (Christ). It has also been suggested that the serenity that is present in Yahweh's character is partly due to influence from the Canaanite god El, while the more violent features which are more akin to Ba'al are genuine and original. At the present stage of our knowledge, however, this is somewhat uncertain.

There has also been indirect and negative Canaanite influences on Israelite religion. The fact that Israel had to defend the unique character of her religion against the influx of Canaanite religion led to the development of certain traits in a more marked and consistent manner. The idea of the one God was marked by the rejection of Canaanite polytheism; the prohibition of making images of Yahweh has a point to Canaanite idol worship, partly represented by the golden calf of Ex. 32 and the bull images of Jeroboam I. Many details of this indirect influence have yet to be worked out.

VII. History of the Study of the Religion

No serious study of Phoenician and Aramaean religion was possible until the disclosure of the authentic material of the inscriptions. Such early works as SELDEN, *De diis Syris* (1629) are based on the classical authors. But even F. C. MOVERS' treatment of Phoenician religion in the first volume of his work *Die Phönizier* (Bonn 1841), is almost entirely based on the same material, though a few inscriptions had been deciphered as early as the 18th century. The French archaeological expedition to Syria in 1860, the results of which were published by RENAN in 1864-74, brought to light new and authentic material. Other discoveries brought new inscriptions to light, later collected and published in *Corpus Inscriptionum Semiticarum I* (1881-1911). Selected inscriptions were published by LIDZBARSKI, in *Handbuch der nord-semitischen Epigraphik* (1898; supplemented by three volumes *Ephemeris für semitische Epigraphie* 1900-15) and by COOK in his *Textbook of North Semitic Inscriptions* (1908).

A comprehensive survey of "the gods of the pagan Semites" was given by Fr. BAETHGEN in his *Beiträge zur semitischen Religionsgeschichte* (1888), based on both the classical authors, the Bible, and inscriptional evidence. Around the turn of the century the various schools of comparative religion applied their theories also to West-Semitic material. W. ROBERTSON SMITH published his *Lectures on the Religion of the Semites* in 1889, in which he tried to show with a wealth of the material that totemism was the origin of Semitic religion and especially of its sacrificial practices. These and other theories were rejected by M. J. LAGRANGE in his *Études sur les religions sémitiques* (1905), a work which is characterized by a thoroughly objective but sometimes overcautious approach. The works of HOMMEL and WINCKLER applied the astral theories of the Panbabylonian school also to West-Semitic material; a late follower was D. NIELSEN in *Der dreieinige Gott* I (1922) who, using also South-Arabian material built up a very speculative theory. From the same basic point of view but with much more critical acumen wrote FR. JEREMIAS in the fourth edition of Chantepie de la Saussaye's *Lehrbuch der Religionsgeschichte* (1925) which is still a most valuable contribution. An important monograph was W. BAUDISSIN's *Adonis und Esmun* (1911). FRAZER dealt with the ideas of dying and rising gods in the fourth volume of *The Golden Bough*. An epoch-making work was R. DUSSAUD's *Les origines cananéenes du sacrifice israélite* (1921) in which he argued the genetical relationship between Phoenician and Israelite sacrifices.

A new era was opened up by the discovery of the Ugaritic texts at Ras Shamra in 1929. The mythological texts were quickly published and interpreted, and were soon utilized for the study of proto-Phoenician religion. Dussaud found his theory of Canaanite sacrifice confirmed. The reliability of Philo Byblius' account of Phoenician religion had to be reconsidered in the light of the new material. The character of the epical texts from Ras Shamra was the object for some discussion: were they historical epics, legends, or myths, and in the latter case, were they purely narrative (literary) myths or ritual texts? Here opinions still differ according to the general outlook of the various scholars. Among those who defended the ritual character of the Ras Shamra texts should be mentioned F. F. Hvidberg (*Weeping and Laughter*, Danish 1938, Engl. transl. 1962) and I. Engnell (*Studies in Divine Kingship* (1943). Some new mythological and liturgical texts are to be published by Ch. Virolleaud in *Ugaritica* V (ed. by C. Schaeffer).

SELECTED BIBLIOGRAPHY

Texts

Cook, S. A., *A Textbook of North Semitic Inscriptions*, 1908
Donner, H.-Röllig, W., *Kanaanäische und aramäische Inschriften*, 1962 (2nd ed. 1967)
Gordon, C. H., *Ugaritic Textbook*, 1963
——, *Ugaritic Literature*, 1949
Ginsberg, H. L., Ugaritic Myths, Epics, and Legends, (In: *Ancient Near Eastern Texts related to the O.T.*, 2nd ed. 1955)
Driver, G. R., *Canaanite Myths and Legends*, 1956
Aistleitner, J., *Die mythologischen und kultischen Texte aus Ras Shamra* 1959
Jirku, A., *Kanaanäische Mythen und Epen aus Ras Shamra-Ugarit*, 1962

General Works

Jeremias, Fr., Kanaaäer, Syrer und Phönizier (In: Chantepie de la Saussaye, *Lehrbuch der Religionsgeschichte*, 4th ed., I 1925)
Dussaud, R., Phéniciens, Syriens (In: *Mana* I: 2, 1945)
Starcky, J., Palmyréniens, Nabatéens et Arabes du Nord avant l'Islam. (In: *Histoire des religions*, publ. sous la direction de M. Brillant et R. Aigrain, 4 s.a.)
Largement, R., La religion cananéenne. (In the same work)
Eissfeldt, O., Kananäisch-ugaritische Religion (In: *Handbuch der Orientalistik* VIII; 1, 1964)
Gray, J., *The Canaanites*, 1964
Harden, D., *The Phoenicians*, 1963
Pope, M.-Röllig, W., Syrien. Die Mythologie der Ugariter und Phönizier. (In: *Wörterbuch der Mythologie*, ed. by H. W., Haussig, I. 1965)
Jirku, A., *Der Mythus der Kanaanäer*, 1966

Monographs

DUSSAUD, R., *Les origines cananéennes du sacrifice israelite*, 2nd ed. 1941
GRAY, J., The Legacy of Canaan (*Suppl. to VT* V), 2nd ed. 1965
EISSFELDT, O., *El im ugaritischen Pantheon*, 1951
POPE, M., El in the Ugaritic Texts (*Suppl. to VT* II) 1955
KAPELRUD, A. S., *Baal in the Ras Shamra Texts*, 1952
DAHOOD, M. J., Ancient Semitic Deities (In: *Le antiche divinità semitiche*, ed.
    S. MOSCATI, 1958)
GASTER, T. H., *Thespis. Ritual, Myth and Drama in the Ancient Near East*, 1950
HOOKE, S. H., (ed.), *Myth, Ritual and Kingship*, 1958
FÉVRIER, J. G., *La religion des Palmyréniens*, 1931
DUPONT-SOMMER, A., *Les Araméens*, 1949
STADELMANN, R., *Syrisch-Palästinensische Gottheiten in Ägypten*, 1967
W. F. ALBRIGHT, *Yahweh and the Gods of Canaan*, 1968.

ISRAELITE-JEWISH RELIGION

Trends in its history down to the Maccabaean revolt

BY

GEO WIDENGREN
Uppsala, Sweden

Dominant in Israelite-Jewish religion is the idea of God. He is seen during the whole period of the development of religious ideas both as the creator of the universe and its master and also as the lord of history in general, and not only the history of Israel. Out of all peoples in the world God has elected Israel as His own people, Israel is His elect one among the nations. This idea of the people's election is associated with the worship of Israel's God from the very beginning of the people's history. But ultimately there emerged the idea that all peoples will turn to God and worship him. There is always a tension between these two lines of thought: Israel's God is the God of all nations, but He is at the same time above all the God of Israel.

God is to be found everywhere and may be worshipped in all places. His place is in heaven and everywhere. In the beginning His worship was located at Mount Sinai, but when David made Jerusalem his capital God's special place was the temple in Jerusalem.

God is worshipped in the temple by means of ritual actions, above all by means of sacrifices. But at the same time God is worshipped also outside all ritual, above all in prayer.

God has concluded a covenant with His people Israel. The outward sign of this covenant is the circumcision of every male Israelite. This means that to worship God in a proper way as a member of His people one has to be circumcised. But on the other hand it is also said that God demands most of all circumcision of heart.

Accordingly we can see in the religion of Israel a tension between ritual practice and spiritual interpretation. The sacrificial system is criticised, when it is taken to be the most important way of approaching the deity. This emphasis on sacrifice is sharply rebuked in some circles. There is thus a tension here between the sacrificial system and an anti-sacrificial attitude.

The temple of Jerusalem with its rich symbolism, its association with various mythical conceptions dating from various periods and quarters, its imposing sacrificial system, its allusion in the cultus to the rich treasure of both mythical and historical events, its music and songs of priestly chorus and temple singers, the marvellous cult-hymns and moving prayers of confession and penitence, all this constituted an enormous source of religious emotions and associations which fully explains the jubilation of the pilgrims when they "go up" to the temple and get sight of Jerusalem.

On the other hand we have the synagogue with its concentration on the word of God, its service, including exposition and teaching, but also sermons and prayers. The synagogue lacks the splendour of the temple, but it is possessed of immense religious value to the pious Jew.

The perspective of history, past and present, but also future, englobes other tensions. Moses is the founder of Israel's religion, but there is a tendency to look back to Abraham as the "ideal" founder of the people and its covenant with God. Moses was the great leader of the people, who brought it out from the serfdom of Egypt, but David's reign was the most glorious period in Israel's history. Expectations for the future are concentrated on the advent of the Davidic ruler, the Messiah, who ultimately is lifted up above the purely human sphere and acquires the mythical traits of a saviour. The Samaritans have elevated Moses to a quasidivine position. The Jews never did. The enigmatic figure of the Suffering Servant marks another, quite different line of thought, pregnant with meaning for the future.

Again, if Moses founded the community of pre-exilic Israel Ezra may be rightly looked upon as the real founder of post-exilic Judaism. The transition from an ethnic group to a religious community is due above all to him and to the help he got from Nehemiah, who prepared the way for him. Without Ezra it is quite probable that Israel would have been lost among the surrounding nations.

Eschatology in the sense of the idea of an individual life after death appeared late in Israel. We can easily see how the way slowly was paved for the hope of an existence *post portem*. Iranian influences offered a solution of the many problems with which the pious Jew had to struggle. The suffering of the innocent troubled all religious thinkers. The idea of an retribution after death, which meant the resurrection of the dead, here seemed the only way out of a hopeless dilemma. This dilemma got its classical expression in the mighty dialogues in the Book of Job.

The period when our exposition of Israelite-Jewish religion stops is a time when nothing yet is definitely settled. Jewish religion in those days was full of various possibilities, rich in varying perspectives. There was, however, one common denominator: the Law. This was the great gift of God to His people Israel through the hands of His servant Moses. The people and its pious members were always living for the Law and in the Law—and that more and more. Here we can see what a radical change there is between pre-exilic and post-exilic periods of Israelite-Jewish religion. The position of the Law is the essential factor in Jewish religion, but what really is implied in that statement needs more qualification than to say that Jewish religion in post-exilic times is a religion of law—as is often said.

Israel settled in Canaan as a confederation of semi-nomadic tribes, possessed of a fairly uncomplicated religion and with ethics marked above all by tribal solidarity. In Canaan the invaders were confronted with a population of farmers and citizens. Theirs was the religion so typical of the western Semites with myths and rites combined into a complicated system of great emotional power, with an elaborate cult including sexual acts, with temples and priesthood, festivals and cult-images foreign to the invaders. There was a violent clash in many quarters as we can see from the writings of the so-called prophets. But after the thesis and anti-thesis there followed at last a synthesis. Canaan gave its contribution to Israel's religion and that not only as a negative stimulus, but also as a positive factor in the development of the people's religion and ethics.

I. Pre-Mosaic Period: General Traits

It is only after the settlement in Canaan that Israel was a real people. Before that period we only meet with single tribes and confederations of tribes. Among the "Sons of Israel", the *beⁿē Yiśrā'ēl*, as they called themselves, we distinguish above all the Northern tribes with the so called Joseph-group, the tribes of Ephraim and Manasseh, from the Southern tribes with Judah as the leading member. With the southern confederation were associated smaller groups like the Calebites and Qenites, originally certainly not belonging to the sons of Israel. All these tribes apparently were pastoral half-nomads, wandering with their flocks freely, but within a comparatively restricted area. They moved on the borders of the cultivated land or even penetrated more or less deeply in it, according to the allowance of circumstances. It is probable that the Israelites were able to cultivate cereal crops at the places, to which they returned at regular intervals (Gen. 18,6), though this may not be taken for granted as a constant trait in their living. At any rate they were chiefly shepherds and not farmers. They were "wandering Aramaeans" as Deut. 26,5 indicates, living in tents, not in houses, drinking the milk of their small cattle (Judges 5,25; Gen. 18,8), not the wine, the product of the vine-yards. The scouts return from Canaan to the children of Israel bringing grapes, pomegranates and figs. This was to them something new and unheard of. They were not sitting "every man under his vine and under his figtree (1Kings 5,5; Micah 4,4; Zach. 3,10)", but were semi-nomads, tending their flocks of sheep (Gen. 46,32).

Their religion was the religion characteristic of this stage of civilization. First of all we find in their proper names a clear indication of the type of their religion. The theophorous elements are such words as 'āb, Father 'aḫ, Brother, 'am, Kinsman and (paternal) Uncle. Such proper names show that there was a strong sense of the solidarity of the gods and their worshippers, members of one and the same social unit, the clan. God and his worshippers together constitute the clan or the tribe, mišpāḥāh. In patriarchal narratives, describing the wanderings of Abraham, Isaac and Jacob, the forefathers of Israel, in whom it is very difficult to recognize individual *historical* personalities, we meet with a deity, frequently called "the God of the father" (Gen. 26, 24; 28,13; 31,5,29,42,53; 32,9; 46,1,49,15,49,24-25; 50,17).

It has been shown that this ephitet indicates a family cult, founded, instituted or taken over by a head of family, where the family also acts as a cultic unity. But this cult is attached to no local shrine (except Beerseba Gen. 46,1), it is associated only with a certain person and his descendants. The deity accompanies the clan of the tribe during its wanderings between the wilderness and settled land. Such a deity was called by the common Semitic generic name of "god" i.e. 'ēl. There were, however, also what we may call house-hold idols, terāfīm, concerning the worship of which we are very much left in the dark.

Several deities with names composed of El are mentioned in the patriarchal stories, though we cannot say with absolute certainty that their worship belongs to this period of semi-nomadic civilization. They are El Shaddai, perhaps meaning "God of the Mountain", El

Rōi, "God of seeing", El'Olām, God of Eternity, El Bethel, God of Bethel" (in itself meaning "House of God"). Probably all these El-names signify local variations of the one highest El, the head of the Canaanite pantheon. The worship of this chief of all the gods is, how-ever, more characteristic of the Sons of Israel after their settlement in Canaan, than before.

The patriarchal narratives speak of various altars constructed by the patriarchs. They also relate that the wandering Israelites worshipped at holy places, trees, sources, stones. These altars were constructed out of unhewn stones (Ex. 20,25; Deut. 27,5; 8,31). But it was the trees or the erected stones that were above all the places of worship. The stone was "the house of God", *bēṯ-ēl*, βαίτυλος. The tree was also a holy symbol of the god's dwelling, e.g. the tamarisk at Beerseba in the Negeb, where the Southern tribes certainly possessed a centre of their cult before their settlement.

There were also minor divine beings, dwelling in the desert, demons called *śeʿīrīm*, in the shape of goats as it seems, though it is uncertain if belief in them dates back to our period. The narratives of the patri-archs have received a strong imprint by the ideas of later generations and it is not easy to disentangle the older layers of tradition from the present context. We are on much safer ground when we descend to the period immediately before the settlement in Canaan. Here above all we get to know something more about the cult. It is clear from the relations of the exodus of Egypt that the sons of Israel, as far as the Southern tribes at least were concerned, possessed a centre of their worship in the oasis of Qadesh, the present 'Ain Qudais, in the north-ern part of the Sinai peninsula. This place obviously was the rallying point of the tribes, who used to undertake a pilgrimage, *ḥāg*, to Qadesh in order to present there their sacrifices to their chief deity (Ex. 3,18; 5, 1-3; 8,27,15,22).

Of the sacrificial festivals we may date in the pre-mosaic period the following three great feasts: the festival of Passover, certainly a nomadic pastoral feast, but of uncertain significance, celebrated in the spring, the festival of Unleavened Bread, the festival of the New Moon.

The ritual of sacrifice must have been rather simple and was carried out by every father of the family. Various types of sacrifice are to be distinguished: the sacrifice of the first-born belonging to the festival of Passover.

II. The Mosaic Period: the Religion of the Sons of Israel

According to Pentateuchal tradition Moses-when as a refugee from Egypt living in the land of Midiān-once came to the Mountain of God called Horeb. Here he received a revelation of a deity who made himself known to Moses as "the God of your father, the God of Abraham, the God of Isaac, and the God of Jacob." "He is the God of your fathers" (Ex. 3,13), but on Moses' question as to his real name he answers: "I am who I am," 'æhiæ 'ašær 'æhiæ, taken as an esoteric pun on the name Yahwæh, from the verb hauā, which may be taken as conveying the meaning of "He is", but in the sense of "He is whatever he wants to be." The narrative leaves the impression of being composed of two different strands of tradition, the historical value of which is rather uncertain. What is of interest is the fact that later generations ascribed the introduction of the name of Yahwaeh, as used of the god of the Sons of Israel, to a personal revelation given to Moses. At any rate, from this moment on Yahwæh appears as the god of Moses, but also of Israel. A covenant, berīṭ is concluded by Moses between his people and this deity. Yahwæh gives to Moses the following promise: "I will take you for my people, and I will be your God" (Ex. 6,7). This deity, Yahwæh, has certain characteristic traits. He is a *holy* God, and he is a jealous God (Ex. 20,5), meaning that he does not tolerate any disobedience or disloyalty from His people, but also that He is full of zeal for Israel. Of course the fact that Yahwæh is the God of Israel does not imply His being the one and alone possessed of a divine status in the whole world. It means that He is the exclusive God of Israel, He and no one else. He is a "jealous God," 'ēl qannā'.

Israelite traditions are full of narratives about the manner in which a covenant was concluded between Yahwaeh and His people, but several facts indicate that these traditions are untrustworthy from a historical point of view, because being coloured by the conditions of later epochs.

The same holds true of the cult in which Yahwæh is worshipped. We can only say that a so-called "tent of assembly," 'ōhæl mō'ēḏ, (Ex. 25,22) designates a sacred tent, appropriate to the conditions of the wilderness, where the people was wandering after the exodus from Egypt. This tent which served the communication of the will of the deity could be carried on a camel (-if such an animal was accessible to the Israelites of our period—just as the *qubbah* of pre-islamic Arabs), from one resting place to the other.

The oracular instruments were the Urim and Tummin, carried in a pouch on the breast of the officiating priest. Still more important is the Ark. This cultobject too, which was—as shown by its name *'arōn* —a chest (made of wood), was also carried by the people in their migrations in the wilderness, though obviously at the outset not on a camel's back or on a wagon, but by some chosen carriers. This doesn't point to a nomadic origin. The Ark, perhaps from the outset thought of as the seat of Yahwaeh, who "was sitting on the Cherubs," who were placed on the Ark, represented to the people the presence of Yahwaeh himself, as indicated in the ancient formula preserved Num. 10,35 f., for here the Ark is addressed in the following words:

> Arise, o Yahwaeh, and let thy enemies be scattered,
>   and let them that hate thee flee before thee!
> Return, o Yahwaeh to the ten thousand thousands of Israel!

It has been surmised that the name originally was *'arōn hā'ᵉlōhīm*, an appellation indicating an origin in Canaan, where it is more in its proper religious context. In the oldest traditions—this has been shown —the Ark and the Tent have no connection. Presumably the Southern tribes took over the use of an Ark from the sanctuaries in southern Canaan.

Tradition gives various accounts of the covenant ceremonies, which confirmed the pact between Israel and its God. Of these only the relation Ex. 24,1, 9-11 would seem to be an authentic report: the covenant-making was accompanied by a sacred meal before the face of God.

The description of the so-called "Tabernacle of Yahwaeh", *miškan Yahwaeh*, on the other hand is so vitiated by details, belonging to the period of kingdom, that it is hardly possible to arrive at a concrete picture of it, consistent with the semi-nomadic customs of the oldest Israel—even after subtraction of the most anachronistic details. (The tent-sanctuary of the united kingdom will be mentioned below, cf. p. 254).

It is remarkable that in the oldest tradition Moses and the seventy elders represent Israel, whereas Aaron certainly, and (Moses,) Adab and Nabihu probably, are later accretions, conditioned by the interests of certain priestly circles.

The God of Israel in the oldest extant extra-Pentateuchal traditions

is called "He of Sinai", *ʒæ Sinai*. This is one of the two names of the
Mountain of God, the other being Horeb. Neither place it is possible
to localize, except that they are to be sought in, or in the immediate
neighbourhood of the Sinai peninsula.

Where actually the covenant between Yahwaeh and Israel was concluded we do not know. The tradition associating the great pilgrimage
festival with Qadesh would presuppose Qadesh as the actual place of
this convenant. And it is expressly stated that Yahwaeh came from
Sinai to Qadesh, Deut. 33,2 (reconstructed text, based on the LXX).
That by the covenant concluded with Yahwaeh Israel made Him its
own deity is evident, which means of course that before the convenant
He was not held to occupy this position. In the present tradition,
however, Qadesh has been relegated into the background in favour
of the Mountain of God, either Sinai or Horeb. *Yahwaeh* was a *new* God
to His people, or else no covenant would have been necessary.

That this was the case is incontrovertible shown by the proper names,
for the theophorous names composed with Yahwaeh are extremely
rare in the most remote periods. Typically enough the successor of
Moses according to tradition is Joshua, who is possessed of a Yahwaeh-
name, probably meaning "Yahwaeh rescues". After him until the
period of royal government in Israel we have *only* 5 names composed
with Yahwaeh, among them Jonathan, a priest of Dan, the grandson
of Moses, Judges 18,30. A most striking fact, which can be explained
only by the circumstance that Yahwaeh occupied a position as the god
of the whole confederation, while the single tribes possibly still possessed their own old tribal deities, in essence, but not in name, perhaps
rather identical with Yahwaeh, namely the gods of the fathers.

The worship of Yahwaeh was aniconic, this fact is not to be doubted.
The expression "before the face of Yahwaeh" prior to the settlement
in Canaan met with in the narrative of the covenant-making, must be
understood as meaning "in the presence of Yahwaeh", i.e. the place
where he used to reveal himself. The commandment not to make any
image of God is to be dated to the "nomadic" period, because significant of nomadic religion. At the outmost we may think of some un-
plastic symbol, but no support for this is found in the texts.

The new god Yahwaeh, as we have seen, was identified with the
god of the Israelite fathers. It was natural then, that He was associated
with all the great events that happened in connection with the exodus
from Egypt. Above all with the wonderful salvation of Israel, when
the people at Yam Sūf, the Red-Sea, was rescued from the persecuting

army of Pharao. What *really* happened is difficult to state with exactitude, because there are different strands of tradition, and these composite relations moreover have received nearly mythical colours in later generations, being used more or less as a cultic text, recited in commemoration of Yahwaeh's greats deeds at the festival where this wonderful act was celebrated. That much would, however, seem to be clear that an Egyptian military contingent, composed chiefly of chariotry, was drowned in the sea and that this event was ascribed to the activity of Israel's new God Yahwaeh. A very ancient song, said to have been recited by the priestess Miriam, glorifies the wonderful deed of Yahwaeh, Exod. 15,21:

> Sing to Yahwaeh,
>   for He is vastly elevate.
> Horse and its driver
>   He hurled into the sea.

By this deed Yahwaeh had shown Himself the Lord of history as later generations saw it. He was, however, also the Lord of nature, for to tradition it was His command of wind and sea that had caused the annihilation of the Egyptians. As a deity of nature, as a god of sky and atmosphere all the ancient descriptions depict his theophanies. He is *not* a god of a mountain, the mountain Sinai (or Horeb) being the place where He is dwelling, but He is wandering freely and was worshipped also in other places, above all at Qadesh.

We have seen that Moses gave the *tōrōt* to Israel, but it is impossible to reconstruct from the present mass of traditions what regulations could be qualified "Mosaic". It is more easy to say what in the laws ascribed to Moses is *not* of Mosaic origin. Most of the cultic and social regulations date from the time after the settlement, especially from the period of kings and is accordingly antedated.

They show that the priestly circles of that period were eager to give a legitimate character to their whole *corpus* of laws by dating them to the time of Moses and making Moses responsible for them. These circles have also introdused Aaron, a representative of the Jerusalem priesthood, as a leading figure at the side of Moses.

The Mosaic traditions have been preserved both in the Southern and the Northern tribes. There is, however, a clear distinction, for the Qadesh-traditions were associated with the Southern tribes for obvious reasons, while traditions about Moses and Mosaic institutions were spread above all among the Northern tribes, chiefly Ephraim and Manasseh, "Israel" in its restricted sense. We may point to Shechem as a special place, where a circle of traditionists collected these traditions and handed them down to subsequent generations.

The covenant between Yahwaeh and Israel also meant that the rather loose confederation of the Sons of Israel now possessed a rallying point in a common deity, with a common cult symbolized in the two cultic objects: the Tent of meeting and the Ark, though it is uncertain when the Ark was introduced into the cult. It also meant a common festival in which the act of covenant-making was memorialised and renewed every year, at a given time of the year. However, it is obvious that the confederation of tribes, led by Joshua after the death of Moses, chiefly were the central part of the Northern tribes, i.e. Ephraim and Manassah. Thus the Southern tribes were split off and went their own way, infiltrating themselves from the south into the land of culture and associating with them some non-Israelite groups such as Calebites and Qenites.

III. The Mosaic Period: Moses and his work

The Sons of Israel went down into Egypt where for some generations they lived in Gosen, the northeastern territory bordering on the Sinai peninsula. For some reasons they left Egypt, not unmolested by the Egyptian government, and went eastwards to Sinai, where they obviously for some time dwelt in the oases in Qadesh (cf. above). They were under the guidance of Moses, who was the leader of the confederation. But it is a much disputed point what tribes actually took part in the descent to Egypt and the emigration from there. The narratives about the role played by Moses, as well as about the political and religious conditions in the Israel of this time, have been transmitted to us in later collections, where different strands of tradition are embedded.

However, it is at least possible to present a minimum formula of the activity of Moses, as it can be defended from a purely historical point of view. First of all it calls for notice that the name of Moses is Egyptian, being a form of the Egyptian verb *mśi*, to bear. Also other members of this clan have Egyptian names, a strong argument in favour of his attachment to Egyptian civilization. Here we should contrast the true Hebrew names of the two nurses of Moses, which show them to be later additions to the authentic tradition. The name of his father-in-law is given either as Hobab, the Qenite (in a notice independent of Pentateuchal tradition) or as Jethro from the tribe of the Midianites. It is obvious that the oldest traditions did not know more than that the father-in-law was either from the tribe of the Midianites or the Qenites. To this tribe modern research has ascribed a decisive influence in Israel's taking over the worship of Yahwaeh. As to his wife the most authentic tradition did not know anything but that she was a woman of foreign origin, Zipporah being no individual, historical figure. The Pentateuchal tradition further gives to Moses as his brother and sister Aaron and Miriam, but it can easily be shown that they originally had nothing to do with Moses: Aaron moreover, probably is only the eponymous ancestor of a priesthood of later times, the Aaronites. Miriam on the other hand would seem to be a historical figure, probably of southern Judaean extraction, attached to Qadesh, where her tomb was situated.

The parents of Moses both belonged to the tribe of Levi, according to a tradition which there is no reason to doubt. We further know from traditions outside the Pentateuch that Mose had a son, Gershom, carrying on the priestly traditions of the tribe of Levi. The priestly family of the tribe of Dan carried its ancestry back to this Gershom, the son of Moses. There is also no reason to reject the tradition about Mose's death and burial, Deut. 34,6.

Genealogies in Ex. 6 and Num. 26 tell us that Moses belonged to the tribe of Levi. While the historical value of such genealogies may be doubted the notice in Judges 17,7 says that Gershom was a Levite. Accordingly also his father Moses must have been a Levite (confirmed by Ex. 2). Here we touch upon the difficult problem of the term "Levite". What does this term mean? There was in Mosaic times surely no secular tribe "Levi", for this term denoted already Ex. 4,14 a priest. That Moses was a Levite means in our period not at all that he had any exclusive rights of sacrifice, but that it was he who communicated the will of the Godhead in the form of a *tōrāh*. Moses as a Levite was a proclaimer of *tōrōṯ*. These were communicated by the Levite by means of the oracular instruments, the Urim and Tummin as Deut. 33,8-10 explicitly states. This being the case it would *a priori* be probable that the tradition is right, when ascribing to Moses the original Law, given to Israel by Moses after the exodus from Egypt. The socalled "Ten commandments" would then be authentically Mosaic. Many scholars are of this opinion, but other reject it. After the latest careful analysis it can not be doubted, however, that in their *present* form these commandments cannot date from the time of Moses. The most we are able to say with some certainty is that they may posses a Mosaic inspiration.

Moses as a Levite acts as a priest and lawgiver, and this position of his is conspicuous everywhere in tradition. As a proclaimer of the divine *tōrōṯ*, he could also be characterized as a prophet, *nābī*. The passage Hos. 12,14 may therefore echo an authentic tradition.

Pentateuchal narratives depict Moses as the great leader of his people. Traditions outside the Pentateuch confirm the authenticity of this tradition (Judges 1,20). He is the chief of the confederation of tribes.

That Moses in some way or other was attached to the oasis of Qadesh has been the opinion of many scholars. In Qadesh the older strata of tradition place some of the events with which Moses was associated. Here it was that the Bᵉnē Yiśrā'ēl wanted to celebrate their pilgrim-festival, for which they asked permission to leave Egypt. And in the original tradition, of which only traces are left, Moses led them to this place. This is the authentic tradition (Ex. 5, 1-3; 15,22-25b; 17, 1b-7; Num. 20,2-12 "P"), showing that there was a sanctuary in Qadesh, where the Hebrew tribes celebrated their *ḥāg*. Here Moses officiated as a priestly Levite, here he gave the *tōrōṯ* to the tribes (Ex. 18).

Who was the deity worshipped at Qadesh? This question is the next problem to occupy us.

The problem of the origin, the "pre-history", of this deity has been much discussed and many hypotheses suggested. Of all the suggestions offered, there is obviously only one to be taken seriously, the Midianite origin of this god. This surmise is founded on the relation Ex. 18, where the father-in-law of Moses, Jethro, acknowledges the might of Yahwaeh, added to the fact that according to Ex. 3 Yahwaeh revealed himself to Moses in the land of Midian. On the other hand (as we have seen above p. 233) the notice Judges 4,11 associates his father-in-law, here however called Hobab, with the Qenites. It has been surmised that the Qenites were Yahwaeh-worshippers, the ancestor of the tribe, Qain, wearing the sign of this deity, Gen. 4,15. The Qenites were attached to the tribe of Judah and this fact may explain that Yahwaeh was worshipped among the southern tribes of the Bᵉnē Yiśrā'ēl. However, it need not be emphasized that these combinations rest on rather uncertain premises. We are on equally uncertain ground when the name itself is considered. We do not even know whether the longer form Yahwaeh or one of the shorter forms Yāhu, Yāh or Yo is the original name. Hence it is rather meaningless to speculate on the sense of the verb *hwy*, underlying the form Yahwaeh, which may be taken as the imperfect of it. It is equally uncertain to speculate on the possibility that the original name might have been Yahwaeh'ēl (in analogy with e.g. Yiśrā'ēl).

We are thus left in the dark and can only state that the worship of Yahwaeh is not attested in any part of the ancient Near East before the entrance of the tribes of Israel into history.

IV. The Period of Settlement: Joshua and the Judges

The settelement in Canaan in the latter half of the 13th century took the form chiefly of a gradual conquest of Central Palestine under the leadership of Joshua, the chief of the Northern tribes, above all Ephraim and Manasseh. Because Canaan politically was divided among a great number of petty princes, each one ruling over a town and its adjacent territory the invaders were at an advantage. On the other hand the Israelite confederacy of tribes were lacking in the decisive military arm, the chariotry. This is expressly stated as far as Judah is concerned in Judges 1,19. The same is said of Dan 1,34. They therefore mostly had to fight in such a country where chariots could not be used: hill country and mountains. The reliable accounts of the conquests given in Judges Ch. 1 show that Manasseh *e.g.* was not able to dislocate the original inhabitants from such towns as Bet-Shean, Taanak, Dor, Jibleam, and Megiddo, but the Canaanites were still living there in these towns. Likewise Gezer was not taken by Ephraim. And the same picture presents itself in the whole country: substantial areas with a Canaanite population remained outside the control of the Bᵉnē Yiśrā'ēl.

Joshua, as already stated, was the leader of the Northern tribes, whereas the Southern tribes, Judah, Simeon, Caleb, and Benjamin seem to have operated on their own, infiltrating themselves gradually from the South. The city of Jerusalem was not conquered. It is expressly related that the Sons of Benjamin were not able to expel the Jebusites from Jerusalem, Judges 1,21 (contrary to 1,8 which is a later addition).

The confederation held together by Moses accordingly would seem to have been split up after his death. The traditions now to be read in the Book of Joshua try to give the impression that the confederation was a closely knit unit of 12 tribes under the command of Joshua. There are, however, a great many instances speaking against the historical truth of these late traditions. For that reason it doesn't seem very probable that the convocation of a diet at Shechem, described in Josh. 24, really concerned the whole of Israel. It is more probable that only the Northern tribes met there. Shechem certainly was of old a central place in Israel, in a later period a city where the diet of all Israel used to meet (I Kings 12,1), but the story of Abimelek (Judges 9) shows that Shechem politically was independent of the Israelites and religiously not a city where Yahwaeh was the most prominent, let alone the one god. Ba'al Berīt was instead the city-god, possessed of a temple in Shechem, where obviously a great temple treasure was stored up (Judg. 9,4).

This existence of the city-god Ba'al Berīt at Shechem leads us to considerations of the religious situation in Israel after the conquest.

On the whole the settlement meant a radical change in Israel's life, from the political, economic, cultural, and religious points of view. From the political point of view it meant a considerable disintegration of the confederacy. The tribes operated rather isolated and settled down in various parts of the country, often without a common leader or a central sanctuary, where all tribes could worship the god of the confederation, Yahwaeh, with whom they once had made their covenant. How difficult it was to assemble the confederacy even in times of great danger, this fact the Song of Deborah (Judg. 5) testifies to us in eloquent words. Of the theoretical 12 tribes of Israel the following tribes took part in the great battle against a Canaanite confederacy, fought in the Yizreel-plain about 1100 B.C.: Sebulon, Naphtali, Ephraim, Makir, Isaschar, Beniamin, 6 tribes among whom Makir is not generally counted as one of the 12 great tribes. On the other hand Gilead is mentioned as not taking part, as also Dan, Asher, Ruben. The House of Joseph does not exist as a tribe or tribal confederation, but we have Ephraim and Makir, a subtribe of Manasseh. Not even mentioned are Gad, Simeon, Levi, Judah, i.e. the Southern tribes, plus Gad in the territory southeast of Jordan (Judges 4): This fact shows the system of a confederation of 12 tribes to be a fiction, or rather an ideal never attained. This doesn't mean of course that there was no unity. But though there was a sense of unity there was no leadership of all the tribes, the traditions about "Judges" of all Israel being a later fiction. And there were several important local sanctuaries, but no central sanctuary, where the whole confederation met with a representative cult assembly. The traditions now collected in Josh. 24 may possess a kernel of truth, in so far that Shechem without doubt was one of the most important Israelite sanctuaries, where a great yearly festival was celebrated. But there were other important sanctuaries beside Shechem which appear to have played a perhaps even greater rôle during certain periods. Thus we have among the Northern tribes: Shiloh, Gilgal, Bethel, Rama, and Dan (formerly Laish) high up in the north at the same latitude as Tyre. Among the Southern tribes we find *inter alia* the following sanctuaries: Beerseba, Hebron, Arad (known as a sanctuary thanks to modern excavations), Nob, and Gibeon.

Now, if Shechem had been the dominating sanctuary as the place where the confederation met already in the time of Joshua we must expect it to be the place of the Ark, the most important cult-object of the Sons of Israel, obviously possessed of pre-conquest traditions as we have seen. But actually we have no traditions about the Ark's being placed there. On the other hand we know that it was placed at Bethel (Judg. 20,27) and at Shiloh (I Sam. 4,4), Beth-Shemesh (I Sam. 6,15), Qiryath-yearim (I Sam. 7,1). The Ark thus ultimately got its place in the territory of Judah. This according to tradition. But it would seem impossible not to assume that the great local sanctuaries had an Ark of Yahwaeh and we are more or less forced to assume the existence of several arks. At any rate, the fact that there was a great Canaanite temple at Shechem, that there were other equally or more important cultcenters, that we have no indications of the Ark's being placed at Shechem, that there was no 12-tribes confederation in reality in oldest times, and last not least, that there was no leader of all the Sons of Israel, all these facts seem to speak against the hypothesis that Shechem was the national sanctuary of the Israelite confederation, where the great festival of the year was celebrated by the chief of the confederation and its cultic assembly. As already stated this doesn't mean that no such festival was celebrated there. It certainly was, and most probably Shechem enjoyed a great reputation, but nothing speaks against the assumption that such festivals were celebrated at all important sanctuaries of the country, and that it is thanks to a certain tendency that we have in the present relation in Josh. 24 a counterpart of the covenant-making at Sinai. As Moses made his covenant at Sinai between Yahwaeh and His people (actually probably at Qadesh!) during the desert wandering Joshua made a covenant after the settlement at Shechem. What is remarkable here is that in the long speech laid in the mouth of Joshua nothing is said about the covenant once concluded by Moses, so that we must ask ourselves, if this covenant was unknown to the author-collector of the traditions about a diet at Shechem. At any rate we may sum up in the following way: there was at Shechem—and at other great local shrines too—a yearly festival where the covenant-making between Yahwaeh and Israel was celebrated and this festival, which meant a renewal of the covenant, was presided over by a tribal chief or chief of a tribal confederation—not by a priest.

V. The Period of Settlement: religious Consequences

The settlement carried with it important consequences. The settlement to a great extent meant a break with the people's earlier life. They still to some extent were shepherds, especially among the Southern tribes and in territories east of Jordan, but the majority soon went over to be farmers. Now they had houses, vineyards, fields to grow crops, and fruit-trees. Some of them settled in towns and were artisans, labourers, and merchants. The more or less class-less "democracy" of the semi-nomadic tribes gave room to a growing emergence of various classes. A real priesthood by profession now also developed at all the local sanctuaries and places of worship, where Israel now approached its God. Architecture and art were cultivated, especially in the field of religion. Regulations of law, brought by the Sons of Israel as a heritage from their pre-conquest times, were now being codified and reformulated, for new conditions needed new laws. Israel took over the use of writing, for even if writing not was totally unknown among the wandering tribes its use was certainly restricted.

Perhaps most important of all was the change of language. Israel now learnt to speak with "the lip of Canaan" (Is. 19,18), abandoning its former "proto-Aramaic" language. This shift of language is demonstrated in the Israelite proper names as *en vogue* after the settlement. There was, however, a rest left from older times, so that Hebrew has been qualified a "mixed" language.

Conquering several Canaanite towns the Israelites inherited also the local sanctuaries there, sometimes not insignificant temples, where we have to assume the existence of scribal schools, where the temple-scribes were trained, employed also for administrative duties. At the sanctuaries the sacred texts were studied and copied. Taking over the sanctuaries and the scribal schools also meant taking over the sacred literature of Canaan.

We may say that on principle all important Israelite places of worship were inherited from the Canaanites. The most famous of them were already mentioned. Now, it was of course necessary to the immigrants to give these sanctuaries a legitimacy within their own religion, to motivate their use. This was done in that way that the wanderings of the great ancestors were associated with these shrines. Abraham was claimed by the sanctuaries of Shechem, Bethel, Beerseba and Hebron. Isaac, a more pale figure, is associated with Beerseba, and Iacob above all with Bethel. With these sanctuaries all the local traditions too, were taken over and blended with the true national Israelite traditions, so that there emerged what we call "the Patriarchal traditions."

With the cult-places among which we also have to count with the more simple places of worship, a height, *bāmāh*, a stone, *maṣṣēbāh*, and a holy tree, an *'ašērāh*, the entire cultic apparatus of Canaanite origin was taken over: temple architecture and religious art, the use of idols, i.e. plastic images of the deities, calendars of religious festivals, cult-lyrics and mythical epics, rituals, especially sacrifices, priesthood and cultic prophets, cultic servants, among them prostitutes, both male, and above all female, yea, even several deities.

As to temple architecture and religious art excavations have provided a rich material, they have also in the case of Hazor *e.g.* demonstrated the continuity in the use of the sanctuary. The House of God passes from Canaanites to Israelites without any observable sharp break. When speaking of the temple in Jerusalem we shall consider more closely the Canaanite influence in this special domain. Let us note only that *e.g.* Shiloh is called a *hēkāl*, a temple. Here the *bāmāh*, *maṣṣēbāh* and *'ašērāh* call for notice. The word *bāmāh* means a "high place", but as a term for a cultic site not necessarily indicates a location on a hilltop. It was probably either a natural or artificial mound or a raised platform. There we find the three most important cultic objects of a Canaanite-Israelite sanctuary: the stone pillar, a symbol of the male deity and called *maṣṣēbāh*, the wooden pole or tree called *'ašērāh*, representing the female deity, and the altar, *mizbēaḥ* ($<*maẓbaḥ$), all three Canaanite in both names and functions. It cannot, however, be disputed that the Israelites also before the settlement knew the use of an altar, though it was insisted in the ritual commandments that it should be constructed out of unhewn stones. Archaic usage may on the other hand be reflected in the sacrifices of Gideon (Judg. 6,21 f.) and Manoah (Judg. 13,19 f.) where the sacrificial victim, in both cases a kid, is placed on a rock and then consumed by fire from heaven. This looks like the sacrifice of nomadic people.

Sacrifices were of different kinds. Because sacrifice was considered a gift to the deity a common term in more remote times was *minḥāh*, gift, later specialized to denote a specific kind of sacrifice, namely vegetables.

Sacrifice of firstlings could be called *mattānāh*, also meaning "gift". So called *nᵉḏāḇōṯ* were "voluntarily" offered sacrifices, and *tōḏāh* an offering of thanksgiving. All three sacrifices possessed the character of a gift to the deity.

The burnt offering, *ʿōlāh*, and the "total" sacrifice, *kālīl*, were sacrifices where everything was given to the deity, without anything being consumed by the sacrificer or the priest. They were accordingly gifts to the Godhead without any restriction.

The breads lying before the deity in the sanctuary, *læḥæm pānīm*, are mentioned in the story about the early shrine of Nob (I Sam. 21). It is to be supposed that originally these breads were thought to serve as food for the deity. But the deity could also enjoy the sacrifice, when it was burnt and a sweet smoke ascended towards heaven (I Sam. 2, 16, 28). Yahwaeh feels the agreable smell of the ascending sacrificial smoke (Gen. 8, 21).

There was, however, a distinct type of sacrifice, the sacrificial meal, in which both God and His worshippers took part. The common name of a sacrifice connected with such a meal was *zæḇaḥ*, a term denoting something slaughtered (*zāḇaḥ*, to slaughter).

It is rather difficult to say what the term *šælæm* or in plural *zᵉḇāḥīm šᵉlāmīm*, properly signifies, except that it was a sacrifice of slaughtering, associated with a sacrificial meal. Probably it aimed at preserving the harmony, "peace", *šālōm*, in the society. Eating and drinking, music, song, dance and licentious practices were associated with such sacrificial meals (attested by Ex. 32, 6, 19 and many passages in prophetical literature). The participants were generally drunk and this explains that the priest Eli could take Hannah for drunken, when she was directing a prayer to Yahwaeh in the sanctuary of Shiloh, after that she and her husband "had eaten in Shiloh and had drunk" (I Sam. 1, 9). It was namely the custom of her husband every year to undertake a pilgrimage to Shiloh to sacrifice there to Yahwaeh, *lizḇōaḥ* (I Sam. 1, 3), i.e. to celebrate the sacrificial meal, *zæḇaḥ*.

Sacrifice could also serve as an a tonement. When the deity was irritated, when his anger was arosed, man tried to appease the godhead by presenting him with a sacrifice called "sacrifice of sin (or "guilt")", called '*āšām* (or *ḥaṭṭāṭ*, this distinction being of a later date). The general form for "atone" is *kippēr* but this term—which doesn't occur in the early texts—would seem to be a loanword from Assyro-Babylonian technical cultic language (< *kuppuru*). To present a sacrifice was called *hiqrīb* (hif. from *qārab*), "to offer" and *hae'ᵃelāh* (hif. from *'ālāh*), "to bring". Corresponding terms found in Ugaritic are *šqrb* (from *qrb*) and *š'ly* (from *'ly*).

That the first-born was sacrificed to Yahwaeh during this period also implied that in some cases human sacrifices, common in Canaan, were offered to Yahwaeh. So in the case of Hiel who is said to have sacrificed his oldest son when rebuilding Jericho (Jos. 6, 26; I Kings 16, 34).

Firstlings, *rēšīṭ* or *bikkūrīm*, were offered not only to the deity but also to the priests and the sanctuaries. They received in that way a considerable part of their income.

Various occasions in the life of man and society were accompanied by a sacrifice or a sacrificial meal. War was introduced in such a way, peace too (I Sam. 7, 7-10; 13, 8-9; Gen. 14, 17-20). All covenant ceremonies were sanctified by the offering of a sacrifice (Gen. 15; 31, 45; Ex. 24, esp. v. 11).

The sacrificial terminology was taken over by the Israelites from Canaan, not only the special kinds of sacrifices they didn't bring with them from nomadic times. The texts from Ugarit have confirmed this view, proposed already before their discovery.

Of the great cultic festivals three of them, Passover, the feast of the Unleavened Bread, and the New Moon days, were of course still observed as a heritage from the semi-nomadic times. To these festivals others were now added. First of them came *ḥag haqqāṣīr*, also called *ḥag šābū'ōṭ*, the (pilgrim) "festival of harvest" or "of Weeks", celebrated seven weeks after *maṣṣōṭ*, the Unleavened Bread. During the autumn there was celebrated the *ḥag hā'āsīf* the (pilgrim) "festival of ingathering" also called *ḥag hassukkōṭ*, the (pilgrim) festival of Booths", the celebration of which fell in the month of Tishri, the month introducing the new year (originally in Būl, the eigth month of the year). This was like *maṣṣōṭ*, *šābū'ōṭ*, a typical agrarian festival. It got its name from the custom to live in huts erected in the vineyards. With this festival was associated the ritual of the Highgod's *hieros gamos*, celebrated in the *sukkāh*, regarded as his marriage chamber. An echo of the practices connected with this festival is found in Judges 21, 19 ff., where it is related how the girls are coming out of Shiloh to the vineyards to dance, participating in the festival. The Sons of Beniamin there unite themselves with the girls of Shiloh, in such a way acquiring wives. Another interesting and important passage is found in Mishnah Ta'aniyyot IV 8, where the young girls in a chorus-song dancing in the *māḥōl*, the dancing ground, invited the young men to contract a marriage in connection with this festival. The festival of *sukkōṭ* was —as we may well understand—characterized of an atmosphere of jubilation, *hillūlīm* (Judg. 9, 27).

The Feast of Booths was as the Festival of the New Year the great festival of the year. Many motifs were associated with this festival, called *ḥæḥāg*, *the* Festival of Pilgrimage, and accordingly implying a pilgrimage from the villages to the local sanctuary. They will be treated in connection with the analysis of the festivals during the period of the united kingdom. That the idea of a renewal of the covenant between Yahwaeh and His people was a dominating idea at this festival seems certain, even if we do not accept the idea that this festival was celebrated only at a (nonexistant) central sanctuary under the (non- existant) leader of a (non-existant) 12 tribes confederacy. Instead we surmise that the festival was celebrated at the various local shrines. A difficult problem is connected with the institution of a day of rest and joy, the seventh day of the week, called *šabbaṭ*. Its origin is highly uncertain and it is possible that its place among the Ten Commandments may be due to a Mosaic origin.

Yahwaeh is holy and everyone and everything dedicated to Him and therefore belonging to Him is holy, *qāḏōš*. The sanctuary was *qōḏæš*, a holy thing, and the priest was *qāḏōš*, holy to his god (Lev. 21, 7). The priests, *kōhᵃnīm*, are called with the name used in Canaan, but it is probable that already the Levites in Mosaic times were so called (= Arabic *kāhin* who could be not only a seer, but also a priest). The levites in this period still preserved their position and the descendant of a house of Levi (ef. I Sam. 2, 27) was priest at the chief sanctuary of the central tribes in Shiloh, his name being Eli. It calls for notice that his both sons carry Egyptian names, Hofni and Pinehas, not theophorous names composed with Yahwaeh.

There were to be found at the sanctuary a great cultic personnel including temple slaves and prostitutes of both sexes. The story of Judah and Thamar throws some light on prevalent conditions (Gen.

38). Also the constant polemics in later times on the side of the prophets clearly demonstrate the role played by the prostitutes, attached to the sanctuaries and high places. Deuteronomy 23, 17 expressly forbids the institution of sacred prostitutes.

In the sanctuary also the oracles of the deity were asked for. The Israelites "sought" Yahwaeh, *biqqēš*, or "asked" him, *dāraš* (I Sam. 9, 9; II Sam. 21,1) in order to get a *tōrāh* from him. The answer from Yahwaeh was chiefly given by the Urim and Tummim, manipulated by the priest who carried them in the efod, obviously a sort of pouch or bag, attached to his breast and making part of the priestly garment (I Sam. 2, 28; 22, 18 ef. I Sam. 14, 3; 23, 9 f.; 30,7 f). The efod was sometimes called *'ēfōd bad*, *bad* designating an oracular priest, a cultic prophet (Is. 44, 25; Jer. 50, 36 used of "false" prophets; Mari *baddum*) who "recited" (Ugarit. *bd*, to sing) his oracular pronouncements. Urim and Tummim as oracular instruments were manipulated by the levites, as the old song Deut. 33, 8 teaches us.

This "technical" manner of communicating the will of the deity went side by side with the oracles given by so-called "profets", *nebī'im*, they might be cultic, i.e. attached to a sanctuary, or not. The prophets were organized in guilds (I Sam. 10, 5 f.; 19,20), living together under the direction of a leader. Samuel in some traditions is depicted as such a prophetical leader (I Sam. 19, 20). Samuel, typically enough was both a prophet and priest (I Sam. 3, 19-21). The prophets could be seen streaming down from a *bāmāh* in an ecstatic procession, proceeded by psalter, tambourine, cither and flute (I Sam. 10, 5). The ecstasy was their dominating characteristic, caused by the Spirit of Yahwaeh, who "jumped" upon them, or the Hand of Yahwaeh, which "seized" them. Music above all was used to call forth this ecstatic state. From the time of the kingdom we learn that their exterior appearance was especially marked by a sign in the front and that they carried a tonsure (I Kings 20, 41; II Kings 2, 23 f.). Their ecstasy was a mighty contagion (I Sam. 10, 5 f.; 19, 18-24).

More quiet were the seers, whose services were sought by the people for various reasons, often rather trivial. The *rō'æh* or *ḥōzæh* possessed the gift to "see" secret and hidden things. The seer may be both priest and prophet, there are no strict borders here. We must assume that this category was found in Israel already before the settlement. Samuel is the most wellknown example of a seer in old Israel. Ultimately they merged with the prophets and in later usage "prophet" and "seer" signifies the same function (Amos 7, 12).

A special category which could be attached to a sanctuary, as Samuel was (I Sam. 1-2), or living outside it as Samson (Judg. 13-16), were the nasiræans, who were subjected to certain taboo regulations: they were not allowed to drink wine, their hair was not cut or razed, and they couldn't touch any dead corpse. The commitment not to drink wine signifies a return to nomadic ideals. The name, *nāzīr*, means that he was dedicated, "promised" to the deity (*nāzar*, a by-form of *nādar*).

All these various categories could be called "men of God" (sg. *'iš* *'ᵉlōhīm*) because they were in constant contact with God, often filled with His Spirit, this also may be a designation from older times (Arabic *ḏū'ilāh*).

There were to the Israelites two distinct spheres, that of holiness and that which was not-holy, profane: *qāḏōš* against *ḥōl, ḥalīl*. Everything belonging to the domain of Yahwaeh was holy: the sanctuary, the cultic servants, the cultic assembly, the sacrifices and other ceremonies, the whole cultic apparatus. Also the festivals and the sabbaths are holy. Holy is everything consecrated to Yahwaeh from the nasir to the warrior, who has consecrated himself to take part in "the wars of Yahwaeh" (I Sam. 18, 17; 25, 28; Num. 21, 14). In these wars of Yahwaeh prisoners and prey were dedicated to the deity, a process called *hæhᵊrim*, to set apart as *ḥēræm*, as holy to Yahwaeh and therefore vowed to destruction. The books of Joshua, Judges and Samuel give many illustrations of this practice, which could mean a wholesale massacre of prisoners (cf. I Sam. 15). The warrior, being a holy person, was subjected to a great many taboos (II Sam. 11, 9-13) and had his hair arranged in a special way (Judges 5, 2: "when in Israel the hairs were growing freely"). All this belongs to an archaic stage of culture.

The blend of Canaanite and Israelite culture led to a syncretistic religion in Israel, often in an unconscious way. The attitude towards Yahwaeh was of course of a various character in various quarters. Some people altogether abandoned the worship of Yahwaeh, they "chose new gods" (Judg. 5, 8). The Sons of Israel abandoned Yahwaeh and served the Ba'alīm, the local Ba'als, the Ba'al worshipped at the many local shrines temples and high places. This Ba'al we know from Canaanite religion as the appellation of the young god, whose proper name was Haddād (cf. above pp. 200). His symbol was the bull, especially the young bull, *'ēgᵊl*, bullock. It is also said in the same passage (Judg. 2, 11-13) that they worshipped Ba'al and the Astartes, the many local forms of 'Astart, the *'aštārōṭ*. This is the extreme form of break with the old religion. It is to be explained by the ancient idea that a country belonged to a certain god (or gods). When Naaman had been cured from his leprosy he asked for some earth to be carried on a couple of mules away to Damascus in order that he might be able to worship Yahwaeh in that city (II Kings 5, 17). And on the other hand David, when driven into exile, complains that accursed people had said to him: "Depart, and serve other gods" (I Sam. 26, 19). When Israel settled down in Canaan they were dependent on Ba'al and Astarte for their well-being, for getting good harvests, rich cattle, and plenty of wine. It was but natural that many turned away from Yahwaeh, the god of Sinai, far away from Canaan.

Other were content to put other gods at the side of Yahwaeh. We find in much later times among the Jews in Egypt, of whom several must have come from Northern Israel, such deities as Betel, Harambetel, 'Ashambetel and 'Anāt worshipped alongside with Yahwaeh (cf. below p. 305). These deities are easy to recognize as Canaanite gods: Behind the names composed of Betel and Haram or Ašam there must be found the High God El (cf. above p. 226). What is startling is the fact that 'Anāt, the Canaanite goddess known from Ugarit was still worshipped in Israel when these Jews left for Egypt.

VI. The Settlement:
Traces of Canaanite Myths in O.T. Literature

Interpretation of what scholars have called Hebrew myths has demonstrated that there once existed in Israel a rich treasure of myths, real, ritual myths, playing a central rōle in the religions system and life of Israel. Here the finds of the Ugaritic epic myths have proved most illuminating, for thanks to the close linguistic affinity between Ugaritic and Hebrew it was possible to show that not only motifs of the same kind, but even whole mythical sequences, of the same or nearly identical wording, had been taken over by the Israelite tribes after their settlement in Canaan. This Canaanite heritage in the majority of cases must have been taken over by the Hebrew invaders when they entered into the possession of the many sanctuaries of worship, as indicated above. However, we also have to count with the possibility of minstrels and story-tellers, mōšᵉlîm, wandering freely from one tribe to another, from one cultic centre to another, reciting and singing stories and songs which later were collected into collections of poems, such as "the Book about the Wars of Yahwaeh" (Num. 21, 14) or "the

Book of the Honest" (Josh. 10, 13; II Sam. 1, 18; I Kings 8, 53 LXX). These songs glorified the national wars fought by the Israelites, but such a passage as Josh. 10, 13 shows that the mythical element not was lacking. More important from our point of view are the fragments of mythical epics still to be discovered in the O.T., e.g. the traditions of creation and paradise as well as about the Great Flood. To what extent these epical traditions have been collected and unified to what has been called "the National Epic of Israel" is still a problem to be investigated.

The Israel of later generations was unfavourably disposed towards myths and why this must be the case we will see in the sequel, but we nevertheless meet with a great many passages in the O.T. containing allusions to cosmological myths. Actually there is rather often a confusion between the O.T. and Israel itself. We must not forget that the O.T. as it is handed down to us, is only one part—we do not even know if the greater part—of Israel's national literature. The references just made to the two last collections of poems is highly instructive as is also the sad loss of the "Chronicles of the Kings of Judah" and the "Chronicles of the Kings of Israel", so often mentioned in the Book of Kings. And, moreover, this preserved part has in many passages quite obviously been exposed to censorship and correspondingly purged. An especially illuminating example concerned with the mythical element in the religion of Israel will be quoted in the following. In such circumstances the remarkable thing is not that there are so few traces left of mythology in the O.T., the remarkable thing is on the contrary that we are still able to detect so *many* traces of myths in the O.T. It surely calls for notice that O.T. poetry *e.g.* has kept intact some ancient Near Eastern myths to a considerably greater extent than its prose narratives. To these poetical parts must, however, be added Genesis, although some arguments would favour the hypothesis that Genesis, as far as its mythical material is concerned, is largely based upon the epic traditions of a mythical character just referred to.

First of all when treating of Israelite myths we should not forget that the descriptions of the appearance of Yahwaeh himself is based upon mythical notions and very often possess a definite mythical-anthropomorphic colouring. Thus we have a number of passages describing God as surrounded by His royal household or His assembly:

El is a terrible master in the great council of the Holy Ones,
and awe-inspiring above all those round about him.

Ps. 89, 8.

Here we note that the God of Israel is called El, a name we met with before and to which we shall return in the following.

These Holy Ones in Ps. 16, 3 too appear as independent, divine beings as in a late prophet, Zech. 14, 5 where we read:

> And Yahwaeh my God, will come,
> all thy Holy Ones with thee.

There are other passages which could be invoked in this connection but we pass to another idea. Just because the Holy Ones constitute the assembly of Yahwaeh He is glorified as unsurpassable among them:

> Who is like thee among the gods, Yahwaeh,
> who is like thee, glorious among the Holy Ones?
>
> Exod. 15, 11.

This passage is especially valuable when compared with Ps. 89, 6 f., where in the two stichoi immediately preceding the already quoted passage it is said:

> The heavens praise thy miracle, Yahwaeh,
> yea, thy faithfulness in the assembly of the Holy Ones.
> For who in the clouds is equal to Yahwaeh,
> can be like to Yahwaeh among the sons of the gods?

Here we can clearly see that "the assembly of the Holy Ones" is the same as "the sons of the gods", i.e. according to usual Hebrew idiom "the gods".

The cosmic perspective present in these hymnal praises of Yahwaeh returns in the so-called Song of Moses where we read in the Hebrew text of TM in translation:

> Rejoice, O ye nations, whith his people!

The LXX gives a more complete text for it has preserved a verse preceding the just quoted one of, the following wording:

> Rejoice, O ye heavens with him
> and let *all the angels of God* worship him!

A manuscript from Qumran, however, gives this passage of Deut. 32, 41 ff. in the original form:

> Rejoice, O ye heavens with him
> and *all ye gods* worship him!

This illustration couldn't be more instructive, for here we can see how LXX has attenuated the original "gods" to "angels of God", whereas the definite Masoretical recension found the whole passage so suspicious that it was blotted out altogether.

The scene depicted in Ps. 82 is very impressive for there God, here called El, is standing in the assembly of the gods, judging them. Yahwaeh is accordingly, as we have seen, the highest god in an assembly of gods, called "the Holy Ones", or "the Holy Ones of God" or "the sons of the gods" or simply "the gods".

This assembly of the Holy Ones, the gods, has been taken over from Canaanite mythology, where we find it in some Phoenician inscriptions and in the Ugaritic texts, where this conception recurs very often. This assembly there too is clearly thought of as being under the leadership of El.

It is well known that Yahwaeh is a god associated above all with storm, lightning and thunder. His epithets or the invocations of him indicate His character, for He is the rider of the clouds, Ps. 68, 5, or "the rider of heavens", Deut. 32, 26, or "the rider on the cloud", Is. 19, 1. With a still stronger mythical colouring it is said that He is riding on the Cherub, a mythical, mixed figure associated with the Ark, II Sam. 22, 11; Ps. 18, 11. In Hab. 3, 8 Yahwaeh is even depicted as borne on His horses. Of these passages Ps. 68, 5 is of considerable interest for the Hebrew expression *rōkēb bā'arābōt* agrees perfectly with the Ugaritic epithet *rkb 'rpt* given to Ba'al. If in this and similar cases we reconstruct the phonetic forms to be assumed in the period from about 1200 to 1000 B.C. the agreement will be still greater.

In the magnificent picture of Yahwaeh's epiphany in Hab. 3, the Canaanite background of which was demonstrated 30 years ago, we read:

> Before Him Pestilence marched,
> and Plague went forth at His feet.

We find here two of the bodyguards of the Israelitic High God, Rasaf and Dabar. Of these Rašaf is a well-known west-Semitic deity, and presumably Dabar is another, minor deity. Other traits too in this description of the epiphany point to a Canaanite background. The same image of Yahwaeh as the thundering and lighting god (Hab. 3, 11) is met with in Ps. 18, 14-15, the Canaanite background of which has long been recognized.

To the retinue of Yahwaeh there also belong other divine beings met with in Canaanite mythology, namely the hypostases Ṣædæq and Mišpāṭ, Šaḥar and Šālēm (Šālōm). The two first beings have their counterparts in the Canaanite Sydyk and Misor (mentioned by Philo Byblius), while Šaḥar and Šlm appear in the same form in Ugarit.

The oft-repeated saying that the monotheistic spirit of Yahwistic religion did not tolerate any mythology, as we have seen, certainly needs qualification. Israelite religion was in older times a rather complex entity, leaving room for the idea of God surrounded by His divine assembly and accompanied by His bodyguards. In this polytheistic trend there was a tendency to express more fully all the richness of divine essence and to get it more concretely visualized.

Yahwaeh originally had his habitation at Sinai as we already have seen. When ultimately Jerusalem was elevated to its position as the capital of Israel—the implications of which will occupy as in the following—He took His seat on Mount Sion. Now this mountain of Sion is explicitly identified with Ṣāfōn in Ps. 48, 3. Here, according to Semitic mythology in the west, the earthly paradise was situated, surrounded by the four paradise rivers which stream forth from below it. The top of this mountain is the seat of God, it is, as it were, His throne. Ṣāfōn plays a central rôle in Ugaritic epics, for here we have the place of the divine assembly where Baʿal is enthroned as a ruler. This mythical geography was taken over by the Israelites.

The Hebrew Paradise story (Gen. 2-3) exhibits the distinctive features of an original myth, though in its new context it has lost much of its original colouring and become somewhat emasculated. There is, however, another description of paradise, preserved in Ezek. 28, where more of the mythical colour is still found. Here we should note the following important points: in the Garden of (the) God(s), situated "on the holy mountain" there was once dwelling a divine being, anointed by God, thus being of royal status. His garment reflects his wonderful nature—for he is also a cherub, a guardian of the garden (cf. Gen. 3, 24)—being set with twelve precious stones, and he was walking in the midst of "stones of fire", i.e. most probably the stars. He was full of wisdom and accomplished in beauty. This garment in the O.T. is said to be worn by the High Priest, but it can be shown that originally it belonged to the ruler (a point taken up in the following, cf. below p. 260).

Primordial Man was conceived of as the guardian of paradise. He is therefore the Gardener *par excellence* and this mythical idea is widely spread, especially associated with royal ideology. That this figure is also a divine being is at least partly explicable from the fact that El in Ugarit is called *ab adm*, "the father of Man (Adam). Adam, Primordial Man is accordingly the son of God (El).

One of the most important traits in West Semitic mythology was God's activity as a creator, manifest in his fight against the Primordial Dragon—the rebellious waters of Primeval Chaos. He split it asunder, creating the world out of its corpse, thus making cosmos out of chaos. This is one of the dominant themes in Ugaritic myths, where the Primordial Dragon is named Lotan (< Lawtan), described as having seven heads and further called *ltn bšn brḥ bšn ʿqltn*, either: Lotan, the *fleeing* serpent, the crooked serpent, or: the primordial (or evil) serpent. This Dragon is rebuked, *gʿr*, by the victorious god, who also conquers his "helpers", his following.

These mythical motifs recur in several O.T. passages. First of all it calls for notice that the Dragon conquered by Yahwaeh here has the same name, Leviathan, described as having several heads (Ps. 74, 14) smashed by Yahwaeh. We also hear of the "helpers" of the Dragon, here called Rahab; there are also other names such as Tehom, "the Deep", Yam, the Sea, Nahar, the River, some of them found in Ugarit.

Yahwaeh too "rebukes", *gāʿar*, the Sea, before drying it up (Nah. 1, 4). Above all it calls for notice that Leviathan is the *nāḥāš bāriᵃḥ* *ʿᵃqallāṭōn*, thus exactly the same terms as used in Ugarit.

The mythical battle in the O.T. is described as ending in Yahwæh's victory over His enemies, followed by His creation of the world (Gen. 1 and many other passages!).

We may leave out another myth of creation, connected with the fertilization of the soil and the creation of earthly Man, where the Canaanite background is likewise easily descernible and may be content with the statement that the whole Creation story in Genesis is thoroughly Canaanite.

Loosely attached to these stories of creation are other myths, now partly extant only in fragments, as e.g. the Fall of the Angels, where the allusions in Genesis recieve a much needed supplementation from the Ethiopic Book of Enoch 6, 1 ff. Especially valuable in this passage is the fact that the angels are located on Mount Hermon, thus furnishing us with a local background of the myth, indicating in this case a Sidonian or Tyrian origin.

All these Canaanite myths in their original setting in life were possessed of a ritual background, they were part of what has been called a "Myth and Ritual pattern". This pattern in the ancient Near East, including the western Semites, has been held to include at least four main themes:

1. The fight against the powers of Chaos.
2. Death and resurrection of the young god.
3. Holy Marriage.
4. Enthronization of the young god on the mountain of gods in the north.

These main mythical motifs found a ritual expression at the great festival of the year, the New Year's festival when they were enacted in a dramatic form.

If the fact that the first motif has been taken over by the Israelites on the soil of Canaan is an undisputable fact, the second and third motifs have been the subject of much discussion and controversy. The *pros et contras* in this case, however, are better understood in the light of the history of political and religious development of the Israelite people after the introduction of kingship, because that institution is intimately bound up with the existence of the whole Myth and Ritual pattern in the ancient Near East.

VII. Period of United Monarchy:
Saul, David and Salomon

The time of the Judges was a period of disintegration of the Israelite tribes, who recognized no capital and no central shrine for all Israel. There was no leader wielding an authority outside his own tribe, except in case of emergency. "In those days there was no king in Israel, every man did what was right in his own eyes" (Judg. 17,6; 21, 25). Endeavours, such as that of Gideon and Abimelek, to create a kingdom had no lasting consequences.

This tribal autonomy led to a serious military and political situation, when about 1175 the so-called "sea peoples" of Aegean origin started a migration, which ultimately brought one of their components, the Philistines, to settle down in the country named after them Palestine. From south of Carmel to the Egyptian border they dominated the coastal plain, but spread also to the territory of Beth-shean in central Canaan and penetrated to the hill-country, possessing a fort at Michmash. The central tribes of Israel, living in these regions, were exposed to violent attacks from the Philistines, who owed their success to their possession not only of chariots of war like the Canaanites, but above all to a superior armament—they brought the new metal, iron, thus introducing the iron age—possibly also to superior military organization and tactics. The stories about the exploits of Samson give an echo of the border warfare between Israelites and Philistines.

The first half of the eleventh century saw a violent pressure of the Philistines against the Israelites. At the sanctuary of Shiloh the Ark was standing at this time (as noted above). From there it was sent to the decisive battle at Eben-ha-ezer, to support the Israelite warriors through the presence of Yahwaeh among His people. But the battle was a crushing defeat of the sons of Israel and—worst of all—the Ark itself was captured by the enemies and carried away to Ashdod, one of the five Philistine cities. It is impossible to date this event with certainty, but it must have occured about 1050. The Philistines now were in control of central Palestine, and the Israelite people from Beth-shean to approximately Bethlehem (II Sam. 23,14) was under strict supervision, partly disarmed, by them. The sanctuary at Shiloh was destroyed by the Philistines, as shown by excavations there.

From this state of things Israel was rescued by Saul, who succeeded in defeating the Philistines and creating a small kingdom in the central part of the country. This was a position somewhere between the so-called Judges and the later kings. Obviously associated with the pro-phetical fraternities Saul himself has been said to be, like the Judges, a "charismatic" leader, exercising his authority thanks to a certain charisma, the gift of Yahwaeh's spirit. At the same time he in many respects introduces a new epoch, with some kind of central adminis-tration and the beginning of a standing army.

The defeat suffered by Saul on the Mount Gilboa means a new period of Philistine hegemony. It didn't last long. David, originally one of Saul's men, who was married with his daughter Mikal, had been suspect to the king for various reasons. It is probable that he was supported by the priest and prophet Samuel, whose real personality is extremely difficult to disentangle from the mass of traditions cluster-ing around him. He was obviously an influential leader of the pro-phetic fraternities, at the same time being a priest.

David was brought to undisputed authority in Southern Israel after the time of Saul's death. The men of the tribe of Judah anointed him as king in Hebron. Meanwhile Saul's surviving son Ishba'al (we note the Ba'al name!) was exercising some authority as king over at least some parts of Israel. However, a series of circumstances paved the way for David, so that after the death of Ishba'al he was duly acknowledged by the elders of Israel as their king. Both Ishba'al and David were the vassals of the Philistines, but during his time in Hebron David started his wars against them, after a series of victories over them and other neighbouring peoples leading to the creation of a small empire. He controlled the inland territories, it is stated, from Qadesh, on the river Orontes in Syria, to Ezion-geber at the Gulf of Aqaba. Also the territories and tribes of Transjordan acknowledged his suzerainty. A central administration and a standing army were created. Israel entered international politics as a very considerable power, the strongest among the Semites of the West.

The most decisive step, however, was the choice of a new capital. David succeeded in conquering Jerusalem from the Jebusites and transferred his government to this place and constructed there his palace. He added considerably to his already respectable harem. And, most important of all, he transferred the Ark to Jerusalem from Qiryat-yearim, where it had its place after its stay in Ashdod (I Sam. 7,1).

By choosing Jerusalem as his capital and calling it the "City of David" the king had given himself an intermediate position between Israel and Judah. He was anointed king over both the Northern and the Southern tribes, but his capital with its immediate territory was his own. Here he established the central sanctuary of Yahwaeh by transferring to Jerusalem the Ark and all other cultic apparel. However, he had to acknowledge the fact that Jerusalem already had its own city-god, the mighty El 'Elyōn, "God the Highest", figuring in the tradition about Abraham and Melchizedeq. The notion of ṣædæq, righteousness, actually was especially associated with Jerusalem, its king at the time of the conquest being one Adonizedeq (Josh. 10,1). The priest appointed by David to be one of his two priests was Zadok, the son of Ahitub. But David already had another priest, Abiathar, the son of Abimelek (the names must change place II Sam. 8,17), who had accompanied him and brought the ephod to him (I Sam. 23,6). It has been surmised that Zadok was the last priest-king of Jerusalem, who had been given, or rather kept, his position as a priest (of David) as a compensation. It is important to observe that it is Zadok who is in charge of the Ark, not Abiathar (II Sam. 15, 24-29). This fact shows him to be the more influential of the two priests. But it should be noted that there is no real high priest. Another fact calling for notice is that sons of David were priests too (II Sam. 8,18).

When David sent and brought the Ark up to Jerusalem from Qiryat-yearim he himself acted as chief priest, playing the central role in all the cultic ceremonies. Dressed in the priestly ephod (perhaps already now the elaborate garment later worn by the high-priest) he carried out the necessary sacrifices, he danced before the Ark a whirling cultic dance, and he placed the Ark in the tent, which he had pitched for it—obviously the ancient "Tent of Assembly". The whole ceremony was concluded by David's sacrificing burnt-offerings of thanksgiving, and blessing the people in the name of Yahwaeh, thus reciting the blessings, which were in later times the prerogative of the High Priest (II Sam. 6).

It was but natural that David had the intention to build a temple for Yahwaeh as a manifestation of his own glory and as a tribute to his god. But his court prophet Nathan, closely attached to the king during his whole life, told him that Yahwaeh had refused him this undertaking, for Yahwaeh had sojourned in a tent and not in a house, thereby indicating Yahwaeh's nomadic nature. Nathan must have been associated with the reactionary tendencies represented by the Rechabites (cf. below). But the refusal is coupled with a solemn promise: to the king who wanted to build a house to Yahwaeh, to him Yahwaeh will build a house, i.e. establish a dynasty. And the son to be born to David will build the temple. This oracle is given in a poetical form, but as the whole chapter is preserved in a late redaction it is not always easy to reconstruct the original wording of it. However, the oracle said:

> Thy house and kingdom shall stand firm,
> Forever in my sight,
> Thy throne shall be established for ever.
> II Sam. 7, 16

The whole oracle has been the starting point of several prophecies, included in royal psalms glorifying the Davidic dynasty (cf. below) and promising a future full of happiness. They introduce a theme which plays a great role in later prophecies about the Davidic king as the ideal ruler, a theme we shall return to, as it is one of the most important ideas of Israelite-Jewish religion (cf. below p. 283f.).

In spite of the fact that David, as we have seen, was an enthusiastic worshipper of Yahwaeh it has been surmised that for political reasons he had to pay regard to the mighty city-god of Jerusalem, El 'Elyōn. Attention has been drawn to the fact that of the sons born to David in Jerusalem (II Sam. 5, 14-16) not less than four posses names composed with El, one, Solomon has a name alluding to Šālem, the epithet of El 'Elyōn, and another, Nathan, a hypocoristicon which probably in its fuller form was Nathanael, "El has given". There is another hypocoristicon Yibchar, which also may be composed with El, meaning "El chooseth". The absence of Yahwaeh-names is indeed most remarkable, especially against the background of the fact that of his sons born to him in Hebron there is not a single name composed with El (Abshalom need not mean anything but "the (divine) Father is Peace"); but on the other hand of six sons there are at least two carrying Yahwaeh-names (II Sam. 3, 2-5). This fact would seem to indicate that David accepted El ʿElyōn as the highest god, the god of the country, the overlord of the gods as he was of old, while still worshipping Yahwaeh as his own god, the deity of his family, of his tribe and of the people of Israel. In the cult-lyrics of Israel, as preserved in the Book of Psalms, Yahwaeh is gloryfied as El ʿElyōn, a fact showing that a syncretistic process had set in, ultimately leading to an identification between Yahwaeh and ʿElyōn. Another, short name of ʿElyōn was ʿAl, testified in Amoritic proper names, and it has been made probable that some of the polemics of the early prophets were directed against him. The syncretistic process—if this is true—did not pass unnoticed then.

The later years of David's reign were marked by dissension and revolt. Intrigues of court and harem had the succession of the ageing king in view. Two parties ultimately faced each other: Solomon, supported by his mother Bathseba (whom David had taken from one of his officers, Uriah, whom he ordered his commander-in-chief Joab to have killed in battle, for which crime David was rebuked by his prophet Nathan), the priest Zadok, the prophet Nathan, and Benayahu, the commander of the royal guard, had as their adversaries Adoniyah, after the death of Ammon and Abshalom probably the oldest surviving of the sons born to David in Hebron, the priest Abiathar, and the old commander-in-chief Joab. Solomon, with the support of "the new men" succeeded in gaining the throne. The leaders of the opponents were murdered with the exception of Abiathar, who was exiled to his estate in Anatot. This meant the exit of the "conservative" party. The case of Joab is instructive, because he had taken refuge to the tent of Yahwaeh and seized the horns of the altar. Nevertheless Solomon ordered the hesitating Benayahu to stab him, in the midst of the sanctuary—a flagrant crime against all laws of asylum and sacred customs.

VIII. Temple, Cultus and religious Syncretism

After his succession to his father (about 960 B.C.) Solomon in the fourth year of his reign (I Kings 6,1,37) started to build the temple, which was "finished in the eleventh year in the moon Būl (the eighth month)". The dedication was celebrated by the king, acting like David as the high priest, offering immense sacrifices (of course exaggerated in the present, late redaction of the text) and reciting the blessing of the people, pronounced by him from a tribune (II Chron 6, 13). In this case again we note that the high-priestly blessing is spoken by the king. The Ark was introduced into the shrine of the house, where Yahwaeh now was to have his habitation. The king spoke at this occasion the following poem (I Kings 8, 12-13):

> Yahwaeh said, he would dwell in the dense-cloud.
> Built indeed have I an exalted house for thee,
> a place for thy dwelling forever.

In the Ark were placed, according to a later notice, the two Tablets of the Law (I Kings 8,9), but this notice cannot be valid for the time of Solomon. The inauguration of the temple in accordance with the dates given (I Kings 6,37; 8,2) was celebrated at the Sukkōt festival, the New Year's Festival. We may assume some processional hymns to have been sung at this occasion, of the type found in the Psalter (Psalms 47-48, 96-98), glorifying the enthronement of Yahwaeh on Mount Sion. The chorus says: "Yahwaeh is king, "*Yahwæh mālak*! His kingship is praised and it is emphasized that he is more mighty than all gods. Important is the exhortation in Ps. 47, 1-2:

> Clap your hands, all ye peoples,
> shout to Yahwaeh with voice of jubilation!
> For Yahwaeh, the Most High, is to be feared,
> a great King over all the earth.

In this hymn we accordingly find Yahwaeh glorified as Yahwaeh 'Elyōn. This means that the syncretistic process has come to an end. 'Elyōn is no longer the overlord. He is indeed nobody else than Yahwaeh, being completely identified with him as the Highest God among all gods. The process by which identification has been possible for the most part escapes us, but we can observe that not only in Gen. 14, but also in such ancient texts as Deut. 32, 8 and Num. 24, 16 (Song of Bileam) 'Elyōn is still an individual deity and not an epitheton of Yahwaeh. Remarkable and significant is the absence of 'Elyōn in the desert traditions. He is obviously attached to the country of Canaan. Especially interesting is Deut. 32, 8, for here 'Elyōn is giving the people of Jacob as inheritance to Yahwaeh, as we pointed out many years ago (extant translations misunderstand this text, which in v. 8b has to be corrected after the LXX):

When the Most High made the peoples an inheritance,
when he separated the sons of Adam,
He set the territories of the peoples,
according to the number of the Sons of God,
For the portion of Yahwaeh is His people,
Jacob the lot of His inheritance.

Israel is accordingly the inheritance of Yahwaeh, for it was given to him as His inheritance, when God the Most High once portioned out the peoples to the various gods in his assembly. Israel, the inheritance of Yahwaeh, this is a very important notion which is found in many passages (Deut. 4,20; 9, 26,29; Ps. 28, 9; 74,2; 78, 62; 71, 79, 1; 94, 5; 14; 106, 5, 40). A late development of this idea is the position of the archangel Michael as the special protector of the people of Israel. Michael has now inherited the position once accorded to Yahwaeh, as the protector of His inheritance, His own people Israel.

The division between the god of the country and the tribal or personal god, in the formulas of the Ancient Near East was marked out in that way that the highest god was introduced only by name, but the subordinate deity received the qualification "thy god". It is really remarkable that Saul in his address to Samuel speaks of "Yahwaeh, thy God". Here obviously an older formula is used (I Sam. 15, 30).

The temple was built by Solomon after the pattern of the Syrian-Palestinian temple as we know it from excavations. The temple was called *bēṯ Yahwæh*, the House of Yahwaeh, or *bēṯ hā'ælōhīm*, the House of God, as in Ugarit it was called *bt il* (corresponding to Bethel) or *bht 'nt*, the House(s) of 'Anāt. It comprised three parts: a vestibule, called the *'ēlām*, a main room, *hēḵāl*, or "Holy Place", and *debīr*, the "Holy of Holies". The measures of the temple were the following: The vestibule was 20 cubits long and 10 cubits broad, the "Holy" was 40 cubits long and 20 cubits broad. The most interesting measures we find in the "Holy of Holies", for it was 20 cubits long, 20 cubits broad and 20 cubits high, thus forming a square. The names of the *'ēlām* and *hēḵāl* derive ultimately from Mesopotamia (*illamu and ēkallu*), but at least *ḥēkāl* is found in Ugarit and Phoenicia too, *ḥkl*. The name of *dᵉëïr* is probably Canaanite (loanword in Egyptian: *dbᵓr*, Copt. *tabir*) too. The measures of the *dᵉbïr* indicate that it was (like in Mesopotamia) a symbol of the square of heaven. Of a square form was also the altar, where burnt-offerings were given to the godhead. It was constructed of three square levels, the lowest 16 cubits, the middle 14 cubits, and the highest 12 cubits. The lowest was based on a platform, called "the bosom of the earth", *ḥeq hāᵓāræṣ*, while the highest part had the much discussed name of *harᵓēl* or *ᵓarᵓēl*. The latter form is probably the correct one (*arallu* in Mesopotamia), but it was later interpreted as "Mountain of God", i.e. *harᵓēl* (= the *siqurat* in Mesopotamia). Both the Hebrew name of *ḥeq hāᵓāraes* and the (originally Accadian) term *ᵓarᵓēl* indicate the symbolical connections of the temple foundation with the nether world.

The tribune from which Solomon, as we have seen, recited his blessing in his capacity of high-priest, was called *kiyōr* being a square of 5 cubits, possessing a height of 3 cubits (II Chron. 6, 12-13). In this case too, there is ultimately Mesopotamian symbolism, which explains its name and function. The name is *ki-ur* (in Sumerian), meaning "the entrance into the nether world (in Accadian *nērib erṣeti*).

Another cosmic symbol is the so-called "Sea", *yam*, with a diameter of 10 cubits and a height of 5 cubits (I Kings 7, 23-26). This huge vase corresponds to the *apsū* found in Mesopotamian temples, a symbol of the sweet-water ocean. But the term *apsū* itself is found in Hebrew too, especially in the expression *ᵓap̄sē ᵓæræṣ*, the ends of the earth (because the ocean surrounds the earth and thus marks its end).

The two pillars Jakin and Boaz have been the subject of much speculation, both as to their names and as to their function. The readings of the LXX in this case would seem to have preserved more authentic traditions, reading Ἰαχούμ and Βάλας, providing the meaning "May he be firm" and "Baʿal is strong", two designations probably introduced by the Phoenician worksmen, who constructed the temple (I Kings 5; 7, 13 ff.), for it is said that the Tyrian artisan Hiram gave them these names (I Kings 7,21).

Not only the temple itself was characterized by a rich symbolism with mythical associations, but also the place of the temple possessed its cosmic significanse. It was situated on Mount Sion, which was looked upon as the *ṭabbūr* (Ezek. 28,12), the "Navel" of the earth, this also an ancient conception in Mesopotamia, for there the holy city was called *rikiṣ mātāti*, "the umbilical cord of the countries". This is actually the centre of the world, where in myth the mountain of the gods, with Paradise, Tree of Life, and Water of Life, is situated. The temple therefore has a garden, a well and a sacred tree, as cultic correspondences of these mythic conceptions. That the temple in Jerusalem was conceived of in the same manner, this is amply proved by a reference to Ezek. 47,9 12 where the prophet speaks of the water of life and the trees of life (cf. also Revel. 22,2).

The Tree of Life had another cultic symbol in the seven-branched candlestick, which was first in use in the temple. This is a symbolical representation of the Tree of Life, its shape showing remarkable agreement with ancient Mesopotamian pictures. This rather realistic shape of a tree has obviously been preserved to the very last, as shown by the picture of Titus' triumphal procession.

If we add to all this the two huge cherubs, 10 cubits high and with a breadth of their wings of 10 cubits, both entirely overlaid with gold, the venerable Ark, the symbol of the presence of the Deity in the Holy of Holies, we may understand that the temple was not only a beautiful specimen of sacral architecture and resplendent of gold, overlaid with gold everywhere as it was, it was above all extremely rich in cosmic symbolism and mythical associations. But this symbolism and these associations were Canaanite, not Israelite. Therefore it may well be that the temple of Solomon only gradually won the place in the heart of the Israelite people, which we gather from the Psalms that it must have possessed.

This temple must have demanded a great priesthood and many cultic servants, but we do not learn in the O.T. anything about Solomon's organization of the temple service. Only, that he himself three times a year sacrificed burnt-offerings and sacrifices of thanksgiving to Yahwaeh on the altar he had built, as well as burning incense before "the face of Yahwaeh" (I Kings 9, 25).

This expression probably does not mean that there was any cultic image of Yahwaeh to be found in the temple. This and other expressions of a similar kind ("Thy wings") found in the Psalms presumably indicate the symbolical presence of the deity in temple. This does not mean that there were no images at the local shrines. There certainly were, e.g. at Dan (Judg. 17-18). But we have no indications, that there were images representing Yahwaeh in the Jerusalem temple. On the other hand other plastic representations of divine beings were found there, as the cherubs, but above all the image called Nehushtan. That was a snake, made of copper, the existence of which was motivated by its introduction by Moses, obviously an aetiological legend invented in order to render its worship legitimate, because serpent-worship or rather worship of a serpent as a symbol of the deity was characteristic of Canaan.

Another cult-image was the *pæsæl hā'ªšērāh*, "the statue of the Ashera", the Canaanite goddess Aširat, whose cult-symbol—carrying the same name—we already have met with (cf. above p. 239). This image was, at least in the later preexilio time, standing in the House of Yahwaeh (I Kings 15, 13; II Kings 18,4 compared with II Kings 21, 3,7), and the repeated failures to abolish this practice shows its place in worship to have been firm. The goddess was indeed the consort of the highest god El and must have enjoyed high reputation.

Another Canaanite female deity was also worshipped in Jerusalem from the days of Solomon, the goddess 'Aštart (I Kings 11, 5). In theory, but probably not in practise, she was distinguished from Aširat. Both, together with 'Anāt, were only differentiated manifestations of the same type of the Semitic Mothergoddess.

Solomon is also accused of having constructed high-places for Kemosh, the god of the Moabites, and for Milkom, the god of Ammon (I Kings II, 5, 7), probably more for political, than for religious reasons, because he was their overlord.

The House of Yahwaeh was essentially the habitation of God, who was thought to have His dwelling there, though on principle He was not restricted to one place, but still had many local shrines where he was worshipped.

When the Davidic king officiated in the cult of the Jerusalem temple he was in all probability dressed in the richly elaborated priestly garment, full of symbolical allusions (cf. above p. 249 on Hesek. 28), which was later to become the cultic robe of the high priest (cf. Exod. 39).

IX. Aspects of the Myth and Ritual pattern

We left the so-called "Myth and Ritual pattern" by stating that it has been a matter for dispute, whether the death and resurrection of the young god and his holy marriage were ever celebrated in Israel. Now, having seen to what extent religious syncretism had gained the upper hand in Jerusalem, the capital of the united monarchy, we may proceed to an investigation of the second mythical theme, while postponing the treatment of the third motif, holy marriage, to a later occasion (cf. below p. 272).

In the Psalms we find descriptions of the situation, prevailing when the sanctuary of Yahwaeh has been destroyed. While the background of Ps. 78 is clearly Northern Israel, with Shiloh as its sanctuary, Ps. 79 is concerned with Jerusalem, Ps. 74 being more difficult to locate. Ps. 78, 61, 65-66 occupies indeed a place in the focus of our interest, for there the mythic situation is described, when God's wrath causes His whole people to be delivered up into the hands of the enemies, the "state of chaos" as it is called with reference to the myth and ritual pattern, cf. Ps. 78, 61 and vv. 62-64. But when the visitation is at its most terrible, then the situation is suddenly completely changed:

> Adonai awaked like a sleeper,
> like a hero, overcome with wine.
> He smote his adversaries backward,
> an everlasting shame he made them.
>
> Ps. 78, 65-66

While the "state of chaos" is reigning on earth, and above all in the courtyard of the temple, the god is slumbering the heavy sleep of death. In this case also the epithet *gibbōr*, hero, is given to Adonai —this name is the Canaanite Adōn, Lord—for "hero" is the epithet associated with the young god, who like a hero sets out for battle, when descending into the nether world. We find accordingly in Ps. 78, 65-66 a description of Yahwaeh as emerging from his stay in the netherworld, depicted as a sleep. It should be noted that the two Hebrew expressions for "to sleep" and "to awake" exactly correspond to those used of the Tyrian Ba'al of Carmel in I Kings 18, 19 ff. (on which passage cf. below p. 268), *yāšan* and *yqṣ*.

Against the background of Ps. 78 we are in a position to understand another mythical passage in the Psalms, where Yahwaeh is exhorted to arise and take vengeance on his enemies:

> Arise, oh Yahwaeh, in Thine anger,
> lift Thyself up in outbursts of rage against mine adversaries,
> and awake, oh my God,
> judgement Thou hast commanded!
> May the congregation of peoples surround Thee,
> and Thou above it, return to the height.
>
> Ps. 7, 7-8.

The leading themes are perfectly clear. First we have the awakening and the arising of the deity. Secondly we meet with the idea that God

is surrounded by the congregation of the peoples. Thirdly we have
the notion that Yahwaeh, enthroned on this congregation, returns to
the height, where He has His throne (Ṣāfōn in Ps. 48, 3). All these
three themes are well-known mythical motifs in the Ugaritic epics. In
this case too, linguistic parallels call for notice. The Hebrew *mārōm*,
height, corresponds to the Ugaritic *mrym*, just as the Hebrew *šūḇ*,
return, appears in the Ugaritio *ṯb* (tha same verb), and the peoples,
leʾummīm, have their correspondence in Ugaritic *lʾimm*. Finally we
note the technical meaning of the verb *ʿālā*, ascend, used of Yahwaeh.
It has its exact equivalent in Ugaritic *ʿly*, used of Baʿal, when he
"ascends" to the height of Ṣāfōn, the North.

The motif of the awakening of God returns in other passages, of
which the most profitable for our main theme certainly is Ps. 44:

> Awake! Why dost thou sleep, oh Adonai?
> Wake up! Do not reject for ever!
> Why dost thou hide thine face,
> forgettest our misery and our tribulation?
>
> Ps. 44, 24-25.

Here again we have an allusion to a cultic situation, where the deity
is sleeping the sleep in the nether world, having thus withdrawn from
his temple. The praying community feels itself deserted by the godhead. In this case too the Canaanite name Adonai is used.

Polemic on the side of the prophets has been directed against the
adaption of such Canaanite motifs, for Habakkuk says 2, 19:

> Woe to him who says to the tree: Wake up!
> Awake! to the silent stone.

A ritual background is furnished by the formula "Yahwæh liveth",
as a cry of triumph coming from the mouth of the praying Davidic
king in Ps. 18, 47, where he rejoices that Yahwæh has given him victory over his enemies. This is the next act in the cultic drama: God
has awakened and like a hero is gone to battle against the enemies of
Israel. The political situation as always in ancient Near Eastern religion is seen as a concrete illustration of the cultic actions. This cry
of jubilation, *ḥay Yahwæh*, agrees perfectly with the jubilant outburst
in Canaanite religion: *ḥy ʾlʾyn bʿl*, "Aliyan Baʿal liveth", when the dead
god returns from his stay in the nether world. It calls for notice that
Ps. 18 is one of the Hebrew psalms most filled with Canaanite expressions.

There are other passages, where the same formula recurs. In one of his attacks on the syncretistic cult in Northern Israel the prophet Hoshea says:

> Yes, do not come to Gilgal,
>> and do not ascend to Beth-Awen,
>>> and do not swear: "Yahwaeh liveth".
>>>> Hosh. 4, 15

The prophet thus declines the use of this Canaanite formula. In this connection we may also refer to the bitter irony found in the prophecies of Amos, who rebukes the maidens and young men,

> who swear by the "guilt" of Samaria,
>> and say: Thy god liveth, oh Dan,
>> yes, thy darling liveth, oh Beer-sheba",
>> they will fall and not rise up again.
>>> Amos 8, 14.

The point is that these virgins and young men, who raise the triumphant cry that their god is living, as a guarantee for their own life, they will fall down for thirst and not rise again, although they think that their god has arisen, is living and gives them plenty of water by sending the rain. We may compare here Hos. 6, 1-3 too.

We cannot analyze all passages of relevance in this connection (e.g. I Sam. 26, 16; Zeph. 2, 8-9; Jer. 12, 16; 14, 8-9; Hiob 19, 25), but shall instead refer to an important moment in the life of David already mentioned, namely his bringing up the Ark to Jerusalem. Reproached by his wife Mikal that by dancing, dressed only in the ephod, he has shamelessly uncovered himself he answers (text reconstructed after the versions of LXX, Ms. Vercellone, and Vulgate):

> Before Yahwaeh I dance,
>> Yahwaeh liveth, He who hath chosen me...
> I dance and I play before Yahwaeh.
>> II Sam. 6, 21.

Here we find that David at this moment of the festival, the date of which unfortunately is unknown to us, expresses his joy that Yahwaeh is living, and therefore is dancing and playing. Why should he be glad that Yahwaeh is living? Because Yahwaeh with His ark has returned from His staying far away from the king and His people. It is as God were returning from His stay in the land of the enemies—and actually His returning from there had not been appropriately celebrated. It is significant that the *TM* has blotted out the essential thing here, the cult-cry "Yahwæh liveth", obviously because it has taken offense at it.

In this case we meet with the cultic jubilation, expressed by means of the verb *śāḥaq*, found also in Ugaritic *ṣḥq*. "Play" is only an inadequate translation of this verb, which definitely has also a sexual connotation. It marks one of the two points of culmination of the festival: the joy over the god's return to life after his stay in the nether world, in the grip of his enemies. The other, the opposite point of culmination, is the weeping, *bākā*. There is another couple of opposite verbs, namely "seeking" and "finding". One seeks the disappeared, because dead, god, and one finds him, when he returns to life. Here the two verbs in Ugaritic are *bqṭ*, to seek, and *mġy*, to find. These two expressions have their correspondences in Hebrew in the two verbs *biqqēš* and *māṣā'*. The Hebrew verb *bākā* is of course the same as Ugaritic *bky*.

The allusions to a ritual weeping and laughing found in the O.T. are generally so intertwined that it is difficult to isolate them from each other. Passages including both jubilation and sorrow are e.g. Hos. 10, 5-8 and Ps. 126, 4-6. This psalm has been invoked as a cultic reminiscence of the mythical situation, depicted in the Ugaritic texts (with its presupposed jubilation over the resurrection, as it is told in another context):

> Restore, Yahwaeh, our fate like that of the streams in Negeb!
>> They that sow in tears, they reap with jubilation.
> Weeping he goeth forth, bearing the bag of seed,
>> he cometh home with jubilation, bearing his sheaves.

We cannot pass in review all the O.T. passages of relevance in this connection, but must be content to refer to Hos. 10, 5; Judges 11, 30-40 (Jepthah's daughter); Micah 1, 10; Isa 15, 1-9; 16, 7-12; 17, 10-11; Jer. 9,9; 50, 5.

Very significant is the exhortation in Joel 1, 8, in the midst of the catastrophes in nature, implying a terrible vastation of all fields and vine-yards:

> Lament like a virgin, sackcloth-girt,
>> for the husband of her youth.

Here we meet with the terms *beṭūlāh* and *ba'al ne'ūraehā*, both reminiscent of the Ugaritic texts, where we have *b'l* and *btlt* as the two partners in the holy couple. The whole book of Joel is full of such reminiscences, as has been shown in recent years. Especially striking is the fact that in O.T. lamentation texts the lack of rain is so often alluded to, and that the withering away of plants is so often mentioned (cf. Joel 1-2; Jer. 9, 9, and Is. 15, 6).

According to the myth and ritual pattern, however, the death of the young god is characterized also by the fact that he has deserted his city and temple, which are left in a "state of chaos". When treating of some passages in the Psalms this theme was expressly noted. By referring to this motif it is possible to place the ritual weeping for the god in a wider perspective. In the Psalms, in the collection called "Lamentations", as well as in Isa. 24-27 we find many such motifs. The question *when* this ritual mourning for the deity took place in Israel will be treated in connection with the problem of the holy marriage as a ritual, once celebrated in Israel (cf. below p. 272f.).

There were still in late post-exilic times a category of cultic servants, who used to recite the verse Ps. 44,24:

Awake! Why dost thou sleep, oh Adonai?

The existence of these "Awakeners", *m^e'ōr^erim*, as a special category is expressly stated in rabbinic sources (Tosefta Sotah XIII 9; T Jer Sotah IX 11, 24a; T Babli Sotah 48a) and is in itself an interesting fact, because testifying to the ritual use of this verse, which was accordingly taken in a literal, *not a figurative* sense. Still more interesting and important is the fact that the Hasmonæn High Priest Johanan abolished the "Awakeners". This abolishment has been explained because of its resemblance to the Egyptian ceremony at the opening of the temple in the morning, when the god was invoked with the words: "Awake in peace!" Johanan, it is said, apparently abolished the ceremony of the "Awakeners" singing Ps. 44, 24, because it sounded like a pagan service. This may be so. It may also be that there in some circles from of old had been opposition against the ceremony, because it sounded like a repetition of the Canaanite ritual for the awakening of the god Adonis, slumbering in the sleep of death. Adonis was intensely worshipped in Hellenistic times, so Johanan at very close quarters had an illustration of what the "Awakeners" really meant. The whole affair is highly instructive, for it shows that in spite of repeated abolishments of Canaanite practices in the temple there nevertheless remained for a long time some of such customs in the temple-service.

X. Period of Divided Monarchy:
Northern Israel, Syncretism and Reaction

Already during the reign of Solomon signs of dissatisfaction had
not been lacking. His building activities had demanded much forced
labour and heavy tributes. Central administration menaced both the
tribal customs of Israel and the feudal trends of Canaan. The Northern
tribes especially felt themselves pushed into the background. The head
of the malcontents was an Ephraimite, Jeroboam, one of the king's
officials. There was some kind of revolt on his side—easily crushed—
whereupon he fled to Egypt. After the death of Solomon he was
recalled by his compatriots and turned up at Shechem, where the
assembly of Israel was called for a diet. The fact that the assembly met
at Shechem, and not at Jerusalem, shows that the Northern tribes had
the upper hand, the capital obviously still being regarded as little
representative and looked upon as the Davidic king's private property.
At Shechem the final result of the negotiations was complete dis-
rupture—Israel, including ten tribes, and Judah, supported only by
Beniamin, went different ways. Rehabeam, Solomon's son was king
in Judah, whereas Jeroboam was elected king over Israel (I Kings 12,
18-20). This took place around the year 925 B.C.

Jeroboam, who took his seat at Shechem, carried on the traditions
of the charismatic leaders, the so-called "Judges". The kings of Israel
were designated, like once Saul and David, by an oracle from Yahwæh,
given by a prophet, and elected by the people, no dynasty comparable
to the Davidic family ever being established. When Jeroboam had
seized power he was confronted with the serious problem of providing
his people with something comparable to the impressive temple in
Jerusalem (with its venerable Ark possessed of Mosaic traditions), in
order to prevent his subjects from undertaking a pilgrimage to that
city and get attached to its sanctuary—and in that way to Judah.
Political reasons above all must have induced him to certain measures,
in order to make the shrines of Israel more attractive. We are told that
he erected two bulls of gold as cult-images, at Bethel in the south and
Dan in the utmost north. The original cult-legend ascribed their
origin to Mosaic times, but the priesthood in Jerusalem perverted this
legend into the tendentious story in Exod. 32 of how the rebellious
people induced Aaron to fabricate a golden calf, which was afterwards
duly destroyed. It is important to note the perfect agreement of Exod.

32, 4: "This is, oh Israel, thy God who has brought thee up from the land of Egypt", referring to the golden calf, and the words ascribed to Jeroboam concerning his two cult-images. Exod. 32 shows the theriomorphous idol to be a representation of the deity, and not, as has been argued, only the pedestal of the deity. The young bull, *'ēgæl*, is chosen because of the ancient symbol of Ba'al, called *'gl* in the Ugaritic texts. Since the time of the settlement there was a syncretistic tendency to identify Ba'al and Yahwæh (cf. above p. 244). Jeroboam celebrated his cultic reforms by means of instituting a pilgrim festival at Bethel on the 15th of the eight month, nothing but the ancient New Year festival, which he probably celebrated at its old regular date (I Kings 12, 32). At this occasion the King officiated as high priest, ascending the altar to burn incense to Yahwæh. What in all this is difficult to explain, is the choice of the two sanctuaries (but if Dan is a later addition, then only Bethel). While having his residence at Shechem, where the tribes had their diet and where there was a sanctuary of great reputation, he nevertheless preferred Bethel as his chief sanctuary. This may be due to the fact that this shrine already had got the name of the ancestor Jacob attached to it, where according to the now current traditions God had revealed himself to the patriarch (Gen. 28, 11-22). Accordingly—it has been surmised—Bethel must have been the chief sanctuary of Ephraim, the tribe of the King!

After a series of mostly bloody usurpations the power was at last seized by Omri, one of the great rulers in Israel, as testified by the Assyrian annals, which call the kingdom "the House of Omri", *bīt Ḥumri*. He conquered Moab, as we learn from the Moabite inscription of Mesha. But of all Omri's great deeds the Judean author of the Book of Kings has nothing to tell us—a striking illustration of how fragmentary and tendentious are the notices given there, when political history is concerned. But we may be sure that religious history is treated in a way at least equally tendentious.

Omri transferred his seat of government from Tirza, to which place it had been moved by Jeroboam, to Samaria, which he rebuilt and enlarged. His heir Achab, also a very capable monarch, married Jezebel, the daughter of Ittoba'al, ruler of Tyre. For his queen he built a shrine to Ba'al at Samaria, including an Asherah as the god's consort. This was not more and not less than what Solomon did for his foreign wives, and meant no desertion of Yahwæh on the side of Achab; actually all his children bore Yahwæh-names. However, there are hints of violence on the part of his queen against the more enthusiastic worshippers of Yahwaeh (I Kings 18, 4, 13; 19, 10, 14), but these notices are embedded in historical legends of highly uncertain reliability.

The most fanatical champions of the case of Yahwaeh were found in the prophetical fraternities (cf. above for Samuel p. 243), representatives of whom now dominate the scene. Organized more or less on a military basis, absolutely obedient to their leader, they constituted a real political factor, not only a religious one, in Northern Israel. The orally transmitted legendary traditions of such "Sons of the Prophets" $b^e n\bar{e}$ $hann^e b\hat{i}'\hat{i}m$ (= simply: prophets), constitute one of the sources of the Book of Kings. In these tales of a very popular character the two great leaders of such prophetical fraternities, Eliyah and Elisha, and their exploits are glorified. The king must have fully seized the importance of such fraternities (I Kings 18, 17 he reproaches Eliyah for "disturbing Israel"), because he kept at his court not less than 400 such prophets, meaning 8 companies of each 50 members (I Kings 22, 6 compared with I Kings 18, 4, 13; I Kings 18, 19). They were dressed in a special way, had tonsure and special marks on their body. In ecstatic frenzy they were capable of astonishing achievements.

There occured in the time of Achab a violent clash between such Yahwistic prophets, represented by Eliyah, and the Ba'al prophets, organized probably on the same lines, being an ancient Canaanite institution (exstatic Canaanite prophecy is met with in the relation of Wenamun, cf. above p. 215).

There was in Achab's reign a terrible drought (this fact is attested from Phoenician history, cf. Josephus, Antiq. VIII 13, 2), lasting for a year. To Eliyah and the real Yahwaeh-worshippers this meant that Yahwaeh had withdrawn from His people, being offended by the Ba'al-worship. In order to challenge the Tyrian Ba'al and to demonstrate the superiority of Yahwaeh Eliyah obtained the king's permission to have a trial of strength between Yahwaeh and Melkart, the Tyrian Ba'al (there can be no other Ba'al, the hypothesis that an unnamed local Ba'al is concerned is gratuitous and lacks motivation: Two *great* gods measured their strength!). The mountain of Carmel is chosen as the place of contest, for here there had been an altar to Yahwaeh, which had been pulled down (I Kings 18, 30). Yahwaeh accordingly had to show His might, in order to regain his lost shrine. The Ba'al prophets in spite of lashing themselves with swords and spears, according to their custom, did not succeed in bringing their god to activity. Eliyah's mocking words show the author of the story to be well acquainted with Canaanite mythology—it is necessary to wake up the sleeping god, sleeping, because the drought is a sign that Baʿal is dead and slumbering in the Nether world (as we learn from the Ugaritic texts), which causes burning heat and drought in nature. When Baʿal is alive the wadis flow again with water. Yahwaeh on the other hand sends fire from heaven consuming the burnt-offering given to Yahwaeh by Eliyah. The assembled people cries a confession to Yahwaeh as God: "Yahwaeh, He is *the* God!" Whereupon the victorious Eliyah orders the Baʿal prophets to be seized, led down to the rivulet Kison and duly slaughtered, we may say, sacrificed to Yahwæh. After this first manifestation of Yahwaeh's power comes the next one: rain is falling in streams. Achab, who has witnessed the whole scene without interceding, in his chariot drives back to his capital, while Eliyah, seized by the hand of Yahwaeh and therefore in exstatic frenzy, runs before the chariot as far as to the city of Jezreel!

What historical realities there are behind this dramatic story we have no means to ascertain. But it gives us a vivid and probably perfectly true picture of what passed in those days as the clash between Yahwaeh and Baʿal was at its height.

The prophetic fraternities in Northern Israel exhibit many features, well known from the Near East of later periods. It is interesting to see how the position of the leader, surrounded by his circle of faithful and obedient disciples, has created an atmosphere of a special kind. As the head of such fraternity, the prophetic leader was both revered and feared, though by outsiders mocked at and called a "madman, $m^e \check{s} ugg a^c$ (II Kings 9, 11). But the dominating factor is respect, yea, awe, for this man is in possession of Yahwæh's spirit. He is also capable of aquiring this Spirit by external means, chiefly by music. Elisha could transfer himself into the exstatic state, filled with the spirit of Yahwæh, by listening to a harp-player (II Kings 3, 15). We remember the scenes in I Sam. 10, 5 or 19, 18-24 (cf. above p. 243). This possession of the Spirit was demonstrated by the prophet's power of exercising acts, falling within the department of parapsychic faculties. These actions, illustrated in the Book of Kings, include the following categories: visions and auditions, far-hearing and far-seeing, rain-making, production of food, neutralizing of poison, far-range acting, healing of sickness, causing of sickness, raising from the dead, occasioning death or its prediction, sudden disappearing, walking on water, flying in the air.

With such faculties at their disposal, we cannot wonder that the leaders of these fraternities excercised such a great influence as they

did. This influence is seen especially when Jehu was revolting against
his king Joram (II Kings 9). Presumably the cooperation of the fraternities with the association of Jonadab and the Rechabites (cf. II
Kings 10, 15 ff. and above p. 254) paved the way for the usurper Jehu.
It is characteristic of the free and independent position occupied by
the "individual" prophets that Jehu's treacherous murder of the royal
family, though committed in the name of Yahwæh, was condemned
by Hoshea (cf. 1, 4).

XI. NORTHERN ISRAEL:
FESTIVAL OF BOOTHS AND THE RÔLE OF THE KING

The Israelite Festival of Booths as celebrated in the autumn marked
the end of the old and the beginning of the new year. As pointed out
here before it was the New Year Festival. In the ritual performances
of this festival the king was the central figure, both in Jerusalem
(David, Solomon) and in Northern Israel (Jeroboam), as we had
opportunity to see (cf. above p. 253f. 256, and 267). However, for the
most part we are dependent on short notices and indirect witnesses,
when we try to reconstruct the active role played by the King. Fortunately there are, as far as the northern kingdom is concerned, some
texts outside the O.T., which furnish us with more material, namely
the Samarian liturgies, dating from various periods, mostly very late
and written in a debased form of Hebrew. In this Hebrew language
of the Samaritans, however, some older traits have been preserved and
the same holds true for their literary traditions. Closer analysis has
revealed that the ritual directions for the festival day, concluding the
sukkōṯ-festival, the mōʿēḏ haššᵉmīnī, possess a rather archaic character
(cf. Cowley, *The Samaritan liturgies* II, p. 782 ff.). Here it is stated that
the king of Israel on that day takes a basket, making a pilgrimage to
Bethel, the most holy of the places of worship (masgᵉḏim, sāḡaḏ attested
in Hebrew, probably a northern dialect term). When the king arrives
at the sanctuary he is greeted by blasts of trumpets. The priest meets
him at the door of the miškān, the "Dwelling" (a term for the allegedly
Mosaic "Tabernacle"). He gives him announcements, in this place not
specified, and takes the basket from his hand and places it before the
altar (mizbēaḥ). The king having given his tithe is filled with joy,
arises and prays to his Lord (mār, an Aramaic term, but the root mrʾ
exists in Ugaritic). He then recites the confession of his freedom of

guilt, in accordance with Deut. 26, 13-15, but with an added wish that the enemies might be dispersed.

The ritual directions given Deut. 26, 1ff. are addressed to every Israelite, as is clear from the context. The Samaritan liturgies clearly show that the "place which Yahwæh chooseth", the common designation of the central sanctuary (cf. below p. 281), is Bethel, the royal temple of the northern kingdom. The Samaritan liturgy further demonstrates that these ritual directions originally are given to the king as the leader of the cultus. The tithe-giving is introduced by the ruler as the representative of the people. This tithe-giving, moreover, was especially associated with Bethel, for according to tradition it was to this place that the ancestor of the people, Jacob, once had made a pilgrimage and given tithe (Gen. 28, 19-22 and 35, 1-7). The king of Israel thus carries on the cultic tradition handed down by his ancestor Jacob. The laws found in Deuteronomy accordingly have democraticized the once royal ritual.

But there is more to be found in the Samaritan texts. There we also read an interesting dialogue between the king and the priest, exchanging blessings and invoking "peace" *šālōm*, for each other. In this dialogue the priest says (Cowley, *The Samaritan Liturgies*, II, p. 786, 9-12):

"Peace on thee, oh King, whom He has designated,
for he has answered me with the rain thou causest to descend."
And the king prostrates and worships,
and his heart is glad as his mind,
and he knows if Yahwaeh has chosen him
and received his offerings.

The most important thing to observe here is the announcement of the priest—probably one of the announcements referred to before—that Yahwæh has answered the questions addressed to him by giving the rain, *gæšæm*, which the king causes to flow. The idea recurs in Ps. 72, 6, where the king is compared to the rain. The fact that Yahwæh has designated and chosen, *bāḥar*, the ruler also calls for notice.

The king's joy over the rain is alluded to in a third passage, where it is said of Yahwæh (Cowley, *The Samaritan Liturgies*, II, p. 791, 17-19):

And he opens his treasure,
the heaven, and gives rain.
And the king is exceedingly glad in his heart,
and Yahwaeh sends him glad tidings through His acceptance.

The cultic situation is then, that Yahwaeh by sending the rain announces that he has accepted the offerings of the king, and accordingly recognized him as the king chosen by God. Yahwæh, it is said, sends him "glad tidings, *biśśar*, an idea to which we shall return in the following.

The Samaritan liturgy also solves some problems in the present text of Deuteronomy, which have been duly pointed out. Thus the text itself presupposes a cultic situation (not at all indicated) according to which the worshipper has undertaken a pilgrimage to the central sanctuary. It has been surmised that the confession was recited, when the tithe was given as a gift to Yahwaeh, and not to the poor of a certain place. All these problems, as we see, are easily solved by a reference to the Samaritan text, which established the original setting in life of Deut. 26; 12 ff., at the same irrefutably demonstrating the northern home of the Deuteronomy.

Of the ritual of the *sukkōṭ*-festival the living in huts is surely one of the most important traits. The hut has played a great rôle in Semitic religion in connection with the Holy Marriage. We know that there was in Charran in the *adyton* of the temple a tent, set up for the Mother Goddess. This tent, called the "bridechamber", was bedecked with all kinds of fruits, plants, and dry roses. We further know that for the marriage between Aphrodite and Adonis in Alexandria a kind of leafy chamber was constructed, in which were found the socalled "gardens of Adonis", known also from Israel (Isa. 17, 10-11). In Southern Mesopotamia such marriage huts are still found among the Mandæans. Such a hut is alluded to in a Gnostic Syriac poem, found in the Acts of Thomas (Chapt. 6-7).

We have spoken of the young girls dancing in the vineyards at this feast (cf. above p. 242) and their union with the young men. Here we focus our interest on the hut itself. There is a passage in the Song of Songs describing it (1, 16):

> Behold, you are handsome, my beloved, yes, lovely,
>   and our bed is green.
> The beams of our house are cedars,
>   and our rafters are cypresses.

The word for bed used in this place is ʿæræś, said to be green. This agrees with its basic meaning, which is both bed and hut of leaves. The hut, where the lovers repose, is clearly a *sukkāh*. This circumstance takes us to the ritual background of the Song of Songs. These poems are a collection of North Israelite love songs in the northern dialect, originally possessed of a cultic background, probably rather early lost, and later spread as folk songs. The lover is the "King" and his bride the "Queen", as in 19th Century Syrian marriage ceremonies. These royal designations would be impossible to understand, without assuming an original place of the songs in a cultic setting in life, where the king and the queen were playing the roles of the god and goddess, the divine king and his divine consort. Opponents of the cultic interpretation do not explain why the terms "seek" and "find", *biqqēš* and *māṣā'*, express one of the main themes of these love poems (cf. above p. 264). Thus the bride's seeking of her bridegroom is reminiscent of the goddess 'Anāt seeking the disappeared and dead Ba'al, roaming the valleys and mountains. It calls for notice in this connection that there are clear allusions to localities north of the territories of Israel. But the songs have been sung and danced for centuries and in a few passages have received Judaean additions. This fact accounts for the mentioning of both Jerusalem and Solomon.

Against this popular religion, by now so intimately bound up with the life of Israel and finding its most intense expression at the great festivals, there was a violent reaction, not only from the prophetic fraternities, but also from individuals, loosely or not at all attached to such societies.

XII. NORTHERN ISRAEL:

TWO GREAT PROPHETS, AMOS AND HOSHEA

In the reign of king Jeroboam II around 750 B.C. there appeared at the sanctuary of Bethel a man from Teqoah in the kingdom of Judah, south of Jerusalem. He was a shepherd, who also occupied himself with cultivation of sycamores. He must have belonged to the lower classes of the people. The more astonishing is his highly polished style and his perfect mastery of poetry. His language is clear, vigorous and trenchant, his sayings belong to the classical passages in the O.T. He was not only a speaker, but also a great poet. His name was Amos.

His leading ideas are of great importance in the history of Israel's religion. He is entirely opposed to the general conviction that Yahwaeh, being the god of Israel was bound to protect his people under all circumstances. To Amos Yahwæh is above all a sovereign lord, not only in nature (4, 6-11; 8, 8; 9, 5), but also in history. Not only did he bring up Israel out of Egypt, but also the Philistines from Kaphtor and the Aramæans from Kir (9, 7). It is true that he has chosen Israel, but then He will also punish the people for its sins (3,2):

> You only have I known
> of all the clans of the earth,
> therefore I shall visit upon you
> all your iniquities.

These sins of the people are various and many. Urban life brought with it a disintegration of the simple society of semi-nomadic and early settelement periods. There emerged social differences, a sharp cleft between rich and poor. The merchants rise the price of corn and falsify the measures. The poor are forced to sell themselves as slaves to get a living (8, 4-6). Justice is not meted out to the poor, because the judges are bribed and the poor suppressed. To this moral evil come the sins of popular religion. The prophet as a saying from God exhorts the people to abstain from its pilgrimages to Bethel, Gilgal and Beerseba and to "seek", *dāraš*, Yahwæh himself. The temple cult in these places is immoral: father and son visit together a temple prostitute. The popular religion is seen by the prophet as a desertion from Yahwæh. We have already found that Israel practised a ritual, where the deity is worshipped in Samaria, Dan and Beerseba as a dying and resurrecting god, like the Canaanite Baʿal (8, 14, cf. above p. 266f.), in the shape of a bull.

Amos reacts sharply against the popular idea that cultus and festivals, songs and sacrifices, all the costly ritual *in itself* could make good for all these iniquities. Yahwæh speaks through his mouth (5, 21-24):

> I hate, I despise your pilgrim festivals,
> I will not smell your feast-assemblies.
> For if you bring up to me burnt-offerings,
> and your meal-offerings, I will not take delight,
> and the peace-offering of your fatlings I will not regard.
> Take away from me the noise of your songs,
> and the melody of your lyres I will not hear.
> Let justice roll as waters,
> and righteousness as an ever-flowing stream!

Yahwæh asks wether the House of Israel brought him bloody sacrifices and offerings in the desert during the 40 years. The answer is of course expected to be "no". But this doesn't mean that the prophet rejects all sacrifices. It means that sacrifices and ritual ceremonies are not enough, if moral and justice are lacking. Amos has an extremely strong sense of righteousness, he is the herald of social justice.

Because of the sins of Israel the people is condemned. Again and again the prophet raises his cry of woe to the people. He takes up a dirge, imitating the wailing over a dead (5, 2-3):

> Fallen is she and cannot rise any more,
>   the virgin Israel!
> Thrown away upon her own soil,
>   with none to raise her up.

The "Day of Yahwæh", the New Year day, when the great pilgrim festival was celebrated, was to be darkness and not light (5, 18). Woe to them who long for it! This day was a celebration of Yahwæh's great deeds in ancient times: victory over the powers of chaos, creation, the liberation of the people from Egypt. It was also held to be a guarantee that He would be victorious and give victory to His people also in coming days. This hope is entirely smashed by the prophet.

Does that mean that there was no expectation of more happy days to come, in a distant future? There are in the collection of oracles and prophecies, as they now are read, some much discussed passages. Especially the authenticity of 9, 8-15 has been denied. It has, however, been rightly pointed out that the possible existence in Amos of prophecies, proclaiming a happy future for Israel after God has punished the sinners among it, is no isolated problem, but must be treated in connection with similar passages in later prophets. We will therefore only state here provisionally, that there is no reason to doubt that Amos cherished some expectations that Yahwæh would not altogether abandon his people.

The absence of all references to Moses and the covenant at Sinai, the more striking as Amos refers to the exodus from Egypt, is quite remarkable. This is to be explained by the fact that Mosaic traditions were spread among the Northern tribes, to whom Amos did not belong.

Amasyah (a Yahwaeh-name!), the priest of Bethel, sent a message to his king that Amos was conspiring against him and that the country couldn't stand all his words. On his own initiative—or having received an order from the king, the text doesn't tell us—the priest then forbids Amos to proclaim his message at Bethel, because it is a royal sanctuary, *miqdaš mælek*, and a temple of the kingdom, *bēṭ mamlākāh*. He ends by saying:

> Oh, you Seer! Go, flee you to the land of Judah,
>   eat bread there and prophesy there!
> But at Bethel you shall no longer prophesy,
>   for it is a royal sanctuary,
> and a temple of the kingdom.

The priest addresses Amos as a "seer", the same term as given to Samuel. Actually Amos *was* a visionary, his visions being collected together with his oracles (7, 1 ff.; 8, 1 ff.). Amasyah also exhorts the prophet to depart to Judah and there to earn his living by prophesying —against Israel, that must be tacitly understood. Amasyah uses the expression *šām tinnābē'*, "speak there as a prophet", *nābī*. But Amos protests, not against being a seer—he hardly could, because he had explicitly referred to his visions—but against being a *nābī*, replying: "I am no prophet and no prophet's son", meaning that he was no prophet by profession and no member of the prophetic fraternities (*bæn nābī* is the sing of *b^enē hann^ebī'īm*, cf. above p. 268). Instead he refers to himself as a shepherd, who has received the call of Yahwaeh to prophesy for His people Israel. Amos obviously wants to free himself from the charge that he belonged to those professional and revolutionary societies, who had caused the downfall of Omri's dynasty.

With this clash the activity of Amos was probably ended. But the ideas he had expressed in so eloquent words were to live on. In a way he seems to have been ahead of his time, for the prophet who appeared after him, perhaps only some decade later, Hoshea, looks as representing a more archaic stage of religious thinking. His theme was the love of Yahwæh. The relations of Yahwaeh and Israel were seen as a marriage between the god and the country, in symbolic imagery spoken of as a "wife", *'iššāh*, who has Yahwaeh as her husband, *'īš*. Hoshea is emphatic in rejecting the Ba'al worship in Israel. He doesn't accept the term Ba'al as used of Yahwaeh. No, Israel will call Yahwaeh *'īšī*, my "man", and not *ba'^alī*, my "husband" (2, 17). The term *ba'al* is disqualified, because Israel didn't keep the faith to her husband Yahwæh, but was a whore, *zōnāh*, who went after her lovers, the Ba'alīm (2). But Yahwaeh will call her away to the wilderness, he will abolish the name of the Ba'alīm from her mouth. He will contract a new marriage with her and peace and happiness will reign in a country, where corn, wine and oil will not be lacking. The perspective of the fertility of the country is a consistent theme in the prophetic oracles— and rightly so, because it was essential to the prophets to make clear to the people that Yahwaeh was the real giver of the fertility to Israel.

This motif of Yahwæh's love for Israel, His election of His people, the lack of faithfulness on the side of Israel, her "whoring" with the Ba'alīm, her return to the God who pardons her, these ideas recur again and again with a certain monotony.

More at random Yahwæh appears as the mighty lord of nature and history. He is the giver of fertility, He brought Israel up from Egypt. But unlike Amos this prophet shows no interest in the activity of Yahwæh outside Israel. It calls for notice that he gives an allusion to Moses (12, 14), and moreover as a prophet, but does not allude to the covenant of Sinai, in spite of his speaking of the time in the desert.

Hoshea is the prophet of love, 'ᵃhābāh, as Amos was that of righteousness and justice, ṣᵉdāqāh and mišpāṭ. In his own unhappy marriage he found a symbolical correspondence of the relations of Yahwæh and Israel. His perspective is that of the farmer, who critizes the kings and the priests, who do not communicate the proper tōrāh concerning the "knowledge of Yahwaeh", da'aṭ Yahwæh, an important notion, to be further developed by later prophets, as also the motif of Yahwæh's love as opposed to His wrath. There is here the constant conflict between judgement and salvation.

Hoshea like Amos is a great poet. But his prophecies, being originally delivered in the northern dialect, though preserved in a Judaean recension, have proved one of the most difficult pieces of O.T. literature to translate, and the Hebrew text has been exposed to reckless emendation.

XIII. Northern Israel:
Oral Tradition and Literary Fixation

In the northern kingdom as well as in Judah there was a lively interest in collecting tribal traditions, customary laws and cult legends. The interest of the local sanctuaries is conspicuous in a great many traditions and we may surmise that such places as Bethel, Shechem, Gilgal were centres of traditionist circles, where the sagas and cycles of narratives, as well as collections of laws, were clustering. Among the great themes were creation stories, narratives about the patriarchs, chiefly the ancestor Jacob, the eponymic hero of the northern tribes, and above all the traditions about Moses and the Exodus, the covenant at the Mount of God, and finally the settlement in Canaan under the leadership of Joshua. Above all important was the figure of Moses.

Southern traditions about Moses had been spread by the Levites, members of his own tribe Levi, to the tribes and shrines of the Northern kingdom, where they were active as priests. This means that the Mosaic traditions were at home chiefly in Northern Israel. It has been pointed out that the close connection between Yahwæh and Mount Sinai is indicated in ancient poems, or in prophetic stories of northern provenance.

It has since the hey-days of the so-called Graf-Kuhnen-Wellhausen theories of Pentateuchal criticism almost always been accepted as an acquired result of literary criticism that these northern traditions first were collected in a written document called "E" (because of its use of the word for God, "Elohim" but also with association to Ephraim). Though it has been denied that "E" is a separate stratum modern research seems disposed to assume the existence of a continous separate written source "E". In practise, however, such a stratum is often extremely difficult to disentangle from the present text. This fact, however, does not affect the theory that there were collections of northern traditions, later finding their way to what we today call the Pentateuch, for this we may call next to an established fact, because the local northern background is so easily discernible in these stories.

A northern origin ("E") has also been ascribed to the so-called Book of the Covenant (Exod. 20,22-23,33). Earlier analysis wanted to find in this code of law a clear distinction between an Israelite heritage from before the settlement, characterized by the categorical form "thou shalt" or "thou shalt not", called "apodictic law", and the "casuistic law", well known from the ancient Near East, where we read the formula "if a man" or "if thou". This casuistic law would have been taken over in Canaan by the priests and the elders of the tribe, who were in charge of communicating the *tōrāh* from God (the priests) and passing judgement "in the gate" (as is said of the elders). However, modern research has proved this clear-cut distinction too simple, because apodictic law is found in the codes of the ancient Near East.

This case is of fundamental importance for the much disputed problem of the origin and date of the Ten Commandments, as we read them Exod. 20, 1-17 and Deut. 5, 6-21. A comparison between these two passages must give the priority to the Exodus formulation of the small code. But even the Exodus text has suffered some additions and alterations. Several reconstructions of the original code have been attempted, of which the apparently best one runs like follows (with insignificant changes):

1. Thou shalt not bow down thyself to another god.
2. Thou shalt not make to thee a graven image.
3. Thou shalt not take up the name of Yahwæh for insincerety.
4. Thou shalt not do work on the day of the sabbath.
5. Thou shalt not despise thy father or thy mother.
6. Thou shalt not commit adultery with the wife of thy neighbour.
7. Thou shalt not spill the blood of thy neighbour.
8. Thou shalt not steal a man from thy neighbour.
9. Thou shalt not answer as a false witness against thy neighbour.
10. Thou shalt not desire the house of thy neighbour.

The six last commandments are rhyming, the five last actually having the word *rē'æḵā*, "your neighbour", which may easily be put at the end of the sentence.

The apodictic form of this code doesn't guarantee any Mosaic origin of the Ten Commandments, even if we subtract all later additions and alterations, undertaken in the course of generations. It has been made extremely probable that there was in the northern kingdom a certain endeavour to have the principles fixed, according to which the king as the highest judge had to mete out justice. The Israelite people, and perhaps above all its leading representatives in the cities and villages, the elders and the feudal lords, wanted to possess a basic law as a canon for every Israelite, including the king. This was the Decalogue. That behind its formulation we have to see both priests and elders would seem to be probable. But even if the date and origins of the Decalogue not is to be found in the Mosaic period, it has been rightly stressed that the spirit of the Ten Commandments agrees well with the little we are able to say about the religion of Moses, above all with the conception of Yahwæh as a "jealous God".

There were, however, some special circles in Northern Israel, cultivating special ideals, which they expressed in a special langage easily recognizable. A concrete result of their activity is left in the present Book of Deuteronomy. Recent research has proved that there is a code of law embedded in the present book, characterized by the address in the second pers. sing. "Thou", in contrast to the additions added by the later collector and editor of the great so-called "Deuteronomistic History" (cf. below p. 297). This collection of laws dates from early times in Northern Israel. It comprises small professions of faith, called "credos" by modern scholars, further sermons introducing and accompanying the commandments, solemn proclamations as the Deu-

teronomic Decalogue (Deut. 5, 6-21), curses, laws of casuistic character, apodictic laws, cultic laws. The northern background is easy to
trace in many passages. One interesting trait, to which attention has
been drawn, is the warlike spirit that pervades this law, where the
principle of *ḥēræm* (cf. above p. 244) is rigorously observed (cf. Deut.
7,1 ff.). There is on the whole a marked anti-Canaanite tendency,
directed against worship of foreign deities (cf. Deut. 7, 26; 12, 29-31;
13, 1-3, 6-18; 18-9-12). There is an express commandment not to plant
an *ᵃšērāh*, or to erect a *maṣṣēbāh* (Deut. 16,21-22). This fight against
syncretism is characteristic of the northern kingdom.

It has been surmised that the warlike spirit would be connected
with the military reorganization undertaken by the king Josiah in
Judah, who, as we will see in the following, accepted the Deuteronomy
as his own code of law (cf. below p. 294). In that case we would have
to ascribe this aspect of the law not to Israel, but to Judah. This seems
rather uncertain, in view of what we know about the practice of
ḥēræm in the northern kingdom. It looks more like the influence of the
prophetic fraternities, where such ruthless ideals were cherished (cf. I
Kings 20,42).

In a marked contrast to this warlike spirit we meet with a humanitarian atmosphere. The humanitarian laws aim at counteracting all the
dangers, menacing the tribal society and its inherited ethics from conditions after the settlement, with its passing to a farmer's life and ur-
banization. We have met drastic illustrations of them in the prophecies
of Amos. Here we note the special care taken of the levite, the *gēr*(man
of foreign extraction living in the land), the orphan and the widow
(cf. Deut. 16,14).

Deuteronomy in many respects marks a renewal of old traditions,
as they were preserved in the North. The law in Deut. 17, 14-20 has
been attractively explained as a kind of charter to be accepted by the
king, either at his designation or his coronation. We remember that
the spirit in Northern Israel was different from that in Judah, and that
the king had to accept the more "democratic" traditions from the
premonarchic period, because Northern Israel lacked the Davidic
dynastic legitimacy, so characteristic of Jerusalem and Judah. And
above all: the Samaritan liturgies have shown that many ritual regulations must have concerned the king, so that the "Thou" of these
laws actually was directed to the king. In the Samaritan directions for
the Feast of Tabernacles Bethel was expressly mentioned as the place,
where the ritual was enacted. This agrees well with a recent hypothesis

that one of the sanctuaries of Northern Israel—and Bethel is expressly mentioned together with Shechem—may have been Deuteronomy's place of origin.

In Deuteronomy we find some of the classical formulations of Israel's faith. So the famous confession in Deut. 6,4-5:

> Hear, Israel! Yahwaeh, our God, Yahwaeh, is One.
> And thou shalt love Yahwaeh, thy God,
> of all thy heart and of all thy strength!

Deuteronomy has also introduced some ritual practices, equally characteristic of Israelite-Jewish religion. So the order to carry the commandments of the law as phylacteries, *ṭōṭāfōṭ*, at the fore-head, and to write them at the door-posts, *mezūzōṭ*. Here Deuteronomy in both cases fore-shadows post-exilic Jewish religion.

Another theme of great importance in the present Book of Deuteronomy is the centralization of the cultus. But it has been shown that the original northern law only says that "the place which Yahwaeh chooseth in one of thy tribes, there thou shalt sacrifice thy burnt-offerings" (Deut. 12,14), a formulation not absolutely excluding the worship at other places, as a comparison with other passages, where the same expression is used, can teach us. The original law accordingly did not expressly command the use of only one single sanctuary in the northern kingdom, even if Bethel was the chief sanctuary.

XIV. Judah: Oral Tradition and Written Literature

In accordance with a custom prevalent among nomadic and semi-nomadic Semitic tribes their traditions were collected and handed over to posterior generations by word of mouth only. But when entering the land of Canaanan the Sons of Israel were confronted with the scribal culture of the Ancient Near East. For that reason some categories of literature, both secular and religous, were presumably taken into the pen. We may assume that from the beginning of the united kingdom royal annals were kept at the court in Jerusalem, that collections of law were produced in a written form, and that psalms and hymns, partly inherited from the Canaanæans, or composed after Canaanite patterns, were written down by professional temple scribes at the great sanctuaries.

There is also some reason to think that there once existed in Israel

various poems of an epic character, glorifying the deeds both of
Yahwaeh and His people, the Sons of Israel. Only fragments of such
an epic literature, partly of the same character as the great epics of
Mesopotamia (Creation epics and XIth Tablet of the Epic of Gilgamesh describing the Great Flood) and Ugarit (the Keret and Aqhat
epics) have been preserved (e.g. Creation story in Genesis, the story
of Noah and the Flood, the birth of Isaac to Abraham, cf. below p.
284), but these fragments are sufficient to show the close affinity between older Hebrew and Canaanite literature.

Epic literature also most probably included description both of the
heroic adventures of the people just before and after the settlement, as
well as glorifications of single heroes, both among the "Judges" and
the first kings, Saul and David. Quite especially David must have been
the central hero of such epic narratives.

The traditions of various kinds were collected in Judah and written
down at an early stage, presumably in the first century of the united
kingdom or shortly after the disruption of unity. Various smaller
collections based upon traditions, handed down orally, were brought
together, reworked and harmonized, and then written down. In such
a way a great literary work was created, perhaps at Jerusalem, perhaps
at Hebron (as far as its older parts are concerned), which included the
Creation Story, the Story of the Flood, the Patriarchal narratives, the
Exodus from Egypt, the wanderings in the desert under the leadership
of Moses, leading up to the time immediately before the settlement,
but hardly including the relation given of the settlement itself. Because
the name of the Godhead is "Jahwæh" this fundamental historical and
religious source has been called "J", which stands both for Yahwæh
and Judah. Many indications of a southern origin are actually found,
but interest is taken not only in Judahite traditions. "J" is therefore
to be classified as a corpus of common Israelite traditions. It is not
always easy to separate the traditions of "J" from other traditions. In
this regard the present generation of scholars is less optimistic than
scholars some 40 years ago. To base conclusions concerning religious
development on the hypothetic dating of this source is also extremely
precarious, though this has been done (far too much) in older days.

Of quite another type are the collections of psalms, which in our
days generally are dated in the pre-exilic period. Many of these psalms
moreover are possessed of such an archaic character that it is tempting
to ascribe their composition to the early days of the Davidic kingdom.
This may be the historical reality behind the authorship's being as-

cribed to David himself in many cases. Other psalms, however, clearly have a northern background and must have been incorporated into the Jerusalem collections, together with the great mass of literary traditions of northern Israel, after the fall of the kingdom of Israel (cf. below p. 294). In this way the literary heritage of Judah included also much, perhaps even most of the northern literature.

XV. JUDAH:
THE POSITION OF THE DAVIDIC KING AND THE CULTUS

The Davidic king, because of the prophetic oracles given to David (cf. above p. 254) promising an eternal *covenant* between Yahwaeh and the House of David, occupied a much stronger position than the royal chief of the northern tribes, continuing as it where the traditions of the charismatic leader. The Judaean king, like the Israelite ruler in the northern kingdom, played a central role as the leader of his people, but there is no doubt that he was much more in the focus of national hope and expectation, because he was the representative of the House of David, to which had been promised by God an everlasting throne, and because Yahwæh proclaimed the king His own son (II Sam. 7,14). This promise was taken up as a solemn declaration in the royal psalms, in which the ruler was glorified in the Jerusalemite cultus and where Yahwæh himself proclaimed the Davidic king on Mount Sion as His son:

> Thou art my son, to-day I have begotten thee.
> Ps. 2,7 (cf. Ps. 110,3 LXX)

Whether we understand this proclamation in a more juridical sense as an adoption formula, or in a more mythical sense as reflecting a natural birth—there were in Canaanite mythology many analogous cases—it is evident that the Davidic king was hailed as the son of Yahwæh. This fact explains that in Ps. 45, where his marriage is praised in glowing terms, he is addressed as "God", v. 7, a unique expression! Interpreters have tried in vain to explain it away, as it has been said. It fits in exactly with what we know about the position of the king.

We know nothing about a divine consort of Yahwæh of Israelite origin. The Mosaic Yahwaeh certainly was alone. In Canaan he could be given various brides, e.g. the Ašērāh, ʿAštart or ʿAnāt, all of whom we know to have been worshipped. The prophetic and deuteronomic polemics are especially directed against the Ašērāh. On the other hand, as goddesses both ʿAštart and ʿAnāt would seem to occupy a more important position. There was in later times a goddess called the "Queen of Heaven", to whom official sacrifices were offered by kings and princes, both in Jerusalem and in other cities of Judah (Jer. 44,17), a fact mostly ignored in discussion. As late as c. 600 this goddess, probably ʿAštart, accordingly enjoyed official worship in the kingdom of Judah. She also appears in some Aramaic letters found in Egypt as *malkat šamin*. It is rather easy to surmise that in the cult the queen must have been thought of as a representative of this divine consort. We refer to what has been said concerning the ritual background of the Song of Songs (cf. above p. 272f.).

In the myth and ritual pattern the *hieros gamos* brought as its fruit the birth of the Saviour-King. The O.T. has preserved some passages relating a super-natural birth, where this mythical background would seem to be demanded to explain the situation. We refer here to such texts as the birth-oracles in the cases of Sarah, the wife of Manoah, and the Immanuel-oracle to which we shall revert (cf. below p. 288). In these passages, Gen. 17,19 + 18,1 ff. + 21, 1-3; Judges 13, 3-5; Isa. 7,14-17, we meet in all the oracles with three stylistic elements, always recurring in this connection: 1. communication concerning the conception, 2. order concerning the child's name, 3. prediction concerning the coming deeds of the child. The model of such an oracle, given by the deity or his messenger, is found in Egypt, but also in Canaan, where the Ugaritic Aqhat text and the Keret legend provide us with the motif of the birth of the royal child. The agreement as usual is also of a linguistic nature. In the legend of Isaac's birth there is a pun on the root *ṣḥq*, leading up to the explanation given of the name Yišḥāq "he laughs". Daniel "laughs", when a son is born to him, 2 Aqhat 2,10, and this detail shows that Gen. 17,17, where Abraham "laughs" has preserved the original concrete motivation for the name. That Sarah, laughs, *tiṣḥaq*, doesn't agree with the name of the son to be born. Sarah, however, is certainly the same word as Accad. *šarra-tum*, queen, princess.

The birth is announced by the "good tidings", brought in Ugaritic epics to Baʿal in several passages. These "good tidings" recur in a great many O.T. passages, where, however, the situation is that God is returning to His temple (Mal. 3,1), or that the Evil Power Belial is "wholly cut off", or that God is King (Isa. 52,7). This means that the "good tidings" are brought, when the "state of chaos" is ended and God has ascended His throne on Mount Sion. That the new force of the returned Ba'al and his enthronement is followed by the holy marriage and the birth of his son, would seem to be generally admitted. Such being the case it is but natural that "good tidings" (found also in the Samaritan liturgies, above p. 272) meet in the O.T. passages, in the context referred too. That the same root *bśr* is found both in Ugarit and Israel is only what we might expect.

We mentioned the idea of Yahwaeh's kingship. This notion, which possesses cosmic significance, is constantly recurring in the psalms of enthronement, where Yahwæh's victory over the powers of chaos, leading up to His creation of the universe and His enthronement is glorified (e.g. Ps. 93, where I AB V 1-6 solves a philogical problem).

The Davidic king, however, not only represents his divine father as the triumphant cosmic ruler, he also represents a suffering and dying figure, carrying as it were the sins and sufferings of his people. This aspect is admittedly one of the less known in the Israelite kingship, and one of the most enigmatic and most disputed.

We shall here present only the material to be found in the royal psalms of lamentation. Here Ps. 88 and Ps. 89 especially claim our attention. Even if possibly not being "liturgies" in "the ritual of the suffering king", as has been claimed for Ps. 89 in a well-documented study, the ritual background in both psalms is sufficiently clear to allow some conclusions as to the cultic situation of the praying subject. At the New Year festival the king obviously represented the young god, when suffering in the nether world. As it has been admirably expressed: "The Davidic king is the Servant of Yahwæh, but at the New Year Festival he is the suffering Servant. He is the Messiah of Yahwæh, but on this occasion he is the humiliated Messiah. The fact is that we are here dealing with a ritual humiliation of the Davidic king which in principle is not unlike that suffered by the Babylonian king in the analogous New Year Festival."

The psalm 88, which presumably, at least in part, was originally recited by the king at that moment of the ritual, when his humiliation was enacted, starts by depicting the situation where he finds himself. He is crying day and night to Yahwæh:

> For my soul is sated with evils,
>   and my life they have brough near to Sheol.
> I am reckoned with those who descend to the pit,
>   I am like a man without help.

> Among the dead is my miserable state,
>   like the slain who lie in the grave,
> whom Thou dost no longer remember,
>   because they are cut off from Thy hand.
> Thou hast placed me in the pit of the nether regions,
>   in the dark regions, in the lower chambers.
> Thy wrath lieth heavily on me,
>   and with all Thy breakers Thou hast afflicted me.
> Thou hast removed my friends from me,
>   Thou hast made me an abomination to them.
> I am bound and cannot go out,
>   my eye is languishing from affliction...
>
> Wretched am I, and expiring from youth,
> The fires of Thy wrath go over me.

The situation here is clear: the speaker is in the nether world, where he is in danger of being drowned by the waters of Sheol. This is a trait found in the misery descriptions of the psalms of lamentation in Israel as well as in Mesopotamia. Similarities in language between this psalm and Ugaritic literature were early observed (cf. II AB VIII 7-9). It has been said of the "author" of this psalm: "His language carries more than one echo of the descent of Mot (cf. above p. 202) to the underworld." The motifs found in the misery description of the psalm are four: 1. The stay in the nether world, 2. The imprisonment, 3. The suffering. 4. His being an abomination, *tōʿēbāh*. This last term leads our thoughts to the suffering Servant in Deutero-Isaiah of whom we shall speak later (cf. below p. 299f.). The three other themes are common in the Mesopotamian liturgies, describing the suffering of Tammuz in the realms of the underworld.

With all this there is no explicit indication that the speaking "I" of this psalm is the king. In order to make this probable we must compare this psalm with other psalms of lamentation, above all Ps. 89, where it is quite evident that the psalm is concerned with the Davidic king, who is referring to the promises given to David and the covenant, *bᵉrīṯ*, made with him. These oracles are extensively quoted, and it is obvious that they have their setting in life in the royal cultus, spoken to the king by a cultic prophet. From there they found their way to prose traditions in II Sam. 7 (cf. above p. 254). In spite of these promises there is a complaint of the king's present situation, for the covenant has been broken and Yahwæh's Anointed rejected, his throne cast to the earth. How long will Yahwaeh hide his face? a question recurring in the psalms of lamentation.

The misery description here does not, however, evoke associations of the mythic colours of Ps. 88. There are rather allusions to military defeats. On the other hand Ps. 69 in its "mythic" language agrees with Ps. 88, but there again there is no clear indication of the supplicant's position. Fortunately there is one royal psalm—though attested in a late context, even if not necessarily of a late date in itself—namely the Psalm of Manasseh, where we once more find the supplicant's situation to be a stay in the realm of Death. This fact shows that the misery descriptions most probably had their context originally in royal psalms.

In the ancient Near East the king's life was given a framework of ritual actions and this being so, it is not astonishing that also a poem glorifying his marriage was included in the Book of Psalm, Ps. 45.

Two most impressive psalms are Ps. 2, where his coronation on Sion is praised and his triumph over his enemies alluded to, and Ps. 72, in which the royal ideology finds an eloquent expression. The king rules from Sea to Sea, the rulers of all countries pay homage to him. In his kingdom he reigns with peace and rightousness, gives justice to the poor and oppressed. He may be like the rain, watering the earth, the corn may be plenty. His name may live for ever. All these themes are well-known motifs in all Near Eastern royal idology, an eloquent witness of the extent to which it had found its way into Israel. Not the least remarkable is the emphasis put on the moral aspects of kingship. This shows that kingship was of great positive value to Israel and foreshadows future developments (cf. below p. 312).

XVI. JUDAH: THE GREAT PROPHETS

Isaiah was a citizen of Jerusalem, who lived somewhere about 740, and he was proclaiming his prophecies in politically difficult and dangerous times, when Judah was near losing its independent state. His call is received in a vision in the temple of Jerusalem (Is. 6, 1-4). He sees Yahwæh sitting on a high throne, his mantle filling the temple. Heavenly winged beings called Seraphim—the notion dates perhaps from Mosaic times—were standing around him, one crying to the other:

Holy, Holy, Holy is Yahwaeh of the Hosts,
His glory filleth all the earth.

The name given here to God, Yahwæh Sebaoth, is from the beginning closely associated with the Ark. When the Ark was transferred to Jerusalem this name is therefore especially connected with the temple of Jerusalem. The three times repeated "Holy" is reminiscent of a corresponding Egyptian formula. What is important to note is the fact that Yahwaeh is seen above all as the mighty king, enthroned in the temple. The kingship of Yahwaeh, as glorified in the cultus, is the dominating trait in the prophet's idea of God.

His preaching is full of well-known themes, for he attacks both cultus without moral, and social injustice like Amos. The Prophet Isaiah has been famous for the stress he lays on faith, as in his saying 7,9: "If you have no faith, you will have no security," with a typical wordplay on the verb 'āman, to have faith. With bitterness he attacks the sinfulness of the people and proclaims the judgement, which will be passed on it. However, as sure as he is that Judah will be condemned, as sure he also is, that a remnant of the people will be saved. Here we meet with this immensely important idea of the "remnant", *še'ār*, which will be converted and be saved. In a symbolical way this idea was expressed by means of the name given to the eldest son of the prophet, called by him *še'ār yāšūb*, "A remnant will return". This remnant is for the time being represented by the prophet's disciples, a faithful circle, who has collected his prophecies and handed them down to later generations.

Isaiah hoped for the advent of a Davidic king as the saviour of his people. He has given eloquent expression to his hope in two prophetic oracles in Ch. 7 and 9, which belong to the most famous of all existant prophecies and have played an enormous role in Jewish and Christian religion. In 7: 1ff. he proclaims the birth of ʿImmānūel, "God-with-us", a mysterious being, who forebodes salvation of the land, depicted as he is in mythical colours. His birth is proclaimed in wordings reminiscent of the birth oracles used in the cultus (cf. above p. 284). In 9,1 Isaiah contrasts the present dark situation with the change to be brought about by the coming "prince of peace". The oracle 7,1ff. must be quoted in its entirety. The situation is that the prophet promises the king a sign from Yahwaeh to assure him that he has nothing to fear from the two rulers of Aram and Israel, who are preparing to attack him:

> Therefore the Lord himself will give to you a sign:
>> Behold, the young woman is pregnant and beareth a son,
>> and calleth his name "God-with-us" (ʿImmānūel).

Curds and honey shall he eat.
when he knoweth to reject the bad and choose the good.
For before the boy knoweth to reject the bad and choose the good,
shall be deserted the land, of whose two kings thou art in dread.
Yahwaeh shall bring upon thee and upon thy people and upon the
house of thy father,
days such as have not come since the day, when Ephraim with-
drew from Judah.
Isa. 7, 14-17

That this oracle belongs to the same category as the mythical royal birth oracles treated here before (cf. above p. 284), was stated long ago. We find in this oracle the three stylistic elements referred to above i.e. 1. Communication concerning the conception. 2.(Order) concerning the child's name. 3. Prediction concerning the coming deeds of the child, in only a slightly altered form. The young woman, ʿalmāh, is found in Ugarit in a poem where we read: "Behold, the young woman beareth a son", Nikal and Košarot, line 7, where the word ǵlmt corresponds exactly with the Hebrew ʿalmāh. That this woman in the actual case must be the queen and the child the heir of the throne was seen more than 40 years ago. The wonderful food, creme and honey, is a symbol of the fertility of the country, as it will be found in coming days. But the prospect of happiness goes farther, for the prophet promises a restoration of the rule of the Davidic dynasty in the northern kingdom. Thus the mythical motif serves to interpret a present and near-future situation. The same is obviously the case also in 11,1ff., where it is prophesied that "there shall come forth a shoot out of the trunk of Isai", i.e. of the royal House of David. He is described as the ideal ruler, faithful and righteous, and introducing a period of peace, when "the wolf shall dwell with the lamb". He shall be possessed of the spirit of Yahwæh, which implies a spirit of wisdom and knowledge.

The oracle 9,3 ff. says that the people dwelling in deep darkness will see a great light. The yoke of its burden, the rod of its oppressor is broken. Peace will reign and the warrior's apparel be burnt as fuel of fire.

For a child is born unto us,
a son is given to us.
The government shall be upon his shoulder
and his name shall be called:
"Wonderful Counsellor, God, Hero, Everlasting Father, Prince of
Peace."
Of the increase of his government
and of peace there is no end,

> upon the throne of David and upon his kingdom,
> to establish it and to uphold it
>   with justice and righteousness,
> from henceforth and to eternity.
> The zeal of Yahwaeh of hosts shall perform this.

Here it is clearly stated that the coming Prince of Peace shall sit on the throne of David, the covenant with David will be kept by Yahwæh, the Lord of Hosts (the specific Jerusalemite designation of Yahwæh, cf. above p. 288). The five names of this future Davidic king in a symbolical way express his wonderful character, they make him a figure floating between myth and history. At the same time it is most probable, as has been persuasively argued, that the five names here mentioned correspond to the 5 names of the Egyptian throne-names, the "royal protocol". We actually know that in several cases the Judaean king received a throne-name at the occasion of his coronation. The names given to the Prince of Peace would then correspond to this usage, being a symbolical interpretation of it. At any rate these prophetic oracles, proclaimed by Isaiah, demonstrate the extent of the influence exercised by royal ideology in prophetic circles in Jerusalem and Judah.

The prophet Micah was a contemporary of Isaiah but obviously—in contrast to Isaiah—a man belonging to the broader layers of the people, perhaps a farmer. He attacks the higher classes and urban life in Jerusalem. Of the capital he has no high opinon, but also Samaria in Israel gets its fulls share. The temple of Jerusalem to Micah doesn't represent any value at all, it will be destroyed. "Sion shall be ploughed as a field, and Jerusalem shall become heaps." (3,12). He turns against the prophets, who only prophesy luck and happiness to the people. In his strong sense of social justice he continues the ideas of Amos. So also in his disregard of the whole sacrificial system. Shall Israel come before Yahwæh with burnt offerings, "with calves of a years old"? No, says the prophet, God has proclaimed what He really wants of man (6,8):

> He hath showed thee, oh man, what is good,
>   and what doth Yahwaeh require of thee,
> but to do justice and to love mercy,
>   and to walk humbly with thy God.

Micah in strong words foretells the destruction of both Israel and Judah. And yet in his prophecies we find promises that there will be a "remnant", *š⁰ʾērīt Yiśrāʾēl*, the dispersed captives will be assembled to Mount Sion (4,6-8; 5,7-15 cf. 2,12-13). But how much of these prophecies we really should attribute to Micah, remains a disputed problem.

One prophet, Nahum appearing at the end of the seventh century, prophecies the fall of the Assyrian empire. From his prophecies—they have been labelled "nationalistic", but we could equally well call them "patriotic", we get an impression of the exultant joy caused by the destruction of the hated, oppresive Assyrians, with their incredibile cruelties against the subjugated peoples. This prophet is a great poet, he evokes in the reader even to-day an immediate impression of the atmosphere of those days.

The prophet Zephaniah was active during the reign of king Josiah. The collection of his prophecies is arranged in accordance with a pattern found also in the books of the great prophets: judgement on Israel, judgement on the nations, promise of restoration. Zephaniah links up with Amos and Isaiah in his descriptions of the Day of Yahwæh, while on the other hand his condemnation of pagan practices in Judah (1, 4-6, 8-9) shows that not only old Canaanite cultus was still alive, but also that Mesopotamican influence made itself felt in the worship of the "Host of Heaven". Part of the prophet's activity, at least, must therefore be placed before the great reformation undertaken by Josiah (cf. below p. 293f.).

Whether Habakkuk is to be placed before or after the Exile is a disputed question. At any rate the content of his oracles (called *massāʾ*) and prophecies, both against Israel and the neighbour peoples, are rather traditional. Original is on the other hand the so-called "Psalm of Habakkuk". Ch. 3, where the theophany of Yahwæh is depicted in mythical colours, e.g. 3,8 His fight against the Sea. The language is archaic and therefore partly difficult to understand.

Around 650 was born one of the greatest prophets, Jeremiah. His prophecies are on the whole not original in their content, but by and large agree with those of Hosheah and Isaiah. Attacks against the unrighteous in the people are coupled with oracles, predicting the fall of the kingdom of Judah. A new and original idea is, however, his rejection of the traditional view of the relation between sin and retribution, expressed in the famous saying Deut. 5,9:

> I, Yahwaeh thy God, am a jealous God
> visiting the iniquity of the fathers upon the sons,
> and upon the third and fourth generations of them who hate me.

This idea of God's retribution—based on the old tribal solidarity—had found an expression in the popular saying quoted by Jeremiah, 31,29-30:

> The fathers have eaten a sour grape,
> and the teeth of the sons get blunt.

But Jeremiah says:

> No, a man that eateth the sour grape,
> his teeth will be blunt.

This is because Yahwæh will make in future days a new covenant with the House of Israel and the House of Judah—the distinction here calls for notice—not such a covenant as He made, when He brought them out of Egypt, a covenant which they had broken. This notion of the New Covenant is an idea pregnant with importance for the future (cf. below p. 293f.).

Also in another respect Jeremiah has been of remarkable importance to posterity, Circumcision, in itself from the beginning just a social rite of initiation, marking the entrance into the age of sexual maturity, ultimately—probably as a consequence of the contrast to the not-circumcised Philistines—was seen as something characteristic of Israel as a people, and hence also of religious significance. This opinion of the meaning of circumcision found an expression in the tradition of the covenant made by God with Abraham (Gen. 17), when circumsion was made the sign of this covenant. Jeremiah, following in the steps of the prophets before him doesn't attach much weight to ritual and sacrifice (cf. 7,22; 14,12). He can therefore say to his compatriots (4,4):

> Circumcise yourselves to Yahwaeh,
> and take away the foreskins of your heart,
> ye men of Judah and Jerusalem!

This "circumcision of the heart" was to have great consequence in later times. What the prophet demands is a change in the attitude of man. The sin he condemns more than anything else is the hardness of heart (7,24; 9,13; 11,8,13 etc.). Exterior reforms were not enough. When he met the Rechabites, who demanded a return to nomadic customs, condemning the agricultural life and what accompanied it, living in houses, sowing of seed, and drinking of wine, he praised their fidelity to principles, but not the principles themselves.

XVII. JUDAH:

THE REFORMS OF JOSIAH AND THE PROMULGATION OF A NEW LAW

The northern kingdom fell for the Assyrians in 722. The situation of the southern kingdom was in the following period highly precarious. Hiskiah after accepting the suzerainty of Assur ultimately joined the rebellion against Sanherib. He managed to save his capital and his kingdom, but had to pay a great indemnity. Under the reign of his son Manasseh things went still worse for the national cause. For political reasons Manasseh had to introduce some Assyrian astral religion (cf. II Kings 23,5: compared with II Kings 21,3: he worshipped "all the host of heaven", including the Zodiacal signs, Hebrew *mazzā-lōṭ* Accadian *mazzaltu*), moreover—obviously of his own—practising popular religion, such as worship of Ba'al and Ašērāh, and human sacrifices. The prophet Zephaniah fulminates against this revival of popular religion and syncretism, as we have seen (cf. above p. 000).

During the reign of Manasseh's grandson Josiah the national party again got the upperhand, and political prospects seemed much brighter. Assurbanipal died 626 and after his death Assyrian power declined rapidly. In the year 622, the eighteenth year of Josiah, a law-code was found in the temple by the priest Hilqiah. He handed over this book to the royal chancellor Shaphan, who read it before the king. When Josiah heard the words of the book he rent his clothes—so violent was the impression made on his mind and so great his sorrow over prevailing conditions—obviously strongly condemned in the Law. After a comforting oracle concerning his own fate, given by the prophetess Huldah, the king ordered a great assembly to meet in the temple: all the elders, all the men of Judah and Jerusalem, and the priests and the prophets. In accordance with the ritual for the king at the occasions of covenant-making (cf. I Kings 8, above p. 256, and II Kings 11,17) the king stood on a dais, reading the stipulations of the new code, establishing the covenant and making the whole people enter the covenant and accept the stipulations of the new code. The festival was concluded by the celebration of the Passover, celebrated as a feast of innovation hence corresponding to the New Year Festival when otherwise such a renewal of the covenant used to be celebrated. The king Josiah here carries on the royal tradition. The new and startling fact is that a new law-code is accepted and promulgated, for we must assume that the older collections of law in the Pentateuchal tradition since centuries were written down, such as the Book of Covenant of an early date (beginning of united kingdom) from Northern Israel (Exod. 20,22-23,33), and the Code of Holiness (Levit. 17-26), probably from Judah at the end of preexilic period. But it is obvious that the king had been won for a great programme of religions reformation, based upon the old kernel of laws in Deuteronomy (cf. above p. 279f.). After the fall of Samaria in 722 presumably some religious people, levitic priests, prophets and temple scribes had taken their refuge to Judah, where under the reign of Hiskiah conditions were favourable to them. Jeremiah, who as a Beniaminite was near to the North, was deeply attached to Northern Israel and must have been influenced by Deuterononic circles, for his language betrays many influences of its ideas and style. That Jeremiah thought favourably of Josiah we know (cf. Jerem. 22,15-16). He also engaged himself in the propagation of the law's commandments and leading ideas among the cities of Judah (Jerem. 11,1-6, 18-23). Therefore it would not seem too bold to assume that the New Covenant originally was the law-code introduced by Josiah as the basis of his covenant, which was actually a "New Covenant". But after the reforms, necessitated by the code, had been carried through, Jeremiah recognized that much had not changed. The people claimed to possess "the tōrāh of Yahwæh", but in reality they had rejected the "Word of Yahwæh", because they were clinging to exterior commandments (8, 7-9; cf. 4,3-4).

The reforms, probably inaugurated already before the finding of the code and making of the covenant, were otherwise so radical as to satisfy all traditional enemies of syncretistic worship, especially when Josiah started to rid himself of Assyrian government and extended his influence to Israel. This purification of the sanctuaries in the northern territories thus was an act also of political significance. In the midst of this undertaking we probably have to place the renewal of the covenant and the celebration of passover in Jerusalem 622.

What was the code of law, made the basis of this covenant and at any rate in its later stages influencing the work of reforms? This is one of the major problems in the history of Israelite religion, though the present situation would seem to indicate that there is general agreement on this point.

Since De Wette it has been argued that the code in question was Deuteronomy. To-day this opinion holds the field. Josiah's reform is obviously inspired by the programme advocated by Deuteronomy, for all his measures are in conformance with the prescriptions given there. Some points need to be emphasized. 1) The cult was centralized to Jerusalem and its temple, and all the high-places destroyed, a measure which clearly exceeds the programme of the original North-Israelite code (cf. above p. 281), but is in keeping with its later re-working and expansion (the exhortations in "you"-style, 2. pers. plur.). 2) The Levites according to the later programme were to be placed as priests at the temple in Jerusalem (Deut. 18). This, however, was not possible to realise, but the Levites were put in a subordinate position as cultic servants. In the following we have two separate categories: the Priests and Levites (cf. II Kings 23,8-9).

The centralization of the cult to Jerusalem must have been inspired by the priests of Jerusalem, who most of all had the benefit of it. This centralization has mightily enhanced the reputation of Jerusalem, its temple from now on being the goal of all the pilgrims, who had before undertaken their pilgrimages to the local sanctuaries. Jerusalem really corresponds now to the mythical conception of its being the centre of the world (cf. above p. 258f.).

Josiah, contrary to what had been proclaimed to him in an oracle (II Kings 22,19-20), fell at Megiddo when trying to stop Pharao Necho, who was coming to the help of the last Assyrian ruler. The New-Babylonian empire with Nebuchadnezzar got the hegemony in Meso-potamia and Syria. A wavering policy from the kings of Judah ulti-mately led to two rebellions, which were bad failures. The whole affair ended in the tragedy of 586, when Jerusalem was taken, the temple destroyed and the leading layers of the population carried off to Babylonia. Thus the kingdom of Judah had ended its existence in the same way as the kingdom of Israel. How could now the God of Israel be worshipped when His House was laid waist, His priests gone in deportation, and His sacrifices and festivals suspended? This prob-lem is significant of the posxteilic period, between the destruction of Jerusalem in 586 and the return of the exulants in 538, having as its consequence the rebuilding of a small temple about 515. Meanwhile, however, we can see how the heart of the deported was attached to the now destructed Jerusalem temple. This attitude is conspicuous in the great prophet, who was active among the deported Jews in Babylonia, Ezekiel.

XVIII. Ezekiel and the Exulants

Ezekiel was a priest and as such a member of the priesthood of Jerusalem. When in 598 Nebuchadnezzar occupied Jerusalem for the first time, he was one of the captives, who were deported (II Kings 24, 14-16 doesn't mention the deportation of any priests). All his activity was spent among the exulants in Babylonia, whose situation to some extent is reflected in his prophecies. These may be attributed to three periods. The first period is characterized by his prophesying doom and judgement over Jerusalem and Judah, besides giving answers to his deported compatriots. The second period prophesies judgement for the unrighteous, salvation for the pious, and doom over the heathen peoples. Among these oracles is the 28th chapter with its mythological background, directed against the king of Tyrus. The third period comprises only prophecies of luck to Israel, and depicts the coming age of happiness to the people. Here we find the much discussed description of the new temple. It is not a direction how to build it, it will already be there—as the prophet has seen it in his vision—when the deported return. What they have to do is to observe the proper cult there.

Ezekiel is a great poet and a fascinating writer. A great many literary categories are found in his book, and the breadth of his preachings and announcements is so incredibly great that it is no wonder that repeatedly it was tried to show, that a great many of the prophetic oracles and announcements couldn't be attributed to him. But closer analysis has demonstrated that the only satisfactory solution is to maintain the essential unity of the book.

His passionate temperament leads him sometimes to descriptions of drastic details, which a modern taste may find repulsive, but no one can deny the terrible vigour and consequence in such diatribes as that against Jerusalem as the great prostitute (16, 1-43), or his violent attack on the two sisters Ohola and Oholiba, where he has seized the motif of an unfaithful, beloved girl and applied it to Israel and Judah (23,1-49). His phantasy may appear to us somewhat morbid, it certainly was not so at his own time, when the tradition of erotic imagery from the time of Hoshea was still unbroken.

Another aspect of Ezekiel's personality, which makes him so important in the history of prophecy, is his psychic disposition. There was always in the equipment of the prophets a certain amount of ecstasy, their visions and auditions being received in a state of trance. But with Ezekiel we find also some parapsychic experiences, reminiscent of the parapsychic powers of the prophetic leaders of Northern Israel (cf. above p. 269).

Especially impressive is the prophet's vision of his calling. Like the visions of calling of Isaiah and Jeremiah it is a true visionary experience, including both auditions and visions. What gives it a special character of its own is the Babylonian colour of it. The influence of the surrounding civilization of Mesopotamia makes itself very much felt in the prophet's language, also in so far that there is a high percentage of words in his Hebrew coming from Accadian.

This ecstatic visionary and inspired poet is at the same time a rational systematic, a casuistic lawgiver, and a pedantic priestly ritualist. One of the greatest figures in the religious history of Israel he has been called the father of Jewish religion and the first apocalyptic. Onesided as these designations are for such a mighty personality, they nevertheless point out rightly that Ezekiel marks a definite break in tradition. Something new is here. This will be clear, if we read the Ch. 37 describing the fascinating vision in which the prophet sees the dried bones get life again—the theme of one of the most important scenes in the paintings of the synagogue at Dura-Europos. Such a vision, as also his vision of calling, forebode really the apocalyptic descriptions of much later periods.

XIX. The Exile: the collecting of priestly traditions and the creation of the Synagogue

To this and the closely following period we have to date two works of traditions, not only collections of traditions but also unified literary products, the results of the planned efforts of an author. One is the deuteronomistic work of history including the historical books from Deuteronomy to Kings, characterized by the deuteronomic outlook on history, according to which all the misfortunes, which befell the chosen people, were the result of its lack of faithfulness to its God, its defection, and its manifold sins. The other literary work is the Priestly Source ("P") which, however, most probably was not given its final shape before the first return of the exulants.

The atmosphere among the deported, their longing for Jerusalem, got an eloquent and touching expression in Ps. 137.

However, everyday's life may have occupied many of them, so as to forget their home-land. From Babylonian documents, as well as from Jeremiah and Ezekiel, we know that their existence was more than tolerable and that at least some of them brought it to considerable wealth. So the famous bankers Murashu & Sons in Nippur. Such Jews were more or less assimilated.

But the majority obviously clung to their nation and religion—one and the same thing at this time. They needed and wanted instruction in the Law, in order to be able to obey the commandments of God. Because the cult was associated with Jerusalem they were cut off from it. Therefore other customs, in themselves not so important and not necessarily cultic, acquired an increased importance, because their strict observation showed the Jews to be the people of Yahwaeh—and not Babylonians. Such a custom was the Shabbath, to be kept holy (cf. Ezek. 20,12 ff.; 22,8,26; 23,38). On this day presumably the assembled of a Jewish colony could read a "credo" and listen to homiletic exhortations of the type attested already in Deuteronomy. The Levites and priests could carry on the traditions from pre-exilic times (cf. above p. 294). Probably also texts from the historical traditions were read to them, glorifying Yahwaeh's great deeds with His people. Perhaps some of the psalms were also sung or recited. In such a way the institution of the Synagogue was created, carrying on an existing tradition, and yet something new. In the centre of worship, from now on, the *word* was placed, because ritual action on the whole was made impossible. This meant that attention had to be paid to the collection and fixation of the traditions, in which the word was communicated. The laws got more importance than before (as indicated), because they tended to keep the Jewish nationality and religion intact. Among the regulations of the law was now counted also circumcision, to which importance was attached as the sign of the covenant, concluded by God with Abraham (Gen. 17, cf. above p. 292). And lastly, another important point. The Jews in Babylonia were from now cut off altogether from the syncretistic Canaanite cult, to which moreover a heavy blow had been given by the great reform. Therefore the exulants were prone to be orthodox in belief and practice, as we will see in the cases of Ezrah and Nehemiah.

XX. The Return of the exulants:
Deutero-Isaiah, and the rebuilding of the Temple

The Neo-Babylonian empire fell in 539 for Cyrus the Great, the builder of the Persian empire. The Persian policy towards the peoples belonging to their empire was characterized by far-reaching religious tolerance, an altogether new phenomenon in the ancient Near East. Cyrus in accordance with his principles permitted the exulants to return and to rebuild the Temple. Judah however, for the time being was only a sub-province of Samaria, where now a Persian governor was installed.

The advent of Cyrus had been waited for with great expectations among the Jews of Babylonia. These hopes have found an eloquent expression in the prophecies, announced by the great unknown prophet, whose proclamations are now read in the book of Isaiah and who is therefore called Deutero-Isaiah. He is a great poet, announcing to his people the immediate return to Jerusalem in prophetic oracles, where nationalistic expectations are blended with a universalistic outlook. Deutero-Isaiah uses many literary patterns, based on the liturgies of the New Year Festival. In the centre of his oracles about the approaching return stands the ingathering of the dispersed (a typical feature of royal ideology), to be effectuated by Cyrus, whom the prophet calls the Servant of God. Cyrus accordingly occupies the position of the royal saviour, so eagerly waited for already in the days of the Kingdom of Judah, but at that time belonging to the Davidic dynasty. It is remarkable that these hopes, which we call "Messianic" after the designation of the king as *mᵉšiaḥ Yahwæh*, the Anointed of Yahwaeh, were now concentrated on a foreign ruler. Among the so-called Servant-Songs in Deutero-Isaiah there is, however, one now to be read Is. 52,13-53,12, which is altogether different from the other songs and has created more problems to scholarly analysis and historical evaluation than perhaps any other O.T. text. Here the Servant is described in such words that he can by no means be Cyrus. But who is he? He is clearly a Suffering Servant. He is suffering for the sins of the people or rather, the prophet says: "He was wounded for our transgressions, he was bruised for our iniquites... Yahwaeh hath laid on him the iniquity of us all" (53,6). By his humilation (*bᵉḏaʿtō* means here "humility or "humilation", cf. Arab. *wadaʿa* as has been proposed) he, who is the righteous Servant shall make many righteous. His suffering has a vicarious character. He is also said to make intercession for the transgressors (v. 12).

The language in this poem, where some passages are difficult to understand and translate correctly, carries an echo of both O.T. and Phoenician language. So the phrase "he was cut off from the land of life" (v.8) is reminiscent of both the Eshmun'azar inscription and of Ps. 27,13; 116,9, and Is. 38,11. This is the language of the psalms of lamentation. Further the simile of the lamb carried away to be slaughtered recurs Jerem. 11,19, moreover in connection with the expression "to cut him off from the land of life." It is obvious that in both cases the prophet makes use of well-established cultic wording. In both prophets we further meet with the symbol of a tree, or root, which is cut off. This is an old symbol of the dying and resurrecting deity, as also the lamb. It has therefore repeatedly been surmised that Deutero-Isaiah uses the cultic language of lamentations over the suffering and dying deity, in the cult represented by the king. When speaking of Ps. 88 we found that the speaker there said, that he was made an abomination to them who know him (cf. above p. 286). This is another point of contact, for the Suffering Servant is really made an abomination. These reminiscences of royal ideology account for the Servant's suffering, but not for his *vicarious* sufferings for the people's sins. This is another line of thought, expressed by the Servant's being an ' āšām (v. 10), a sin-offering (cf. for this type above p. 241). He was *sacrificed* as a sin-offering by God for the sake of the many. Here the prophet links up with sacrificial language and ideology. But ultimately, because the Servant was carrying the sins of many, God will give him a lot among many, and with the mighty he will give the booty as a lot —enigmatic words, but pointing to some kind of remuneration (v. 12).

Is this Servant a single individual or a collective entity? Many have voted for the latter alternative, thinking of Israel, but how could a collective entity, Israel, fulfill the vicarious suffering exactly for Israel, for what else could be the "we", who are spoken of as those, who had the benefit of the Servant's sufferings? That in this case the outlook is universalistic, is often maintained, but difficult to prove. It seems more probable then, that the Servant is an individual person, depicted in the colours of the king, who is suffering in the cult for the sins of his people. This must be the prophet's own interpretation, for it is difficult to find a precedence of it in Near-Eastern religion, even if we often meet there with the royal sufferer, especially in the psalms of lamentation to be recited by the king.

Also in 61,1 ff. the Book of Isaiah uses a text from the royal ritual, the proclamation that the king has been the Sent one, who has come to bring the Good Tidings. He has God's spirit, because Yahwæh has anointed him, a clear sign of his royal status. He has come to free all imprisoned and to comfort all mourners. This is perfectly in keeping with the motif of "the ingathering of the dispersed". But this passage has been ascribed to another prophet, although its style would not seem to be much different.

Deutero-Isaiah is also known for his ironical polemics against the gods of foreign peoples. He especially attacks all forms of idolworship, mocking at the ridiculous ineffectiveness of the idols. His is a firm monotheistic belief, coupled with a universalistic perspective. Here he has set a mark for coming developments. His hope of the future restoration of Israel is associated with a belief in the whole nature's being as it were a street of procession for Yahwæh and His people, returning to Mount Sion. Here the influence of the New Year Festival liturgies is strongly felt.

That the prophet is dependent upon this ritual was shown many years ago. The leading motifs of this festival recur in so many passages that it is impossible to give illustrations. The endeavours to prove the opposite view, *viz*. that the psalms are dependent upon Deutero-Isaiah, have proved impossible, because we have been able to date the majority of the psalms in pre-exilic times.

The returning exulants—about 3.0000 men, we do not know how many women and children-found Jerusalem completely devastated and most parts of Judah very sparsely populated. Neighbouring peoples had moreover annexed several territories. This means that *e.g.* the Edomites had occupied Negeb. The Calebites, already in ancient times in near association with Judah, were now accepted as part of the people. More difficult were the relations with the inhabitants of the province Samaria, where the Assyrians had settled many non-Jewish people from Mesopotamia and Elam, who worshipped their own deities but also accepted the worship of Yahwæh (cf. II Kings 17,24 ff.), which led to a strenghtening of the syncretistic type of religion in the northern territories. The returned Jews had as their governor Šešbasar (= Šamašapaluṣur), a son of the deported king Jojakin. He had been appointed by Cyrus and had received from him the temple apparatus, which Nebuchadnezzar had robbed from Jerusalem, with the commission to rebuild the temple. He had laid the foundations of the temple, but in the year 520 it was yet unfinished. In that year, how-

ever, the Persian empire, after Darius had seized power, was shaken
by a series of revolts in nearly all the provinces of the empire, which
was accordingly in danger of falling into pieces. Under the impression
of these agitated happenings there were great expectations among the
Jews, who were of course in close connection with Babylonia, where
one usurper after the other revolted against Darius. Two prophets'
first Haggai, and then Zechariah, now took up the word and proclaimed a bright future. They went even so far as to promise that Yahwaeh
would shake heaven and earth and crush kingdoms. The new governor
Zerubabel (Zērbābili, again a Babylonian name), who was a Davidic
prince he too, a son of She'altiel, who was a son of Jojakin (accordingly a nephew of Šešbasar), was proclaimed as chosen by Yahwæh, kept
by him as His signetring. The end will draw near, it was said, and
Zerubabel will obviously be the king on Mount Sion, the Shoot as he
is called (Zech. 6,12 is now adapted to suit the person of the High
Priest Josua) after an old "Messianic" designation (cf. above p. 289),
and with a play on his name which means "Shoot of Babel". The
temple must be built, in order that the new state of things might be
celebrated, and Yahwaeh return and take his habitation on Sion (Zech
8,3). But Darius chrushed the revolts, his empire stood firm, the
prophetic voices were silent, and Zerubabel disappears from history.
The governor of Syria, who got report of the undertaking, tried to
stop the temple-building, but Darius made researches and found in
Ecbatana the edict of Cyrus concerning the building of the temple. He
therefore ordered his satrap not to stop it, and moerover gave the
command that from the tribute from Syria necessary means should be
given for the sacrificial service. The building activities were finished
in 515, when the temple-alas, only a small and insignificant one as
compared to Solomon's temple—stood ready for the temple service,
to be conducted by the returned priests and levites of whom we have
lists preserved.

XXI. Post-exilic period:
Ezra and Nehemiah, the Samaritan schism

The Jew Nehemiah was the cup-bearer of the Persian king Artaxerxes I (464-424 B.C.) and hence one of the higher officials at the Persian
court. While staying with the Great King in Susa in the year 444 he
received sad news about conditions in Judah, the wall of Jerusalem

still being broken down and the gates of the city destroyed by fire. Nehemiah, using a suitable occasion, obtained from Artaxerxes the commission to do the necessary repairs and was sent away, provided with royal letters to the Persian governors in the province Abar-naharā and the superintendent of the royal *pairidaisā* (where he could get the necessary wood for the building activities). Accompanied by officers and horsemen Nehemiah arrived at Jerusalem. With great skill and vigour he tackled the task of reconstructing city-wall and gates. After only 52 days Nehemiah had brought his undertaking to a succesful end. But the governor of Samaria, Sanballat (= Sinuballiṭ, a Babylonian name meaning "Sin made alive") together with an Ammonite, called Tobiah, conspired against Nehemiah and even threatened to attack Jerusalem before the construction of the wall was finished. Nehemiah therefore had one half of his followers keeping watch, while the other half devoted itself to the work. Under such difficulties was the construction finished.

Nehemiah also proceeded with characteristic vigour against the Jew's mixing with foreign people, with whom they had intermarried. These mixed marriages provoked the irritation of Nehemiah (Neh. 13, 23-25). A grandson of the high priest Elyashib was married with a daughter of Sanballat. This son-in-law of his enemy Nehemiah, when returning from a visit to Mesopotamia, expelled from the Temple together with Tobiah the Ammonite (13, 8,28). Moreover, in various ways Nehemiah purified the people from foreign influences and surveyed the strict keeping of sabbath regulations. His actions demonstrate that Nehemiah represents the Jewish religion in its exclusive character, as it had taken shape in the exile in Mesopotamia.

Nehemiah was followed by Ezra, who is said to be both a "priest" and a "scribe of the Law of the God of Heaven" (Ezra 7,12). It is related that in the seventh year of king Artaxerxes he went up to Jerusalem, accompanied by priests, levites, temple singers, and temple servatns, and part of the exulants. Who is then Artaxerxes? This is one of the most vexed problems in O.T. history. However, probability would seem to be on the side of those who think that the king in question is Artaxerxes II. The year when Ezra went up to Jerusalem would in that case be 398 B.C.

Ezra was given a royal rescript, according to which he was commissioned to bring to the temple in Jerusalem gold, silver and precious vases, given by the Great King for the temple service. At his arrival Ezra found much the same conditions prevalent as in the time of

Nehemiah. Ezra celebrated therefore a festival, at which he recited
from "the Book of Law of Moses which Yahwaeh had given to Israel"
(Neh. 8, 1-4). At this occasion Ezra acts in the same way as the Davidic
king, reading the Law from a high tribune. The festival celebrated was
the Sukkōt, which was celebrated during seven days, concluded by a
solemn reunion on the eight day. On the 24th day in the same month,
the seventh, Ezra organized a festival of fasting and confession, at
which the whole congregation confessed their sins. Then a renewal of
the covenant was enacted in the same way as Josia once had promulgated the Law and concluded a covenant (cf. above p. 293f.). The
result was that the foreign elements were expulsed from the Jewish
community (Ezra 10). We do not know what the Law was, which
Ezra made the basis of his purification, but obviously it was a collection of laws generally acknowledged. The problem is complicated by
the fact that as a result of Ezra's work there was a break between the
Jews of Judah and those of Samaria. The Judaeans had their central
sanctuary in Jerusalem, the Samaritans theirs at Shechem, where ultimately a new temple was built on Mount Garizim—we do not know
when.

Now the fact is that the Samaritans acknowledge as holy Scriptures
the whole Pentateuch, and moreover in a recension very little different
from the official Massoretic recension later accepted by the Jews.
Hence the conclusion is inevitable, that this recension of the Pentateuch was known and accepted in Palestine both by the Jews and
Samaritans before the definite breach, introduced by Ezra, though not
necessarily absolutely definite in his time.

That there was no break before the end of the fifth century is shown
by the most remarkable Elefantine Papyri. There was at the fortress
of Yeb (Elefantine) in Upper Egypt a Jewish colony of mercenaries
and their families, probably dating back to the days of Jeremiah (Jer.
41-44), possibly even the time of king Manasseh, including not only
Judaeans but also Jews from Northern Israel. They had a temple
which had been destroyed at the instigation of Egyptian priests. Not
unnaturally the Jews of Yeb invoked the help of the authorities of
Jerusalem. When they got no answer they sent a new letter to Jerusalem, in which they told the governor Bagoas and the High Priest
Johanan that they also had set forth the whole matter in a letter to
Delaiah and Shelemiah, the sons of Sanballat, governor of Samaria.
Now this Sanballat is of course the old enemy of Nehemiah. Accordingly the Jews of Egypt in the year of 407 B.C. seem to be quite un-

aware of any break between the Jerusalem and the Samaritan communities, or else they would hardly in all simplicity have told the Jerusalem authorities of their demarche in Samaria. However, the strong measures taken by Ezra certainly aggravated the situation considerably, for Samaritan tradition is outspoken in its hatred of Ezra.

The Jews in Yeb ultimately got an oral command from Bagoas that their temple should be rebuilt on its former place. They were allowed to sacrifice there *minḥāh* and *leḇōnāh* (gift-offering and frankincense), but not the *ʿōlāh* (burnt-offering), for which they also had asked. Various explanations of this restriction have been offered: one has thought both of a wish not to hurt too much the feelings of the Egyptian priests and of an endeavour to keep more contact with the regulations of Deuteronomy. Neither explanation seems satisfactory.

From the year 419, before the destruction of the temple of Yeb we possess a famous papyrus regulating the celebration of the Festival of the Unleavened Bread and Pæsah, as ordered by a certain Hananiah. He gives directions both concerning the proper days in the month Nisan, when these two festivals are to be celebrated, and concerning the modalities. What is most remarkable is that Hananiah says in his letter that the Great King Darius (II.) has sent a letter to his satrap Aršām in Egypt, giving orders for the two festivals. Hananiah therefore was commissioned by the Persian authorities to transmit their orders. The official authorities on the other hand follow the policy inaugurated already by Cyrus and Darius I. From a Jewish point of view the non-observance of the law of Deuteronomy calls for notice, and it is indeed probable that Deuteronomy in its final Judaean redaction was unknown to the Jews of Yeb. This ignorance of Deuteronomy is associated with the whole religious attitude of the community of Elefantine. First of all the very existence of a Jewish temple, with its sacrificial service, is against the Deuteronomic regulations, according to which sacrifices could be offered only at Jerusalem. But still worse: at this temple of Yeb there were worshipped at the side of Yāhū (as the name of God is there) other deities: Betel, a manifestation of the High god El, further Ḥarambetel, the hypostasis as it were of Betel, indicating the sacred enclosure, *ḥaram*, of the deity, and last not least the goddess ʿAnāt, so well known from Beisān. More enigmatic is the figure of the god Ašambetel, either the divine name, *šem*, or a form of the Canaanite god Ešmūn. This polytheistic attitude, and quite especially the existence of a female paredros, ʿAnāt, at the side of Yahwæh is explicable only on the presumption that the Jews of

Elefantine carried on in Egypt the worship they had practised in Israel. That this worship with its emphasis on the god Betel had a strong northern accent cannot possibly be denied.

Also in Palestine itself syncretistic tendencies were not yet annihilated. We find in the third part of the book of Isaiah sharp polemics against those who still practise Canaanite rites of worship, implying sexual acts "under all green trees", and who "slaughter their children in the valleys" (Is. 57,5). The deity they worship they call Mælaek, "King". This is a name of Yahwaeh (cf. above p. 256), but the fact that it is said that they send messengers to the nether world would seem to indicate that he was thought of as a dying and resurrecting deity in the old manner (Is. 57,9). Other deities are worshipped at the side of Yahwæh, who can in no wise be identified with him, but are gods of fate and luck, Gad and Meni (Is. 65,11). Of these two Gad is a well-known Aramaean deity (his name is "luck"). Our impression that Canaanite religion had received new vigour is strengthened, if we take into account the fact that in the so-called apocalyptic literature we come across many ideas, belonging to what has been called "popular religion". It is very difficult to think with an older generation of scholars that these traits are due to literary influences—chiefly from abroad. The fact that many conceptions, agreeing with what we know from Ugaritic texts, make their appearance in some of the youngest texts of the O.T. would seem to make it natural to assume a certain continuity of development. From this point of view the polemics in the book of Isaiah look highly significant. If more of prophetical polemics were preserved we would certainly have a clearer conception of religious conditions in this period.

What is most typical is that the prophets cease to be an active factor in the people's religion. Considerable changes of accents are discernible in the early post-exilic prophecies. There was more emphasis on the universalistic trend and this trend was now accentuated.

XXII. Post-exilic period: Development of religious ideas

The loss of political independence brought with it also several consequences of religious importance. The religion of the Jewish people after the exile differs in many respects from that of pre-exilic times. Something of this development has already been alluded to. The Jews in order to preserve themselves as a nation, worshipping their own God, Yahwæh, and no one else, had to isolate themselves from the surrounding peoples, among whom they were living and with whom they nevertheless had to mix in innumerable ways. This development was introduced during the period of the Babylonian exile (cf. above p. 298) and the strong measures taken by Nehemiah and Ezra served to strengthen this tendency towards isolation by emphasizing the distinctive features in Jewish life and religion, above all circumcision, dietary rules, and rigorous observation of sabbath. These methods of isolating the Jews from the surroundings are acts of self-defence. In sharp contrast to this exclusiveness of the people we meet with a marked universalistic conception of God. Yahwæh is the god of all the world. The heavens are His throne and the earth His footstool" (Is. 66,1). Moreover, Yahwæh is also the king of the earth who overthrows the thrones of the earthly kingdoms (Hag. 2,23). He disposes freely of the rulers of the world and we have seen that the Persian Great King Cyrus could be looked upon as the Servant of the Lord and His Anointed, who carries out His will (cf. above p. 299). The place where Israel's God is worshipped is not only the cultic centre of God's own people, Israel. No, in a near future the foreigners who have given their adherence to Yahwaeh will be brought by Yahwæh to His holy mountain. He will accept their burnt-offerings, and victims on His own altar, for His house shall be called a "house of prayer for all peoples". There is a compromise here in a double sense, for both is the God of Israel also the God of all peoples, but Israel has the place of predilection, and further is Jerusalem both the place of sacrifice *par excellence* and also, as it were, the central Synagogue where all peoples will worship him. The postulate, clearly expressed in this passage in the Book of Isaiah, is, however, that these "foreigners", *bᵉnē hannēkār*, will keep the Sabbath and keep to Yahwæh's covenant and love His name. This obviously means that in some way or other they must turn Jews—as the following development shows (cf. below II, p. 585). The compromise between sanctuary and synagogue is moreover typical. The temple, once rebuilt, was both a national and religious symbol, the visible sign of all the expectations of the Jewish people. But the temple owed its existence to the rituals of sacrifice, hence an enormous increase of reputation, as far as the bloody sacrifices are concerned. It is significant that the prophetical message of the last prophet, whose name is known, Malachi, is much concerned with the ritual irreproachability of the victims to be slaughtered at the altar (1,8).

That the opposition against the bloody sacrifice was not silenced is nevertheless clear from the subsequent history of Jewish religion and worship.

Yahwæh's position as the creator of the world is further emphasized and His deed of creation is seen as a manifestation of His might. His both one-ness and uniqueness are always stressed. There is no God but Him. The confession Deut. 6,4, is now understood in that way, that all the so-called gods of the nations are but vain idols. The polemic on the Jewish side carries on the theme once played upon by Deutero-Isaiah. Monotheism is now for all times absolute.

In the view of man and world we note a change of attitude too. There is always expressed the hope of the ingathering of the dispersed tribes. The accent is placed on Yahwaeh's promise to His people. Israel will be united with Judah and they will again constitute one common kingdom (cf. Ez. 37,15f.). Within this united people the emphasis, however, is put on the pious individual. Israel has definitely passed from an ethnic group to a religious congregation. And this congregation is centred around the pious and righteous. "Righteousness" begins to be the central religious conception. It is the foremost duty of every pious Jew to be righteous, which means that he should observe the precepts given in the Law of Moses. We have seen that Ezra in the impressive celebration of the Feast of Tabernacles put the cultic congregation under the obligation to keep in the strictest way the commandments given in the Law of Moses. It is of great significance that Malachi ends his prophecy by saying:

> Think of the Law of Moses, my Servant,
>   whom I ordered,
> on Horeb for all Israel
>   commandments and rights.
>   Mal. 3,22

The Law of Moses is from the post-exilic period on the great duty of every Jew—but also the great gift of God to His chosen people.

From Moses the thoughts go back to the Patriarchs, the promise given to them and the covenant made with Abraham (Gen. 17).

But even the pious Jew, scrupulous about the fulfillment of the demands of the Law was confronted with serious problems. The art of these problems is illustrated in the Book of Job, to be dated probably not before 450 B.C., but based on an ancient tale. We have seen that already in preexilic Israel the problem of collective and individual responsibility was actualized: the individual was responsible for his own transgressions only (cf. above p. 291f.). There was another aspect of the same problem: if collective responsibility is declined and only the individual has to suffer the consequences of his actions, then the righteous who has committed no, or only insignificant sins, will lead a happy life whereas the unrighteous will be punished. But both psalms (e.g. Ps. 73,3) and prophetical literature (Jer. 12, 1-2) complain of the happiness of the unrighteous.

The Book of Job discusses the problem of suffering. Job, the ideal of a pious man, was suddenly subjected to a series of misfortunes. He lost both family and richness, he was exposed to disease. The friends visiting him offered the traditional explanation: Job had sinned and therefore an evil fate had befallen him. Job, however, refused to accept this conventional view, offered by the orthodoxy of his times. He was unaware of any serious transgression and therefore he accused God of being unjust to him. He was not willing to confess the sins he had not committed, though pressed by his friends to accept his evil fate as a punishment from God for his sins. Instead, with great boldness he is hurling his complaints against God, who is thus provoked to enter upon a dialogue with Job. God refers to His majesty and inscrutable might and wisdom. He asks Job whether he actually will litigate with the Almighty, but Job answers that he is too slight, so what could he answer Him (Job 40, 1-2). This of cource is no satisfactory solution, it only refers to the difference between the Almighty God and the humble human individual. But also the weak has a claim to be treated in a just manner, for we must realize that the underlying idea is that there is a covenant between God and His people. If Israel, or a single Israelite, fulfills his duty in accordance with the covenant he has a claim on God to be given his share of happiness, as God has promised when establishing His covenant. The problem thus gets no theoretical solution, only a practical: man is commended resignation to the inscrutable will and majesty of God. Man is not entitled to judge about the actions of God.

A step further along the way of resignation, a step leading to absolute pessimism, is taken in the book that bears the name of Ecclesiastes. The atmosphere of the author's teaching is the lack of meaning in life "below the sun". Everything is purposeless. "Vanity of vanities, all is vanity", this is the melancholy "Leitmotif" in this treatise (1,2), where there is no reason to presume editorial revision, or a composition of various sources of a different attitude. Actually God is here thought of as an inscrutable Fate, we have advanced beyond the ideas in the Book of Job, but the germ is to be found already there. This does not mean that the ideas of Ecclesiastes *per se* must be much younger than those developed in the Book of Job. The language, however, indicates a later stage of the Hebrew language, and for that reason we cannot date the book before 200 B.C.

Both Job and Ecclesiastes belong to what we call Wisdom literature. This literary category has a marked international character, still more observable in the collections of Proverbs, where also much old, pre-exilic material is embodied. From the days of Solomon it is assumed that the Egyptian and Mesopotamian Wisdom literature exercised a strong influence on the circles of scribes and teachers to be found in Israel. Undoubtedly a large portion of the Egyptian book "The Teaching of Amunemhope" has been included in Hebrew remodelling in Proverbs (chapt. 22, 17-23,11). The outlook in Wisdom literature is international, the characteristically Israelite attitude being more or less absent. God is seen above all as the Creator, the God of world and mankind. Wisdom teaches man how to act in order to be pleasing both to God and men. It therefore includes not only the religious sphere, but all aspects of human life.

Pre-exilic Israel saw Yahwæh as the master of both history and world. He was ultimately the agent of all what happened. In the Myth and Ritual complex He had as His adversaries certain monsters, Tᵉhōm, Tannīn, Rahab, or Leviathan as they were called, figures possessing their correspondences in Canaan and Ugarit (cf. above p. 201). They represent the sea of primordial chaos, seen as an opponent of God, who created the cosmos out of chaos. Such purely mythical figures in Israel could be seen also as representatives of historical powers, so that Rahab was a name of Egypt as the adversary conquered by Yahwaeh. But we cannot say that these antidivine powers were seen as responsible for the evil things which happen. In post-exilic times, however, we find other figures, as it were, in a concentrated way as real persons incarnating the evil. Such figures are Satan, Belial, and Beelzebub, all of whom are found in O.T. texts already in the pre-exilic and early post-exilic periods, but at that time in a less pregnant form. Satan is only an angel of Yahwæh's, one of the Sons of God (cf. above p. 247), who in correspondence with the meaning of his Hebrew name, "the Opposer", appears as the prosecutor of man before God (Zech, 3,1 ff.). In the Book of Job he tries to arouse suspicions against the pious Job. The subsequent tribulations, to which

Job is exposed, arise from the fact that Yahwæh hands over into the hand of Satan everything possessed by Job. It should be observed here that Satan, when originating the evil, in this case only is a servant of Yahwæh, who cannot act contrary to the will of God. That the evil was traced back to Yahwæh is evident from such passages as I Sam. 16,14 ff.; Amos 3,6; Is. 45,7. For the later development the difference between II Sam. 24,1 and I Chron. 21,1 is typical, for in the first passage David is incited by Yahwæh to undertake a census of Israel, but in the second passage it is said that the incitation comes from Satan. This instance is the only one, where in the O.T. the name of Satan has no definite article, having passed from an appellation to a real proper name—from *haśśāṭān* to only *Śāṭān*. Belial and Beelzebub are not concrete figures in the O.T. passages, where they appear, but in later post-exilic times they are alternating names of the adversary of God. In that period another name is much used too, viz. Maśṭēmāh (cf. Hos. 9,7 f.). The Devil—as we may now call him—is conceived of as a mighty opponent of God—and this is a new conception, intimately associated which a new orientation of religious belief.

When descending in time into the period of 200 B.C. and thereafter we note a radical change in the religious attitude. Compared with above all the pre-exilic period altogether new problems have come to the fore. The outlook on the world is dominated by a dualistic view of the universe: God and the Devil, good and evil powers, struggle for the sovereignty of this world, God being supported by His angels, the Devil by his evil supporters. The outlook, however, is not confined within the boundaries of this world, for this world *hā'ōlām hazzæ*, will be succeeded by the future world, *hā'ōlām habbā*. This idea of '*ōlām* as meaning "world" is a novelty in Hebrew and indicates a foreign, *i.e.* Iranian influence. This influence is still more accentuated in the dualistic outlook on the present universe with its strong opposition of God and Devil, of good and evil, light and darkness. It calls for notice that the *physical* contrast between light and darkness is interpreted as revealing an *ethical* contrast. This again is a typically Iranian idea. And the fact that Satan, or what he may be called, is seen as the great adversary of God cannot be explained as due to anything but a strong Iranian influence, for it runs counter to the true O.T. notion of God, so well expressed in Isaiah 45, 6-7. The world then, is seen as a battlefield between good and evil, and history is viewed as a drama, advancing towards its climax, a final judgement when sentence will be passed on all people. The good will be rewarded, the evil punished.

These various perspectives emerge from the Book of Daniel, which is something of a water-shed in Israelite-Jewish religion. Here we also meet with the enigmatic figure the "Son of Man", *bar ᵃnāš*, the proper meaning of which is but "Man". In Dan. 7, 13f. he is coming as a transcendent being with the skies of heaven, is brought before the throne of God and given an eternal dominion over all peoples. The interpretation given in 7,27 says that this "Man" is "the people of the holy of the Most High". But this must be a secondary, not a primary interpretation, for in the scene described it would be more natural to take him, not as a collective, but as a single individual, who is enthroned and given power to reign over the earth. This means that he corresponds to the figure called "the Anointed of Yahwæh" in the older texts of the O.T. Originally a king of the Davidic dynasty (cf. above p. 299) he in later times very often is seen, not as a national figure, but as a metaphysical being. Behind the enigmatic title *bar ᵃnāš* we surmise an influence from Iranian and Mesopotamian ideas of a God-Man, who is a saviour of mankind and at the same time identical with mankind. This conception, however, is still very imperfectly known, so that for the present rather little can be said with any degree of certainty. At any rate we may state that the "Messiah" of the period of the second temple is a complex figure, appearing in different texts in a different context.

What also has to be stressed is the fact that the "Messiah" does not always belong to the necessary requisites of eschatology, for often God alone is the chief actor in the final act of the drama of the world, conquering and judging the evil powers—without the assistance of His Anointed. This weakening of the position of the Messiah goes hand in hand with the disappearance of a ruler of the Davidic dynasty and his being substituted by the High Priest—not found in pre-exilic times (cf. above p. 253)—as the leader of the community. The immense increase of the High Priest's reputation is seen in Jes. Syr. Ch. 50, with its enthusiastic description of the glory of his appearance.

The Book of Daniel doesn't count with a general resurrection of the dead, but we can clearly see that this idea is rapidly gaining ground (Is. 24-27 compared with Dan. 12). This idea has grown out of inner-Israelite religious problems concerning recompense of righteous and unrighteous, but the idea of a general resurrection is due to Iranian influence. For this reason it was felt in some quarters as an innovation and not accepted.

BIBLIOGRAPHY

General works

ALBREKTSON, B., *History and the Gods*, Lund 1967.
ALBRIGHT, W. F., *Archaeology and the Religion of Israel*, 2nd ed, Baltimore 1946.
——,*The Biblical Period*, Reprint from: *The Jews*, ed. L. Finkelstein, Pittsburgh 1950.
ANDERSON, G. W., *The History and Religion of Israel*, Oxford 1966.
BARR, J., *The Semantics of Biblical Language*, Oxford 1961.
COOK, S. A., *The Religion of Ancient Palestine in the Light of Archaeology*, London 1930.
DANELL, G. A., *Studies in the Name Israel in the Old Testament*, Uppsala 1946.
DE VAUX, R., *Les institutions de l'Ancien Testament*, 1-2, Paris 1958-60.
DHORME, ED., *Recueil Édouard Dhorme*, Paris 1951.
GALLING, K., *Biblisches Reallexikon*, Tübingen 1937.
HAHN, H. F., *The Old Testament in Modern Research*, London 1956.
HEMPEL, J., *Gott und Mensch im Alten Testament*, 2nd ed. Stuttgart 1936.
——,*Das Ethos des Alten Testaments*, Berlin 1938.
LODS, AD., *Israel des origines au milieu du VIIIe siècle*, Paris 1932.
PEDERSEN, J., *Der Eid bei den Seniten*, Strassburg 1916.
——,"Die Auffassung vom Alten Testament", *ZAW* N.F. VIII-1931, pp. 161--81.
RINGGREN, H., *Israelitische Religion*, Stuttgart 1963.
ROWLEY, H. H., *The Faith of Israel*, London 1956.
——,ed., *The Old Testament and Modern Study*, Oxford 1951.
WELLHAUSEN, J., *Israelitische und jüdische Geschichte*, 5th ed. Berlin 1904.
——,*Prolegomena zur Geschichte Israels*, 6th ed. Berlin 1905.
——,*Grundrisse zum Alten Testament*, Repr. München 1965.
WIDENGREN, G., "Myth and History in Israelite-Jewish Thought", in: *Culture in History, Essays in Honor of Paul Radin*, New York 1960, pp. 467-495.
ÖSTBORN, G., *Tōra in the Old Testament*, Uppsala 1945.

Pre-Mosaic and Mosaic periods

ALT, A., *Der Gott der Väter*, Stuttgart 1929.
ARNOLD, W. R., *Ephod and Ark*, Cambridge, Mass., 1917.
AUERBACH, E., *Moses*, Amsterdam 1953.
CAZELLES, H., *Moïse, l'homme de l'Alliance*, 1955.
DHORME, ÉD., *La religion des Hebreux nomades*, Brussels 1937.
GRESSMAN, H., *Mose and seine Zeit*, Göttingen 1913.
LEWY, J., "Les textes paleo-assyriens et l'Ancient Testament," *RHR* CX-1934, pp. 29-64.
MEEK, T. J., *Hebrew Origins*, 2nd ed. New York 1950.
MENDENHALL, G. E., *Law and Covenant in Israel and the Ancient Near East*, Pittsburgh 1955.
MEYER, ED., *Die Israeliten und ihre Nachbarstämme*, Halle 1906.
MOWINCKEL, S., *Le dècalogue*, Strassburg 1927.
NIELSEN, ED., Review of Mendenhall, Law and Covenant, *ThLZ* 84-1959, Col. 592-93.
——,*Die Zehn Gebote*, Copenhagen 1965.
NOTH, M., *Die Ursprünge des alten Israel im Lichte neuer Quellen*, Köln-Opladen 1961.
RAD, G. VON, "Zelt und Lade," *Neue Kirchliche Zeitschrift* 42-1931, pp. 476-498.
ROWLEY, H. H., "Recent discovery and the patriarchal age," *BJRL* 32-1949, pp. 3-38.

——,*From Joseph to Joshua*, Oxford 1950.
——,"Moses and the Decalogue," *BJRL* 34-1951, pp. 81-118.
——,"Moses and Monotheism," *ZAW* N.F. XXVIII-1957, pp. 1-21.
VOLZ, P., *Mose und sein Werk*, Tübingen 1932.
WIDENGREN, G., Review of: Le antiche divinita semitiche, ed. S. Moscati, *JSS* V-1960, pp. 397-410.
——,*What do we know about Moses? "Festschrift Henton-Davies"* (to be published).
WINNETT, F. W., *The Mosaic tradition*, Toronto-London 1949.

The Settlement

ALT, A., *Die Landnahme der Israeliten in Palästina*, Leipzig 1925.
——,"Erwägungen über die Landnahme der Israeliten in Palästina," *PJB* 35-1939, pp. 8-63.
BAUER, H., *Zur Frage der Sprachmischung im Hebräischen*, Halle 1924.
DUSSAUD, R., *Les origines cananéennes du sacrifice israélite*, Paris 1921.
GRAHAM, W. G.-MAY, H. G., *Culture and Conscience*, Chicago 1936.
GRAY, G. B., *Sacrifice in the Old Testament*, Oxford 1925.
GRESSMAN, H., *Der Messias*, Göttingen 1929.
HALDAR, A., *Associations of cult-prophets among the Ancient Semites*, Uppsala 1945.
HOOKE, S. H. ed., *Myth and Ritual*, Oxford 1933.
——,ed., *Myth, Ritual and Kingship*, Oxford 1958.
——,*The Origins of Early Semitic Rituals*, London 1938.
HVIDBERG, F. F., *Weeping and Laughter in the Old Testament*, Leyden-Copenhagen 1962.
JOHNSON, A. R., *The cultic prophet in ancient Israel*, 2nd ed. Cardiff 1962.
NIELSEN, ED., *Shechem*, 2nd ed. Copenhagen 1959.
NOTH, M., *Das System der Zwölf Stämme Israels*, Stuttgart 1930.
OESTERLEY, W. O. E., *The sacred dance*, Cambridge 1923.
PATTON, J. H., *Canaanite Parallells in the Book of Psalms*, Baltimore 1944.
RAD, G. VON, *Der Heilige Krieg im alten Israel*, Zürich 1951.
——,"Das judäische Königsritual," *ThLZ* 72-1947, Col. 211-216.
RINGGREN, H., *Sacrifice in the Bible*, London 1962.
ROWLEY, H. H., "The meaning of sacrifice in the Old Testament," *BJRL* 33-1950, pp. 74-110.
——,"The Interpretation of the Song of Songs," in: *the Servant of the Lord*, pp. 187-234.
SCHWALLY, F., *Semitische Kriegsaltertümer*, I, Leipzig 1903.
WEBER, M., "Das antike Judentum," in: *Gesammelte Aufsätze zur Religionssoziologie*, III, Tübingen 1921.
WETZSTEIN, "Die Syrische Dreschtafel," *Zeitschrift für Ethnologie* 5-1873, pp. 270-302.
WIDENGREN, G., "Early Hebrew Myths and their interpretation, in: *Myth, Ritual and Kingship*, ed. S. H. Hooke, Oxford 1958, pp. 149-203.

Period of monarchy: kingship and cultus

AHLSTRÖM, G. W., *Psalm 89. Eine Liturgie aus dem Ritual des leidenden Königs*, Lund 1959.
——,"Der Prophet Nathan und der Tempelbau," *VT* XI-1961 pp. 113-127.
——,*Aspects of Syncretism in Israelite Religion*, Uppsala, 1963.
ALT, A., "Jerusalems Aufstieg," *ZDMG* N.F. 4-1925, pp. 1-19.
——,"Verbreitung und Herkunft des syrischen Tempeltypus," *PJB* 35-1939, pp. 83-89.

CARLSSON, A., *David, the Chosen King*, Uppsala 1964.
ENGNELL, I., *Studies in Divine Kingship in the Ancient Near East*, Uppsala, 1943.
GOODENOUGH, E. K., "Kingship in early Israel," *JBL* 48-1929, pp. 169-206.
GRESSMAN, H., *Die Lade Jahves und das Allerheiligste des Salomonischen Tempels*, Stuttgart 1920.
——,*Der Messias*, Göttingen 1929.
GUNKEL, H.-BEGRICH, J., *Einleitung in die Psalmen*, Göttingen 1928-1933.
KAPELRUD, A., *Joel Studies*, Uppsala 1948.
MOWINCKEL, S., *Psalmenstudien, I-VI*, Repr. Amsterdam 1961.
NYBERG, H. S., "Studien zum Religionskampf in Israel," *ARW* XXXV-1938, pp. 329-387.
PATTON, J. H., *Canaanite Parallels in the Book of Psalms*, Baltimore 1944.
RAD, G. VON, "Das judäische Königsritual," *ThLZ* 72-1947, Col. 211-216.
RINGGREN, H., "Hohes Lied und hieros gamos," *ZAW* 65-1953, pp. 300-302.
——, *The Messiah in the Old Testament*, Chicago 1956.
——, *The Faith of the Psalmists*, London 1963.
ROWLEY, H. H., "The Interpretation of the Song of Songs," in: *The Servant of the Lord*, London 1952, pp. 187-234.
WIDENGREN, G., *The Accadian and Hebrew Psalms of Lamentation*, Revised ed. Stockholm 1937.
——,*Psalm 110*, Uppsala 1941.
——,*The Ascension of the Apostle and the Heavenly Book*, Uppsala 1950.
——, *The King and the Tree of Life in Ancient Near Eastern Religion*, Uppsala 1951.
——, *Sakrales Königtum im Alten Testament und im Judentum*, Stuttgart 1955.
——,King and Covenant, *JSS* II-1957, pp. 1-32.
——,Aspetti simbolici dei templi e luoghi di culto del vicino oriente antico, NUMEN VII-1960, pp. 1-25.

Period of monarchy, the prophets

ALT, A., "Das Gottesurteil auf dem Karmel," in: *Festschrift G. Beer*, Stuttgart 1935, p. 1-18.
DE VAUX, R., "Les prophetes de Baal sur le mont Carmel," *Bulletin du Musée de Beyrouth*, pp. 7ff.
EISSFELDT, O., *Der Gott Karmel*, Berlin 1953.
ENGNELL, I., *The Call of Isaiah*, Uppsala 1949.
FOHRER, G., *Elia*, Zürich 1957.
GRESSMAN, H., *Der Ursprung der israelitisch-jüdischen Escatologie*, Göttingen 1905.
GUNKEL, H., *Elias, Jahve und Baal*, Tübingen 1906.
——,*Die Propheten*, Göttingen 1917.
HAMMERSHAIMB, E., *Some Aspects of Old Testament Prophecy*, Copenhagen 1966.
HÖLSCHER, G., *Die Propheten*, Leipzig 1914.
KAPELRUD, A., *Central Ideas in Amos*, Oslo 1956.
LINDBLOM, J., *Die literarische Gattung der prophetischen Literatur*, Uppsala 1924.
——,*Prophecy in Ancient Israel*, Oxford 1962.
LODS, AD., *Les prophètes d'Israël et les débuts du Judaisme*, Paris 1935.
NYBERG, H. S., *Studien zum Hoseabuche*, Uppsala 1935.
ROWLEY, H. H., ed., *Studies in Old Testament Prophecy*, Edinburgh 1950.
——,"The Nature of Old Testament Prophecy in the Light of Recent Study," in: *The Servant of the Lord and other Essays on the Old Testament*, London 1952, pp. 89-128.
——,"Eliyah on Mount Carmel," *BJRL* 43-1960-61, pp. 190-219.
WELCH, A. C., *Prophet and Priest in Old Israel*, 2nd ed. London 1953.

WIDENGREN, G., *Literary and Psychological Aspects of the Hebrew Prophets*, Uppsala 1948.

Period of monarchy, oral tradition and literary fixation

ANDERSON, G. W., *A Critical Introduction to the Old Testament*, London 1959.
EISSFELDT, O., *Einleitung in das Alte Testament*, 2nd ed. Tübingen 1956.
GUNKEL, H., *Die Sagen der Genesis*, Göttingen 1901.
——,*Das Märchen im Alten Testament*, Tübingen 1917.
HEMPEL, J., *Die althebräische Literatur und ihr hellenistisch-jüdisches Nachleben*, Potsdam 1930.
LODS, AD., *Historie de la littérature hébraïcque et juive*, Paris 1950.
MINETTE DE TILLESSE, G., "Sections "tu" et sections "vous" dans le Deuteronome," *VT* XII 1962, pp. 29-87.
NOTH, M., *Überlieferungsgeschichte des Pentateuch*, Stuttgart 1948.
RAD, G. VON, *Das formgeschichtliche Problem des Hexateuchs*, Stuttgart 1938.
ROWLEY, H. H., *The Growth of the Old Testament*, London 1950.
WIDENGREN, G., "Oral Tradition and Written Literature among the Hebrews in the Light of Arabic Evidence," *AO* XXIII 1959, pp. 201-262.

Exilic and post-exilic periods

ALBREKTSON, B., *Studies in the Text and Theology of the Book of Lamentations*, Lund 1963.
BAUMGARTEN, W., *Israelitische und altorientalische Weisheit*, Tübingen 1933.
CAZELLES, H., "La mission d'Esdras," *VT* IV 1954, pp. 113-140.
CAUSSE, A., *Du groupe ethnique à la communauté religieuse*, Paris 1937.
DHORME, ED., *Le livre de Job*, Paris 1926.
ENGNELL, I., "The 'EbedYahweh songs and the suffering Messiah," *BJRL* 31-1948, pp. 54-93.
ERMAN, AD., "Eine ägyptische Quelle der Sprüche Salomos," *SPAW* 1924, pp. 86-93.
HUMBERT, P., *Recherches sur les sources egyptiennes de la litterature sapientale d'Israël*, Neuchatel 1929.
JANSEN, H. LUDIN, *Die spätjüdische Psalmendichtung*, Oslo 1938.
KELLERMANN, U., *Nehemia. Quellen, Überlieferung und Geschichte*, Berlin 1967.
LINDBLOM, J., *The Servant Songs in Deutero-Isaiah*, Lund 1951.
——,*Die Jesaiah-Apokalypse*, Lund 1938.
——,"Die Vergeltung Gottes im Buche Hiob," *Bulmerincq-Gedenkschrift*, Riga 1938, pp. 80-97.
MOWINCKEL, S., *Studien zu dem Buche Ezra-Nehemia*, I-III, Oslo 1964-65.
NORTH, C. R., *The Suffering Servant in Deutero-Isaiah*, 2nd ed. Oxford 1956.
NOTH, M. *Überlieferungsgeschichtliche Studien*, I Halle 1943.
OESTERLEY, W. O. E., *The Wisdom of Egypt, and the Old Testament*, London 1927.
PEDERSEN, J., *Scepticisme israélite*, Paris 1931.
RAD, G. VON, "Die levitische Predigt in den Büchern der Chronik," *Festschrift Procksch*, Leipzig, 1934, pp. 113-124.
RINGGREN, H., *Word and Wisdom*, Uppsala 1947.
ROTHSTEIN, J. W., *Die Nachtgesichte des Sacharja*, Leipzig 1910.
ROWLEY, H. H., "The Book of Ezekiel in Modern Study," *BJRL* 36-1953, pp. 146.
——,"The Servant of the Lord in the Light of Three Decades of Criticism," in: *the Servant of the Lord and other Essays on the Old Testament*, London 1952, pp. 1-57.
——,"Nehemiah's Mission and its Background," *BJRL* 37-1955, pp. 528-561.

——,"Sanballat and the Samaritan Temple," *BJRL* 38-1955, pp. 166-198.

SCHAEDER, H. H., *Ezra der Schreiber*, Tübingen 1930.

SCHMID, H. H., *Wesen und Geschichte der Weisheit*, Berlin 1966.

SIMPSON, D. C., "The Hebrew Book of Proverbs and the Teaching of Amenophis," *J.E.A.* XII, 1926, pp. 232-239.

TOURNAY, R., "A propos des babylonismes d'Ezechiel," *RB* LXVIII-1961, pp. 388-393.

WEINGREEN, J., Rabbinic-type Glosses in the Old Testament, *JSS* II 1957, pp. 149-162.

THE RELIGION OF THE HITTITES

BY

H. OTTEN

Marburg, Germany

I. The Conception of the Deity

Texts and works of art bear witness to a multitude of deities, in which, generally speaking, a development of the local deities of the individual city-states into the Pantheon of the Hittite realm (14th-13th century B.C.) may be assumed. Very well illustrated from the Ancient Assyrian trading settlement period (19th-18th century B.C.) are a female god, a divine couple with one or two children, especially in small votive figures (AKURGAL-HIRMER, *Kunst d. Hethiter* Ill. 35.).

In each of the various languages of Asia Minor (Proto-Hattian, Hittite, Palaic, Luvian, Hurrian) there is a word for "deity" without differentiation between the sexes and also including demons and numens. The divinity manifests itself under its own name and it is in accordance with the Proto-Hattian belief, that besides this name "amongst the mortals" there is a second "amongst the gods", which partially represents a true second name, partially is only an epitheton.

The earliest known deities of Asia Minor seem to be connected with the agricultural life; repayments of debts are dated on their feast days. Only the name and worship of the god (goddess) Parka are still mentioned in the later Hittite texts. The fusion of various tribes and thus the creation of a large state, leads to the establishment of a multiform Pantheon. The ancient Hittite Anitta-text mentions side by side "the weather god of heaven" as a central ruling figure, to whom also the wordly realm is subjected; the god Šiušummi with a Indo-European substitute name ("our god"), whose statue was stolen by enemies but brought back by Anitta to its place of worship and erected in a newly established temple; the god Ḫalmašuitta of Proto-Hattian origin, with the significance "throne". Finally, Ḫattušili I (16th century B.C.) transported large numbers of Hurrian gods from North Syria to the temples of Ḫattuša.

The Pantheon of the 14-13th century B.C. which resulted from this, is founded on system formation, in which "all weather gods", "all Ištar goddesses", though originally locally different gods, are now grouped together according to their particular function. The official state contracts refer to the resulting total: "the thousand gods of the Hattian realm"; the myth mentions e.g.: "the large and the small gods"; magic combines "the gods from heaven and earth"; finally, the ritual texts of Hurrian origin mention: "the male gods, the female deities (all)".

Moreover, the Hurrian conception of divinities also knows a group of old, former deities, who, exiled by the reigning weather god to the underworld, are available for all kinds of magical appeals. It was supposed that one could recognize various influences when a "sun god (from heaven)", is opposed by a "sun goddess from Arinna" (wife of the chief weather god) and a "sun deity from the earth" (an underworld goddess). Only specialized investigations can properly clarify the many-sided religious representation.

Theology has further combined and arranged the various circles of worship genealogically: the weather god, his wife the sun goddess of Arinna, their children "the weather god of Nerik" and their daughter Mezzulla; the Hurrian Tešub, his wife Ḥepat, their son Šarruma (depicted in the main group of the great rock temple Yazilikaya). The other deities are all provided with a place in this hierarchy as further members of the family (sisters and brothers, grandchildren) or members of the royal household (viziers, messengers, servants and maids). The Pantheon can always be extended; "the deities", "an unknown god" do not cause surprise. One is also prepared to recognize the gods of neighbouring countries: "the gods of the Kaška lands have started a fight" or they are emphatically appealed to in the lists of oath gods for state agreements (Indra, Mitra, etc. in the Mitanni agreement).

God and man are wide apart, the most important difference being eternal life for the gods only. However, the younger generation of the gods have definitely not existed from eternity, but have been procreated, without the texts elaborating such thoughts. They possess a divine power with which they can influence human life. Otherwise the gods are subject to the same emotions as men: happiness, love, and anger.

Besides the anthropomorphous interpretation there is the representation of the weather god as a bull, the naming of Šarruma as "calf" of his father. The combination of other deities with animals is frequent: Ištar on the lion, the hunting god on a deer. Animal-shaped containers, as well as weapons and cult-disks can serve as image of the divinity and be worshipped. A clear genetic development from e.g. a "stone of worship" or a theriomorphic representation of the deity to the anthromorphous image cannot be found. Mountain deities are usually represented as males, the genii of rivers and springs as females.

II. Worship

Worship is mainly designed for the daily provision of the deity with food and drink. These offerings are defined according to kind and size: cattle and sheep, bread, beer and wine are the main gifts. Furthermore the (half) monthly celebrations and the great annual feasts have to be observed; these are mostly fixed to a time and their correct execution is an essential task of the king in his function as supreme priest. They also include pilgrimages lasting several days, mostly accompanied by the court.

The deity requires further attendance: she has sleeping accommodation in the temple, where dressing takes place in the morning and by the light of a lamp she is put to sleep at night. Both the temple and the articles for worship require regular renovation; there are precise service directives for both priests and priestesses of different grades. In less well equipped places the worship can take place in other rooms when the god possesses no temple of his own. Negligence often occurs in this connection.

Magic plays a major part as means of influencing the deity. Mostly an "old woman" acts as sorceress; magic action and spells usually go together, in which symbolic and analogic enchantment play an essential part. According to Hittite Law, black magic is punished with the death penalty, consequently, the rituals we know consist of spells of protection, of magical purification in cases of sickness, family quarrels, death in the country, defeat of the army. Here in magic, appear also the dog and the pig, animals which are otherwise considered to be unclean for ritual purposes, and which are slaughtered; occasionally people are chosen as substitute for the person concerned (especially the king in the substitute rituals).

Many of the extant prayers are literary creations, partially with derivations from the Babylonian language; they also partially show a specific formal stiffness. Man feels himself not only a servant, but also a protégé of his god. It is therefore perhaps not only a *topos*, when it is said: "Father and mother I do not possess, you, my God, are my father and mother."

The deity has several ways of making his will known: —"and now my God shall make known to me completely his innermost will; He shall reveal my sins to me and I shall recognize them. Either my God shall speak to me in dreams ... or the prophetess shall speak to me or the priest of the sun god shall speak to me through the liver oracle, and my God shall make known to me completely his innermost will and reveal to me my sins and I shall recognize them."

And so besides the outward act of worship there exist signs of true piety in the confession of sins and readiness to make good. By these declarations the deity is addressed as ethical being, as a principle of order and justice: —"Do not let the good perish with the bad! O gods, when it is a town, a house or a man, let (only) this one perish."

It is popular to direct oneself to a mediator of the prayer, usually one of the nearest relatives of the great god; especially close to the individual is his tutelary deity. This concept is illustrated in the relief of king Tudhaliyas IV in the embrace of the god Šarruma, to be seen in the side chamber of Yazilikaya.

The myths of Asia Minor were handed down in relation to ritual texts, e.g. aitiologic for the purulli (New Year) feast is the story of the weather god and the snake Illujanka. The connection between deity and man has been conceived here as so close, that they enter into sexual relationship. In the myths of the lost and refound god (Telepinu myth), the wrath of the god is partially traced back to a human mentioned by name (queen or recorder Pirwa). Myths of Hurrian origin spread in Hattuša and beyond: —the history of the kingdom of the gods shows parallels with the "Theogony"; the song of Ullikummi, who was procreated as rock giant by Kumarbi against the reigning world of the gods, shows some connection with the Typhon tales.

III. Conception of Man

God is the ruler, man his servant. In the myths of Asia Minor, there is no mention of the creation of man, but the idea that man consists of body and soul is present to a somewhat different conception. "Whereas in the past I was born from my mothers womb, afterwards my god planted my soul in me." This division into two-even though the particulars are not yet distinct—makes it understandable that the royal corpse is burnt, the ashes put aside and that, independent from this, his "soul" is thought to be present and is cared for by offerings.

Only the king and his nearest relatives become gods at death. They are thereby accepted in the heaven of the gods, receive from then onwards offerings in front of their statues, and are invoked that thus accept graciously their descendants.

However, the simple mortal has his abode in the underworld, which is not even brightened by the light of belief in the life hereafter. Such a fate may even befall the king, when he dies prematurely during a replacement royal ritual: "Sun god of heaven, my Lord, What have I done? Thou hast taken away my throne and hast given it to someone else ... yet, Thou hast called me to the dead (ghosts) ... Let me now enter my divine fate with the gods of heaven and set me free from amidst the ghosts".

SELECTED BIBLIOGRAPHY

GOETZE, A., Kleinasien, in: *Handbuch der Altertumswissenschaft*, second edition, 1957, pp. 130-171

Handbuch der Orientalistik, Vol. 8, Religion, 1964, pp. 92-116 (H. OTTEN)

Wörterbuch der Mythologie, edited by A. W. HAUSSIG, Kleinasien, pp. 143-215 (E. VON SCHULER)

Historia, Einzelschriften Heft 7, 1964, Neuere Hethiterforschung, pp. 54-73 (H. G. GÜTERBOCK)

KÜMMEL, A. H., *Ersatzrituale für den hethitischen König*, 1967

Reallexikon der Assyriologie, Vol. 3, 1968, s.v. Gott, Hatti (G. STEINER)

THE RELIGION OF ANCIENT IRAN

BY

J. DUCHESNE-GUILLEMIN
Liège, Belgium

I. A Short Description of the Essence of the Religion

In trying to follow the order of questions imposed for all the religions in this *Historia Religionum* the difficulty immediately becomes apparent, in the case of Iran, of dealing with the first one without some reference to the second. To give a short description of the essence of the Iranian religion presupposes that this religion never varied, or varied so little that it is possible to define its essence in a few sentences. In fact, although its historical development is only a matter for conjecture, as will be seen in the next chapter, it does seem fairly certain that the religion of ancient Iran changed a great deal in the course of time. The term 'essence' might also be misleading, for it is doubtful if a religion has any essence at all except in the eyes of the believers. We shall then have to operate with notions, such as "monotheism", which are familiar to us from the history of other religions but of which the adepts of this one may very well not have been cognizant—an obvious source of misunderstanding.

The Iranian religion has never been as aggressively monotheistic as are, for instance, Judaism and Islam. But it does represent, in some of its sources, an attempt at monotheism, with one god, Ahura Mazda (later Ohrmazd) dominating a series of abstract entities. In other sources, other gods exist also, whose relationship with the main god is not always clearly defined. They can be equivalents of the saints in Roman Catholicism or in Islam; or they can, as in the case of Mithra or Zurvan, tend to rob Ahura Mazda of his supremacy; or else they are simply, besides Ahura Mazda, "the other gods".

Iranian monotheism is thus tempered by polytheism; it is also, in a more characteristic way, tempered by dualism. Here again there are variations. In the "classic" picture, Ahura Mazda's power is limited by that of Anra Mainyu, who is the author of part of the creation and is hostile to Ahura Mazda and *his* creation, but will finally be vanquished. (A pure, rigorous Dualism, with a God and a Demon equal to each other and indefinitely fighting each other with no predictable outcome, has never been known to Iran.) But another solution of the problem of evil had been propounded—against the general background of the opposition between gods and demons—by Zarathuštra, for whom Ahura Mazda was the father of two twin-spirits, Spenta Mainyu and Aŋra Mainyu, the "holy" and the "destructive" spirits, of which more presently. Later, Ahura Mazda was identified with the "holy Spirit" and this was the "classic" picture referred to above. In yet another system, Ahura Mazda was replaced as the First God by Zurvan, who had Ahura Mazda and Aŋra Mainyu as his sons.

The notion of free choice is a further characteristic feature of the Iranian religion. It is by choice that the holy and the destructive Spirits, in Zarathuštra's doctrine, became partisans of good and evil, respectively, and man, in turn, has to make his choice and thus take sides in the struggle which forms the very fabric of existence (the metaphor is *not* Iranian!). Even the demons, who are all on the side of evil, under the destructive Spirit, are there by choice.

This vast, all-pervading struggle, has nothing to do with another universal cleavage, that between spirit and matter. (Only in Manicheism is spirit identical with the good, matter with evil). Every being in the material, corporeal (Iranians say "bony") creation, has its spiritual or celestial counterpart or patron. In the explicit cosmogonies in Middle-Iranian, the world itself, before it became material, existed first in a spiritual state only. Man, then, being composed of matter and spirit, must not neglect either part of his person. Spiritual values, it is true, are superior to material ones, but these, as recalled earlier, are not evil: man must strive for goodness as part of this material world. Fasting and celibacy, far from being recommended as virtuous, are proscribed—except as part of the purificatory ritual—for fasting diminishes the strength of the faithful in his struggle against evil and celibacy is contrary to the work of life. And life is good, death is evil.

Fighting for the forces of life against the forces of death may summarize morality. It has a ritual aspect, which is very important. All contact with dead matter or with any other source of "impurity" must be avoided or, if not, made good—in purificatory rites or ceremonies, ranging from simply washing one's hands to undergoing elaborate rituals of purification lasting several days and nights. There is, even in the cult of the god or gods, an obsession with the fight against the ever-present demons.

II. Historical Development

It would be pleasing to be able to describe the historical development of the Iranian religion, but it is impossible, owing to the paucity
and variegated character of our sources, the peculiar geography of
Iran and its lack of political unity. Our chief text, the Avesta, in its
earliest part—Zarathuštra's gâthâs—does not mention any single
place or person known otherwise, so that it has been maintained—it
was MOLÉ's main thesis—that they cannot be utilized at all in a historical reconstruction. Although it is possible to deduce from a later
part of the Avesta, as well as from the particular dialects (two in
number) in which the Avesta was written that Zarathuštra lived and
preached in Eastern Iran, some time before the rise of the Achaemenid
power, no archaeological evidence has yet been found—in Afghanistan
or Transoxiana or Sistan—to bear out this conjecture. The origins of
the Iranian religion still float in mid-air. When the Iranians emerge
into the light of history, it is, owing to the cuneiform records, in
Western Iran, from which Eastern Iran was isolated by the great
central desert of the Iranian plateau, except for the series of oases
south of the Caspian.

The northwest was the country of the Medes, whose King Deioces
founded the first Iranian empire (Herodotus, I, 96), with Ecbatana for
its capital. They are cited for the first time in 835 B.C. in a cuneiform
document reporting a campaign of Salmanassar III, king of Assyria,
against them. The Magi, according to Herodotus, were a Median
tribe. The presence of Persians, under the name *Parsua*, was first attested in the same region, south of the Caucasus, in chronicles of
Adad-nirari III (809-782) and Tiglat-pileser III (745-727), then further
to the southeast in one of Sargon II (722-705) until they settled in that
part of the plateau lying along the Persian gulf which was named after
them: Parsa. It was only under one of them, Cyrus the great (558-530),
that Eastern Iran and Western Iran were politically unified. But the
scanty evidence that can be culled from the Achaemenid inscriptions,
and other contemporary documents, about the Iranian religion gives
a picture of it which has very little in common with that of the Avesta:
indeed only the name of the supreme god, Ahura Mazda, is common
to both sources. And since we cannot at all be sure that this god was
Zarathuštra's invention, we do not know whether the Achaemenids,
Cyrus or Darius or their successors, ever heard of the prophet and his
reform. And if so, when did it occur? Under Cyrus? (unlikely, despite

several attempts to prove this) [.] Under Darius? (GERSHEVITCH's first theory). Under Artaxerxes I?(GERSHEVITCH's second theory). For some time, a clue seemed to be provided by the supposed adoption, at a certain moment in the Achaemenian period, of the "Zoroastrian calendar" (with month-names obviously reflecting the Avestan pantheon). But it has now been shown by BICKERMAN that this line of argument has to be abandoned.

As for HERODOTUS, his testimony on the Iranian religion in the latter half of the 5th century can only confuse the issue a little more, for not only does he ignore Zarathuštra, he even does not name Ahura Mazda either. These uncertainties made it possible for MOLÉ, in a passionate reaction against evolutionism and historicism, to disregard the current problem of the origin and development of the Iranian religion and to assemble the evidence from the gâthâs, the Achaemenid inscriptions and Herodotus into a single static picture. According to him, the three sources belong to the same religion, only to three different levels of initiation into its mysteries: the gâthâs to the highest level, that of the initiates proper, the inscriptions to the more mundane, political religion of the kings, Herodotus to the religion of the common people. There was never any such thing as Zarathuštra's reform, later on more or less adapted to pre-zoroastrian, pagan surroundings. Indeed, for all we can ascertain, he might as well not have existed. This, we must object obviously leaves intact the main problem: what made the Iranian religion what it is? What, in particular, made it so different from the Indian religion?

The Iranians perhaps owed something, in religious matters, to the peoples with whom they came into contact on penetrating into Iran: first the Urartaeans (south of the Caucasus, near Lake Urmiya), then the Elamites (to the West of Parsa). But they certainly brought a certain religion with them. Before invading Iran—a term which is shortened from Iran-šahr and means "land of the Aryas"—these Aryas formed a single group with the future occupants of India, who also called themselves Aryas. This kinship is proved not only by the identity of names, but also and above all by the comparison of the two languages; and it is likewise reflected in their religion.

Where did these Indo-Iranians live, this offshoot of the larger Indo-European nation? They have left no identifiable material trace. It is known only that they entered India from the northwest, for they first occupied the Panjāb (the land of the Indus river and its tributaries) before reaching the Ganges and swarming off into the rest of the Indian subcontinent and beyond. As for the invasion of Iran, we have no knowledge of how it took place, apart from the mention of Mada and Parsuwa or Parsa in cuneiform texts, referred to above.

The presence of Aryas, recognizable by the names they bore, is attested in western Asia from the middle of the second millennium B.C. on, among the Kassites, who held sway over Babylonia at that time, among the Mitanians, who reigned in Upper Mesopotamia, and as far as Palestine. It seems fairly certain that these Aryas were closely akin to those who invaded India. An important, if laconic document about their religion has survived at the end of a treaty concluded in the first half of the 14th century B.C. between King Kurtiwaza (formerly read Matiwaza) of Mitani and his Hittite suzerain Supiluliuma: the gods of the Mitanians are enumerated and their names are practically those of wellknown Vedic gods, namely Mitra and Varuṇa, Indra, and the two Nāsatyas. The order of this enumeration is, as will be seen below, revealing.

Since these and other Indian gods, though ignored by Zarathuštra (in his gâthâs), are found in other Iranian sources, it seems safe to infer, despite MOLÉ's scepticism, that:

1) the Iranians had inherited a number of gods from their Indo-Iranian past;

2) Zarathuštra, in his gâthâs, ignored them all except for one, called Ahura Mazda;

3) his reform spread but did not eliminate the ancient religion, with which it had to compromise;

4) we do not know whether another reform, parallel to Zarathuštra's, was the basis of the religion of Darius and his successors, with Ahuramazda as the supreme god, or, if the Achaemenids came to know of Zarathuštra, when this happened.

The first evidence of the use of the Zoroastrian month-names occurs on a Parthian ostracon at Nisa in 90 B.C. By then, as a consequence of Alexander's conquest of Iran, the whole country had been more or less hellenized, but the Iranian gods did not die and as the Hellenic wave began to subside in the middle of the 1st cent. A.D. they emerged again, while Pahlavi characters and fire-altars appeared on Arsacid coins. Already one century earlier, on the monument erected on the Nimrud Dagh by Antiochus of Commagene towards 50 B.C., the chief Iranian gods are mentioned, but in close connection with Greek gods with whom they are "contaminated": Oromazes with Zeus, Mithra with Apollon-Helios-Hermes, Artagnes with

Herakles-Ares. In Eastern Iran, it is in the 2nd century A.D., under the Kuṣana king Kaniṣka, that the gods get back their Iranian names —on the coins.

Anāhitā is a very popular deity in that period, notably in Armenia and, under the Greek form of her name, Anaitis, in Asia Minor. The chief god seems to have been, not Ohrmazd, but Mithra, and it is in Asia Minor also that his mysteries probably originated. The Mysteries of Mithra contained a considerable Greco-Roman element which, in the absence of explicit texts, it is difficult to gauge. However, they are the only aspect of the Iranian religion known in some detail in that period, whose history is particularly obscure. As in the Achaemenid period, Greek sources (now also Latin ones) are a great help, but on the whole the evidence remains extremely scanty.

Only with the advent of the Sassanids in the 3rd century does a sufficient amount of archaeological, epigraphical, historical evidence begin to accumulate; still, a proper history of Iran in Sassanian times has not yet been written, let alone of the Iranian religion. We do learn a few facts here and there about the cult, the clergy, the religious policy of a Šāpur the first—who reigned from 241 to 272 and was, at least for a time, favourable to Manichaeism—, of a Šāpur II (309-379) who persecuted the Christians with particular zest, of a Kavad, 488-531, the patron of a socio-religious revolutionary movement, Mazdakism, of a Xosrau Anošarvan (531-578) who finally established Mazdeism, etc. But all the bits of evidence put together would only, at best, give an outline of the *external* history of the Iranian religion; it could not teach us anything of the actual beliefs, of the religious controversies, the existence of which can be barely surmised, as in the case, for instance, of the Zurvanite views. The reason for this void is simple: although some religious books were almost certainly written during the period, not a single one of the Pahlavi works extant can be dated before the Muslim conquest in the 7th century, nay more, before the 9th or 10th century! One of them, it is true, the Dēnkart, provides information on how Šapur I collected dispersed books of the Avesta (an information difficult to interpret) and how Xosrau Anošarvan vanquished irreligion and heresy, but it hardly tells us what heresy meant and although additional data can be culled here and there from Arabic or Greek or Syriac or Armenian historians, we do not on the whole have even the beginning of a critical history.

Only some of the Manichaean and Zurvanite material is dated (the latter in Armenian and Syriac authors of the 5th and following centu-

ries) and even with their help, to extract from the bulk of undated
Pahlavi writings a picture of the religious development is a hazardous
undertaking: if ZAEHNER, who has made such an attempt, trying to
show the oscillation between Zurvanism and Mazdeism in the course
of the Sassanian period, has only partly succeeded, it is not for lack
of patience or ingeniosity, and it *is* tempting, as will be seen below,
to explain many features of the Mazdean orthodoxy as reflections of
some previous Zurvanite doctrine.

Thanks to the royal and official protection, under the Sassanids,
the Mazdean religion was able to hold its own against its many
rivals in Iran: Manichaeism, Christianity, and (in the East) Buddhism.
Artaxšer stemmed from a priestly family and, according to the
Pahlavi tradition, he founded the Mazdean Church and built several
temples to the "royal fire" Varhrān, perhaps with the help of a high-
priest, Tosar.

Šāpur I had a high-priest, Kartēr, whose activities are recorded in
several inscriptions and who served also under Šāpur's successors.
While Šāpur tolerated, at least for a time, Manichaeism, Kartēr worked
to restore Mazdeism in former provinces of the Persian Empire, now
reconquered by Šāpur. The religious hierarchy was organized. Under
Varhrān I (273-276), Kartēr succeeded in destroying his great rival
Mani. Under Varhrān II he, "as *magupat* and judge of the whole
empire", persecuted "Jews, Buddhists, Brahmins, Nasoreans, Christians, Muktiks (? perhaps the Jains) and Zandiks (heretics, perhaps
Zurvanites)".

During the reign of Šāpur II, Christianity became, under Constantine, the official religion of the Byzantine empire: from then on, there
were two reasons for the Iranians to persecute Christians. Šāpur II
was helped in his defence of Mazdeism by Aturpāt, son of Mahraspand, who, to prove his faith, submitted himself to an ordeal by
molten metal.

Varhrān V or Gūr (420-438) was apparently the first Sassanid to be
crowned at Šīz, a sanctuary in Media where, according to the Pahlavi
tradition, Šāpur I had deposited a complete Avesta. Under his reign,
the Christian Church in Iran severed itself from the Byzantine Church:
from then on, it was possible for an Iranian to be a Christian without
being ipso facto an enemy of his country. It was under the same king
also that the highest rank in the Mazdean Church was created under
the name of *mobadān mobad*.

Mihr-Narseh, who was prime minister to Vahrān V's predecessor,

to him and to Yazdakart II, seems to have followed a personal religious policy with Zurvanite leanings.

Yazdakart II (438-457) tried to impose Mazdeism on Armenia,
against Christianity.

After a sort of parenthesis in which Kavād (488-531) favoured the
revolutionary doctrines of Mazdak, who wanted to abolish social
inequality, the throne and the altar were restored at the same time by
Kavād's son, Xosrau "of the immortal soul", Anošarvan, who crushed
Mazdakism, completed the organization of Šīz as a politico-religious
centre, reinforced the four-caste system and upheld Mazdean Orthodoxy against all forms of heresy, including, perhaps, Zurvanism and
Greek philosophy. When the famous school of Athens was shut, in
529, by order of Justinian, the last philosophers found a refuge at the
court of Xosrau but they soon wanted to go home and Xosrau ne-
gociated their return with the Byzantine emperor.

Xosrau II Parvez (590-627) married a Christian wife and was
perhaps himself a Christian. Like several of his predecessors, he was
particularly devoted to Anāhitā. It was in Anāhitā's temple at Istaxr
(near Persepolis) that Yazdakart III, the last Sassanid, was crowned
king.

Iran offered little resistance to Islam, and whatever the reasons for
this collapse, the disappearance of the Sassanian rule deprived Mazdeism of an important support. May be there was never a real and
profound religious unity, even under the most orthodox kings.
Judging from all the evidence, other gods besides Ohrmazd were in
great favour: not only Anāhitā, as mentioned before, but Mithra and
Varhrān (Verethraghna, Artagnes in Commagene). Those are the
same four gods who were dominant already in the Arsacid period.
To them must be added Zurvan, also mentioned before, and theoretically the supreme god, father of Ohrmazd and Ahriman.

III. Conception of the Deity

A. *Zarathuštra (and before)*

a) *The Religion of the* Ahuras

Mazda was an *ahura*, not a *daēva*. The distinction between *ahuras* and
daēvas was an old one, since in India also *asuras* are opposed to *devas*.
Already in Indo-Iranian times the *asuras* or 'lords' constituted, among
the *daivas* or 'celestial ones' a special category, with occult, moral
powers.

In India, after the Vedic period, the *asura* notion deteriorated through the stressing of its occult, hence baleful side, and the *asuras* went down to the rank of demons. In Iran, on the contrary, the *ahuras* were extolled and the *daēvas*, by contrast, were devalued. The existence of a worship of ahuras has been demonstrated by ZAEHNER: "First the Gâthâs themselves speak of a plurality of ahuras: secondly the Seven Chapters (a part of the Avesta in the gâthic dialect but in prose) speak of both one and many *ahurānīs* or female ahuras, and thirdly the title *ahura* 'lord' is still retained by the gods Mithra and Apām Napāt, 'the Child of the Waters', both of whom are of common Indo-Iranian origin".

As for the term *daēva*, it seems in the Avesta to have three meanings.

1) In the phrase *daēvāišcā mašyāišcā* 'by daēvas and men' used three times in the gâthâs the old gods-men dichotomy seems to survive, and it is not clear whether *daēva* is taken in an evil sense;

2) In most case *daēva* means non-ahura. It is in this sense that, in the later Avesta, ancient gods are designated as *daēvas*, namely Indra, Saurva (in India Šarva, another name of Rudra), Nånhaiθya (in India Nāsatya, an epithet of the Aśvins). On the other hand neither Mithra nor Airyaman are ever called daevas, although Zarathustra ignored them also. This must be because they were ahuras;

3) Finally, daēva designates demons which were *not* formerly gods. Such are Aēšma 'Wrath', Druj 'Lie' (skr. druh), Apaoša, Gandarǝwa (skr. Gandharva), etc. They represent a class of beings which, already in Indo-Iranian times, existed beside the asuras and the other daivas.

b) *Apām Napāt and the life-principles*

Apām Napāt, who is called an ahura, is a fire or brightness in the waters, corresponding to the Vedic Apāṃ Napāt who shines without fuel in the waters which surround and nourish him. As his Vedic counterpart "has created all beings" (RV 2, 35, 2), so he is said to have created and formed mankind (Yast 19, 52). He is therefore a principle of life. So is the *xvarǝnah*, a fiery emanation from the celestial light and, like Apām Napāt, abiding in waters, *awǝdātǝm* (Yt 8, 34). Indeed it is said (Yt 19, 51) that Apām Napāt covets and seizes the *xvarǝnah* in the Lake Vourukaša.

In India, Apāṃ Napāt was sometimes formally identified with Agni, the god of fire, whose name had almost completely disappeared in Iranian, being replaced by ātar.

Another close associate of fire, especially sacrificial fire, was *Nairyō.*

saŋha, a name corresponding to skr. *Narāśaṃsa*, meaning 'Human Message' and alluding to fire as conveyor of offerings and prayers to the gods. (He also became in Pahlavi, conversely, a divine messenger sent to the men.)

Another life-fluid and, as an ingredient of sacrifice, perhaps as important as fire itself, was the sacred liquor, *haoma*, in skr. *soma*. It was a juice obtained by pounding the stalks of a certain plant. It had intoxicating, exhilarating properties which led to its being regarded as a divine drink bestowing immortal life. Preparing it, offering it to the gods and partaking of it constitutes the chief ceremony of the Zoroastrian cult, up to the present day. Zarathuštra condemned this rite in association with orgiastic blood-sacrifice, but, as ZAEHNER has argued, he must have tolerated or even encouraged it in a purer form, otherwise it could hardly have become the very core of the Zoroastrian cult. The haoma or soma is said to be dwelling or growing on the mountains, but its true origin and abode are farther up, in heaven, like those of the fire, the *xvarənah*, and (as the lightning form of the fire, as a fire from above) Apām Napāt. It was divinized: sacrifices were offered to it, both in India and in Iran. In the Iranian legend, heroes had worshipped him—this is the chief object of the Hom Yašt, Yasna 9—in order to get an offspring. This underlines its fertility character.

Yet another life-principle was: plain water. It also, like the others, came from heaven—in the form of rain. Although no name of a river-goddess survived in India *and* in Iran (for Harahvatī, the Iranian counterpart of skr. Sarasvatī, is a province, not a goddess), there is such a similarity between 'motherly, heroic, pure' Sarasvatī and 'humid, strong, undefiled' Arədvī Sūrā Anāhitā that a substitution of name must have taken place, probably on the Iranian side.

The soma or haoma's healing power also characterized a couple of deities, the Nāsatya, who were known to Vedic India and to the 'Para-Indians' of Mitani mentioned above. They must have existed in Indo-Iranian times already, for their name survives also in Iran. But here it designates (in the singular) a daeva: Nanhaiθya.

It seems therefore that the category of life, fertility, healing, once patronized by the Nāsatyas, is in the ahura religion represented by Apām Napāt.

c) *Vərəθrayna and war*

The name of this Iranian god is almost identical with *vṛtrahan*, an epithet of Indra in India. India attributes the killing of a dragon to Indra, whom it then calls *vṛtrahan* 'killer of Vṛtra'. In Iran, Vərəθraγna has many features of Indra, except for—precisely—dragon-killing. Iran knows no dragon by the name of Vərəθra. This word in the Avesta is neuter and means 'defence'.

According to a theory revived from Mgr DE HARLEZ by BENVENISTE, there was in Indo-Iranian times a god of victory *Vṛtraghan*, meaning literally 'defence-slaying', and a dragon-killing hero. Iran kept the former, who only by chance become, in Armenia, a dragon-killer; and made Indra a demon. India raised Indra to the rank of a god and gave him several of *_Vṛtraghan's_ features, including the capacity for metamorphosis.

It must be said against this theory, first, that Indra was from the outset a god and not a mere hero, as proves his presence in the Mitani treaty. Then, supposing Vṛtra only subsequently came to designate, in the Veda, the dragon, this does not prove that his name, as the first term in the compound *Vṛtrahan*, only designated so abstract a notion as "the adversary's defense". It seems therefore preferable to go back to a more traditional view, according to which Indra *vṛtrahan*, is of Indo-Iranian date, is a war-god and a dragon-killer; if he survives in Iran as Vərəθraγna who does *not* kill a dragon, it is, as writes WIKANDER, because "the sacred book of the Zoroastrians shrank from attributing to a god the murder of a dragon, but did not mind telling of several dragon-killing heroes". Outside Zoroastrianism, in Armenia, Vahagn kills a dragon, and even in orthodoxy, at a relatively late rate, Varhrān is entrusted with fettering Ahriman.

This traditional view should only be modified, taking into account KUIPER's remark that "the epithet *vṛtrahan*, in India, is given to several mythical figures taking part in the work of creation, for instance Soma as well as Indra and Agni. Since the Avesta gives the same title to Haoma, we are led to conclude that there was a time when the Iranians also must have known the notion of *vərəθra* as a cosmogonic obstacle, conceived or not as a dragon".

Vṛtraghan referred therefore, already in Indo-Iranian, to the cosmogonic performance of a god striking down the obstacle or agent that had been holding back the waters. India made it more precise by identifying this obstacle or agent with the dragon Dahaka, which it called Vṛtra. Mazdaean Iran did away with the cosmogonic rôle of the god, probably in order to reserve for Ahura Mazda everything that had to do with creation, as will be seen below, and kept for Vərəθraγna the meaning Victory, interpreting it as a victory over evil, carried out in the form of a warrior, a wild boar, a rutting camel, etc.

Since Indra was a daeva, he was lost to the ahuric pantheon; but part of his functions were taken over by Vərəθraγna. However, this deity could not be called a ahura; but, in order to mark his belonging to the ahuric world, he was called ahuraδāta "created by an ahura". (The same epithet applied to the earth serves also to 'ahurize' it, relating it with the sphere of the ahura Apām Napāt.)

Indra, in the Veda, had sometimes for his companion Vāyu, the wind-god. Both had to do with war, but, according to WIKANDER's analysis, while Vāyu was brutal and furious, Indra had beauty and dexterity. The same distinction is seen in Iran between brutal Kərəsās-pa armed with the club and connected with the Vayu cult and his more attractive heroes such as Θraētaona.

Like Indra in the Veda, Vayu is situated in the intermediate space, which means that he reigns between this world and the next: the path which the dead must follow into the hereafter is, according to an Avestan text (the Aogəmadaēca), "the path of merciless Vayu". He is also, thanks to his position between heaven and earth, the first god to receive the offerings that rise towards the gods. However, since he was not an ahura, how is it that he did not become a demon? It is probably because he split into two halves. This is attested in Zoroastrian times: Vayu is said in Yašt 15 to come in part from the Holy Spirit, and the splitting is later completed into a good Vāy and a bad Vāy, in the Pahlavi texts. But it may go back to the (pre-Zarathuštrian) ahuric religion. Indeed, as the first god to receive the offerings, as the god of beginning, generally, he was more or less, since an action is always, to start with, ambiguous, a kind of Janus, therefore predisposed to halving. (According to MARY BOYCE, Vayu's halving was consecutive to the Zoroastrian dualistic reform.)

d) Miθra and the Ahura, and sovereignty

The two main ahuras, corresponding to the Indian Mitra and Varuṇa, were cited in the ancient metric formula miθra ahura bərəzanta "the two great ones, Mithra and the Ahura", in which 'the Ahura' either stands for Varuna (not attested in Iran) or, less likely, represented some other ahura who replaced Varuṇa. This seems less likely because there is no obvious reason for such a substitution.

Mitra, the Contract, formed with Varuṇa "the pair most frequently mentioned (in the Veda) next to Heaven and Earth" (MACDONELL) and heading the Mitani list. But Varuṇa has no clear etymology: THIEME's 'True Speech' is sheer conjecture. However, there is a similarity between his Vedic epithet *médhira* 'wise' and the Ahura's *mazda*, with the same meaning.

In addition to his association with Varuṇa, Mitra had two companions, Aryaman and Bhaga. It emerges from the Veda as proved by DUMÉZIL, that Aryaman was especially concerned with persons, with marriage, etc., whereas Bhaga had to do with riches. This would be confirmed by etymology, Aryaman deriving from Arya and Bhaga meaning literally 'distributor'. In Iran, the distinction is blurred: Airyaman is invoked in a Zoroastrian prayer "to help the men and women (disciples) of Zarathuštra", which seems quite in character, but Baga also, as recently shown by HENNING, is the god of marriage. He occurs in Sogdiana at a relatively late date, and since there is no mention of Airyaman there it seems probable that his characteristics had been taken over by Baga, an explanation which would reconcile the Veda, etymology, and the Iranian facts. It would also provide a nice parallel to another extension of Baga's power, to the detriment of Mithra this time, a process finally elucidated by HENNING: "the feast of Mithra which was called *Miθrakāna* in Persia was dedicated to Baga in Sogdiana and hence named **Bagakāna*; etc."

Apart from designating this particular god, a companion of Mithra and Airyaman, the word *baga* was, in several Iranian dialects, an appellative, a near synonym of ahura. In the (later) Avesta, it was applied to Mithra (who was said to be the most intelligent of the bagas), to the moon-god (who was also 'full of riches') and to Ahura Mazda. In Old Persian, baga was, as far as our sources go, the only word for 'god'.

When, therefore, Ahuramazda is on the one hand said in the Achaemenian inscriptions to be the greatest of the bagas and is the only one to be named there amongst "all the bagas that exist" and on the other hand Ahura Mazda in the Gâthâs is the only ahura to stand out from "the other ahuras", the two facts are evidently parallel and are likely to be historically connected, though we cannot say how. On both sides we have the rudiments of monotheism, if more elaborate with Zarathuštra than with Darius.

Ahuramazda has created heaven and earth, he has made Darius king, he protects the righteous, who act according to his will, against the evils which threaten the three levels: a bad harvest, an enemy at war, injustice or bad rule (*drauga*, akin to skr. *druh*, see below).

Ahura Mazda not only has created all things but is also the father of Entities with abstract names, later collectively called Aməša Spəntas 'Holy or Beneficent Immortal Ones', which help him animate and govern the world. They have supplanted the other ahuras and the daevas. Most of them can be traced back to the Indo-Iranian period.

e) *The Entities*

In our review of the entities, we may start, as we have done for the ahuras, with the 'lowest' level, that of 'life', and proceed upwards.

Armaiti.

RgVeda V. 43, 6 invokes "the great consenting Aramati, the divinf woman". On the other hand, if Sāyana's gloss identifying her with the Earth is in itself worthless, it tallies with the unanimous evidence oe the Iranian texts which associate Armaiti with the earth. It seems therefore that there existed already in Indo-Iranian times a goddess Aramati of Piety, Devotion, etc. (according to her name's etymology: 'agreeing thought'), but also of the Earth.

Haurvatāt and Amərətāt

In the Avesta these two Entities are patrons of the waters and plants, and already one Gâthâ (Yasna 51, 7) significantly parallels both couples: "O thou who hast fashioned the cow and the waters and plants, give me Immortality and Integrity." The ideas that waters and plants are apt to procure health and to rescue from death goes back to the Indo-Iranian period. Moreover, there are, between the Indian myths of the Aśvins and the Muslim legends of Harūt and Marūt (medieval forms of our two entities) traits of similarity too precise to be attributable to chance. One must conclude that if not with the Indo-Iranians, at least in Iran before Nanhaiθya's downfall to the rank of a demon, Haurvatāt and Amərətāt were conceived as persons, as subjects of myths.

Xšaθra

In the Veda, *kṣatra* has its primary sense of 'power, might'; its derivate only means 'sovereign'. But one passage (VIII 35, 17) already shows the specialization which in classical Sanskrit will cause *kṣatriya* to designate the warrior class: "favour the *kṣatra* and the warrior." That this is not a late development, peculiar to India, is proved by the name of one family, in the Ossetic legend, the *Æxsaertaegkatae*, who distinguish themselves by their bravery.

Vohu Manah

Vedic *manas* lacks the epithet 'good' which would make it parallel to *vohu manah*. The latter's nearest correspondent in the Veda is *sumati*. "The concept of good mind had already attained personification in the Indo-Iranian period," wrote GEIGER, but it does seem that, of all the Entities, this one is most likely Zarathuštra's own creation. As noted long ago by MOULTON, Vohu Manah 'significantly replaces Mithra as lord of cattle' in the Gâthâs, a correspondence which CHRISTENSEN had also indicated. It is the most active, helpful intermediary between God and man.

Mithra's associates, Airyaman and Baga, were also replaced in the Gâthâs, the former by Sraoša, 'Discipline' the latter by Aši 'Retribution, Windfall.'

Aša

This was the most important Entity. Its correspondent in India, Ṛta, was personified, and it was prominent, as Arta, in names of the 'Para-Indians' in Western Asia. It seems to have meant originally 'true order.' It had in the Veda a cosmic, a moral, and a ritual value. Varuṇa is, par excellence, its guardian. It materializes itself in light and is situated in the uppermost heaven. In Iran, Aša is one of the poles between which the great choice takes place, as will be seen below. It has the nearest connection with Ahura Mazda and through it the Creator filled the space with lights. It must be appreciated not only as the 'Gegen-Pol' of *druj*, see infra, but in its differences with Vohu Manah. These differences, which can be classified under six headings, may be summarized as follows: Aša is nearer to God, Vohu Manah to man. This corresponds to the late Vedic distinction between Varuṇa and Mitra. This, added to the fact that Vohu Manah, as we have seen, superseded Mithra, proves that Aša has taken the place of Varuṇa.

Spǝnta Mainyu

This is the Entity whose 'prehistory' seems the least simple, may be because it had a dual role, as the chief agent of creation and as one of the chief characters in the primeval drama of the Choice. In Vedic *manyu* means 'impetuosity, ardor, spirit,' etc. Thus in the hymn I 139,2 Mitra and Varuṇa keep disorder away from order "by the liveliness (*manyunā*) of their will." Another hymn is addressed to Manyu personified. Manyu is the psychic force, a divine force which gives triumph in battle, etc. This does not bring us very far.

On the other hand there seems to have been in the Indo-Iranian period a god *Twarštar, who became in Vedic Tvaṣṭar and in the later Avesta θwōrəštar. Zarathuštra, apparently because he did not want to reject this god altogether, but could not adopt him as he was either, designated him with a synonym, tašan, 'Fashioner', adding to it gəuš 'of the ox' and sometimes identifying him with Spənta Mainyu, sometimes with Ahura Mazda himself.

Spənta Mainyu is thus perhaps, insofar as he is creator, another substitute for θwōrəštar. But the splitting of the original Manyu into the two actors of the Choice, Spənta and Aŋra Mainyu, respectively the Holy or Beneficent and the Destructive Spirit, recalls the splitting of Vayu into a good half and a bad one. In this respect Mainyu would have succeeded Vayu and taken over from him his character of a Janus-like god of the ambiguous origins.

f) The Poles of choice

The primeval choice made by the two Spirits and, after them, by every man (and even by the daevas, who choose wrongly) is between Aša and the Druj. This couple of opposites goes back at least to the Indo-Iranian period: in the Veda, the druh is opposed to the ṛta. It is true that the contrast is less marked there than in the Avesta. But the main point is that it existed and that in some cases Ṛta has for his adversary the sorceress Druh, an incarnation of deceit; that rtāvan (in its liturgical sense) is opposed to abhidruh 'deceitful' and that derivates from the root druh are often used in contrast with ṛta.

It is owing to a specially Iranian evolution that, in the Avesta, druj and drəgvant are constantly opposed to aša and ašavan. In Old Persian, the opposition between drauga and arta is less formally marked.

Dualism in Iran has probably distant origins that go back well beyond the Indo-Iranian period. Dualistic features which are observed with several peoples of Asia and America whose history largely escapes us may either be traces of borrowings from the Greek and Iranian Dualisms, or, on the contrary, form the common back-ground, the primitive soil out of which the historical Dualisms have sprung. These dualistic features, as shown by BIANCHI, consist mainly of the opposition between a rival-demiurge and a basic creator who does not pretend to be the universal creator or sovereign; hence, usually, a certain cult addressed to his rival. They are found with peoples who are the least suspect of having undergone the influence of the historical Dualisms: the ancient Siberians and the Indians of America.

g) *Ahura Mazda and the Entities*

Zarathuštra's Gâthâs are manifestly a meditation on the Entities, and it seems that the prophet's original experience and the subject of his day-to-day mental life consisted in thinking them over, in insistently formulating their relationship with the supreme god. The initial illumination, which was to lighten up for him all this spiritual itinerary, might well have been the one chanted in Yasna 43 and which according to tradition he underwent at the age of thirty: "I acknowledge Thee as holy (beneficent), O Wise Lord...," he chants, and the ray of light spreads itself. Holy-beneficent is also one of the two primeval Spirits; holy-beneficent is Armaiti.

Another epithet, *vohu*, 'good', is also applied to several Entities; that half of the *manah* which takes sides with the Beneficent Spirit is said to be *vohu*. Vohu Manah is a kind of Providence, God turning toward man, revealing himself to him and helping him. And it is also, on the other hand, the human 'good mind.' The same epithet is affixed to the Xšaθra, 'Empire or Dominion', Indra's former appanage, which becomes Ahura Mazda's Good Dominion. The same adjective again, in the superlative, extols Aša, henceforth 'the Best Order', Aša vahišta.

A last qualification, *vairya*, 'desirable, to be chosen', transmutes the meaning of Xšaθra 'Dominion' and projects it into an eschatological perspective. This Good Dominion is a kingdom to come, which is announced and for which one must take sides. It will be the reward of the just.

In this way, through the revelation of novel epithets, Ahura Mazda's escort is organized over against the forces of evil. Thanks to Ahura Mazda and his 'family' of Entities, thanks especially to the doctrine of the twin Spirits and the choice they make, Zarathuštra propounded a monotheistic solution to the old Aša-Druj dualism. Each Entity had a special adversary in the universal fight: Spənta Mainyu has Aŋra Mainyu, Aša has the Druj, Vohu Manah has Aka Manah, Armaiti has Tarō-maiti, etc.

In this fight, the whole material universe is, thanks to the Entities, at least potentially enrolled, Spənta Mainyu being the patron of man, Aša of fire, Vohu Manah of the Ox, Xšaθra of the metals, Armaiti of the Earth, Haurvatāt and Aməṛatat of the Waters and Plants.

The doctrine of the Entities also allows Zarathuštra to put every faithful one in communion with the Wise Lord, since they are at once divine and human. Suffice it to cite some of the rarer cases where the human sense is at least predominant: "I who desire, o Wise Lord, to approach you with a good mind..."; "the one (Zarathuštra) who upholds Justice"; "whoever robs the evil one of power or life"; "those who will lend me devotion,", etc.

After Zarathuštra, this supple, delicate system was lost.

2. The later Avesta

a) Effacement of the Entities

The Entities were reduced to mere deities, which were even separated into male and female. Nevermore was their name used to designate a human faculty. Spənta Mainyu has even almost reabsorbed himself into Ahura Mazda.

b) Ahura Mazda and Aŋra Mainyu

Whereas in Yašt 19, 46 Spənta Mainyu and Anra Mainyu are fighting each other for the possession of the Xvarənah, Ahura Mazda tends, as early as the 'Seven Chapters', to eclipse his own Beneficent Spirit, for he himself creates all things. In the Videvdat, first and last chapters, this is an accomplished fact: Ahura Mazda and Anra Mainyu fight each other by creating, respectively, the good and the bad things, for instance the provinces of Iran and the plagues and diseases that pester them.

It can be said, as seen by GERSHEVITCH, that this alteration in the theology dates back at least to the fourth century B.C., for it is mentioned in a fragment of the *Peri Philosophias* of ARISTOTLE that the Magi preached the existence of two principles referred to as Spirits (daimones), one of whom, the good one, was called Oromasdes, the other, evil, Areimanios. This meant a profound perturbation of Zarathuštra's system, for Ahura Mazda was no longer, as implied by the prophet, the father of the twin Spirits: he now faced, on equal terms so to speak, a sort of anti-God.

c) Resurgence of the ancient gods

In the later Avesta, many gods of Indo-Iranian origin, but whom Zarathuštra had ignored, are mentioned and invoked, most of them in special hymns called Yašts. They seem to have developed independently and do not form an organised pantheon.

Airyaman is invoked, as mentioned before, in a gâthic prayer to help the Zarathuštrian men and women; then he is said in the Videvdat to have cured, at Ahura Mazda's request, the diseases Aŋra Mainyu had introduced into the world.

Anāhitā, corresponding with Vedic Sarasvatī, is the goddess of the waters, the fair maiden, strong, beautiful, high-girt and straight, shod with gleaming golden shoes, who presides over generation and birth and furthers creatures, the land, the herd, and wealth.

Apām Napāt, 'Child of the Waters', portions out the waters and is said to have created and formed mankind.

Haoma blesses those who brew him and drives foes afar; he belongs to the righteous, not to the wicked, and he curses with sterility those who fail to do him honour. He possesses healing remedies. The first four mortals who offered sacrifice to him in order to get an offspring were Vivanhan (skr. Vivasvant, an epithet of the sun), who got Yima; Aθwya, who got Θraētaona, who killed the serpent Dahāka; Θrita, who got two sons, a legislator (Urvāxšya) and a dragonslayer (Kərəsaspa); Pourušāspa, who got Zarathuštra. The portion of the sacrificial victim due him is the cheeks, the tongue, and the left eye.

Hvarə is the sun, shining and immortal.

Māh is the moon.

Mithra, the god with the wide pastures, the guardian of contract, is also a god of war; a god of dawn, who rises on Mount Harā and embraces at a glance the whole country of the Aryas; terrible to perjurers but providing others with victory and prosperity; surrounded with spies at his service; whose chariot, fashioned by spirits and adorned with stars, is pulled by four immortal white horses, with gold and silver hoofs, etc.

Nairyō-sanha, 'Human Message', is mentioned in company with Atar 'Fire', Apām Napāt, etc.

Pārəndi is the equivalent of Vedic Puraṃdhi and a goddess of abundance and wealth.

Rašnu aids the innocent and strikes down the thief; is in all parts of the terrestrial and celestial worlds; goes to and fro between the opposing hosts with Vərəθraγna and Mithra to give victory to the right; attends Mithra on his left, while Sraoša is on his right. He has been explained by DUMÉZIL as a sublimation of the Indo-Iranian ancestor of Viṣṇu, whose name was understood as containing the prefix vi, meaning dispersion. The substitution of ra- 'exactly' for vi seems in accord with the Zarathuštrian ethics, but may have been anterior to Zarathuštra.

Vayu 'Wind' should be invoked in time of peril; when proper

sacrifice is made to him, he averts danger, and he teaches magic spells potent against demons; unmarried girls make offerings to him to obtain husbands.

Vərəθraγna, the best-armed of all the gods, conquers demons and assumes the forms of a bull with golden horns, of a white horse with golden ears and bridle, of a rutting camel, of a wild boar, of a handsome youth, of a falcon, of a wild ram, of a wild goat, and of a warrior. When battle is in suspense, the army which first invokes him gains the victory.

Besides all those gods, there are many whose origin, for lack of clear Vedic correspondents, is unknown:

Daēnā, 'Religion' is closely associated with the Wise Lord, with whom she contracted next-of-kin marriage. According to the Seven Chapters, Armaiti will come to those to whom Daēnā is proclaimed. She possesses, like the 'Creator', an Upamana or 'double'. To her is also associated Cistā 'Intelligence'. Bound in fetters, Daēnā was released by Vištāspa, who set her as an invisible ruler on high.

Drvāspā, the goddess 'Possessing Sound Horses', gives health to cattle and has healing powers.

The Fravašis are guardian spirits, whose name seems to have meant originally 'champions': they are invoked in battle and give victory over demons and all kinds of enemies. The stars, the moon, the sun, and the infinite light, long paralysed by the demons, have been set in motion by them and it is with their help that Ahura Mazda maintains the sky, the earth, and Anāhitā, who presides over all the phases of life, be it the semen of males, children in the womb, birth, nursing. They also send the rain, through the star Satavaesa, and make the plants grow.

Rāman 'Rest' is closely associated with Mithra.

Tīra appears only once in the Avesta as part of the name of a faithful one: Tirō.nakaθwa. He seems to have been an archer-god, and was identified with the planet Mercury. He should not be confused with Tištrya.

Tištrya is Sirius, the rain-producing star, who in the shape of a white horse fights the demon Apaoša as a black horse and conquers him.

Θwāša 'Space' share with Anaγra Raocah 'Infinite Light' the adjective xvaδāta 'autonomous'.

Xvarenah 'Glory', whose closest cognate in Sanskrit is svarṇara 'ether, etc.', seems to have been a fiery, life-giving emanation of the outer light. He dwells in the waters. He caused Yima to prosper until the monarch's sin caused Xvarənah to depart from him. Spənta Mainyu and Aŋra Mainyu, as mentioned above, strove with each other to win him. He is the protector of the Aryan lands, of animals, of righteous men, and of the Mazdean religion. He can assume the shape of a falcon.

Zrvan 'Time' shares with Vayu the epithet *darəyō.xvaδāta* 'long-autonomous' and has exclusive use of the adjective *akarana* 'boundless'. He created the path which leads to the Bridge of the Requiter.

These gods do not form a system and there is no distribution of powers between them: for instance, fertility is not reserved to Anāhitā or the Fravašis; both Mithra and Vərəθrayna are gods of war; etc. But there is an attempt at creating some unity by relating them to Ahura Mazda and his Aməša Spəntas. Thus, as has been mentioned above, Ahura Mazda marries Daēnā. Or the Fravašis are instruments of Ahura Mazda in maintaining the sky, the earth, and Anāhitā. Or Ahura Mazda has created Anāhitā, is the father of Rašnu and of Mithra, for whom he has built a dwelling on Mount Harā, with the help of the Aməša Spəntas. He made Tištrya lord of all stars and equal in honour to himself. He is also the father of Haoma. Parəndi is one of his wives. Nairyō.sanha is his messenger. He possesses the Xvarənah, thanks to whom he can create all things; and so do the Aməša Spəntas (and so will do, ultimately, the Saošyant). This represents various efforts to assimilate alien gods to the gâthic religion, when this spread to new provinces and had to come to terms with existing cults. In the same way, Zarathuštra is pictured conversing with Haoma (whom he never mentioned in his gâthâs) or obtaining from Vərəθrayna (also ignored in the gâthâs) strength of body and marvellous keenness of vision; etc.

This process was facilitated by the adoption, as the appellative for 'god', of a term, *yazata*, literally 'worthy of sacrifice', which was first applied (in the Seven Chapters) to Ahura Mazda but was extended to the Aməša Spəntas, the ahuras, the bagas and superseded the last two as the generic term.

This enables the gâthic doctrine, by a process which is the converse of the one described above, to adapt itself to the ambient polytheism in that several beings mentioned in the gâthâs are made into yazatas. Such is the case with Atar 'Fire', who is said in the Seven Chapters to be Ahura Mazda's and identified with Spənta Mainyu, whose messenger he is later called, being especially opposed to the dragon Dahāka, whom he overcomes. In the same way Gəuš Urvan, the 'Soul of the Ox' is listed in the later Avesta with other yazatas. Aši and Sraoša, who in the gâthâs seemed to have superseded Baga and Airyaman, survive in the later Avesta as deities rather more defined than the Aməša Spəntas. Aši has a Yašt devoted to her: she grants both wisdom and material blessings; the sterile and the immature may not share in her oblations; she guards chastity; she is, in the form of a noble maiden, invincible in battle and grants victory; she possesses healing for waters, animals, and plants, and overcomes both demonic and human enmity.

Sraoša has not only a Yašt devoted to him, but a chapter of the Yasna as well. He was the first of Ahura Mazda's creation to offer prayer and to spread the sacred twigs and to chant the gâthâs; bearing an uplifted weapon, he has kept sleepless watch over the universe of Ahura Mazda, battling day and night—but especially after sunset—with the demons, whom he drives back into darkness. He dwells in a splendid mansion on Mount Haraiti. Ahura Mazda created him to overcome Aēšma.

d) *The demons*

Parallel to what happened to the ancient gods, the demons crop up again in the later Avesta, but there is no compromise with *them*.

Dahāka is the name of the ancient Serpent or Dragon which has three heads, three mouths, six eyes, and a thousand skills. He offered sacrifice to Anāhitā, but it was in vain and he was overcome by Θraētaona.

Gandarəwa, corresponding to Sanskrit *gandharva*, is associated with water; he was slain by Kərəsāspa on the shore of Lake Vourukaša.

Indra occurs only twice, as a daeva, in the Avesta; so does Nanhai-θya, the only survivor of the Indo-Iranian Nāsatyas; and so is Saurva, whose name corresponds to Sanskrit Śarva, an archer-god and deity of destructive lightning.

Other demons have no traceable Indo-Iranian origin. Such are Apaoša, a demon of drought and the adversary of Tištrya, Astō.viδatu, a demon of death, whose name means 'dismembering of skeleton', Aži 'Greed', Bušyastā, a demon of procrastination, Nasu, the demon of dead matter, Pairikā, a witch who can assume the form of a shooting star; she is then conquered by Tištrya.

As in the case of the gods, there are signs of adaptation of the demons to the gâthic system of thought dominated by Ahura Mazda.

For instance, the serpent Dahāka is said to be the mightiest druj created by Anra Mainyu to destroy the world of Aša.

Then again, just as some beings appearing in the gâthâs were in the later Avesta made into yazatas, others were made into demons. Aŋra Mainyu, mentioned only once in the gâthâs, is in the later Avesta the 'demon of demons'. Aēšma 'Fury' is the demonic antithesis of Aša. Against him the pious invoke the aid of Sraoša, who conquers him; and he is also overcome by Mithra. Asrušti is the antithesis of Sraoša and is also conquered by him. The Druj, already very much characterized in the gâthâs as the special foe of Aša, seeking to overcome all goodness, whose house is a synonym for hell, is said in the later Avesta to dwell in the north, to seek to destroy life and the creation of Aša and to be conquered by Aša, Sraoša, and others. Tarōmaiti is, according to the Seven chapters, conquered by Armaiti.

The amalgamation of the gâthic religion with the previous cults does not seem, on the whole, to have been a simple process. In the confrontation of Ahura Mazda with other deities, it was not always the former who got the upper hand, for we see that, in the case of some, instead of their paying homage to him, it is on the contrary Ahura Mazda who offers sacrifice to Anāhitā, to Tištrya, to Vayu. It does not seem, therefore, that the great amalgamation was due to the initiative of a single person, powerful enough to impose it, such as an Achaemenid monarch.

3. *The later Achaemenids*

From the reign of Artaxerxes II onwards, not only is Ahuramazda mentioned in the inscriptions, but Anāhitā and Mithra as well. The possibility that this triad may reflect the Mesopotamian pantheon must not be discarded, though it is difficult to prove. Ahuramazda resembles Bel-Marduk; Mithra was later (on the Nimrud-Dāgh inscription) identified with Hermes, perhaps because he had previously been assimilated to Nabu. But the chief point of contact would be between Anāhitā and Ištar, if it could be proved that the war-like character later assumed, according to PLUTARCH's testimony, by the Iranian goddess, which made her strongly resemble Ištar, dated back to Achaemenid times. We only know, through the testimony of BEROSSUS, that Artaxerxes II "was the first to set up an image of Aphrodite Anaitis (he does not say Pallas Anaitis) in Babylon and Susa and Ecbatana and among the Persians and Bactrians and in Damascus and Sardis, and to inculcate her worship."

4. *under the Seleucids and Arsacids*

After Alexander's conquest, Hellenism swept over Iran. Greek gods replaced Iranians gods, but it is difficult to ascertain to what extent this substitution was not purely nominal. Of the Iranian religion under the Seleucids, nothing is known. Under the Arsacids, Semitic cults are found in Mesopotamia under Greek or partially Greek names, but the Iranian element is elusive. Has the sculptured figure of Hades-Nergal in Hatra borrowed any feature from Ahriman? There are names in Nisa (the first capital of the Arsacids, east of the Caspian sea) which seem Zoroastrian, such as Ohrmazdik, Artavahištak, Spandarmatak, Denmazdak, Farnbag, but "there is no evidence of a flourishing Zoroastrian cult in Nisa," (FRYE) and rhytons found there were decorated with scenes of Greek mythology.

However, from the first century B.C. onwards, the Iranian element gradually asserted itself again. The two most characteristic cases are the monument of the Nimrud Dagh—a case of Graeco-Iranian contamination—and the replacement of Greek divine names on the Kuṣana coins by Iranian ones.

The monument erected on the Nimrud Dagh about the middle of the first century B.C. by Antiochus of Commagene gives list of gods with Greek and Iranian names:

Zeus Oromazdes

Apollon Mithras Helios Hermes

Artagnes Heracles Ares,

to which is added "Commagene my all-nourishing country," a plausible periphrase for a goddess of fertility. If one bears in mind that Vərəθraɣna (Artagnes) had replaced Indra and that Ahuramazda and Mithra were the ancient Mitra-Varuna pair, the resemblance of this list with the one found in the Mitani treaty is striking. It would seem to be a reflection of DUMÉZIL's 'tripartite ideology.' On the other hand, it appears to be only a modification of an older list, the one given in Arsameia on the Nymphaios by Mithradates, the father of Antiochus, a list in which the only goddess is Hera.

Under Kaniṣka, the great Kuṣana king, the coinage showed at first deities which were Greek both in figure and in name, such as Hephaistos, Helios, Selene. Then, as the king had extended his sway to all the peoples of his empire, he could afford to assert his own religion, that of Iran. Only the script and the artistic type remain Greek; the language is Iranian and so are most of the gods, when not Hellenistic (Nana) or Indian (Śiva, Buddha, or Uma).

Although Ahuramazda appears twice on Kuṣana coins, comes first on the Commagene monument, and was worshiped (Aramazd) in Prechristian Armenia, he seems to have been second, in popularity and importance, to Mithra. In Manichaeism, he was the Primal Man.

Mithra appears in the name of several Arsacids, including Mithradates I, the real founder (171-138) of the Arsacid empire. He is the god most frequently named on Kuṣana coins. In the Videvdat, a relatively late part of the Avesta, the cult described in Chapter 3 as performed in the first sojourn of happiness is a sacrifice to Mithra. It is then by no means surprising that the god whose cult spread throughout the Roman empire was Mithra, prominent in the Mysteries named for him. And it is probable that he was the 'great king from the sun' or 'from the sky' announced as the coming saviour by the so-called Oracles of the Sibyl, of Hystaspes, and of the Potter. In Manichaeism also, in its Parthian and Sogdian forms, Mithra played a not inconspicuous role as the Tertius Legatus.

It is therefore impossible to decide whether the god called Bel in the inscription of Arabissos (probably 2nd c. B.C.) stating that he married the Mazdean religion was Mithra or Ahuramazda.

Vohu Manah, the 'substitute' of Mithra, was not replaced by him. His cult is mentioned by STRABO in Asia Minor and he was to play an important part in Manichaeism, under the name of Manwahmed.

Vərəθraγna survives as Vahagn in Armenia, as Ošlagno with the Kuṣanas and as Artagnes in Commagene, and he may lurk behind the Heracles with whom Antiochus' father, Mithradates, shakes hands on the relief at Arsameia, although Heracles was, anyhow, the favorite deity of the Seleucids.

Anāhitā, whom the Greeks identified with Artemis, was very popular in Asia Minor and elsewhere, notably in Armenia.

An 'immortal fire' was reported to be burning at the crowningplace of the first Arsacid, and Aθšo was represented on Kuṣana coins. Such was the case with Farro (the Xvarənah) Ardoxšo (Aši vanuhī 'the good Aši'), Lrooaspo (Drvāspā), Oado (Vāta), and Mao (Māh).

Tīra 'Mercury' was conspicuous in Arsacid names, and Narisaf (Nairyō.sanha) was, in Manichaeism, another name of the Tertius Legatus.

Zrvan 'Time', although not directly attested in Arsacid Iran, must have been prominent at least in the theology, if not in the cult, and at least towards the end of the period, for not only was he identified with Aion (and Kronos-Saturn) and often represented in the Mysteries of

Mithra (as a lion-headed god), but he was also, in one of the adaptations of Mani's pantheon destined for Iran, the supreme god, the equivalent of the 'Father of Greatness' of other versions.

5. *Under the Sassanids and after*

There must have existed throughout the Sassanian period a three-cornered rivalry between Mazdeism, Zurvanism, and the non-gâthic cults. But it is very difficult indeed to assign the respective importance of these elements and to discover a line of evolution.

According to the Dēnkart and other Pahlavi sources, the founder of the Sassanian dynasty, Artaxšēr, was also the founder of Mazdean orthodoxy, and it would appear, as ZAEHNER writes, that "the Sassanian kings saw in Zoroastrianism the only answer to the rising dogmatisms of both Christianity ans Manichaeanism. They came into power in the third century, and they were thereby faced with a challenge which their 'irreligious' predecessors had not had to meet." The tradition names a Tosar (formerly read Tansar) as the artisan of this reform under Ardašir. On the other hand, the rock inscriptions, which have the merit of authenticity, start only under Šāpur and ignore Tosar, but speak of the high priest Kartēr, formerly known only as the inquisitor who did Mani to death. It now appears that "he was the principal agent in the Zoroastrian revival that took place in the first century of Sassanian rule. Under him Zoroastrianism appears for the first time as a fanatical and persecuting religion." But although, among the persecuted religions enumerated, Jews, Christians, Manichees, Mandaeans, Buddhists, Brahmans, there are "Heretics within the Magian community," we hardly know in what orthodoxy consisted. Particularly, what part did Zurvanism play in it?

It was certainly exaggerated to say that "foreign sources for the late Achaemenian and Sassanian periods represent Persian Zoroastrianism as Zurvanite, whereas the native texts (almost all composed after the Muslim conquest) embody a predominantly Mazdean orthodoxy." For even the Christian texts do not always designate Zurvan as supreme god of Mazdeism, but sometimes, under the name of Zeus, or of 'the great Zeus', Ohrmazd, sometimes Mihr, or both. On the other hand, the theory, put forward by WESENDONK and revived by ZAEHNER, that the two schools of Zoroastrianism dominated alternately during the Sassanian period has been convincingly combated by Dr. MARY BOYCE who showed that the evidence is sufficient only for the alleged Zurvanite periods: there seems a lack of proof for that

Mazdeism of any Sasanian king. There is, to begin with, no proof for Kartēr persecuted Zurvanites. For even "if it were admitted as proved that Kartēr persecuted materialist Zurvanites, there is nothing in the evidence to exclude Kartēr from the ethical Zurvanites, who appear to have been the better known and more influential."

It is likely, then, that Zurvanism was dominant throughout the Sassanian period. And although the Avestan and Pahlavi texts reflect a Mazdean reaction, Zurvanism has left traces in it, direct and indirect as will appear when Cosmogony is dealt with. That Ohrmazd was conceived by the Mazdeans as a four-fold god, bearing the names of Ohrmazd, Time, Space and Religion respectively, seems due to a Zurvanite precedent in which Zurvan had three associates, Light, Power, and Wisdom.

Three varieties of Zurvanism have been distinguished by ZAEHNER. First the Zandiqs derived all creation from infinite Space-Time, denied heaven and hell, did not believe in rewards and punishments, and did not admit the existence of the spiritual world. Secondly the astrological fatalists believed that not only man's earthly lot, but also his character were determined by Fate, itself ruled by the (good) twelve Signs of the Zodiac and the (evil) seven planets. Lastly the Zurvanites proper regarded Infinite Time, in its personification as the god Zurvan, as being the father of the twin spirits of good and evil, Ohrmazd and Ahriman.

Whereas the Zurvanites insist on God's infinity, the Mazdeans see him above all as good, and therefore limited by Evil, with which he has nothing in common. Ohrmazd is Light, Ahriman is Darkness.

To judge from contemporary documents, as distinct from the Pahlavi writings, which in so far as they are datable, are post-Sassanian, Ohrmazd is only one of several gods. Many kings, notably the first two of the dynasty, Artaxšēr and Šāpur, owe him their investiture.

There appears, attested for the first time under Šāpur, the term Yazdān, originally the plural of *yaẓata*, an Avestan word designating, as we saw above, any god as worthy of cult.

It is to Mithra that Ohrmazd I and II and Artaxšēr II owe their investiture. Varhrān imitates his crown. A great minister is called Mihr-Narseh. An intaglio belonging to a certain Humihr shows an aureoled Mihr on a two-horse chariot, who appears also on a post-Sassanian fabric. The great feast of the Mihragan is named for him, and so is the fire Burzēn-Mihr.

Varhrān is the generic name of the royal fires; Šāpur, then Kartēr have founded many Varhrān fires. Several gods kings call themselves Varhrān, and the second of them has on his crown a pair of wings, symbolizing Varhrān's winged incarnation. This type is later to be frequently followed.

Anāhitā bestows investitures on most kings up to Šāpur III, and many of them imitate her crown. Her temple at Istaxr is tended by Artaxšēr and his successors, probably up to Varhrān II, and in it Yazdakart III, the last Sassanid, is elected. Šāpur II founds a temple to the Waters, which means probably Anāhitā. Under the name of Nanai she appears in the Martyrdom of Mu'ain (under Šāpur II) and is attested in Sogdian. Without a name, but unmistakably, she appears on several intaglios, holding a flower, a bird, a child.

It will be seen that those four gods, Ohrmazd, Mithra, Varhrān, Anāhitā, correspond to the four in the list of Commagene.

Other gods are less conspicuous. Zurvan appears only once, in the name of a son of Mihr-Narse, Zurvāndād. Narse is the Middle-Iranian form of Nairyo-sanha, in Parthian Narisaf. Xvarr or Farn, the royal fortune, gives its name to one of the great fires, Farnbāg, and is found in personal names.

IV. Worship

1. Cult *(Magic, divination, prayer, sacrifice, sacrament, holy persons)*

a. *Magic.* Although its name was coined (by the Greeks) after that of the Magi, magic, as the method of constraining occult, often evil forces, in contradistinction to the cult of the gods which tries to influence them not by way of compulsion, but by securing their powerful goodwill, was formally condemned by Zoroastrianism, which treated sorcerers (*yātu*) and witches (*pairikā*) as criminals. According to the Videvdat and the Bundahišn, for instance, a plague created by Ahriman against one province of Iran was sorcery. And it was known to the Greeks, notably to ARISTOTLE, that the Magi did not know magic in the vulgar sense of the term, *their* magic being a 'service of the gods'. All the same, there are magic elements, either as survivals or degeneracies or corruptions, in many cult-practices, and prayers are often used as spells. Even the means of averting a magic influence may be itself magic. For instance, according to Yašt 14, 34 sq., if a spell has been cast against somebody he should take a feather of the widewinged falcon and with it rub his body; this will curse back the enemy.

b. *Divination*. Several methods of divination were in use in Iran. The hero of the Book of Arda Viraf, a Pahlavi work, when he decided to visit the hereafter, took a narcotic that was named after Vištāspa, Zarathuštra's protector. This recalls shamanistic practices, attested, on the other hand, amongst the Scythians by HERODOTUS. Besides other means such as rhabdomancy, cylicomancy, prophetic animals, the chief ones are oneiromancy, astrology, and ordeal.

The Magi of HERODOTUS were famous as dream-interpreters (and astrologers). For examples of oneiromancy, we have only Greek testimonies about Cyrus and Xerxes. Later it is attested in the Gesta of Artaxšēr, in the Shāh Nāmeh, and in the Book of Zoroaster.

Astrology, although Zoroaster was, in Greek eyes, an astrologer and worshipper of heavenly bodies, is absent from the Avesta. It first appears, in literature, in the Gesta of Artaxšēr, but its introduction into Iran must date as far back as the Arsacid period. The Arabissos inscription, in which is celebrated the wedding of Bel (Ahura Mazda or Mithra) with the Mazdean religion, ends with an astrological text. There is an astrological figure on the monument of the Nimrud Dagh. Lastly, in the Mysteries of Mithra astrology played a conspicuous part.

In the Mazdean system, as expounded in the Bundahišn, the planets, as opposed to the stars, are maleficent. But their names, far from being demoniac, are divine, resulting from an *interpretatio iranica* of the Babylonian names. If the Bundahišn deals with astrology, it is because a history of the creation (the general subject of the book) naturally includes a horoscope of the world or *thema mundi*, i.e. the position of the heavenly bodies at the beginning of the world, and the horoscope of the first man, Gayōmart.

Astrology plays also an important part in the Shāh Nāmeh.

The ordeal is abundantly attested in the Pahlavi books as well as in at least two passages of the Avesta. In Yašt 12, the preparation of an ordeal is mentioned, in which fire, sacred twigs, butter, and the juice of plants are mentioned. The Videvdat mentions two other kinds of ordeal, one with boiling water, the other with sulphur and gold water. The gâthâs contain one reference to ordeal as an actual practice, besides several to a future ordeal at the end of time. According to ZATSPRAM (a Pahlavi writer), the prophet subjected himself to the fire-ordeal in order to prove the excellence of his religion. That is no doubt a projection backward into the legendary past of a use for which we have at least one historical testimony: in the reign of Šāpur II, Aturpāt son of Mahraspand, to prove the truth of his doctrine, caused molten metal to be poured on his breast. The fact is reported in the Dēnkart and other Pahlavi texts.

c. *Prayer*. The efficacy of prayers is warranted by numerous precedents recorded in the Avesta. Ahura Mazda is said to have himself pronounced the prayer *Ahunavar*, and according to the Bundahišn he triumphed for three thousand years over the Evil Spirit. When the latter tempted Zarathuštra, it is by reciting this prayer, which he had learned from Ahura Mazda, that the prophet vanquished the Evil Spirit.

The Avesta knows one attitude of prayer. And the word designating it, *ustānazasta*, is very ancient, for it is found also in Vedic India: *uttānahasta*. It is represented on reliefs at Naqš i Rustam, Daskyleion, etc.: one hand is held vertically towards the deity.

Prayers were chanted or psalmodized, but the most characteristic way was for the Zoroastrians to murmur or drone.

The gâthâs are hymns adressed by Zarathuštra to the Wise Lord and his escort of Entities. Zarathuštra's attitude towards them is almost entirely made up of questions and demands. He needs him, he calls him to help, he tries to engage in a dialogue in order to obtain enlightenment, instructions, and also victory over his enemies. He also asks for his salary, as did the Vedic bards in the *danastuti*.

The four short gâthic prayers very often repeated are, besides the *Ahunavar* mentioned above, and the *Airyemā išyō* to which we alluded a propos of Airyaman, the *Ašem Vohu* and the *Yenhē hātām*. They are difficult to translate, and the Parsis have but a vague idea of their meaning.

In the Seven Chapters (in gâthic) are embedded a prayer to the Waters and one to Fire.

The Yašts consist essentially, besides the praise of the deity, in relating how such and such a favour was obtained, or in explaining how it should be asked for.

The efficacy of prayer greatly depends on the time in which it is recited. There are five moments in the day in which prayer is compulsory: they are those in which the priest tend the sacred fire. The first one, Avestan *havani* 'pressing (of the haoma)' takes place at sunrise; the second one, *rapithwina*, at the midday meal; the third, *uzayeirina*, in the afternoon; the fourth, *aiwisruθrima*, at dusk; the fifth, *ušahina*, literally 'at dawn', from midnight to sunrise. The prayers at these different moments include hymns to fire, the waters, the sun and the moon.

Prayers are also recited at various moments of the day, when rising, washing, before and after eating, or when performing natural functions. The hymn to the moon is recited once a month. And there are many circumstances of life, such as beginning any enterprise, in which prayers are prescribed. A long list of them is given in the Pahlavi Šayast ne Šayast; another one in recent Rivāyāts in Gujarati.

Sacrifices and sacraments, to be dealt with presently, are of course steeped in prayer.

d. *Sacrifice*. The three chief instruments of sacrifice, in the Iranian religion, were blood, haoma, and fire.

α) blood-sacrifice. Zarathuštra seems to have disapproved of a certain sacrificial rite, but it is by no means certain that he condemned blood-sacrifice as such. Anyhow, sacrifices of animals are attested in several parts of the Avesta. The term *myazda* designates an offering of meat and wine. In Yasna 11 the parts of the victim are mentioned to which Haoma is entitled. In Yašt 8 and Videvdat 18 sacrifices of sheep are prescribed.

The sacrifice of bulls is still mentioned in the Avesta (together with that of horses and sheep). Under the Achaemenids blood sacrifice was widely in use. HERODOTUS describes it. So does, under the Parthians, STRABO. PLUTARCH also speaks of blood sacrifices, but it is in the cult of Ahriman: a wolf is immolated. Under the Sassanians, the inscription of Šāpur tells us that the king, as he founded fires, assigned one lamb a day for the sacrifices. The Armenian historian ELISAEUS says that Yazdakart II celebrated his victory over various peoples by sacrificing on the fire-altar many bulls and long-haired goats. Five Pahlavi texts deal with blood-sacrifice. The memory of sacrifices of bulls survives in the Pahlavi term for sheep: *gospand*, which stems from the Avestan words *gav* 'ox' and *spanta* 'sacred'. When bulls ceased to be sacrificed and were replaced by more economical sheep, the name of the former was transferred to the latter.

The central act in the Mysteries of Mithra shows the god slaying the primeval Bull, from whose tail a corn-ear grows. This must be added in anticipation of the next chapter, which will deal with Cosmogony, to the evidence from the Pahlavi books about the bull-sacrifice which is three-fold, namely: Ahriman's slaughter of the Bull, which resulted in the production of all animal and vegetable life (so too, apparently, on the Mithraic monuments); the Bull-sacrifice at the end of time, which is to bring immortality to all men (it was almost certainly the principal purpose of the Mithraic sacrifice to secure

immortality); the Bull-sacrifice of Man's first parents, as told in the
Bundahišn. The presence of a dog and a carnivorous bird at the sacrifice and the participation of the daevas indicate, as ZAEHNER has well
seen, that this sacrifice is indeed the original of the bull-sacrifice celebrated in the Mysteries of Mithra.

β) haoma.   The preparation of the haoma is itself a whole ceremony. Twigs of the haoma plant are washed in the sacred water; they
are then pounded in a mortar, the sides of which have been struck
repeatedly by the pestle whilst apotropaic formulas were uttered. The
juice is collected and filtered through a sieve made up of hairs of the
sacred bull. The haoma sacrifice is a life-giving operation, analogous
to the soma sacrifice in India. One of the aspects of its action is
revealed in procreation. The heroes who first pressed the haoma,
according to the Hom Yašt (Yasna 9-11), always obtained, as sole
favour, an offspring. For the same reason Zurvan offered sacrifice
during a thousand years, and in India Prajāpati offers *ghee* to the fire.
And as Prajāpati's most eager adversary is *Mṛtyu*, 'Death', so is Haoma
the enemy of the daevas and death. Haoma was until recently given
to the dying as a viaticum, the aliment of immortality. In the same
fashion, the Vedic bards who have drunk the soma are immortal. The
Yasna, or sacrifice of the haoma, is often performed for the sake of
the deceased—for an obvious reason. And it is to the deceased that
the offering of the bread and *ghee* is destined, a rite which can constitute a special ceremony, in that case addressed to Sraoša, conductor
of the dead souls.

γ) fire.   A fire is present at most rites. The Nirangistan expressly
states that the offerings of flesh and fat are made to the fire. In the
Yasna, it receives no solid or liquid offering, but the priest faces it
during the whole ceremony and at several moments he explicitly
addresses it, looks at it, presents it with the haoma, etc.

The fire of the highest grade, Varhrān or Bahrām fire, is kept in the
principal temples and treated as a king: a crown is hung over it;
several Pahlavi texts call it the king of fires; its installation is called
enthronement.

That the sacred fire should constantly be kept burning, that it should
be considered criminal to let it die, is not a peculiar trait of the Iranian
religion. The same rule prevails, for instance, in the cult of Vesta, and
it seems probable that the cult of the domestic fire had already developed in this way in the Indo-European period. The care with
which the Mazdeans tend the fire is, at least in part, older than the

Iranian nation. Thus, when they 'purify' it, they designate this action by a word of Indo-European origin: *yaoždā*.

Two traditions seems to have coalesced in the Rivayats (either in Pahlavi or Persian) which deal with the fire-ritual. A first rite is a purification of fire by refinement, with transfer of the flame only and its reunion with others similar to it, with a view to founding a superior fire, the other is a regeneration of fire through transfer of the worn-out fire (viz. of its glowing embers, without the flame) to a superior fire already existing. The inferior fire is brought back to its master, so to speak, in order to renew its virtue. This recalls the custom, current all over the world, of the renewal of fires on New Year's eve; and indeed it seems probable that, to give the rite its full meaning, it had to be completed by returning the fire once again to the hearth from which it had been taken. This rite seems to have been important under the Sassanids.

Apart from the distinction between the *Bahrām* fire, second-rank fires or *Adarān*, sufficient for a village with a dozen families, and the third-rank or domestic fires, *Dādgāh*, there existed under the Sassanids a distribution of fires according to social classes: the *Farnbāg* was connected with priests, the *Gušnasp* with warriors, and the *Burzēn-Mihr* with husbandmen. The three fires are not named in the Avesta, but they are alluded to in the section of it called *Sīrōza*. There is yet another classification, already attested in the Avesta and in which a physical speculation is reflected: a physical doctrine of the universal presence of fire. It distinguishes between five fires, and it is certainly no mere chance if India also knows three sacrificial fires (roughly corresponding with Iran's three 'social' fires) and five natural ones.

The sun's rays must not fall on the fire, whose power would thereby be diminished. For the same reason, fire may not be brought to a fire, only 'cooled fire' may. The faithful would content themselves with filing round the fire, in the corridor surrounding the room where it was burning. But there also seems to have been ceremonies where the fire was displayed, if one may judge by the *tetrapyles*, open on all four sides and placed on the summit of hills, as if to be seen from all points around by night—and from as far as possible. No text mentions such a rite, but there seems no other way of justifying the choice of high places.

e. *Sacrament.* This term may be reserved, for convenience's sake, to ceremonies in which one faithful at a time is personally involved. One must distinguish between ceremonies of initiation, of purification, and of funerary character.

α) initiation. Every Mazdean had to be initiated, in his youth, in a ceremony consisting essentially in investing him or her with the thread and the shirt. The thread or girdle is the obligatory emblem of every Mazdean, who ties and unties it several times a day. A multiple symbolism is attached to it. In the universe its counterpart is the Milky Way. On the other hand, the girdle which Ahura Mazda offered to Haoma symbolizes 'the good Mazdean religion'. The shirt should be white, a symbol of innocence, but above all, a symbol of religion. The soul after death dons a white, luminous garment which, like the shirt worn by the living, is the garment of Vohu Manah. This garment of the soul is a frequent theme in Pahlavi literature: the virtues that help combat evil are the garments, the weapons, and the armour of the faithful, etc.

More complicated ceremonies of initiation operate the admission into the priestly state. Priests will be dealth with infra, p. 351.

β) purification. The main ceremony of purification, called barə-šnum, is described in the Videvdat. The candidate places himself successively on holes made in the ground. They are obviously destined to receive and pass on to the soil the impurities of which the man strips himself by means of gōmēz (bull's urine), sand, and water. These holes are surrounded at some distance with furrows traced in rectangles, the aim of which is clear: it is to limit the zones of pollution in which the disinfection is carried on. What is sacred, like what is impure, is circled off, for the two notions are originally one.

The barəšnum requires the presence of a dog, which is led up to the candidate several times to be touched by him with his left hand, on the left ear. This dog must be 'four-eyed', viz. he must have two spots underneath the eyes, a peculiarity supposed to double the efficiency of his gaze. In the funeral rite also a four-eyed dog is led into the presence of the deceased person. One can scarcely separate the funerary sagdīd ('dog's gaze') from the belief in the two dogs which, according to the Videvdat, keep the Bridge of the Retributor and which in turn have their opposite numbers in India in the two 'four-eyed' dogs, messengers of the death god Yama.

γ) funerary ceremonies. A well-known feature of the Mazdean religion is the method of disposing of the dead by means of towers, described in the Videvdat which calls them daxma, in which the bodies are abandoned to birds of prey. The origin of this usage, in which the Mazdeans see a means of avoiding the defilement of either the earth or water or fire, is not known. We read only in HERODOTUS that the

Magi neither buried their dead nor burnt them, but exposed them to birds and dogs. On the other hand Cyrus had himself buried in a sarcophagus on top of a kind of tower, and the other Achaemenids had their bodies covered with wax and buried in rock-hewn tombs.

After the bodies had been long enough esposed, the bones would be collected and preserved in ossuaries called *astodan*.

f. *Holy Persons*. It seems appropriate under this heading to deal successively with Zarathuštra and the priests in general.

α) Zarathuštra called himself a *ẑaotar*, the equivalent of Skr. *hotṛ*, which must have meant that he was competent in invoking deities and presenting them with liquid offerings. Seven other kinds of officiants are named in the Visprat (a section of the Avesta), and such is also the case in the Veda. But since the names do not coincide, one must conclude that only the role of the *hotṛ-ẑaotar* is securely attested for the Indo-Iranian period.

β) The gâthâs mention *usigs* and *karapans*, apparently priests of condemned cults, and the term *kavi*, which has its exact counterpart in India and must have meant originally a seer, is taken in a pejorative sense, except in the case of Kavi Vištāspa. In the later Avesta, it is the title of the sovereigns of a certain dynasty. The term for 'priest' in the later Avesta was *athaurvan*, which can hardly be separated from Skr. *atharvan*, on the one hand, and from the Iranian word for 'fire', *ātar*, on the other.

The term *magu* is attested in Old Persian but occurs only once in the whole Avesta, which must therefore, for some unknown reason, have expressly avoided it. But the gâthâs had the term *magavan*, which may have been somehow connected with *magu* but whose exact meaning is far from clear. Etymologically, it corresponded nearly exactly with Skr. *maghavant*, which meant 'generous'.

A priestly hierarchy does not seem to have existed in Iran until after Šāpur's reign. Under him and his predecessor Artaxšēr there were simply *magus* or *mogmarts*, generic terms found on intaglios and in the Gesta of Artaxšēr. *Erpats* were a special kind of priest, in Avestan *aēθra-paiti* or 'master of instruction'.

When rudiments of a hierarchy were created—probably under Ohrmazd I and to the benefit of Kartēr—a term was coined to signify the subordination of several magi to one, namely *magu-pat* 'master of magi', whose resemblance with *ēr-pat* 'master of instruction' is only superficial. Later, perhaps under Varhrān V, a supreme ecclesiastical dignity was created and its title was copied from that of the King of Kings, *šāhān šāh*, hence *mōgpatān mōgpat* (today *mōbadān mōbad*).

2. *Ethics*

The precepts of Mazdean ethics can be seen from two angles: maintenance of life and fight against evil. In order to maintain life one must earn one's living by means of cattle-raising and agriculture, and one must procreate. To fight against evil is to combat the demons and whatever beings, men or animals, belong to them. In a sense, the two points of view seem to coincide, considering that the forces of evil are the forces of death: good is opposed to evil as light is to darkness, as life to non-life. In fact the life-precepts can be transposed into fight-precepts: for instance, eating and drinking are interpreted by ZāTSPRAM as a struggle against the she-demon Āz 'Concupiscence'.

In another sense, the two points of view are contradictory: how can we fight the forces of evil without suppressing certain lives, for instance baleful animals? It is then the second viewpoint that prevails: Iran ignores, even in theory, the universal respect of life which is preached by Buddhism or which justifies the vegetarian diet of Brahmanic India.

If human lives are at stake, which viewpoint will prevail? Must one kill the enemies of life? On this point, Zoroastrianism varied. Zarathuštra urged that the forces of the Lie should be combated by force of arms. Under the Sassanids, from the time of Kartēr onwards, Manichaeans, Christians, Buddhists, etc. were persecuted. Under the Muslim rule, Mazdeism lost all aggressiveness. There is only one case in which death is to be preferred to life; that is when a Mazdean dies in order to avoid apostasy. There remains the duty to treat the wicked badly, a duty expressly proclaimed by Zarathuštra.

The 'vitalistic' viewpoint contains moreover its own condemnation: each living being feeds on another living being, whom it must kill. And Aturpāt, son of Mahraspand, enjoins: "Abstain rigorously from eating the flesh of kine and all domestic animals... For though you eat but a mouthful, you involve your hand in sin, and though a camel be slain by another man in another place it is as if you had slain it with your own hand." This interdiction is in line with Zarathustra's for-bidding of at least some form of the ox-sacrifice. One could live on bread, milk, plants, and water, and one must in any case till the earth and raise cattle and milk it. Forsaking animal food will be the prelude to Resurrection. But Mazdeism in no case tolerates fasting, which is considered as weakening the faithful in their struggle against evil. And there are in the Avesta several references to animal food, perhaps a survival from nomadic times when flesh was only eaten when it had been sacrificed.

Since sexual activity is subordinate to the duty of procreation, it is understandable that homosexuality should be banished, as well as intercourse with courtesans or prostitutes, personages who were typified in the Primeval Whore, whose action was interpreted in dualistic terms: she mixed up the seed of the wicked with that of the good, instead of keeping them apart.

It will also be seen that celibacy and absolute chastity are to be proscribed: the human kind ought to be perpetuated, as an indispensable auxiliary to Ohrmazd in his struggle against Ahriman. Mazdeism condemns the asceticism of the Christians, Manicheans, etc.

It is less easy to see why adultery and polygamy should be condemned in the name of the same principle. On the contrary, if by indulging in a desire one stills it—as the demon of hunger is combated by eating—this method should be authorized. In fact, Mazdak, the fifth century 'communist' reformer who claimed to interpret Zoroastrianism aright, recommended the sharing of women. Marriage—conjugal truthfulness—has owed its victory to social and economic reasons.

Social reasons also explain, it seems, the development of consanguineous marriage. This, according to the Rivayats, is almost the most meritorious deed: it is only outranked by commission of all the rites to one priest. In the Rivayats it is a question of unions between first cousins, an interpretation also found in the Dēnkart. But it has not always been so. GRAY's excellent study of the subject in the Encyclopaedia of Religion and Ethics, VIII, 456, is worth being summarized: the Avesta mentions xvaētvadaθa in five passages only, all of them recent, and without defining the term. Zarathuštra ignores it. Greek and Latin authors notice marriage between parents and children or between uterine brothers and sisters, not only in the royal family of Persia but among the Persians generally, and particularly among the Magi. The use is continued in Sassanian times. The Pahlavi texts warmly recommend it and leave no doubt as to its definition. In the Dēnkart its origin is justified by the will to preserve the purity of the race, and to increase the chances of mutual understanding between consorts and affection for their children. The Pahlavi Rivayat remarks —perhaps rightly, given the Muslim rule—that exogamy might foster religious laxity and even apostasy. This usage seems to have been alien to Zarathuštra's doctrine, but it was perhaps an old Indo-European practice, for it had its counterpart amongst the Old Prussians and Lithuanians, who permitted marriage with a parent (except the mother), and amongst the ancient Irish. In Iran it seems that the Magi tried to impose 'this extreme form of endogamy' (GRAY) under the Sassanids and in the first centuries of Muslim rule. But it was resisted by the mass of the faithful and has disappeared.

Distributive justice was regulated from on high by the principles of veridicalness and respect of contracts. A salary that had been promised must be paid, says Zarathuštra. More particularly, hoarding and usury are condemned in the Rivayats as grave faults. A just interest is permissible (*Sad Darband Hōš*, 38).

ZATSPRAM disapproves of covetousness and avarice. To be charitable is a source of merits: "He who will give (to a faithful one) a quantity of meat equal to this bird of mine Parodars (the cock)," says Ahura Mazda (Videvdat 18, 29), "I shall not question him twice on his entering Paradise." It is even a duty, for the one who refuses even a very small part of his wealth to a just one who is asking for it makes pregnant the she-demon of Lie, "as the other males make the females pregnant by laying their seed into them."

The interests of religion are those of the establishment: religious law dominates, at least theoretically, the whole life (as in Islam). Artaxšēr the Sassanid king is supposed to have said that religion and kingship are brothers, neither of which can do without the other. Religion is the foundation of kingship, and the latter protects the former. Now, whatever lacks foundation must perish and whatever lacks a protector vanishes away. It is important for the good march of the world that everyone should keep his place, viz., accomplish the duties of his class. (Dēnkart 45, 15-19, and Letter of Tosar).

The economic order, threatened by the 'communist' preachings of Mazdak, was restored by a king, Xosrau Anošarvān. What the Evil Spirit mostly fears is the union into one person of kingship and the good religion (Dēnkart 129). In fact, at the end of time, the work of the Saviours will be preluded by that of a king, Vahrān the Splendid.

A theory of virtues and vices is sometimes found with the Iranian moralists, for instance, the one studied by Father de MENASCE, which recalls to us a well-known Greek model, the *Ethics to Nicomachus*. MENASCE compares several passages, which he designates with letters, and whose doctrine he summarizes as follows: Text A, dealing with the repression of vice, points out that it must not entail the suppression of the virtues which the vices resemble. In B, the formula requires that the virtues should be pure of any mingling with the vices which, according to C, seek to supplant them. The health of the soul implies therefore an exact measure insuring the adjustment of the powers, and safeguards them from the intrusion of antagonistic elements that would alter them."

This doctrine presupposes another one, namely that of the Mean (*patmān*), which Iran vindicates as its own—as Islam does as well: "Iran has always lauded just measure and blamed excess and default," says Dēnkart 429, 11. "Amongst the Byzantines the philosophers, in India the scholars, and elsewhere the specialists have in general praised the man with a subtle speech, but the realm of Iran has approved the sages." In fact, it is difficult to decide whether it was a borrowing from ARISTOTLE or a genuinely Iranian notion. It may be of use to remark, at all events, that the Chinese had also their Doctrine of the Mean.

This notion collided in Iran with a cosmogonic notion designated by the same term of *patmān*, namely the pact concluded between Ohrmazd and Ahriman to fight each other during a limited number of years—a formula of non-peaceful coexistence!

Anyhow, as a maxim it does not belong to a rough or primitive nation, but to a civilized one, capable of mild mores like those advocated by Aturpāt, son of Mahraspand, who writes: "Do not harbour vengeance in your thoughts lest your enemies catch up with you. Consider rather what injury, harm, and destruction you are liable to suffer by smiting your enemy in vengeance and how you will (perpetually) brood over vengeance in your heart." (ZAEHNER's translation). This is a far cry from Zarathustra's preaching holy war and enjoining to treat the wicked badly!

Ethics finally soar up to the notion of disinterestedness: "Do good," says Aturpāt, "simply because it is good." Man's destiny depends on the choice he makes each moment, and in the smallest details of his life, between truth and lie, between good words, thoughts, and deeds, and evil ones. And this choice is free. Zarathustra already said so, and there is a term in Pahlavi for those 'whose will is free': *āzād-kām*.

How are we to explain that, as often happens, the just are unhappy? How can fate's omnipotence be reconciled with the freedom of the will? The Mazdeans have asked themselves the question. Their most striking solution is that expressed in the Pahlavi Vidēvdat: *gētē pat baxt, mēnōk pat kunišn* ("the material is according to fate, the spiritual according to action"): in other words, we depend on fate only for the

material things, whereas in the spiritual order our action is autonomous. The Iranians may have found this formula unaided. Nevertheless, it cannot be ignored that the Neo-Platonists had found a
similar one, at least as far as the content is concerned. They had found
this means to 'escape determinism', as we would say: they identified
the heimarmene with the physis, and so left the soul free. However,
if the Iranians were perhaps attracted by this formula, they did not
borrow it as it was. PLOTINUS used to say that the soul, when without
the body, is free. The Iranians, unless they were Manicheans, did not
despise matter, and thought little of the soul separated from it.

This conception safeguarded human responsibility by limiting the
efficacy of human endeavour to the moral domain, the *mēnōk* sphere,
future life. But, as it was, it was too hard, and in practice it underwent
two compromises. On the one hand, it appeared superhuman to
abandon all things of this world to a Fate on which one had no grip.
Was it really not possible in the material domain to influence fate? It
must be in certain cases. The gods must be swayed. In order to sustain
such a hope a distinction was drawn in the Pahlavi books between
baxt, which is simply fate—which even the gods cannot change—and
bagōbaxt, which is 'fate allotted by the gods', who remain able to
modify it according to the prayers or merits of everyone.

On the other hand, future life should be determined by the balance
of the good and evil deeds, words, and thoughts of the whole life:
this principle is propounded in all its strictness, so much so that a
special dwelling-place—*hamēstagān*—is provided, as will be seen in the
Eschatology, for those whose good deeds exactly balance their evil
ones. In fact, this principle also is tempered to allow for human
weakness. All faults do not have to be registered or weigh for ever in
the scales. There are two means of effacing them. One is confession,
with contrition and penance: "I have made this penance," says the
Patēt-formula translated by ZAEHNER, "in order to wipe out my sins,
obtain my share of reward for good deeds done, and for the comfort
of my soul," etc. The second means is the transfer of supererogatory
merits (the equivalent of the Christian 'Communion of Saints'):
"Should it happen to me that I leave this world without having done
my (final) penance and someone from among my near relations should
do penance on my behalf, I agree to it." This transfer of merits is the
justification of the prayers and ceremonies for the dead; but these are
deemed efficacious of themselves, independently of the merits of those
who perform or sponsor them. These rites can indeed be performed

in the lifetime of the beneficiary, be he or not considered *in articulo mortis*. According to the Sad Darband Hōš, one may have sinned much: if the rites have been performed *in articulo mortis*, the soul at the moment of death, when passing the Bridge of the Requiter, is assisted by "the Spirit of the gâthâs," who supports her and prevents her from falling into hell and into the hands of Ahriman. As to the ceremony performed when one is not *in articulo mortis*, its advantages are subject to a tariff: it is, namely, seven hundred times more profitable to have the Yasna performed, not in a discontinued way, but by four priests taking turns two by two for three days and three nights.

Mazdeism is therefore not the purely moral religion it may seem. And even the picture we have sketched is still likely to be deceptive, owing to the stress put on free choice. In practice the Mazdean is constantly involved in such a meticulous struggle against the contamination of death and a thousand causes of defilement, against the threat, even in his sleep, of ever-present demons, that he would not often feel to be leading his life freely, morally.

Apart from this Mazdean attitude, the belief in the power of destiny sometimes exasperates itself into fatalism. This is a major theme and life-spring of the Epics. Fatalism easily associates itself with Zurvanism, itself sometimes tainted with materialism. And we read in the *Mēnōk-i-Xrat* that "though one be armed with the valour and strength of wisdom and knowledge, yet it is not possible to strive against fate. For once a thing is fated and comes true, whether good or the reverse, the wise man goes astray in his work, and the man of wrong knowledge becomes clever in his work; the coward becomes brave, and the brave cowardly; the energetic man becomes a sluggard and the sluggard energetic. For everything that has been fated a fit occasion arises which sweeps away all other things."

But it remains true, on the whole, as ZAEHNER writes, that "the theological premisses" of Mazdeism "are based on an essentially moralistic view of life."

V. MYTH, DOCTRINE

1. *Cosmogony*

a. *in the gâthâs.* Yasna 44 asks who created the sky, the earth, etc.: a rhetorical question, for Ahura Mazda is clearly implied. But as he appears lastly as the lord of time, it may be that a belief in the supremacy of Zurvan was implicitly aimed at. A second moment in the

beginning of things is the Choice (cf. Yasna 30 etc.) made by the twin
Spirits between good and evil, life and death, etc., and followed by a
similar decision of the daevas and of man. A third moment is the
'social contract', Yasna 29, in which man and the ox mutually bind
themselves under the rule of Zarathuštra and of a good chief, still to
come: this man will complete the work of creation and extend the
realm of the divine justice. A pre-Zarathuštrian, at least Indo-Iranian
back-ground to the lament of the soul of the ox has recently been
sought (by DUMÉZIL) through comparison with the Mahābhārata, the
Rgveda and other texts.

   b. *in the later Avesta, and in the Pahlavi writings.* The *fravašis* are said,
in the Yašt 13, to have played a role in the cosmogony, not only in
helping Ahura Mazda to keep the sky and earth separate, but in 'de-
freezing', as we would say, not only the waters, but the plants and the
heavenly bodies.

   Yima, according to the Videvdat, extended the earth three times,
which recalls in India the three steps of Viṣṇu. He must have been one
of the figures of 'primal man' current in the Indo-Iranian mythology:
Yama became in India the king of the dead. He is, on both sides, the
son of Vivasvant-Vivanhan, who is in India identified with the sun.
Gayōmart, whose name seems made up of two gâthic words (meaning
'mortal life') has been compared with the Vedic solar god Mārtāṇḍa.
He seems on the other hand to have replaced Yima as the primal man
in Zoroastrianism. According to the Bundahišn, he is as broad as he
is tall, meaning probably spherical. This is the ancient idea of the
microcosm. Another Pahlavi text, the Rivayat, states that Infinite
Light produced a giant body, whose different parts became the sky,
the earth, the water, the plants, the ox, etc.

   The history of creation is fully developed in the Bundahišn, in
which it spans, from beginning to end, twelve thousand years. But
another narrative is more anciently attested, thanks to Christian
authors in the Sassanian period: it is the Zurvanite myth told by
EZNIK and others and which probably represents an earlier stage in
the development of the doctrine. It comprises only then thousand
years. During the first millennium Zurvan, as we saw above, offers
sacrifice in order to get an offspring. A doubt occurs to him as to the
efficacy of his sacrifice. At the end of the period twins are born to him,
Ohrmazd as the effect of the sacrifice, Ahriman as the result of his
doubt. Ohrmazd should normally have been born first, but Ahriman
managed to take his place and Zurvan, deceived, gave him the do-

minion of the world—but only for nine thousand years, at the end of which Ohrmazd will reign.

In the Pahlavi cosmology, several traits are difficult to account for except as adaptations from the Zurvanite system. We saw earlier that the Mazdean quadrinity seems indirectly to reflect the Zurvanite one. Zurvan had three associates, Light, Power, and Wisdom: the Mazdean simply substituted Ohrmazd for Power, called Light Space and Wisdom Religion, and kept Zurvan as Time.

Ohrmazd and Ahriman are shown, in the Bundahišn and other Pahlavi books, as two adversaries with contrary and mutually incompatible natures, one light, one dark, one above, the other underneath and separated by Space or the Void (Vāy, the ancient Vayu): they seem to have ever existed in that state—the question of their origin is ignored—until Ahriman gets to know of Ohrmazd's existence, envies him and attacks him. It is in order to vanquish him that Ohrmazd creates the world, as a battle-field. Ohrmazd knows that this fight will be limited in time—it will last 9.000 years—and he offers Ahriman a pact to that effect. But why this pact? Only in the Zurvanite perspective was it justified, for it is there Zurvan who offers it, as a means of distributing power between his two sons.

The pact or treaty is given to Ahriman in the form of an implement or a garment. The myth was again coherent only in the Zurvanite version, when Zurvan gave his sons a white and a dark robe.

The one thousand years of Zurvan's sacrifice are replaced by a period of three thousand years preceding Ahriman's assault on the universe. During this period the world does not yet exist except in a 'spiritual' (*mēnōk*) state which neither moves nor thinks nor can be touched. Whereas Ahriman fashions many demons to help him, Ohrmazd is said to create a spherical 'form of fire', from which all things are to proceed. But when we read that this form of fire was called Ohrmazd it becomes apparent that we have to do with a remnant of a Zurvanite myth, in which Zurvan gave birth to Ohrmazd.

It is then said that after the twin Spirits have created their respective material worlds, Ahriman from the endless darkness creates Lying Speech and then Ohrmazd creates True Speech. This peculiar order of succession recalls Ahriman's birth preceding that of Ohrmazd in the Zurvanite cosmogony.

Ahriman's first attack had been defeated by Ohrmazd with the help of the Ahunavar prayer. He lay prostrate for a period of 3.000 years, which is the second in the total of four. At the end of this period he is stirred up by the Prostitute and goes back to the attack, this time on the material universe. He kills the primal Bull, whose marrow gives birth to the plants and whose semen is collected and purified in the moon, from whence it will produce the useful animals. This may be an adaptation of the cosmogonic sacrifice of the Bull by Mithra, as we mentioned earlier, p. 354

Ahriman then kills Gayōmart, the primal man, whose body produces the metals. (It must not be forgotten that Gayōmart is a cosmic giant, and it is natural to consider the veins of metal, in the earth, as the earth's skeleton). The semen of Gayōmart is preserved and purified in the sun by the god Neriosang. A part of it will produce the rhubarb from which the first human couple will be born.

The first human couple, Mašya and Mašyane, are perverted by Ahriman and it is only with the advent of Zarathuštra, after 3.000 years, that Ahriman's supremacy comes to an end. From then on, and for the last of the four periods, Ohrmazd and Ahriman fight on equal terms until Ohrmazd finally triumphs. But before we deal with this general eschatology, the individual eschatology must be considered.

2. *Eschatology*

a. *individual.* Indian and Iranian beliefs in the after-life have many features in common, probably dating back to the Indo-Iranian period: the feminine encounter, the bridge, the dogs watching it, the heavenly journey. In the Upaniṣads, the soul is welcomed in heaven by five hundred apsaras. In Iran, the soul meets his own Religion in the form either of a beautiful damsel if he has lived justly, otherwise a horrid hag.

Either before this encounter or after, according to the various texts, the soul must cross a bridge. This, with the young girl and the dogs, is attested in the Yajurveda and the Upaniṣads. In the gâthâs it is called the Bridge of the Requiter. It leads the good souls to Paradise, but the bad ones fall into Hell. Pahlavi texts say that it is broad and easy to cross to the former, but to the latter as narrow as a razor's edge.

The soul has also to undergo a judgment: she appears before Mithra and his two companions Sraoša and Rašnu. These three judges, not mentioned in the gâthâs and unknown to India, have as their closest parallel the Greek, or rather Pre-Hellenic Minos, Aeacus and Rhadamanthus.

The soul finally ascends through three successive stages representing respectively his good thoughts (the stars), good words (the moon) and good deeds (the sun), to the Paradise (of Infinite Lights). In the Veda it is only said that the sojourn of the good deed is beyond the path of the sun. In Paradise, the soul is led by Vohu Manah to the golden throne of Ahura Mazda.

Hell has also, symmetrically, four levels. And there is, for the souls whose good actions exactly balance their evil ones, an intermediate place called in Avestan *misvan gātu*, in Pahlavi *hamēstagān*. It is misleading to translate this by 'purgatory'. In fact, as ZAEHNER observes, it is the Mazdean hell which is to be compared with the Christian purgatory, for it is temporary. It will last only until the final resurrection.

b. *general.* Zarathuštra used in his gâthâs to invoke Saviours who, like the dawns of new days, would come to the world. And he hoped himself to be one of them, who would render this world *fraša*, probably meaning 'renovated'. It is not known whether he believed in the resurrection of the body.

After his death the belief in coming saviours developed. Zarathuštra was expected to return, if not personally, at least in the form of his three sons who, born at intervals of a thousand years from the semen of the prophet, miraculously preserved in the Lake Kansaoya, and three virgins, would come to save the world. This was to be the last turning in the history of the world, and the *frašōkərəti* or 'Renovation'. The last of these saviours, Astvat-ərəta or Justice incarnate, was also simply called the Saviour (*Saošyant*). Armed with the weapon of Thraetaona, he would slay the Druj and put Fury to flight; his gaze would render the creation imperishable; following his example, Vohu Manah would destroy Aka Manah, and Hunger and Thirst would be suppressed by Haurvatāt and Amərətāt.

It is only in the Pahlavi books that this theme is systematically dealt with, but we can more or less fill the gap between the Avesta and these books by means of foreign testimonies, mainly Greek and Latin. The Sibylline books, the Oracle of the Potter (a Greek text in Egypt), the Oracles of Hystaspes (preserved in Lactantius), and Virgil's Fourth Eclogue bear witness to the wide-spread belief, in the last two centuries before our era, in the coming of a saviour king from heaven or from the sun. This probably corresponds to the rôle of Mithra as saviour or mediator in the Mysteries and it may well be that this god played a prominent part in Eschatology in Arsacid Iran. He seems indeed, judging from a Pahlavi text, the Bahman Yašt, to have usurped one feat which the Avesta attributed to Astvat-ərəta: it is he who puts Fury to flight. But his role is otherwise very secondary in the Eschatology of the Pahlavi books: he is but a lieutenant of Ohrmazd at the head of his host, and is sent to help one of the Saviour's precursors, Pešōtan.

An idea dominates the Eschatology in the Pahlavi books: it is that of a final return to the initial state of things. The first human couple had at first fed on water, then also on plants, on milk and at last on meat: the people in the last millennia will, at the advent of the three successive saviours, abstain, in the reverse order, from meat, milk, and plants, to keep finally only water.

Gayōmart was the first man. He will also be the first to ressuscitate. That will be his only function. He will not, as if he were a reincarnation, in the Gnostic fashion, of a pristine saviour, repeat the sacrifice of his own body which had given birth, as we saw, to the metals and to the human race.

The idea is present, however, of the final revival of a cosmogonic sacrifice, but it concerns the sacrifice of the bull. Echoing the killing of the primal bull by Ahriman (previously, perhaps, by Mithra, as seen above), the ox Hadayōš is sacrificed: from his fat and marrow, as well as from the white haoma a drink is made which will be given to the newly-ressuscitated men and secure them immortality.

The primeval combats have also their counterpart at the end of time. The dragon which Θraetaona had killed in order to liberate the emprisoned waters appears again at the Resurrection to be killed by another hero; otherwise fire would not spread, water would refuse to flow. In a great last struggle the host of good and the host of evil are at grips, and each soldier of Ohrmazd defeats and kills his special adversary. This restores the state of peace that had prevailed initially. The wicked are then submitted to an ordeal of molten metal and fire. Fire and Airyaman cause the metals of the mountains to melt, and to flow down as a river of fire. The whole ressuscitated mankind must traverse it: it burns only the wicked, whereas to the just it is as sweet as warm milk. But the suffering of the wicked will only last three days, after which all mankind will enjoy happiness. On the flattened earth (for the metal has filled in all the valleys), men and women, henceforth shadowless as they are sinless, taste the bliss of family life. Hell has also been sealed for ever. Ahriman is for ever powerless, or annihilated.

V Influences of the Iranian Religion

The Iranian religion has perhaps influenced the development of Judaism, and of Greek philosophy, and contributed to the rise of Gnosticism.

1. *Iran and Israel*

The debt of Israel to its Eastern neighbours in religious matters is easy to demonstrate on a few precise points of minor importance; it is less so in other, more important points like dualism, angelology, and eschatology.

Yahweh was raised so high and so purified by the prophets that the need was felt to bridge the void between his transcendence and the world. The Logos, borrowed from Greek philosophy, was the solution that occurred to PHILO. Otherwise, the wisdom of God is mentioned in Proverbs, Ecclesiasticus, the Book of Wisdom, Enoch, etc. It is the beloved and counsellor of the Lord, the friend and guide of men. Its intrusion into Judaism is so abrupt that one is prompted to imagine a foreign influence. But it is most difficult to find its prototype in Iranian religion. Is it Vohu Manah, or Armaiti?

The Spirit is comparable to Spənta Mainyu, and so are the six powers of God in Philonian speculation to the Iranian Entities. Since the latter were known to the Greeks, it is by no means impossible that PHILO had heard about them. In fact, he mentions as quite familiar the Persian doctrine of God's virtues. But the likeness is limited to general analogy.

The case of post-exilic soteriology is quite different. After the Exile, the traditional hope in a Messiah-king of the house of David, who would re-establish Israel as an independent nation and make it triumph over all enemies, gave way gradually to a concept at once more universal and more moral. The salvation of Israel was still essential; but it had to come about in the framework of a general renewal; the appearance of a Saviour would mean the end of this world and the birth of a new creation: his judgment of Israel would become a general judgment, dividing mankind into good and evil. This new concept, at once universal and ethical, recalls Iran so strongly that many scholars attribute it to the influence of that country, all the more because there is no strong personality to be found in Israel during the last few centuries before our era who could have provoked such a profound change.

May the Son of Man be compared to Gayōmart? The former, as he appears in Daniel, Enoch, etc., seems a purely eschatological figure, quite distinct from the primeval being alluded to by Job and Ezekiel. On the Iranian side, Gayōmart is, as we have seen, an essentially cosmogonic figure, whose role in Eschatology is limited and late. The fact that the Avesta places him in the same series as Zarathuštra and the Saošyant by no means implies that all three were considered to be a single being, or even to belong to the same line of descent.

Did Iranian Dualism colour Israel's beliefs? A considerable change came about in the conception of Satan. Whereas in the prologue of Job and in the mouth of Zacharias he was no more than the humble servant of God, whose function was to act as prosecutor, he afterwards became God's adversary. Two successive versions of the same story, in Samuel and in Chronicles, show Satan literally taking the place of God. Samuel tells us that the anger of the Lord was kindled against Israel and he stirred David to number his people. Instead of which, in Chronicles we read, "And Satan rose up against Israel and moved David to number Israel."

In apocalyptic literature, too, it is possible to follow the progress of the newcomer. The Jewish apocalypses—which are not part of the Old Testament—spoke at first of a judgment of rebellious angels, of the sons and spirits of Belial and Mastema, as well as of those angels who had misused their power of punishment; later in the Assumption of Moses, the final decision is conceived as a struggle between God and the Demon; then, in Sibylline literature and the Assumption of Isaias, Belial appears as God's adversary. All this implies a pessimistic view which may be due partly to the misfortunes of Israel under Greek and Roman domination, but it would be rash to deny that the example of the Iranian Demon helped the Jews to transform the old public prosecutor into the adversary of God. A still more exact parallel is provided by the doctrine of the Two Spirits, amply attested in the Dead Sea Scrolls.

Of all the other points of comparison between Iran and Israel, namely the doctrine of millennia, the last judgment, the heavenly book in which human actions are inscribed, the resurrection, the final transformation of the earth, the ecstatic ascent of Enoch and Arda Viraf into the heavens, hell, the souls of the animals accusing man in the Slavonic Enoch like the soul of the ox in the gâthâs, and finally, in Tobias, the demon Asmodeus, alias *aēšma daēva* or Demon of Fury, the last two are the most characteristic.

2. *Iran and Greece*

Whereas the Jews, the chosen people, never acknowledged any foreign influence in their religion, the Greeks aspired quite early to the title of heirs of the ancient wisdom of the east. But the more remote in time are the references of their authors to these pretended borrowings the more accurate they are. PYTHAGORAS was finally supposed to have been Zoroaster's pupil in Babylon, a city to which, probably neither had ever been. However, there are striking likenesses of doctrine between Iran and Greece.

ANAXIMANDER's world picture corresponds to that of the Avesta, with the stars nearest to the earth, then the moon, then the sun, beyond which there is in Iran the Paradise of Infinite Lights, in Greece the *apeiron*. But it is impossible to account for this resemblance in precise historical terms.

HERACLITUS' notion of the Logos as a true utterance corresponding to the order of the universe, and related with universal fire, may be compared with the Entity Aša. He may have been impressed, in Ephesus, by the practices of the Magi, if not by any explicit theory of theirs on the fiery nature of the soul. This was then passed on to EMPEDOCLES and the Orphics and would account for the emergence, in the Greece of the 5th century, of the belief in the heavenly fate of the soul. In the same century the notion suddenly appears in Greece of a parallelism between different parts of the body and different parts of the universe. It is likely, as demonstrated by GOTZE, that some Greek physician employed at the Persian court brought back the doctrine from there.

With PLATO, the distinction between mind and matter was typically Greek, being derived from a multiple tradition—Ionian, Pythagorean, Eleatic, and Sophistic. The opposition of mind and matter had already been transferred to the epistemological sphere, between physical science and mathematical science. Here, PLATO's position differed essentially from Zarathuštra's. For the Iranian prophet, the distinction was only between visible things and the superior realities to which his ecstasies, meditation and devotion provided access. He certainly had no idea of the critical problem.

The Platonic doctrine of the soul, set out in mythical form in the Timaeus, was taken in a monist, optimistic sense: evil is the absence of God and the individual is free to choose. PLATO would never hear of two spirits, one god and the other evil. He expressly rejects this idea in the course of his myth in the Politic. The world goes between good and evil like a wheel turning forwards and backwards: this cannot be due to the action of two different gods, since a god cannot be evil, but only to the fact that the world now obeys divine impulse, now obeys itself. PLATO may allude to Iranian doctrine, but it is only to refute it. In the Laws in fact he seems to believe for a moment in the possibility of an evil soul, but this is more a plurality of human souls than the soul of the world, for the latter can be nothing but good.

PLATO frequently tends to be judged through Gnosticism. It is true that he had the stuff of a pessimistic, anticosmic dualist in him: the Phaedo, for instance, is tinged with "Weltflucht." But one cannot proceed from there to consider that he poses the Soul of the world purposely as a bridge over the gulf between God and the world; PLATO never felt so great a distance between God and the world as to warrant a third term to link them; for him, the Soul of the World, a traditional idea, was to be deduced from contemplation of the world order, as was God; it was, once more like God, the reason, the *nous*, the harmony of the spheres without which the world order—demonstrated in the regularity of the movements of the planets, the great discovery of the Greek mathematicians—would remain inexplicable.

However, a dualism more ancient than PLATO himself does subsist in PLOTINUS and all the Neo-Platonists: matter or evil is a separate principle, irreducible to God. The Neo-Platonists could therefore legitimately find the roots and seeds of their own attitudes in the "Weltflucht" and profound dualism of the master. The problem is what importance to assign this feature in a general appreciation of PLATO's doctrine.

A parallel problem occurs with Zarathuštra: is it possible to trace the origin of the Gnostic movement back to him and to the gâthâs?

3. *Iran and Gnosticism*

The problem of the Iranian origins of Gnosticism has been tackled, firstly, by comparing the notion of salvation in Iran and India. It appears to be essentially the same in both, coming from man's desire to transcend the world and unite his soul with the Great Soul. But, on the Iranian side, the proofs of this pessimistic and anti-cosmic tendency, which is not usually attributed to Iran, are indeed scanty, and it must be admitted that it was largely overlaid or arrested by Zarathuštra's optimistic and ethical dualism.

The means of salvation were present in the gâthic system itself in the form of man's union with the Entities, especially Vohu Manah.

The rôle of Vohu Manah has been stressed above: this Entity receives the soul into heaven and leads it to the throne of Ahura Mazda.

It has recently been recognized that the Syriac allegory of the Pearl goes back to an Iranian original of the Parthian period. But this does not exclude the possibility of a western or Babylonian origin. The Gnostic myth owed something to the story of Tammuz, who comes down, fights, suffers, and is imprisoned before rising again.

However it may be, traces are found in Iran of an attitude surviving from the Indo-Iranian past, obscured by the active and ethical dualism of Zarathuštra, but capable of revival. Iran, then, like Greece, possessed besides a more optimistic conception an anti-cosmic tendency which could give rise to Gnosticism. However, this tendency had on each side distinctive features: in Greece, first of all, the spirit was identified with good and matter with evil, and secondly, the world was seen as a scale of degrees going from pure ether down to pure matter, a ready-made framework for the idea or myth of the fall, be it fall of the angels, fall of the soul, descent of the saviour, and the corresponding re-ascent into heaven. On the Iranian side the drama was enacted between two poles, two co-eternal spirits. But although the spirit-matter distinction was never identified, before Manicheism, with that between good and evil, there is to be found in Zarathuštra the notion, analogous to the Platonic conception of the spirit-matter relationship, that the evil spirit is purely negative and destructive, a sheer limit to God's power.

Later on, this conception was to coarsen when Ahriman was increasingly conceived as the counterpart of Ohrmazd in the rigid dualism reflected notably in the Videvdat. However, although Manicheism may have been the only Gnostic movement to adopt this extreme form of dualism, this may have combined with the pessimistic, anti-cosmic tendency which subsisted on the fringe of Zoroastrianism, and given rise to Gnosticism.

The latter, with its asceticism that sometimes turned into ethical indifference, certainly seems to have been derived from the meeting of Greek and Iranian elements partly similar and partly complementary to each other, not excluding Babylonian features and other Semitic elements. The meeting may have taken place on Semitic ground, in Samaria, for instance, but it probably occurred independently in several places: we simply do not know.

Gnosticism, once it had become the powerful movement it developed into in the second and third centuries, was soon reflected in

Iran, not only in Manicheism but also in orthodox Mazdeism. According to at least two cosmogonical texts, when beings receive material form, Ohrmazd is moved to perform this creation in reply to Ahriman's attack: therefore, the initiative in material creation belongs to the evil Spirit.

The end of the world is sometimes conceived, not as the beginning of a new world, with happiness for the good and punishment or destruction or conversion for the wicked, but as a return of creation to God, or rather as reabsorption into him of what had emanated from him.

In cosmology there is a remarkable and manifest compromise between the ancient Iranian religion which made gods of the heavenly bodies and Gnosticism or Manicheism which makes them demons. Mazdeism regarded only the planets as demons, the sun, moon and stars remaining gods.

Finally, when under Islam mysticism invaded Iran from east and west, it found there favourable ground after all. Did not Sohravardī (who died in 1091) feel himself to be at once the heir of Iran and Greece?

VII. SHORT HISTORY OF THE STUDY OF THE IRANIAN RELIGION

Classical Antiquity, for various reasons, was very much interested in Iranian religion. Through the Middle Ages, the memory of Zoroaster survived as that of a prince of the Magi: he appears as such in the Faust legend. The Renaissance saw in him a sort of counterpart of PLATO. From then on, interest in his religion never ceased.

BARNABÉ BRISSON in 1590 published his *De regio Persarum Principatu*, entirely based on ancient sources. The next important work was THOMAS HYDE's *De vetere religione Persarum*, 1700, in which a synthesis is attempted between those sources and what had come to be known of contemporary Zoroastrianism, either in Iran or in India. In 1771 ANQUETIL-DUPERRON brought back from India the Avesta and the Bundahišn, but it was not until about 1830, when comparative grammar had been founded, that a scientific study of those texts could be initiated. The first attempt at a historical approach based on such a study is MARTIN HAUG's lecture given in Poona in 1861. This started the vast, collective work of a legion of scholars in Germany, France, England, etc., in which a few landmarks may be pointed out. DARMESTETER's monumental translation of the Avesta towards the end of the 19th century was based on a direct knowledge of the cult and usages of the Parsis. At the same time CUMONT published his great study of the Mysteries of Mithra. Meanwhile, Iranian philology reached a new stage with the *Grundriss der Iranischen Philologie* and BARTHOLOMAE's *Altiranisches Wörterbuch*.

In the first years of the 20th century Central Asia yielded an unexpected harvest of Middle Iranian texts, which was gradually to transform our knowledge of Pahlavi. Archaeology, Numismatics, etc., had their share in helping to reconstruct a still sketchy picture of the historical development of the Iranian religion. Of the two chief Pahlavi texts, the Bundahišn and the Dēnkart, no complete critical edition and reliable translation exists as yet. And Zarathuštra's gâthâs, although several times edited and translated, are still obscure and do not provide a sufficient basis for a historical and biographical approach to Zarathuštra, whose personality still evades us. In 1937 NYBERG tried to interpret him in the light of Central Asian shamanism. Ten years later HERZFELD built a fanciful *Zoroaster and his world*. Meanwhile, DUMÉZIL's progressive reconstruction of the Indo-European tripartite Ideology shed light on the prehistory of Zoroastrianism. His views have been accepted by such scholars as BARR, WIDENGREN and WIKANDER, rejected by ZAEHNER, GERSHEVITCH, LENTZ, HUMBACH, etc. Consensus on any point between Iranists remains a rarity. Progress in the study of the Middle-Iranian period is due mainly to the work of NYBERG, BAILEY, ZAEHNER, and MENASCE.

The part played by Parsi scholars, some of them trained in European or American universities, is invaluable.

SELECTED BIBLIOGRAPHY

a) *General*
Bibliographical data will be found in the only manual available:
DUCHESNE-GUILLEMIN, J., *La Religion de l'Iran ancien*, Paris, Presses Universitaires, 1962. A list of errata and additional remarks has appeared in the *Revue de l'Histoire des Religions*, July-Sept. 1967, p. 87 sq.
ZAEHNER's *Dawn and Twilight of Zoroastrianism*, 1961, appeared too late to be fully taken into account in the manual just mentioned. But a long, critical review of it has been given in *Indo-Iranian Journal*, 1964, p. 196-207;
WIDENGREN's *Die Religionen Irans*, 1965, is a new version of a useful bibliographical work published in *Numen*, 1955, under the title of *Stand und Aufgaben der iranischen Religionsgeschichte*;
MOLÉ's thesis has been published as *Culte, Mythe et Cosmologie dans l'Iran ancien*, 1963. It cannot be recommended to beginners;
JACKSON's *Zoroastrian Studies*, 1928, gives all the facts it would be useful to memorise;
GRAY's *Foundations of the Iranian Religions*, Bombay 1929, is an excellent alphabetical repertory and should serve as the basis for any serious study;

HASTINGS' *Encyclopaedia of Religion and Ethics*, 1908-1926, with its 95 articles or sections of articles bearing on Iranian religion, is still very useful; DHALLA, M. N., *History of Zoroastrianism*, 1938, 2nd printing 1963, is uncritical.

b) *Particular*

Several attempts have been made to prove that Cyrus was acquainted with Zoroastrianism: W. HINZ, *Zarathustra*, 1961; HILDEGARD LEWY, in *A Locust's Leg*, 1962, p. 139; MORTON SMITH, *JAOS*, 1963, p. 415.

GERSHEVITCH, *The Avestan Hymn to Mithra*, 1959, Introduction; 'Zoroaster's own Contribution', in *JNES*, 1964, p. 12.

BICKERMAN, *Archív Orientálný*, 1967.

On the Aryas in Western Asia: MAYRHOFER, *Die Indo-Arier im alten Vorderasien*, 1966.

On the Xvarenah: DUCHESNE-GUILLEMIN, *AION, Linguistica*, 1963, p. 19

The similarity between Anāhitā and Sarasvatī has been proved independently by DUMÉZIL, *Tarpeia*, 1947, and by LOMMEL, *Festschrift Weller*, 1954, p. 405.

On Vərəθraγna: BENVENISTE-RENOU, *Vr̥tra et Vr̥θragna*, 1934; MENASCE, *RHR*, 1947, p. 5; DUMÉZIL, *RHR*, 1938, p. 152.

On Vayu: WIKANDER, *Vayu*, 1941.

On Baga: HENNING, 'A Sogdian God', *BSOAS*, 1965, p. 242; DUCHESNE-GUILLEMIN, *Festschrift Eilers*, 1967, p. 157 sq.

On ARAMATI: WESENDONK, 'Arəmati als arische Erdgottheit', *ARW*, 1929, p. 61.

On the Am. Sp.: B. GEIGER, *Die Aməsa Spentas*, 1916.

On the difference between Vohu Manah and Aśa: DUCHESNE-GUILLEMIN, *Western Response to Zoroaster*, 1958, p. 47.

On Dualism: UGO BIANCHI, *Il Dualismo Religioso*, 1958.

Resurgence of the ancient Gods: for the material used in this section I am greatly in debt to Gray's *Foundations*, from which I have quoted freely, without quotation-marks.

On Manwahmēd: WIDENGREN, *The great Vohu Manah and the Apostle of God*, 1945.

On Arsameia: F. DÖRNER, 'Die Entdeckung von Arsameia', *Neue deutsche Aus-grabungen im Mittelmeergebiet und im vorderen Orient*, p. 71. Picture in R. FRYE, *Heritage of Persia*, fig. 87.

On Anāhitā in Armenia: DUCHESNE-GUILLEMIN, *La Religion de l'Iran ancien*, p. 324.

On Zurvanism: MARY BOYCE, 'Some Reflections on Zurvanism', *BSOAS*, 1957, p. 304.

MENASCE, *Une Encyclopédie mazdéenne, le Denkart*, 1958; on the Mean: BRANDON, *Man and his Destiny*, 1962, p. 370; on *āzād-kām*, JACKSON's study, 'The Zoroastrian Doctrine of the Freedom of the Will', *Zoroastrian Studies*, p. 219, must be supplemented and corrected by means of Tavadia, *ZII*, VIII, p. 119, and by forthcoming studies by F. B. KUIPER.

On the Soul of the Ox: G. DUMÉZIL, 'A propos de la Plainte de l'Ame du Bœuf', *Bulletin cl. des let. Acad. Roy. de Belgique*, 1965, p. 24; B. SCHLERATH, 'Opfergaben', *Festgabe Herman Lommel*, 1960, p. 129.

On Mārtāṇḍa: K. HOFFMANN, *Münch. St. z. Sprachw.*, 1957, p. 85

On Iran and Israël: DUCHESNE-GUILLEMIN, *Ormazd et Ahriman*, 1953; FRANZ KÖNIG, *Zarathustras Jenseitsvorstellungen u. das Alte Testament*, 1964.

On Iran and Greece: J.D.-G., 'D'Anaximandre à Empédocle', *Atti del Convegno sulla Persia e il Mondo greco-romano*, Accad. Lincei, 1966, p. 423.

On Gnosticism: WIDENGREN, 'Der Iranische Hintergrund der Gnosis', *Z. f. Religionsgeschichte*, 1952, Heft 2; *Atti del Convegno sul Gnosticismo* (Messina 1966).

GREEK RELIGION

BY

A. W. H. ADKINS
Reading, England

I. The Essence of the Religion

The editors of this handbook have very wisely laid down the categories and subdivisions in terms of which each religion is to be discussed. The selected categories accurately reflect the questions which the modern reader naturally asks, and expects to find answered, on approaching the study of a religion with which he is unfamiliar. Some of these categories, in fact, are not those which a writer on Greek religion would propose to himself in beginning the exposition of the subject: Greek religion was a phenomenon far different from the religions called to mind by them. Yet the categories are useful, provided they are not used in a Procrustean manner: the explanation under each heading of the reasons why the data of Greek religion do not fit into any given category will serve to focus the differences between that religion and those which are more familiar to the reader, and should not prevent the exposition of the nature of Greek religion.

Even this first category, which seems general enough to cover almost any kind of material, is suitable only in that it demonstrates what Greek religion was not. Anything which has an essence must have some coherence, some degree of unity. We may readily describe the essence of a religion which has a founder, a limited corpus of sacred books, a creed (and hence orthodoxy and heresies), and some means of assuring that the adherents of the religion observe its tenets. Greek religion has none of these. One or two of the cults which will be described below have; but these are not separate religions in the sense that membership of them entails rejection of all other beliefs current in the Greek world. In fact, 'Greek religion' refers to no simple phenomenon whose essence can be briefly characterized, but to the totality of religious beliefs and practices observable among the Greeks during the period under discussion, from the Mycenean period down to the third quarter of the fourth century B.C. The closing date must be arbitrary; but the battle of Chaeronea in 338 B.C. marked the end of the importance on the political level of the Greek city-state, with which many Greek religious observances were closely linked; and this change was not without relevance to the history of Greek religion.

The essence of Greek religion, then, defies description, not for any ineffability it possesses, but because of the kaleidoscopic and ever-shifting nature of the phenomenon. There is no dogma, and no heresy: each writer who chooses can leave his mark on it. It will be a comparatively small mark, for the fabric of Greek religion is large, complicated, and at times self-contradictory, and no man can hope to impose order on it. Furthermore, it will be written on sand; for no writer has any more religious authority in the Greek world than any other. True, we possess some hymns and prayers; but the version of a myth which they contain acquires no added religious status, though it may have attained wider currency, by its inclusion therein. True, Homer was an important part of the literary culture of the Greeks, and any account of a myth or of the nature of a deity which appears in the Homeric poems must have become well-known throughout Greece; but local variants both of myth and of attributes of deities persisted alongside the versions of Homer. It would be misleading to say 'in defiance of Homer'; for this phrase would by implication impart to the Homeric poems a religious authority which no Greek accorded to them. HOMER, and other writers, or artists in other media, may have sometimes caused the modification of local myths or of local attributes of deities, for these too were guaranteed by custom, not by creed or dogma; but there was no feeling that any god or goddess should have precisely the same attributes, or perform precisely the same role in the same myths, all over the Greek world. Though there were important religious centres in Greece, in matters of religion as of politics the Greeks of this period were organized in small autonomous units. Even had there been creeds and dogma within individual city-states, they could not have been imposed beyond the borders of those states; but the idea of orthodoxy of belief was in fact absent from the official cults of the city-states. Prosecutions for 'blasphemy' do admittedly occur, and that too at Athens in the late fifth century; but these are extreme actions in extreme circumstances. If everyone believes the sun to be a god, in a political crisis a philosopher may be prosecuted for asserting that it is a stone. But only in a crisis: at other times he need fear nothing worse than the ridicule of the comic poet. Further, provided that the divinity of the deity is acknowledged, virtually any other characteristic of the god may be affirmed or denied without imputations of blasphemy: current myths attributed such contradictory behaviour to the same god that almost any statement could be justified from them.

As a result, we can rarely, if ever, ascribe a belief, except in the most general and uninformative terms, to the Greeks as a whole at any period. Caution demands that the belief should be ascribed to the author in whose works we find it; and even here we must make qualifications. None of the Greek writers of this period was a systematic theologian: any may exhibit contradictory religious statements, not merely in works written at different periods, but in different parts of the same work. There is naturally broad general agreement on many topics; but we may not conclude that a particular belief which is found in AESCHYLUS was necessarily widely held in the Athens of AESCHYLUS' day; and still less may we conclude that such a belief was held by the Greeks in general at that time. It is only when, as is rarely the case, we have documents from other cities that we can have any knowledge of what even some of the inhabitants of those cities believed. We may be able to establish from archaeological evidence that these cities worshipped particular members of the Olympian pantheon; we know that different cities, for historical reasons, gave prominence to different members of that pantheon; but we cannot know, save where documents are available, what beliefs were associated with those deities. It must always be remembered, in discussing any aspect of Greek thought or belief, that we know incomparably more about Athens than about any other Greek state; and that the history of the thought and belief of most Greek cities is, and must remain, virtually a blank.

In these circumstances, it will be necessary throughout the discussion to make detailed references to many authors; and an essential preliminary is to list, and briefly describe, the sources for this period. Until recently, the Homeric poems were the earliest documents in Greek; but since 1952 the decipherment of the Linear B tablets has furnished material from the later part of the second millenium. The tablets are stocktaking records, but furnish what appear to be some names of deities and certain other information of interest to students of religion. Unfortunately, the information is scanty, and the interpretation of almost any tablet can be challenged; but they may be used, with great care, to supplement the archaeological data of the period.

The Homeric poems remain our earliest major source of information. The result, as is now universally agreed, of a long oral poetic tradition, they present a remarkably homogeneous (by Greek standards) picture of religious belief and observance. One might argue that the picture is representative only of the latest stages of the tradition, the eighth century B.C.; but the pattern of religious belief changes slowly, and it seems reasonable to treat the data of these poems as valid for at least the previous century; though on the other hand certain parts of the poems seem to reflect changes that were just beginning to take place when the poems took on their final form. It is difficult to determine how far the poems portray the actual practices and beliefs of any existing society: HOMER certainly did not invent any of the gods, nor any of the attitudes, social or religious, of the society he depicts, for these are found elsewhere; but the portrayal of life on Olympus, while it accurately reflects the human society of the poems, is likely to be a contribution to literature rather than the description of actual religious belief. Nevertheless, it reveals the attitude expected by men from their gods at the period, and the attitude of men to their gods; and this closely resembles attitudes found in later writers. HESIOD, our next source, who wrote in Boeotia at about the time when the Homeric poems were taking their final shape on the other side of the Aegean, furnishes in his *Theogony* much information about the genealogies of the Greek gods, and aspects of belief which seem more primitive than those of HOMER; but the Homeric tradition seems to have been selective in its choice of material suitable for epic. HESIOD's *Works and Days* makes more ethical demands of the gods than do HOMER's characters, and also provides details of some magical beliefs. To this period, or rather later, belong some of the Homeric hymns, which increase our knowledge of the attributes of certain Olympian gods at certain cult-centres. In the next period, roughly the sixth century, emerge writers with more sharply-defined personalities, such as THEOGNIS, SOLON and XENOPHANES. Their poems are short, and those which concern religious thought debate moral problems posed by religion as they found it. XENOPHANES, indeed, attacks both the anthropomorphic nature of the Greek gods and the immorality of some of the myths told of them. The earlier lyric poets, such as SAPPHO and ALCAEUS, some at least of whose works were composed for festal occasions, add something to our knowledge both of the Olympian gods and the ethos of their worship, as do SIMONIDES, whose work extends from the later sixth century into the fifth, and the fifth-century poets PINDAR and BACCHYLIDES. The former, like XENOPHANES, was critical of the immorality of some myths, and refused to believe those which he considered unworthy of deity. The Attic tragedians provide an abundant source of material, extending over much of a century of rapid change. It is impossible to characterize any of these poets in a sentence, and what is said here must be modified in the light of more detailed comments which will follow. AESCHYLUS, a devout man and a moralist, did not, in the manner of XENOPHANES and PINDAR, reject myths which he found offensive, but in at least some of his plays attempted to rework the mythical material which he accepted into a more ethically acceptable form. Some decades ago, on the grounds of certain passages taken out of context, AESCHYLUS was credited both with monotheism and a remarkably 'advanced' ethic; but this modern myth has now been exploded, and AESCHYLUS can be seen more clearly, as a considerable thinker wrestling in some of his plays with individual problems presented by Greek religious belief, and furnishing solutions which are, as is inevitable, governed by his own presuppositions and those of his period. These individual solutions do not, and could not, impose an ethical pattern on Greek religious belief as a whole: the nature of Greek myths renders this impossible. SOPHOCLES appears to be the least adventurous thinker of the three extant tragedians, and may perhaps be taken as more typical of the beliefs of his day; though this should not be overemphasized, since the *Philoctetes* and *Oedipus at Colonus*, the last two of his extant plays, are influenced by the intellectual speculation of the latter part of the fifth century. No label fits EURIPIDES, who was the youngest of the three, though the long-lived Sophocles died slightly later. An intellectual sponge, he absorbed and reproduced in his plays virtually all of the ideas, religious and other, which were being discussed in a period almost unsurpassed for the vigour of its speculation. He is the best of sources, though to determine his own beliefs is probably impossible. The sophists, the instigators of this speculation, survive in disappointingly small quantity; but their ideas are frequently reflected in the dramas of EURIPIDES. The historian HERODOTUS of Halicarnassus, said to have been a friend of SOPHOCLES, wrote his history in the framework of the religious ideas of his day, for which he is a valuable source. THUCYDIDES, the contemporary historian of the Peloponnesian War at the end of the fifth century, has interest for the present discussion chiefly in that his history does not invoke divine causation. In the fourth century, religious ideas and critique are found in PLATO, and to a lesser extent in ARISTOTLE. The former gives some interesting testimony concerning current belief, but his own religious ideas are certainly peculiar to himself, and perhaps a small circle of pupils. Earlier philosophers, such as PYTHAGORAS and EMPEDOCLES, are sometimes relevant. The orators of the later fifth and fourth centuries frequently throw light on religious categories of thought, and are very valuable, since these categories must also be those of their audience. These writers provide much evidence about Greek religious thought and some religious practices; but there is little reference even in Athens to religious festivals, which were the basis of the religious year all over Greece. For information about these we must rely on later authorities, on the early Christian fathers, on learned antiquarians in the ancient Greek world, on the fragments of their learning which appear in the scholia of Greek manuscripts, and on the ancient lexicographers. Consequently, the festivals of early Greece pose some of the most vexed questions in Greek religion.

Among non-literary sources, inscriptions from many places in Greece furnish us with details of organization of cult; while vase-paintings and sculpture illustrate the manner in which these anthropomorphic deities were imagined by the Greeks, and sometimes throw light on particular myths or rituals. Some scholars have attempted in addition to base conclusions about the ethos of Greek religion on the nature of their portrayal in the visual arts; but this is hazardous. FARNELL says that 'the Zeus Olympios of Pheidias transcended the portrait of the High God as given by HOMER or even by AESCHYLUS; for the chryselephantine statue impressed the later Greeks as the ideal of the benign and friendly deity...; an image that appeared "to add something to the traditional religion," embodying, as DIO CHRYSOSTOM says, a conception of the God so convincing and complete that "having once seen it one could not imagine him otherwise"'. FARNELL's quotations are from ancient writers, but from writers far later than the period we are discussing here: they are of use only as testimony that the statue was benign in appearance. FARNELL also overestimates the benignity of the Zeus of HOMER and AESCHYLUS—a deity sometimes beneficent, sometimes malevolent, sometimes capricious; more important for my present point, he forgets that the sculptor and the worshipper of such a deity will naturally in his prayers and worship emphasize the beneficent aspect of the deity to whom he prays, in the hope that the deity will manifest that facet of himself in his response. A statue can only portray one aspect of a deity, while one play may reveal several: we may not use the statue to argue that the other aspects which appear in the play are irrelevant. The Greeks called the turbulent Black Sea 'hospitable' (*euxeinos*), and sometimes termed the Furies 'kindly' (*eumenides*); but this is persuasion, not description; and the motives which prompt a sculptor to portray a multi-faceted deity as kindly may well be similar. At all events, the other facets are certainly present in the writers of our period, and must not be overlooked.

It will be convenient to close this section by enumerating the principal categories into which the Greek gods may be divided. It must not be assumed that all Greek deities fit neatly into these categories; but they will serve as an initial broad classification. The Olympians are the Greek deities most familiar to the non-specialist from later European art; but before them there were two generations of other gods, who may be referred to as pre-Olympian. The Olympians are the gods of the upper air, the surface of the earth and the sea; and may be distinguished from chthonic powers, powers beneath the earth. These may themselves be divided into two, the powers which ensure the earth's fertility and the gods of the underworld and the dead. The same gods appear in both roles, but the distinction of function is convenient, as will become apparent. 'Heroes', the powerful earth-bound spirits of men who were outstanding in certain respects in life, received cult, as did the dead in general to some extent. The powers of nature were also acknowledged to be divine; and these, as well as the idea of 'Fate', will be discussed in their appropriate place.

II. HISTORICAL DEVELOPMENT

Most discussions in this work will begin from a period not earlier than HOMER; for though Greek-speaking peoples practising a religion had long been settled in Greece when the Homeric poems took on the form and content which they now possess, and considerable quantities of the archaeological remains of these peoples are now accessible, the attempt to infer religious thought and belief from archaeological remains alone is hazardous; and the Linear B tablets give no aid here. However, it will be relevant to include here a few words on what little can be inferred of the pre-Homeric sources of the various streams of belief and practice which appear later.

The Greek-speakers arrived, in the first half of the second millenium B.C., in a Greece occupied already by a settled agricultural society; and it is tempting to derive all the elements of agricultural and fertility religion in later Greece from the earlier population, all elements suited to a fighting aristocracy from the religion of the incomers. An added inducement is given by the apparent worship of a great fertility-goddess or goddesses in pre-Greek Crete. In broad terms, there is doubtless truth in this hypothesis; but it requires many qualifications. It demands the assumption that the incomers arrived in raiding parties who lived by booty and were concerned only with booty; not only that they grew no food-grains, but that they raised no animals themselves for any purpose; for early societies are wont to invoke religious aid, and to employ magic, to ensure the fertility of their animal stock no less than to ensure that of their fields; while the fertility and continued existence of their own race stands in no less need of supernatural assistance. It also demands the assumption that the earlier inhabitants of Greece took thought for farming to the complete exclusion of defence; for if the need for self-defence is no more than a possibility, such a society will expect its gods—or one of them—to take an interest in this aspect of its needs. Unless both of these assumptions are certainly correct—and neither is—it is impossible to assign any aspect of later Greek religion to a particular element in the earlier population with confidence. One may speak of different emphases: when Zeus, the old Indo-European sky god, arrived in Crete, he became metamorphosed, at least in one aspect of himself, into the type of male fertility deity who is consort of a fertility-goddess, and is born and dies annually at appropriate periods in the agricultural year. It is possible to argue from this that the role was the most important one for a male deity in Crete, and that fertility-cults had precedence; but it is not possible to argue either that there were only fertility cults in early Crete, or that there were no such cults among the incomers, even if their most important deity was not primarily concerned with them. (The Indo-European Zeus was concerned with fertility to some extent, for he was the god not only of the bright sky, but also of rain; but he was certainly not a vegetation-spirit.) It is certainly incorrect to suppose that the Olympians as we first find them in Homer, the gods of a fighting aristocracy, are for that reason drawn exclusively from the gods of the incomers. Only Zeus undoubtedly belongs to this group. HOMER's Olympians are the gods of a fighting aristocracy because the poems reflect the attitudes and beliefs of a particular fighting aristocracy in Greece; and in the undogmatic Greek religion the gods take on the characteristics which seem most relevant to those who are at any time worshipping them. When the city-states develop, the Olympians become gods of the city-state. In literature, they are then mostly concerned with defence in war; but they are also the gods who preside over the festivals of the sacral calendar; and these are fertility festivals. This is not a new, bizarre function for these deities, but a basic original one.

The rites at the core of these festivals are mysterious in the everyday sense of the word, and at least part of the source from which 'myster-ies' in the technical sense developed in later Greece. The appearance of these 'mysteries' is the most striking religious development in the period under discussion; and it is sometimes stated almost without qualification that they represent a resurgence of the beliefs and prac-tices of the aboriginal population. This is a possibility: it can only be a certainty if it can be shown that the incomers never arrived gradually and peacefully, by a process of slow infiltration, bringing agricultural practices of their own and religious beliefs and practices which would be mingled, in time, with those of the earlier population. That the mysteries developed from agricultural ritual seems certain. To say more is mere conjecture: when Demeter, in the Homeric *Hymn to Demeter*, our earliest document concerned with 'mysteries', says, when disguised as a mortal, that she has come from Crete, this is not merely untrue in the immediate context of the poem, but the usual pretence of disguised persons in Homer who do not wish to be caught out in a lie: Crete was remote, Greeks lived there, and if a man said he came from Crete it was difficult to prove that he did not.

We cannot confidently assign sources to the different aspects of Greek religion. Nor can we trace a simple line of development, whether in the direction of greater sophistication of thought, belief and practice, or merely of greater complexity of gods worshipped and cults practised: there is, as has already been said, no entity to develop. Nor is there a converse process towards homogeneity; there was never anyone with the authority, or the superhuman intellectual power, needed to impose a uniform pattern on the anarchic confusion of Greek belief and cult. New, more 'advanced' beliefs are evolved by a number of thinkers; but earlier beliefs, even on the same topics, are not ruled out thereby: the more advanced and the more primitive exist side by side, not merely in the same society, but in the same writer: even an AESCHYLUS may simultaneously hold beliefs on the same subject, or about the same god, which cannot logically coexist.

In this situation, many topics discussed below must necessarily be treated historically, and generalization is impossible: a separate treatment of historical development could only be vague and inaccurate, and would require detailed correction in the remainder of the work. It has been pointed out, notably by M. P. NILSSON, that the agricultural festivals of the farming year form a constant and unchanging background of cult, in country and city alike; but here too we cannot speak of development, and these, together with their links with the remainder of Greek religion, will be discussed in their appropriate place.

Nor can one speak of development in the sense of territorial expansion, except in so far as the Greeks colonized wider areas. The Greeks did not proselytize non-Greeks, and in all periods to which the documents give us access all Greeks believed in gods with the same names, even if there were numerous local variations of belief and cult, and different deities had prominence in different places. The Olympian and agricultural cults of the Greeks had no content on which a proselytizing religion could have been based. The Eleusinian mysteries had such a content, for CICERO can say that they were the greatest gift of Athens to the world; but they were only made available to the world in general after the period under discussion here, and since they were mysteries, the content could only be revealed after initiation and an oath of secrecy—though the kind of benefit the initiate would enjoy could be made known.

The Greeks themselves were not exclusive in their attitudes to deities from other lands, and had no belief that all other gods were necessarily false or inferior. The Athenian state furnished a festival for the Thracian deity Bendis, and PLATO in his *Republic* is willing to portray SOCRATES as going to the festival and—possibly—praying to Bendis; and other foreign deities were admitted in the historical period. The Greek, after all, knew that Dionysus had originally come from abroad; and the Greek gods themselves, while jealous in other ways, did not insist that their worshippers should not worship other gods at the same time.

To admit them to the native pantheon is one method of acknowledging foreign gods. HERODOTUS displays another: he identifies foreign deities with Greek ones, and says, for example, that the Assyrians call Aphrodite Mylitta, the Arabians, Alitta. HERODOTUS' attitude to foreigners was more liberal than that of most Greeks; but Greeks in general did not despise foreign deities merely because they were foreign: they were wont to worship divine power wherever they felt it to be present.

III. Conceptions of Deity

Several separate discussions will be necessary; for the numerous deities and supernatural powers worshipped by the Greeks may be divided into a number of categories.

1. *The earlier generations of gods*

The Greek did not believe that 'in the beginning, God created the earth'. The gods who ruled in his own day had not existed from the beginning, and no god of any kind had created the universe *ex nihilo*: they merely ordered and apportioned the cosmos in which they found themselves.

HESIOD's version of the earlier stages of divine government was probably the most generally believed. (There was also an 'Orphic' cosmogony.) Chaos came into being first, followed by Earth, Tartarus (the infernal regions), and Eros (Love). From Chaos sprang Erebus and Night, and from Night, Aether and Day, Erebus being the father. Earth first bore Uranus (the starry heaven), the mountains and the sea, who was conceived without a father; but afterwards Earth lay with Uranus and bore Oceanus...and Hyperion...and Rhea, Themis and Mnemosyne (Memory)... After them was born Cronus, who hated his father Uranus. Earth also bore the Cyclopes and three hundred-armed giants, Cottus, Obriareus and Gyes. Earth was angry because Uranus used to hide his children in her depths, and exhorted the children to punish him. Cronus, who alone dared to do so, ambushed and castrated Uranus. The drops of blood fell upon Earth, who bore the Furies and Giants...; and from the genitals, thrown into the sea, Aphrodite was born. Uranus in reproach called his children Titans (strainers).

To Cronus, who now held supreme power, Rhea bore Hestia (the hearth), Demeter, Hera, Hades, Poseidon and Zeus. Cronus, informed that his own son would overthrow him, swallowed the earlier children as they were born; but at the birth of Zeus, Rhea gave Cronus a stone wrapped in swaddling clothes instead, and he swallowed this. Zeus grew up secretly, overthrew his father, rescued his brothers and sisters, and the rule of the Olympians began.

War now broke out between the children of Cronus and the Titans.

Zeus, however, had allies from the earlier generation: Cottus, Obri-areus and Gyes, whom Cronus had imprisoned. Zeus freed them and with their aid overcame the other Titans, whom he bound for ever in Tartarus, guarded by the three giants.

The thought of this account is primitive, but it contains presup-positions which were not abandoned by the Greeks of our period. Greek gods were immortal, but were not eternal: there was a time at which they came into existence. They were not omnipotent, and had no guarantee of continuing power: two supreme gods had fallen violently before the age of the Olympians in which the Greeks of the historical period believed themselves to be living; and Zeus himself was no more firmly established than his predecessors.

Even in the simplified form given here, this is a confused account. However, it should not be underestimated. HESIOD (or the poetic tradition of which he is the culmination) is trying to harmonize in-tractable and at times contradictory myths: the accounts of the rule of Uranus and Cronus seem to be doublets in some respects, and in the *Theogony* as a whole conflicting accounts are given of a number of deities. One certain element of this amalgam is a cosmogonic myth of a kind found elsewhere: its resemblance to some middle-Eastern versions is close enough to suggest direct borrowing. The existence of *two* pre-Olympian stages, however, seems unnecessary; and pre-sumably results from the conflation of two versions, neither of which the tradition felt itself able to discard. The battle of the Olympians and Titans has been seen as a reflection of the triumph of the religion of the incoming Greeks over that of the earlier inhabitants. If so, the Greeks had no inkling of it. The whole of the *Theogony* is presented genealogically, and Zeus is no more and no less Greek than Cronus or any of the Titans, some of whom have transparently Greek names, while the cosmogonic stage of the myth naturally uses Greek words for the original principles. The Greeks thought of the succeeding generations of gods as one big unhappy family, and sometimes drew moral, or rather immoral, conclusions from their behaviour. PLATO in his *Laws* expresses his fears of the bad effects such theogonies have on the attitudes of children to parents. He does not reject them as false, however,—though he had done so in the *Republic*—and it must be emphasized that they form the background to Greek religious belief, even if they are rarely mentioned in extant literature.

2. *The children of Night*

Though some of them were imprisoned later in Tartarus, most of the foregoing deities were once gods of daylight and the upper air. Very different are those whom HESIOD lists as the children of Night: Doom, black *Ker*, Sleep and the tribe of Dreams, Blame and painful Grief, and the Hesperides, together with the *Moirai* and *Keres, Nemesis*, Deceit, Friendship, Age and Strife. Strife in her turn bore Toil, Forgetfulness, Famine, Woes, Fights, Battles, Homicides, Man-slaughters, Quarrels, Lies, Disputes, Lawlessness and Blind Folly, and Oath.

This is a grim and grisly crew ('Friendship', if the text is sound, is a strange exception), not surprisingly held to be the children of Night; though the *Moirai* are said by HESIOD elsewhere to have been the daughters of Zeus and Themis. Most of these deities have no person-alities, but they should not be dismissed as colourless abstractions. In the time of HESIOD it is too early to speak of abstractions, for primitive man readily sees such phenomena in the guise of malicious demons. Certainly all these words are frequently used in early Greek in contexts where no thought of a malicious demon is brought to our mind, but at a period before philosophy and rigorous categorization, we cannot say that Blind Folly must be either a state of mind or a demon, for it is both at once, just as Earth is both a personalized deity and a visible, tangible substance. As we shall see in the separate discussion of *keres* —and the 'abstracts' here could be regarded as *keres* by the Greek— Blind Folly and the rest, since they affect a man in particular situations and produce particular effects in his behaviour, may be treated as a multitude of individual supernatural beings.

A clear example is furnished by the *Moirai*. (HESIOD's account shows signs of conflation: Clotho, Lachesis and Atropos are usually—even elsewhere in HESIOD's poem—the names of the *Moirai* when vividly personalized, but HESIOD has given the names to a small group of similarly personalized *Keres*.) *Moira*, like the other names of deities in this section, is also a common noun in Homeri, its basic usage is not 'fate' or 'destiny'—both misleading translations in any context—but 'share': one's share of booty after a raid, of food at a banquet, or of anything divided, as Zeus, Hades and Poseidon divided the cosmos among themselves. In a society without money, one's share of land, booty, food and other commodities delimits one's position in society, and, in a stratified society like that of HOMER, one's rights and privi-leges or lack of them. Accordingly, one may speak or act 'according to one's *moira*' or 'in excess of one's *moira*'. Since Homeric society is both stratified and static, the distribution of *moirai* within society is held to be the right one, and such phrases express what one ought or ought not to do in the situation. Death is something which comes to every man as his share, and so is seen in terms of *moira*; and anything else which happens to one clearly 'was to' happen, was part of one's share, not to be changed any more than, in normal Homeric circumstances, one's share in other things can be changed. Position in society, life as a whole in its most important aspects, is governed by a number of *moirai*. The early Greek gave such powerful influences on his life the status of individual invisible powers. Already in Homer, Agamemnon ascribes the folly which led him to deprive Achilles of Briseis to 'Zeus and *moira* and the fury that walks in darkness'. Such a statement could be made in 'real life'. In literature, and at times in life—for the arts must have affected the religion of everyday to some extent—the *moirai* may be three in number, and imagined as three old women spinning, measuring and cutting the yarn of life at one's birth, but in saying '*moira* (or "a *moira*") caused this', the Greek is simply ascribing the event to an 'allotting spirit' seen in personal terms; and sometimes he is not thinking in personal terms at all when he uses the word. The attitudes blend into one another, and one cannot draw clear distinctions where none exist in the material.

3. *The children of the Sea and the Nymphs*

The 'children of Night' are sprung directly from an earlier generation of deities. The children of the Sea, in HESIOD's scheme, are collateral with the Olympians. Pontus, the sea, is an elder brother of Cronus; from him are sprung the sea-deities Nereus, Thaumas, Phorcys, Ceto and Eurybia, who are of the same generation as Zeus and the older Olympians. From these sprang a host of sea-goddesses, coeval with the younger Olympians, and also Iris (the rainbow), the Harpies (the storm-winds seen in personal terms) and the Gorgons. Some of these have a role in Greek literature: Iris, Medusa the Gorgon, Thetis the mother of Achilles, and Galatea the sea-nymph loved by Polyphemus, are well known. In cult they must have been of most importance to sailors, and of the cults of Greek sailors we know little. They must have had much the same status as the nymphs of streams and trees, who will be discussed next.

The river gods and nymphs, according to HESIOD, were sprung from Oceanus and Tethys. HESIOD lists the more important ones, but adds that there are three thousand in all, spread over the whole earth. PLATO describes a beautiful plane tree by a stream, and SOCRATES says that he supposes it to be sacred to Achelous and some nymphs, from the presence of statuettes and other offerings. STRABO records that the land at the mouth of the river Alpheus was full of shrines of Aphrodite, Artemis and the nymphs, in groves full of flowers. In a land deficient in water, any spring or river with its attendant lush vegetation was likely to be held sacred to the powers which ensured its flourishing condition, and these powers were the nymphs. They were individual, female and anthropomorphic, though they might in many cases be indefinite in number and nameless: offerings were merely made to 'the nymphs' of a place. Their powers were local, parochial; little need be said of them here, but their existence, and that of their numerous shrines, should be borne in mind, since they lend even greater variety to the complex pattern of Greek religion.

4. The Olympians

Throughout Greek literature, the Olympians receive more attention than the other Greek deities. HERODOTUS, indeed, almost ascribes the creation of the Olympians to literature when he says that HOMER and HESIOD constructed a theogony for the Greeks, gave names to the gods, allotted to them their appropriate functions, and described their appearance. This is misleading: the bardic traditions which culminate in the works we possess under the names of HOMER and HESIOD cannot be shown to have invented the name of any god or goddess, and certainly did not invent any of the more important ones. Yet HERODOTUS' statement is not without point. The gods who appear together on Olympus in Homer and Hesiod were originally unrelated deities, some deities of individual Greek states, others imported from abroad. In cult practice, different states continued to favour different Olympians: Athens worshipped all of them to some extent, but Athena—her local deity—had first place in her affections. The bardic tradition must have been one of the influences which led to the gradual assembling of these scattered deities into the divine household on HOMER's Olympus; and must have helped to perpetuate in literature at least the personality and certain attributes of the Olympians.

HOMER and HESIOD, then, give an 'Olympocentric' tendency to the gods of the upper world. The stories of the amours of Zeus and some other Olympians with other deities, nymphs and mortals are one result of this. Early Greece contained a multiplicity of local goddesses who once possessed locally—worshipped consorts, whose names are frequently unknown to us. As Olympus gained in importance, they were furnished with Olympian consorts, usually Zeus. This is true even of the most important deities: Hera was not originally the wife of Zeus, nor were Apollo and Artemis brother and sister, or children of Zeus. Again, local noble families traced their ancestry back to a divinity. In a number of cases an Olympian takes over this function. The ruling house of Sparta derived its ancestry from Zeus, the Ionians, through their ancestor Ion, from Apollo, and thence from Zeus. Little feeling of Greek unity resulted: the Olympians themselves were quarrelsome, and the god with whom the family or race was linked was not the god of epic poetry, but the local variant of the deity. Cleomenes, the king of Sparta, was forbidden to enter the temple of Athena on the acropolis at Athens, and justified his doing so by the claim that he was not a Dorian but an Achaean. The Athena of Athens had no love for Dorians.

Since Homer and Hesiod do not contain dogma, they do not furnish a definitive list of Olympians. There is no such list: though the number twelve is associated with the major Olympians, the same twelve deities do not always occur. One list is: Zeus, Hera, Poseidon, Apollo, Artemis, Athena, Aphrodite, Hephaestus, Hermes, Ares, Demeter and Hestia (the hearth). Associated with them are Helios (the sun), Selene (the moon), Leto (the mother of Apollo and Artemis), Dione, Dionysus, Themis (law) and Eos (the dawn), Iris (messenger of the gods), Hebe, Ganymede (the cupbearer), the Horai, the Muses and the Graces.

Of these deities, Zeus, Hera, Poseidon, Artemis and Athena have been recognized on the Linear B tablets. Hera is already linked with Zeus, but *Diwia*, in form the feminine of Zeus, also occurs. Ares and Apollo are absent, but Enyalios and Paeon, who coalesced with these deities, are found. Hermes and Hephaestus are possibly attested, and Dionysus seems to occur once, though possibly not as the name of a god. The tablets contain merely names of gods and offerings made to them: their attributes need not resemble those of later literature, vases and sculpture. Their visual attributes cannot, for later artists gradually created them. Archaeology indicates that some deities of the Mycenean period were conceived aniconically, some in human, and some apparently in animal form; but interpretation is hazardous where texts are absent. The bardic tradition may preserve an element of earlier belief: the epithets applied to Hera and Athena clearly mean 'ox-eyed' and 'grey-eyed' to the poets, but their literal sense is 'cow-faced' and 'owl-faced'.

HOMER and HESIOD, then, exerted an influence on later literature. It is difficult to estimate the extent to which literature affected the manner in which worshippers visualised the object of their cult. One might expect sculpture to be even more influential; our response to Greek sculpture is purely aesthetic, however, and we may not assume that what we, and some Greeks, have found most beautiful was necessarily invested with greatest sanctity in the eyes of all worshippers. When PHEIDIAS, a renowned sculptor, made a new statue of Athena for the Acropolis in the later fifth century, the Athenians in general continued to venerate most highly the ancient olive-wood *xoanon* of Athena there, as they had long been accustomed to do. We may not identify the characteristics of Greek gods and goddesses as we find them represented in the arts with those of the deities actually worshipped by the majority of the inhabitants of any Greek state; as will become clearer in the discussion of cult below.

In literature, however, the Olympians present vivid, rounded personalities. In Homer and Hesiod they live in a group on Olympus, whether the Thessalian mountain or some more vaguely localised 'heaven', under the headship of Zeus. They are anthropomorphic, and have the same standards of behaviour as the Homeric heroes. Their organization is roughly equivalent to that of a small agglomeration of noble households in Homer, meeting in assembly to discuss questions which affect all of them. Zeus has a wife, Hera, and among the lesser Olympians Hephaestus is married to Aphrodite; and in Homer and Hesiod a very complex network of relationships binds all these deities together. This fact may give rise to very human motives: in the *Iliad*, Zeus tries to conceal from Hera the help he gives to Achilles, for fear of her sharp tongue.

In such a situation, many attributes familiar to us as divine have no part to play. In the first place, there can be no omnipotence; and indeed, no deity of any kind is omnipotent in the religion of the period under discussion. Zeus not only is not omnipotent in Homer, he ought not to be: Poseidon says that he, Hades and Zeus drew lots, and were apportioned the sea, the underworld and the heavens as their spheres of influence. Where the major deities divide the cosmos —which none of them has created—among themselves, there can be no question of omnipotence. Zeus has, however, more power than Poseidon and Hades in Homer: only he can exert his will from a distance; and though he may find it politic to placate the other gods, his plans triumph in the end. The other Olympians can only help, or harm, men in Homer when they are present; and when they come to earth and take part in battles, they differ from men only in being stronger and immortal. (They can be wounded.) These lesser gods may be prevented from helping favoured mortals by Zeus, whose superior power they fear, or by the necessity of deferring to one another: Athena does not appear in visible form to Odysseus throughout much of the *Odyssey* in deference to the anger of Poseidon against him.

There is no significant change after Homer. The Olympians remain plural; and polytheism entails, and is occasioned by, a departmentalization of the functions of deity. True, many of the Olympians have, even in literature, no clearly defined sphere of influence, as their Romanized equivalents have later; and in the cities where they were worshipped, blessings of all kinds might be sought from any of them. But there is no sign that, even before the assemblage of the Olympian pantheon, any Greek community was ever monotheistic: in this sense, supernatural power was never ascribed to one source alone. It used to be held that AESCHYLUS was virtually a monotheist, and that Zeus was his god; but this view, based on a few striking passages taken out of context, is untenable. Other writers give no encouragement for a belief in omnipotence: the explanation that one god defers to another appears in Euripides; and in the *Eumenides* of AESCHYLUS, where Zeus and Apollo prevail over the Furies, the latter have to be placated: Zeus does not carry the day by omnipotence. (Even were he omnipotent among the Olympians—and he is not—the Furies belong to the realm of Hades; and Zeus' writ does not run there.) In Euripides, the lesser gods can now exert their power at a distance: he ridicules the story of Aphrodite coming in person with Paris to Helen.

Nor is *moira* a greater power behind, and sometimes opposed to, the Olympians. We have seen that a man may speak or act in a manner not in accordance with *moira*, for *moira* represents what a man ought to do, or what is to happen to him. In the second category fall many events which a man has no power to avert; but when Zeus knows that something 'is to' happen to a human character in the Homeric poems, he knows merely that this *ought* to happen to him at that moment. On two occasions when he proposes in the assembly of the gods to save a man whose *moira* it is to die then and there, the reply is not that it is impossible, but that the other gods will not approve. Similarly, the power of Zeus is delimited by his having only one third of the cosmos as his *moira*; it is not, however, impossible, but wrong, for Zeus to encroach on the other gods. Later, in AESCHYLUS' *Eumenides*, the Furies claim that Apollo is depriving them of Orestes, who is their rightful prey, since *Moira* allotted them the function of haunting matricides; and it is clear throughout that the Furies do not believe it to be impossible, but wrong, for them to be treated in such a manner. *Moira* is still merely the system of apportionment of divine functions treated in personal terms: the Greeks of this period had not the conceptual material wherewith to create a system of determinism.

Nor are the Olympians, individually or as a group, held to be omniscient. Not only the lesser gods, but even Zeus, may be deceived or fail to notice something important to them: a successful deception of Zeus by Hera affects the fortunes of the human characters in the *Iliad*. HOMER says 'the gods know all things' of such deities as the sea-god Proteus. He knows all things in the sense that he can answer any question, however difficult, if it is put to him; but he does not know everything actually, as opposed to potentially, all the time, so that it is possible to capture Proteus while he is asleep. The situation is unchanged in later writers, for the old myths remain. In AESCHYLUS' *Prometheus Vinctus*, unless Zeus placates Prometheus, whom he has chained to a rock, Prometheus will not reveal to him how he might prevent himself from being overthrown, as Cronus overthrew Uranus, and Zeus, Cronus; and though Prometheus himself has the power of seeing into the future, he did not realise that Zeus would punish him so terribly for helping mankind. Oracles flourished at this time, the best-known being that of Apollo at Delphi. We need not suppose that omniscience in a 'theological' sense was ascribed to Apollo: this idea is too sophisticated for the period. As in Homer, the all-knowing god can answer any question, however difficult.

5. *Dionysus*

Dionysus is a deity of a very different stamp from those so far discussed. True, a tamed Dionysus presided over certain Athenian festivals in the same manner as other gods presided over theirs. To Dionysus belonged the festivals at which tragedies and comedies were performed; and in one comedy, ARISTOPHANES' *Frogs*, he is portrayed on the stage as an effeminate and cowardly deity on whom all manner of indignities may be heaped, and who is involved in grotesque comic situations: he is even flogged. It would be rash to assert that this was the characteristic picture of Dionysus even in Athens in ARISTOPHA-

NES' day: comedy has its licence, and Greek religion would readily admit of a wine-bibbing, cowardly, genial Dionysus of comedy side by side with very dissimilar and to us quite incongruous aspects of the deity in other contexts. It is certain that a different, much wilder deity was worshipped, and long continued to be worshipped, elsewhere in Greece. EURIPIDES' *Bacchae*, written when the poet was resident in Macedonia, portrays this wilder deity. One source from which the Dionysiac cult came to Greece was almost certainly Thrace, and the cult had a strong hold in Thrace and Macedonia, particularly among the women. The play is concerned with its arrival in Thebes. The Greeks, while acknowledging that the cult came from elsewhere, yet believed that Dionysus was the son of Zeus and Semele, a Theban princess. Semele, tricked by the jealous Hera, asked Zeus to manifest himself in the form of a thunderbolt. He did so, and Semele was killed. Zeus put the still unborn Dionysus in his thigh, from which he was in due course born. In the *Bacchae*, the sisters of Semele deny the divinity of Dionysus, are driven mad by him, and dance in frenzy on the mountains. Pentheus, the king of Thebes, son of Agave, one of Semele's sisters, believes that they have gone to the mountains to indulge in sexual orgies; and when a long-haired young man, on the question of whose identity—Dionysus or his priest?—scholars have spilt much ink, arrives with a train of Bacchantes, Pentheus arrests and imprisons him as a foe to public order. There is an earthquake, and the Stranger escapes from the prison. By playing on Pentheus' prurient curiosity, he induces him to disguise himself as a woman and spy on the dancers in the mountains. He is caught by them. In their frenzy they suppose him to be a wild animal, which they tear to pieces with their bare hands.

The play, while set in the remote past, naturally reproduces aspects of the Dionysiac cult known in EURIPIDES' own day, and later. Dancing on the mountains—in the depths of winter—whether in a maddened ecstasy like that of the Theban women, or with a joyous sense of release, such as that evinced by the Bacchantes who are the chorus of the play, is characteristic. So is the *omophagia*, the tearing to pieces and devouring of an animal raw: the women of Thebes merely tear Pentheus to pieces, but the joyous Bacchantes of the chorus speak of the delight in eating the raw flesh of a goat during their rites.

To scholars who clove to their picture of the Greeks as rational in all things, EURIPIDES' play, and the Dionysiac cult as a whole, posed many problems; but DODDS' discussion, on which this brief account is based, both gives a clear account of the cult in Greece and relates it to similar phenomena in other cultures.

Dionysus is a god of many names, one of which is Bacchus; and Bacchus, in the neat compartments of the Roman world, is the god of wine. The Greek Dionysus is the god of wine, but of much else besides: he is the god of the 'life force' in all its manifestations, plant, animal or human. To those who acknowledge him, as the Bacchante chorus do, he is a god who gives a sense of release (and the poet emphasizes at length that this is not to be identified, as Pentheus identifies it, with sexual licence); to those who deny him, as Pentheus and the women of Thebes deny him in different ways, he brings madness and disaster. He enters into each: each becomes *entheos*, possessed by the god, in different ways. Those who acknowledge him *wish* to become *entheos*, possessed by Dionysus; and a method of attaining this end is by devouring an animal raw. For Dionysus, though he may be portrayed on the stage, or in art, in human form, is far more than this: he is not merely the god of the 'life force', he *is* the life force in all its manifestations. In tearing apart a goat or a bull (which is in itself only possible to those who are already 'beside themselves') and eating it raw, the worshippers are taking the god into themselves. In such a cult the god may enter into his priest: the Stranger may be priest and Dionysus at one and the same time.

In those parts of Greece of which we know most, such outbursts of dancing had been given an approved safety-valve at regular festivals: at Delphi there was a regular biennial festival of Dionysus, to which other states sent delegations of women who danced on the heights of Parnassus along with the women of Delphi in the depths of winter, even in the days of PLUTARCH; but at other times and in other places, including, in all probability, Macedonia in the days of EURIPIDES, such outbursts of dancing fever must have struck as suddenly, and spread as infectiously, as in the *Bacchae*. Athens had long tamed Dionysus (though she sent a contingent of women to Delphi); but in the late fifth century similar gods, such as Sabazius and Bendis, were arriving in Athens from abroad. EURIPIDES may have observed wilder religious practices of a Dionysiac nature before he went to Macedonia. As DODDS points out, most references to these gods in the authors we possess are hostile; but these authors are drawn from a small segment of society, and it seems clear that many found a need for, and welcomed, such practices. PLATO was willing to represent SOCRATES going to watch the festival of Bendis and, on one interpretation of the Greek, offering a prayer to the goddess.

It is clear that such gods as these differ radically from the Olympians. The latter were in some respects all too human, and the relationship into which one entered with them had many resemblances to that between a vassal and his lord. In Homer, an Olympian could 'infuse strength' into a man, but could not himself 'enter into' a man. (One can be *entheos* with Ares or Eros, the gods of war and love, but though these deities appear on Olympus, they are special cases, as being confusedly gods and human passions.) The Olympians influence a man from without, sending success and prowess, disaster and disease; Dionysus enters into his worshippers. The Olympians, and Apollo in particular, are gods who impose limits and rules. Dionysus, while equally jealous of his prerogatives and equally ruthless towards those who slight him, gives release. It is not surprising that there were legends of clashes between the Apolline and the Dionysiac cults in early times. All had been settled before the historical period, however, and Apollo and Dionysus each given their place. At Delphi, for example, Apollo held sway for nine months of the year, Dionysus—a Dionysus worshipped at appointed festivals—for three.

It is mistaken to attempt to base any estimate of the Greek character on the fact that Dionysus was not originally a Greek god. Apollo, the epitome of 'Greekness' in the eyes of scholars of an earlier period, was no more Greek than Dionysus in origin; and the Greeks themselves regarded Dionysus as the son of Zeus. We are concerned here not with national characteristics, but with the universal springs of human nature.

6. *Deities of fertility and deities of the underworld*

Ancient Greece had gods of the living and gods of the dead; at death, a man passed from the realm of Zeus to that of Hades. The Olympians became more sensitive to the fact of death after Homer: in Homer, they fight on the battlefield amid corpses; but in later writers corpses are 'polluted' and 'polluting', and an Olympian must withdraw when a death is imminent.

A man must be either in the realm of Zeus or that of Hades: but this does not entail that the two groups of deities cannot communicate, nor yet that there are only two groups, to one of which any god may be assigned, whether in literature or in cult. Two early poets agree that Hades carried Persephone off to the underworld with the permission of Zeus, his brother; and Tantalus, Ixion and Sisyphus, who had insulted the Olympians in various ways, were punished eternally in Hades for their insults. No Greek of the period had tried to systematize such individual beliefs, or even to formulate them clearly: the question whether an impassable gulf existed between Olympians and gods below had never been asked. This requires emphasis, for the two groups in general hold aloof from one another in literature; and it might be supposed that the instances which do occur require special explanation.

Among gods who do not fit these categories we find Hermes, who is on Homer's Olympus, but also conducts the dead down to Hades in literature and in cult; while 'triple Hecate' is a confused amalgam of chthonic, Olympian and lunar elements. These, and similar, deities do not offend against rigid Greek theological categories, for no such existed. Literature furnishes us with broad groupings of deities. Cult is always more flexible, for the deities in cult have not equally clear-cut personalities; but, as will appear later, the type of ritual used indicates, in the case of deities with more than one aspect, which is in the mind of the worshipper.

I include in this section deities of the earth and of fertility. The most important underworld deities are also concerned with fertility; but among fertility deities are found also some whose role, if we derive our picture of them from literature alone, will appear surprising.

Underworld deities, however, are concerned with fertility in both literature and cult. Hades and Persephone, god and goddess of the underworld, may once have been distinct from Pluto and Kore, the corn-maiden, daughter of Demeter, the corn-(or earth-) mother. But Greek writers treat them as different names for the same pair; and here literature reflects the attitudes of daily life. Had the Greeks believed only in the remote Homeric underworld, such a union of functions might be difficult to understand, for such deities could have little concern with the fertility of the earth. However, the Greeks of the historical period also believed, confusedly, that the dead were in some sense close by in their graves. In early Greece the dead were buried, and the seed-corn was stored, in jars of similar design, immediately below the surface of the earth, from which at the due season sprouts the year's vegetation. To the worshipper confronted by the mysterious powers of the dead and those of the fertilising earth, both located just beneath its surface, it was natural to place both under the aegis of the same deities; and literature presents the same picture, for the Greek imagination did not endow the infernal gods with well-defined personalities, which might have conflicted with one or other aspect of their functions.

Literature and the visual arts, however, furnished the Olympians with clear-cut personalities, functions and interests; and here we must distinguish literature from cult and practice. The calendars of Greek states contain numerous festivals concerned with fertility. Literature would suggest that Demeter, Kore, Dionysus or lesser fertility-deities should preside over these. This occurs in some cases; but among the most important at Athens are festivals of Athena, Apollo and Artemis. The festivals certainly antedate their link with the deities: their names refer to the rituals performed, not to any deity, and the rituals contain agricultural magic which is likely to be older than the anthropo-morphic Olympians. These rituals are the most important element of the festivals, for they give their names to the months in which they were performed: the Anthesteria, Thargelia and Skira took place in the months Anthesterion, Thargelion and Skirophorion respectively. However, in historic times the festivals were associated with Olympian gods, and though Demeter and Kore were the deities of the Skira, and Dionysus of the Anthesteria, Apollo and Artemis were linked with the Thargelia, while Athena had an important fertility festival, the Arrephoria. If we identify the latter with their presentations in literature, we may find bizarre the link of the prophetic deity, the goddess of hunting and the virgin warrior goddess with agricultural fertility magic. We should not. At Athens, these gods have not merely the qualities which they possess in literature: Athena is the patron deity of Athens, while Apollo and Artemis are among 'the city's gods'. They are concerned with every aspect of the city's welfare: not only with the successful defence of the city and its crops, but also with the quality of those crops. The Athenian worshipper can have seen no reason why 'his' Athena should not concern herself with his pros-perity as well as with his success in war. Athena was at Athens before she was on Olympus, and *this* Athena is not merely the Athena of HOMER, AESCHYLUS and PHEIDIAS—though she is that too—but also the revered *xoanon* of olive-wood (a significant material, in view of the importance of the olive-crop) which PHEIDIAS' Athena failed to sup-plant in popular reverence.

7. 'Heroes'

Of the deities so far discussed, 'heroes' resemble nymphs in that their power is localised, but differ from them in not being fully divine.

The idea must be treated historically, for it underwent a development, at least in literature.

In Homer, describing an age gone by, 'heroes' are prominent living warriors. Some, like Achilles, are sprung from one human and one divine parent. For HESIOD, the 'heroes' belong to the age before his own, the race which fought before Thebes and Troy: they are necessarily no longer among men. Terming them 'demigods', he says that some of them died in battle and went to Hades, while Zeus placed others in the Islands of the Blest: a favour which was promised to Menelaus in Homer.

In Homer or Hesiod, 'heroes' have no supernatural powers. Such a belief was impossible: the later 'hero' acquired—or exercised—his powers only after death, and for HOMER and HESIOD a dead 'hero' was in Hades, a living one in the Islands of the Blest, in their own day. In either case they were too far away to help or harm anyone. However, in the historic period of Greece the dead were believed to be nearby in their graves, and sentient to some degree. Any dead man who retained considerable powers could now be a powerful influence; and in essence the 'heroes' of the historical age were mighty dead men, whose superabundant power had survived death. We are far from the strengthless and gibbering shadow which even the Homeric 'hero' became at death. Some 'heroes' revered later, like Theseus, Hercules and Orestes, belong to the age of the Homeric 'heroes'. Some, like Theseus and Hercules, have one human and one divine parent. In historical times, however, neither qualification was essential. Heroization might be accorded to anyone whose great powers in life led his fellows to believe that even after death he would be able to help them.

The later 'hero' had power in the land where his bones were buried. In consequence, the remains of the past 'heroes' were eagerly sought. The Spartans carried off the bones of Orestes from Tegea to Sparta; and thereafter were able to defeat the Tegeats. In 475 B.C. the Athenians transferred the bones of *their* 'hero' Theseus from Scyros to Athens; and in drama, SOPHOCLES' *Oedipus at Colonus* turns on the question whether Oedipus, soon to become a powerful 'hero', is to be buried in Theban or Attic territory.

If the Spartan lawgiver Lycurgus ever lived, he is the first known *historical* example of heroization. But such 'heroes' do not belong only to early times: in the late fifth century the Amphipolitans heroized the Spartan general Brasidas, who had died bravely in their defence, and deprived the Athenian Hagnon of the similar honours he had previously enjoyed as founder of the city. They did this partly, no doubt, as a compliment to Sparta and an insult to Athens, but also because Brasidas would be more powerful in their defence.

'Heroes' gave help in time of danger, especially in battle, but some in other ways. Some 'heroes' were healers, notably Machaon and Podalirius, the sons of Asclepius, himself probably once a 'hero', later the god of medicine; but Hercules too was a healer in Boeotia. Others gave help appropriate to their natures: Helen, worshipped as a 'hero-ine' in Sparta, changed an ugly child into a beauty. Some had prophetic powers, notably Trophonius at Lebadeia. Here too we must not schematize: if a Greek was in dire trouble, he would be likely to pray to any power which might help; and all 'heroes' probably received prayers for help as varied as those addressed to the gods.

The status of 'heroes' is quite clear: they are midway between the human and the divine. Some never existed at all, but all were believed by their worshippers to have been men once, and to have attained their status by their outstanding powers. Men were not heroized for 'goodness' in the usual English sense of the word: Oedipus becomes a 'hero' not because he has been morally rehabilitated, but because he is a strange, awesome old man. The Greek worshipped supernatural power where he found it; and finding it in some men, he accorded them due reverence after their deaths.

8. *Daimones*

Any attempt to present a clear picture of a *daimon* would falsify the material: the idea is quicksilver, elusive and manifold, sometimes even in a single writer.

HESIOD, however, has a simple belief. *Daimones* have two qualities: they are the spirits of the dead of the Golden Age, and 'are kindly, ward off harm, and watch over mortal men'. They are distinct from 'heroes', who belong to the Age immediately before HESIOD's own, and have no concern for men on earth.

The two qualities of HESIOD's *daimones* are not found linked else-where. In tragedy, some dead are referred to as *daimones*. Such dead have high status: their tombs receive honours like those due to the gods, and they may be invoked in the manner of a 'hero'. Indeed, in this usage *daimon* and 'hero' seem virtually synonymous.

Such *daimones*, like 'heroes', are bound to their tombs: they cannot watch over the affairs of mankind, nor accompany an individual through life, as other powers termed *daimones* were believed to do.

THEOGNIS, PLATO and ARISTOTLE all reflect this last belief; HERACLI-
TUS' equation of character with *daimon* is probably uttered in rejection
of it; and when SOCRATES claimed that his *daimonion* always restrained
him from actions harmful to himself, his contemporaries probably
understood *daimonion* in this sense, whatever SOCRATES himself may
have meant. MENANDER asserts that such *daimones* only benefit their
possessors; but the tone of voice suggests that some believed that
one's *daimon* might harm one.

Certainly some *daimones* cause harm; but it is often difficult to
determine whether the *daimon* is the personal *daimon* of the man affected. The question should not be pressed: it is doubtful whether an
ancient Greek could have given a clear answer, and there was an
abundance of *daimones* who were not personal *daimones*. In a Greek
household libations were poured to the 'good *daimon*'; while a baneful
daimon falls on the House of Atreus in Aeschylus. The former seems to
be assigned to the household, not to an individual; the latter comes
at a particular time to harm and punish.

In fact, *daimon* can be applied to practically any supernatural power.
At its vaguest, it refers to a divine agency, specific but unidentified
and unidentifiable. Authors differ in their usage: HOMER even uses
daimon of the Olympians, while PLATO distinguishes *daimones* from
gods on several occasions as an inferior class of supernatural beings,
with the function of interpreting between gods and men. Eros is given
this function as his prerogative in the *Symposium*; but elsewhere they
are nameless and numberless. Their function recalls that of HESIOD's
daimones.

HESIOD and PLATO use *daimon* more precisely than most writers. In
under thirty lines of AESCHYLUS' *Persae*, *daimon* is used of a guardian
spirit, of the powerful dead Darius, and of the chthonic powers Earth,
Hermes and the king of the dead; and other writers behave similarly.
We need not look for some abstruse common characteristic in these
usages: the range is explicable in terms of the function performed by
the idea in daily life. It is not that the Greeks have abstracted and
generalized the idea of divine potency, as some of the less precise
usages might suggest: *daimones* are individual but innumerable. The
ancient Greek saw divine causation everywhere. Some events he
ascribed to specific named deities, Olympian or other; but in the case
of many events the answer to the question 'why has this happened to
me?' was 'A *daimon* has sent this'. Popular belief might assign particular functions to some *daimones*—each human being might have his

own—but an infinity of these unseen powers remained for causing good or harm in general; and since the word denoted merely a divine power, particular but otherwise undefined, in its characteristic usage, its range could easily encompass a variety of deities of different functions. The word well illustrates the tangle of supernatural causation within which the ancient Greek passed his life.

9. *Keres*

Keres are portrayed in two passages of early literature. On the shield of Achilles in Homer, a *ker* drags off a man slain in battle; and on the shield of Hercules in Hesiod *keres* 'gnashing their white teeth, terrible to look upon, grisly, bloody and unapproachable, struggled for those who were dying; for they wanted to drink the black blood'. Faced with the problem of representing the invisible, the visual artist must employ a particular image, however vague and indefinite the idea may be in the minds of men; and here HOMER and HESIOD may be describing, or preserving the memory of, actual works of art. It is not surprising that *keres* in general are less clearly defined, though no less terrible, beings; nor that their functions are wider than those appropriate for portrayal on a shield.

The *keres* of daily life are believed to cause death. In this respect they resemble *moira*; and indeed in the *Theogony* HESIOD calls the *Keres*, here three in number, Clotho, Lachesis and Atropos, usually the names of the *Moirai*. *Keres*, however, are a quite different phenomenon: one's *moira* is a personal thing, allotted to oneself, while *keres* are more general. True, Achilles in Homer says that he has two *keres* of death, depending on whether he lives a quiet life (when he will die old) or the life of a warrior (when he will soon be killed); but this is 'literature'. Achilles' mother, the goddess Thetis, told him this; and such sources of information are denied to the ordinary man. For him, the *keres* of death are countless, and he knows merely that he must succumb to one of them. Nor do *keres* cause death alone: MIMNERMUS regards old age as a *ker*, and THEOGNIS agrees; but he also says that there are two *keres* connected with drinking, thirst and drunkenness, between which he will try to steer his course. The philosopher DEMOCRITUS lists jealousy, emulation and enmity among *keres*; while PLATO says that most good things are spoiled by 'as it were, *keres*'; and he instances the effect of rhetoric on justice. THEOPHRASTUS holds that each place has its own *ker* which mar the plants that grow there; but he adds a naturalistic explanation of this.

The last two examples may be figurative; though in early Greek one mode of thought does not necessarily exclude another. However, they illustrate the belief in *keres* generally held even in the fourth century. *Keres* are a host of invisible powers which cause discomfort, misery, old age and death. They either are these states of affairs, or cause them: the Greek does not draw a sharp distinction. They are not personifications of abstractions: abstract nouns are used of them, but they are felt as concrete and particular in the life of the individual; and the Greek ascribed the states of affairs to causes equally concrete, particular and malignant. It is possible that the little creatures which escaped from Pandora's box were *keres*, though this depends on an emendation of the text.

The Athenians seem to have banished the spirits of the dead under the name of *keres* at the end of the Anthesteria; but certainly not all *keres* are ghosts. We must not attempt to force Greek religious phenomena into a strait-jacket of clearly defined terms. The Greek felt himself surrounded by supernatural influences in a world in which his existence was precarious; and certain of these invisible hostile powers he termed *keres*.

10. *Erinyes*

The function of *keres* is to harm; that of *erinyes* to punish. In Homer, Oedipus, Telemachus and even the god Ares are either punished by the *erinyes* of their mothers, or punishment from this source is threatened; the father of Phoenix invokes the *erinyes* against him; while Poseidon is reminded that *erinyes* protect elder brothers. In Aeschylus, Clytemnestra threatens Orestes with her *erinyes* if he kills her; while Orestes fears those of Agamemnon if he does not. The function of the *erinyes* is to guarantee the rights of members of the household in need of such protection: a wife was separated from her own kin when she married, a father's rights might be threatened by an adult son—or in Agamemnon's case, by his wife; and in a country where land was scarce an elder brother might need protection against his younger brothers. The *erinyes* have other functions. In Homer, when Achilles' horse prophesies his master's death, they cut short his words; while HERACLITUS says that the *erinyes* would punish the sun if he left his allotted path in the heavens. They are also associated with oaths and curses: HOMER—most uncharacteristically, for punishment after death is not usual in the Homeric Hades—says that the *erinyes* punish below the earth anyone who swears a false oath. In Hesiod, they were present at the birth of *Horkos* (Oath). In Aeschylus, *erinyes* and 'curse' are used in apposition, while the *Erinyes*, characters in the *Eumenides*, say of themselves that they are called Curses beneath the earth.

The pattern of belief now becomes clearer. Scholars have pointed out the link between *erinyes* and *moira*. In the household, each has his due *moira*: if this is upset, the *erinyes* restore the correct apportionment, if the individual cannot do this for himself. Again, the sun has his path in the heavens, a horse an appropriate mode of behaviour, to which they should keep: the *erinyes* will check any deviation. Similarly, an oath creates a pattern of behaviour which ought to be followed. The *erinyes* 'sent' by the wronged may be seen as objectified curses, given a life of their own. No-one has cursed the sun or Achilles' horse, but the function of the *erinyes* is similar; and it is similarity of function in the different situations which determines the range of the *erinyes*' activity. Even in saying that the *erinyes* punish transgressions of *moira* we need not suppose that any Greek, if asked, would have given an explicit answer in these terms; but the two ideas form part of the same pattern of thought.

IV. Worship

1. *Ethics*

The relationship between the ancient Greek and his gods, and the demands made on each by the other, can only be understood in the wider context of Greek values and society; for the Greek, particularly in Homer, credited his gods with values similar to his own; and these are closely linked with the nature of his society.

In Homer, the largest effective social unit, the only one capable of defending the weaker members of society, was the *oikos*, the noble household under the sway of its head, to whom the commendatory adjective *agathos* was applied. Such a man possessed and controlled the property of the *oikos* (in kind, for there was no money), and belonged to a class of hereditary landowners. In war, he and his like, being able to furnish themselves with full armour, were the most effective fighting force which this society possessed, and in the uneasy peace experienced by such small virtually autonomous units, he was the only one capable of defending his dependants. In these activities success was of the highest importance, for failure meant annihilation or slavery. As a result, *agathos* denotes and commends prosperity, high

birth, and courage leading to a successful outcome. The members of
the group defended by the *agathos* regard this successful defence,
naturally enough, as his most important function. By comparison, his
justice or injustice appears of less importance to their survival. His
justice is thus less highly commended than his success, his injustice
less severely decried than his failure; and different words are used to
commend justice and decry injustice from those used to commend
success and decry failure. The latter are naturally emotively more
powerful: if the *agathos* is successful though unjust, society cannot
effectively censure him for his injustice, and the *agathos*, valuing
success most highly, will take the means, just or unjust, which lead
most directly to that end. These values persist into the historic period:
the later city-state, and the later household, continued to feel a stronger
need for the success of the *agathos* than for his justice, if the former
could be pursued without the latter. Nevertheless, the wronged individual had a strong interest in the effective maintenance of justice. To
achieve this it was necessary to ensure, by means human or divine,
that one could not be unjust and prosper, that justice was a necessary
means to being successful and so *agathos*.

The *agathos*, if powerful enough, might be able to resist the attempts
of his fellow-men to punish him. The onus then fell on the gods; and
since punishment after death was reserved for those few men who
wronged the gods themselves, not their fellow-men, punishment must
be exacted by the Olympians in this life. This function they were
singularly ill-fitted to perform. Homer says of the gods that they have
more *arete* (the excellence of the *agathos*), status and strength than men;
and save for the fact that they do not die, this indeed seems to be the
only distinction between Homeric god and Homeric *agathos*.

Accordingly, when in the *Iliad* Agamemnon robs Achilles of his
prize, the slave-girl Briseis, Achilles is showing himself deficient in
arete, for he has been worsted by Agamemnon; and the situation is
aischron (the most powerful word available to decry it) for Achilles,
but not for Agamemnon, whose *arete* remains unsmirched by the
transaction. Provided Agamemnon can lead the army whose commander-in-chief he is successfully against the Trojans, he remains
agathos; and this is so much the most important aspect of the situation
that even when Agamemnon later recompenses Achilles, he does not
evaluate his earlier action as unjust. Agamemnon had two purposes,
to capture Troy and to deprive Achilles of Briseis. He thought it
possible to achieve both: finding it impossible to do so, since the

absence of Achilles sulking in his tent and the hostility of Zeus to the Greek cause had seriously weakened the Greek army, he acknowledged that he had *miscalculated* and recompensed Achilles to bring him back into the fighting.

Nor did the wronged Achilles threaten Agamemnon with just punishment from Zeus. Zeus did indeed take a hand in Agamemnon's discomfiture, but not because it was just to do so: as we shall see in the discussion of prayer, Achilles was able to obtain this *as a favour*, for his mother, Thetis, had the ear of Zeus. An ordinary mortal could not hope for such favoured treatment, for the gods endorse human values and esteem *arete* most highly. When Nestor realises that Telemachus has been escorted by Athena in disguise, he infers that Telemachus will not prove to be *kakos* (the opposite of *agathos*). A deity would not favour anyone who was *kakos*: his justice or injustice is comparatively unimportant.

Only strangers, beggars, suppliants and guests can hope for justice from heaven: Zeus Xeinios, the Strangers' Zeus, should protect them. Stranger, suppliant and guest are three stages through which the Homeric traveller must rapidly pass, for his own safety. The household is the largest effective social, political and economic unit in Homer, and a man has no rights *qua* human being, but only as a member of a particular social unit. The traveller is in an exposed position; and in a society with no coined money, no readily portable wealth, he cannot purchase assistance. He is dependent upon an *agathos*, a head of household, for protection, status, and the necessities of life which the *agathos* alone controls, in the society into which he has come. The stranger (*hiketes*, 'suppliant', means 'one who comes') must supplicate an *agathos*; and if he does so successfully, he becomes a guest. The *agathos* must then protect him against others, for *arete* requires a man to protect his dependants. It does not, however, require him not to harm his dependants himself; and here Zeus Xeinios' function begins. He will punish the host who harms his guests. This may appear at first sight to be a strange activity for the Zeus we have seen so far; and indeed Xeinios may have originally been a separate deity—'the power who protects guests'—taken over by Zeus. Nevertheless, this function could be represented as part of the *arete* of Zeus: if all strangers and beggars are, as it were, part of the household of Zeus, who has undertaken to protect them, his *arete* requires that he should do so with all the means at his disposal.

In general, the gods make no wider ethical demands than these in

Homer. (The prayer and sacrifice which they expect will be discussed below.) Their worshippers assume that they will sometimes be capricious, even in the acknowledgment of *arete*. Two jars stand at the threshold of Zeus, from which he allots good and ill to mankind at his whim, without regard to merit. This belief may be turned to moral ends: Odysseus observes that a man should be moderate in prosperity, for the gods may bring him low one day, when he will need just treatment from others.

In so far as the *agathos* feels himself at all insecure, the very caprice of the gods may underwrite morality; but as his security increases, more will be required of heaven. In a society in which justice and similar qualities are the highest ethical goods, to forsake these in search of success is immoral; but in HOMER's Greece and much later, to pursue success at the expense of justice, if injustice is a surer means to that end, is simply to act in accordance with the accepted values of society. HESIOD understands the situation perfectly: "Now may neither I nor my son be just among men any more; for it is a bad thing to be just, if the unjust man is to come off better."

Such 'coming off better', whether for just or unjust, must occur in this life. There is no reward or punishment for the ordinary man in the Homeric after-life; and this remained the usual view later. HOMER's expectation that heaven would be just was too marginal for him to be shocked when heaven was not. But, though they preserved all the myths which portrayed the gods as capricious, HESIOD and later writers hope that Zeus will punish wrongdoers: a punishment which must be seen to be inflicted in this life, if justice is to be valued. Despite his outburst above, HESIOD believed that the unjust are always punished in this life. THEOGNIS and SOLON were more clear-headed. They realised that an unjust individual sometimes prospers throughout his life, and record the solution which had been offered: the gods may punish the children, or even the remote descendants, of a man who is unjust. As a formal explanation of observable phenomena, this belief is admirable: if a man is just and prospers, he deserves to; if he is unjust and comes to ruin, he is rightly punished; if he is unjust and prospers, his descendants will suffer; and if he is just and comes to ruin, he is paying for the misdeeds of some ancestor. So long as the kinship-group is held to be of more importance than the individual, the belief also has ethical validity; but in proportion as the individual gains in importance, the possibility that one should be just oneself and suffer for an ancestor's crimes will appear to be the rankest injustice.

This stage has been reached by the time of THEOGNIS, who complains bitterly that Zeus should see to it that the wrongdoer should pay for his misdeeds at once; 'but as it is, he escapes, and another man comes to harm thereafter'. For the individual, there is no necessary link between being just and being successful: he may be doomed to ruin anyway for the crimes of his ancestors. In the context of Greek values, there must be a strong temptation to pursue success by whatever means, and chance the vagaries of divine retribution.

THEOGNIS cannot solve this problem; and writers in the fifth century who hold the view—the usual view—that this life is all fare no better. Only those who believe, as AESCHYLUS may have done, that the unjust are infallibly punished in this life feel no problem. (AESCHYLUS also holds occasionally that there is punishment after death, but most of his extant work reflects the normal Greek view.) Indeed, it is desirable that reward and punishment come not only in this life, but quickly: in the *Oedipus at Colonus* Oedipus maintains that the gods reward the pious and punish the impious; but when Ismene says that the gods are about to rehabilitate him, he replies 'It is an empty thing to raise up an old man who fell when he was young.' This life is all, and Oedipus has little of it left.

Since reward and punishment must come in this life and the individual, not the kinship-group, now has priority, the Greeks believe that the gods' attitude to a man can be empirically ascertained from his successes or disasters. In AESCHYLUS' *Seven against Thebes*, though Oedipus' ultimate fate is known, it is held that the gods were honouring him while he was prospering in Thebes. And yet the gods knew that Oedipus was an incestuous parricide; and that he was not so deliberately was irrelevant at this period. The pious Greek, seeing a man prosper, held that the gods were granting him success: when the evil-doer flourished, the gods were not merely failing to punish him, they were positively favouring him.

The 'Problem of Evil' related to belief in a just and omnipotent god does not usually result from this. True, EURIPIDES' Electra thus argues that Orestes must be successful in avenging Agamemnon: 'If injustice is to get the better of justice, we must no longer believe that the gods exist.' If there were gods they would be just, and reward and punish men in this life; but they do not: therefore there are no gods. This remark is uncharacteristic, not merely of ancient Greeks, but also of EURIPIDES. The Greek did not believe that his gods were omnipotent, and numerous myths portrayed them as capricious and amoral. The

Greeks' problem was not to explain the existence of evil in a world governed by benevolent gods but, under the sway of very different gods, to render justice preferable to injustice nevertheless.

The Greeks also believed that the gods might harm a whole group (city, army) which contained an individual of whom they disapproved, for whatever reason. The belief is based on observable fact: cities and armies may be ravaged by pestilence, cities suffer from drought, flood, earthquake, bad harvests. Such disasters are sent by gods, and harm groups as a whole: the gods must be punishing the group as a whole. Sometimes the group is at fault; but sometimes the culprit is an individual. Therefore the gods may punish a group for the offences of an individual. Where the gods are concerned with their own status, the offence may be failure to sacrifice. In Homer, Oeneus forgot to sacrifice to Artemis when he did so to the other gods; and she sent a wild boar which ravaged the countryside. That he forgot, that the slight was not deliberate, is irrelevant. The gods too are concerned with *arete* and *time*; and a prominent element of each is wealth actually possessed. Sacrifice confers such *time* on the gods; and its absence, whether caused deliberately or accidentally, lowers the status of the god concerned, and will be punished severely. Where the gods are held to be just, a famine or earthquake may be believed to be punishment for an individual's injustice; and 'pollution' admits of similar arguments.

'Pollution' must be discussed separately. It concerns the supernatural, and in some cases affects ethical judgments; but here we leave the Olympians, for these were believed to withdraw from any situation in which 'pollution' was involved. The phenomenon requires definition; and the best-known occurrences of the idea are not the most illuminating. Orestes kills his mother and is 'polluted'; Oedipus kills his father and marries his mother, and is 'polluted'. One might conclude that 'pollution' was a representation of moral guilt in concrete, material terms. But homicide of (almost) any kind, including accidental homicide, occasions 'pollution'; as do a bad dream, contact with death—any human death, not merely homicide—childbirth, and certain diseases of a repellent and unnatural kind. The Greeks were capable of distinguishing morally between deliberate and accidental homicide; and the remaining examples do not raise moral issues at all. 'Pollution' does not conform to ethical categories.

'Pollution' is dangerous, for the 'polluted' man 'pollutes' his whole group; and supernatural disasters may result. Such occurrences lead

Oedipus to seek advice from Delphi; and the oracle pronounces the cause to be the presence in Thebes of the unpunished murderer of Laius. This is an everyday belief in the sixth, fifth and fourth centuries. To the Ionians, Delos was a sacred island. Accordingly, Pisistratus in the sixth century purified as much of Delos as was visible from Apollo's temple. Later, in the sixth year of the Peloponnesian War, all the corpses on Delos were disinterred, and it was decreed that no birth or death should occur there; and four years later the Athenians expelled the Delians on the grounds that there was some reason from former days why they were not pure. Athenian solicitude for the island's purity may well be linked with their lack of success in the war: 'pollution' is dangerous. The removal of the corpses and the expulsion of the Delians show that no distinction is drawn between kinds of 'pollution'. The former kind cannot be moral: accordingly, neither is moral.

Such dangers cannot be ignored. If his 'pollution' requires time for its removal, or is indelible, a 'polluted' man should be exiled; if this is not done, he must be shunned until he is purified, where this is possible; and though one should, in EURIPIDES' opinion, welcome a guest-friend even if he is 'polluted', one should keep him in quarantine.

Since 'pollution' is non-moral, so is purification. A bad dream requires a wash in a spring; homicide is purified by fire and the blood of a pig; while an object touched by a 'polluted' man should be washed, preferably in the sea.

Indelible 'pollution' is equally non-moral. The homicide of a member of the same family, or the killing of a suppliant at an altar, entails a stain which cannot be washed out. There can be no question of justification: justice demanded that Orestes kill his mother, yet the Erinyes claim that he is indelibly 'polluted'; while even had Creusa poisoned Ion as she intended, to kill her at the altar would entail indelible 'pollution' as surely as would an unprovoked attack upon an innocent person in the same circumstances.

In one sense, the reason for the belief in 'pollution' is clear enough: disasters occur, and society looks round for a supernatural cause. The Greek did not suppose that only intentional acts could occasion supernaturally-caused disaster, and need not search only among those who had intentionally done wrong or given offence; and once a disaster had been ascribed to the 'pollution' caused by a homicide, and appropriate measures had been taken, the same measures might be taken in future lest homicide, through 'pollution', might cause disaster.

However, Homeric man would have ascribed such disasters to the wrath of a god; and it may appear strange that later Greeks sought a different cause. Only hypotheses can be offered in explanation, for no writer records the beginnings of the belief: 'pollution' is not found in Homer in this form, occurs only in the form of a few taboos in Hesiod, and suddenly emerges fully-fledged in later writers. However, some things are certain: it is a non-rational phenomenon, and has two distinguishable facets in the individual's own feeling of 'pollution' and society's feelings that an individual is 'polluted', whether by the same or different actions. In some cases, the individual alone is concerned: only he can know whether he has had a bad dream, with consequent feelings of unease or non-rational guilt. Such feelings may exist independently of any later disaster; but society's attitude is clearly linked with disaster, whether actual or, when the belief has become established, possible; and society's attitude too is, to put it no more strongly, one of unease. Now HOMER's attitude to the supernatural is confident: one must beware of the anger of his gods, but there is nothing eerie about them. But in the ages which followed life became harder and narrower, and literature reflects perplexity in the face of many new problems: conditions were suitable for development of a very different kind of belief.

The case of homicide may have furnished one of the seeds from which it sprang. In Homer, homicide of whatever kind is followed by flight: not because of 'pollution', for such 'pollution' is unknown to Homer, but to escape the wrath of the victim's family. A later practice, however, already depicted on the shield of Achilles, permitted the family to accept a blood price in lieu of the killer's exile or death. This may at first have appeared to have social advantages; but communities are not moved only by economic considerations; and as cities developed and more households lived close together, the victim's relatives might see every day the killer walking among them unharmed. True, he had paid compensation, but *arete* really demands more rigorous reprisals. They may not be taken, but a society containing such a killer and the emotional stresses he generates is likely to be uneasy; and in time of famine or pestilence, he is well marked out to be a Jonah. The practice of accepting indemnity for homicide does not in itself lead to a belief in 'pollution': straitened conditions heighten the sensibilities of the homicide's fellows to such an extent that they project their anxieties and hatreds on to him, and on to other situations which appear strange and awesome to them, to such an extent that they seem to them to acquire an objective character.

A remedy for such a situation is urgent; and this may explain the close association of Delphi with 'pollution'. If we regard Delphi as a civilizing influence, and 'pollution' as the blackest of superstition—and both attitudes are reasonable—the association may appear *prima facie* surprising. But of course Delphi did not invent 'pollution', which had arisen from tensions and anxieties within communities faced with disasters: it prescribed remedies for the situation, and though the remedies, like the supposed causes, were in fact unlinked with those disasters, at such a time any remedy is reassuring.

The result, however, cannot be held to be an ethical advance. 'Pollution' adheres to persons involved in certain kinds of action or situation, without regard to intention; and the horror aroused by these actions or situations is not a moral horror, but one derived from the fear of disaster which the presence of 'pollution' was believed to entail. The belief cuts across the categories of ethics, and is so powerful that it prevents the application of these in several important fields. Athenian law in fact succeeded in distinguishing categories of homicide: homicide in self-defence, or death caused accidentally in practice for the games or war, and homicide in certain other circumstances, carried no penalty, though accidental homicide entailed temporary exile. The simple fiat of the early lawgiver seems to have sufficed until the later fifth century, when fine-drawn justifications of this fiat were offered; but no moral reformer could root out the belief, or completely annul its effect upon Greek ethics.

In early Greece, then, supernatural sanctions for ethics posed many problems not only when Greek deities were held to be capricious: their behaviour as moral agents posed problems no less severe. It was necessary that the just individual should prosper, if justice was to be valued and pursued; and empirical observation led the Greek to conclude that the gods sometimes punished a man's descendants for his crimes, sometimes brought a whole city to disaster for the misdeeds of an individual. When it is remembered that the gods were also believed to confer good and ill fortune capriciously, whether on the individual or the group, that they took no account of intentions where their own status was concerned, and that 'pollution' was similarly unconcerned with intentions, Greek perplexity in these matters is entirely comprehensible.

The belief of a minority, associated with mystery-cults, in a more real existence after death has ethical implications: these will be discussed below, under 'Personal Eschatology'.

Worship: Cult

2. *Magic*

Magic rites which are directly linked with the cult and worship of deities form only a part of magical phenomena found in Greek society, as in other societies, for magic need not be associated with any god. In societies with little or no knowledge of natural laws, such 'independent' magic is not and cannot be distinguished from medicine: in Greek *pharmakon* is used to denote what we should distinguish as medicinal drugs and magical material, and also the use of spells and incantations in magic and medicine. These different methods of affecting the well-being of others are not distinguished. Doctors made use of incantations: Pindar lists them with *pharmaka* (here restricted to exclude spells) and surgery among the methods used by Asclepius, the god of medicine. The methods were not interchangeable: at all events, Sophocles says that it is not the mark of a good doctor to use incantations on a disease which requires surgery.

The foregoing are *pharmaka* used for a definite purpose. Hesiod reflects fear of magical influence accidentally suffered as a result of the nature of certain objects with which one comes into contact: a boy at the age of puberty should not sit on a tomb, nor should a man wash in water used by a woman. He also warns against cutting one's nails at a festival of the gods: the fear that an enemy might gain possession of the nails and so power over oneself is presumably present, though the restriction to festivals indicates that this has developed, or is developing, into a religious prohibition. (One might compare the English superstition, still found, forbidding the cutting of fingernails on Fridays and Sundays.)

This last is the first indication that magic may be linked with the gods in Greece at all. The methods used by a young girl in Theocritus to win back her lover make the matter clearer. One invocation shows that the use of verbal magic need not involve the gods: the *iunx*, a wryneck used as a prayerwheel or a prayerwheel itself, is invoked in its own right. However, the girl also calls upon the Moon and Hecate to make her spells more powerful than those of Circe; and other deities appear later in the poem. Nevertheless, sympathetic magic is also used, with full knowledge of the means by which it is believed

to work: 'as I burn this laurel, so may Daphnis waste away.' Supernatural aid is sought from every source available. Extant Greek
magical papyri also show the invocation of gods to preside over
magical rites and guarantee their efficacy.

THEOCRITUS' poem is Hellenistic in date, and the magical papyri
much later; but they are almost certainly relevant to our period, for
magic is the most conservative of all the arts; and exactly similar
processes of thought can be discovered not on the fringes of Greek
religion, but at its core, the agricultural festivals of the Greek calendar.
We have seen already that many Olympians presided over these in
their capacity as gods of the city; and their power in itself might have
sufficed to ensure fertility. One example will show that this was not
the case. At the Athenian Arrephoria, a festival of Athena, two young
girls, selected each year and given quarters near Athena's temple,
were given boxes containing mysterious objects which they carried
down into a natural cavern, bringing something else with them when
they returned. This ended the duties of the girls. We are informed that
neither they nor the priestess knew what the objects were; but other
sources mention models of snakes and phalli made out of bread-dough,
and pine branches, selected because of the fertility of the tree. This
must be a fertility-ritual; and analogy with other festivals, notably the
Thesmophoria, at which the remains of pigs left to decompose underground were similarly used, suggests that what remained of the dough
and pine branches when brought up again was mixed with the seed
corn to ensure a good harvest. The earth is the source of new vegetable life each year; the material, selected for its magic fertilising
power, was further charged by contact with the life-giving earth until
such time as it was needed for its vital function. These are only two
of many agricultural festivals found in the calendars of Greece. Like
the Arrephoria and Thesmophoria, they are linked with the names of
gods, whose powerful aid was hoped for; but the festivals bear the
names not of gods, but of the rituals performed; and the heart of
these rituals is pure fertility-magic, which probably precedes belief in
personalised gods and is not displaced by the belief in Greece. The
Greek tried to harness every supernatural power available to ensure
the success of his harvest, on which so much depended.

3. Prayer

In the Homeric poems, the Greek gods are little concerned with
justice, and in general regard mankind as of little account. In the

Trojan War, different factions of the Olympians support Greeks and Trojans, but they are not concerned with the justice of the cause of either side, and reflect in the *Iliad* that it will be intolerable if strife breaks out among them on behalf of mortal men, for the gods will no longer be able to take their pleasure in feasting.

To obtain the attention of such gods as these, some claim is needed; and various claims are possible. Those who, like Achilles, have one divine parent, have preferential treatment. Apollo (a supporter of the Trojans) is shocked when Achilles drags the corpse of Hector round the walls of Troy; but Hera points out that Hector is a mere mortal, whereas Achilles' mother was Thetis, a sea-goddess, whose marriage to Peleus was attended by all the gods. Achilles has superior status: the gods should not be angry. Similarly, when Polyphemus, son of Poseidon, was blinded by Odysseus, though Odysseus acted in self-defence and Polyphemus had behaved in a shocking manner by devouring Odysseus' companions, he had only to pray to Poseidon and vengeance on Odysseus was granted to him. Even Chryses, Apollo's priest, has to remind Apollo of sacrifices he has offered him to ensure that he will punish the Greek army for the wrong that Chryses has suffered. In Homer in general, if one has claims one will not be punished for wrong-doing; and the ordinary man must mention claims in the form of sacrifices offered and similar benefits conferred in order to obtain justice against those who have wronged him.

This type of prayer is frequent in the fifth century too. Where the prayer is made to the gods of the city, it should be remembered, when the god is not reminded of sacrifices performed, that such gods received regular and abundant sacrifices as their festivals came round; and this may be taken for granted by both sides. SOCRATES in PLATO's *Euthyphro* terms conventional Greek piety barter between god and man; and other Greeks would have been no more able to deny this than is Euthyphro. AESCHYLUS' *Seven against Thebes* shows the inducements which were still offered to the gods in the fifth century. The chorus is afraid that Polynices may conquer Thebes; and they try every means available to persuade the gods to help. They pray to Zeus, Earth and the gods who are the guardians of the city not to allow them to fall into slavery; for a flourishing city gives much *time* (in the form of sacrifices and other offerings) to the gods. They say that they are suppliants, which gives them a special claim to protection; and they ask the gods not to betray them. They remind Cypris—Aphrodite—that she is the ancestor from whom they are descended. (Cadmus, founder of Thebes, married Harmonia, the daughter of Ares and Aphrodite). They beg the gods to be *philopoleis* —the ordinary word for 'patriotic'—and to remember the many sacrifices from which they have benefited in the past; and they ask what city there is more pleasant than Thebes to which the gods could migrate, should Thebes fall.

These prayers show the attitude of the citizen to his gods. He knows that the same gods—gods with the same names—are worshipped throughout Greece; but when he prays, he prays to them as the gods of his city; and in the last resort, the gods' attitude should be 'My city, right or wrong'. The claims of kin and patriotism can readily be exemplified from poems composed in urgent, real-life situations: Tyrtaeus, amid the stresses of the Messenian War, reminds the Spartans that their kings are descended from Zeus through Hercules, so that Zeus will not let them be defeated; while Solon tells the Athenians that no deity will ever bring Athens to ruin, since Athena is their mighty protector. The patriotic motif raises no questions of right or wrong, for the *arete* of the god is concerned.

Prayers to the infernal powers are similar. In the passage of AESCHYLUS already discussed, the Chorus reminds Earth, Curse and the Erinys of Orestes that a prospering city will furnish them with *time*. Electra in AESCHYLUS' *Choephori* utters a more complex prayer to the gods below. She asks the chthonic Hermes, in his role as herald and messenger, to request these gods to hear her prayers, and calls upon the shade of Agamemnon to pity Orestes and herself. She reminds him that they are shut out from their royal inheritance by his murderer and the adulterous Aegisthus, and prays to him that Orestes may return with good fortune, and that she may be more virtuous than Clytemnestra. May Agamemnon be avenged, as is just, and may he send benefits to them, together with the gods, and Earth and Justice that brings victory. After this prayer she pours an offering.

This appeal is partly to Agamemnon's self-interest—his murder at the hands of a woman was shameful for him, for if an *agathos* dies violently, he should die bravely in battle—but also to justice. Since supernatural powers are sometimes moral, prayers may be addressed to their moral aspect, and not only when, as in this case, the power has a personal interest in exacting a penalty. Even in Homer, where the ties of hospitality have been broken, the wronged Menelaus can pray to Zeus that he may be able to avenge himself on Paris 'in order that men even of future generations may fear to harm a host who treats them well'. In Aeschylus, suppliant maidens, strangers in a possibly hostile land, pray to the Suppliants' Zeus, and ask the gods of their own race to look upon what is just and hear their prayer; though they naturally add all the inducements which occur to them: they remind Zeus that he is the father of their race, and pray to the maiden daughter of Zeus, Athena, to help them, for they are maidens, and to Apollo who was once an exile to help them who are exiles.

Greek practice in prayer naturally reflects the Greek confusions of belief in the nature of their gods. Sometimes the gods, Olympian or chthonic and 'heroes', are held to be amoral powers concerned only with their own *time*, whose ear can only be obtained by those who have a specific claim on them. Sometimes they are held to be moral, and justice is expected of them; but it is not surprising that as many claims as can be thought of are frequently added in addition, as a guarantee that these confusing deities will make some response to prayer. Indeed, even in prayer to gods, as opposed to magic rites, elements of magical means of binding the gods to the will of the worshipper persist. In the *Agamemnon*, AESCHYLUS begins a prayer to Zeus, in a passage which contains much religious thought that is 'advanced' by Greek standards, 'Zeus, whoever he may be, I address him by the name which is most pleasing to him'. This is not agnosticism but a mixture of faith and magic: it is widely believed that to address a supernatural power by its 'real' name gives one the means of binding that power to one's will. This is found, naturally, in magical documents, for it is a magic belief; but it is reflected here, in a 'religious' passage.

4. *Sacrifice*

Sacrifice as a means of obtaining the attention of Greek gods has already received passing mention; but the matter requires fuller discussion. When sacrifice is concerned, the non-moral aspects of Greek deity are usually to the fore. In the *Odyssey* Athena reminds Zeus that Odysseus offered abundant sacrifice while at Troy: what reason could Zeus have for being angry with him? If sacrifice furnished a claim on heaven, and disaster in itself betokened divine displeasure, the disaster of a man who had offered outstanding sacrifice or had sent magnificent gifts to a god's shrine (an activity which may be classed with sacrifice, since the god receives *time* in either case) creates a problem. Croesus, the richest man in the world, had made splendid offerings to Apollo; yet his kingdom fell to the Persians. Though

Croesus was long dead, fifth century writers still discuss him. BAC-
CHYLIDES contrives a happy ending: when the king ascended the pyre
with his family and ordered it to be lighted, Zeus extinguished the
flames with a shower of rain and Apollo carried Croesus and his
family off to the Hyperboreans 'on account of his piety, because he
had, more than any other mortal, sent gifts to goodly Pytho'. HERO-
DOTUS maintains that Apollo had already staved off disaster, which
was bound to come, for as long as he could in virtue of Croesus' gifts.
BACCHYLIDES advises a living tyrant 'Do holy things, and be of good
cheer, for that is the greatest of benefits'. He adds 'Continue to give
gifts to Apollo; and then you may have many more years of wealthy
life'. To give gifts to Apollo is to do holy things. The prosperous
tyrant is in the best position to do this: who should be more assured
of the favour of heaven? Not that the belief is invented for the tyrant's
convenience: as has been shown, it is generally held that sacrifice is
necessary to gain the ear of these amoral deities.

The manner of sacrifice, and to some extent its purpose, varies in
accordance with the type of god to which it is offered. Sacrifice of
both food and drink is made, but the Olympian and chthonic sacrifice
differ in method. HOMER describes in detail the sacrifice of a pig to the
Olympians. Hairs from the animal's head are thrown into the fire as
first offering. Then its throat is slit and it is cut up. A piece of meat
from each limb is wrapped in fat and thrown into the fire, with barley-
grains sprinkled on it. The rest is then roasted, divided into portions
and eaten by the worshippers, one portion on this occasion being
reserved for Hermes and the nymphs. The informality is characteristic
of HOMER: the sacrifice is offered not at some festival of the gods, but
as an integral part of supper. A portion of the animal goes up in
smoke as *time* for the Olympians, the rest becomes a meat meal.
HESIOD already found it strange that the gods only received a portion,
and explained the practice by an aetiological myth: Prometheus tricked
Zeus by covering the meat of an animal with an ox paunch, arranging
the bones artistically with a covering of fat, and inviting Zeus to choose.
Zeus chose the bones and fat, and discovered his mistake too late; 'and
so men burn white bones to the gods on their altars'. Olympian sacrifice
remained a meat meal of which the worshippers ate the larger part:
public sacrifices, performed on altars set outside large and beautiful
temples, later added pomp and magnificence, but the essentials remained the same.

Very different in kind and in vocabulary were sacrifices to the gods below. To sacrifice to the Olympians is *hiereuein* or *thuein*: to offer burnt sacrifice to infernal deities or 'heroes' is *enagizein*. HERODOTUS says of Hercules, in some traditions an Olympian, in others a 'hero', that those Greeks are right who both *hiereuein* and *enagizein* to him. (The terms are not always as carefully used as they are in this passage.) Again, while Olympian sacrifice was made on a raised altar, *bōmos*, in later times (Eumaeus in Homer simply used his hearth, and indeed called it an *eschara*), sacrifice to infernal gods and 'heroes' was performed on a low hearth, *eschara*. The ritual was quite dissimilar: black victims were used, and the whole animal was burned, for no-one would eat food with the gods below or with the dead; and 'heroes' were the greatest of the dead.

It is a simplification to say that Olympian sacrifice is concerned with the 'tendance' of beneficent powers, chthonic sacrifice with the 'aversion' of malevolent ones. When they chose, the Olympians could match any infernal deity in malevolence, and 'tendance' of infernal powers has already been mentioned. The earliest recorded sacrifice to the dead, in the *Odyssey*, is offered to summon them: Odysseus allows the animals' blood to flow into a trench so that the dead may drink it. In tragedy, several sacrifices are made to 'heroes' to ensure their aid: Polyxena is sacrificed to Achilles since he has made this the condition of granting a fair wind home to the Greeks, and Electra and Orestes, in pouring out offerings to Agamemnon's shade, ask for his help. True, Clytemnestra had sent the offerings to avert the anger of Agamemnon; and Achilles withheld the fair wind until Polyxena was sacrificed. But the anger of Olympians had to be averted too, and sacrifice was an appropriate means; while the Olympian Artemis withheld a fair wind from the Greeks on their way to Troy until Iphigeneia was sacrificed to her. The gods below and the dead were indeed awful and mysterious in a manner quite un-Olympian; but all Greek deities could be malevolent and capricious; and those below could be powerful helpers, if they received their own kind of 'tendance'.

Non-animate offerings played a part in both Olympian and chthonic ritual. Barley-grains accompanied Olympian sacrifice both in Homer and later. These may once have stood alone as offerings from worshippers whose diet was vegetarian, meat being added when this was added to the diet of the Greeks. Libations—a drink-offering of wine poured on to table, hearth or altar—similarly accompanied drinking. *Choai*, liquid offerings to the infernal gods and the dead, like their meat-sacrifices, were not shared. Atossa in Aeschylus tells us of their content: milk, honey, water, 'and an unmixed draught from an ancient wild vine'. To reach their recipients, they were poured on the ground. Their purpose is naturally the same as that of other sacrifices: the shade of Clytemnestra reproaches the sleeping Furies, who have received such offerings from her when she was alive, and yet now are relaxing and allowing Orestes to escape. The Furies have received *time* from Clytemnestra, and should help her: one may wish to 'avert' the Furies from oneself, but even a Fury may be 'tended' in case her services may be needed.

5. *Myth*

Greek religion was so rich in myths that the barest outline would require more space than is available here for the whole subject. However, those which are most relevant to the Greek's picture of the world and his place in it necessarily appear under other headings in this work; and I shall confine myself to a brief resumé of these.

The Greek gods and goddesses cared more for the *time* that was offered to them than for what was believed about them. It was unnecessary to believe any particular myth as part of the demands of religion; though the worshipper on his side naturally derived his belief in the nature of his gods from the myths in which these frequently quarrelsome, jealous and capricious deities appeared.

Some myths form the framework within which most Greeks lived. No penalties attached to a refusal to believe in the truth of the Hesiodic or 'Orphic' cosmogonies; but the Greeks, save for the few who could comprehend the numerous competing cosmologies offered by their philosophers, had to accept one of these cosmogonies or nothing; and they doubtless furnished an unquestioned background for most Greeks. Some of these 'framework' myths are in competition: HESIOD's myth of the five Ages, with its picture of inevitable degeneration, and the myths associated with Prometheus, with their message that much progress had been made in despite of the Olympians, cannot logically be accepted by the same person; though much in Greek religion suggests that many Greeks may have held both, according to their prevailing mood of pessimism or optimism, without noticing any incongruity. Each portrays the same capricious gods. The myth of the Flood, too, furnishes a framework; deriving the majority of mankind from stones, the nobility from an earlier race of men, it could be invoked to justify a particular organization of society.

Other myths furnish an origin and explanation of particular human customs, as Prometheus' deception of Zeus explains mankind's retention of the best parts of an animal sacrificed to the Olympians; or customs and practices in individual cities, as the myth of Orestes' trial on the Areopagus explains the institution of the Areopagus as a homicide court in Athens.

In general, the myths, involving both gods and men, which form the subject matter of Greek epic and tragedy (if it may be permitted to include some saga and folk-lore among myths for the present purpose) furnished the Greek with accounts of relationships between men and gods, the kind of behaviour which could be expected from the latter, and the respective status of both. As has been seen elsewhere, the myths spoke with a confused and confusing voice; as did those concerned with the ultimate destiny of man after death.

At this period, only an unusually clear-headed man will have noticed, and attempted to select a coherent view of the world from this confusion. Most Greeks will have accepted juxtaposed contradictions: we can see even AESCHYLUS doing this. The function of such myths is to furnish solutions for particular problems; that all myths taken together should present a coherent picture is beyond the resources of the myth-makers and the requirements of the believers.

Though myths were not dogma, and disbelief was not heresy, an aetiological myth is likely to have been accepted by most Greeks as being an explanation of phenomena for which no other explanation was offered; while the subject matter of epic and tragedy, with its implications for the nature of the gods, would be accepted by most as early history. Most rejection of myth has an ethical basis: XENOPHANES, PINDAR and PLATO reject myths which portray divine behaviour which they find ethically shocking. Some is based on commonsense: HERODOTUS refuses to believe that Cyrus was suckled by a bitch, EURIPIDES—who was sceptical of many Greek myths—that Dionysus was born from Zeus' thigh. (In each of these cases the explanation offered is the same: one word has been confused with another in the transmission of the story.)

To reject even the whole of Greek mythology did not necessarily constitute atheism whether in the ancient or the modern sense. XENOPHANES believed that man created the gods in his own image; but he nevertheless believed in a god—a quite different kind of god—himself. SOCRATES' case is similar. The cosmologies of Ionians like ANAXAGORAS made possible explanation without invoking divine causation, and some Ionians may have been atheists in the modern

sense of the word. For the Greek and his gods, however, the criterion
was not belief but cult practice, the touchstone whether or no a man
offered sacrifice. Prosecutions for atheism seem usually, as in the case
of ANAXAGORAS and SOCRATES, to have had other motives; and this
charge against SOCRATES seems to have been less vigorously pressed
than the other indictments against him, possibly because, as portrayed
by PLATO at all events, he was scrupulous in his religious observances.

6. *Priests*

There was no distinctive priestly class in Greece, and no type of
function in the dominant stream of religion which only a priest could
perform. The principal ritual act of the priest was the offering of
sacrifice; but from HOMER onwards anyone might offer sacrifice to
the Greek gods on behalf of himself and his family, whether to Zeus
and Hermes in their role as protectors of the household, to the other
guardian powers of the house, such as the *agathos daimon*, or to any
other deity. To his household gods he would naturally sacrifice in his
own house; to other deities at the temple appropriate to each. The
priest of the temple would perform the sacrifice if required; and would
have the right to superintend, and to receive certain perquisites, such
as a portion of the meat, the skin of the animal, and a fee. The religious validity of the sacrifice, however, was in no way impaired if
the priest did not participate.

Larger social units than the family had their own officiating priests.
For example, the four Attic *phulai* (tribes) and the twelve *phratriai*
(subdivisions of *phulai*) each had its own cult and priest. When the city
as a whole offered sacrifice, the functionary appointed by law, usually
the priest or priestess of the appropriate temple, performed the sacrifice, as being the functionary authorized by the city to do so. Sometimes the city had not only authorized but also appointed the functionary: the 'king-archon' at Athens, one of the nine magistrates appointed
by lot every year, had important religious functions, including the
organization of those aspects of the Eleusinian mysteries which took
place in Athens, and the performance of certain sacrifices. Many
priesthoods, however, were confined to the members of particular
families: here the function of the state was merely to record the necessary conditions and to establish that these had been fulfilled, and to
lay down the appropriate perquisites and ceremonies. The rites themselves, being hallowed by tradition, were not and could not be controlled by the state. Where priesthoods were confined to the members

of one family, it is reasonable to assume that the cult had originally been peculiar to that family, and only later, with the development of the city-state, widened into a city cult.

Other priesthoods were filled by election or lot, or even by purchase in certain places, mostly in the islands and Asia Minor. A priesthood at a temple at which many sacrifices were offered must have been financially attractive. In addition to his perquisites in the temple, a priest might be accorded a front seat at theatrical and musical performances, exemption from taxes, and meals at the public expense by the state; but few priests received a salary from their city.

The 'king-archon' at Athens performed religious functions; and the kings at Sparta offered the public sacrifices. The ideas of priest and king are linked in Greece, as elsewhere, but the surviving links are few in historical times. Already in Homer not only King Nestor but also Eumaeus the swineherd can offer sacrifice; and there is nothing to indicate that kings had ever had the sole right to offer sacrifice in Greece.

A Greek priest was not a priest of the gods in general, nor even a priest of one god or goddess in general: he was the priest of a particular god or gods at a particular temple, and could exercise no priestly functions elsewhere. There being no dogma concerned with deity, he had no duties of exposition and interpretation, and no concern with matters of ethics: difficult questions of religious observance or procedure were decided by *exegetai*, either at the major oracular centres such as Delphi, or in individual cities. Having no function beyond sacrificing, ensuring that worshippers behaved in a seemly manner, and keeping the temple in good repair (usually with funds supplied by the city), and exercising even these functions only in his own temple, the Greek priest could not feel himself as part of a priestly class.

Some priests have different characteristics derived from their function. The priests of the Eleusinian and other mysteries possessed secrets transmitted to them by word of mouth from their predecessors; and these discharged functions which no-one else could perform. Others had powers of divination and soothsaying; of these, some were priests at oracular centres, others not linked with any temple. There were also wandering 'purifiers', ranging from the renowned (if mysterious) Epimenides and similar figures who seem to have possessed shamanistic qualities (see DODDS, *The Greeks and the Irrational*, 141 ff.) to the mountebanks castigated by PLATO in the *Republic*. Like every other aspect of Greek religion, the priesthood is characterized by its multiplicity, variety and lack of large-scale organization.

V. Man

1. *Creation. Progress or degeneration? The Flood*

In Hesiod's *Works and Days*, the earliest Greek account of the creation of man, we have not one creation but five. First of all 'the gods who dwell on Olympus' made a golden race or generation, who lived in the time of Cronus 'like gods', did not grow old, and whose death was like falling asleep. When they had all died and become *daimones*, the Olympians made a silver race; their children took a hundred years to grow up, lived only a short adult life, wronged one another and refused sacrifice to the gods. Zeus in anger 'hid them away'; and they became blessed spirits of the underworld. Then Zeus made a bronze race, terrible and strong, who used bronze weapons and tools. They destroyed one another and left no name behind. Next Zeus made the race of 'heroes'. Some fought against Thebes and Troy, and died; but the rest are still alive in the Islands of the Blest at the ends of the earth. Lastly, Zeus made an iron race, that of Hesiod's own day; and this is the most miserable of all.

Hesiod has inserted into a schematic list of metal-races an account of the Heroic Age of Greece. The list is basically mythical, not historical; but this aspect should not be overemphasized. The bronze race, like the men of the historical Bronze Age, used bronze weapons and tools. The metals in the account of the earlier races have merely symbolic value—the gold and silver races seem not to have used gold and silver weapons and tools—to characterize progressive deterioration; but the treatment of the bronze and iron races (for Hesiod need not mention that the iron race used iron tools, since his contemporaries knew this) suggests that in his mind the account is in part an extrapolation from known history. Hesiod may for this reason have found it easier to disrupt the scheme of the metal-races (which occurs elsewhere, and is presumably not his own invention); for Hesiod knew that a Heroic Age had occurred. No-one thinking entirely mythologically would have made this concession to history.

However, much myth is present. The races are distinct creations: indeed, 'the gods who dwell on Olympus' who created the golden race in the time of Cronus were not the same 'Olympians' as the later ones. Here myth has overcome tradition: Hesiod knew that there was no unbridgeable gap between the last two races, at all events, for many Greek families traced their ancestry back to 'heroes'.

The myth portrays degeneration, but without sustained moral intent. The silver and bronze races deserved their ends; the golden and 'heroic' did not. No reason is given why the gods should create successively worse races: the myth simply expresses the belief that they in fact do so. The discontinuities are mythical: they do not represent historical changes of population.

The story of the Flood forms a pendant to this account. PINDAR, our earliest authority, is allusive: when the Flood ebbed away, Pyrrha and Deucalion came down from Parnassus and made the people (*lāos*) from stones (*lāas*). From Pyrrha and Deucalion themselves were sprung the brazen-shielded ancestors of the Locrian rulers (in honour of whom PINDAR's poem is composed), young men sprung 'from the daughters of the race of Iapetus and from the mighty sons of Cronus'. Later writers supply more detail. According to APOLLODORUS, Deucalion, Prometheus' son, married Pyrrha, daughter of Prometheus' brother Epimetheus and Pandora, the first woman. When Zeus wished to destroy the bronze race by a flood, Deucalion and Pyrrha embarked in a chest. Everyone was drowned save a few who took refuge on the highest mountains. When the rain ceased, Deucalion and Pyrrha landed on Mount Parnassus, and both threw stones, those thrown by Deucalion becoming men, those by Pyrrha, women. Hence mankind was called *laos* from *lāas*.

These accounts are set in a Hesiodic framework, at the point where the bronze race perished. (The 'heroes' also used bronze weapons: the 'brazen-shielded' ancestors of the Locrian kings are 'heroic'.) But the thought is more historical: this tradition is concerned to demonstrate continuity from the bronze age onwards, at least at the highest levels of society. PINDAR only mentions the ancestors of the Locrian kings, for they are his audience; but in Apollodorus Hellen, the eponymous ancestor of the Hellenes, whose children were Dorus, Xuthus and Aeolus (ancestors of the Dorians, Ionians and Aeolians), was the child of Deucalion and Pyrrha. The derivation of *laos*, 'the people', from *lāas* shows that only noble families were supposed to be sprung from Pyrrha and Deucalion. (Many such families did in fact claim descent at least from 'heroes'.)

Though the Flood is set in the Hesiodic framework of degeneration, it is linked also with Prometheus, the culture-hero of the alternative tradition, that of progress. Men, according to this version, were created helpless and weak, and remained so until Prometheus stole fire from heaven for them. Different writers treat the myth rather differently. This tradition too occurs first in Hesiod. The gods keep the means of life hidden from men. Were it not so, a day's work would suffice to keep a man for a year. Zeus, angry because Prometheus had deceived him, hid fire from mankind; but Prometheus stole it back again for them. In anger, Zeus devised Pandora's Box, from which all the woes and plagues of the world escaped to vex mankind: previously men had no hardship, toil, or sickness.

HESIOD's account has to be fitted into the pessimistic framework of the Five Ages. For him, accordingly, life was at its best *before* Prometheus. Men already had fire: Prometheus merely restored it to them; and Pandora's Box made their situation incalculably worse than it was before.

In the *Prometheus Vinctus*, AESCHYLUS not only presents human history as progress but seems to refer to, and reject, the other view. Prometheus says that when Zeus ascended his throne he wished to destroy the human race and create a new one. He, Prometheus, alone saved them. The human race, then, is the same today as it was under Cronus: there is no break. Men were witless and unintelligent at first, and 'like dreams did everything at random during their long life'. (Their longevity is perhaps derived from Hesiod.) They lived in caves, and knew nothing of the seasons. Prometheus taught them the arts: to tell the season by the stars, to read and write, to domesticate animals, to practise medicine, interpretation of dreams, divination and the use of metals.

Witless, helpless mankind, then, bettered itself by means of the skills furnished by Prometheus in the teeth of a hostile heaven. PLATO ascribes another version to PROTAGORAS the sophist. The gods created man and the animal species and gave them to Prometheus (Forethought) and Epimetheus(Afterthought) to equip with the qualities (speed, claws, prickles, and so on) which would enable them to survive. Epimetheus persuaded Prometheus to allow him to equip the species; but on coming to man last of all, had nothing left to give him. When Prometheus discovered this, he stole fire and the skill in arts and crafts from Hephaestus and Athena, and gave it to mankind; and men thus developed their skills. At first they did not live in cities, for they had not the political art. In their isolation, they used to be destroyed by wild beasts; but when they assembled into cities for safety, not having the political art they were for ever wronging one another, so that these associations broke up. Zeus, accordingly, fearing lest the human race should perish utterly, sent Hermes to give them reverence and justice, so that societies might come into existence; and whereas other skills are not allotted to the whole of mankind, everyone must have reverence and justice if there are to be cities at all.

The sophist is more optimistic than AESCHYLUS. The gods want man and the animals to be equipped for survival; Zeus does not want the human race to perish, and himself takes steps (in which Prometheus is not concerned) to prevent this. However, Prometheus still has to steal from the gods for man, though when the theft has occurred Zeus gives man another skill in addition: it is not that Zeus wants mankind to exist, but only on the same level as the other animals. Possibly the theft-motif could not be discarded from the tradition; possibly PROTAGORAS—if PLATO correctly ascribes the myth to him—could not entirely disassociate himself from the idea of the Olympians as jealous.

There is, then, a world-picture of inevitable degeneration, whether discontinuous or (in part at least) continuous; and one of ascent or progress by the efforts of man himself, whether with the disapproval or with the aid of the Olympian gods, relying on the powers or skills stolen from these gods with the aid of the culture-hero Prometheus. Neither is much concerned with any qualities inherent in human nature as such. The four metal-races and that of the 'heroes' in Hesiod are simply endowed by the gods with the characteristics which they in fact possess. They are said to be all human, despite the five independent creations, but it is only their differences which are emphasized: what they have in common is not considered by the poet. Again, in the myth associated with Prometheus men are characterized merely as helpless before they are endowed with skills. This is not surprising, for though myth presents such things in a temporal sequence, it is really concerned to abstract the distinctive characteristics of man. Not surprisingly, what remains is not clearly differentiated.

A third belief, which certainly existed later, may have occurred in our period. It is concerned with original sin, a tenet absent from the main streams of early Greek religion. It derives from 'Orphism'. The myth relates how the Titans (in DODDS' words) 'trapped the infant Dionysus, tore him to bits, boiled him, roasted him, ate him, and were themselves immediately burned up by a thunderbolt from Zeus: from the smoke of their remains sprang the human race, who thus inherit the horrid tendencies of the Titans, tempered by a tiny portion of the divine soul-stuff, which is the substance of the god Dionysus still working in them as an occult self'. PAUSANIAS ascribes the invention of this myth to ONOMACRITUS in the sixth century B.C.; but there is no clear reference to it until the third century B.C., and it was held by WILAMOWITZ to be an invention of that date. DODDS cites passages from PINDAR and PLATO which may be allusions to such a myth, and a report that PLATO's pupil XENOCRATES 'somehow connected the notion of the body as a "prison" with Dionysus and the Titans.' DODDS concludes, in cautious terms, that the complete story was known to PLATO and his public. This may be so; but 'Orphism' as a whole belongs to the strand of belief which is little represented in extant writers, and this aspect of it, if known at all, has an even more tenuous existence in our sources. To say this is not to assert that such beliefs were unimportant in society as a whole; for PLATO makes it clear that they had considerable influence in society; but we can only form a clear impression of beliefs which are represented in the writers which we possess.

2. *The nature of man*

The dominant stream of Greek thought about man's nature contains much that is pessimistic. 'We are as leaves', said HOMER; and SIMONIDES echoed him with approval. Life, except for the rich man, is hard; yet better the meanest lot on earth than to rule among the dead, a mindless twittering shadow.

Bleak indeed; and yet HESIOD introduces the Five Ages itself as the tale 'of how the gods and mortal men sprang from one source'. He does not explain this: in his account the gods do not beget, but create, mankind; and the five races are quite distinct from one another. Elsewhere in early Greek Zeus is termed 'father of gods and men'; but the reference is to the analogy between the *function* of Zeus as head of the community of gods and of men and that of the human head of a household, not to any belief that the blood of Zeus flows in the veins of all mankind. Nevertheless, there are close links between gods and men: children may be born of one human, one divine parent, and the divine parent may be either the father or the mother. (Zeus, and other gods, were believed to be the ancestors of some Greeks: for example, the Spartan kings traced their descent from Hercules, child of Zeus and the mortal Alcmena.) As a corollary, the excellence (*arete*) of man is the same quality, though usually manifested to a much lower degree, as the *arete* of a god. Consequently, a man who displays sufficient *arete* may become a god. Granted, the most famous example is Hercules, who had one divine parent; but men in the full light of history were 'heroized', and had the power to give supernatural help (or hindrance); and the ordinary dead, when believed to be in their graves rather than far away in Hades, were at least worth propitiating.

Traditional Greek *arete* is a vigorous, active, and competitive quality, which enjoins on a man that he should strive upward. Moderation has no part in it. Accordingly, although HOMER holds that man is like grass that grows up and withers, and his gods regard it as foolish to quarrel among themselves over such ephemeral creatures, those same gods fear that, if men can achieve their ends without offering sacrifice, or in despite of the gods' wishes, they will never offer sacrifice again. After HOMER, the Olympians become more remote and more powerful; but the spur of *arete* remains, encouraging men to ever greater efforts.

It is for this reason that, leaf-like though he may be, the ancient Greek does not fold his hands and passively lament his unhappy lot. Some may have reflected that it is best not to be born at all and even that, if born, it is best to die as soon as possible, but the Greek writer clearly found that, once born, his fellows required less consolation than warning against excess. PINDAR says to an *agathos* 'Do not seek to become Zeus. ... It befits mortals to have mortal thoughts.' The rich and powerful man, who has *arete*, is drawn ever onwards and upwards by the *arete*. To go too far will invoke the wrath of the gods, who will consider it *hubris*, an overstepping of the bounds; and the fact that there are no clear bounds between man and god renders the gods more jealous of their prerogatives. The moralist warns that such *hubris* will cause *ate*, 'blindness', leading to disaster (though we have seen that the idea of divine punishment posed insoluble problems; and the ideas of *hubris* and *ate* did not render a solution easier). 'Know thyself' and 'Nothing in excess', the precepts of Delphi and its god Apollo, emphasize the distance between god and mortal, for 'Know thyself' has the implication 'that thou art mortal'; but one does not repeatedly urge moderation and self-restraint on a people to whom moderation and self-restraint come naturally, and who freely acknowledge the existence of bounds. The fear that the gods may punish *hubris* will have acted as a check on many an *agathos*; but it is a check on *arete* and abundant energy, not a yoke on an ox.

Apollo and the Olympians are concerned with their own status, with keeping man in his proper place, with drawing a line beyond which *arete* advances only at its peril: prowess, success, prosperity must observe proper limits. The end of man is to be just and to offer *time* to his gods in the form of sacrifice; and these gods require *time* consistently, justice only intermittently. Dionysus, however, though equally jealous of his privileges and as quick to punish those who do not acknowledge him (which is to deny him his *time*), offers release from bounds and limits to the worshippers into whom he enters. No distinctive doctrine of human nature can be ascribed to the Dionysiac cult: it was simply a fact of experience that human beings could be 'possessed' by Dionysus. (It is interesting to note, however, that in the 'Orphic' doctrine discussed earlier, in which there is a definite theory of human nature, it is Dionysus who is responsible for the 'divine spark' in man.)

The mystery-cults offer a different doctrine of the nature and destiny of man; but this will be discussed below.

3. *Destiny; path of salvation; personal eschatology*

The ultimate destiny expected by most of the articulate Greeks of our period has already become apparent: not annihilation, but a dim existence beyond the grave. In Homer, the *psuchai*, ghosts, can only speak to Odysseus when they are given blood to drink, and they are referred to as mindless creatures who flit and gibber aimlessly; but they retain sufficient mind to conduct a pale shadow of their earthly existence: Orion continues to hunt, Minos to be an arbiter of disputes, in death as in life; while the 'heroes' are portrayed as reminiscing over earthly triumphs and failures. Only these are relevant in the shame-culture of the dead: AESCHYLUS' Agamemnon is shamed in Hades, for he was killed ignominiously by his wife; but he would have enjoyed status in Hades had he died gloriously in battle. Achilles tells Odysseus that it is better to live the life of a landless man on earth than to rule among the dead: better, certainly, but to enjoy status and prestige among the dead is better than to bear the stigma of failure there, derived from one's experiences on earth. There is in this Hades no reward for the just, no punishment for the unjust. The only 'damnation' is suffered by Tantalus, Sisyphus and Ixion, punished not for injustice to their fellow-men but for insulting and harming the gods. The only 'salvation' possible in Homer is that offered to Menelaus: he is to be transported living to the Islands of the Blest at the ends of the earth. His qualification for such privilege is that, as the husband

of Helen, he is the son-in-law of Zeus. HESIOD extends the privilege
to more 'heroes', but only to those who were not killed in battle, for
this is not better life after death, but an alternative to death; and it is
reserved for a few 'heroes' *qua* 'heroes'.

The rest of mankind cannot pursue 'salvation': they must flit and
gibber in Hades. The dominant belief of the historical period maintains either that the dead are in Hades, or that they are close by in
their graves, enjoying an existence equally dim, but with more power
to affect the living. These beliefs are not strictly alternatives, for they
exist confusedly together: AESCHYLUS can pass from one to the other
in a few lines. The 'hero' in the later sense, essentially a very powerful
dead man, can do more good or harm from his tomb, and benefits
from more lavish rites, than the ordinary man. Tragic poets can point
to heroization as a reward and consolation for woes suffered in this
life: Oedipus and Hippolytus are thus consoled. Save for the very
few like Hercules, whom *arete* raised to the ranks of deity, no greater
consolation is possible.

For anything more than this we must turn to the mystery-cults.
Our earliest reference, the Homeric *Hymn to Demeter*, which can hardly
be later than the sixth century, says of the Eleusinian rites founded by
Demeter 'Blessed is he who has seen these things; but he who is not
initiated and has no part in the rites never has a share of similar good
things when he is dead, down in the dank gloom'. Here salvation is
to be won by seeing certain objects: no change of heart, no way of life
is prescribed; and this continued to be the case at Eleusis, the most
famous centre of mystery-cult in Greece. Similarly, PINDAR in the
Laments for the Dead accounts blessed 'him who has seen these things'.
Elsewhere in the *Laments* he enumerates the blessings of such men:
they are to have their own sun after death, and live as gentlemen of
leisure in beautiful rural surroundings. Gold tablets found in the
graves of adherents of a Greek mystery cult in southern Italy give a
similar picture. These tablets contain information and formulae to be
used by the shade, *psuche*, on its journey to Bliss. It is to avoid a spring
by a white cypress; but it is thus to address the guardians of another
spring, which flows from the Lake of Memory: 'I am the child of
earth and starry heaven, but my birth is heavenly.... Give me straight-
way water from the Lake of Memory.' This being done, the *psuche*
will then 'reign among the other "heroes"'. The shade is thus to
address Penelope and the other infernal deities: 'I come pure from
pure. I claim to be of your blessed race, having paid the penalty for

unjust acts committed when *moira* and other gods overcame me...But now I have come as a suppliant before the Lady Persephone, that she may graciously send me to the abodes of the pure.' Persephone will then reply: 'Blessed and fortunate being, you shall be a god instead of a mortal. You have fallen as a kid into milk'; and the *psuche* presumably receives its reward.

These documents may well be derived from different mystery-cults; but they share a feature likely to be found in such cults. Emphasis is on rites performed and on knowledge obtained, not on the necessity of leading a just life. This is not surprising, since in the dominant stream of belief too justice could not be rewarded after death: the gods below were not held to care for such things. The gold tablets show how these beliefs could arise from, and be harmonized with, the dominant stream; a harmony which was desirable at least in the Eleusinian cult, which was officially sponsored by Athens. In Homer only a relative of Zeus by marriage, in Hesiod only those 'heroes' who had not died in battle and had been translated before death overtook them, could enjoy the bliss here offered to the initiate. These initiates died, but in other respects resembled the undying 'heroes' of the earlier period. By avoiding one spring—presumably water of forgetfulness—and drinking water from the Lake of Memory, the *psuche*, unlike the mindless twitterers, retained its wits and could enjoy the benefits of the life to come. It was then to proclaim its purity—a purity doubtless ensured by ritual abstentions, for *katharotes* has no moral connotations in its other usages—and its heavenly birth. It is expressly said that it then 'reigned among the other "heroes"'.

The additional belief here, not found in the dominant stream, is that the *psuche* is of heavenly origin. Knowledge of this fact—preserved by not drinking from the wrong spring on the way to Hades—and ritual abstention seem required to ensure that the *psuche* receives favoured treatment. The favour can be justified in the context of traditional Greek beliefs and values by the relationship with the divine which the *psuche* enjoys: the privileges of Zeus' son-in-law and some of the demigod 'heroes' can be extended to all adherents of the cult. This knowledge and ritual practice suffice: the *psuche's* presence on earth may be due to some pre-natal wrongdoing, but its cleansing requires non-moral means. If this is illogical, it is an explicable illogicality. Life is hard, and we must have done some unspecified wrong in another existence to justify our being condemned to it. Death is terrifying, and some means of alleviating the terror is needed. In

Greece, the terrors do not usually include a Last Judgment: initiation, and a vegetarian regimen (in some cults) may suffice to ensure a pleasant existence beyond the tomb.

However, some passages in Greek authors of our period make 'salvation' dependent on moral behaviour in this life. Except in the *Laments*, PINDAR usually takes the view that this life is all, with values appropriate to the belief; but in *Olympian II* he says that 'all men who have had the courage three times...to keep their *psuche* free from injustice have accomplished the road of Zeus to the tower of Cronus: in the islands of the blest sea breezes waft about them and golden flowers blaze'. Similarly, in AESCHYLUS' *Suppliants*, Danaus says 'In the next world, it is said, another Zeus (Hades, whose position below is analogous to that of Zeus above) pronounces judgment among the dead for wrongdoing'; while in his *Eumenides* the Furies say '[Below the earth] you will see all other mortals who have impiously wronged a god, some guest-friend or dear parents, each receiving his due punishment. For Hades is a mighty judge of mortals beneath the earth, and watches everything with faithfully recording mind.'

In such passages, the pre-eminent importance of moral behaviour is clear. The belief depends on that in a 'real' future life for the *psuche*: the shadowy *psuchai* of HOMER and the dominant tradition are too tenuous for reward or punishment. However, in order to have knowledge of such a belief it was unnecessary to be oneself an adherent of a mystery-cult. The cults held that certain arcane knowledge, carefully guarded from the uninitiate, was necessary to 'salvation'. However, the nature of that 'salvation' was not a secret, and the belief in the nature of the *psuche* on which it depended was available to a moralist who held it. AESCHYLUS in fact seems to have been an initiate of some—presumably the Eleusinian—mystery-cult: PINDAR in *Olympian* II probably mirrors the beliefs of his patron, Theron of Acragas.

None of the foregoing passages mentions both initiation and judgment. This is perhaps not surprising, for it is *prima facie* illogical to make 'salvation' dependent both on initiation *tout court* and on a judgment of moral behaviour which everyone must undergo. (Of course, *knowledge* that there was to be a last judgment might be one of the 'saving' mysteries.) However, we cannot sharply distinguish between a moral belief associated with a last judgment and that of the mystery-cults, in which initiation alone mattered. PLATO, in *Republic* II, ascribes initiation ceremonies without moral requirements to

Musaeus and Orpheus, while saying that 'Musaeus and his son' offer extravagant benefits *to the just*. Like other branches of Greek religion, 'Orphism' can have had no systematized theology: these are two aspects of the same tradition.

PLATO himself sweeps away all ideas of initiation, and in his myths insists on a moral last judgment. In the *Gorgias*, Minos, Rhadamanthus and Aeacus judge after death 'the soul in itself' with *their* 'soul in itself', and only justice is taken into account. For PLATO, as for PINDAR and AESCHYLUS, justice in life is the way of salvation. PLATO, however, like PINDAR—or Theron—believed in reincarnation, and also held that only philosophy would render a man certainly just throughout a series of lives; for in his Myth of Er in the *Republic*, the important choice is made just before rebirth, and only the philosopher will correctly choose his lot in life. In the last resort, then, philosophy is the way of 'salvation' for PLATO; and only a tiny minority of men is capable of philosophy in PLATO's sense. Only the philosopher will attain *lasting* salvation over a series of lives; but what is judged after death is one's justice, not one's intellectual attainments; and the man who in any incarnation, because his environment was favourable, has behaved justly receives the same reward after death as the philosopher.

That ideas of existence after death were confused is evident also from PAUSANIAS' account of the painting at Delphi commissioned from Polygnotus by the Cnidians. POLYGNOTUS portrayed Homeric heroes at play; Tantalus and Sisyphus' eternal punishment for insulting the gods; the apparently allegorical (and un-Homeric) Ocnus plaiting a rope which a donkey perpetually devoured; a father throttling a son who had been unjust to him in life; 'some of the women who were not initiated' carrying water in broken potsherds; and a family, supposed by PAUSANIAS to be representative of those who scorned the Eleusinian mysteries, pouring water into a (presumably) perforated jar. POLYGNOTUS has juxtaposed in one picture all the attitudes and beliefs about the next world (save that of AESCHYLUS and *Olympian* II) which had existed up to his own time, with no thought of consistency: a Hades neutral for all except those who insult the gods cannot logically coexist with one in which simple failure to be initiated may be eternally punished. It is indicative of the confusion in belief that neither POLYGNOTUS nor his employer—a whole state, not an individual—seems worried by this.

It is difficult to estimate the extent to which these different beliefs were held. Extant Greek writers favour, on the whole, the Olympian tradition, in which neither salvation nor damnation is possible; while AESCHYLUS, who presumably believed in a 'real' existence after death for the *psuche*, also treats the dead as being in a neutral Hades and as nearby in their tombs. All three beliefs occur in the *Oresteia*, the latter two in adjacent lines on one occasion. The plays give us no reason to conclude that any of these beliefs was more favoured by AESCHYLUS than the others: we have, as in POLYGNOTUS' painting, mere juxtaposition without thought of logical compatibility.

Most writers do not mention 'salvation' or 'damnation' after death at all; and one might conclude that the belief was not widely held. No definite conclusion can be drawn: the aged Cephalus in PLATO's *Republic* mentions 'damnation' as a fear which troubles the old; but the philosopher DEMOCRITUS of Abdera attacks it as a belief which renders the whole of life a misery. Certainly in the class whose beliefs are represented in literature it has little currency; but this class is a small part of the whole, and we know of the beliefs even of this class in only a small minority of Greek cities: the extent of these beliefs in the remainder of society, and in other cities, cannot be known.

4. *General eschatology*

No Greek of our period believed in a god who created the world *ex nihilo*: the earliest generations of gods, who simply 'came to be', are confusedly gods and goddesses and the material of the universe endowed with form; and the later generations of gods merely administer the cosmos. Similarly, no Greek of our period believed that the cosmos would simply cease to exist, leaving nothing behind. In general, the ultimate fate of the universe is not discussed.

There was, however, a theory—or theories—of the life-cycle of the cosmos. PLATO in his *Politicus* relates a myth of two alternating periods of rotation, each apparently lasting for a Great Year (36,000 terrestrial years). In one, 'the god' guides the cosmos, and it travels in one direction: in the other, 'the god' removes his controlling hand, and the cosmos 'being a living creature, with the power of reason', goes its own way—the opposite way; and this is a necessary, innate quality of the cosmos. Accordingly, neither 'the god' nor the cosmos is responsible for both rotations. PLATO believed himself to be living in a period when 'the god' had removed his hand. When 'the god' is in control, all fares well, and all natural processes are reversed: men are born—from the earth—old, and gradually become younger, until they dwindle away to nothing. This recalls HESIOD's statement in the

Works and Days that Zeus will destroy the iron race when they have grey hair on their temples at birth; but for HESIOD, whose picture is entirely pessimistic, this is a sign of the ultimate degeneration of the iron race, not a change to better things: HESIOD does not consider what happens after the iron race has perished. The myth found in the *Politicus* appears only in PLATO, and is there imbued with much Platonic thought; but HESIOD may be alluding to a popular version of the same myth, adapted to fit HESIOD's unwavering pessimism. EMPEDOCLES, one of the pre-Socratic philosophers, held that the cosmos passed through alternate periods of Love and Strife, and a whirling movement was somehow instrumental in this. This account too is imbued with the personal philosophy of its author, but may echo a more widely held belief.

VI. SUBSEQUENT INFLUENCE OF GREEK RELIGION

Greek religion, like virtually every other aspect of Greek life, had a considerable effect on Roman religion, and had a great influence on the manner in which the Romans portrayed their gods in literature and the arts; but this can be treated most conveniently in the discussion of Roman religion.

VII. THE STUDY OF GREEK RELIGION

The ancient Greeks themselves studied their religion in a variety of ways. XENOPHANES, PINDAR and PLATO scrutinised Greek myths and censured their ethical inadequacies. XENOPHANES also held that men made the gods in their own image; while sophists such as CRITIAS maintained that the gods were mere inventions designed to bolster up conventional morality. In the late fourth century B.C. EUHEMERUS put forward the 'euhemeristic' theory that the gods had originally been great men, to whom men had accorded worship as a result of their illustrious deeds. In the context of Greek belief, one could arrive at this theory by extrapolating from a few well known instances, supported by many more cases of heroization; but despite this, and the practices of the Hellenistic monarchies, the theory seems never to have been popular in Greece. The scholars of Alexandria collected and studied myths; and learned men like PLUTARCH and PAUSANIAS made observations on practices that seemed strange to them. The writings of the early Christian fathers are naturally polemical towards pagan belief and practice, but sometimes contain interesting observations.

Effective modern study of Greek religion begins in the nineteenth century, largely under the influence of anthropology and the study of folk-lore. Many anthropologists of this period turned to anthropology from classical studies, and in the late nineteenth and early twentieth centuries there were close links between the two disciplines. USENER, ROHDE, ANDREW LANG, J. G. FRAZER, JANE HARRISON, A. B. COOK, L. R. FARNELL, R. R. MARETT, and GILBERT MURRAY were all acquainted with both the classics and anthropology. The predilections of the evolutionary and comparative anthropology of the day led them to study for the most part the prehistory of Greek religion and the evolutionary process which had resulted in the religion of classical Greece. The evidence for this is naturally scanty, and was then even scantier; and many scholars succumbed to the temptation of trying to explain the manifold phenomena of Greek religion in terms of one theory. Most of these led to some insights into certain aspects of Greek religion, but far more limited insights than those claimed for them by their authors.

More recent anthropologists have rarely had knowledge of the classics; and the priorities of anthropology have led them to devote their attention to the study of still existing primitive cultures. As a result, contact between the two disciplines has largely ceased, and many classical scholars equate anthropology with anthropology of the time of FRAZER. Of these most, finding distasteful the speculative nature of the conclusions of evolutionary and comparative anthropology, have turned their backs on the subject; while the majority of those scholars who continue to make use of the findings of anthropology ignore subsequent developments in this field. A distinguished exception is E. R. DODDS, whose *The Greeks and the Irrational*, which draws on both anthropology and psychology, is an indispensable work for the study of Greek religion.

Other disciplines have been drawn into the study, particularly in the field of Greek mythology, where interpretations have ranged from the psychoanalytic to the Marxist. (K. KERÉNYI has published work jointly with JUNG.) In some cases, one key has been used to unlock all doors; but more balanced works exist: MICHAEL GRANT's *Myths of the Greeks and Romans* has seventeen distinct index-entries under 'Methods, Theories and Interpretations of Mythology,' and the author draws on the method which seems to him most appropriate to the phenomenon under discussion. However, books devoted to one line of explanation continue to appear.

Modern scholarship has also produced numerous excellent studies of topics, wider or narrower, in this field, which owe less to disciplines outside classical studies. Here classical archaeology has had its part to play. Despite the decipherment of Linear B, most of our inadequate knowledge of Mycenean Greek religion is still drawn from archaeological material; while at Eleusis, whose mysteries might not be represented in art or set down in writing, excavation has at least served to confute some of the wilder theories. Finds at shrines, temples and tombs in many parts of Greece have contributed much to our knowledge of everyday cult practice; and inscriptions have furnished most of what is known of the administration of temples, priesthoods and cults. In the study of Greek religion, as in every other branch of classical studies, the collection and attempted elucidation of fragmentary material, literary and other, is frequently the first task; and all the techniques of classical scholarship have been devoted to this.

The subject can probably be approached most conveniently through the works of H. J. ROSE and M. P. NILSSON, a selection of which will be found in the bibliography. The latter's small 'Greek Folk Religion' portrays with great sensitivity the interplay of cult and life.

SELECTED BIBLIOGRAPHY

COOK, A. B., Zeus, Cambridge 1914-1940
DEUBNER, L., Attische Feste, 1932, reprinted Berlin 1956
DODDS, E. R., Euripides' Bacchae, Oxford 1944
——, The Greeks and the Irrational, Berkeley 1951
EHNMARK, E., The Idea of God in Homer, Diss. Uppsala, 1935
FARNELL, L. R., The Cults of the Greek States, Oxford 1896-1909
FESTUGIÈRE, A. J., Personal Religion among the Greeks, Berkeley 1954
GRANT, M., Myths of the Greeks and Romans, London 1962
GREENE, W. C., Moira, Harvard 1944
GUTHRIE, W. K. C., Orpheus and Greek Religion, London 1935
——, The Greeks and their Gods, London 1950
HARRISON, J., Prolegomena to the Study of Greek Religion, Cambridge, 3rd end., 1922
——, Themis, A Study of the Social Origins of Greek Religion, Cambridge, 2nd edn., 1927
KERÉNYI, K., The Gods of the Greeks (translated from German), London 1951
——, The Heroes of the Greeks, London 1959
——, The Religion of the Greeks and Romans, London 1962
KERN, O., Die Religion der Griechen, Berlin 1926-1938
LANG, A., The World of Homer, London 1910

MARETT, R. R., *Anthropology and the Classics*, Oxford 1908

MURRAY, G., *Five Stages of Greek Religion*, Oxford 1925

MYLONAS, G. E., *Eleusis and the Eleusinian Mysteries*, Princeton 1961

NILSSON, M. P., *Geschichte der Griechischen Religion*, (Handbuch der Altertums-wissenschaft, V, 2), Munich 1941-1950

——, *Greek Folk Religion*, New York 1940

——, *Greek Piety*, translated by H. J. Rose, Oxford 1948

——, *Griechische Feste von religiöser Bedeutung*, 1906, reprinted Stuttgart 1957

——, *History of Greek Religion*, translated by F. J. Fielden, Oxford 1925

——, *Homer and Mycenae*, London 1933

——, *The Mycenean Origin of Greek Mythology*, Berkeley 1932

ONIANS, R. B., *The Origins of European Thought*, Cambridge 1951

OTTO, W. F., *The Homeric Gods*, translated by M. Hadas, New York 1954

PARKE, H. W. and WORMELL, D. E. W., *The Delphic Oracle*, Oxford 1956

ROSE, H. J., *Gods and Heroes of the Greeks*, London 1957

——, *A Handbook of Greek Mythology*, London, 6th edn., 1958

——, *Some Problems of Classical Religion*, Oslo 1958

ROHDE, E., *Psyche*, in German, Tübingen and Leipzig 1903, translated into English, London 1925

SNELL, B., *The Discovery of the Mind*, translated by Rosenmeyer, Oxford 1953

USENER, H. K., *Mythologie*, Archiv für Religionswissenschaft, Band 7, Leipzig 1904

THE ROMAN RELIGION

ROBERT SCHILLING

Paris and Strasbourg, France

I. The Originality of the Roman Religion

One particularly important fact concerning this subject stands out from the beginning: the term *religio*, which has passed into most modern languages in the West, is of Latin origin. It is a specific word which has no equivalent in Greek; one can have recourse to analogous expressions: τὸ σέβας (respect for the gods), ἡ προσκύνησις (adoration), ἡ εὐλάβεια (reverent fear), ἡ θρησκεία (cult), but these only serve to emphasize the impossibility of translating *religio* into Greek.

This fact is all the more remarkable as the Romans prided themselves on being the most religious people in the world: "if we compare ourselves to foreign nations," writes Cicero (*N.D.*, II, 3), "we appear equal or even inferior in various spheres, except that of religion, meaning the cult of gods, where we are by far superior." ("...religione id est cultu deorum, multo superiores"). The same writer makes the same declaration elsewhere (*De Haruspicum responsis*, 19) in a more pithy fashion: "in piety and religion we have outstripped all nations" ("pietate ac religione omnes gentes superauimus").

One is therefore led to believe that this term was still a valued one at the end of the first century B.C. An interesting detail is that it was occasionally used as a term of praise to a particular individual. An example of this is when the author of the *Laudatio* of a Roman matron known as Turia (end of the first century B.C.) mentions among the qualities of this lady, "her religious nature free of superstition" ("religionis sine superstitione").

What, therefore, is meant by this term coined by the Romans to define a situation of which they were so proud of being the best qualified representatives? A word which we have inherited from the Latins and which has taken its place in all the languages of the Western world. While the philologists may agree in seeing in *religio* a structure resulting from a verbal root (such as *legio* or *regio*), they differ immediately in their choice of verb. Some link the word with *relegere*, giving the prefix an intensive value which gives the expression the sense of "*scrupulous observance.*" Others favour derivation from *religare*, with the meaning of "to bind oneself with regard to the gods." Texts are quoted in support of both hypotheses. In the first case, the ancient verses quoted by NIGIDIUS FIGULUS are referred to (in AULUS GELLIUS, IV, 9, 11): "*religentem* esse oportet, religiosus ne fuas" ("it is proper to be religious, but not to be superstitious"). In the second case, one recalls the ritual use of sacred bands (*uittae*) as well as the numerous allusions to the idea of religious bonds, for example in LUCRETIUS, I, 931: "Religionum *nodis* animum exsoluere" ("Deliver the soul from religious bonds"); LIVY, V, 23, 10 "Se domumque religione exsoluere" ("Free oneself and one's household from religious obligation").

Therefore it seems to be difficult to decide between the two etymological explanations, the more so because each of them offers a complementary aspect of the meaning of the expression. For it is quite true that the Latin term *religio* implies at the same time the concern for a *scrupulous observance* in the cult and the idea of the bonds which unite gods and men.

One can say that the conviction of an unavoidable *interdependence* between heaven and earth forms the foundation of Roman worship, of which the purpose consisted in assuring the *pax ueniaque deum*. Without the friendship and the grace of the gods, the Roman felt himself to be helpless. Thus he would show himself to be assiduous in maintaining this "state of grace" by a meticulous worship, so meticulous that it often appeared to be merely formal. He was attentive to the signs from heaven, and if unfortunately, the gods would manifest their anger—"Iamque irae patuere deum..." (Already the anger of the gods is revealed), LUCAN, II, 1—he would not rest until the peace had been reestablished. The Romans never entertained the idea of rebelling against the gods: this theme has been the prerogative of the Greeks, illustrated particularly by the myth of the Titan Prometheus. It was not until LUCRETIUS that the first signs of blasphemy appeared in Latin literature, and moreover when this epicurean poet raised the flag of revolt against religion and denounced the crimes committed in its name—"tantum religio potuit suadere malorum" (I, 101)—he took his example from the Hellenic religion when condemning the sacrifice of Iphigenia.

If reverent fear of the gods is the basis of Roman religion, the concern for efficacity explains many of the characteristics of the *cult*. In the first place, the cautious wording of the prayers, when the Roman ignored the precise identity of the god to be appeased, for instance in the case of earthquakes (the example is quoted by AULUS GELLIUS, *N.A.*, II, 28,2-3) he would employ the prudent formula: "whether you be god or goddess" ("si deo, si deae"). When the Roman pledged himself to the deity, he would have recourse to precise stipulations of which the *carmina* handed down to us by CATO THE ELDER, give a faithful rendering. This contractual approach has often been interpreted in a pejorative sense, whereas it only expressed a concern for establishing an irreproachable contract between men and gods. "Piety is justice towards the gods" says CICERO (*N.D.*, I, 41: "est enim pietas iustitia aduersum deos") and similarly in the prayer of CATO's peasant to the deity of the woods about to be thinned (*De agricultura*, 139), this significant formula appears: "*uti tibi ius est*" ("according to your rights").

This preocupation often appears with excessive emphasis to our taste: CATO's peasant had no compunction about tediously repeating the exact clauses in the limits of which he intended to commit himself with the deity. Perhaps one should attribute an even more practical connotation to certain adjectives which appear to be merely descriptive: thus the addition of the epithet *inferium* to *uinum* would, according to TREBATIUS (quoted by ARNOBIUS, *Aduersus nationes*, VII, 31) prevent the consecration of all the wine in the cellar, the prayer referring only to the offered wine. Thus some people have believed themselves justified in condemning the juridicial dryness of Roman piety which would have been always supported by the principle "*dabo cum dederis*" ("I will give when you have given"). Thus, the gods were given notice of the conditions necessary so that the Roman state would carry out within a fixed delay its vow of consacrating the first produce of spring, the *uer sacrum* (LIVY, XXII, 10).

It is certain that the Roman's liking for precision became more and more active in the drawing up of contracts, and that this juridical spirit is also reflected in their prayers. We will have the opportunity of coming back to this point when we examine later OVID's fictional negotiation between King Numa and Jupiter. Nevertheless one must not be led by this into ignoring the other aspect of Roman piety which expressed itself by an unconditional appeal to divine benevolence. When the Roman general "dedicated" himself together with the enemy army, in the midst of battle, according to the procedure of the *deuotio*, he addresses an urgent supplication to the gods— "uos precor ueneror ueniam peto feroque"... (LIVY, VIII, 9)—and he puts himself entirely into their hands, without concern for restrictive clauses. This type of unconditional *votum* recurs often in Roman history, for example, when promises were made to raise a temple. Doubtless, the Roman following this course of action was not fully disinterested, (but then, except in the case of the Quietist, what believer is disinterested in his devotion?); he always implied his hope that his prayer would be answered, *do ut des* ("I give so that you might give"). Is it not well known that "the gift is the archaic form of exchange" (MAUSS), and that it implicitly provokes restitution from the receiver, perhaps an increased restitution, where gods are concerned? In fact, the Romans never ceased to put into practice this unconditional form of piety, which also appears to be the most ancient. They expected some profit in return, in the name of the reciprocity of "good offices" which formed the basis of the *pietas*. Thus we can understand better why the Romans so loudly proclaimed their religious nature: HORACE on one occasion (*C.*, III, 6,5) eulogized the Roman in the following revealing manner: "dis te minorem quod geris, imperas" ("it is because you submit to the gods that you control (the world").

The word *religio* thus effectively conveys the specifically Roman point of view. Perhaps it would be profitable at this point to expose the different traits which throw into relief the originality of this position. The first characteristic of this religion is its purity (*castitas*), at its origins. VARRON (in the work of St. AUGUSTINE, *C.D.*, IV, 31) wrote this often discussed phrase: "for over a hundred and seventy years, the Romans honoured their gods without statues; if this practise had been continued, the cult would have been more pure" (..."castius dii obseruarentur"). Attempts have doubtless been made to diminish the significance of this declaration, by referring to the discovery of small statues in the cremation tombs of Latium, which would date back to the ninth century B.C.: however there is an increasing tendency nowadays to identify these small figures as being representations of human beings and not small deities (MULLER-KARPE considers them to be *praying-figures, Betende*. PUGLISI considers them as a corrective to the ritual of cremation, a modelled representation affirming the physical integrety of the dead person).

The consequence of this state of affairs is important: the absence of statues preserved the Latins from the antropomorphism which characterized the Greek pantheon since HESIOD and HOMER. To represent a divinity by a statue is to create a god more or less in the image of man, contrary to the Biblical formula. It means—as the Greeks demonstrated abundantly this process—lending the gods the characteristics, the passions, even the vices of man. The attitude of the Romans is totally different, as they dreaded far too much the power (*numen*) of the invoked divinity to dress it up with scandalous legends.

Yet is this attitude due to reverent fear, or is it rather due to technical incapacity? It is known that the Romans began to erect temples from the sixth century onwards under the influence of the Etruscans, and that they placed therein statues sculptured by artists from Etruria and Magna Graecia. In any case, the psychological reason seems to predominate, if it is true that the desire to create effigies has always been manifest, even in the most primitive forms (and the latial tombs corroborate precisely this figuration on the *human level*).

There is another fact to support this: the Latin pantheon had no hierogamy which was a common tradition in Greece. The divinities are male or female, but they are never paired off in couples. We have seen how the Roman might hesitate over their identity, and therefore he would use the circumspect formula "si deus, si dea est," as did CATO's peasant when he wished to implore the divinity of the copse (*De Agricultura*, 139). Occasionally the same supernatural forces are recorded as masculine and elsewhere as feminine: for example, while *Pales*, the shepherd deity, honoured at the *Palilia* or *Parilia* may generally be accepted as a goddess,("*Te quoque, magna Pales*"...,VIRGIL, *G.*, III, 1), the god Pales was still known to VARRO (SERVIUS, *Ad G.* III, 1). *Faunus* and *Fauna* appear on those lists of parallel deities which show an initial indecision later on settled in favour of the one sex or the other; the goddess *Pales* finally eclipsed her masculin namesake, just as the god *Faunus* ousted his feminine counterpart.

When one reflects that the Romans were surrounded by peoples such as the Etruscans and Greeks who freely attributed to their gods the customs of their own human society, (for instance, the important role of women in society is reflected in the Etruscan pantheon), the resistance of the Roman mentality appears all the more remarkable. Let us consider that another Indo-European nation which established itself at the beginning of the second millenium B.C. in Asia Minor, namely the Hittites, became very quickly influenced by their neighbours the Semites, from whom they borrowed their hierogamy. On the contrary, the Romans showed themselves to be quite indifferent to the idea of the "divine couple," even when they had accepted Greek ritual. The first *lectisternium* (399 B.C.) which introduced into Rome the Hellenic rite of venerating statues lying on ceremonial beds, paired together "heterogeneous" couples: Apollo was associated with Latona, his mother, Hercules with Diana, Mercury with Neptune. It was only in 217 B.C. that a new lectisternium presented twelve Greek divinities grouped in real couples (Jupiter and Juno, Neptune and Minerva, Mars and Venus, Apollo and Diana, Vulcan and Vesta, Mercury and Ceres). It is significant that this ceremony was to take place for the last time in Rome, and even more significant that the memory of it only survived to inspire Octavius one day with the idea of organizing a playful mascarade—the *cena* δωδεκάθεος—in the course of which the twelve guests disguised themselves as gods and goddesses (SUETONIUS, *Diuus Augustus*, 70).

Indeed, the idea of the "couple" never flourished in the Roman pantheon: even when the Romans appeared to be adopting the idea in a particular instance, they completely reshaped it in order to adapt it to their needs. The most outstanding example of this is provided for us in the association of Venus and Mars, which allowed the uniting of the Trojan traditions with Romulean traditions, an association which did not by far represent the couple Ares-Aphrodite, who were still glorified in immortal verses by LUCRETIUS in his philosophical transposition.

Thus, in the beginning there were no statues, no hierogamy. We may even add: no semi-gods. Greece had been able to give birth to heroes, who often owed their birth to divine follies; in Rome, on the other hand, the frontiers between gods and men were clearly defined, although the former were necessarily bound to the latter by the ties of the *religio*.

A second characteristic of the Roman religion is that it presented gods under a strictly functional aspect. In Greece the divinities were practically always enveloped by legends, which varied with the caprices of the poets. This rich mythology which so quickly corrupted Greek religious customs, is absent in Rome. The Roman deity was always defined by his precise office and it was according to this function that he held the veneration of the worshipper.

This functionalism may be limited. The list of minor deities assigned to the different tasks of the field has been much discussed. *Veruactor* was associated with the digging up of the stubble, *Redarator* with the second ploughing, *Imporcitor* with the cross ploughing, *In-*

sitor with the sowing, *Obarator* with the ploughing for the covering up of the seeds, *Occator* with the harrowing, *Sarritor* with the hoeing, *Subruncinator* with the weeding, *Messor* with the harvest, *Conuector* with the transport of the grain, *Conditor* with its storage, *Promitor* with its utilization (This list comes from Fabius Pictor, quoted by SERVIUS *Ad G.*, I, 21). It is possible that these are for the most part artificial creations due to the analysis of the Roman pontifices who took pleasure in decomposing the various rural operations. Likewise, one must no doubt take into consideration the polemic intentions when, in another context, St. AUGUSTINE ironically enumerates the different divinities who are reputed to further the marriage union: *Virginensis, Subigus, Prema, Pertunda*: "...What has the goddess *Pertunda* got to do here? Let her blush, let her go away! Let her leave something to the husband!" (*C.D.*, VI, 9). However, this is only a caricature of a very real tendency, which is the tendency to assign a precise function to each deity.

This function can, in extreme cases, correspond to a single manifestation, the essential point being that it is historically substantiated. One characteristic example is provided us by *Aius Locutius*: the deity with the transparent name ("the voice that talks") who only once made himself heard, to announce the approach of the Gauls (390 B.C.): he was duly honoured by having a temple dedicated to him in token of gratitude (LIVY, V, 50).

Pure aesthetism had therefore no part to play in the Latin pantheon, which admitted no deities without any precise function. WISSOWA nevertheless believed this to be the case with *Venus*, in whom he saw the incarnation of "the charm and bounty of nature," but this poetic dream was no more than an illusion, for the word *uenus* is deeply rooted in the semantic family of *uenerari*, (**uenes-ari*), in which it refers primarily to the power of seduction capable of subjugating the gods. The word changed from its neuter gender into the feminine, when this power was personified to become the goddess *Venus*. (An analogous metamorphosis changed the feminine *cupido* into the masculine, when the common word was promoted to the divine by becoming the god *Cupido*. Nobody would blame the Latins for their choice of the feminine to personify seduction, and the masculine to incarnate desire, in imitation of the Greek Eros).

A third distinct trait of this religion is its clearly political character. In Rome, everything was subordinated to the control of the State which would not tolerate any alienation of its power. There were no oracles as in the Greek territories, where the sibyl replied to the consultations of cities and individuals. There was also no revelation as there was with the Etruscans, where Tagès is believed to have taught the science of the haruspex and the nymph Végoé the interpretation of lightning. Doubtless, the Romans had the books of the sibyls in trust, of greco-etruscan origin, which are reputed to have come from Cumae; they had entrusted this collection of oracles and prescriptions for the averting of prodigies to the care of specialists, the *uiri sacris faciundis*. However, these books, preserved for a long time in the temple of Jupiter at the Capitol (before Augustus had them transferred to the Palatine temple of Apollo) were only accessible under the order of the senate; likewise their prescriptions did not come into effect but with the official sanction of the senate.

The sovereignty of the state manifests itself not only by the control of the religion, exercising itself through the intermediary of special colleges, in particular the college of pontifices. It expressed itself above all through the concept of the deity. When VARRO, in the first century B.C., wished to write a work of theological reflexion, he suggested a classification which has since remained famous, distinguishing the "gods of the city," the "gods of the philosophers" and the "gods of the poets." Rome only knew the first category; she honoured her gods after an hierarchical order: the cult was celebrated on the different levels of society—public worship provided by the h'ghest magistrates, worship within the *curiae*, worship presided over by the *paterfamilias* within the *gentes*.

A *personal* religion is inconceivable in a society where the individual only exists in so far as he integrates himself completely within the framework of society. Within each cell of society the religious bond re-enforced the feeling of belonging to the community. The citizen was controlled by religion from his birth to his death. To say that this religion did not address itself to the *man* as such, would be almost an anachronistic standpoint, at a time which did not concern itself with either metaphysics or eschatology, and when the "problems of the individual" were unknown. The only thing that mattered was the temporal wellbeing of the city,... and its development. This theme is not devoid of grandeur: it animated the Romans with a powerful dynamism (reflected in the epics of VIRGIL), which lasted until the time when it was overcome by vehement attacks from the wave of eastern religions.

One last characteristic of the Roman religion is its antithetic nature. One could compare it with a sort of *Janus bifrons* who looks to the past and to the future simultaneously. On the one hand, a scrupulous conservatism strongly maintains tradition under the authority of the *Pontifex Maximus*. He carefully attended to the execution of public ceremonies which are the means of maintaining the *pax ueniaque deum*, indispensable to the prosperity of the city. He honoured the national gods according to the necessities of ritual... When VIRGIL exclaims (*G.*, I, 497): "Di patrii indigetes...," one can sense the emotion felt at addressing those gods who had protected the city since its beginnings and throughout all its vicissitudes: being the gods of the native country (*patrii*) they are thought to have for it a particular affection, which one could perhaps not expect from the more recently established gods. The Ancients liked to contrast the *di indigetes* with the *di novensides* or *novensiles:* in their minds, this last expression means "recently established gods," although one cannot propose a certain etymology. (The explanation "the nine gods" definitely ought to be dismissed, it seems). As gods invoked from times immemorial (*indigetes*) in those official litanies called *Indigitamenta*, they were discreetely invited to reply to this fervent *pietas*. There was a special statute to confirm their privilege: only the gods called *indigetes* could be established by right within the consecrated precincts, in the area of the *pomerium*, while the gods of foreign origin had to be installed outside the "pomerial" area of Rome, for example on the hill called the Aventine, or on the field of Mars.

On the other hand, a spirit of open-mindedness counterbalanced this traditionalism, which, if let to itself, would have threatened to petrify the religion. On the level of institutions, the *uiri sacris faciundis* (whose numbers increased from two to fifteen in the time of Sylla) cannot be compared with the college of *pontifices*, although their influence which worked in the opposite direction took on a growing importance: they were in fact charged with the introduction of the foreign gods. This question came up above all in times of crisis, when confusion of the minds induced the senate to consult the sibylline books: the answer was nearly always a recommendation to admit a god from abroad. At one time an epidemic spread to disturbing proportions and the sibylline books designated the healing god Esculapus to be brought from Epidaurus (in 293 B.C.) and to be installed on the island of the Tiber. When Hannibal was at the gates of the walls of Rome, the Romans, remembering their Trojan origins, by order of the same books, welcomed in 204 B.C. the arrival of Cybele, the *Magna Mater Idaea* from Pessinus, who saw herself offered a temple on the summit of the Palatine in 191 B.C.: the Trojan links even caused the Romans to disregard the strict observance of the statute of the *pomerium*, which forbade a foreign goddess to reside within the confines of the *Vrbs*, much less on the most sacred hill of Rome.

It is in this way that the Roman pantheon expanded in the course of history. This attitude, furthermore, is in conformity with the spirit of polytheism, which is characterized by its hospitable spirit. It was not only epidemics and crises which were the cause of the increase in the number of gods, but equally the spirit of conquest. The Romans thus proceeded along two paths. On the one hand, they pretended more or less to confuse foreign deities with their own native gods, and this interpretation (*interpretatio Romana*) enabled them to pass over the differences. When, in 248 B.C., the Roman consul Lucius Iunius succeeded in placing himself on the rocky peak of Mount Eryx in Sicily, face to face with the Carthaginians, he put himself under the protection of the goddess of that place, who possessed a famous sanctuary there, namely Aphrodite, whom he likened to Venus; by right of this title, Venus Erycina, the Roman goddess with the Sicilian aura, had a temple erected in her honour on the Capitol in 215 B.C., within the boundaries of the *pomerium*.

On the other hand, the Romans respected the foreign identity of the god. They could hardly disown it, when in time of war they found themselves faced with the tutelary deity of an enemy city. In this situation the ritual provided a prayer which permitted the Roman general to call upon (*euocare*) the deity to join the Roman camp, while promising him solemnly a temple in Rome. It was in this way that the Roman dictator Marcus Furius Camillus "called upon" Juno of Veii at the end of a ten years' war (396 B.C.: cf. LIVY V, 21). This *Iuno Regina* kept her foreign identity and her temple was consecrated outside the *pomerium*, on Mount Aventinus (392 B.C.). She was placed into the category of the *foreign gods* who retained the original status of their cult, (cf. FESTUS, p. 268, L.).

History has thus progressively provoked a renovation within the Roman pantheon. Certain autochtonous deities might fade away to the point of disappearing altogether: thus, the *diuus pater Falacer*, who, although provided with a priest of his own, a *flamen*, had lost all substance by the time of Varro (*L.L.*, V, 84). Others might change their image by the means of circumstances: we shall see what a brilliant career awaited Venus, thanks to the Trojan legend. Later, in the last century of the Republic, the foreign deities penetrated Rome in greater and greater numbers: this trend did not present any serious threat to the national religion as long as the control of the senate was able to guarantee a reasonable intake. Under the Empire the equilibrium was gravely broken only when syncretism caused the prestige of the national gods to fade in favour of that of the eastern gods. Then the Roman religion was impaired in one of its essential aspects, and its strength (its political character) became weakness. Leaving behind the concept of a national god, people slowly began to be seduced by the idea of a universal god. From that time, the balance was broken, the Roman religion had received a fatal blow, even though its agonies had yet to last a few more centuries.

II. The Historical Development

This religion suffered of course various vicissitudes from the moment of the birth of Rome until the establishment of the Empire. It is even possible to find reflected in the liturgy the phases of the development of the primitive city. Indeed the characteristics of certain festivals enable us to draw conclusions about the relative size of the area of Rome.

In this sense the three festivals which we shall mention correspond to three successive stages. The first, the *Lupercalia*, a public festival occuring every year on the 15th of February, reveals its archaic character in its conception of the god (*Faunus*, a sort of wolf-god) and his priests (*luperci*, a sort of wolf-men, clad in loin-cloths). The main feature of the ceremony consists in a race of these *luperci*, who, armed with strips of goat-skins, used them to strike passers-by, this flagellation being reputed to have the effect of making women fertile. Now this prophylactic race followed a precisely circumscribed course around the Palatine: in other words, it took place on the boundaries of the ancient *oppidum Palatinum*, which was the cradle of the *Vrbs*. This feature alone would enable us to consider it as one of the oldest festivals in the Roman calendar, without speaking about other characteristics which can only be explained by the pastoral customs of bygone ages.

With the feast of the *Septimontium* of the 11th of December, we have to deal with a ceremony which concerned only the inhabitants of the *montes* ("feriae non populi, sed montanorum modo", says VARRO, *LL.* VI, 24). By chance the ancient scholars have preserved for us the list of those seven *montes* (which one must not confuse with the seven hills of the future city of Rome): the list includes the hills of Palatium, of Cermal, of Velia (which later will form the Palatine), the Fagutal, the Oppian, the Cispius (which will be absorbed by the Esquiline) and the Caelian. (See in particular FESTUS, p. 458 L., who while confirming the number of hills as being seven, adds to this list *Subura;* SERVIVS, *ad Ae.*, VI, 783.) It is obvious that this new topographical definition corresponds to a later stage, an intermediate state between the isolated villages and the final organization of the city. It is interesting to note the use of the word *mons* to name these small hills, excluding the word *collis*, which will be applied to the northern hills.

The ceremony of the Argei brings us to the last period. This festival, which was celebrated at two different times of the year (on the 16th and 17th of March and the 14th of May), comprised first of all a procession carrying the *Argei,* or rush dolls to the twenty-seven chapels intended for this purpose. On the 14th of May they were taken from these *sacraria* to be thrown into the Tiber from the *Pons Sublicius.* The meaning of this ceremony has given rise to discussion: WISSOWA considered it to be a sort of rite of substitution in which the dolls replaced human figures, whereas LATTE prefers to compare them to the *oscilla* (tiny figures that were hung from trees), to make them absorb all the impurities of which they wished to rid the city.

In any case this festival includes some elements of interest for our study. The reference to the *Pons Sublicius,* the oldest bridge in Rome, which was built on piles, according to its definition, would give an initial date: it is traditionally attributed to the king Ancus Marcius (LIVY, I, 33, 6). But the itinerary of the procession along the twenty-seven chapels, such as VARRO records it *(L.L.,* V, 45-54) provides the most precise information: it follows in fact the hills of the Caelian, of the Esquiline, of the Viminal, the Quirinal and the Palatine, circling the Forum which is henceforth part of the city. Thus this topographical definition corresponds to the inclusion of the Forum in the city, to the decisive stage of the urban transformation, the Rome of the *quatuor regiones.*

Thus we have seen from lustration to lustration, the circle expanding: it enclosed at first the *Roma quadrata* of the Palatine, then the seven small hills, finally the *Vrbs* centered around the Forum. Thanks to the conservatism of the Roman liturgy, we can observe this progression as the city gradually develops. At the last stage, the Forum has become the religious heart of the city, with the sanctuary of Vesta and the abode of the Vestals. The hill which is situated at its western extremity will constitute the higher sanctuary of this recent unity. Indeed it is on the Capitol that the most important public temple was to be built dedicated to the triad of Jupiter, Juno and Minerva. This building which tradition attributes to the Tarquins, reveals incontestably Etruscan influences, as we shall see. We have now reached the end of the sixth century B.C.

Do these religious traditions go back only as far as the birth of Rome? Must we take this date as the absolute initial state? A certain "primitivist" school of thought formerly upheld this attitude, that the comparative studies of GEORGES DUMÉZIL have made intenable. An indo-european heritage seems to be quite evident at the origins of Rome. This explains many points of the legend. Thus the distribution of the political and the religious initiatives between the first two kings: to Romulus was attributed the founding of the city, to his successor Numa, the organization of the religion.

This stylization, according to comparatist teaching, takes up the indo-european concept of a two-sided sovereignty: on the one hand, the bellicose and *ferox* aspect of Romulus, and on the other, the juridicial and pacifying aspect of Numa.

Can traces of this indo-european legacy be found in the institutions? Incontestably: both in the survival of rites which appear as "aberrant" if one refuses to elucidate them in the light of the indo-european ideology and in the existence of hierarchical structures which can only be explained through reference to the same ideology.

Through the confrontation of several latin goddesses and Vedic myths (*Déesses latines et mythes védiques*, Collection Latomus, Vol. XXXV, Bruxelles 1956.) GEORGES DUMÉZIL presented the most inspiring results of his research. These goddesses formerly seemed to offer no ground for a satisfactory interpretation and were the subject of conflicting discussions among scholars: thus, *Mater Matuta* had ultimately lost its meaning of "Goddess of Dawn" and become a "Mother-Goddess" or "Good-Mother". She was honoured by two strange rites on the day of the festival of the *Matralia*, the 11th of June; in the course of the ceremony, the roman matrons carried in their arms and nursed not their own children, but those of their sisters; they also made a servant enter into the temple of *Mater Matuta* whom they beat with rods before chasing her outside. Apparently curious rites... Now, the goddess of Dawn is "one of the most outstanding female figures in the Rig Veda," in which she appears suckling and licking the child which is either" jointly her child and that of her sister the Night" (we know that India is not embarrassed by contradictory conceptions) either "only that of the latter."

Everything seems to suggest that the most logical form of the theological idea—"The Dawn nursing the child of her sister the Night"—had reached Rome: but here the *myth* has disappeared, only the *rite* has survived which ascribes to the matrons the behaviour of the deity. Thus the mothers behave with their sisters' children in the same way as the Dawn, sister of the Night, behaves with the Sun, the child of Night.

As to the rite of the expulsion of the servant, it may also be explained by a Vedic parallel. In order to be beneficial, the Dawn must make a short apparition and give way to the day: thus Indra is praised because he expels the Dawn which is "too slow." In Rome, the *myth* of the Rig Veda transposes itself once again into a *rite*: in driving from the temple the female slave (a slave, as is natural for an abused person), the roman ladies reproduce, by a sympathetic action, the same symbolic gesture. "Once a year they take on the duties that the Indian hymns attribute in the far reaches of the Great Time to their God of Thunder, the expulsion of the Dawn, which is as necessary as is in the spring, the expulsion of the *"old March"*.

By having recourse to the same method based upon analysis of structural correspondences, the comparatist scholar has succeeded in bringing to light the meaning of *Diua Angerona*, "who saves the sun from the crisis of the winter solstice by the power of silence"; of *Fortuna Primigenia* a primordial goddess both "mother and daughter of Jupiter," of *Lua Mater*, "Goddess of Dissolution at the service of the roman order."

These *rites* had become unintelligible in Rome merely because they had been separated from their *mythological* context: in bringing to light their symbolical meaning by confronting them with indoeuropean data, comparatism has at the same time given a brilliant proof of its legitimate value.

And yet this concerns only "marginal" deities which more and more appeared as merely "survivals" in historical times. The indoeuropean heritage in Rome is even more strongly manifested in the fundamental structures. Indeed a tripartite ideology inspired the political system in its origins as well as the hierarchy of the three principal gods, Jupiter, Mars and Quirinus.

Tradition has kept the memory of the three tribes which were supposed to have provided the structures of the original society: the *Ramnes*, the *Luceres* and the *Tities* or *Quirites*. Probably it conferred upon this distribution an ethnic value: The Ramnes passed for the companions of Romulus, the Luceres for the Etruscan allies under the command of Lucumon, the Tities for the Sabines of Tatius. CICERO has given a precise expression to this tripartite distribution: "Romulus had divided the nation into three tribes... giving them his own name, that of Tatius, as well as the name of Lucumon, the ally of Romulus, who had perished in the battle against the Sabines" (*De republica*, II, 8, 14). The memory of this tripartite division had never been lost: its existence has been admitted by the great scholar Varro (quoted by SERVIUS, *ad Aeneidem*, V, 560), taken up as a text-book fact by the abridger FLORUS (II, 5, 6) "The Roman nation is constituted by the mixture of Etruscans, Latins and Sabines."

Now this ternary articulation can hardly be the result of a chance addition. What can we think of the explanation provided by the ethnic components? If it were valid, we could be surprised by its limitations: for other peoples, the Umbrians for instance who stand out among the Italics, or again the Greeks from Magna Graecia, could, (perhaps with greater reason) have aspired to the honour of providing "valences" to Roman society.

Inreality, the ethnic colouration of this ternary sum can barely conceal its functional source: is it not remarkable that the Ramnes should correspond exactly to the companions of the Priest-King, the Luceres, to the soldiers 'par excellence', the Tities, to the farmers-breeders according to their traditional vocation? This thought led GEORGES DUMÉZIL to recall the fact that similar structures existed in Vedic India, with the difference that, in the case of India, this distribution became fixed in hereditary classes: every Aryan belongs by birth to one and only one of the three groups, brahmins, warriors or farmers-breeders. This difference can be explained because India remained a monarchy of the feudal type whereas Rome in the course of its history was in a constant state of evolution towards a democracy of the citizens.

This functional tripartition is reflected also in the hierarchy of the three principal gods, which preceeded in Rome the existence of the

Capitoline Triad. Indeed, it can be discerned by implication, in the ancient *ordo sacerdotum*, handed down to us by FESTUS (p. 198, L.) and which specifies the following hierarchical order: the king, the flamen *Dialis*, the flamen *Martialis*, the flamen *Quirinalis*, the *Pontifex Maximus*. The three flamens, framed on either side by the king and the Pontifex Maximus, were respectively attached to the service of Jupiter, Mars and Quirinus. It is of interest to note that once a year these three flamens set forth, in an open charriot, to the chapel of *Fides*, the goddess of *Good Faith*, who presided over, so to speak, harmonious relations between these three representatives. This divine triad can only be explained by the conceptual structure which GEORGES DUMEZIL has called "the ideology of the three functions" (and which can be found in most of the ancient indo-european societies with particularities and variants peculiar to each one).

The same triad appears in the religious institutions of the archaic period. Thus, the *Regia*, the former "King's dwelling" which has become at the time of the Republic, the seat of the *Pontifex Maximus*, protected three different types of religious cults (besides the cults of Janus and Juno, who were honoured as presiding over the introduction of the year and of the month): the first principally concerns Jupiter; the second, concerns Mars, in the *sacrarium Martis*; the third, in another sacrarium, *Ops Consiua*, who belongs to the group of deities represented in the canonical list of the trilogy by Quirinus (in fact, as the powers of Quirinus—god and leader of the community of the *Quirites*, given up to the productive occupations of peace time, as opposed to the *milites* subjected to Mars—can be extended to the whole field of his jurisdiction, his flamen on occasion may intervene if there is no specialized priest: thus, OVID (*F.*, IV, 910) informs us that the *flamen Quirinalis* officiates at the ceremonies of *Robigus* (or *Robigo*)—a deity that was invoked for protection against the blight of the wheat).

The same three gods, Jupiter, Mars and Quirinus are associated, after Janus, the introductory god, and before the particular deities invoked by reason of circumstances, in the ancient *carmen* of the *deuotio*: a solemn prayer by which the commander in chief of the Roman army "vowed" himself and the enemy's army with him (see LIVY VIII, 9, 6). It also inspires the ancient law concerning the *spolia opima*, recorded by FESTUS (p. 204, L.), which provides that the *prima spolia* should be offered to Jupiter, the *secunda* to Mars and the *tertia* to "Janus Quirinus" (the ternary schema remains, whatever interpretation one adopts for *prima*, *secunda* and *tertia* and whatever the meaning which must be given to the expression "Janus Quirinus", which I have attempted to elucidate in *MEFR*, 1960, p. 116 sq.). Lastly it can be discerned once again in the triple leadership of the college of the Salii whose members are under the protection of the three deities, "in tutela Iouis Martis Quirini" (see SERVIUS, *ad Aeneidem*, VIII, 663).

Finally these Roman facts are confirmed in a remarkable way by the parallel offered by the Umbrian pantheon: in Iguuium as in Rome, a triad binds together three gods *Iou-Mart-Vofiono-*, endowed with the epithet *Grabouio-* (in this list, *Vofiono-*, has been interpreted by some linguists as being the etymological equivalent of *Quirinus*: see G. DUMÉZIL *RRA.*, p. 155, n. 3).

There appears to be no doubt as to the existence of a "tripartite ideology" which reflects ancient indo-european concepts, at the origins of Rome. It postulates that a society can only operate harmoniously on the condition that there be established a hierarchical structure of three functions which are the sovereignty (both magic and juridicial) strength (physical and military) fertility and prosperity (with its pastoral and agricultural variants).

But everything seems to suggest that this schema had been constantly degenerating from the moment when the Latins settled in the Italic peninsula. They passed from prehistory to history when they ceased to be itinerant and became sedentary.

Their history was to be marked by the tensions of internal rivalries and by the pressure exerted by external influences. If one is to believe the tradition according to which three monarchs of Etruscan origin appear at the end of the list of kings, namely—Tarquinius Priscus, Servius Tullius and Tarquinius Superbus—the Etruscan influence has been predominant at the dawn of Roman history. In fact, Etruria which allowed women a more important social role than indo-european society, was certainly no stranger to the substitution of two goddesses, Juno and Minerva, to the male paredros of Jupiter (gods associated to Jupiter): from the end of the sixth century B.C. the new association of Jupiter, Juno and Minerva, to which was dedicated a temple at the summit of the Capitol, permanently replaced the old triad Jupiter, Mars and Quirinus.

There can be no question of our following the religious history of Rome in all its convolutions. But it is worth mentioning the main events which constitute landmarks in its development. The expulsion of the kings which according to tradition dates from 509 B.C., is an important event as it marks the collapse of the keystone which guaranteed the cohesion of the old system. Of course, in a manner of speaking, the figure of the king survived on the religious level, in the person of the *Rex Sacrorum* or *Rex sacrificulus*, who inherited the liturgical functions of the former king (by this device, the Romans hoped to escape the just anger of the gods—*ira deum*—who would not have accepted an upheaval in the religious traditions). But this fossilized character no longer had any part to play in the life of the city. In the absence of any supreme arbiters, two social classes were to start a rivalry which was to last for centuries, the patricians and the plebeians. If their confrontation was mainly expressed by a social, economic and political conflict, which can be explained by the opposition of respective interests, it also revealed itself on the religious level. At the origins, patricians and plebians were far from enjoying religious equality. Only the patricians were entitled to assume the highest traditional religious dignities such as the offices of pontifex or augur. It was only in the year 300 B.C. that the Lex Ogulnia proclaimed the religious equality of both classes, and set aside for the recruitment of each college half the seats for the plebeians. (however, the ancient priesthoods such as *Rex sacrorum*, the *flamines maiores*, the *Salii*, were still reserved for the patricians).

This rivalry between the two classes explains certain cultual initiatives. Thus one can notice that at the beginning of the fifth century B.C., a sort of balance was struck in a compensating manner. At a few years' interval, two temples were established, in the honour of the triad Ceres-Liber-Libera (493 B.C.) near the Circus Maximus in the first case, and in the second case, the temple of Castor in the centre of the Forum (484 B.C.). The vow *(uotum)* to erect these temples originated from the same man, A. Postumius, the victor of the famous battle of Lake Regille that the Romans won in 499 B.C. against the Latins. This was a famous battle in Roman annals: it had gone through a critical phase, overcome only thanks to the entry of the Roman cavalry. While giving the order to his cavalry to enter the turmoil, the dictator Postumius vowed at the same time to have a temple built in the honour of Castor (LIVY II, 20, 12). The reason being that Castor, originally a Greek god, (the presence of whom in Lavinium, outside the bounds of the ancient city, has been confirmed by the recent discovery of an archaic inscription associating him with Pollux) was, according to the hellenic tradition, itself based upon the indo-european tradition, more particularly the protector of the cavalry. A. Postumius had then added to "human" ressources "divine" ressources, to use the expression of LIVY, in pledging a *uotum* to Castor, while simultaneously calling upon the *equites*. From the "historical" event of Lake Regille the god protector of the patrician class of cavalrymen became a national Roman god.

Now the same dictator, before starting upon this military campaign, had taken another religious initiative which was of a nature to satisfy the plebs. Dionysius of Halicarnassus (*Rom. Antiq.* VI, 17) relates that, as he was at that time worried because of difficulties in obtaining food supplies, he vowed to build a temple in the honour of the triad Demeter-Dyonisos-Core. This temple was dedicated by Postumius, immediately after his victory, as a token of gratitude for the exceptionally abundant harvest (the temple of Castor was dedicated nine years later by his son). Knowing that the cult of Ceres-Liber-Libera was directly entrusted to the care of the plebs, there can be no doubt as to the intentions of A. Postumius: by bringing in a plebeian cult to counterbalance the patrician cult, the dictator had wished to ensure a sort of dosage likely to satisfy both classes... while maintaining the hierarchical order: the temple of Ceres and of her associate deities is raised outside the *pomerium*, near the Circus Maximus, the sanctuary of Castor was to be erected inside the *pomerium* in the heart of the Forum. (Cf. our study, "Les Castores romains à la lumière des traditions indo-européennes", Hommages à G. DUMÉZIL, Latomus Collection, Brussels 1960.)

Besides the internal factors, external influences have set their mark on the development of the Roman religion. This process can be explained firstly because this religion was not a closed system but an open polytheism, then by the fact that Rome was in direct contact with the Greek world and the Etruscan world—let us not forget that Magna Graecia bordered upon the Roman territory as did the Etruscan Confederation. These contacts will become yet more extensive later on, with the conquest of metropolitan Greece and of Asia Minor. The Greek and Etruscan influences certainly contributed to give a more anthropomorphic character to the cult: tradition has it that the first terracotta statue of Jupiter, in the temple of the Capitol, was the work of an Etruscan sculptor, Vulca of Veii (PLINY, *HN*, 35, 157) and that the bronze Ceres as well as the ornamentation of the plebeian temple were carried out by Greek artists, Damophilus and Gorgasus (PLINY *HN*, 34, 15). Once the deity had assumed human form, it followed logically that it should also acquire a "dwelling": in this way, to the consecrated place *(fanum)* which was often a sacred wood *(lucus)*, was substituted a sanctuary *(aedes)* which was held to be the dwelling-place of the deity. Usually the sanctuary was established at a later date in a site which had previously been dedicated to the deity: thus LIVY (III, 63, 7) points out that the sanctuary of Apollo *(aedes Apollinis)* was built in 431 B.C. in the Flaminian Fields, in a place which already bore the name of "enclosure of Apollo" *(Apollinare)*.

New deities were not introduced on impulse but on the occasion of a serious incident, likely to shake the faith of the Romans in their national pantheon, or at least to make them seek out further help with some new deity. In this respect, the introduction of the Greek Apollo is most enlightening. It was not the god of the Muses or the sun-god which drew the attention of the Romans, nor the prophet god who later was to sponsor the "sibylline books" (these titles will be solemnly evoked in the *Carmen Saeculare* of HORACE at the time of Augustus) but, most probably following an epidemic, the healing god (See J. GAGÉ, *Apollon Romain*, Paris 1955, p. 158 sq.; 167). Thus, the oldest invocation recorded in the prayers of the Vestals, was addressed to the "doctor": "Apollo medice, Apollo Paean" (MACROBIUS, *S.* I, 17, 15). The circumstances of the building of his first temple in the Flaminian Fields confirm the significance of that introduction: a severe epidemic caused the sanctuary to be dedicated *pro ualetudine populi* to the god who bore the official name of *Apollo Medicus* (LIVY, IV, 25, 3; XL, 51, 6).

No less interesting are the circumstances of the arrival in Rome, at the beginning of the fourth century B.C., of the Etruscan deity Juno of Veii. It is worth dwelling upon these facts. The war that the Romans waged against the above mentioned city was prolonged beyond all expectation, in the midst of alarming reports (you will recall that the siege of Veii was to take up to ten years: LIVY, V, 22, 8... as did the siege of Troy). Then the Romans, following certain prodigious events, ("the waters of the Lake of Alba had risen to an extraordinary level, with no rain or any other cause": LIVY, V, 15"), appointed M. Furius Camillus as dictator. The new leader that the Latin historian names *fatalis dux* ("for the ruin of the Etruscan city") did not merely take measures to improve the army, he obtained a settlement by directly calling upon the tutelary deity with this prayer: "Juno Regina, who now resides in Veii, I beseech you to follow us, after our victory, in our city which will soon be yours: you will receive there a temple worthy of your majesty." (LIVY, V, 21, 3). The anecdote handed down by the latin historian stresses the favourable intentions of the goddess: to the question "do you wish to come to Rome, Juno?" asked by a young Roman, the goddess is said to have eagerly acquiesced (LIVY, V, 22, 5). Thus Rome became the seat of two "Juno Regina": the one enthroned in the temple of the Capitol, at the side of Jupiter, as national deity; the other was established on the hill of the Aventine as deity of foreign origin.

Let us also come back to the introduction in Rome of Cybele, the eastern goddess, at the end of the third century B.C. This example offers proof that the Romans from then on looked beyond the Greek or the Etruscan world. But it also reveals a certain constancy in their method of procedure. Following the dramatic vicissitudes which punctuated the second Punic war, it was not until 204 B.C. that hope dawned for the Romans, the hope of putting an end to this war after more than fourteen years of military campaigns. LIVY, the historian, notes the series of prodigious events which stimulated religious conscience: "two suns had been seen; intermittent flashes of light had streaked across the night; a fiery trail had been seen stretching from east to west. Lightning had struck a door at Terracina, a door at Agnani and in several places a wall; in the sanctuary of Juno Sospita, in Lanuvium, a terrible crash had been heard" (LIVY XXIX, 14, 3). In fact, hope had dawned as early as the previous year, thanks to the proclamation of an oracle drawn from the sibylline books. It set forth the conditions for redressing the situation: "the day when an enemy of a foreign race should carry war into the territory of Italy, he could be vanquished and driven out of Italy, if the Mother of Mount Ida were carried from Pessinonte to Rome" (LIVY XXIX, 10, 5).

We have already noted that this innovation which led the Romans to turn finally to an asiatic deity of a primitive nature (let us remember the black sacred stones which were supposed to be the incarnation of the deity, the galli, eunuch-priests attached to his cult) can, in reality, be explained in the light of Trojan treatment which transformed the wild *Magna Mater* of Mount Ida into "the ancestor of the Roman people." Ovid has underlined this treatment when he attributes to the goddess a miraculous intervention which triumphed over the reticence of Attalus, the king of Phrygia: "It is I who have desired to be sought: do not delay; send me, I wish it; Rome deserves the presence of every deity." And the king, terrified by this awful voice cries out: "go, you will always be ours, for Rome goes back to Phrygian ancestors." (OVID, *Fasti*, IV, 269-272).

The installation of Cybele, in 204 B.C., in the temple of Victory at the summit of the Palatine (pending the building of her own temple in 191) came, eleven years after Venus of Eryx had been established in a temple erected on the Capitol. The introduction of both cults had been brought about by the military setbacks that the Romans had suffered at the hands of the Carthaginian enemy: both referred to the same Trojan legend. The very order of their introduction can be explained in the most natural way. The Romans had indeed already come across Venus, the mother of their legendary ancestor, Aeneas, in the course of the first Punic war: the consul Lucius Junius had not hesitated to "recognize" her in the Aphrodite of Mount Eryx which he had succeeded in occupying definitely from 248 B.C. until the victorious conclusion of the war. Thus the Romans resorted *first*, in the course of the second Punic war, to the Venus of Eryx, who would appear to them to be a sure token of victory, in front of the *same* enemy. Later, in order to increase their chances, following the same Trojan line of thought, they sought to welcome the "Great Goddess" who enjoyed great prestige in the land of their "ancestors".

These innovations at the end of the third century B.C. offer proof that the roman religion to which, originally, Greek mythology was so foreign, came under the influence of syncretism. The Trojan legend, which was doubtless present in Etruria from the end of the sixth century B.C. (statues have been found in Veii of Aeneas carrying Anchises), had from that time been incorporated into the religion to the point of providing an ideological schema capable of justifying the importation of new cults. This was no ordinary legend: it was to become a sort of national dogma with Julius Caesar who claimed descent from Iulius-Ascanius, son of Aeneas. According to this myth, the Romans-Aeneades were the priviledged beneficiaries of a propitiatory Venus who intervened to ensure the grace of the gods in their favour, *pacem ueniamque deum* (we shall come back to the full significance of these religious expressions). The whole of VIRGIL's Aeneid is based upon this theological principle, which promises the Romans-Aeneades, on condition that they conform to the *pietas* of their famous ancestor, the blessing of the gods in all their enterprises.

The success of the Trojan legends also offers proof that the Romans, far from succumbing to some sort of syncretic fascination, managed to be selective. Events seem to show that the Romans welcomed suggestions from the outside... *ad maiorem gloriam populi Romani*. Nothing could be more significant in this respect than the way in which Augustus managed to exploit the Greek idea of the Ares-Aphrodite couple for Roman ends. Indeed if the emperor reserved a place of honour for this divine couple in the Pantheon (built in 25 B.C.) as well as on the pediment of the temple of Mars the Avenger (erected in 2 B.C.), he did not intend to take up the hellenic symbol (Aphrodite, principle of love, pacifying the principle of Discord). Quite on the contrary, he wished to "associate" "the father of the founder of Rome to "the mother of the people of the Aeneades" in the service of a dynastic mission: Mars has assumed a "Julian" character as *Vltor parentis patriae* ("Avenger of Caesar, father of the homeland") whereas Venus, while still remaining *Aeneadum Genetrix*, has assumed a more military character in order to get closer to Mars. Thus it is no longer the hellenic myth of their loves, but the mutual commitment to the service of Rome and its emperors which justifies the couple Mars-Venus. This metamorphosis is most instructive as to the reaction of the Romans to foreign influences.

III. The Official Cult

If it is true that the Roman religion presents itself in the manner of a *Ianus bifrons*, with one face turned towards the traditions of the past and the other towards the perspectives of the future, this dual character can also be found in the public cult: indeed the Ancients established a distinction between the national liturgy *(Sacra Romana)* and the Greek rite *(graecus ritus)*. And yet, this distinction leaves in the shade the Etruscan influence, which, it is true, was exercised in a more restricted and technical manner, particularly by haruspicy.

The Greek rite characterizes first of all the cult of deities which retained their original features in spite of an ulterior romanization: such is the case with the Roman Hercules, worshipped at the 'Great Altar' *(ara maxima)* which stood in the 'cattle market' *(Forum Boarium)*. If the legend, taken up by Virgil, relates the establishment of his cult to the stay of Evander of Arcadia on the future site of Rome, history (See the fundamental work of J. Bayet, *Les origines de l'Hercule Romain*, Paris 1926), explains his arrival in Rome through the intermediacy of Magna Graecia. This cult was at first privately assured by two Latin families, the *gens Potitia* and the *gens Pinaria* until 312 B.C.: at this time, the Roman state annexed it, on the initiative of the censor Appius Claudius Caecus. Despite this romanization, the sacrifices were still celebrated *graeco ritu*: thus, when the praetor urbanus, the representative of the state, officiated at the altar of Hercules, he was bare-headed and crowned with laurels and he mentioned in his prayers no other deities apart from Hercules (as opposed to the Roman practice, which insists that the officiant's head be veiled during the ceremony and which provides for a general invocation 'to the other deities', *di deaeque omnes.*)

More generally speaking, the Greek influence manifested itself by innovations in the official liturgy. We have already mentioned the introduction in Rome of the custom of the *lectisternia*, which consists in worshipping the statues of deities placed on ceremonial beds. This presentation of the deities on *puluinaria* which one could approach, lent itself to a more emotional type of worship, the *supplicatio*. This was prescribed in the case of a major crisis, generally after consultation of the *uiri sacris faciundis*: it was intended for all citizens, men and women who came to beg the gods in all their temples, to deliver them from their distress. LIVY (XXVI, 9, 7) described the dramatic 'supplication' which took place in the year 211 B.C., when Rome found itself at the mercy of Hannibal: 'the wailing of the women was heard not only in private houses, but from all directions the matrons spread across the public way, they run around the sanctuaries, sweep the altars with their dishevelled hair, prostrate themselves on their bended knees, stretch out their palms *(supinas manus)* towards the gods of heaven begging them to save the City of Rome from the hands of the enemy and to save from violence the Roman mothers and their small children.'

The spectacular ceremonies of the Secular games which aimed at obtaining a general lustration, in exceptional circumstances, also belonged to the *graecus ritus*. Their institution goes back to the year 249 B.C., according to the evidence of Varro (quoted by Censorinus, *De die natali* 17, 8): "following numerous prodigious events—in particular, the wall and the tower, between the porta Collina and the porta Esquilina, had been struck by lightning—the decemuirs, consulted the Sibylline books and announced that the Tarentine games *(ludi Tarentini)* should be celebrated for three nights in the honour of Dis Pater and Proserpina in the Campus Martis, as well as a sacrifice of dark-haired victims; these games were to take place every hundred years." Augustus drew inspiration from these arrangements for the organization of his Secular games, although he gave to them a totally different orientation. In fact, although he preserved the site of the ceremony—*Tarentum* referred to land situated in the northern part of the *Campus Martis*, along the Tiber—as well as the three nocturnal ceremonies (while adding to them three diurnal celebrations), he substituted to the computation of a hundred years a new saeculum of a hundred and ten years based on different traditions; above all, he relinquished the idea of an expiatory sacrifice, reserved for the funeral gods Pluto (or Dis Pater) and Proserpina, in favour of a solemn liturgy which was to lay the foundations of the new golden Age. The official hymn which was commissioned from HORACE, the *Carmen Saeculare*, and sung during the ceremonies by twenty-seven youths and twenty-seven virgins, expresses this sentiment when it appeals to the various protecting deities, particularly Apollo and Diana. It shows no hesitation in announcing the signs which promise the benediction of the gods (verses 57-60).

> 'Already the Loyalty, the Peace, the Honour, the ancient Modesty and Virtue, so neglected, dare to return: joyous Abundance appears with its overflowing cornucopia.'

Doubtless, personal reasons can explain here the choice of the Greek liturgy which entrusted the ordering of the festivals to the *uiri sacris faciundis*, (the expression *Achivo ritu* appears explicitly in the official record which has reached us through epigraphy: *CIL*, VI, 32.323): in 17 B.C. Augustus was not yet *Pontifex Maximus* as this dignity still belonged to Lepidus, exiled in the south of Italy, the Emperor did not receive this title until 12 B.C., after the death of the former Triumvir); on the other hand, he was president *(magister)* of the college of the *uiri sacris faciundis* and professed a personal devotion to Apollo, to whom HORACE's hymn had been principally dedicated. But this choice can be explained also for general reasons: in any case this magnificent celebration extended beyond the traditional framework of the national liturgy. It established a 'holy period' lasting three nights and three days. It invoked not a particular deity but all 'the gods who love the seven hills', and especially in the diurnal liturgy, Jupiter and Juno of the Capitol, Apollo and Diana. Most of all, it did not hesitate to address to all these deities a prayer of unusual scope, formulated by Horace at the beginning of his *Carmen Saeculare* (verses 9-12):

> 'Beneficient Sun who, on your fiery chariot, give and take away the day from us, according to the regular sequence of your births, may you never see anything greater than the city of Rome!'

Let us now come to the ordinary liturgy, such as it is arranged in the Roman tradition. Let us recall the supreme aim of the *religio*: to ensure for human beings the 'benevolence and the grace of the gods' *(pacem ueniamque deum)* through the observance of pious duties. If religious prescriptions are neglected or carried out in a faulty manner, the gods may express their resentment *(iram deum)* particularly by sending prodigious events. It is therefore logical that the cult should provide regular festivals *(ferias)* which recur periodically and celebrations arranged exceptionally *(ferias imperatiuas)* for expiatory purposes.

The word *feriae* corresponds certainly to the idea of 'concerning oneself exclusively with the service of the gods,' leaving aside all profane occupations: it is significant that the characteristic of the most important priest of the city, the *flamen Dialis*, should be that of being *'cottidie feriatus'* (Aulus Gellius, X, 15, 16) or in other words being pledged every day to the sole service of the god (Jupiter).

The festivals taking place in normal circumstances are divided into two categories: some fall on fixed dates *(feriae statiuae)*, others on movable dates *(feriae conceptiuae)*; among the latter appear in particular the agrarian feasts which depend more or less upon the variations of the seasons (thus the festival for the sowing, the *Sementiuae*, takes place on varying dates in January, the festivals of the fields, celebrated by the Fratres Arvales on varying dates in May: note however that the month itself remains unchanged). The fixed festivals have been entered in large capital letters in the calendar (which, according to tradition, was published for the first time in 304 B.C. by Cn. Flavius): this remark was made by Theodor Mommsen who undertook the publication of the different epigraphic calendars found in Italy in the *Corpus Inscriptionum Latinarum*, I² (Berlin 1893 and 1918). Today, one can have access to the full edition, comprising both the calendar previous to Julius Caesar's reform and the calendar following this reform (46 B.C.) in the publication provided by A. Degrassi, *Inscriptiones Italiae*, XIII, 2 (Rome 1963).

As the old established *feriae* (which go back at least to the VI cent. B.C.), stand out from later inscriptions by the size of their capital letters, it becomes easy to acquire a panoramic knowledge of the Roman liturgical year. Thus, the month of January appears as the opening month of the twelve-month year (tradition has kept besides the memory of a 'romulean' ten-month year, which started on the first of March). Only three public ceremonies took place during this month: the *Agonium* of the 9th of January", offered by the *Rex Sacrorum* to Janus; the *Carmentalia* of the 11th and 15th of January, taking place before and after the Ides, that concern *Carmentis* or *Carmenta*, the goddess whose name indicates her competence for the carmen (<* *carmen*). In other words, during the month of January, one venerated the god who was necessarily first in all Roman liturgy as well as the deity in charge of the liturgical instrument that is the *carmen*—a rythmic formula which is, so to speak, the mould of ancient prayer. (If the main function of Carmentis particularized itself in Republican times—she became the goddess of birth—the original legend always attributes to Carmentis a more general function: she is the great prophetess of the Roman Fate in VIRGIL, *Aeneid*, VIII, 339-341.)

As for the month of February, it is dedicated, as its name indicates (*februare* is glozed by *lustrare* or *purgare* by the Ancients: see FESTUS-PAULUS p. 75. L.), to the purification of the living and of the dead. It is during this month, that take place in a sort of compensatory perspective, the festival of the *Feralia* (21) which crowns the days consecrated to the dead *(dies parentales)* and the *Quirinalia* (17) which include, with the *Fornacalia*, the purifying rite of the parching of the grain intended for the living. The field of rituals of purification extends as far as the institutions and structures of the city. At least it is in this perspective that the *Lupercalia* (15)—purification of the basis of archaic Rome, the *Regifugium* (24)—purification of the royal institution? the *Equiria* (27)—purification of the tribes by chariot races? seem to regulate themselves. (See on this topic, the study of the *albati*, *russati*, *uirides* by G. DUMÉZIL in *Rituels indo-européens à Rome*, Paris, Klincksieck, 1954, p. 55 sq.)

In the succession of the months, the festivals distribute themselves according to the successive needs of the city and the exigencies of the season. One can note the correspondences which exist between certain festivals in March and in October: in the month of March, which coincided with the beginning of military operations, several festivals are rituals for the opening of the military season, whereas in the month of October are entered symetrically closing ceremonies. Other connections depend upon the rythm of nature: most of the festivals concerning the growth of vegetation are held in April, whereas those concerning the maturing and preservation of crops take place respectively in August and in December.

What is perhaps the most striking feature in the general picture, is the contrast between certain liturgical positions and their importance in historical times: thus the *Lucaria* which take up two days in the calendar, the 19th and the 21st of July, have a definite relationship with a cult celebrated in a sacred wood *(lucus)*; but their exact significance was already lost to the Romans of classical times: just as the sacred wood had long been overshadowed in the cult by the temple, in a Rome which had been becoming more and more urbanized from the VIth century B.C.

In what does the cult consist? In prayers accompanied by the sacrifice: 'without prayers the sacrifice is useless,' states PLINY THE ELDER (*H. N.*, XXVIII, 10). The association of these two elements forms in effect the basis of the Roman liturgy. For the sacrifices, one usually establishes a distinction between the bloodless and the bloody forms of sacrifice, granting a sort of priority to the first. This conception, it is true, rests upon a tradition passed on by the Ancients: PLINY THE ELDER (*H. N.*, XVIII, 7) takes pleasure in recalling that 'Numa established the custom of honouring the gods with the produce of the earth *(fruge)* and the sacred flour *(mola salsa)*.' In fact, matters present themselves in a somewhat different way. It seems that one must establish a distinction between the offerings which can be simple (first fruits, libations of wine, offerings of sacrificial cakes) or copious (the *epulum Iouis* of the 13th of September during the Roman games, and of the 13th of November, during the Plebeian games, is a veritable feast organized in the honour of Jupiter of the Capitol) from the liturgical sacrifices which always require, leaving aside a few exceptions, animal victims. Thus Pales, the goddess of the flocks, was honoured at the Parilia of the 21st of April, according to the testimony of OVID (*F.*, IV, 743 sq.) solely with sacrificial cakes, or grains of millet and libations of milk. This liturgy of an exceptional character which goes back to remotest antiquity (G. DUMÉZIL has pointed out the similar case of the Vedic god of cattle, who 'mythologically and ritually is nothing but a gruel eater') can be explained for a deity which is invoked precisely to ensure life and vitality for the herds. (Doubtless similar reasons explain why Ilithya, goddess of human procreation, alone among all the deities honoured in the Secular games of 17 B.C., and who is assimilated by Horace to (Juno) Lucina is offered sacrificial cakes instead of an animal victim: cf. DESSAU *I.L.S.* 5050, § 117.) In the prayer composed by OVID for use by the shepherd (*F.*, IV, 771-772), appears this explicitly worded request:

> Sitque salax aries conceptaque semina coniunx
> reddat et in stabulo multa sit agna meo.

("May the ram be ardent, may the ewe receive the seed to become fertile: may my stable number many lambs!")

A similar concern for perfection can be recognized in the execution of the prayers and the performance of the sacrifices. This concern explains the punctilious regulations which have sometimes surprised the moderns. Let us hear the testimony of PLINY THE ELDER (*H. N.* XXVIII, 11) concerning prayers: "...words differ according to whether one wishes to obtain favourable omens *(impetritis)*, to ward off ominous auguries *(depulsoriis)* or to present supplications *(commendationis)* and we see the highest magistrates using precise formulae in their prayers; to prevent any word from being omitted or inverted, someone first reads out the formula from a written text, another is responsible for careful supervision, a third must give orders for silence *(fauere linguis)*, while a fluteplayer is heard to cover all other noises..."

As far as the officiant is concerned, he must be in a state of physical and moral purity (CICERO, in the treatise *De Legibus*, I, 10, 24 recalls these two requirements when quoting the law: "caste iubet lex adire ad deos"—"the law ordains that the gods be approached in a state of purity"). To this end, he avoids all impure contacts, such as contact with the dead. He must wash his hands, take care to wear immaculate clothes *(pura uestimenta:* see PAULUS-FESTUS, p. 293 L.) and, during the ceremony, his head must be veiled *(capite uelato)*: this last form of dress characterizes the Roman rite as opposed to the Greek custom of being bare-headed *(capite aperto:* see FESTUS p. 432 L).

The sacrifice is subjected to a meticulous ritual. First, it is necessary in the choice of victims to respect the legal prescriptions (see CICERO *de Legibus* II, 12, 29: depending on the deity, one must offer adult animals *(hostias maiores)*, unweaned animals *(lactentes)*, male animals *(mares)* or female animals *(feminas)*. These animals are subjected to a preliminary examination *(probatio)* which not only ascertains their good state of health, and good appearance, but which also sometimes goes as far as to require the unexpected detail: 'the calf is only accepted, we learn from PLINY THE ELDER (*H. N.*, VIII, 183) if its tail reaches down to the articulation of the hock.'

Pulcher is the adjective which in religious language refers to the flourishing animal, a choice victim (see FESTUS, p. 274 L.). Thus we can read in the records of the Secular games of 17 B.C. that Jupiter and Juno of the Capitol are offered a sacrifice consisting respectively in a magnificent bull—"tibi hoc boue mare pulchro sacrum fiat" (DESSAU, *I.L.S.*, n. 5050 § 105)—and in a magnificent heifer—"tibi boue femina pulchra sacrum fiat" (*Ibidem*, § 121).

Once chosen, the victim is led to the altar crowned with bands *(in-*

fulae) and strips of cloth *(uittae)*. It is consecrated by the *immolatio*—a rite which consists in pouring over the victim's head some sacred flour (cf. PAULUS FESTUS, p. 97 L.: "immolare est mola, id est farre molito et sale, hostiam perspersam sacrare"), also some wine (cf. SERVIUS, *ad Aeneidem*, IX, 641), once the sacrificer had drawn the flat of the knife blade over its backbone from the head to the tail (cf. SERVIUS, *Ibidem*, XII, 173): this triple operation corresponds to the expression *immolauitque uino mola cultroque* which can be found in the records of the Arvals (3rd of January of the year 87 A.D.: *C.I.L.*, VI, 2065). It is obvious that all these ritual gestures symbolize the withdrawal of the victim from the profane world: from then on it belongs exclusively to the deity.

The logical consequence of this is the putting to death of the animal (in classical times it is done by the assistants of the priests, the *ministri* or *uictimarii* otherwise called *popae*). It is then that occurs the examination of the internal organs *(exta)*, which must determine whether the deity accepts the sacrifice, in other words, whether there is a *litatio*. Indeed, in the Roman sacrifices the internal organs *(exta)*, and the blood are set aside for the gods, only the flesh *(uiscera)* is given up for profane uses: in making this distinction, the Roman conception differs from the Greek which shares out between the gods and the celebrants the flesh (κρεά ὑπέρτερα) as well as the pluck (σπλάγχνα) .These *exta* with the blood were held to be the seat of life: now only life itself *(anima)* can be of interest to the Roman deity, according to the precept formulated by the jurisconsult TREBATIUS: "sola anima deo sacratur." (TREBATIUS quoted by MACROBIUS, *Saturnalia* III, 5,1—See the pertinent commentary of A. MAGDELAIN, *Essai sur les origines de la sponsio* Paris, 1943 p. 34 sq.)

The *exta* comprise several elements that CICERO *(De Diuitanione* II, 12, 29) enumerates in the following order: the gall blader *(fel)*, the liver *(iecur)*, the heart *(cor)*, the lungs *(pulmo)* (let us make clear on the one hand the fact that it seems the heart was not included in this general list before 274 B.C. according to information given by PLINY THE ELDER *H. N.*, XI, 186 and that on the other hand, LUCAN, I, 621 sq. also mentions the membrane of the peritoneum *omentum)*. In principle, the examination of the *exta—inspicere exta*—was a simple process: if they were in good condition, the goodwill of the deity was supposed to be obtained. Then the officiant cooked them in a cauldron *(aula)* or, more rarely, roasted them on a spit *(ueru)* in order to offer them later (exta *porricere* or *dare* or *reddere)* to the deity. (In fact, the

processes are generally more complex. To the *exta* sprinkled with
sacred flour *(mola salsa)* was added, apart from a few exceptions—
thus, the regulations for the altar of Narbon, erected to the divinity of
Augustus in 11 A.D. provide for the omission of the *magmentum*: cf.
DESSAU, *ILS.* 112—the *magmentum* or *augmentum* (cf. VARRO, *L.L.* V,
112), a sort of supplement formed from various elements taken from
other parts of the victim. *Exta* and *magmenta* were then cut up, *prosecta*,
to be presented to the deity.) A resume of this procedure can be found
for instance in the terms of a record from the Arvals dated 29th May
240 A.D. (cf. DESSAU, *ILS*, 9522): "Ad litationem exta inspexerunt et
reddiderunt". If on the other hand, the inspection showed an abnormal
condition of the *exta*, the officiant did not lose courage: he renewed
the sacrifice by the means of some victims of substitution *(hostiae suc-
cidaneae)* until he succeeded, *usque ad litationem.*

In reality, the examination of the *exta* was seldom restricted to this
verification. This is due to the fact that the Roman conception, which
is limited, on the whole, to a mere report, was contaminated by the
Etruscan doctrine of the divinatory sacrifice: now the *haruspices* consult—*consulere*—the *exta* in order to make predictions, by virtue of a
postulate according to which the *exta*, and more particularly the liver,
constitute a sort of microcosm in 'sympathetic' relation with the universe (CICERO alludes to this exegesis in his treatise *De Divinatione* II,
12, 29). From then on, it is no longer a rapid report of validity, but a
methodical consultation which studies the more remarquable parts of
the liver: the upper lobe or protuberance of the liver, *caput iocineris*,
the part concerning the consultant, *pars familiaris*, the part of the
enemy, *pars hostilis.*

The interference between the Roman and the Etruscan traditions
soon entered into use. It seemed so normal in the Ist century that
PLINY THE ELDER mentions only extispicy for divinatory purposes.
(*H. N.*, XXVIII, 10). And yet, the jurisconsult TREBATIUS had clearly
established the distinction between the two types of sacrifices, the one
of divinatory character ("unum in quo voluntas dei per exta disquiri-
tur"), the other of sacred character ("alterum in quo sola anima deo
sacratur"). It is true that if the pure Roman tradition is respected in the
liturgy of the Arvals, elsewhere the facts are mostly presented in a
syncretist light. (We mention here the essential aspects of our observations published under the title "A propos des '*exta*': l'extispicine
étrusque et la 'litation romaine," *Collection Latomus*, vol. LVIII, 1962,
Hommages à Albert Grenier p. 1371-1378.)

This is notably the case with LIVY, when he describes the sacrifice offered respectively by the consuls Decius and Manlius in 340 B.C. before the great battle waged by the Romans against the Latins near Vesuvius. Let us quote the passage (VIII, 9, 1): "Romani consules, priusquam educerent in aciem, immolauerunt. Decio caput iocineris a familiari parte caesum haruspex dicitur ostendisse; alioqui acceptam dis hostiam esse; Manlium egregie litasse. 'Atqui bene habet', inquit Decius, 'si ab collega litatum est'." ("The Roman consuls offered a sacrifice before setting out their troops in battle order. According to the tradition, the haruspex pointed out to Decius that the protuberance of the liver showed a lesion in the 'part of the concultant'; otherwise the victim was accepted by the gods; as to Manlius his sacrifice had been remarquably favourable.—'Then, all is well', said Decius, 'since my colleague obtained an favourable sacrifice.'"). In this text, the word *litare* evokes the Roman ritual: Manlius obtained *at the first attempt* the approval of the gods for his sacrifice, as is suggested by the adverb *egregie* which reinforces the verb *litasse*. His colleague experiences a less fortunate situation, which is interpreted by the haruspex as follows: his sacrifice is accepted by the gods, with the reservation that the protuberance of the liver shows a lesion in the *pars familiaris*: the sequal shows that the prophecy of the haruspex announces the death of Decius but his army's victory. (Decius will offer himself the to Manes by a solemn *devotio* in the course of the battle.)

This subtle reply would have been inconceivable from the strictly Roman point of view, which admits only of a categorical reply, either affirmative or negative. It also shows that in a complex situation, it was tempting to have recourse to the 'Etruscan consultation' which could be superimposed without difficult on the Roman ritual.

The sacrificial techniques just described represented in some way a sort of assurance for the officiant. The ultimate end was to obtain the approval of the gods. This approval was not only necessary for the public *feriae*, distributed over the course of the religious year; it had to be sought even more fervently when the Roman was conscious of having lost the good graces of the gods, *pacem ueniamque deum*. It is therefore necessary to distinguish between votive sacrifices and expiatory sacrifices.

The *uotum* is a solemn promise by which a magistrate pledges himself to the deity in the name of the State. He becomes, by this vow, the debtor of the gods, *uoti damnatus*, until the moment when he fulfills it (*uotum soluere*). These vows may become traditions: during the time of the Republic, it became customary for the new consuls to go to the Capitol on the first of January. There they sacrificed some white oxen to Jupiter, doubtless carrying out a vow made the previous year and, in their turn, they addressed a new *uotum pro reipublicae salute*. This ceremony was perpetuated under the Empire and Ovid recalls it during his exile (*Pont.* IV, 4), imagining his friend Pompeius, dressed in the purple of a consul in the process of making the gods accept his *uota* on the first day of the year: *(cernere iam uideor … et fieri faciles in tua uota deos)*.

Exceptional circumstances can be responsible for the *uota*. A famous vow was made at the beginning of the second Punic war, in 217 B.C., after the disaster of Trasimene: renewing an ancient Italic tradition, the Roman authorities promised an *uer sacrum*, that is to say the sacrifice of the whole spring litter represented by the species of pigs, sheep, goats and cows ("quod uer attulerit ex suillo, ouillo, caprino, bouillo grege"): the exceptional importance of this *uotum* is underlined by the fact that the *Pontifex Maximus* thought it necessary to consult the people before allowing the praetor commissioned by the senate to enter into this contract (cf. LIVY XXII, 10).

As for the expiatory sacrifice, it answers an urgent need: it aims to establish once again peace with the gods which has been threatened by the fault of men. In this respect, the Romans have a significant reaction: in their eyes, a calamity or a disaster are always more or less the sign of divine anger. It is in this way exactly that the disaster of Trasimene was interpreted; thus, the first concern of the Roman dictator Q. Fabius Maximus was to consult the Sibylline Books so as to discover which expiatory sacrifices would be suitable to stave off the resentment of the gods ("quaeque piacula irae deum essent": LIVY XXII, 9, 7-8). As might be expected, it was discovered that "a *uotum* made to Mars in view of this war had not been correctly fulfilled and should be renewed more magnificently": this measure of redress was followed by an impressive series of other religious measures among which appears the *uer sacrum*.

The obsession to avoid the *ira deum* went so far that people secured themselves against it, by offering in advance an expiatory sacrifice *(sacrificium hostiae praecidaneae)* on the eve of a solemn sacrifice (cf. AULUS GELLIUS, IV, 6, 7). Generally speaking, all prodigious events were a danger signal and gave rise to a serious enquiry to find out which deity had to be appeased: there existed a real right of claim *(postilio)* to the credit of that deity (see CICERO, *De Haruspicum responsis* X, 20). Should the enquiry turn out to be too difficult, as in the example (quoted by AULUS GELLIUS II, 28, 2) of an earthquake which does not allow the identification of the deity? Then, in order to avoid any risk of addressing themselves to the wrong deity, the Romans sacrificed the victim 'to the god or the goddess' *(hostiam 'si deo si deae' immolabant)*.

In our analysis of the Roman pietas (see p. 444 and 445), it appeared to us to be justifiably seen in a double light: it assumes sometimes an unconditional and sometimes a contractual aspect. The *uota* are consequently connected with either one or the other of these two extremes of piety. Let us refer once again to the articulation of the famous *uotum* by which Decius 'vows' himself to the Manes and to the Earth (cf. LIVY, VIII, 9, 6 sq.). Without concerning himself with any condition, he invokes directly 'Janus, Jupiter, Mars Pater, Quirinus, Bellona, the Lares, the Nouensiles gods, the Indigetes gods, the gods which have authority over us and over the enemy, the Manes' (one can recognize in this list, in particular, Janus the introductory god to all liturgy, the archaic triad Jupiter, Mars, Quirinus, the technician of war Bellona, the Lares, gods protecting the soil: he begs them 'to grant strength and victory to the Roman people and to inflict confusion, terror and death on the enemies of the Roman people'. It is here that the expression "uos precor, ueneror, ueniam peto feroque..." takes all its value (with the restitution of the authentic lesson of the manuscripts *feroque*, which had been corrected arbitrarily into *oroque* by the publishers: the credit for this restitution and the exegesis of the real lesson must be given to G. DUMÉZIL, *RRA*, p. 124.) Decius is not satisfied merely with praying *(precari)*, he has recourse to the seductiveness of the venusian vocabulary *(uenerari)*, and what is more, he presumes to obtain the grace of the gods, the *uenia* which is the divine correlative of the **uenus*, of the human *ueneratio (ueniam peto feroque* = I beg for and I already carry away your favour) (The analysis of the vocabulary belonging to the semantic family of Venus has been made in our study: *La religion romaine de Vénus depuis les origines jusqu'au temps d'Auguste*, Paris 1954, pp. 30 sq.: *uenus* is an ancient neutral form from which derives the verb *uenerari*: 'to seek to seduce, to charm (the deity)'; *uenia* is the symetrical notion—'the favour, the grace, granted by the deity').

It is because he has an unconditional faith in the gods that he 'vows' at the same time his own person and the enemy armies to the

Tellurique deuoueo). Henceforth he is no longer a mere mortal ("aliquanto augustior humano uisus") but a sort of lightning conductor entrusted with turning the wrath of the gods onto the enemy ("sicut caelo Manes and to the Earth *(Legiones auxiliaque hostium mecum deis Manibus missus piaculum omnis deorum irae*, qui pestem ab suis auersam in hostes ferret"): therefore he flings himself upon the enemy to die with the certainty that he will drag down the enemy to his own destruction.

If this unconditional gift—in this case, the gift of his own person—can remind sociologists of the *potlatch*, "a total prestation of agonistic type," it refers, in the Roman ideology, to the famous precedent of Aeneas. Indeed in the etiology of the festival of the *Vinalia*, the son of Venus, is presented in a light which exalts his piety in contrast with the impiety of Mezentius (see OVID, F., IV, 889 sq.). As the price of his alliance, Mezentius demanded from his Rutulan allies the new wine of the future wine harvest. And the Rutuls accept this ... Immediately Aeneas made this higher bid to Jupiter: "the wine harvest of the enemy has been promised to the Etruscan king, the wine from the vineyards of the Latium shall be yours!"

Jupiter's answer is immediate: "The best vow wins, the great Mezentius falls"—In order to understand the brief drama staged by OVID, one must remember the exegesis of the Ancients: it is an impiety for a mortal to claim the first fruits of the wine harvest, it is a wish to arrogate to oneself the honours reserved for the gods (see CATO quoted by MACROBIUS, *Saturnals*, III, 5, 10). That is the reason why the two protagonists have assumed perfectly symetrical roles. If Aeneas is the very incarnation of piety *("sum pius Aeneas"* in VIRGIL, *Ae*, I, 378), Mezentius is designated as impious *("contemptor diuum Mezentius"*: VIRGIL, *Ae*., VII, 648). The rapid conclusion of the joust between the two adversaries is only all the more interesting for religious philosophy.

This myth traces clearly the border line between piety and impiety for the Aeneas-Mezentius diptych. It suggests that piety 'pays' even at the very moment when it seems the most disinterested. Far from encumbering itself with contractual clauses, Aeneas's initiative assumes an unconditional aspect. It presents no explicit requests, but no sooner has Aeneas offered the new wine of the Latium to Jupiter, than the grace of the gods grants him a lightning victory over his enemies. For Aeneas, no less than the practician of the *potlatch*, is ignorant of the implicit virtues of his gesture: "any gift implies restitution ... and an increased restitution." Instead of formulating a request in return, he trusts to the *ueneratio* alone...

If the vow of Aeneas, as well as all the *uota* of this type imply the tacit belief *do ut des*, they never include conditional clauses. It is on the contrary on the pattern *dabo cum dederis* that are built the prayers of contractual type. The text for the solemn promise of a *uer sacrum* (LIVY XXII, 10, 2-6) submitted to the approbation of the people is particularly enlightening in this respect: "Velitis iubeatisne haec sic fieri? Si res publica populi Romani Quiritium ad quinquennium proximum, sicut uelim eam saluam, seruata erit hisce duellis, quod duellum populo Romano cum Carthaginiensi est, quaeque duella cum Gallis sunt, qui cis Alpes sunt, tum donum duit populus Romanus Quiritium: quod uer attulerit ex suillo, ouillo, caprino, bouillo grege, quaeque profana erunt, Ioui fieri, ex qua die senatus populusque iusserit. Qui faciet, quando uolet quaeque lege uolet, facito; quo modo faxit, probe factum esto. Si id moritur, quod fieri oportebit, profanum esto neque scelus esto; si quis rumpet occidetue insciens, ne fraus esto; si quis clepsit, ne populo scelus esto, neue cui cleptum erit; si atro die faxit insciens, probe factum esto; si nocte siue luce, si seruus siue liber faxit, probe factum esto; si antidea quam senatus populusque iusserit fieri, faxitur, eo populus solutus liber esto." ('Do you wish, do you command that these arrangements be made? If the State of the people of the Roman citizens, after the space of five years, emerges safe and sound, as I wish to be it sound, from these wars, from the war that the Roman people are waging against the Carthaginian people, from the wars against the Cisalpine Gauls, then let the people of the Roman citizens make the gift of sacrificing to Jupiter all the pigs, sheep, goats and oxen to be born in the spring and which shall still be profane, from the date which shall be fixed by the Senate and the people. Let the sacrificer make the sacrifice when and how he wishes: whatever the rite, let the sacrifice be valid. If the animal, promised for the sacrifice, dies, may it be considered to be profane, and that there be no fault; if unconsciously it is wounded or killed, let there be no fault; if it is stolen, let the fault fall back neither on the people or on the stolen owner; if unconsciously, the sacrifice is made on an inauspicious day, let the sacrifice be valid; whether the sacrifice is made by day or by night, by the hands of a slave or of a free man, let the sacrifice be valid; if the sacrifice takes place before the date that will be settled by the Senate and the people, let the people be released from it." (In connection with the execution—at the least costs—of this *uotum*, see J. HEURGON, *Trois Etudes sur le Ver sacrum*, coll. Latomus 26, 1957.)

Without doubt, the first fruits of spring constitute an important stake ... But with how many precautions is this extraordinary promise accompanied! It assigns a precise delay of five years for the restoration of the public well-being, it identifies with precision the enemies aimed at by Rome, the Cisalpine Gauls and the Carthaginians. It enumerates the list of irregularities which in normal times would render the sacrifice null and void and which, in this case, must be considered in advance as being nonexistant. In fact, this *uotum* is a veritable legal contract. And, last but not least, it provides that the promise shall be fulfilled only after the sollicited favour has been obtained.

Has the juridicial spirit prevailed over the spontaneous confidence? The invention of this new style has been attributed by the Ancients, not to Romulus who, in the manner of Aeneas, applies directly to Jupiter (according to the tradition handed down by Livy, I, 10, 5 and I, 12, 5, he founds successively a cult to Jupiter Feretrius and another to Jupiter Stator), without concerning himself with stipulations, but to his successor the king and lawgiver Numa. Let us resume our former considerations (See our study *RRV* p. 57-58.) about Numa who is held to be the founder of organized piety. "The improvisation of Romulus gives way to hierarchical organization. Henceforth religious acts require a procedure which is essential to their efficacity. It is no accident if tradition attributes to the same king the creation of the cult of *Fides* (see Livy I, 21, 4). This innovation is more important than the creation of the various priesthoods (Livy I, 20, attributes to Numa the creation of the three flamines maiores, of the Vestals, the twelve Salii, the Pontifex Maximus): the cult of *Fides* establishes the relations between men and the gods on the juridicial level of respect for one's commitments. This is a radical change in the religious climate: to religious spontaneity succeeds the spirit of barter.

Let us reflect over this contrast: whereas Romulus inaugurates the cult with an act of sheer gratitude (the offering of the *spolia opima* to Jupiter *Feretrius*), Numa will have recourse to the stratagems of crafty procedures, in order to acquit himself with the least costs. Indeed such is the sense of his discussion with Jupiter to obtain the expiation of thunder without human sacrifice. (See Ovid, F., III, 339 sq.; cf. Plutarch, *Numa*, 15. In his *Mitra-Varuna*, Paris 1948, pp. 73-74, G. Dumézil has compared the latin story and a similar legend from India, concerning Manu and Indra). "The deity demands a head— agreed, an onion head, replies the king. No, the head of a man, says the god—you shall have his hair, retorts Numa—No, it must be a living being—I shall put a fish, concludes Numa." In short, Numa's reform introduces a sort of religious rationalism: it bases the piety on respect of one's commitments (hence CICERO's expression, *N. D.*, I, 41: "est enim pietas *iustitia* aduersum deos")."

What is the situation in the first century? Are the *uota* drafted in an unconditional style or in the form of a contract? It seems that the contractual form prevails, save on exceptional occasions. Thus the solemn prayer that Augustus addresses to each deity, invoked at the time of the Secular games in 17 B.C., presents itself in the following way (see DESSAU, *ILS.*, 5050. This stereotyped expression crops up for each deity, so that the *Acta* confine themselves to refer to it once and for all, by mentioning *cetera uti supra*.):

"I pray you and I ask you to increase the power and the majesty of the Roman people, in time of war and in time of peace, to protect always all the Latins, to grant forever salvation, victory and prosperity to the Roman people, to be favourable to the Roman people, as well as to the legions of the Roman people, to preserve safe and sound the State of the Roman people, to be benevolent, favourable to the Roman people, to the college of the XV priests, to me, to my house, to my household" ... While it sets forth with precision the various requests —in which it differs from the spontaneity attributed to Aeneas or to Romulus—this *uotum* nevertheless corresponds to an unconditional act: it does not subordinate the performance of the sacrifice to the fulfillment of the requests. Besides, it is a matter of gaining the favour of the gods for the duration of a *saeculum*!

It is otherwise in the ordinary liturgy. Here the *uota* bear the mark of the style of the imperial chancellery. The *Fratres Arvales* which were recruited in the senatorial class and missed no opportunity of manifesting their loyalty towards the prince's household, provide us with some remarquable examples of this sort. Here is, by way of an example, the *carmen* which was delivered on the 3rd January of the year 91, intended for the reigning emperor Domitian: "Iupiter optime maxime, si imperator Caesar diui Vespasiani filius Domitianus Augustus Germanicus pontifex maximus tribunicia potestate censor perpetuus pater patriae et Domitia Augusta coniunx ejus, quos me sentio dicere, uiuent domusque eorum incolumis erit ante diem III nonas Ianuarias, quae proximae populo Romano Quiritibus, rei publicae populi Romani Quiritium erunt, et eum diem eosque saluos seruaueris ex periculis si qua sunt eruntue ante eum diem, euentumque bonum ita uti me sentio dicere, dederis, eosque in eo statu, qui nunc est aut eo meliore seruaueris, astu ea ita faxsis *(sic)*, tunc tibi nomine collegi Fratrum

Arualium bouem auratum uouemus esse futurum"(*CIL.*, VI, 2068, l.1-9).

"Jupiter Optimus Maximus, if the Emperor Caesar, son of the divine Vespasian, Domitian, Augustus, Germanicus, Pontifex Maximus, holder of tribunicial power, censor for life, father of the nation and Domitia Augusta his wife, whom I consciously name, remain alive and their house remains safe and sound on the third of January which falls due, next year, for the Roman people and for the Roman State, and that you watch over that day and their persons so as to preserve them from the perils which may exist or occur before that day and that you grant a happy issue, as I am conscious of saying, by watching over their persons so as to keep them in their present state or again in a better state, if you consent to answer this request, then, in the name of the college of the Fratres Arvales, we enter into this commitment, we shall offer you an ox with gilded horns."

Obviously, not only is this *uotum* no longer inspired by the irresistible impulse which inspired a Decius giving himself up with full confidence to the gods, but it is encumbered with clauses in which prudence contends with artfulness (thus, while asking Jupiter to maintain the present situation—*eo statu qui nunc est*—one does not refuse the possible improvement of a better situation—*aut eo meliore*). As in any good contract, a date of payment is fixed, the 3rd of January of the following year—for the contracting parties: the safe-keeping of the imperial couple will then be 'renumerated' by the sacrifice of the ritual ox with gilded horns.

IV. The Place of Man

In the official prayers which we have quoted, there is a constant expression recurring like a sort of common denominator, through the ages, in spite of the diversity of styles: *populus Romanus Quiritium*. At the most the construction with the genitive *Quiritium* seems to have been prefered at the time of Decius (4th century) and at the time of the vow of the *uer sacrum* (3rd century) whereas at the time of Augustus (at the Secular Games of 17 B.C.) and of Domitian (in the year 91 A.D.) the construction with the apposition *Quirites* is preferred. Is ancient man anything more than a citizen submerged in the mass of the *Quirites*? It is significant that the word *Quirites* is hardly ever used other than in the plural as if the language implicitly condemned the tendency towards the singular. More precisely, it becomes evident in the singular only at that moment when the citizen faces the test of inevitable solitude: death. Thus, the grammarians have taken care to point out this "exception": 'the word was formerly used in the singular, as the declaration made by the funeral herald proves: "this *quiris* has passed away"—*ollus Quiris leto datus*—(FESTUS p. 304 L., with the correction of AUGUSTINUS: *ollus* for *illius†*). Is man therefore an unknown quantity for the Roman religion? The question is put even in this highly communal society.

Indeed this religion seems to offer neither ethic nor metaphysic for the use of the individual being. Doubtless, it recognizes moral reprobation: in particular it condemns the *impietas*, a deliberate sacrilege which has nothing in common with the fault committed by inadvertence or clumsiness against the ritual. Whilst the latter can be redeemed by an expiatory sacrifice, *piaculum*, the former perpetually stigmatizes the culprit, without hope of redemption. The impious one no longer has the right to approach the altar of the gods, or to try to appease them by offerings. The law is implacable: *impius ne audeto placare donis iram deorum* (CICERO, *De legibus*, II, 9, 22). There exists "no purification for crimes committed towards men, nor for the impieties committed towards the gods" (... *scelerum in homines atque in deos inpietatum nulla expiatio est:* CICERO, *De legibus*, I, 14, 40). Thus the culprits are given over to the verdict of the tribunals, or to the remorse of their consciences: when making this distinction, CICERO *(Ibidem)* counts less on the *iudiciis* than on the *angore conscientiae*.

We are forced to state that in the two hypotheses, the sanction leaves no hope of salvation for the reprobate. Neither law nor religion provide for an ethic of redemption any more than they have provided for rules of practical morality.

What of doctrinal teaching? We know, thanks to the testimony of St. AUGUSTINE *(De Civitate Dei*, IV, 27 and VI, 5), how the *Pontifex Maximus* Mucius Scaeuola and VARRO, author of the *Antiquitates rerum diuinarum*, considered the problem. They distinguished three categories of gods—the gods of the poets, the gods of the philosophers, the gods of the city—to which correspond three kinds of theologies— mythical theology, "physical" theology, and civic theology. As good Romans, the two authors reject the first two categories—the first because it comprises a number of fables unworthy of the majesty of the gods, the second because it contains knowledge capable of harming the people *(aliqua etiam quae obsit populis nosse:* cf. *C.D.* IV, 27) only retaining the gods of the city. Let us quote the judgment of Varro *(C.D.* VI, 5): "the third kind (civic theology) is that which the citizens, particularly the priests should know and practise in the cities. It teaches what gods each man must honour in public, what ceremonies and what sacrifices he must fulfill." This concordant judgment from two eminent Romans is in itself revealing: it exalts the tradition, the *mos maiorum*, not without putting the minds on guard against the dubious fictions of the poets or the dangerous teachings of the philosophers. This is finally CICERO's position, such as he has it exposed by COTTA, the mouthpiece of tradition in the *De Natura deorum* (III, 17): "...I shall show that I have been better informed on the cult of the immortal gods by pontifical law *(iure pontificio)* by the customs of the ancestors *(maiorum more)*, by the liturgical vases *(capedunculis)* which come to us from Numa, than by the theories of the Stoics."

We can understand that this religion, founded essentially upon the respect for traditions and civic loyalty, has not aroused mystical fervour. However, an exception must be pointed out: it is to the credit of the Roman who, appointed as proconsul in dark days (211 B.C.), at the age of 24, was to be the future conqueror of Hannibal: P. Cornelius Scipio. This early appointment to this high office was due to his prestige surrounded by an aura of religious mystery. "As soon as he took the *toga uirilis*, reports LIVY (XXVI, 19, 5 sq.), he undertook no public or private act without first going to the Capitol: on entering the sanctuary, he would generally remain there alone, for some time." This habit of meditating before the Supreme god has something undefinably modern which is surprising in the ancient world: it is true that the Latin historian seeks some sort of explanation in the fable according to which Scipio was of divine origin: as in the case of Alexander the Great, he was said to owe his birth to a monstrous serpent...

Such was not, assuredly, the situation of the ordinary citizen. He could find no salvation outside the structures of the city. He was taken in hand, at birth, by the family group which was itself an integral part of the *gens*, that line of generations issued from the same ancestor. The importance that FUSTEL DE COULANGES has given in la *Cité Antique* to the domestic cult must not be questioned: the young Roman was really steeped in an atmosphere which was likely to instill him for ever with the great national traditions. He was introduced into the city at the age of seventeen, when he took the *toga uirilis*. From then on, according to his birth and to his merits, he embarked upon a more or less brilliant political career.

This career did not prevent him from assuming at the same time a priesthood, with the exception of the archaic priesthoods (the *rex sacrorum* and the *flamonium*) that were incompatible, particularly the dignity of *flamen Dialis*, with political duties. (These lasting regulations, in spite of a few attenuations, explain the fact that, for seventy-five years the post of *flamen Dialis* remained vacant at the end of the Republic). Thus, the young Roman, whether patrician or plebeian by birth, could gain access to the four great religious colleges, *quatuor amplissima collegia*: the college of pontifices, presided over by the *Pontifex Maximus*, the college of *Augures*, the college of the *uiri sacris faciundis*, the college of the *Epulones*. (Let us note the dates from which plebeians had acess to these: it became possible for plebeians to be admitted to the *uiri sacris faciundis*, who were in charge of consulting the Sibylline books, from 367 B.C. when the *Lex Licinia* was passed, to get admission to the pontifices or augurs, by virtue of the *Lex Ogulnia* 300 B.C. As for the college of the *Epulones*, it was instituted in 196 B.C., in order to relieve the pontifices of some of their sacred obligations, particularly from the celebration of sacred feasts, *epula*, at the Roman Games and at the Plebeian Games.)

What idea could the Roman, drawn by all the sollicitations of ambition, have of death? Doubtless, a confused image. Upon leaving this life—*uita defunctus*—he entered the deified community of the *Manes* who were also called the *Di parentes*: here again he could not escape from the community. Lost among the shadows of the ancestors, he had to depend upon the piety of his descendants. This need explains the frequent use of adoption in families which would have disappeared through lack of legitimate sons: indeed, only the legitimate son (by ties of blood or of adoption) was qualified to take over the duties of the *pater familias* in the cult of the ancestors, at his death. This need also explains the concern to rest in an inviolable place, *locus religiosus*. What they feared above all was to be deprived of burial: instead of becoming part of the *Manes* who were worshipped at the family tomb during the festivals of the dead from the 13th to the 21st of February —the *dies Parentales*—one ran the risk of becoming a tormented shadow, one of those evil spirits—*Lemures*—that the head of the family expelled from his house, according to the ancestral rite, at the *Lemuria* of the 9th, 11th and 13th of May. This belief allows the scope of the terrible curse made by Aeneas over the corpse of a presumptuous enemy to be understood: "...a fond mother will not come to lay you into the ground; she will not lay your body under the weight of the tomb in your country. You will be abandoned to birds of prey or thrown into the abyss of the sea where the voracious fish will come to lick your wounds." (*Aeneid*, X, 557-560).

The idea of a personal immortality had probably come to light in the last century of the Republic. But this was the exclusive privilege of great men. It is at least in this way that CICERO presents the new doctrine, marked by the influence of Plato, which he attributes to the illustrious Scipio Africanus (*De Republica*, VI, 13): "all those that have helped to maintain, to safeguard, to develop the motherland have a place assured for them in the heavens: they will enjoy there perfect bliss for all eternity; indeed nothing is more agreeable to the supreme god who reigns over the universe, at least for that which takes place on earth, than the formation, founded on law, of associations and human communities that are called cities: having descended from heaven, their chiefs and leaders return to heaven"—We know what was to be the destiny of this idea of astral immortality under the Empire: the apotheosis of the Emperors, who became *diui* at their death, was based upon the belief in the migration of their souls to the celestial spheres.

But this new teaching escaped the national religion: it denoted the ever-increasing influence of philosophical doctrines on cultured minds. In fact, Rome had become a cross-roads for philosophical currents: Platonism, stoicism, epicurism competed for the interest of the leading classes. The best minds tried to find, more or less successfully, a compromise between the invasion of new ideas and fidelity to the past. Stoicism, which tried to interpret the deities of the traditional Pantheon as symbols of natural forces represents an interesting attempt in this respect: this may explain, at least in part, the greater influence that it exerted in Rome, in comparison with that of epicurism, hostile to any religious traditions. But scepticism, for its part, had no scruple about showing itself out in the open: in his work, dedicated to the Emperor Vespanian, PLINY THE ELDER (*H.N.*, II, 14-18) does not hesitate to attribute to stupidity *(socordia)* the belief in the multiplicity of gods, and to put forth a profession of faith in which theology confines itself to a social programme: "For a man, god is to help men: that is the path towards eternal glory"—"*Deus est mortali iuuare mortalem et haec ad aeternam gloriam uia.*"

What became of the lower orders in this general upheaval? They could hardly indulge in the luxury of studying more or less difficult philosophical systems. They dimly apired to a less *political* and more *personal* religion. For in spite of official interdictions—for instance, against the cult of Isis, under Augustus and Tiber—an increasingly strong wind of influence was blowing from the east. It warmed the souls which were a prey to latent nostalgia. Book XI of the *Metamorphoses* of Apuleius in this respect constitutes an interesting document: the isiac religion was not only attractive because of the picturesque character of its rites and the warm atmosphere of its ceremonies, but because of its doctrinal and moral innovations. It offered to its adherents an eschatology, enabling them to make sure of their salvation in the after-life thanks to initiation; it proposed to them a self-discipline, by assigning rules of conduct in their daily life. The Roman world was moving towards profound changes...

V. THE INFLUENCE OF THE ROMAN RELIGION

It is a well-known fact, that of the progressive invasion of the Roman Empire by the eastern religions; over all these, Christianity was to triumph in the 4th century. It may be best to present this fact with a few nuances: on the eve of its victory, Christianity directed its polemics less against the traditional Roman religion than against the scandalous fictions of the Greek mythology and the extravagant beliefs of the mystery religions. This is at least the impression given by an anonymous pamphlet written in 394, the *carmen contra paganos* which directs its most virulent darts against the cults of Isis, of Mithra and of Magna Mater, which were—let us remember this—only foreign cults, *sacra peregrina* in Ancient Rome (leaving aside Magna Mater who is *also* a Roman "relation" in the name of the Trojan legend).

At all events, the agony of the Roman religion was prolonged during the whole of the 4th century from 313 when Constantine, in the edict of Milan, declared himself to be the protector of Christianity, without however abolishing paganism. Various episodes marked the confrontation of the new religion and of the ancient institution. The incident of the statue of Victory, which brought into conflict the pagan prefect of Rome, Symmachus, and the Bishop of Milan, Saint Ambrose, is perhaps symbolically the most significant of all: as we know, the statue of Victory ultimately was removed from the altar of the Senate. More serious blows were to be delivered against the ancient religion by the Emperor Gratian who gave up in 375 A.D. the title of *Pontifex Maximus* and who abolished around 382 A.D. the subsidies given to pagan temples as well as the payments given to the priests.

The decisive blows were given by the Emperor Theodosius. He had already ordered the closing of the temples, the interdiction of cele-

brating public sacrifices, and the suppression of the domestic cults
rendered to the Lares, the Genii, and the di Penates, when his victory
over Eugene in 394, ensured definitively the triumph of Christianity.
Around 400, Saint Jerome was able to write (*Ep.* CVII, 1) "the gilding
of the Capitol is flaking away, soot and spider's webs cover all the
temples in Rome...". At about the same time, Stilichon, the minister
of the Emperor Honorius, whom the poet Rutilius Namatianus *(De
reditu suo,* II, 41 and 52) called "the sinister Stilichon" *(dirus Stilicho)*
had the books of prophecy of Ancient Rome burnt, i.e. the Sibylline
books.

Therefore, has one the right to speak of influence with respect to a
religion in decline for some fifteen hundred years? The length of time
it took in its deaththroes shows however how deeply rooted it was.
Indeed, surprising resurgences prove that the legal sentence of death
passed by Theodosius at the end of the 4th century had not marked
the end. Thus the calendar of Polemius Silvius, dated 449 A.D., still
mentions 'pagan' feasts, in spite of the Christian appartenance of the
author: he notes, for example, the *Carmentalia* in January and the
Lupercalia in February (cf. A. DEGRASSI, *I. I,* XIII, 2, p. 264-265). At
the end of the 5th century a pope found himself obliged to protest
against the celebration of the Lupercalia in Rome... (Usually the
treatise on the *Lupercalia* is attributed to Pope Gelasius. Recent criticism has tended to attribute the authorship of it to Pope Felix III: cf.
P. NAUTIN, *Dict. d'hist. et de géogr.,* n. 32, Felix III, col. 894.) Moreover,
in the 6th century of our era, when Belisarius, General of Justinian,
was maintaining a difficult siege against the Goths, some Romans
remembered the archaic rite which ordained the opening of the doors
of the sanctuary of Janus Quirinus, in time of war: they secretly
undertook to force the doors of the temple which had been closed
since the abolition of paganism, in order to conform to the ancient
prescription. (Cf. PROCOPIUS, *Gothic Wars,* I, 25, ed. Comparetti, Rome,
1895, I, p. 184-185.)

Therefore Christianity found itself at grips with pagan survivals
which were rooted strongly enough to suggest to it some solutions of
substitution. These *mutations* testify in their way for the ancient institution. That is the reason why a whole school of research could arise in
the wake of *Antike und Christentum* by E. J. DÖLGER. Let us take a few
examples. The idea of purification which inspires the feast of the
Lupercalia has been taken up in the feast of the Purification of the
Virgin. The *Ambarualia* which were to ensure the lustration of the

fields have been transposed into the processions of the Rogations. Even the cult of the dead has retained from ancient piety, not the taste for libations (that was still practised by Monica, the mother of St. Augustine) but the use of flowers—OVID (*F*, IV, 539) recommended violets. And we know that the cult of saints often took over from such and such local deity.

Another legacy of the Roman religion lies in the sacred vocabulary. From the time when Latin replaced Greek, since the 2nd century, in the liturgy of the western church, the riches of the Latin language were at the disposal of the Christians. No doubt, the transfer did not take place directly. (There are no rules without exceptions: the invocation *Regina caeli*, addressed by APULEIUS to Isis, was taken up in the Paschal anthem in the honour of the Virgin Mary). Besides, it often happens that the adopted word no longer exactly reflects the original meaning; it takes on a new sparkling iridescence, like a bronze patinated by time. Thus the word *religiosus* evokes in classical language an idea of a taboo or of a scruple, according to whether it is applied to an object (a *locus religiosus* is inviolable) or to a subject (a *religiosus* man is scrupulous to a fault). Already, in the language of Apuleius, the word seems to have lost this purely negative value. The author of the *Metamorphoses* (XI, 13, 6) takes pleasure in contrasting the common people *(populi)* or the impious *(inreligiosi)* with the *religiosi* who are the faithful worshippers of the goddess Isis. This "positive" meaning has remained linked with the word, when it came to Christian usage: JEROME(*Ep.*, CVII, 2) is certainly making a compliment to his correspondent when he calls her *religiosissima in Christo filia*.

Another word merits our attention: *sacramentum*. Here again, APULEIUS, a veritable magician in the art of extending vocabulary, seems to have played the part of intermediary: talking about the holy *militia* of Isis which his hero is about *to join*, he calls this engagement *sacramentum* (*M.*, XI, 15, 5): used in this way, the word still retains a link with the military meaning which is consistent with the classic use, while revealing through the context its religious vocation: *sacramentum*, in the mystical sense, has now become possible for the Christian language.

This example shows also that Christians have occasionally succeeded in transposing to the holy register words which were originally profane. However, the method of "re-use" seems to be just as frequent in the vocabulary as in the paleochristian architecture or sculpture. Research into the Leonian sacramentary is most instructive in this respect.

(We retain the denomination "Leonian Sacramentary" which is the most widespread to refer to the collection of prayers containing the oldest prayers of the Roman Church. It is under this title—which attributed it to the Pope and Saint Leo the Great—that it was published, particularly in Tome LV of Migne's *Patrologie Latine*. A more recent and more learned edition has been brought out by L. C. Mohlberg with the title of *Sacramentarium Veronense*—in the collection *Rerum ecclesiasticarum documenta*, constituting the first tome of the *Fontes*, Rome, Herder, 2nd. Ed. 1966. — This new denomination refers to its source, a manuscript from Verona, Hn. LXXXV of the Capitular library which, written in uncial characters, would date from the first half of the 7th century and would originate from Italy, probably from Verona.). Here reappear the *uota* that one begs God to receive favourably, the *hostia*, which ceases to be bloody to become *salutaris* or *spiritalis*, refers to Christ. (Cf. *Sacramentarium Veronense*, ed. Mohlberg[2], Rome 1966, p. 33, l. 10 sq. = MIGNE, *P.L.*, LV, c. 46: "Remotis obumbrationibus carnalium uictimarum, *spiritalem* tibi, summe Pater, *hostiam* supplici seruitute deferimus..." "Abandoning the dark sacrifices of bloody victims, we offer you, O Supreme God, as humble supplicants, a spiritual host"). Even the most sacred vocabulary of Rome reappears with the specific words *uenerari* and *uenia*, without mentioning the ritual custom of associating prayers and sacrifices: "Ecclesiae tuae, quaesumus, Domine, *preces* et *hostias* apostolica commendet oratio ut quod pro illorum gloria celebramus prosit ad *ueniam*" (Cf. *Ibidem*, p. 43, l. 9 sq. = MIGNE, *P.L.*, LV, c. 53-54): "O Lord, may the intercession of the apostles recommend to you the prayers and the sacrifices of your church, so that the feast that we celebrate in their honour shall serve to gain us your favour."

But Rome did not restrict itself to a lexicographical legacy of which the most illustrious term remains the term *religio*. It seems certain that the Roman spirit put its mark on the style of Christianity. A style which is apparent in the structure of the prayers which have retained the qualities of restraint and clarity which characterized the former *carmina*, avoiding all murky sentimentality in order to establish a clear and confident relationship between man and heaven. According to an expression of St. Augustine (*De. Doctr. christ.*, III, 11) Christianity had succeeded in carrying away "the gold and silver vases" of its adversaries to use them in its own way. A style which is perhaps even more remarkable, when it manifested itself, if not at the beginning, at least at the time of turmoils and heresies, through its sense of order and spirit of organization. One fact seems to me to assume a deeply symbolic value. It is well established that the first popes bore only the name of bishop (ἐπίσκοπος): but it may not be entirely due to chance that tradition later revived the title of *Pontifex Maximus*, to grant it to the head of Christendom. Consciously or unconsciously, this was to pay a magnificent tribute to the traditions of Ancient Rome.

VI. OUTLINE OF A HISTORY OF STUDIES ON THE ROMAN RELIGION

The importance of religion in the Ancient World now appears to be an indisputable fact. This assertion has only recently been established. Let us not talk about the 17th century which mainly took pleasure in annexing indiscriminately the deities of Greece and Rome for the "fêtes galantes" of the Court. When, in the 18th century, a man such as Montesquieu wrote his *Considérations sur les causes de la grandeur des Romains et de leur décadence* (1734) he was thinking merely of politics and customs. One must wait until the 19th century, with Fustel de Coulanges, to see religion given its real place in the heart of ancient society: devoting the lectures which he gave in the University of Strasbourg 1862-1863 to the "history of a belief", this scholar was to publish in the following year (1864) the classic text of *la Cité antique*: for the first time, it was vigorously asserted that a study of the religion was indispensable for an understanding of the institutions of the Ancients. There is no doubt that this investigation did not take place without some trial and error. In their eagerness to offer global explanations, several theoreticians yielded to systemization. Thus religious studies were subject to fashions amongst which we may quote, as an example, the system of MAX MULLER for whom the deities were nothing but the names *(nomina numina)* given to the various impressions, created by the light of the sun—or again, the naturalistic theory of Wilhelm Mannhardt, which was expressed mostly in the book which bore the evocative title of: "The cult of the tree among the Germanic peoples" (1875). Nowadays, one is more wary of systematic explanations: we prefer the straightforward examination of facts.

It is incontestable that sociology renewed the methods towards the end of the last century, by proposing the principle of a comparison between ancient societies and modern "primitive" societies: ÉMILE DURKHEIM's book, *Les formes élémentaires de la vie religieuse* (1912) is a comparatist study which proposes to circumscribe the definition of the religious phenomenon in general. A wise injunction stated that "only the comparison of facts of identical nature has any demonstrative value." This advice has not always been heard: imperceptibly one has fallen into a "universal" comparatism which all too often mistook the *"ancient"* fact for the *primitive* fact (in the sense of *inferior*). Is it possible to say that the remarkable work of JAMES FRAZER is safe from this criticism? Thanks to his vast erudition, this scholar rendered enormous services to the history of religion, of the roman religion in particular, by his monumental commentary of the *Fasti* of OVID. However, he set forth a dangerous postulate ("Human nature is much the same all the world over and in all ages") which prompted him to make dangerous parallels. In any case, the arsenal of sociological *exempla* is vast enough to provide almost always a case which is apparently similar: if the Hottentot does not suit, let the Zulu take his place!

It is thus that one has cast a "primitivist" back-cloth over the beginnings of Roman society, by a process of excessive assimilation. One had recourse to the Polynesian *mana* to explain a religion of indoeuropean tradition, the gods and goddesses were made to emerge from some dim nebula in the name of a progressive evolutionism.

Reaction was not long in coming. Already GEORG WISSOWA firmly established in his *Religion und Kultur der Römer* (first edition: 1902; second edition: 1912) the necessity of respecting corresponding areas in the field of religion and attempted to draw up a precise and clear picture of the facts. But a mere description, however faithful, does not suffice to render them comprehensible. Very soon, historians realised how much they could gain by drawing comparisons between analogous religious structures, such as for instance the Latin triad of Rome, "Jupiter, Mars and Quirinus", and the Umbrian triad of Iguvium, "Jupiter, Mars and Vofionus" (designated by *Grabouio-*). But it is on a larger scale that comparatism was to derive its best results thanks to the enlightening works of Georges DUMÉZIL, who used as a starting-point the existence of the original community of the Ancient Indians and the Ancient Italics (the probable equivalente of the Sanscrit terms *bráhman* and the Latin *flamen* to describe the priest is one sign of this among others). It results from this that the indo-european legacy in Rome can no longer be denied. In opposition to the opinions of evolutionism, it appears that personal gods disposed according to a functional hierarchy which recalls a distribution of similar functions in India, existed in Rome from the origins. Contrary to the teachings of the "primitivists", the Romans are discovered to be the inheritors of a millenary ideology, which underwent with them a sort of metamorphosis: for the *myth* was substituted *history*, so that the same character can appear in *divine form* in a mythology of indo-european inspiration and in *human form* in the Roman history. A forcible example is provided by a double pair of "homologues": the Roman heroes Horatius Cocles, the one-eyed, and Mucius Scaevola, the one-handed, who correspond to the Scandinavian couple Odhinn, the one-eyed magician god and Tyr, the jurist god, who sacrificed one hand. The findings of this vast enquiry have been recorded by G. DUMÉZIL in his work *La Religion Romaine Archaïque* (Paris, 1966). The comparatist perspective should not however lead us away from the main objective of the historian of the Roman religion: he must determine with as much precision as possible the originality of that religion. Not that all the facts have been explained, despite the efforts made by scholars. But research extending over a hundred years or so enables us to pose the problem with more accuracy.

In what measure may one speak about an originality of the Roman religion? G. WISSOWA had tried to define it by chronological criteria: he thought that the Romans had managed to keep their institutions free from foreign influences until roughly the 3rd century B.C., after which syncretism would have exerted a disturbing action. This distinction did not hold out against the facts: in any case, it would have been surprising, had Rome managed to live sealed off from the outside world, when it only constituted in the 6th century B.C. a small group in comparison with its rich neighbours, the Etruscans (who contributed to its urbanisation under the dynasty of the last three kings of Rome, who, according to tradition, came from Etruria) and the settlers of Magna Graecia, who had founded opulent settlements in the Southern part of Italy.

F. ALTHEIM therefore thought it possible to take the opposite view to his predecessor: he denied any Latin originality, laying down as a principle that foreign influences and especially Greek influences had come into play from the earliest times. In one sense, his treatise *"Griechische Götter im alten Rom"* (1930) is even more a book of programmes than a collection of particular studies.

It goes without saying that this extreme view does not fail to expose itself to criticism. Attempting to reduce the Roman Pantheon to a sort of transfer of the Hellenic Pantheon is a doubtful wager, whether one admits a direct influence through Magna Graecia or an indirect influence through the intermediary of the Etruscans. If it is true that some Hellenic deities such as Apollo or the Dioscuri were known in Rome as early as the 6th century B.C., they were incorporated in the Latin Pantheon by reason of circumstances, in conformity with the welcoming spirit of the polytheism of the Ancients. These admissions do not implicate the autochtonous traditions.

Therefore we shall always be fascinated by this mystery: why and how did the Latins, established since the 8th century on the site of the future city of Rome, manage to preserve the vital part of their religious heritage, while lending themselves to external influences? It is in this spirit that Jean Bayet has undertaken a fruitful study in a book, the title of which is most revealing: *Histoire Politique et psychologique de la religion romaine* (Paris 1957). The intention of K. LATTE, *Römische Religionsgeschichte* (Munich 1960) has been to take up the original matter of Wissowa, while benefitting from the acquisitions of philology and archeological and epigraphic discoveries. Whatever the appreciation one gives to the value and the success of his efforts, the materials placed at the disposal of the researcher render incontestable services.

SELECTED BIBLIOGRAPHY

I. *Principal ancient sources*

Fasti: The Roman calendar (ed. TH. MOMMSEN, *CIL*, I², 1893: for the Julian year; ed. G. MANCINI, *N.S.*, 1921 p. 73-141: for the pre-Julian year; complete: ed. by ATILIO DEGRASSI, *I.I.*, XIII, part II, 1963).

Acta fratrum Arualium (ed. HENZEN, Berlin 1874; ed. PASOLI, Bologna 1950): records (First to IVth cent. A.D.) of the college of the Arvales Brethren. The record for the year 218 includes the *carmen Aruale*, which probably goes back to the end of the 6th cent. B.C.).

Carminum Saliarium reliquiae, ed. B. MAURENBRECHER, *J. Ph.*, 1894, Sup. Band 21, p. 314-352 (fragments of the ancient Carmen of the Salii).

CATO, *De agricultura* (for the prayers and sacrifices of the private cult).

M. TERENTI VARRONIS *Antiquitatum rerum diuinarum libri I, XIV, XV, XVI:* ed. R. AGAHD, *J.Ph.*, 1898, Sup. Band 24, p. 3-220 (Reconstitution of Varro's lost treatise thanks to the quotations given by the Christian authors).

Acta ludorum saecularium, *CIL*, VI, 32323 sq. (Records relating to the Secular Games, particularly those of 17 B.C.).

OVID, *Fastorum libri VI* (Commentary of the liturgical calendar).

All the Latin authors, primarily Virgil, should be consulted by the historian of the Roman religion.

II. *Encyclopedias of Reference*

DAREMBERG ET SAGLIO, *Dictionnaire des antiquités grecques et romaines*. 10 volumes including one volume of tables (Paris, 1877-1929).

DE RUGGIERO-CARDINALI, *Dizionario Epigrafico di antichità romane* (Rome, 1885 sq.).

ROSCHER-ZIEGLER, *Ausführliches Lexikon der griechischen und römischen Mythologie* 10 vol. (Leipzig, 1884-1937).

PAULY-WISSOWA, *Realencyclopädie der classischen Altertumswissenschaft* (Stuttgart, 1893 sq.), nearing completion (77 volumes published).

III. *Modern treatises*

JOACHIM MARQUARDT, *Le culte chez les Romains*, 2 volumes, (translated by M. Brissaud) (Paris, 1889-1890).

W. WARDE FOWLER, *The Roman Festivals of the Period of the Republic* (London, 1899).

———, *The religious experience of the Roman people from the earliest times to the age of Augustus* (London, 1911: 2nd edition, 1922).

GEORG WISSOWA, *Religion und Kultus der Römer*, 2nd ed. (Munich, 1912).

FRANZ CUMONT, *Les religions orientales dans le paganisme romain* (Paris, 1909; 4th edition 1929).

CYRIL BAILEY, *Roman Religion and the Advent of Philosophy in* The Cambridge Ancient History, VIII, pp. 423-465 (1930).

———, *Phases in the Religion of Ancient Rome* (Berkeley, Calif. 1932).

NICOLA TURCHI, *La religione di Roma antica* (Bologna, 1939).

FRANZ ALTHEIM, *Römische Religionsgeschichte*, 2nd ed. (Berlin, 1956).

JEAN BAYET, *Histoire politique et psychologique de la religion romaine* (Paris, 1957).

KURT LATTE, *Römische Religionsgeschichte*, (Munich, 1960).

GEORGES DUMÉZIL, *La religion romaine archaïque* (Paris, 1966).

AGNES KIRSOPP MICHELS, *The calendar of the Roman republic* (Princeton, 1967).

ABREVIATIONS

CIL	*Corpus Inscriptionum Latinarum* (Berlin, 1863 sq.).
DEGRASSI, *I.I.*	Atilio DEGRASSI, *Inscriptiones Italiae*, vol. XIII, part II: *Fasti anni Numani et Iulani* (Rome, 1963).
DESSAU, *I.L.S.*	Heinrich DESSAU, *Inscriptiones Latinae selectae* 3 volumes (Berlin, 1892-1916).
DUMÉZIL, *RRA*	Georges DUMÉZIL *La Religion romaine archaïque* (Paris, 1966).
J.Ph.	*Jahrbücher für classische Philologie* (Leipzig).
MEFR	*Mélanges de l'Ecole Française de Rome*.
N.S.	*Notizie degli Scavi di Antichità* (Rome).
SCHILLING, *R.R.V.*	R. SCHILLING, *La Religion Romaine de Vénus depuis les origines jusqu'au temps d'Auguste* (Paris, 1954).
WISSOWA, *Ruk²*	Georg WISSOWA, *Religion und Kultur der Römer*, 2nd. ed. (Munich, 1912).

LIST OF ANCIENT AUTHORS QUOTED

APVLEIVS, *M.* = L. APVLEIVS, *Metamorphoseon libri XI*.

ARNOBIVS = ARNOBIVS, *Disputationes aduersus nationes*.

AUGUSTINE = AVRELIVS AVGVSTINVS
  C.D. = *De ciuitate Dei*
  D.C. = *De doctrina Christiana.*
GELLIUS, *N.A.* = AVLVS GELLIVS, *Noctes Atticae.*
Carmen contra paganos: in *Poetea latini minores* III p. 286-292 (ed. Baehrens, Leipzig 1881).
CATO = M. PORCIVS CATO, *De agricultura.*
CENSORINVS = CENSORINVS, *De die natali.*
CICERO = M. TVLLIVS CICERO
  De diuinatione.
  De haruspicum responsis.
  De legibus.
  N.D. = *De natura deorum.*
  De republica (ed. K. Ziegler, Leipzig, 1929).
DIONYSIUS OF HALICARNASSUS = ΛΙΟΝΥΣΙΟΣ ΑΛΙΚΑΡΝΑΣΣΕΥΣ, ῾ρωμαικὴ ᾽αρχαιολογια (*Roman Antiquities*).
FESTVS, L. = S. POMPEIVS FESTVS, *De uerborum significatu, cum Pauli Diaconi epitoma* (ed. W. M. Lindsay, Leipzig, 1913).
HORACE, *C.* = Q. HORATIVS FLACCVS, *Carmina.*
JEROME, *Ep.* = EVSEBIVS HIERONYMVS, *Epistulae.*
LUCAN = M. ANNAEVS LVCANVS, *Belli ciuilis libri (Pharsalia).*
LUCRETIUS = T. LVCRETIVS CARVS, *De rerum natura.*
MACROBIUS, *Saturnales* = AURELIVS MACROBIVS, *Saturnalia.*
NONIUS = NONIUS MARCELLUS, *De compendiosa doctrina* (ed. W. M. Lindsay, Leipzig, 1903).
OVID, *F.* = P. OVIDIVS NASO, *Fasti.*
  Epistulae ex Ponto.
PLAUTUS = T. MACCIVS PLAVTVS.
PLINY, *H.N.* = C. PLINIVS SECVNDVS, *Naturalis Historiae libri XXXVII.*
PLUTARCH = ΠΛΟΥΤΑΡΧΟΣ, ῾Ο Νουμᾶς (*Numa*).
PROCOPIUS = ΠΡΟΚΟΠΙΟΣ ΚΑΙΣΑΡΕΥΣ, ῾Η ῾ιστορια τῶν γοτθικῶν Πολέμων (*Gothic Wars*).
RUTILIUS NAMATIANUS = RVTILIVS NAMATIANVS, *De reditu suo.*
SERUIUS, *Ad Aeneidem* = SERVIVS (et SERVIVS DANIELIS, interpolator), *commentarii in Vergilium ad Aeneidem.*
SUETONIUS = C. SVETONIVS TRANQUILLVS, *Diuus Augustus.*
TACITUS = C. CORNELIVS TACITVS, *Annales Historiae.*
TERTULLIAN = Q. SEPTIMIVS TERTVLLIANVS.
LIVY = TITVS LIVIVS, *Ab urbe condita libri qui supersunt.*
VARRO, *L.L.* = M. TERENTIVS VARRO, *De lingua Latina.*
VERGIL = P. VERGILIVS MARO
  G. = *Georgica*
  Ae. = *Aeneis.*

HELLENISTIC RELIGIONS

BY

M. J. VERMASEREN
Utrecht, Netherlands

I. The Essence of Hellenistic Religion

It may seem strange but it is nevertheless true that in periods in which cosmopolitism or universalism is widespread we also find that individualism shows an increase. While religion, philosophy, and government policy are all apparently doing their best to shape an all-embracing uniformity that the most various peoples will feel at home in, there are some in all layers of society who, though accepting the great unifying ideas of their time, feel impelled by the very existance of these same ideas to lay more stress on their own individuality. And so, in a paradoxical way, universalism may be said to strengthen individualism. This paradox finds excellent illustration in the period of Alexander and his successors (hellenism I) and that of the early Roman Empire (hellenism II). Under Alexander and his immediate successors the hellenic spirit, in its widest sense, was brought into closer contact with the various civilizations of the eastern Mediterranean, and though the conquest of the East at first resulted in the spread of Greek influences among the subjected peoples, it was not longer before hellenism itself—which was already a compound formed from the whole Greek world—began to absorb at an ever increasing rate the conceptions of those who, in accordance with the testament of their great leader Alexander, were to be treated not as uncivilized and barbarous members of subject races but as equals with whom one must live in concord (ὁμόνοια). The characteristic traits peculiar to the Asiatic, Egyptian, Syrian and Persian cultures now had to be fully recognized, accepted and re-worked. Alexander himself was the representative example —often in disaccord with his best friends and followers—of these progressive ideas, as he showed in Troy, during his visits to the oracle of Jupiter Ammon in the oasis of Siwa and the Apis at Thebes, and shortly before his death in Babylon at the wedding ceremonies of Macedonians, Greeks, and Asiatics. As the heir of Greek tradition he granted liberty and freedom as far as was possible—naturally less in political than in cultural and religious respects.

But Alexander did not have time to incorporate the western peoples in his projected worldwide empire. The immense task of organizing the western and the eastern world under one central sceptre was the destiny of Rome. After preparations lasting several centuries in which the Scipios, Pompey, and Caesar played the foremost roles, the first centuries before and after the beginning of our era saw the developments we may refer to as hellenism II. But more than in hellenism I east and west felt the presence of imperial rule as a result of the strong political organisation of Rome, and one of the most striking features of Roman power was the official State religion with the increasingly important cult of the Emperor. The indigenous religious creeds of the various peoples were respected on two conditions—that the Roman State-cult was recognized and respected (especially on official Roman festivals), and that the indigenous cults did not lead to disorder. The approved middle way was that of identifying one's own deities with those of the Romans—a syncretism which one also finds in hellenism I where (as it seems to me) it proceeded in a more natural and less forced way. In hellenism I one also remarks that the *Diadochi* themselves, and especially the Ptolemies, tried to put forward a flexible solution for their subjects by promoting cults able to combine the creeds of both Greeks and other peoples. In hellenism II however, and indeed long before, the Romans accepted foreign deities only with the greatest difficulty, though Ovid—to give an example—in the *Fasti* joyfully exclaims that the Asiatic Cybele has finally returned from Troy to Rome, the usual attitude was very different. Especially in the Capital the *pontifex maximus* and the priestly societies remained cautious and suspicious of newly-introduced cults.

Since the whole varied heritage of the Greeks had come into the possession of the Romans, there were great differences between the religious traditions in many provinces not only in the east but also in the west. It is only in this century that scholars have begun to distinguish the various varieties, using both literary and archaeological sources. Much study will still be necessary before the real facts of the diffusion of the eastern mystery cults over the Mediterranean world can be established. The great cosmopolitan cities such as Alexandria, Athene and Rome deserved especial attention and though in hellenistic times they formed with their large conglomerations of people and culture a section apart, there are as yet no monographs that describe their complicated religious characteristics with any precision.

The Greek City-states that founded colonies in the east and in the west were accustomed to export their own deities and heroes at the same time. This immediately explains the differences between the religious cults in the various Greek cities, whose inhabitants because of their worship of the Greek gods felt themselves to be Greeks amid foreigners. The foreign cults were indeed adopted but their minor shrines usually gave way very soon to imposing Greek temples. In hellenistic times however the Greeks going abroad as founders of a new city came no more from an especial City-state but from the whole Greek nation. Moreover the Greek no longer encountered only uncivilized peoples but he now went to countries with a high civilization of their own, which was often more ancient than that of the Greeks. Together with these peoples they founded the many new cities of the *Diadochi*, and these cities must from the very beginning have had a more mixed and less purely-hellenic character, which in the religious sphere finds its expression in the cult of Tyche as goddess of the new City and link between the various creeds. The Greeks (and Macedonians) now came into contact with certain great, traditional oriental deities, who had such individual and impressive cults, that they could not be forced to yield any ground to the gods of the Greeks. One therefore sees that e.g. in Egypt the Greeks worshipped their own deities but at the same time did not neglect the Egyptian gods. It seems that the Greeks were less inclined to impose their own ideas on other peoples, and were more adaptable than the Romans, who immediately built new Capitols for the Roman triad everywhere.

As a result of international diplomatic relations, trade, and culture, as well as the racial mixture and the army, the oriental cults had excellent opportunities to start their spread over the hellenistic world. The decisive period was hellenism I during which some of these cults became officially accepted in Greece and Rome (Isis, Cybele, Dea Syria), the new cult of Serapis arose, and some others seem certainly to have been transformed into mystery-cults (Mithras). Their largest diffusion however took place during hellenism II and especially in the second and third centuries A.D. During the Roman Republic and under the first two Roman Emperors religious politics were uncertain, sometimes hostile; but from Caligula, Claudius, and Nero on the eastern cults soon demolished the walls of the old *pomerium*.

What then finally was happening in the hellenistic beliefs? We have
just seen that old traditional cults did not disappear, since they were
representative of a race, a nation or a state. Nor did magic or astrology
disappear. Both of them always flourished in Antiquity not only in the
country on the peasant's farm, and among simple people of the larger
cities, but also in the villas of the upper classes. What indeed took
place, just as in modern times, was that an ever-increasing number of
people were able to make acquaintance with foreign beliefs hitherto
unknown, with new philosophies and forms of knowledge. During
such periods of rapid evolution the human mind is inclined to doubt
much that seemed established forever; old traditions are thrown overboard, sometimes too quickly; the new, attractive as it always is, is
preferred to the old. Others conclude a treaty between the old and
new. These gradations can also be seen in hellenistic religion. The
assimilation of various deities (such as is found in the Isis' hymns, and
in Lucian's the Dea Syria) led to unification; the worship of the many
solar gods led finally to henotheism; the eastern and later the western
monarchs were emanations of gods, mostly of solar gods, hence they
too found their worshippers; the choice of deities was larger and
since ancient man was not bound by dogma his choice was also much
more free; the individual had the opportunity to worship his personal
deities outside his own country also. This means that besides the
more-or-less official cults supervised by the city or state priests, there
was much more place for a personal deity and for those deities whose
cults were of more restricted appeal. Indeed all the mighty gods of
Greece, Egypt, Asia, Gaul, and Germany who seemed only to notice
mankind when worshipped by the whole people, now began to lose
their hold on people's minds. There were however other deities who
by a dream or some other sign personally called their own devotees;
they drew them away from their former evil ways to close personal
contact with their new god (conversion); their life-stories furnished
patterns of behaviour for their worshippers; they were sure guides
through the difficulties of earthly existence, and they also promised a
happy after-life. The most faithful and fervent of their followers were
sometimes privileged to have a vision of the deity, even during their
life-time. They were, in short, individual Saviour gods. For the Greeks
and Romans this meant that many exchanged the majestic temples of
the all too human Olympian gods for the simple chapels of divinities
who were equally human but nevertheless immaculate. These included
those of the old gods, such as Asklepios, Artemis and Heracles, who

had similar characteristics and whose presence was the most felt.

These various cults competed with each other and one after another seemed about to become the State-religion. The cult of Isis and Serapis was particulary succesful, and forced its way into many other sanctuaries. (It is also, of course, possible that these other gods welcomed the Egyptian deities into their temples in order to strengthen their own position and spread their own influence yet further afield.) However all these attempts, including those of the Emperors, to create a single imperial cult from those of the whole empire shipwrecked on the unwillingness of the Roman to accept something that was so different from his ancestral traditions (Caesar, Antony, Caligula, Nero, Heliogabalus and Aurelian), and it was not until Constantine that one religion was able to unite the East and West.

II. HISTORICAL DEVELOPMENT

Through their contacts with the East the Greeks became acquainted with the oriental gods long before the beginning of hellenism I, but in Greece itself these deities generally remained foreigners—the Isis sanctuary in the Piraeus known from an inscription of 333-332 B.C. was intended more for Egyptian traders in the Athenian harbour than for the Greeks; the same document authorizes Phoenician traders from Cyprus to build a temple for Aphrodite i.e. for Astarte. There is however one exception made—for Cybele, mother of the gods, whose cult statue in the old *bouleuterion* of the Agora was attributed to either Pheidias or his pupil Agorakritos. A relief from the Piraeus, dated to the fourth century B.C. even shows Agdistis = Cybele together with her favourite, Attis, and this goddess was soon assimilated to Rhea and the mighty mistress of the animals. The impulse to the spread of the oriental cults was given by the *Diadochi* and their successors, and as early as the end of the third and the beginning of the second centuries B.C. the documents start to reveal the conquest of the eastern cults in ever clearer terms.

It is curious that the cult of Men, another Phrygian deity, does not seem to have been known in Attica before hellenism I; on the other hand it must be due to the innate hatred of the Greeks for the Persian peoples that Mithra did not find any acceptance in Greece before the second century A.D.—the Iranian goddess Anaïtis was not accepted at all.

Study of the archaeological documents makes it clear that the cults of Cybele, Isis, and Serapis were the most popular of the eastern cults in the Greek Mediterranean world as early as hellenism I. In hellenism II the Iranian Mithras and the various Syrian Ba'als and their consorts spread their influence over the hellenistic world, but with the difference that this group of gods seems to have been largely restricted to the west while the Egyptian and Phrygian cults continued to be popular also in the eastern provinces of the Roman Empire.

As for the Egyptian cults—Isis was, like Cybele, one of the easiest foreign deities for the Greeks to accept; but this did not mean that the Greeks were willing to adopt the Egyptian veneration for holy animals. This created a difficulty, since the deified Osiris was represented by the bull, Apis! And so Ptolemy I Soter decided to create a new god, by fusing Osiris and Apis to form Serapis. The introduction of this new deity is known from various traditions mentioned in Tacitus (*Hist.*, IV, 83) and Plutarch (*De Iside et Osiride*, 28). The new cult was a political, religious, and artistic reform. Modern scholars like P. Fraser do not consider that the statue and the cult of Serapis originally came from Sinope on the Black Sea, from Babylon, or from Seleucia in Syria, but are of the opinion that it arose at Memphis and found its centre in Alexandria, where a large temple was built in his honour. The last statue of the Greek artist Bryaxis was the embodiment of this new conception of the deity in precious metals. The god was portrayed seated on a throne and his bearded face was similar to those of Zeus, Hades, and Asclepius. As a fertility-god he wore on his head a *modius* or *kalathos* adorned with olive-branches and sometimes filled with fruit. In his left hand he held a sceptre (Zeus) and at his right hand-side was seated three-headed Cerberus of the Underworld. Later on many other artistic types of the god (standing and reclining figures; arising together with Isis from snakes etc.) are to be found. Tradition agrees that Ptolemy was advised on the formation of the cult by two religious scholars: the Egyptian Manetho, high priest in Heliopolis, and the Greek Timotheus, high priest in Eleusis, known as theologian of the cult of Demeter and Cybele.

Many details of the story are still obscure, but, the evidence shows that the new cult under the protection of the first Ptolemies and favoured, as it was, by the aristocratic families, was soon spread throughout the Greek world by traders and the army. One also notices that in the earlier representations of the divine couple Serapis is a more important figure than Isis. In the later mystery-cult, however, as we know it from the classical authors, Isis is the principal Egyptian deity. But the spread of the worship of Isis and Serapis in the West was not to be as easy. From the excavations of the Iseum at Pompeii it appears that here the cult must have been introduced as early as the second century B.C., and an inscription from Puteoli proves the existence of a Serapeum here in 105 B.C. But when Isis, advancing from Campania tried to conquer the Capitol, the Senate took sharp measures. The position of her cult was for the next few years influenced by Roman politics and national feelings—Augustus and Tiberius who favoured the official and traditional Roman cult were especially hostile to the Isiac devotees, who were regarded as traitors and followers of Cleopatra. But from Caligula onwards the Egyptian cult began to flourish over the whole empire. Isis appears in the imperial palace on the Palatine, and the first large Iseum and Serapeum is built on the Campus Martius, to be followed by a second on the Quirinal during the reign of Caracalla (211-217). Serapis and Isis now entered the temples of other oriental deities (Jupiter Dolichenus, Mithras) also, and were influenced but not superseded by them, as is proved for the end of the fourth century when the Egyptian deities (A. Älföldi) appear on coins as a medium of propaganda for the aristocratic pagan party against victorious Christendom.

The emperor Julian (*Or.*, VIII [V], 159) mentions that according to the tradition it was on the instigation of the Delphic oracle that the Athenians built the temple of Cybele; the Metroon at Thebes is supposed to have had the same origin (*schol. ad Pind., Pyth.*, III, 137). This would mean that the cult of the Mother of the gods was accorded official recognition. When the Roman Senate and the aristocratic families introduced the cult into Rome about two hundred years later (204 B.C.), they did this in an official manner also, only taking the step after having consulted the Sybilline books and the Pythian oracle. This goddess was already a well-known personality to the Greeks. In her statues and cult Greek traits superseded the oriental ones, and the Phrygian Attis was consequently pushed into the background. For the Romans however, the goddess was a Prygian deity with a wild, ecstatic cult and she came, just as theyselves did, from Troy. The goddess who was to bring victory over Hannibal was finally home; hence her temple was built on the Palatine next to the place where the original Roman huts dating from the eighth century B.C. (the foundation of the city) have been found. And so the Trojan cult was finally accepted inside the *pomerium*; in her honour official feasts were instituted, but it seems that certain asiatic rites especially connected with Attis were limited to the Palatine only.

P. Romanelli did indeed find terracotta figurines of Attis dating from the Republican period during his excavations of the temple of the Magna Mater on the Germalus, but, on the other hand, on the coins of the Republican age Cybele is represented alone. We know from Joh. Lydus (*De Mensibus* IV, 59), a byzantine author of the sixth century A.D., that the emperor Claudius reorganized the cycle of feasts in honour of Cybele during the month of March. He is supposed to have instituted on the 22th of March the feast of *Arbor intrat* (see below), at which the collegium of the *dendrophori* (tree-bearers) brought a pine-tree to the Palatine. J. Carcopino consequently concluded that the cult of Attis, connected with the pine-tree, had also gained a measure of official recognition; P. Lambrechts is however of the opinion that the veneration of Attis as a god does not appear before the middle of the second century A.D. But the Belgian scholar does nevertheless lay stress on an evolution in ideas about the nature of Attis, and he does not accept the theory that the god is one of the dying and resurrecting deities of the orient. In any case it is clear that from the first century A.D. Attis appears more and more on the monuments and that in the wall-paintings at Pompeii he is even represented alone without the goddess. From the second century A.-D., and especially during the period of Antoninus Pius, the cult of Cybele and Attis became very important in Ostia, were a special sanctuary was built in honour of each of them.

The first *taurobolium* and *criobolium* inscriptions (see p. 518) also date from this period, and continue to be in evidence till the end of the fourth century and the last pagan resistance against the new Christian State-religion.

Studying the arrival of Mithraism in the West one finds the same periods in its history. It is possible that Iranian ideas were introduced into Greece in the time of Plato, but the "barbarous" oriental religion was not admitted. On the other hand Fr. Cumont and J. Bidez have shown that it was especially during hellenism I that the priestly-class of the *Magi* or *Magousaioi* were busy transforming the adoration of Mithra into the Mithras-mysteries.

Plutarch (*Vita Pomp.*, 24) tells us that the Romans came into contact with Mithras through Cilician pirates who after their defeat by Pompey the Great were settled in Italy. Once again, just as in the history of the cults of the Egyptian Isis and the Phrygian Attis, the first century

B.C. seems to have been the period in which this oriental cult with its oriental rites was waiting before the City gates to receive official acknowledgement from the Senate. Once again the successors of Augustus and Tiberius were its first promotors. In the case of Mithras it is probable that Nero favoured the cult of this Iranian Sun-god, and in A.D. 66 the Armenian king Tiridates I arriving at Rome for his coronation adored Nero as Mithras. Pliny (*Nat. Hist.*, XXX,1,6) mentions that during this visit the oriental king initiated Nero at a magic repast. Not a single representation of Mithras has been found in Pompeii; Statius (about A.D. 80) does however describe a statue of the god. But from the second century A.D. one finds the invincible god in all provinces of the Roman Empire, brought by soldiers and traders.

These followers were not only foreigners but also Roman citizens from among the highest ranks, and in the second century the god even penetrated into the Imperial palace on the Palatine. These few scattered indications together with the archaeological documentation are almost all we have on which to base our knowledge of Mithraism— one is, however, able to follow the attempt of the Mithraists to make their religion the official State-cult, in which the secret mysteries had nevertheless to be reserved for an exclusive community. At the beginning of the third century A.D. one notices the tendency, favoured by the Severan house, towards a henotheistic belief in one general Sun-god who would satisfy the common religious aspirations and who could unify the most various peoples of the Empire. This impulse came from the Syrian Ba'als. The strength of these gods did not subsist in their myths (see below) but in their developing from weather gods and local protectors of the City into universal Sun-gods. The Ba'al from Doliche (*Jupiter Dolichenus*) was thus able to conquer Rome (sanctuaries on the Aventine and Esquiline) and many of the Roman provinces; the Ba'al of Syrian Heliopolis (Ba'albek), i.e. Jupiter Heliopolitanus, found a residence in the capital (on the Janiculum) and some other cities and countries; for the Ba'al of Hierapolis (Bambyce) and his consort Atargatis a temple was built in Trans Tiberim. None of these Ba'als, however, was able to become the universally recognized Sun-god of the Empire; they were all overshadowed by Mithras and the Egyptian and Phrygian deities, but the cult of many of them did not spread in the West until the Antonine or the Severan periods. It is difficult to disentangle the web of mutual influence that characterizes the history of the oriental religions in the second and third centu-

ries A.D. Malakbel (Sun-god) and Aglibol (Moon) found little acceptance in the West. The Iranian Mithra, also known in Syria, suffered under the severe handicap that women were not admitted as members of his cult. Another disadvantage, which however does not seem
to have influenced the Romans to the same extent as the Greeks, was
that his origin lay in a hostile country. But certainly it was too early
when Heliogabalus (218-222), a young high-priest of the Ba'al of
Emesa and now Emperor brought the holy black stone to Rome. He
made the same mistake as Caesar did when he presented Cleopatra-
Isis to the Roman people. The appropriate time did not come before
the end of the third century when the Emperor Aurelian after his
victory over Queen Zenobia built a temple for the invincible Sun-god
from Emesa on the slope of the Quirinal-hill. From this time on the
Syrian god gradually became more romanised, thus becoming a single
Roman State-god. The various efforts to create one State-religion led
in the fourth century to the last and final struggle between the competing cults which ended in the victory of Christianity.

III. The Conception of the Deity

In classical Greek religion the deities lived on Olympus far removed
from mankind, where they were governed by Zeus who entrusted
special powers to each of them. Their immortality created an immense
gap between their world and that of men. Mortals realized their complete dependence on the almighty gods, to whom they were bound
to pray and bring offerings. The divinities came into contact with
mortals either to help or to punish them. The cosmos was therefore
divided into a happy and an unhappy part. The denizens of the first
almost without exception knew only pleasures and passions, which
were, as it happens, those of this world also but to mankind were
reserved hard daily labour, hunger, and illness, which after a short
period led to death. Hence the Greek sought immortality in famous
deeds; though in the underworld he would still, at any rate, live on in
men's memories. Yet, there were some gods and heroes who had experienced grief, like man, and had pity on him more than the others:
Demeter who lost her daughter and after many wanderings gave grain
to the world; Dionysus who during his wanderings brought wine and
the divine ecstasy that makes man forget his labours (λυσίπονος);
Asclepius who appeared in dreams and restored the sick to health;

and Heracles and Odysseus, the latter because he as a mortal equalled the immortals.

In hellenistic times man sought those gods who seemed to be seeking him. In his misfortune he sought gods who were able to bring good fortune—no longer good fortune due to chance but that which was acquired by personal merit. A man had to be able to follow the divine example, otherwise he would be excluded from salvation; he must have complete trust and faith in the deity, who, in his turn, demanded service as if from a slave or soldier, certain ethical standards, and, from the intellectual, the knowledge necessary to enter into closer contact. And so religious feelings had a tendency to change from materialistic into spiritual; the material offerings which mostly meant *do ut des* were transformed into *impera ut implorem* i.e. the deity commanded no longer primarily material but rather spiritual offerings, and if man was minded to fulfill these commands, the deity was prepared to listen to the requests of his devotee. These devotees organized themselves more and more into closed societies, where they felt at home and found other like-minded persons willing to help each other, even as their god was prepared to save them all.

It should be noted that it was in the fourth century B.C. that the Asclepius-cult at Epidaurus, which had existed from the sixth century, found its greatest period of growth. In the city itself the large temple, the theatre, and the rooms for "incubation" all date from this period; Cos, Pergamum and many other centres with their medical faculties also flourished at this time; and in 293 B.C. this god arrived in Rome. The physician, though in service of the god, worked in a rational manner; the god himself in an irrational way. He was the miraculous god who required complete faith of his patients, so that one of his devotees cried out: "Do not admire the greatness of the offering, but the might of the god." The god himself in a dream or vision personally gave advice to the patient about the cure for his sickness. There is even a mystery cult connected with this god, which we know through the physician Thessalus (first century A.D.), to whom the god appeared in the sanctuary at Thebes, after his preparation by the priests and a period of fasting, and revealed his divine doctrine.

Serapis was also a god of healing as may be seen from the marble and terracotta votive-gifts representing feet and eyes which are found in the temples of both deities. But literary and archaeological documentation lay stress rather on his Zeus-Hades character. Like Zeus he must therefore have been an universal god, reigning over the upperworld. Like so many other deities, he was invoked as ὕψιστος, a possible sign of influence from Judaism, like the epithet κύριος. With other hellenistic gods he had in common the titles of βασιλεύς and σωτήρ which clearly connect him directly with the Egyptian royal house. To Zeus owes his title μέγας, and the formal εἷς θεός to his identification with Helios-Sol. In the same way he was introduced into the cults of Mithras (hence the adjective *invictus*) and of the Syrian Jupiter Dolichenus. From Hades, as a governor of the Lower World, he took his severe look, his companion Cerberus, and his rule over fertility, which is expressed by either a *modius* on his head or a *cornucopia* in his left hand.

Isis, who in hellenistic times nearly always figures together with Serapis, also received more and more might and eventually became a pantheistic goddess, as is clear from the hymns in her honour as well as the artistic representations. As the consort of Osiris-Serapis she is the heavenly queen (*regina*), who governs the elements, the stars and planets. No wonder that she is also able to enter the underworld and help her true devotees. Thus until the end of the fourth century A.D. her powers over the land and the corn, over the sea and the corn traffic, are praised and serve as propaganda for the anti-Christian party. She was in particular identified with the Moon-goddess Selene, with the Eleusinian Demeter, and with Tyche. In all these identifications her relationship with the vegetative life in nature remained important. In the second place she was the representative of female nature. In distress she sought the dismembered Osiris and assisted him to new life; in the same way she will help as a δώτειρα her devotees in the after-life. She is the divine mother of Horus-Harpocrates and it is this aspect of her nature that is stressed in the many representations in which she is suckling her child. Like Cybele she helps women in childbirth and in bringing up a baby. She is like Aphrodite/Venus a particularly womanly goddess and she can therefore be connected with the Syrian Atargatis and Phoenician Astarte.

What has been said about Isis also applies in great part to Cybele. There is however one great difference: Isis is never the mighty and often harsh mistress of the animals, like Cybele with her lions. In a more general way one might say that basically Isis represents the soft and tender feelings in woman's life and Osiris the severe and even hard features. However much she was tortured by the misfortunes of Osiris, nevertheless she remained the ideal wife who lived only for her husband, and will therefore help all other women in distress. She is also the example of a mother who brings up her child to revenge his father. Cybele's story is however quite different. In one tradition Attis is her child, though born in a most miraculous way; usually however he is regarded as her lover, from whom she forever asks eternal love such as Artemis did of Hippolytus. Isis when punishing Seth-Typhon through her son Horus was not able to complete her revenge; Attis on the other hand was driven insane by the goddess after his unfaithfullness and was tormented by her as long as she herself, after her own frenzy, had to kneel before mighty Zeus.

After a long period of development this large gap between the character of the two goddesses gradually narrowed. Cybele then became just such a deity as Juno-Demeter-Venus; she was the mother of life on earth, protector of cities like Tyche, helper of women like Juno and Venus. But those ecstatic and wild asiatic traits, which one also sees in the Dionysiac cult and which play an essential role in her character, never disappeared.

In studying the so-called syncretistic trend in the conception of the male and female deities in general one notices that the original traits often partly fade away; and that not every example of syncretism follows the same course; nor is it always clear how these mutual interchanges precisely took place. But, as we have said, each divinity (especially during hellenism II) seems to have tried to attract as many powers as possible in order to become the universal deity of the Roman Empire. This tendency is clearly to be seen in the epithet *invictus* or *invicta*, which is in fact properly to be applied only to the Syrian Ba'als and to Mithras. The Ba'als were weather gods, protectors of cities and their citizens to whom they brought fertility. They wield the thunderbolt, the lightning, and a sceptre; often they have a warlike appearance. They were soon assimilated to Zeus and Jupiter, but without entirely loosing their originally nature and the masks of their home-countries, where they had already become solar deities. The Iranian Mithras on his arrival in the West was a solar deity too. But among the other oriental deities he has a special place, because his person and his myth have such a strong spiritualty. He is a famous warrior, but in the service of Good and Light against Evil and Darkness; he is guardian of oaths and truth; his battles, in which he is naturally victorious, are not waged only for material welfare but also for ideals. His creation of vegetative life by slaying the bull means at the same time a victory over his own person, since it was against his will that he fulfilled the commandment of the gods. As Sun-god he sees every action of mankind, and consequently he becomes god of justice, in this capacity he also takes part in the Last Judgement.

IV. Worship

A. *Myth*

Apart from philosophical and astrological speculations about the deities and heroes, there are some Greek and rather more oriental divinities whose myth led to a secret doctrine, only accessible to those who had been initiated into the cult and had become true followers. These cults are therefore referred to as the mystery or mysteriosophical cults. In Greece itself the Eleusinian and Dionysian cults were already in existence before our period, but they now began to flourish and developed in the whole Mediterranean world. The cult of Demeter and Persephone was found everywhere that Greeks settled, but the real mystery cult for both goddesses was restricted to Eleusis, and so those who wished to come into the closest contact with these mysteries had to go to the city of the corn-ear whether they were hellenistic kings or Roman emperors. The Dionysiac mysteries however were accessible in many other places also—even in a little village such as Pompeii (Villa dei Misteri). The myths of both Demeter and Dionysus are very old, and both are related to the wonder of the yearly growth of the corn and the vine. This rise of food and drink from the earth after the winter was ascribed to these powerful divinities and became for the initiates a symbol of their own death and resurrection. The vegetation gods of the east represent the same pattern, but each of them has his own myth, sometimes with differences varying with country and time. Of these eastern cults those of Egypt (Isis and Serapis) were the most favoured in Greece but they never overshadowed the native Greek mysteries. During hellenism II all the mystery cults spread over the Roman Empire; yet it is remarkable that the cult of Mithras was practised in Greece by the Romans only. This shows that the Greek religion was able to satisfy individual religious feelings in the hellenistic age also.

Indeed Demeter, who sought her daughter and after much terrible wandering found her again, is very like the Egyptian Isis and Phrygian Cybele. All three belong to the category of mother-goddesses, and all three, on account of their own sorrowful adventures, are deeply moved by the lot of humanity and have therefore become goddesses helpful to mankind.

In archaeological sources Demeter and Isis are sometimes represented together in the same relief, and in literary sources their myths have some close affinities—at any rate in the story as told by Plutarch, *De Iside et Osiride* (second cent. A.D.):

Osiris, king and god, brought the Egyptian people the "fruits of cultivation, by giving them laws, and by teaching them to honour the gods". His sisters were Isis and Nephthys, and his brother was Typhon or Seth. Osiris married Isis. Typhon contrived a treacherous plot and made a beautiful chest of the same size as Osiris' body. During a feast he promised to present the chest to whoever fitted into it exactly, and when Osiris got into it, Typhon and his companions slammed down the lid, carried the chest to the river and sent it on its way to the sea. Isis wandered everywhere looking for her husband. After a time she learnt that the chest had been cast up by the sea near the land of Byblus and that the waves had gently set it down in the midst of a clump heather (ἐρείκη). And now follows a scene which immediately reminds one of Demeter, who was accepted in the house of King Celeus in Eleusis and who nursed the child Triptolemos there in order to make him immortal. In the same way Isis arrived at Byblus "and sat down by a spring, all dejection and tears; she enchanged no word with anybody, save only that she welcomed the queen's maidservants and treated them with great amiability. She thus became so intimate with the queen that the queen made her the nurse of her baby. She nursed the child by giving it her finger to suck instead of her breast, and in the night she would burn away the mortal portions of its body. The queen, who had been watching, when she saw her baby on fire, gave forth a loud cry and thus deprived it of immortality." Isis now removed the wood of the heather (ἐρείκη) (used as a pillar in the king's palace) and found the chest with Osiris' body. She then went off to her son Horus and hid the chest in a place well out of the way; but Typhon found it and recognizing the body divided it into fourteen parts and scattered them, each in a different place. According to tradition the result of Osiris' dismemberment was that there were many so-called tombs of Osiris in Egypt, for Isis held a funeral for each part where she found it. Later Osiris came to Horus from the other world and exercised and trained him for the battle with Typhon. This battle lasted many days and Horus prevailed. Typhon was overcome in two other battles also. Osiris consorted with Isis after his death, and she became the mother of Harpocrates, untimely born and weak in his lower limbs. It was also said that Osiris was buried at Memphis, where his incarnation the Apis-bull was worshipped by the Egyptians.

Like Persephone Osiris also has two realms, i.e. that of the Nether and that of the Upper worlds, in both of which he is life-giving. Osiris in his myth is the consort of Isis; in the myth of Cybele however Attis is only her completely devoted lover. This Asiatic goddess worshipped especially in Phrygia was originally also the mother of all that lives and exists in nature. Demeter is the goddess of the corn-ear and of vegetation. Cybele is in the first place mighty mistress of the animals, and she is therefore similar to some other Asiatic goddesses connected with the lion, the king of animals. The myth of her love for Attis is told both by Pausanias (second century A.D.) and Arnobius, a Christian author (third century A.D.). The myth related by them is the official version such as was told in Pessinus, the centre of the Phrygian cult (the main traits of the story are reflected in the artistic representations):

An enormous rock named Agdus in Phrygia took the form of the great Mother. While she slept Zeus tried to make love to her, but the goddess resisted and in the ensuing struggle Zeus lost his seed. From the rock (= the goddess) a wild bisexual being by the name of Agdistis was born. The gods were anxious and arranged to tame him. Liber or Bacchus mixed the water in the spring from which Agdistis usually drank with wine. When he had sunk into deep sleep, Bacchus tied his virile parts to a tree, with the result that on awakening he deprived himself of his virility. From the blood that he shed a pomegranate or almond tree sprang up and eventually bore fruit. Nana, the daughter of the king of the river Sangarius, took its fruit and put it in her lap; she then became pregnant and after many difficulties, in which the goddess Cybele was her helper, gave birth to a son, Attis. He was exposed by Sangarius, but was found and nourished by a goat. He grew up and became a shepherd. He was so handsome that the mother of the gods herself fell in love with him, and declared him her favourite on the condition that he accepted the favours of his divine protectress only. But fate induced Attis to allow himself to be seduced by a water-nymph, and Cybele took revenge. She drove Attis insane and he emasculated himself under a tree on the banks of the river Gallus. From his blood a spring burst fourth. Some authors say that Attis was changed into a pine tree and in this way never really died, but others relate that he died, and that his grave was to be seen at Pessinus. The archaeological sources show his emasculation, some of them suggesting that he is just about to awake (cf. Plutarch, De Iside et Osiride, 69) one relief shows him already dead. But the goddess felt compassion for Attis and she asked—so Arnobius tells us (V,7;V,14)—Jupiter to bring her lover back to life. But Attis was not permitted to revive completely. Only his little finger will always be in motion and his hair will grow for ever. But from Plutarch (*De Iside et Osiride*, 69) and some of the monuments one can deduce that there was also a tradition that the Phrygian god slept during the winter and awakened in the summer. In any case it is clear from the myth that the passion of Cybele for Attis was closely related to nature, of which the goddess was mistress.

In the myth of the Iranian Mithras however the main god is the creator (δημιουργός) of order in nature. He is better known from the arachaeological monuments of the Roman period than from the classical authors. After the creation of the world, Saturn or Kronos handed his powers over to his successor Jupiter, who is identified with the Iranian Ahura Mazda. This god of light, representing life and good, is engaged in an eternal battle with the might of darkness, representing evil and death. In this war Mithras is the faithful helper of Ahura Mazda or Ohrmuzd. He was born from a rock (*petra genetrix*), a symbol of the celestial vault. At birth he was already provided with bow, quiver, and dagger, which announce his future deeds. He is often represented in a forest with the bow and arrows like a Persian king at a hunt. Sometimes he shoots his arrows into a rock (= heaven) or into the clouds from which water miraculously pours—an eternal spring (*fons perennis*), or nectar. Mithras' most famous deed was the sacrifice of the bull. The sequence of events can be followed in the monuments. At first we see the god hunting the bull, who is quietly grazing in the meadows; after many struggles he finally masters the animal and carries him triumphantly on his shoulders to a grotto (*transitus dei*). In the grotto, against his will and at the command of the supreme god, he kills the bull. From the blood of the dying animal new vegetation arised in the form of corn-ears. After this *tauroktonos* scene there is a series which tells of his relationship with the Sun-god. Mithras concludes a treaty with Sol, who, apparently, first gave him the command of Jupiter (Ahura Mazda) to kill the bull. Then Sol is seen kneeling before the Iranian god who confers the accolade on him. During a sacred repast they eat the meat of the slaughtered bull and drink his blood. At the end of his earthly life Mithras accends to heaven with Sol in a chariot.

B. *Doctrine and Cult*

About the doctrine flowing from these various myths we know almost nothing, except in the case of Mithraism. The mystery cults were secret, and these secrets were mostly handed over (*tradere*) from father to son or by the priests to the initiate. Those who had knowledge of the cult were generally wise old men who were willing to expound their wisdom only after a certain time of preparation. In Mithraism the Magi or the *patres* of the community are sometimes represented with their attributes (ring, staff, and scroll) which assimilate them to philosophers (hence the title *magister sacrorum*). The priest at Memphis, who brought Thessalus (see p. 505) his vision of Asclepius, was old and wise and possessed the art of lecanomancy. The priest Mithra, who in Apuleius' book initiates Lucius into the cult of Isis, consults the holy books before doing so; in the Dionysus-villa at Pompeii one also sees the holy book. But it seems that this sacred literature contained more about the ceremonies, rites, and *formulae* than about the doctrine, which as in most religions of Antiquity, must have been undogmatic. According to Aristotle, *Metaphys.*, A 2 p. 982b 12ff, wondering about things brings man to both philosophy and religion. Consequently various philosophical systems influenced religion; astronomical and astrological theories are common to both of them. Just as in magic, the correct rites have to be followed in order to receive the favours of the deity. The divinity asks complete obediance and faith (*servus; militia*); in the rites one follows the divine example and each member of the community plays his prescribed role in the repetition of this sacred drama, which must end in a psychological climax. In order to exclude the *profanum vulgus*, one was generally bound by an holy oath (*sacramentum*); in this way the members (*socii; sodales*) were bound still more closely together in their community. Sometimes one is able through the ancient sources, either literary or archaeological, to assist at the sacred liturgy and holy services, such as initiation, and purification, the processions the hymns and meals. And so there was for every cult an occasionally large priestly class with various ranks and their assistants.

a. In Mithraism the god was conceived as the defender of righteousness and a victorious leader. The titles which his followers gave to him in their dedications express their own expectations clearly. He was the sun-god, born on the 25th of December, which is called the *natalis dei invicti*. Often in his company are Cautes with upraised torch and Cautopates with his flaming torch downwards. Both are *hypostases* of Mithras himself, who in this way is present the whole day. The god must especially be adored between morning and evening, and also on the 16th of every month. He therefore is also called μεσίτης as the "mediator" between the supreme god and man. His divine deeds are recorded in the cult—especially his birth, the water-miracle, the slaying of the bull, and his sacred repast.

The new *mystes* was born into the cult like a naked child; he began a new life after having endured many trials. Tertullian, *De Baptismo*, 5 speaks of a purification which is compared with baptism, and elsewhere he tells us that this ceremony promised an *expiationem delictorum*, an expiation of faults. In the Mithraic sanctuaries one often finds a water basin, and the sanctuaries themselves are sometimes situated near a river or spring (Mithras' birth took place near a spring (*fons perennis*)). On the other hand two lines of a hymn in the Sa Prisca Mithraeum on the Aventine record that the water coming forth from the rock into which Mithras shot his arrows was the same as nectar or the beverage of immortality.

The adepts of the Sun god venerated the four elements which are often represented on the monuments by the symbolic group of bird, snake, vessel, and lion. It is probable that the initiates, just as in the Isiac mysteries, went in a symbolic way through *omnia elementa*. Moreover, as Sun god and *kosmokrator*, Mithras reigned over the seven planets and the twelve signs of the zodiac. Some of the ceremonies are therefore to be connected with both elements and planets. Mithras' heroic deeds before killing the bull and his *transitus* (see p. 511) are also reflected in the cult: his followers carried a burden on their shoulders as Mithras himself once carried the bull and performed the divine task (*maxima divum*). Like the raven that summoned Mithras to slay the bull, an initiate with the name of *corax* and sometimes wearing a raven's mask fulfilled the task of herald (*ceryx*) and assistant. The scene of the bull-slaying is intimately connected with that of the sacred meal. On some large reliefs, especially those from the Rhine countries, these two scenes are represented one on the obverse and the other on the reverse. The importance of the sacrifice of the bull lies not only in the creation of plantlife, but also in the fact that the meat and blood of the animal contain the substance of eternity. In other monuments we see Mithras and Sol, his companion, before they ascend to heaven. They are reclining at a table, sometimes covered with the bull's skin; in the Mithraic community the followers assisted at a meal consisting of either the meat and blood or their substitutes bread and wine. According to Tertullian, *De praescr.haer.*, 40, this sacred meal was a devilish imitation of the Eucharist and was supposed to give eternal life.

A line of verse in the Sa Prisca Mithraeum gives clear expression to this conception: *Et nos servasti eternali sanguine fuso*—And You saved us by means of this eternal blood You shed. In another line of verse the ideas of rebirth and recreation are combined. To those who participated in the meal immortality was given and after death their souls ascended to the eternal light just as Sol and Mithras went in the chariot up into heaven.

The archaeological discoveries (Sa Prisca Mithraeum at Rome; Ostia) make it possible for us to assist at the processions held in the sanctuary. In two of them the bull has a prominent place. He will be slain not only as an offering in the god's honour but also in order to re-enact the most glorious deed of Mithras. In one case the bull forms part of a *suovetaurilia* (pig, sheep, and bull) offering made officially on the occasion of the enlargement of the underground temple (Rome). Some initiates of higher rank are carrying a large vessel, a glass dish with bread, candlesticks, palmleaves, and a cock. Two other processions represent the seven grades of the initiated with their emblems; the latter are also known from mosaics at Ostia. Each of them is placed under the special protection of one of the planets. The arrangement is as follows:

1) corax	raven	Mercury	magic staff and cup
2) nymphus	bride	Venus	torch, lamp and diadem
3) miles	soldier	Mars	helmet, bag and lance
4) leo	lion	Jupiter	fire-shovel, rattle, thunderbolt
5) perses	persian	Luna	sickle, scythe and crescent
6) heliodromus	courier of the Sun	Sol	whip, torch and radiate halo
7) pater	father	Saturnus	ring, staff, phrygian cap, sickle

Each grade brings the devotee into closer contact with Mithras himself and the initiates of the highest are the representatives of the god on earth. The three lower grades are attendants, and the four higher ones are the real participants. In the various grades Mithras' deeds are reflected, as is clear from the *corax*, the *miles* (cf. *transitus dei*), the *heliodromus* (Sol): they are probably also connected with the elements: *corax* (air); *nymphus* (water); *miles* (earth); *leo* (fire). A mosaic floor in one of the Ostian sanctuaries shows the seven planetary spheres. As has been rightly noted these symbolize the Mithraic doctrine of the soul (Origenes, *contra Celsum*, VI,22). The soul, coming from the heavenly light into man's body, passes through the seven spheres and receives various qualities from each of the planets; the soul delivered from the body by death passes once again through the spheres of the planets and lays down her qualities one by one before returning to the eternal light. Already during his life the *mystes* of Mithras is preparing himself for this journey to heaven by taking part in the sacred cult. It is likely that each time he entered a higher grade he had to undergo a special initiation and consecration. According to Tertullian the *miles* was branded with a sign on his forehead, and when he was being initiated in the cave, a wreath offered to him on the point of his sword and then placed on his head must be pushed off the head with the flat of his hand, and then laid on his shoulder with the words that Mithras alone was his wreath. Porphyry on the other hand gives the following details about the initiation of the lion: those who are being initiated as lions have honey instead of water poured over their heads to cleanse them, so that their hands are undefiled by evil, crime, or other contamination, as becomes an initiate. (This is a fitting absolution that is administered to them, since water, the usual cleansing agent, is the enemy of fire, the great purifier). And they also cleanse his tongue from sin with honey.

In this context three lines of verse in the Sa Prisca Mithraeum are interesting:

1) *Nama leonibus novis et multis annis* = "hail to the lions for many and new years." This is probably an acclamation to the lions after their elevation.

2) *Accipe thuricremos pater accipe sancte leones | per quos thuradamus per quos consumimur ipsi* = "receive, o holy Father, receive the incense-burning lions, through whom we offer the incense, through whom we ourselves are consumed." The last words may refer to the Stoic belief in the final conflagration of the kosmos, which was also accepted in the mithraic mysteries, as is clear from a Sol-Phaeton scene in the mithraeum at Dieburg in Germany. Something must be said about the adoration of the Eternal Time-god, many representations of whom have been found in the sanctuaries. Some "lions" during the ceremonies apparently wore a lion's mask, and this is connected with the fact that the Mithraic Time-god is given the head of a ravenous lion (symbol of fire). His body is entwined by a snake that is sometimes decorated with the signs of the zodiac. In his figure are combined the Iranian Zrvan akarana (infinite time), Kronos-Chronos and Saturn; and in one inscription such a statue of Aioon is dedicated to Ahriman, the god of Evil. He sometimes takes the form of a young god and is identified with Mithras himself, but other statues show him as terrible and omnipotent.

b. When the cult of Cybele came to Rome, a temple was built on the Palatine. This sanctuary is known through the excavations of P. Romanelli and a representation on the *Ara Pietatis* of Claudius (41-54 A.D.). It appears that the building, which was burnt down and restored several times, was relatively small and existed till into the fifth century A.D. The façade of the temple had six columns and a pediment decorated in its centre with a throne on which Cybele's mural crown was visible. Romanelli found many terracotta figurines of Attis dating from the Republican period of the temple. Statues were erected of Cybele herself and of the priestess Claudia Quinta, who in 204 B.C. brought the ship with the goddess' statue from Ostia to Rome. Before the sanctuary was a small theatre where dramatic performances were held during the feast of the Megalensia (see below). At the foot of the Palatine is the *circus maximus* with which the victorious goddess of life and death was also connected, and on the *spina* of which she was represented riding a lion. Another sanctuary dedicated to Cybele was situated on the Vatican hill near the circus of Nero; from this so-called *Phrygianum* many taurobolium inscriptions of later date (mostly fourth century A.D.) are known (see below). Her temple precinct at Ostia, which also contained a separate building for Attis and several rooms for the *collegia*, dates from the second century A.D. This vast *campus* has yielded many statues, reliefs, and dedications. The cult flourished especially in southern Gaul with Lyon as centre. But generally speaking these sanctuaries scattered throughout the Empire do not reveal many details about the cult, which had primarily an official character. This is also clear from the feasts held in March and April.

Our main source for the feasts of March is a calendar from 354 A.D. which gives them in the following order:

15th of March	*Canna intrat*
22th of March	*Arbor intrat*
24th of March	*Sanguem* or *Sanguis*
25th of March	*Hilaria*
26th of March	*Requietio*
27th of March	*Lavatio*
28th of March	*Initium Caiani*

From other sources one is able to deduce that the emperors Claudius and Antoninus Pius reorganised both cult and feasts so that more attention was paid to Attis. The ceremony of the "entry of the reed" was performed by the *cannephori*, who after having mown the reed brought it in procession to the temple. This reed symbolized either Attis' exposure on the banks of the river Gallus and miraculous preservation or his emasculation, which the emperor Julian called "the sacred and ineffable harvest"(Graillot even supposes an allusion to Attis' love for the nymph (see p. 510). At this festival a sixyear-old bull was offered by the *archigallus* for the fertility of the mountain meadows.

From the 15th onwards there was a period of abstinence. On the 22nd the *dendrophori* carried a tree, almost certainly the pine as a symbol for Attis, to the Palatine. The tree was set up in the temple and the faithful mourned the dead god. On the following day, the feast of the Salii, who were later connected with the Attiscycle, the priests performed their sacred dance with shields and lances like Corybantes (see p. 502). On the "day of blood" the devotees or *galli* scourged and wounded themselves, commemorating Attis' castration, and others emasculated themselves in order to join their ranks. The pine-tree was then carried into the innermost part of the temple where it stayed till the following year. This *katabasis* symbolized Attis' burial and descent to the underworld. The *hilaria* on the following day were, as the name implies, a festive occasion. The 25th of March is according to Macrobius, *Sat.*, I,21,10 the first day of the year in which the sun makes the day longer than the night (*sol diem longiorem nocte protendit*). It is generally accepted that this feast was like that of the preceeding days, in honour of Attis and commemorates his resurrection. However as Lambrechts points out it is possible that the *hilaria* took place before the *lavatio*, only at a late stage in the history of the rite, and do not refer to the joy of the goddess and her followers at Attis' resurrection, but were held to commemorate Cybele's finishing her mourning after bathing in the Almo. Lambrechts has shown that there was an evolution in the successive feasts. It seems clear that there were two main series: the first concerned with Attis and the second with Cybele. The *hilaria* eventually came to form the transition between the end of Attis' passion and the reunion of Cybele with her lover. The day of rest (*requietio*) consequently took on a more definite character. The feasts of Attis (*Attideia*) in the innermost parts of the sanctuary developed into mysteries; the feasts of Cybele remained more public and official, as is attested by the public processions in which representatives of the state also participated. The concluding *initium Caiani* took place in the sanctuary near the Vatican hill next to the Circus of Gaius Caligula. The word *initium* seems to indicate an initiation of some kind, but this all we can say with certainty about the final ceremony.

In the sixth century A.D. Damascius tells us that at Hierapolis in Syria he had a dream that he had become Attis (ὁ Ἄττης γενέαι), and that the Mother of the gods celebrated the feast of the *hilaria* for him— proof that he was saved from the underworld (τὴν ἐξ ᾅδου γεγονυῖαν ἡμῶν σωτηρίαν). The words "I have become an initiate of Attis" (γέγονα μύστης Ἄττεως) are found in a secret formula transmitted by Firmicus Maternus (fourth century A.D.), and in another form by Clement of Alexandria (second century A.D.). Clement (*Protr.*, II,15,3) mentions four "signs of initiation": ἐκ τυμπάνου ἐφαγον, ἐκ κυμβάλου ἔπιον, ἐκερνοφόρησα, ὑπὸ τὸν παστὸν ὑπέδυν, whereas Firmicus, *De err. rel. prof.*, XVIII,1 gives three in two different versions:

1) ἐκ τυμπάνου βέβρωκα, ἐκ κυμβάλου πέπωκα, γέγονα μύστης Ἄττεως,
2) *de tympano manducavi, de cymbalo bibi, et religionis secreta perdidici*

i.e. after learning the secrets of the mysteries I became an initiate of Attis; the variant of Clement one has generally interpreted as an entering into the παστός, the bridal chamber or shrine. It is not clear what was actually eaten and drunk from the sacred instruments, which were commonly used in the cult. The "carrying of the vessel" is an expression which also occurs in the rite of the *taurobolium* (see below). Its meaning is more obvious in that context, but it is unclear whether the *vires* i.e. the testicles or blood of the bull were carried.

After the feasts of Cybele and Attis in March followed the *Megale(n)-sia* (so-called after the Μήτηρ μεγάλη) for Cybele alone. The fourth of April was the anniversary of the goddess' coming to Rome in 204 B.C.; and on the tenth of April the dedication of her temple on the Palatine was celebrated (*dies natalis*). During these festivities the Roman aristocracy, who had introduced the cult into Rome (see p. 501) played a leading role. They organized the sacrifices, the banquet (*lectisternium*) for the whole people, and the mutual meals, and the *ludi megalenses* consisting both of plays in the *circus maximus* (where the goddess had a statue on the *spina*) and of the plays in the theatre before her temple during which her statue was present. Only free-born Romans were admitted to these *ludi*.

The same evolution recognizable in the March feasts is also clear in the ceremony of the *taurobolium*, as R. Duthoy has recently demonstrated. One sometimes finds the term *criobolium* also. The name derives from the custom of catching a bull or ram, and killing (βάλλειν) and eating him in confraternity—both animals being specially associated with virility. (Later on their virile parts played a leading role in the rite. The epigraphical sources mention the ceremony at Rome in the period of A.D. 295 till 390), but in Ostia and the Roman provinces *taurobolium* inscriptions are found dating from as early as A.D. 160.

The best literary source for this rite is also late. The poet Prudentius, writing A.D. 410 *Perist.*, X.1011ff gives an extensive description: the chiefpriest (*summus sacerdos* = *archigallus*) descends into a pit in his robes. A wooden platform is then laid above the pit and through the holes drilled in it the bull's blood streams down upon the priest who even licks it up. When the bull has pulled away, the *archigallus*, horrible to see, shows himself to the people, who adore him from a distance (*adorant eminus*). It is possible that the pit discovered in Ostia next to the sanctuary of Attis was put to such a use. But what is the real meaning of the ceremony? According to Prudentius the priest was venerated like a god, and Firmicus Maternus (*c*. A.D. 350) remarks that the blood pollutes and does not redeem (*polluit sanguis iste, non redimit*) —in contrast with the blood of Christ. This may point to the fourth century belief that one received a spiritual purification from the *taurobolium*. On the other hand, we also find the idea that the blood of the bull or ram renews man's vitality. Two late data from Rome are especially interesting in this respect. A poem from A.D. 394 contains the line *vivere cum speras mundus viginti in annos*, when you hope to live in purity for twenty years. The effect of the *taurobolium* was clearly now restricted to a certain period. In an inscription from A.D. 376 there is even talk of *in aeternum renatus*. But then we are at the end of the evolution; in the case of the earlier inscriptions one can generally establish that the *taurobolia* (which could be held on most various days of the year and which therefore were not connected directly with the feasts in March and April) were performed for the welfare (*pro salute*) of the emperor, the imperial house, the family, the senate, the city, the army, or the fleet.

c. New excavations have shown that the temple of Serapis at Memphis is older than that at Alexandria. At Memphis the site of the Serapeium proper is known to be near the necropolis of the Apis-bulls but has yet to be explored. A long *dromos* decorated with a series of sphinxes from the time of Nectanebo I (378-360 B.C.), the founder of the XXXth Dynasty, leads to the sanctuary. Ptolemy I (306-285) who re-organized the cult and brought it under strong dionysian influence, built a large *hemicylcus* with statues of philisophers and poets; there are also a small separate building for Apis and a *lychnapterion*, a building for the corporation of the *lychnaptae* i.e. for those who provided the lights in the necropolis and in the funerary cult. In the sacred precinct of the temple lived the κάτοχοι who were not allowed to leave the sanctuary of their god; oracles were given and *incubation* was practised. A recently discovered inscription mentions that Ptolemy III "built the temple and the sacred precinct for Ousor-Hapi." This temple, which was destroyed in A.D. 391 was situated on a hill, which according to the late statement of Rufinus was man-made. The area accessible by a flight of one hundred steps is square and of large dimensions. There are also the propylaea and an enormous square portico in which the Serapeum, a temple for Anubis, and a library were built. In the neighbourhood is a necropolis.

The two large Serapeia in Rome, the first constructed in A.D. 38 on the Campus Martius and the other during the reign of Caracalla on the Quirinal, are well-known. The temple of Caligula was dedicated to both Isis and Serapis. Coins show that this Isis-temple was surrounded by a large portico; the marble plan of Rome gives the Serapeum as a separate building with a large semi-circular apse at its southern end. Small temples were sometimes also erected for Serapis and Isis by private persons (Delos; Pompeii). In Pompeii the Iseum is situated in a rectangular area surrounded by a peristylium of 25 columns. The temple itself consists of a *naos* and a *pronaos* to which seven steps lead up. In the *naos* were probably the statues of both Isis and Serapis. Before the temple is an altar. In the S.E. part of the court is a small subterranean room with a basin, which one may consider as a *megaron* (inscription at Ostia) or as a room reserved for the initiation such as is also found elsewhere. Joined to the temple there are two large and five small rooms. The largest is probably the *ekklesiasterion*, which served for the repasts of the devotees, for the reunions of the *isiaci*, or for the dramatic representations of the sacred myth. The smaller room or *sacrarium* might also have served for initiation-rites. The five other rooms are of minor importance (kitchen, dining-room). There were usually special rooms for the priests such as the *pastophori* (shrine-bearers), and the Egyptian character of the cult was stressed in the paintings and statues. Sometimes the myth of Isis and Osiris was retold; the principal deities Serapis-Anubis-Horus and Harpocrates were also present. In two paintings from Herculaneum one can see the ceremonies before the entrance of the temple. In one of them a priest, assisted by two attendants, holds in his veiled hands a vessel containing the water of the Nile-Osiris. Another priest kindles a fire of the altar before the sanctuary, at his side a priest with in either hand a staff is standing; before the steps a priest, like the others shaven-headed, holds a sceptre in his upraised right hand and a *sistrum* (rattle) in his left. Two groups of musicians—some with musical instruments—acclaim the goddess. The painting probably represents the morning service when the devotees greeted the returning light (Apuleius, *Met.*, XI,20). The other painting represents the temple precinct and another building with columns. On the platform a dark individual in a loincloth and a shoulder-cape, his head decorated with leaves and a lotus flower, and probably wearing a mask, is performing a dance. He represents either Osiris himself or the god Bes. Priests, women, and children accompany him with *sistra*, a *tympanum*, and a flute. Before the building is a smoking altar to which a woman and a child are bringing offerings. In both paintings sphinxes, ibises, or palmtrees indicate the Egyptian character of the cult. Reliefs sometimes show a procession. One, probably from Rome and now in the Vatican museum, shows four persons walking behind each other:

1) a priestess with a lotus flower on her head, holding a *situla* (an urn) in her left hand; a snake is coiled round her outstretched right arm.

2) a priest with a diadem on his head. He holds a scroll open before him with both hands (ἱερογραμματεύς).

3) a priest (προφήτης) *capite velato* who holds the vessel with the holy Nile water in his veiled hands.

4) a priestess holding a *sistrum* in her left hand and a *simpulum* (a small ladle) in her right.

On a relief now in Berlin, Anubis holding a palm branch and dish leads the procession, in which a child playing the double flute also takes part. It should be noted that in all mysteries the pure child is to be found and is often looked upon as a mediator between the divine and human (oracles, prophecies).

Just as in the Cybele-cult there are in the Isiac ceremonies public carnaval-like processions. In the Isiac cult these take place on the feast of the *navigium Isidis* (πλοιαφέσια) on the fifth of March, when the new maritime season opens. The goddess is the protectress of ships, navigation, and harbours (Isis *pelagia*; *pharia*; *euploia*). On this day a new ship dedicated to the goddess is launched into the sea. As Alföldi has shown, the Isis-ship on the coins in the fourth century was even as a propaganda medium connected with the *vota publica* in the beginning of the year.

From 13th-16th November and from 29th October-1st November in the sanctuaries the finding (*inventio;* εὕρεσις) of Osiris' body was commemorated. During these days the story of Isis and Osiris is re-enacted: the wandering of Isis, her lamentations, the finding of Osiris cut into pieces by Seth-Typhon, the resurrection of his body (Firm. Mat., *De err. prof. rel.*, 22,2; *tu iacentia lapidis membra componis*). Firmicus Maternus quotes a sacred formula pronounced by the priest when after the lamentations he has anointed the throats of the initiated and the light is brought out:

θαρρεῖτε μύσται τοῦ θεοῦ σεσωσμένου
ἔσται γαρ ἡμῖν ἐκ πόνων σωτηρία

Keep good heart, initiates, since the god has been saved and we shall be saved from our troubles. Now begin the *hilaria*: εὑρήκαμεν, συγχαίρομεν. The following words of Firmicus are also most interesting: "may You die as he dies, may You live as he lives (*sic moriaris ut moritur, sic vivas ut vivit*).

It is, however, Apuleis, himself an initiate into the Isiac mysteries (*Met.*, XI,19ff), who gives the most helpful information about them. After many adventures in the shape of an ass, his hero, Lucius is transformed again into human shape during the feast of the *navigium* in Cenchreae near Corinth. Completely persuaded of the might of the goddess he now has only one wish, and that is to be initiated into her cult. The goddess gives the sign to him and the highpriest Mithras in a dream. Lucius undergoes the necessary preparation: from holy books the priest reads the instructions for providing the necessary clothes and accessories; Lucius is then bathed and sprinkled with holy water by the priest, *praefatus deum veniam* which Nelson interpretes as an absolution; and follows a period of ten days of abstinence. In *Met.*, XI,23 Lucius tells: *Accessi confinium mortis et calcato Proserpinae limine per omnia vectus elementa remeavi, nocte media vidi solem candido coruscantem lumine deos inferos et superos accessi coram et adoravi de proximo* = I approached the very gates of death and set one foot on Proserpine's threshold, yet was permitted to return, rapt through all elements. At midnight I saw the sun shining as if it were noon; I entered the presence of the gods of the underworld and the gods of the upper-world, stood near and worshipped them" (translation: Robert Graves). The next morning Lucius is shown to the crowd. He is now dressed in twelve *stolae* and a long shoulder-cape, which the initiates call the olympian *stola*. These garments symbolize the sun. The following day the initiate celebrates his *natalis sacrorum* with a festive repast. On the third day he performs the same rites. Lucius then prays to the goddess who is invoked as the queen of the underworld and with epithets also found in her hymns. Isis advises Lucius to go to Rome for an second initiation. And here in the temple of the Campus Martius he is received into the mysteries of the *magni dei deumque summi parentis* Osiris. These mysteries probably consisted of a sacred drama telling the story of the god (see p. 508). Again after fasting and abstaining for ten days and after having shaved his head Lucius "was admitted to the nocturnal orgies of the great god and became his illuminate." (*principalis dei nocturnis orgiis inlustratus*). Finally Lucius is advised to undergo still a third initiation *deis magnis auctoribus*, which wanted seem to imply in the mysteries of both Isis and Osiris. The latter manifested himself in a dream and "now he deigned to address me in his own person, with his own divine mouth." Lucius becomes not only a member of the order of shrine-bearers (*pastophori*) but also a temple councillor (*decurio*) for the next five years.

It is remarkable that Apuleius does not mention the mysteries of Serapis, but only those of Isis and Osiris. And yet the inscriptions also give evidence concerning the *collegium* of Serapiasti, who hold banquets together and who recorded their decrees on official *stelae*. In the second place it is clear that the culmination is the adoption of the initiated in the priesthood. When Lucius prepares himself for the first initiation (Apuleius, *Met.*, XI,21) the priest explains him that "the gates of the underworld and the guardianship of life are in the goddess's hands and that the rites of initiation approximate to a voluntary death (*voluntaria mors*) from which there is only a precarious hope of resurrection (*precaria salus*)." It has been suggested that this scene is shown in a mosaic from a house in Antioch. Before the open door of a temple (Hades) stands the initiate, half-naked and barefoot, and attended by Hermes and Isis. The goddess stretches forth her hand to sustain the devotee who is starting the journey to the underworld. In Apuleius' text he will return safely and he will be *renatus* after having renounced his former life. He now starts a new life and may be sure of enjoying a happy afterlife also.

d. The Syrian Cults

The excavations at Dura-Europos on the Euphrates have revealed the nature of the religion of a hellenistic Syrian city. In hellenism I the official religion was the same as in other Macedonian colonies: Zeus Olympios, Apollo, and Artemis, the gods of the Seleucid monarchy and also the deified Seleucus himself were the principal deities. There were also however gods of Semitic origin, who came from various countries. In hellenism II the Roman soldiers adored the Pantheon, as in Rome, and also the oriental gods such as Mithras and Jupiter Dolichenus. But the Roman religion like the Greek, was much more important for the garrisons than for the civil population of the city. As M. Rostovtzeff remarks: "the real religion of Dura, that of the large majority of the population, was the Semitic religion, or rather the traditional religion of the predominantly Semitic part of the Near East. The Greek inhabitants were certainly aware of this tendency towards unification. They understood that behind the variety of gods and goddesses, most of them Semitic, there was a unity. They knew that in fact it was one and the same god who was worshipped under different names in most of the large temples of Dura—the great sky god of solar henotheism and they showed their knowledge by giving this god one and the same name—Zeus."

The great goddess was venerated under the name of Artemis. Rostovtzeff has also shown that in Dura there is found "a kind of religious κοινή, familiar to all the Semites and to the semitized Greeks and Iranians throughout Babylonia, Mesopotamia, Syria and Arabia. The greatest creation of this κοινή was a solar henotheism, which in this period became more and more important. A counterpart to it was the creation of the dominant figure of the Great Goddess, whose worship became the religion of women not only in Syria but all over the Roman Empire."

It was especially at Byblos that the cult of Adonis flourished; past this city flowed the river Adonis which yearly became red, a sign for the celebrations of the god's death. It was said that he stayed four months in the underworld and then returned to earth in order to live together with Aphrodite. His cult and his feast, in which the women commemorated his violent death by a boar and his return to the upperworld, were already spread over the hellenic world long before hellenism I.

Later the "Adonis-gardens" (vases in which grain was planted) remained popular, though in Rome itself one has only scanty evidence of his worship. The very location of the *Adonaea* recorded in both the Severan marble plan of Rome and in Philostratus (*Vita Apollonii*, VII, 32) is uncertain.

The signification of the name Adonis is Lord. In Syria there were many local 'Lords' or Ba'als, who were originally the Lords of heaven, the protectors of the harvest and of the city. They generally formed a couple with a goddess who was the protectress of fertility and love, and who belonged to the type of "mistress of the animals". Some of these cults spread into the Western world. In the city of Hierapolis (= Bambyce) to the north-east of Aleppo the goddess Atargatis had a large temple. Her cult and her sanctuary are especially well known through a book περὶ τῆς Συρίης θεοῦ attributed to the Syrian Lucian (second century A.D.). The temple was situated on a hill; in a court were several statues of gods, kings, and mythological figures.

There was also a large altar of bronze, and in the court animals (even bears and lions) lived peacefully together. A number of enormous *phalloi* also stood there. Twice a year a man climbed to the top of one of them and prayed there during seven days for the devotees. There were many priests, some of whom were eunuchs or *galli*; sacred prostitution was also practised. In the innermost shrine of the temple, into which only certain priests were permitted to go, there stood three golden images. The statue of Atargatis is compared with that of Hera by Lucian, but she has also traits of Athena, Aphrodite, Selene, Rhea, Artemis, Nemesis, and the Moirae. She was represented seated upon lions, and her consort Hadad who may be compared to Zeus was seated upon bulls. Between them was a golden statue which Lucian denotes by σημήιον. This had a dove on its head. It is certainly their son, who was called Simmas or Simmias. In this divine couple the goddess was the most important; the *dea Syria* was even invoked in the distant province of Britannia.

In the other Syrian cults, the male divinity was the more important one. Jupiter Dolichenus had his sanctuary from Hittite times in Doliche, the present-day Tell-Duruk in the province Commagene. This place was connected with the origin of iron (*ubi ferrum nascitur*), and the god himself was consequently represented with an iron axe in his upraised right hand. He is a god of the thunder and lightning and at the same time the lord of the bull. In this latter capacity he is shown on the back of the bull, whereas his consort, identified with Juno, mostly stands upon the back of a hind. Reliable information about the cult of this divine couple in its country of origin is lacking, since their sanctuary on the hill has not yet been excavated. Syrian traders and soldiers brought their god to the West and he is sometimes closely connected with the other god of the bull, the Iranian Mithras. In places where the latter was adored, Jupiter Dolichenus was also found; thus his cult spread over the whole Empire.

In Rome he had two sanctuaries situated on the Aventine and on the Esquiline. The former is the better known (excavations of A. M. Colini). Its construction was completed in A.D. 138 when Antoninus Pius began his reign, which was most favourable for the oriental cults. The temple consists of a large central chamber and two smaller side-rooms. Two elevated benches against the northern and southern sides of the central room suggest its use for sacred meals; the western side-room, which has a large niche with three smaller niches inside, is supposed to have been a *schola*; the eastern room may have been used for lustrations. However, comparison of this temple in Rome with others shows that the Dolichena did not, unlike the Mithraea, have a certain definite groundplan. Moreover, these sanctuaries were mostly only small chapels. The many monuments, among which the silver triangular votive-plates are particularly characteristic, tell more than the literary sources what were the beliefs of Dolichenus' followers. They regarded their god as their supreme ruler and protector,—he wears the imperial military dress, and is even called in inscriptions the *aeternus conservator totius mundi* or the *conservator totius poli et numen prae-stantissimum exibitor invictus*. He had indeed become the king of the cosmos and cosmic powers, and was consequently accompanied not only by the triad formed of the eagle, sun, and moon, but also by the two Dioscuri, sometimes referred to as the *castores conservatores*, who symbolized the two hemispheres. It is therefore quite understandable that his followers, who were organized in a community of *fratres* with a cult consisting of processions, ablutions, meals, and even the practice of oniromancy, saw in such a powerful god the one who could bring salvation to their souls.

The cult of Jupiter Heliopolitanus derives from Heliopolis, the present-day Ba'albek. There was already a temple-complex on the acropolis, but it was not until the third century A.D. that it reached the height of its fame. In its final form, known from the French and German excavations, the enormous temple of the god himself, the architects of which are unknown, was fronted by a large open square with two basins and the altar. Later on the propylaion and a hexagonal court were added with the aid of the Severan house and Philip the Arabian. In the same period a sanctuary in honour of Dionysus, on the southern side of Jupiter's temple, also surrounded by rows of columns, was built. In the interior a flight of steps leads to the baldachino, below which the cult-image stood. On the right there is underneath the floor of the cella, a crypt consisting of two vaulted rooms; and on the left there are seven steps leading into a room in which stood a table for offerings. Two other temples in the immediate neighbourhood of the acropolis are supposed to have been dedicated the one to Mercury and the other to Aphrodite. In this way each member of the heliopolitan triad had his or her own temple and again, just as in nearly all oriental cults, the dionysiac element was very evident.

The name Heliopolis indicates that the Ba'al of that city was already in hellenism I a solar god, formed a couple with Atargatis i.e. Venus, and who had a son, Mercury. Macrobius (*Sat.*, 23,10-20) describes his original statue: "it is in fact a golden statue of beardless aspect, standing like a charioteer with a whip in its raised hand, a thunderbold and corn-ears in the left—attributes which all indicate the combined power of Jupiter and the sun." This sun-god came to the West, especially to Rome and Puteoli, where Tyrian colonists had settled. His cult spread even to Britain and Austria. The cult-images we have do indeed correspond to Macrobius' description, but the god has on either side a bull, and he wears, like Serapis, a *modius*. Sometimes his cuirass-like garment (*ependytes*) is decorated with busts of the planets, still stressing more his solar character. Sometimes the solar disk with two uraeus-snakes also occurs (e.g. on a marble stele from Marseilles). He is at the same time a weather and a vegetation god.

A temple for the heliopolitan triad has been found on the Janiculum in Rome. In this sanctuary, which dates from the Antonine period and was still in use during the fourth century, there are three rooms communicating with each other. The central room has no particular characteristics and was destinated for the official cult. The left-hand room however is divided again in three parts and has in the middle a niche before which a triangular altar stood. Its three sides have representations of respectively a bull, Sol, and Luna. The right-hand room, added in the fourth century, ends in a sexagonal(?) niche in which a basalt statue of a pharaoh has been found (probably replacing a statue of Osiris). In a triangular grave before the niche a small bronze statue was discovered. A male figure, wearing an Egyptian *klaft* and standing in a hieratic attitude, is encircled seven times by a snake. According to Maria B. Felletti-Maj one may recognize here the son of the divine couple, i.e. Mercury identified with Adonis, Dionysus, and Osiris.

In honour of the Syrian triad there was also a mystery cult under the direction of a *pater* and during which in certain ceremonies the grave and dead body of the young god were shown. The titles κίστιβερ and δειπνοκρίτης of one of the devotees indicate sacred cultic meals.

Of the other Syrian gods the sun-god Malakbel and the moon-god

Aglibol came to Rome. They originated in Palmyra, the city from which at the end of the third century Aurelian brought the sun-god of Emesa to be the generally acknowledged State-god, intending that he should now be adored in a more Roman way, and not, as under Heliogabalus, in the Syrian fashion that had proved too oriental for Roman tastes.

V. Short History of the Study of Hellenistic Religion

Since it was during the hellenistic period that many of the mystery-cults and Christendom, from Antiquity onwards the literature reflects the ever-increasing antagonism, which finally led to Christianity's victory. On one side we find the ancient and often oriental gods praised in hymns, speaches and treatises; on the other the revolutionary new Jewish religion. Official paganism, including the oriental cults, was for several centuries at war with this new oriental religion which was not content before it obtained the supremacy. The fierce struggle involved the Christian authors not only in defending their faith with apologetic writings but also in attacking their opponents. The Christians also claimed ancient traditions; pagan rites were ridiculed or branded as devilish imitations of the ceremonies of the one true faith. Even in Antiquity both parties disputed the questions of priority and mutual influences; on a lower level they accused each other of the most various crimes. Both were proud of wonder-workers and both were eagerly doing their best to give to their ideas a philosophical background. In the case of the Church-Fathers we can safely say that they generally knew the official deities of the surrounding hellenistic world very well, but that with few exceptions they could not have been able to judge the secret doctrines of the mystery cults for which an initiation was necessary. And yet much of our information about these cults is derived from these very apologists, since the scriptures of the opposition party are either lost or were intentionally destroyed. Archaeological monuments sometimes fill a part of this enormous gap.

In the quarrel between the two parties Celsus was the first to write against the Christians with any real knowledge of his adversaries' faith. His 'Αληθὴς λόγος was written towards the end of the second century A.D. Celsus' book is lost, but we know his arguments through Origen, who a century later attacked him fiercely in a work in which he treats nearly all the important questions of Christians doctrine from a philosophical point of view. Somewhat later the neoplatonist Porphyrius wrote a treatise κατὰ Χριστιανῶν; this book was later on systematically destroyed after having been attacked by various Christian apologists, Eusebius of Caesarea and Apollinaris of Laodicea. In the fourth century there were many up and downs for both parties: but after the reign of the Emperor Julian, who like the neoplatonist Sallustius wrote books in praise of the ancient gods, and after the disputes between the two parties in the Senate such as that about the statue of Victory in the Curia, the battle was lost and people started to destroy the old sanctuaries. The subsequent fall of Rome, the *caput mundi*, seemed incredible to the whole world. Hence the dispute about its causes, which form a religious point of view might be connected with the abandoning of the traditional gods. In the same period the growing Church had to defend itself not only against paganism but also against the controversies between the various Christian sects. The study of hellenism II largely depends from this complete context of current ideas.

In the following centuries the Church inherited the power of ancient Rome, and tried hard to preserve a certain measure of unity. The old traditions were incorporated into the ever more dogmatic Christian system. Both Edgar Wind, *The Pagan Mysteries in the Renaissance* (London 1958) and Jean Seznec, *The Survival of the Pagan Gods* (1963) have recently demonstrated how the ancient gods lived on, sometimes in disguised forms, and inspired many artists to create masterpieces. Of interest is the fact that the study of Greek and Roman religion increased though not as an independent discipline, since it was almost always carried on within Christian frames of reference. These studies prepared the way for the more independent ones which began to flourish in the 18th and 19th centuries under the influence of rationalism. It is a pity however that many of the books written during this period deal mainly with the old question of the priority and mutual influences of the hellenistic creeds and Christendom. Even at the beginning of the 20th century it seemed that the quarrel of the two ancient parties had been revived. A typical book in this respect is that of Edwin Hatch, *The influence of Greek Ideas and Usages upon the Christian Church* (London 1907); Ernest Renan and Alfred Loisy supported similar views, and influenced the conception of hellenism very greatly, as did James Frazer, who, in his voluminous work *The golden Bough* developed his ideas about the dying and resurrecting gods. For the other side studies such as *Attis et le Christianisme* of J. Lagrange (in *Rev. Bibl.*, XXVIII, 1919, pp. 419-480) and of J. Dey, Παλιγγενεσία (Münster 1937) may be taken as representative.

A new era in the knowledge of the oriental mystery-cults starts with Franz Cumont. In his two volumes about Mithraism he gathered both literary and archaeological sources,—the latter being in this cult the principal documents. G. Lafaye had already performed a similar task for the Isis and Serapis cult and soon after H. Graillot's monograph about Cybele and Attis was published. It was of course Fr. Cumont himself who showed the way in which the problems should be approached by paying great attention to the archaeological finds in his *Religions orientales*. But he also developed the study of many other sources of a better understanding of the religious thoughts of hellenism (astrological texts; alchemy; the intensive influence of Dionysiac ideas; hermetism), as well as investigating the origins and development of the mystery-cults, their mutual influences and their influence on the ideas about the after-life. M. Nilsson, A. D. Nock, and A. J. Festugière are other prominent scholars who have all used the same historical method to lay the foundations of our present knowledge of hellenistic religious thought. It now seems that neither in Antiquity nor in modern times the right moment has come for a definite answer to the always intriguing priority-question. There are still too many areas for which thorough well documented studies are lacking, and it is these that are needed before a satisfactory answer can be attempted. One must not forget that it is only in the last few decades that archaeological methods have become something like what they should be, that especially in the near-eastern countries the excavations are only at the starting-point; that an inventory of former finds has not yet always been made, and that of these documents the exact data or find-circumstances are usually either lost or only to be discovered with the greatest difficulty. Monographs about the propagation of the various cults, about the religious creeds in the cities of countries with such varying populations, about the social status of their adherents and about their mutual influences are still few and far between—an enormous task has still to be completed by the next generations.

SELECTED BIBLIOGRAPHY

General works

In nearly all handbooks of ancient history, philosophy, Greek and Roman Religion the various cults and creeds of the hellenistic age are described. For more serious study one must consult these books and those listed here as well as the many articles in the large encyclopedias (Pauly-Wissowa-Kroll; Roscher; Daremberg-Saglio; Hastings) and in the international reviews. The bibliography is very extensive indeed, and I therefore mention here only the most important studies for each subject.

FR. CUMONT, *Les religions orientales dans le paganisme romain*, Paris 1929⁴.

A. J. FESTUGIÈRE, *Personal Religion among the Greeks*, Berkeley 1954.

F. C. GRANT, *Hellenistic Religions: The Age of Syncretism*, New York 1953.

H. GRESSMANN, *Die orientalischen Religionen im hellenistisch-römischen Zeitalter*, Berlin-Leipzig 1930.

K. H. E. DE JONG, *Das antike Mysterienwesen*, Leiden 1919.

A. LOISY, *Les mystères païens et le mystère chrétien*, Paris 1930.

M. P. NILSSON, *Geschichte der Griechischen Religion*, II, *Die hellenistische und römische Zeit*, München 1950.

A. D. NOCK, *Conversion*, Oxford 1933.

H. W. OBBINK, *Cybele, Isis, Mithras*, Haarlem 1965.

R. PETTAZZONI, *I Misteri*, Bologna 1924.

K. PRÜMM, *Religionsgeschichtliches Handbuch für den Raum der altchristlichen Umwelt*, Rom 1954.

R. REITZENSTEIN, *Die hellenistischen Mysterienreligionen*, Stuttgart 1927³ (1956).

N. TURCHI, *Fontes historiae mysteriorum aevi hellenistici*, Roma 1930.

——,*Le Religioni misteriche del mondo antico*, Milan 1948.

Isis and Serapis

A. ALFÖLDI, *A Festival of Isis in Rome under the Christian Emperors of the IVth Century*, Budapest 1937.

——,*Die alexandrinischen Götter und die vota publica am Jahresbeginn* in *Jb.f.Antike und Christ.* 8-9, 1965-1966, pp. 53-87.

H. I. BELL, *Cults and Creeds in Graeco-Roman Egypt*, Liverpool 1957.

P. M. FRASER, *Two Studies on the Cult of Sarapis in the Hellenistic World* in *Opuscula Atheniensia* III, Lund 1960, pp. 1-54.

——,*Current Problems Concerning the Early History of the Cult of Sarapis* in *Opuscula Atheniensia* VII, Lund 1967, pp. 23-42.

TH. HOPFNER, *Plutarch über Isis und Osiris*, I-II, Prag 1940 (1967).

G. LAFAYE, *Les divinités d'Alexandrie hors de l'Egypte*, Paris 1884.

J. PH. LAUER-CH. PICARD, *Les statues ptolémaïques du Sarapieion de Memphis*, Paris 1955.

P. ROUSSEL, *Les cultes égyptiens à Délos*, Paris 1915-1916.

V. TRAM TAN TINH, *Le culte d'Isis à Pompéi*, Paris 1964.

G. VANDEBEEK, *De interpretatio graeca van de Isisfiguur*, Lovanii 1946.

Syrian Cults

W. ATALLAH, *Adonis dans la littérature et l'art grecs*, Paris 1966.

R. DU MESNIL DU BUISSON, *Les tessères et les monnaies de Palmyre*, Paris 1962.

O. EISSFELDT, *Tempel und Kulte syrischer Städte in hellenistisch-römischer Zeit*, Leipzig 1941.

B. M. Felletti-Maj, *Il santuario della triade Eliopolitana* in *Bull. Comm. Arch. Roma* LXXV, 1953-1955, pp. 137-162.

P. Gauckler, *Le sanctuaire syrien du Janicule*, Paris 1912.

A. H. Kan, *Juppiter Dolichenus*, Leyde 1943.

P. Merlat, *Répertoire des inscriptions et monuments figurés du culte de Jupiter Dolichenus*, Rennes 1951.

——,*Jupiter Dolichenus*, Paris 1960.

P. S. Ronzevalle, *Jupiter Héliopolitain*, Beyrouth 1937.

Cybele and Attis

R. Duthoy, *Taurobolium*, Leyde 1969.

H. Graillot, *Le culte de Cybèle*, Paris 1912.

H. Hepding, *Attis, seine Mythen und sein Kult*, Grieszen 1903.

E. O. James, *The Cult of the Mother Goddess*, New York 1959.

P. Lambrechts, *Les fêtes "phrygiennes" de Cybèle et d'Attis* in *Bull. de l'Institut historique belge de Rome* 27, 1952, pp. 141-170.

——,*Attis, van herdersknaap tot god*, Brussels 1962.

——,*Attis en het feest der hilariën*, Amsterdam 1967.

M. J. Vermaseren, *The Legend of Attis in Greek and Roman Art*, Leyde 1966.

Mithraism

LeRoy A. Campbell, *Mithraic Iconography and Ideology*, Leyde 1968.

Fr. Cumont, *Textes et Monuments relatifs aux Mystères de Mithra*, I-II, Brussels 1896-1898.

——,*Die Mysterien des Mithra*, Leipzig 1923³.

M. J. Vermaseren, *Corpus Inscriptionum et Monumentorum Religionis Mithriacae*, Hague 1956-1960.

——,*Mithras, Geschichte eines Kultes*, Stuttgart 1965.

The new studies about the above-mentioned sections are being collected in the Series *Études préliminaires aux religions orientales*.

GNOSTICISM

BY

J. DORESSE
Paris, France

I. The Sources

The earliest definite evidence we have of the sects which later were to receive the appellation "Gnostics" is to be found in the *Acts* of the Apostles, certain of the *Epistles* of Paul, the *Apocalypse*, the prologue to St. John's *Gospel*, which, in places, confute certain "heresies" and denounce "false prophets", two of whom, Simon of Samaria and the deacon Nicolas, are famous precisely because of this. Between then and the 3rd century, Simon was even to be transformed by the writings of pseudo-Clement and the apocryphal *Acts of Peter* into the figure of a legendary magus. At about the same time Polycarp, Justin, Hegesippus stigmatize certain members of the sect in works of which, unfortunately, only fragments have come down to us. But already the schools of the Satornilians, the Basilidians, the Valentinians have begun to multiply—like poisonous *fungi*, to use again the comparison made by Bishop Irenaeus who, in about the year 180, describes them in his *Confutation of the False Gnosis*. At the beginning of the 3rd century, the *Philosophumena*, doubtfully attributed to Hippolytus of Rome, illustrates with abundant quotations the astonishing diversity of these doctrines. Tertullian, Clement of Alexandria, Origen take it upon themselves to attack certain Gnostics in the name of Christianity. The same sects are attacked by Plotinus, Porphyry and their disciples in the name of pagan Platonism. In the 4th century St. Epiphanius, in his *Panarion* adds his personal observations, taken from life, to what earlier attackers had collected. However the controversies were either to be turned against Manichaeism (see the following chapter) or gradually die down, at least as regards the older Gnostic sects; in the 6th century the Egyptian Bishop John of Parallos denounces some members of the sect disguised as Christians. Theodore Bar Konai (late 8th century), then Michael the Syrian (late 12th century), mention only a few strange oriental sects among which, it is true, the Mandaeans, then called Dositheans or Nasoraeans, figure plainly for the first time.

So, from the period which stretches from the origins to the 3rd century only the voice of the attackers seems to have reached us; for the earliest works of the sects we have only what the heresiologists have summarized and quoted: the *Epistle of Ptolemy to Flora*, tran‑scribed by Irenaeus, the Naassenean hymn reproduced in the *Philo-sophumena*, the fragments of the works of Theodotus quoted by *Clement of Alexandria*. On the other hand, for the period from the 3rd to the 5th century, numerous original manuscripts have been found, as the sects had by then spread to Upper Egypt, where the dry sands preserved until the present day the vestiges, almost all in the Coptic tongue, of certain Gnostic and Manichaean libraries. To the Codex brought back from Thebes by Bruce in 1769 with its two *Books of Ieou* and its precious untitled treatise, to the Askewianus Codex, famous for the *Pistis-Sophia* was to be added in 1896 the Codex Berolinensis 8502 with, among others, the texts of the *Apocryphon* (or *Secret Book*) *of John*, and of the *Sophia of Jesus*. But these texts, all too few, seemed to bear little similarity to the picture of Gnosticism traced by the heresiologists and so posed more problems than they resolved. It was then, in 1947 and 1948 that the late TOGO MINA and ourselves had the extraordinary good fortune to find the 13 Coptic codices on papyrus of a library dating from the 3rd and 4th centuries, at one time buried in an earthenware jar near the ancient Chenoboskion in the region of Nag-Hammadi. This collection, first and foremost, restored to us the writings of the Eastern sects which had been attacked by Irenaeus, the *Philosophumena*, Plotinus and his disciples—sects which Epiphanius had encountered, still in existence, when staying in Egypt. We may mention the *Revelation of Adam to Seth*, several writings attributed to the heavenly Seth—the Allogenes—and to Seth the son of the earthly Adam, to Shem, to Messos, to Zoroaster and to Zostrian, as well as a *Hypostasis of the Archons* which seems to be derived from the *Book of Norea* mentioned by Epiphanius. A treatise on the *Triple Epiphany*, a *Thought of the Great Power*, form a link with the later writings which, according to the *Philosophumena*, may have preserved teachings of Simon Magus. We may also mention for their "Sethian" doctrine an *Apocalypse of Dositheus* and the two works—an *Epistle* and a *Sacred Book of the Great Invisible Spirit* (called a *Gospel of the Egyptians*) attributed to a doctor called Eugnostos. Other treatises show the influence of the Valentinian doctrine: the *Gospel of Truth*, the *Treatise on the Three Natures*, the one "*On the Resurrection*." To these texts which form the core of the library may be added apocryphal writings in which Christianity and Gnosticism are mingled: revelations in the names of James, Paul, Peter, Silvanus; a *Gospel according to Philip*, the *Book of Thomas* "written by Matthias". As for the collection of the *Secret Sayings of Jesus* or the *Gospel of Thomas*, its contents offer only slight traces of Gnosticism; it is, moreover—as H. Ch. PUECH recognised as early as 1953—a complete collection of the *"logia"* (the "sayings") of Jesus, of which the Greek fragments of Oxyrhynchus had formerly only offered incomprehensible shreds. Finally we may mention, in this same sacred library, the presence of a few treatises of pagan Hermetism, which had been lost until now, with the exception of a few pages which had been preserved for us, in a rather different form in the *Asclepius*.

To these vestiges of the literature on which the teachings and the secret practices of the sects were founded must be added other documents, which had long been available but which had not been associated with Gnosis through failure to identify accurately certain of the myths which are foreshadowed in them or used in them. Such is the case for various magic formularies, in the Greek or Coptic tongues. We may mention the magic papyrus I of Oslo; the so-called *Mithraic Liturgy* of the Mimaut papyrus; the formulas of liberation from Fatality studied by E. PETERSON; the treatise of the pseudo-Zosimus *On the Letter Omega*; finally, perhaps, certain of the "Sethian" formulas.

To this literature of the ancient sects must be added the abundant Mandaean literature, the recent manuscripts of which have been brought back from Lower Mesopotamia by European travellers: so, for a century now, scholars have been able to publish the *Treasure*, the *Book of John*, the liturgies, astrological and magic texts, etc. Scholars hesitated for a long time to attribute an ancient origin to these texts. Today, it has been established that certain passages of Mandaean writings were prior to the composition of the *Psalms of Thomas*, Manichaean hymns which date from the 4th century at the latest.

Finally, vestiges of Gnostic works have been preserved, in edulcorated forms, by certain Eastern Churches: the *Gospel of Bartholemew*, so-called homilies on the *Institution of St. Michael and the fall of Samael* in the Coptic church; the *Institution of the Angel Abbaton* and the *Apocalypse of Gorgorios* among the Ethiopian Falashas—a pseudo-judaic sect which adapted to its own faith these two works which came, once again, from Coptic Egypt.

It will be understood, in the light of this inventory, that even today ancient "Gnosticism" can only be known within very narrow limits. Faced with the vastness and complexity of the subject, the Historian has his hands tied by the penury of direct and precise authentic documents. Do the doctors and doctrines about which we have some seemingly precise and concordant depositions indeed represent the most characteristic stages in this religion? Or are they but aberrant examples, isolated cases, maliciously chosen by the Chance which has preserved them for us and from which it would be imprudent to establish any synthesis? If we are to tackle this problem, it is essential that we answer a preliminary question: what criterion have we for drawing together in one definition the many and varied sects to which, more or less hastily, the appellation "Gnostics" has been attached?

II. Definition of Gnosticism

Indeed, the definitions of Gnosticism which were current while we had only the ancient polemics on the sects were hesitating, imprecise, inadequate. Too much attention was paid to the simple fact that all the schools thus listed had claimed to be the custodians of a Gnosis, that is to say, of a Knowledge mysteriously revealed to certain privileged beings in order that to them might be unveiled the mysteries of the world above and the formulas which would allow the chosen, and only the chosen, to win salvation. Such a criterion had its disadvantages. The Christians of the "Great Church", bitter opponents of the Gnostics, had also given the name "gnosis" to a certain form of their teaching. And so, not long since, there was an attempt to define the Gnosticism of the sects in more precise terms. But the most famous, that of Harnack: "the extreme Hellenization of Christianity" brought together two historical hypotheses which cannot be today accepted.

However, a most valuable definition had been formulated in the early days, chiefly by the pagan opponents of the Gnostics: Porphyry and Plotinus. Section 9 of the second *Ennead* in which the sects are confuted is called: "Against those who maintain that the Demiurge of this world is evil and that the Cosmos is evil." Not only does this formula sum up the essentials of what the Creeds and the Christian anathematisms will condemn in all Gnostics (including the Manichaeans and the Priscillianists) but it also marks the gulf which separates the gnosticism of these sects from the less dualist gnoses, which have recourse to myths which are often very similar, but on which they put an optimistic interpretation. In so far as the teachings of our sects can be brought together in an incontestable historic and doctrinal unity, it is because they have as a principle the revelation to the "elect" of a dualism associating the hatred of this lower world and of the perverse inferior God who created it with belief in an invisible superior divine hierarchy to which the Perfect must return.

Is it necessary to clarify and complete this definition? It is sufficient to add that, in order to explain the position of man in this world, the Gnostics assume in each of the elect the presence of a hidden spark, radically foreign to the Cosmos, wrested, at some time in the past, from the eternal world of the supreme deity, but destined to return to its original source. The fall of this spark into the realms of darkness would seem to be the consequence, either of a war between darkness and light, or of an accident which occurred during the production of emanations from on high: from one or other of these deficiencies was born an imperfect and jealous god who, incapable of continuing the production of superior hierarchies, can only clumsily copy the models, drawing from darkness the substance of material heavens enslaved to Time and Fate, and of a carnal man in whom the fire from above is imprisoned. Before finally dissolving this ephemeral lower world, the entities above are endeavouring to recall the fragments of light engulfed in the cosmos: by means of saviours they send to the elect who, until now, have been transmigrating from one body to another in the depths of this prison-house, revelations of the Gnosis and in particular the rites of the great baptisms by "living" water which will allow them to regain the ineffable higher world.

III. HISTORY

The retracing of the history of the Gnostic sects is a difficult task, so difficult is it to co-ordinate in a single precise chronology the information given by the heresiologists and the substance of the original texts. Of these last, we know neither when, nor where, nor by whom they were composed before assuming the form in which they have reached us. Apart from the single case of Eugnostos called Goggessos (a person of whom, incidentally, the heresiologists are completely ignorant, at least under these names), the texts that have been preserved give no acceptable indications of their authors. Often, the writer introduces himself as an incarnation of the Great Seth, or of some other celestial figure, or as one of the Apostles. The titles given to the works are many and often changing: *The Sacred Book of the Great Invisible Spirit* receives at the same time the title *"Gospel of the Egyptians,"* stolen no doubt from a Christian apocrypha with different contents. The very substance of the revelations and the treatises seems to have been constantly re-modelled, as can be discovered from those works of which several copies have reached us: in the *Secret Book of John*, the figure of the heavenly Mother, to whom is attributed in the oldest version the redeeming descent into Hell, is later clumsily replaced by the figure of Jesus! Elsewhere, the substance of the scarcely modified *Epistle of Eugnostos* is to be found incorporated into a fictitious dialogue between the Saviour and his disciples, a modification which receives the title of *Sophia of Jesus*. A number of works seem to have been fabricated by generations of compilers, sometimes anxious to insert their lucubrations into the body of more ancient texts with well-known titles, sometimes ransacking two or three earlier works in order to re-assemble the fragments under a new designation more appropriate to the doctrine of their sect. Under such conditions, in the sixty or so original works of which we today possess the Coptic editions, it is difficult to recognize what represents the original form of the work, when it is a question of a treatise of which the title and certain fragments may have been quoted by a heresiologist of the 2nd or 3rd century. Indeed, we can find, in the beginning of the *Secret Book of John*, long pages already quoted by Irenaeus (*Adv. Haer.* I, XXIX), but this only proves that the *Secret Book of John*, as the contradictions between certain of its pages lead us to believe, has pillaged one or more ancient works amongst which was the anonymous treatise known to Irenaeus. As for the *Gospel of Truth* which was found, without the name of the author, in a 5th century Codex, can we really see in it, by virtue of the title only, that work which Valentinus is thought to have composed under this name, a treatise so thoroughly lost until then that no characteristic detail from it is quoted by the heresiologists who might have known it? Indeed, in so far as we possess original works, we must not blind ourselves to the fact that they represent Gnostic literature as certain sects, from the end of the 3rd century to the beginning of the 6th, adapted it to their needs of the moment. Numerous vestiges of earlier works are incorporated in it: but only a detailed literary and doctrinal analysis, the necessity for which too many specialists have, until now, tried to avoid, will bring these to light and permit us to ascribe to certain pages a date earlier than the end of the 3rd century. Before establishing these facts, any claim that, through their Coptic versions, the *Gospel of Truth*, the *Gospel of Philip* and the *Secret Book of John* can faithfully represent texts of the middle of the 2nd century, would be deceptive; to draw therefrom conclusions about the date of certain works of the *N.T.* which are quoted in them is even more foolhardy!

Christian scholars, beginning with Hegesippus, claimed that the Gnostic sects owed their origins to Judaist schools such as the Essenes, the Samaritans, the Ebionites, the Sampseans, the Elkesaites, etc. Perhaps this affirmation hides more truth than the moderns have believed.

It is in a geographical setting, extending from the valley of the Jordan to Asia Minor that the sects reveal themselves for the first time to the eyes of historians, at the time of the Apostles. The principal centres that can be identified are Samaria, Antioch, Colossae, Ephesus, Pergamum ... Simon, who came from Gitta, in Samaria, probably began preaching after the death of John the Baptist; he claimed to be the Great Power of God. With him we associate a certain Dositheus, his master or at the very least his equal. If we are to believe the pseudo-Clementine works, this Dositheus, like Simon, had with him his "Helen", a fallen woman whom he presented as an incarnation of the Heavenly Mother. Again according to the Clementine work and to the *Acts of Peter*, it would seem that Simon went to Rome where he had to contend with the Apostle Peter; but these late accounts are too full of romance to be believed. The principal heir of Simon seems to be Menander, a native of Capparetia in Samaria, who had as disciples Satornil and Basilides; these two in turn carried their doctrines, the one to Antioch, the other to Alexandria. Antioch was the home of another heretic: the deacon Nicolas; his disciples are denounced at Ephesus and Pergamum, by the *Revelation* of St. John. Of Cerinthus we know very little; Polycarp met him at Ephesus. Asia Minor was invaded by doctrines whose outlines can be glimpsed in Paul's epistles to the *Colossians* and to *Timothy*: false doctors claimed that the Law is evil and that it was not the supreme God who created the world, but certain angels. How close these doctrines could be to Gnosticism can be better seen by the introduction to *St. John's Gospel* which declares itself, point by point, against the teachings according to which the world is not the work of the supreme God, light has been overcome by darkness, the Word has only made a semblance of becoming flesh and has come down to this world only for certain privileged beings...

Under Trajan, the name of Elxai takes us back to the Dead Sea area: Elxai, the head of a Baptist sect, had with him the prophetesses Marthos and Marthana, whose names correspond perhaps to those of Marsanes and Martiades, celebrated later by the Sethian Gnostics.

From Jordan, Antioch and Asia Minor, the sects reached Alexandria (supposing that they were not already in existence there under forms of which we are unaware). It was in the time of Hadrian that Basilides taught there and produced a considerable literary work, many features of which seem to have been preserved in Coptic writings that have been found, and whose influence, according to the *Acta Archelai*, reaching as far as Persia, contributed to the elaboration of Manichaeism. He made use of revelations attributed to prophets named Barcabbas, Barcoph or Parchor, but which he may have composed himself. His son Isidore continued to develop his doctrine, particularly on the "adventitious soul". About the same time as Basilides, Carpocrates was also teaching in Alexandria; the sect he founded actually bore the name *Gnostic*. The son of Carpocrates, Epiphanius, added to his father's doctrine borrowings from Secundus, one of the disciples of Valentinus. Epiphanius died young, at Samos, where the inhabitants erected a temple to him.

Through Valentinus who, born in Egypt, had taught first in Alexandria in the time of Hadrian, a gnosis tinged with Christianity was diffused in Rome; it there encountered the teachings of Carpocrates, introduced by Marcellina in the middle of the 2nd century, and of Cerdo, who some believe to be the master of Marcion. For the heresy of Marcion must perhaps also be included among the gnoses, of which it was the only wholly and completely Christian one.

Valentinus, while giving the Gnosis its most philosophical form, obscured the "Jewish fables" and the oriental myths which formed its original constitution and developed, on this basis, a strange exegesis of Christianity. Its disciples were divided into an "Italic" school, with Heracleon and Ptolemy, and an "oriental" school, to which the *Philosophumena* (VI, 35) attach Axionicos and Bardesanes. It is to this second branch that belong Theodotus, extracts of whose works have been preserved by Clement of Alexandria, and, no doubt, Mark "the magus", who came to Rome from Asia Minor, before travelling up the Rhône valley.

Meanwhile, non-Christian Gnosticisms continued to abound in Rome: about 220, Alcibiades of Apamea introduced the revelations of Elxai. And it appears that it was in Rome also, about the same time, that Plotinus and his disciples Porphyry and Amelius, met the Gnostics among whom they mention Adelphius and Aquilinus; these last based their beliefs on revelations attributed to Zoroaster and Zostrian, Nicotheus, Allogenes and Messos, texts which,—except for that of Nicotheus—have been discovered in the Coptic library at Chenoboskion. It is unfortunate that the revelation of Nicotheus is lost, for it is mentioned in the *Treatise on the letter Omega* and in Manichaean writings, as well as in the anonymous work of Bruce's Codex, which quotes it alongside the revelations of Phosilampes and of Marsanes and Martiades, as a vision of the most hidden of the heavenly secrets.

The Greek islands have been mentioned in connexion with the young Epiphanius who was deified at Samos. It was in Cyprus that Valentinus spent the last years of his teaching. Euboea appears to have been the home of a branch of the Ophite sect—the Peratae—with Celbes of Caryste and with Euphrates, mentioned in the *Philosophumena*.

The most western branch of Gnosis is hidden, it seems, behind the teaching of the Priscillianists of Spain at the end of the 4th century. St. Augustine even accused them of hiding the true nature of their teaching, which seems to have been a combination of Gnosis and Manichaeism: did not they too make use of certain revelations of Zoroaster? Condemned in the middle of the 5th century, the sect had to go underground. It did not disappear completely until after it had been condemned by the second Council of Braga, in 563, a synod whose denunciations represent a brief but precise definition of all that can separate Christianity from Gnosis.

However, the East, from which the first wave of Gnosticism had come to conquer the Roman world, did not cease to produce new men of inspiration. The greatest of these was Mani who collected together the teachings of the Sethians, the Bardesanites and other Gnostics, and of Baptist sects from Mesopotamia, into a vast synthesis enriched with Persian elements. At his death in 273 the religion he had founded spread towards the West as well as towards central Asia, competing everywhere with the unco-ordinated teachings of earlier sects and contributing to their obliteration.

Of the other Asian sectarians it seems we must in particular mention Audi, a Syrian of Mesopotamia who separated from the church after the Council of Nicaea; the doctrine taught in the monasteries of Taurus, Palestine and Arabia which rallied to him was not perhaps originally Gnostic. However, as early as 373 St. Ephraem denounces them as such, in the region of Edessa; three centuries later, Bar-Konai even specifies that the Audians had adopted apocryphas amongst which can be recognized the *Secret Book of John* and the revelations of *Allogenes*. It seems that the same thing happened among the heirs to the doctrine of Bardesanes, who appropriated the same writings. After spreading as far as Khurasan and China, these Bardesanites, if we are to believe An-Nadim's *Fihrist*, had retired to Mesopotamia. And it is still the "Sethian" books which are to serve the Archontics, a school founded in Palestine by the priest Peter, excluded from the church in 347 but who, from the region of Hebron, was to propagate its doctrines as far as Armenia.

Other sectarians from even farther east are mentioned by St. Ephraem, by Theodore Bar-Konai and by Michael the Syrian: Qouqous, founder of the Qouqeans, may have used the *Gospel of the Twelve*. The Kantaeans owed their origins to one Papas, who, like Mani, was a native of the Babylonian locality of Gaukai; later, this sect would seem to have become implanted in Persia where it concealed its doctrines under the typically Persian firecult. But it seems that Bar Konai's account of this sect, which may have been known to Mani and have had connexions with the Mandaeans, is tinged with errors and fanciful information.

We have not quoted, in this list, some sects which the heresiologists mention without saying to which scholars they were attached nor even where they came across them. Names such as "Stratiotics" correspond, in any case, more to grades of initiation (as was the case with the disciples of Mithras) than to separate schools. But certain denominations represent important sects. The Sethians, for example, seem to have preserved certain of the writings attributed to the Simonians by the *Philosophumena*, teachings similar to those of Satornil, revelations attached to the names of Martiades and Marsanes, names which recall the Sampseans prophetesses. The Barbelognostics, said to be derived from the Nicolaitans, the sectarians attacked by Plotinus, the Archontics, the latter-day Audians, seem to have been no more than ramifications of the same powerful current. It is, in any case, to groups of this family that belong the Codex of Bruce, the Codex Berolinensis, the manuscripts of Chenonoskion and the apocryphas denounced later by John of Parallos. In spite of similarities, the Ophites or the Naassenes (of which the Peratae were, perhaps, only a sub-division), seem to be distinguished from the Sethians by a peculiar recourse to certain Greek mysteries, and by a complex astrology in which the constellation of the Dragon (and not the serpent of Genesis!) held a respectable place, as is attested by their mention in the *Philosophumena*. It appears, finally, that there really existed sects animated by an extreme antinomy which, through hatred of the God of *Genesis*, venerated Cain, Esau and the Egyptians of the *Exodus*, and who practised rites in which was expressed their scorn of the flesh and of procreation.

It remains to say a word about the Mandaeans who have survived to the present day in Lower Mesopotamia. Their name means, literally, "Gnostics". Their traditions depict them as the followers of John the Baptist who fled the region of Jerusalem in circumstances which suggest the year A.D. 135. Indeed, the Aramaic dialect used in their books makes this western origin a likely one. And it is in these same regions that the *Psalms* of Thomas the Manichee made use of borrowings from their literature towards the end of the 3rd and the beginning of the 4th century.

We must recognize in them the Mughtasilas, a Baptist sect whose teachings were followed by Mani. Mandaean inscriptions, the oldest of which would seem to date from about 400 A.D., have been found on goblets and on tablets of lead. In the 8th century, Bar Konai specifies that in Mesene they were known chiefly by the name of Mandaeans, while farther north they received the name Nasoraeans or Dositheans. The *Haran Gawaita*, that they present today as the account of their past history, recalls the wanderings of certain of their ancestors, sometimes in the mountains of Media, sometimes in the legendary white mountain of Parwan, in the reign of a Parthian ruler named Artaban. It is known that other sects—Bardesanites, Kantaeans, Borborites—developed in a similar way in these countries, sometimes on the plateaux, sometimes in the valley. Perhaps the ancestors of the Mandaeans were represented by several of these sects: the cosmology and anthropology set forth in their sacred writings in fact represent, albeit with great originality, the fusion of separate doctrines in which various themes of the great Sethian apocryphas are to be found. The appellation "Dosithean" born by some of them reminds us indeed of the companion of Simon Magus, no doubt identical with the Dositheus under whose name is placed a Sethian revelation found at Chenoboskion. We must, however, wait for the complete publication of the manuscripts of the Coptic Museum before we can fully judge the closeness of the ties which they give promise of revealing between mainly "Sethian" Gnosticism and its Mandaean and Manichaean branches.

IV. Principal Stages of Development

Such are the principal figures and the principal sects which it is possible to place in the history of Gnosticism; varied figures, disguised sometimes as Greek philosophers, sometimes as disciples of one or another of the Baptists, sometimes as disciples of a shadowy Christ, sometimes as Persian fire-priests. It is possible to bring some order into this unco-ordinated picture by defining some of the stages which have marked the evolution of these doctrines.

A. The point of departure of Gnosticism can only be the moment at which men thought fit to make a distinction between the supreme deity and the creator of this lesser world. This dualism found one of its pretexts in the double preamble to the Book of *Genesis* (I 1-II 3, II 4ss), in which the creation of Adam is exposed under two different aspects, being first attributed to Elohim (literally: "the gods"), then assigned a second time to Jahweh (cf also *Job*, I, which contains the same duality of expression). Research undertaken round about our own time into Jewish doctrines has probably not yet permitted us to discover and to place precise traces of such a step, although it is foreshadowed in certain of the books found at Qumran; we must await another discovery. We can however state, in favour of these Judaic origins of Gnosis, that the essential part of the Greek philosophic vocabulary of which the sects were to make full use in their treatises appears with Philo. Perhaps even, in the writings of Philo, are to be found almost all the elements of the allegoric exegesises which delight the Gnostics, except that radical opposition to created matter which some of them will soon exhibit by cursing the God of the O.T. and his prophet Moses. Unless, perhaps, there is the germ of this dualism in the *Allegoric Commentary*, Philo's last work, in which he seems to turn away from the idea of an initially perfect Adam, to which idea he held in the *De Opificio*, to relate this perfection to the only model from above, Celestial Man, and to admit that the earthly Adam is, through his flesh, a prisoner of matter. Moreover we find in Philo that allegory which was to have such success with the Gnostics and the Manichaeans: the departure of the soul from the body symbolised by the crossing of the Red Sea by the Hebrews fleeing from Egypt, the land of servitude.

After Philo, the allusions in certain books of the N.T. to false prophets, according to whom this lesser world cannot be the work of the supreme deity—beliefs which the Creeds were to thrust aside with the formula "creatorem coeli et terrae"—give clear evidence that the decisive step had been taken some time before. It is therefore with all the more regret that we must after that wait almost for Irenaeus in order to find, at a precise date, definite details on some of the systems by which this conclusion has been reached. Among these precious milestones we will retain, for example, what is said of the doctrine of Satornil, and the summaries of Ophitian or Sethian works given by Irenaeus in chapters XXIX and XXX of his Book I. The long text which he analyses in chapter XXIX is, almost word for word, the one which was later incorporated in the first part of the *Secret Book of John* of which we have several editions, and which remained till a much later date the favourite work of the oriental Gnostics. Irenaeus knew then a doctrine, already formulated, which will be found again among the Sethians and of which, we also have glimpses behind some Valentinian exegesises.

B. A second fact we must underline is that, although certain exegises suppose myths originally expounded in the Semitic tongue, it is in the Greek language that Gnosticism developed. It seems, moreover, that its development very soon began to follow fairly closely, although by devious routes, the development of a Greek mystical philosophy, of an optimistic Hellenic Gnosis which starts with Philo and which will die out, six centuries later, with Damascius. It is for this reason that we must put certain pages of Eugnostos side by side with the vocabulary and even the ideas of certain treatises of Iamblichus and of Plutarch. It has been pointed out, elsewhere, how close the doctrine of one Numenius of Apamea was to Gnosticism, over which he had some influence. It is possible to examine closely the connexions between Gnostics and Neo-Platonists, principally in the first half of the 3rd century, thanks to our knowledge of the conflict which set Plotinus and his disciples in opposition to Gnostic sectarians. It is to be regretted that we have lost the original works of these sectarians which no doubt constituted the intellectual peak of Gnosticism. Had it not been for that, they would not have been taken so seriously by Plotinus and his disciples, as well as by the anonymous Hermetists to whom we owe the optimistic version of the myth of the first man included in the *Poimandres*. Moreover, one of the sectarians, Aquilinus, was a former fellow disciple of Porphyry and had distinguished himself by a commentary on the Greek myth of Maia, a theme parallel to that of the God-Wisdom pair giving birth to the Word as it is propounded in Biblical terms by Philo. The "father" of these Gnostics was perhaps

Prodicus, of whom only the name has been preserved. What must be especially emphasized is that, in brandishing at that time writings attributed in particular to Zoroaster, these sectarians were directly countering the use made by Porphyry and certain of his predecessors of *logia* doubtfully attributed to the same Persian magus. Proclus alludes to a revelation of Zoroaster—that of the Gnostics, probably, which the Platonist Cronius mentioned as early as the end of the 2nd century. It is true that Zoroaster had given his name, well before our era, to books on plants and stones. But the mystical revelations of Zoroaster that Porphyry and his former comrades bandied between them corresponded to a more recent manner, and the whole of the affair constitutes a very clearly-defined milestone in the history of the evolution of Gnostic systems.

At this point of its history, Gnosticism is clearly distinguished from the philosophical thinking of the time—which in its turn was nourished as much by oriental as by Hellenic myths—much more by the dualist interpretations it gives than by the impedimenta of cosmological, astrological and anthropological notions that it calls into play!

C. Two other characteristic phenomena again illustrate the evolution of Gnosticism but this time in Christian forms.

The theme of a Fate at last vanquished by some intervention from above which fettered the planets, masters till then of fate, was already to be found in the *Book of Enoch* (X-XVI; XVIII). This legendary episode which marks the establishment of a new cycle of visible heavens, delivered from the tyranny of the Archons, would appear, by reference to what *Genesis* says about the episode of the Flood, to be situated in the time of Noah. Pre-Christian Gnosticism was to take up the same theme; it is mentioned with this same signification in the *Sacred Book* of Eugnostos. Christianized Gnosticism, in its turn, was to inherit it, but only after transforming or repeating it in order to link it up with the account of a strange phenomenon which is said to have occurred at the beginning of our era. It assumes particular precision in the works of Valentinus and his disciples, although it is mentioned in the *Pistis-Sophia*. The former order of the stars was overturned so that their influences, to which men had been enslaved, were henceforth neutralized by an alternation imposed upon their movements. We are told that this phenomenon arose from the fact that the Saviour, ascending from this lesser world, forced his way through material heavens and crossed the point of interception of the circles of the "same" and the "other" (to borrow the terms used by

Plato's Timaeus), inscribed like a gigantic X on the heaven of the fixed
stars, the last boundary before the invisible world of Light. This
"boundary" /"Ὄρος, was thus associated with the image of the cross,
Σταυρός, according to the tempting exegesis of the Valentinians. That
would be the true explanation of the "crucifixion" of the Christ of the
Gnostics, impassive and non-incarnate. We meet the outlines of a
similar myth in several of the earlier Christian texts, such as the *Acts
of John*; it is commented on in the works of the pseudo-Denys to explain the eclipse, impossible at that time according to modern astrono-
mers, which took place at the death of Christ. Was this theme the
product of Christian imagination? But an analogous episode already
occurs in Pliny, as having been observed in Rome in his day (*Hist.
Nat.* XXXVI, 15). It seems that we have here a transposition of an
alleged miracle, originally conceived to glorify the new pagan Golden
Age of the reign of the deified Augustus, a figure to whom was already
attributed a miraculous abolition of astral Fate. It is noteworthy that
this phenomenon—this third "parousia" after the flood and the conflagration of the stars mentioned in *Genesis* and *Enoch*—was considered
an authentic cosmic phenomenon by the Gnostics whereas the Christians, for whom the true crucifixion could not be situated elsewhere
than at Golgotha, quickly abandonned the very ambiguous allegorical
interpretation which some of them had accepted. But it was doubtless
this legend, accepted for a time by Christianity at its outset, so close
in many details to the myth that the Gnostics had taken from *Enoch*
and other sources, that contributed most to the acceptance of the
figure of Christ by certain sectarians, despite the fact that evangelical
teaching presented him in a form which could scarcely be reconciled
with the original dogmas of Gnosticism.

   D. A no less essential stage in the formation of Christianised Gnoses
illustrates the effects of this same attitude.

   Valentinus and his disciples, when commenting on the teachings of
Christianity, do so essentially according to the canonical Gospels; this,
with respect to the primary nature of Gnosticism, is so original that
we are almost tempted by it to consider the Valentinians as more
Christian then Gnostic. A similar attitude, even more pronounced, on
the part of Marcion, has resulted in some critics refusing to consider
him a Gnostic, despite his intransigent dualism. There is indeed a
certain incompatibility between the canonical Gospels and Gnosis.
So, when other Gnostic groups claimed for themselves the redeeming
figure of Jesus, it was founded on apocryphal writings which they had

either stolen from primitive Christianity or invented for themselves; to *Matthew*, *Mark* and *Luke* they deliberately opposed *Thomas*, *Philip* and *Matthias*: the vicissitudes of the gospels attributed to these last suggest certain possible stages in the conflict between the sectarians and the Christian Church, the latter being forced, it seems, to condemn and destroy some of the older apocryphal writings from which the Gnostics too readily drew tendentious interpretations. Since the discovery of the Chenoboskion manuscripts, we know that, under the title of the *Gospel of Thomas*, the sectarians made use of the great collection of *logia* of Jesus, some fragments of which we already knew from the Greek papyri of Oxhyrhynchus, and from which innumerable quotations abound in the Patristic literature of the first centuries. Some of these *logia* were tinged with Platonism and it is probably the use that first the Gnostics, then the Manichaeans made of this circumstance that made the Church condemn it very early, and to publish in its place, under the same title of *Gospel of Thomas*, a harmless apocrypha on the childhood of Jesus. It was perhaps the other facet of this rivalry between the Church and the Gnostics which appears in connexion with the *Gospel of the Egyptians:* Clement of Alexandria has quoted some passages of the oldest work which bore this title and in which were some *agrapha* deserving consideration. A work bearing the same title has been found among the sectarians of Thebaid; but it is a revelation of Eugnostos, originally entitled: *Holy Book of the Great Invisible Spirit*. Perhaps the title of *The Gospel of Egyptians* was added to attract the curious after the first work of this name had disappeared? These procedures illustrate the first stages of literary stratagems which, probably after the 3rd century, were to become increasingly summary and audacious. Not content with inventing entire apocryphal works in which Christ was given the characteristics of the imaginary Gnostic Saviour, the sectarians went so far as to disguise their earliest revelations under summary Christian travesties. It is in this way that the *Epistle of Eugnostos to his disciples* was, later, cut up into slices offered to us as the substance of a dialogue between the Saviour and his disciples, the whole bearing the title *Sophia of Jesus*. In the same way the ancient sethian work mentioned by Irenaeus (I, XXIX) was set into a clumsy fabulation which transformed it into a revelation of Christ to the apostle John, then completed by sections on Eschatological subjects and, finally, by an "explicit" taken again from an old revelation, in which the heavenly Mother played the part of the redeemer; stupidly, the compiler forgot to correct some of the characteristics which, in this fragment, obviously cannot be applied to Jesus. At what point can we situate this falsification? It is noteworthy that this work, whose original contents played a considerable rôle among the Gnostics at a date anterior to Irenaeus, is only mentioned as attributed to John by heresiologists or in manuscripts later than the 3rd century. Does not this hasty and artificial Christianizing of texts by the Gnostics, texts which they had earlier put forward as revelations of the Magi or as philosophical treatises with no mention of Christianity correspond, considering its fairly precise date, to the fact that the victory then won by the Church over the Paganism that was persecuting her, incited the sects to hide their doctrines under Christian disguises which were henceforth to be the fashion?

V. Doctrines

It is not possible to set forth here all the variety of Gnostic doctrines. Between extremes such as Mandaeism and the Mesopotamian sects on the one hand, and Marcion and Bardesanes on the other, one can pick out only what was common to the most original sects, those most distinct from other contemporary religions, the most powerful and enduring. Most importance will therefore be given to the teachings, exempt for a long time from Christian influences, of the oriental sects which stem, according to legend, from Simon, Dositheus, Nicolas, Menander, Basilides and Satornil, that is the Sethians, Ophites, Archontics and Audians, whose doctrine was perhaps one of the sources of Valentinianism before fostering the Manichaean synthesis and producing other ramifications up to and beyond the 8th century. This choice can be justified by the very full documentation which both the heresiologists and the original manuscripts have preserved for us on these sects.

Before entering into a more detailed analysis we must point out that the unity of the Gnostic doctrines which will become evident rests more on the interpretation they put on certain Biblical, oriental and —at a lesser rate—Hellenic myths than on the account of these myths themselves. Their chief originality lies in having tried to incorporate these myths within a vast philosophical conception according to which this lesser world is only the counterpart, material, perishable, imperfect to the point of perversity, of an unattainable ideal universe. Making abundant use of the Platonic notion according to which the forms of this world are, in their diversity, only the unstable reflections of the ideal images of a higher unity, arranged in a remarkable system of hierarchy, the sectarians endeavoured to elaborate an explanation of these two contradictory universes, from which nothing was to be omitted; every detail of the superior world must have its counterpart in this world, a theory based on the supposition that the gnostic elect has been enabled, by revelations from above, to have cognizance of the eternal and intangible hierarchies evoked by the philosophers. Platonism in its later form, and the philosophy of Plotinus supply the earliest material for the infinite multiplication of abstract entities which has become, among the Gnostics, the main theme of descriptions of the higher world.

But for these explanations of the universe to be complete it was necessary to establish a precise parallelism between this abstract image of the higher world—the macrocosm—and the description of the microcosm of this world with not only its earthly realities but also its heavens where each one placed a complete hierarchy of gods connected with planets, Powers linked to the signs of the constellations, archangels and angels guarding the doors of every heaven, spirits and demons. Who would deny these beliefs which, apart from the differences in terminology and the discrepancy in the number of the heavens—(three, seven or ten)—the Greeks, the Egyptians, "the Chaldeans" and Judaism (if you look at the *Book of Enoch!*) are in agreement in accepting. So the Gnostics, while adapting certain features of their descriptions of the lesser world to the necessity of showing the material counterparts of certain abstract fictions from the world of ideas, had also to insert into the fine abstract hierarchies drawn from Plato and Philo, the alleged patterns of the heavens and their gods, angels and demons as well as of earthly humanity. The *Epistle of Eugnostos*, the anonymous work quoted by Irenaeus and used again in the *Secret Book of John* and the Valentinian system represent the most complete expression reached by these vain efforts to transform a mythical hypothesis into a complete philosophic doctrine. Inevitably, Gnosticism in all its forms remained enslaved to the myths, from various sources, which it had failed to repudiate.

It is noteworthy that, when it is a question of grouping the myths relating to the origin and development of this lesser world, the Gnostics have hesitated, even within doctrines almost identical in detail, between two or three main outlines, varying from a radical dualism to more optimistic hypotheses. The most common solution avoids stating that the dark matter was pre-existent like the supreme light: the creation of the material world was due only to an accident occuring in the higher world by the production of an imperfect entity, Ialdabaoth, who, ignorant and exiled, created for himself an aeon of darkness—this lesser world—which will dissolve without trace(?), when the act of redemption undertaken by the higher world is completed. A variation to this outline exists, according to which Ialdabaoth has a son Sabaoth; he it is who discovers the existence of the Light from above and, after his conversion, is set by the higher powers to replace his father, at the time of the overthrowing of the heavens and the chaining of the archons, and sets the cosmos on the way to salvation; we will pass over another variant of this last theme in which Ialdabaoth, although ignorant and imperfect, is presented as good and will allow himself to be converted to the works of Light (in Basilides, the later Marcionites, etc). As for radical dualism, to which, according to the *Philosophumena*, the Nicolaitans and Simon had already born testimony, it sets at the very origin of material creation a brutal attack by the pre-existing waters of darkness against the Light from above, an attack which develops in the intervening space of a third element, air or void. This myth is expounded in the same terms, word for word, by the Persian *Bundahishn* and by the *Paraphrase of Shem* used by the Sethians (the *Philosophumena* summarizes it, and the text of it has been found in the library of Chenoboskion). The same Persian theme appears in Basilides, in the Peratae, is called to mind by Marcion and Bardesanes and is finally perpetuated in the Euchites and the Bogomils. But in particular the Manichaeans have made it one of the principal foundations of their system. With the Gnostics it is sometimes interpolated by allusions in the cosmogonical accounts founded on the less dualist schemas to which allusion has already been made.

VI. DIVINITY

For our Gnostics, the notion of divinity is dispersed not only throughout all the hierarchies of the higher world, but also throughout the visible material heavens, since the sectarians have preserved, with all their titles, if not with all their power, the perverse divinities who rule humanity in this world. It is true that in contrast they refuse, or almost refuse, to use the term "god" to designate the infinite, ineffable, supreme Being. "God" is, in their eyes, a word inseparable from the perverse figure of the Demiurge in *Genesis* as also from the Greek divinities who rule the planets; they continue to use the word for these figures. When they use it to qualify certain entities of the higher world it is more especially to designate, in a rank between that of the supreme emanations and that of the angels of light, certain hierarchies on whose model the "gods" of the material world might logically have been formed.

However, we must establish the fact that when the Gnostics, independently of their philosophical treatises on the higher world, wished to describe it within the framework of the visions which transported certain of them—Shem, for example—towards higher "paradises", they did so by having recourse to the classical images of the *Book of Enoch* and to the Jewish visions of the divine Throne—the Merkaba—which, moreover, were associated with the springs and cypresses of the Pythagoreans, and the crowns of an astrology rich in images!

The origin of everything, whether it is according to Valentinus, Eugnostos, or the anonymous work revived in the *Secret Book of John*, is a perfect aeon, eternal, invisible, inconceivable, which does not participate in all the aeons of the higher world, from which it is isolated by its supremacy. This pro-father resides in repose where, alone, he contemplates his own image as in a mirror. With him there co-exists his Thought which is Silence.

From this primordial unity of the pro-Father and his Thought, which has no beginning and no begetting, are to emanate, begotten one of another, "intermediaries", the countless aeons of the Plerome. This transition from the non-begotten to the begotten is set forth in very different ways: even Eugnostos, in the two works attributed to him, proposes two different versions. The first stage is the production of a second image of the pro-Father, freed from the isolation of primordial infinity and capable of engendering. This supreme generative power is qualified, according to the different writings, as the Creative Father, Primal Man, Wisdom, or by proper names such as Barbelo (= Tetrad). This androgynous entity then engenders, one after another, the hierarchical structures of a Plerome, of which the texts give widely differing pictures: in Valentinus, thirty aeons resulting from the association of an ogdoad, a decade and a dodecade; in Eugnostos, a series of couples each associating the masculine aspect of an Anthropos with the feminine image of a Sophia; in the *Secret Book of John*, two series of five aeons; etc. Suffice it to say that these hierarchies include, albeit differently disposed, a certain number of essential figures: Monogene, Logos, the primal Celestial Mother, Man or Adam of the Light, Son of Man or Celestial Seth, the great generation of the

Sons of Primal Man, and finally at least one Sophia called Akhamoth or Prunicos, from whose sin this lesser world stems. We also found, quite often, four mysterious entities, called great Luminaries, perhaps modelled on the four incorporeal Creatures of the Divine Throne: Harmozel, Oroiael, Daveithe, and Heleleth who, each with a complement of two abstract entities, constitute twelve aeons: it is in these four Luminaries that the Gnostics who mention them usually situate Primal Adam, the celestial Seth, the Sons of Serh and finally the souls of "those who have repented"—details which suggest that the Luminaries were spread out like a series of Paradises between the material heavens and the supreme unattainable heavens.

We have used the term *aeons* to which the Gnostics attach a very particular meaning: each hierarchy of the higher world is an αἰών, a self-contained element with its heavens, its sources, its eternity, details which reproduce in the same order of numerical sub-divisions the general order of the Plerome, or indeed the order of the supreme Non-Begotten. Our lesser world, an aeon unique and finite in space and time, cuts but a small figure in comparison with that infinite succession of infinites whose images are multiplied like the repeated reflections in a succession of mirrors.

It is necessary to pass now, without yet leaving the long chain of divine generations, from these "intermediaries", these divine models, to the accident which our lesser world represents, a world which also has its gods, but this time mortal gods.

Whereas the proliferation of the aeons of the higher world should have continued normally through the work of the pairs of powers mentioned above, the feminine aspect of one of these powers—Sophia-Akhamoth, Sophia Prunicos, or Pistis-Sophia, according to the different versions,—was seized by exstasy or frenzy. According to a version to be found in the works of Hermetists *(Poimandres, Balinous)*, and which can be glimpsed in the *Pistis-Sophia*, this Sophia was seized by love for the matter to which she descended and became entangled in it, forgetting her heavenly home. According to the myth in the ancient work utilized by the *Secret Book of John*, this Sophia, carried away by her pride, tried to imitate the supreme power by begetting by herself alone without recourse to her male counterpart. But the result of this attempt is an imperfect, misshapen power, with the head of a lion and the body of a serpent, deprived even of the light shared by all entities which had appeared hitherto. Seized with shame, its mother hides it from the powers of the Plerome under a veil which is to represent in future the ultimate limit of the envelopes of the material world, whether it be the heaven of the fixed stars enclosing the heavens of the planets, or, according to some systems, the envelope of the intermediary heavens opposed like purgatories to the ascent of souls to the Light above.

For the Valentinians the act of extending this veil is represented by the sending out of Stauros and Horos, "Cross" and "Limit", which situates the frontiers of our world on an imaginary sphere where the circle of the ecliptic meets that of the celestial equator. Enclosed beneath this veil, Ialdabaoth—known also as Sacla, Samael, and Ariael—is unaware even of the existence of the world or Light. He has in his possession a heavenly spark which he took from his Mother and which he keeps hidden within himself. He also has—it seems—the waters of the dark abyss which, under the effect of his jealousy, are changing into matter. He possesses a "dark" fire. He hovers over the abyss on which his Mother—exiled from the higher world after her fault—wanders in all directions, for she is the Spirit (the word, in Hebrew, is in fact, feminine) of *Genesis* I, II. Indeed, if we refer to the *Secret Book of John* and to some other works of the same family, it is from now on an exegesis of the first pages of *Genesis* which is offered us, an exegesis in which the Gnostic commentator runs counter to the Biblical glorification of the Creator.

The pro-Father had united with his Thought to create the higher world. Ialdabaoth unites with his own ignorance to create his cosmos made, firstly, from twelve monstrous powers of which seven seem to stand for the planets while five correspond to infernal heavens. Besides their glorious name, these Powers have other secret names by the knowledge of which the initiates can not only escape their power but even overcome it! Angels and archangels are associated with them in a hierarchy which reaches the number 360 or 365, and which gives also the number of days in a year, an image of time to which this lesser world is henceforth chained. Then Ialdabaoth cries: "I am a jealous God and there is no other god but me!"

Meanwhile the repentance and the tears of Sophia (the first part of the *Pistis-Sophia* even puts into her mouth some of the apocryphal *Odes of Solomon*) have touched the supreme powers who take her from the material world and establish her at the lower limit of the world of Light where she finds her partner again and where she will wait to be

more completely rehabilitated after her fall. Such is the version of the
Secret Book of John and the *Pistis-Sophia*. The exegesis of this myth of
Sophia-Akhamoth offered by the Valentinians notes an additional detail: the emotions of Sophia occasioned by her repentance, when excluded from the Plerome and prevented by Horos from returning to
it, become the very matter from which our world is formed. A Sethian
work, the *Hypostasis of the Archons*, ignores the penitance of Sophia to
whom, on the contrary, he attributes the rôle of a redeemer, probably
because the compiler of this work confused Sophia-Pistis-Akhamoth
with the great Sophia, mother of Life (Zoe) to whom certain ancient
systems attributed the redeeming descent into Hell which was later
given to the Christian Saviour.

VII. MAN

After thus resolving the problem of reconciling their faith in an ineffable higher deity with their belief in the reality of other gods, archangels and angels, the Gnostics have to solve the problem of man.
They are convinced that their soul is a spark of light unjustly imprisoned in malicious matter: the mythical history of the universe, as
they imagine it, will continue with the object this time of explaining
our captivity in this world and announcing the next steps towards
salvation. But this salvation is not promised to all men under the same
conditions; only some, the elect, are certain of obtaining it.

The best account of this is still the archaic treatise which has been
revived in the *Secret Book of John*. In it we see the creation of the first
Adam by the Demiurge and his archons which gave rise to the ac-
cusation levelled at the Gnostics of attributing the work of *Genesis*
not to the God of Moses but to Samael and his powers, that is, to the
"angels".

To the blasphemy of Ialdabaoth who proclaims himself the only
God a voice replies, from the heights of the Heavens of Light: "Thou
art mistaken, Samael: Man exists, and the Son of Man!"—words which
can only be clearly understood if one remembers the importance accorded to Anthropos in certain descriptions of the higher world of
Light. This is probably one of the most fundamental conceptions of
Gnosticism, even preceding the elaboration of its artificial schemas of
the higher world. It is the figure of such a man that the prophet
Ezekiel saw on the throne of the Merkaba (*Ez* I, 26). Mystical Judaism

developed at length, in a sense even closer to the Gnosis, the theme of
Adam Qadmon, primal man. This Adam-Kasia (= Secret) with his
heavenly son Seth plays a considerable part in the Mandaean gnosis.
Among our Gnostics, the anonymous treatise of Bruce gives at some
length a description of the celestial Anthropos, each member of which
reproduces the entities of the higher universe. Indeed, the heavens
half-opened to allow the celestial voice to descend, and at the same
moment the archons of Ialdabaoth see the image of the first celestial
Anthropos reflected in the lower waters: everything, even to the very
foundations of the abyss, is shaken by the power of this vision. It is
at this moment that the Demiurge says to his angels: "Let us make a
Man in the image of God and in our own image, so that his image
may supply us with light." The seven powers of the planets and the
other powers of the lesser heavens share among themselves the fabri-
cation of the parts of a "psychic Adam." But they cannot breathe life
into him. So, in order to take back by ruse from Ialdabaoth the spark
of Light which he had seized, the Father in heaven sends his messengers, in disguise, to advise the Demiurge to breathe his spirit into
Adam's mouth. But as soon as Ialdabaoth yields to this advice, the
spark leaves him to enter into the first earthly man who arises, resplendent this time, superior to those who fashioned him. Then the
jealous powers refashion him, enclosing this time the spirit and the
psyche in the prison of a body of mortal flesh which they then cast
down to the lowest level of their cosmos, into the socalled Paradise of
the O.T., with its evil trees. In two of them however, Gnosis and Life
have been hidden by the powers above. Whether in the form of a
serpent or, according to other traditions, of an eagle, the saviour from
the world above incites Adam, and Eve formed by the Demiurge from
his rib, to taste the tree by which the mysteries from above are revealed. Meanwhile, the archons, to enslave Adam, have refashioned
his body with material elements, fire, earth, water and air and have
placed within him a second spirit—the "counterfeit" spirit which wars
with the spirit from above. This idea goes back to Basilides; it is his
"adventitious soul".

Ialdabaoth, furious, expels the first couple from Paradise. But at the
same time he defiles Eve who, as a result, begets Abel and Cain.
Adam's true offspring is Seth, to whose seed alone is promised salvation. It is to escape the Demiurge that Noah, a descendant of the
"kingless race" (thus named because it escapes the tyranny of the stars),
builds the ark and shelters in it with the family whilst the race born of

the daughters of the earth and the angels of the Demiurge is, for the first time, annihilated. To the episode of the Flood we must attach also the burning up of the planets, cast into the abyss by the anger of supreme powers and the subjection of the visible heavens to immutable movements which annul their powers.

The formation of every man, if we are to believe works such as the *Pistis-Sophia* is a faithful reflection of the fashioning of Adam by the powers. Indeed, astrologers in the early centuries of our era taught the same theories and on this point the Gnostics lack originality. Every part of man, physical or moral, belonged to a power in the visible heavens who fashioned it. Into this body, assembled in the womb of the mother before birth, descended the soul which, coming down through every heaven, received from each such dispositions as were appropriate to each: only the coming of the Saviour was to break this hold that the stars had over men by chaining the archons to the celestial sphere and making them turn now in their former direction, now in the opposite—if we are to believe the *Pistis-Sophia*. Finally the powers insinuated into the foetus the "counterfeit", or rather the "counteracting" spirit, destined to thwart all man's impulses towards salvation. This is a revival of the Persian theory of the "two souls", which, moreover, the sectarians of Qumran had already more or less adopted before the Gnostics. On the other hand, reflecting each of the three successive stages which had marked the creation of the first earthly man, one can distinguish three categories of men, according to their degree of perfection: the somatic or *Hylici*, whose purely carnal substance belongs only to this world; the *Psychici*, whose soul strives to return to the higher world; the *Pneumatici*, chosen beings exempt from the Fate of this world.

The Gnostics seem not to have established between man and woman an unshakeable inequality. Eve, like Adam, had within her a spark of light. In the history of the salvation of mankind Noah's wife, the "luminous" Norea, plays an important part. Those of the sectarians who plagiarized Christianity have assigned to Mary, Mariamne and Salome rôles as important as those of the apostles: this belief corresponds, perhaps, to the fact that the principal redeeming entity from above—Wisdom, Mother, Barbelo—was originally conceived as feminine. However, the perfect celestial form to which all were to return was an androgyny in which the masculine principle was to some extent pre-eminent, if only because the fault from which this lesser world emerged had been committed by the feminine aspect of one of the aeons; the lesser world is often designated: "the works of feminity." But, in the earliest versions of the salvation myth the feminine entities play a considerable part, beginning with the celestial Mother, the great Sophia, counterpart of the Father, who will later be replaced by Christ as well as by other entities: Mirothea, Derdekea, Zoe.

We must at this point rapidly add a few words on the form these myths took among the Mandaeans. It is true that, in their abundant texts, later developments have complicated and obscured what the original doctrine may have been. It seems besides that certain important rôles are here repeated, attributed to multiple entities, as if at least two versions of the Gnostic myths had been mixed together when they were added. The redemptive figures, the creative entities of the material world and of man are multiplied. But—although we find in them Seth (Shitil), Shem (Shum) and Norea (Nuraitha)—the forms these fables take and the meaning that is given them are remarkably like those attributed by the Gnoses to Simon, Dositheus, Nicotheus, etc. (Do not the Mandaeans indeed call themselves Dositheans?). According to their books, at the top of the ineffable higher world Mana-rabba—the Great Spirit, the Great King of Light—is seated at the heart of a white and shining expanse of water. Beneath him come the aeons—the Uthras—of Yo-shamin—"Iahweh of the heavens"—and of Abathur; three aeons of Abathur wish to make dwelling-places and a world: the Gnosis of Life—Manda-d'Hayye—descends, to make this project fail, into the Darkness where she chains up Ur. In other versions, this descent is attributed to Hibil-Ziwa. The theme of the creation of Adam beginning from the reflection of the celestial image is repeated: thus was created Ptahil who, on the other hand, is going to play the rôle of a demiurge. As for the fashioning of Adam by the seven archons, this occupies an important central position in this mythology and his descendants—Abel, Seth and Enoch—play the same privileged rôle as in the Gnoses already summarized. Similarly, Abraham and Moses are treated as false prophets: but in addition Jesus is named the "False Messiah" and the "Christ of nothing." The true prophet is John the Baptist, who is said to have at first remained hidden in the "white mountain" before administering the baptism of life in the Jordan. He would seem to have been preceded by Enosh-Uthra who, after the Flood, had revealed the Gnosis to the chosen before bearing witness against Jesus as the "Son of Man", performing miracles similar to those of Christ.

VIII. Personal Salvation

We must perhaps consider separately the vicissitudes which, from one existence to another, bring individuals nearer to or farther from their salvation, and the general redemptive system by means of which the world of Light prepares the final dissolution of the cosmos. Indeed, we shall comprehend more clearly the details of these two subjects if we think on the one hand of the destiny of souls on their way through the cycles of the material world; and on the other hand of the stages by which the Plerome intends to rescue the elect from this universe before proceding to its destruction.

In this world man has been subjected to all the powers of the visible heavens, large or small, which the old astrologers could imagine: when he is born he already belongs to them for it is they who have fashioned him and have left their marks on each of his organs, physical or moral. So, according to the conjunctures which cause these various powers to rule in turn, man must suffer the ills and passions generously dispensed by each of them. He can only defend himself against them by the incantations of magic: we have seen that each power received, besides its own name, a second secret appellation whose effect was to constrain it even when in a position of power. The initiate who knows these names uses them to ward off the corresponding evils. But this only applies to what concerns the body and the soul. To combat the "pneumatic" spark which has been injected from above into the spiritual beings, the archons have fashioned this "counterfeiting" spirit which constantly wars against the Spirit. In order to escape the consequences of the aberrations it causes, of the weakening of the spark of light hidden within the individual, men need the rites revealed by the Gnosis to accompany, if not to take the place of, "repentance".

It is probably from Platonism that Gnosticism has borrowed the belief in the transmigration of souls. It has incorporated this belief into all the fantastic details about calesial and infernal topography that are supplied by the other-worlds of Greco-Egyptian mythology, Pythagorism, and the apocryphal writings of the Old Testament. Thus the fate of the individual exposes it, when it leaves the body, to an infinite variety of judgments and trials. It is true that, in the case of one of the chosen whose purity is guaranteed by all the sacraments of Gnosis, its translation to the gates of Light will take place without fear of return. At each stage, the soul presents to the "frontier guards" powers who guard the heavenly portals, the "seals" and mystic words

which constrain the guards to let it pass; by the "column of light"—
the Milky Way—it ascends towards the moon whose quarters correspond to the periods in which it is filled with the sparks of light ascended from below, before sending them on higher to the world of
light. At the frontiers of this world are to be found the places of celestial baptism with their springs and their trees guarded by figures,
some of which seem to be angels or other fantastic entities, while yet
others (Gamaliel, James, Theopemptos, Samlō) appear to be prophets
of Gnosis elevated to a heavenly function (the same features appear in
Mandaean works); these guardians complete the purification of the
chosen ones before, introduced among the Sons of Light, they join
the Kingless Race of the sons of Seth.

In many of the details of this ascension the Gnostics have only
copied, with some adaptations to their doctrine, notions current at
that time in the Greek and Roman world. We have only to read formularies such as the so-called "Mithraic liturgy" or the prayers for the
liberation of Adam from ἀνάγκη! Let us add that certain privileged
beings were believed to have made this ascension in their life-time,
even reaching the summit of the Plerome. Such was the case of the
Seth, son of the earthly Adam, Nicotheus, Phosilampes, Marsanes and
yet others. Not only Gnosis but also mystic Judaism sought these
visions, from which the apostle Paul, in particular, may have benefited
before his conversion (*II Cor*, XII, 2).

If the "perfect" ascend directly to the Plerome, such is not the case
for those weighed down by diverse deficiencies. There are some, however, who will be purified in the intervening distance and will wait at
the portals of Light for the moment of admission, without returning
below. Others will be cast into the hands of tormentors and into
punishment of which Dante's *Inferno* is only a poetic interpretation.
Then they suffer oblivion of their past life and are recast into new
bodies.

IX. Collective Eschatology

If individuals succeed in thus rising from their material prison
towards the heights, it is because the Plerome contributes to this ascension by a series of steps of which the first image is given by the
episode of the repentance of Sophia-Akhamoth and her return to her
male counterpart.

Indeed, the world of Light has engaged a systematic battle against the Demiurge and his archons. What gives the struggle its strange, absurd character is the fact that the infinite world above has to employ ruses and disguises to operate in the world of darkness and ignorance, imperfect and impotent though this world may be. It is perhaps because, more then at first appears, there is in the background of this drama, the belief in the pre-existence of darkness and the abyss which is inherent in the most radical dualism.

Against the Race of Perfect, the Demiurge and his powers do not cease to send cataclysms—the Flood, from which Noah saves the chosen—and Conflagration—perhaps that which destroyed Sodom and Gomorrha where, in compensation, Seth caused life-giving thermal springs to flow, if we are to believe the *Holy Book* of Eugnostos. Traces of these ideas are already to be found in *Enoch*.

Meanwhile Wisdom from above injects into captive humanity the epinoia of light, the mystic "drop", the Logos, the Gnosis. The power which presides at this operation is the supreme Sophia, counterpart of the Father; the Mother; Barbelo, according to the situation. To arouse the elect by reminding them of their heavenly origins and revealing to them the secrets of baptism, a succession of Saviours and Prophets —some supernatural, others learned doctors risen from mankind,—is sent to them.

It appears that several separate myths have here combined and intermingled their variants: the earliest is that which attributes the work of redemption to the descents of the celestial Mother into the abyss wherein mankind is imprisoned: it goes back to models such as the Sumerian myth of Ishtar. It will merge admirably with the theme of the redemptive Sophia whose existence is implied by, among others, the Biblical *Book of Wisdom*. To that is added the story which brings in the heavenly Seth and his image, the son of the earthly Adam. It will be associated with the legend which makes the Magi the prophets of redemption. Finally, the revelation of heavenly secrets and of baptisms is the work of various prophets—Nicotheus, Marsanes and Martiades, Phosilampes and Theopemptos, to which names is added that of John the Baptist, who plays an essential rôle in Mandaean beliefs.

The redeeming descent of the Mother is reported in the fragment of an early work incorporated in the end of the *Secret Book of John:* this deals with the third and last descent of the power from above who, having twice descended to this world in disguise now appears in it in glory to put an end to this aeon. It is as the "wealth of Light, the memory of the Plerome" that she penetrates the dark abyss that is the "prison of the body," calling Adam who is there chained and asleep and, after awakening him from his heavy sleep, sealing him with five seals (corresponding to the five senses?) of Light and Water so that death has no more power over him. This "descent into hell" in which our Gnostics later replaced the Mother first by the heavenly Seth, and then by Christ, is also to be found, much developed, in Manichaean works.

The version which makes Seth the Redeemer, until he is replaced in this rôle by Christ, brings in also the Magi as guardians and prophets of the mysteries of the redemption. Why? No doubt Zoroaster was inserted there because of Balaam's prophecy according to which there would one day rise the star of annunciation (*Numbers* XXIV, 17). Perhaps also because the *Apocalypse of Hystaspes* had given the model of a prophecy about the overthrow of the kingdoms of this world. The sectarians developed these themes mainly in their Revelation of *Adam to Seth*, the point of departure of a multitude of apocryphal writings which were to become more sober and more Christian as they changed to romantic stories about the "Treasure Cave" where the revelations were kept until the coming of the Saviour. According to the *Apocalypse of Adam* a succession of kingships saw a succession of saviours appear in this world until there grew up a golden age in which at last the perverse Demiurge was replaced by his son; this theme we have already indicated. Was it only a Persian influence which introduced these beliefs into Gnostic mythology? Hellenism knew the same themes of the overthrow of Ahriman by Ormuzd in a form which was abundantly exploited by astrology, the fall of Kronos and his replacement by Zeus at the head of the visible heavens. And yet, considering the precise details which the pseudo-Clementine "*Recognitiones*" and "*Homilies*" give on the Gnostic myth of Zoroaster, of which they give many quotations, it appears incontestable that the myths which came from Persia by a mysterious route—perhaps by the followers of Mithras, for the figures of Ostanes and Zoroaster have been painted on the Mithraeum of Doura-Europos—did indeed penetrate into the oriental circles in which the Gnoses and Christianity developed.

Announced by the stars—whether the star of Balaam, of Seth or of the Magi—the Saviour, the "new star" came down through the Spheres, disguised as an angel of the lesser heavens. His appearance in this world is recounted in different ways: he appears gigantic, sometimes also with three faces, those of a child, an adult and an old man, which intermingle. Even when they give him the person of Jesus, the Gnostics find any suggestion of an incarnation repugnant. This is probably one of the main reasons why they rejected the canonical Gospels, which tell of the earthly life of Jesus and his Passion, and preferred either to use texts which left these subjects in shadow or to make for themselves alleged revelations in which the Saviour does not appear to his disciples until after the Resurrection, then to stay with them for the long period in the course of which he administers his teachings. To treat it otherwise would be in contradiction to their earlier myths according to which an entity invisible to all but the perfect came down through this world to the abyss to deliver the chosen from it. As we have already seen, the passage of the redeeming entity through the visible skies was marked by a veritable upheaval of the ordering of their movements, not only because the Demiurge was dispossessed of his throne and replaced by one or several beneficent powers, but also because the Archons were chained to the vault of material heaven, and thus constrained to rotate in a contrary direction, which destroyed their influence on the creatures of the lower world. This version of the later Jewish legend according to which Satan was vanquished by Michael (the episode took place after the Exodus, according to *Jude* V, 6, or about the time of the Flood, according to *Enoch* X, 11), which is presented here as the "crucifixion" of the Archons, was to find its most complete expression in Manichaeism. As for the last act of the redeeming power, which was to force upwards the barrier of Horos which marked the limit of the material heavens, it is this episode, more or less a reduplication of the preceding one, which the sectarians wish to present as the true "Crucifixion" of the Saviour. When our Gnostics were propagating such a doctrine they believed, moreover, that they had reached the end of the times, the beginning of which had been marked precisely by this episode: the secret books, hidden until then in inaccessible places such as the mountain of Light with its cave of the Magi, the mountain of Seir and that of Charax, had just been brought out by their learned doctors in whom one or other of the higher entities (most usually Seth, the Great Power according to one Simon, the Heavenly Mother according to the companions of certain of these prophets) had established themselves. It remained to await, no longer fearing the Archons who are now powerless, the final judgment of this world and the ascent of the

Perfect towards the higher heavens: the third of the great "moments" already mentioned by the Gnostics, and whose succession Manichaeism was to affirm yet more clearly.

With the help of one of these myths, Gnosis was to give a new force to the comparatively recent Jewish legend of the fall of Satan whose place, as first of the archangels, was taken by Michael. For some time already, Jewish angelology had identified the seven archangels with the planets. The replacing of Satan—Samael—by Michael was the equivalent in Jewish style of the replacement of Kronos by Zeus or of Ahriman by Ormuzd. So, in as much as Gnosis had to hide under a cloak less suspect in the eyes of the Church, it transferred the substance of the episode of Ialdabaoth replaced by Sabaoth to apocryphas in which many of the details of the anti-Mosaic myth became simple incidents in the combat of Michael against Lucifer. After all, the Gnostic interpretation of these legends was already latent, at an earlier date, in the allusions that the Jewish mystics made to them under the cover of commentaries on the Old Testament.

X. ETHICS

It is difficult to develop any clear code of ethics as long as one believes oneself to be subjected, in one's actions, to the domination of the planets and the constellations: it is useless to draw up a code of ethics when, later, one believes oneself endowed with celestial grace which will cause one, whatever one does, to pass without let or hindrance through the judgments of the other-world to attain, through the sacraments, heavenly beatitude. It is true that certain texts such as the *Pistis-Sophia, the Books of Ieou*, the last sections of the *Secret Book of John* or of the *Sophia of Jesus* expose a complete hierarchy of pains and penitences which sinners must undergo, but these are but exercises in literary "padding", lacking any precise psychology, and which serve rather to underline the moral insouciance of the compilers. Have the Christian heresiologists then justly accused the sectarians of many abominations? The testimony of Plotinus is hardly more favourable to them, taken as a whole. Yet Gnosis, in its principal forms, involves an appeal to a rigorous asceticism, and it is indeed thus that Manichaeism was to interpret it and Mandaeism preserve it. It implied the condemnation of the flesh and all its works. And yet certain sects were reputed to be given to the strangest forms of immorality. Mention will be made later of their strange practices. They can be explained, in as much as we are not dealing with calumnies, by various attitudes: for some, they represent the principle of opposing in every way the Biblical Law because this, the work of the perverse Creator, can only be evil and contrary to the way of salvation. To this could be added a glorification of the reprobates of the Old Testament who, for these same reasons, are considered heroes. For others the principle was operative that the flesh belongs to matter and so, since it has nothing in common with the higher elements of man, it is a matter of complete indifference what use we make of it. It follows that, if some sectarians showed a complacency for lewdness which was in no way authentically religious, there may have been others for whom the systematic abuse of the flesh was indeed, as they claimed, a form of asceticism. Finally, in other cases, certain Greek mysteries—among the Naassenes, for example—may have been the origin of mystical interpretations concerning the union of the male and female elements, and fecundation. It is significant that the passage on carnal union in the *Asclepius* (§ 21) was reproduced in full in a codex from Chenoboskion.

XI. Sects and the Faithful

It remains, after this account of the doctrines to say what is known of the organisation of the sects and their practices. These are the points on which we are the least well-informed.

It appears that Simon presented himself as the Supreme Power. The Gnostic compilers, in their writings, often claim to be transcribers of revelations dictated by the heavenly Seth or by Christ, of whom some of them no doubt believed themselves to be temporary incarnations. If indeed these men were honest in thinking themselves inspired, it is a matter of conjecture whether this belief that they were possessed by a higher entity only came upon them at times of visions during which they felt transported beyond this world (according to practices of which Jewish mysticism also had cognisance), or whether they believed, throughout the whole course of their daily activity, that they were the living figures of these entities. If we judge by what we know from one Mark the Magus, there must have been among them more thaumaturges and more theurgy than among the Neo-Platonists. Plotinus makes fun of the practices of certain sectarians who invoked the supreme deity by formulas accompanied by tongue-clicking and strange whistlings. The masters of Gnosticism, taking into consideration their rôle in the transmission of certain sacraments, certain initiations, could not fail to associate a certain sacerdotal character with an inevitable claim to gifts of prophecy. The teaching of some of them appears, whether in Rome or Alexandria, to be addressed to a wider public than the initiates only: although, as in the *Epistle of Ptolemy to Flora*, there was probably no question at that time of what the texts and rites, vowed to the most profound secrecy, literally contained; the prohibition on communication of the most important revelations to the uninitiated, placed at the end of certain manuscripts, is accompanied by curses which are intended to terrify.

Did women have a particular part to play?—Probably yes, since prophetesses are mentioned among the Elkesaites, since it was the female initiates who wished to draw St. Epiphanius into their mysteries. To this may be added the example of Marcellina who brought the teachings of Carpocrates to Rome. Among the Mandaeans, religious functions were, as a rule, open to women.

It seems, in other respects, that the initiates were divided into several classes. We learn, in the *Sacred Book* of Eugnostos, of the elect and of people who are willing to receive them, which perhaps already represent, as in Manichaeism, a dinstiction between the perfect, entirely vowed to the precepts of Gnosis, and the faithful who minister to the needs of the perfect but continue to lead a life that we may call "secular". But—and this was a feature which, at the time of the persecutions, widened the gap still more between the Gnostics and orthodox Christians—it appears that most of the sects made their faith a strictly secret matter, in no way betrayed by the exterior existence of the adepts, and thus not exposing them to any persecution or any martyrdom—far from it! Were certain actions forbidden to them, as was the case for the Manichaeans? We have some indication, in the anathemas pronounced by the Christian Church as well as in the doctrines of Gnosticism itself, of the principle of some abstinences, mainly concerning food and drink. But it is possible that only a few sects really observed rigorous asceticism.

We know, on the other hand, how they carried out their apostleship towards the faithful of the Christian Church. They gradually disclosed, it appears, certain of their particular beliefs, those closest to the beliefs of the Church, complaining of being treated as excommunicates despite the fact that their doctrines were the same. They also asked questions. Once they had shaken the faith of the one they were questioning they drew him aside and revealed their secrets to him. The female initiates used other wiles: in Egypt, the most seductive of some of the Gnostics tried to seduce St. Epiphanius in his youth: "I am a chosen vessel, and I can save those who are in error..." they claimed (*Panarion* XXVI, xvi).

Finally the sects could attract others to them by the lure of magic formulas, and amulets able to protect against the manifold powers of the planets. These subjects held in their writings, a place both so precise and so wide that they could, by making use of their knowledge of them, satisfy a very wide "clientèle".

XII. Worship

A. *Sacred Objects*

If there remains any vestige of a place of worship of Gnosticism, no archeologist has yet recognized it as such. There are no precise details in the texts: what was the temple erected at Samos to the honour of the Gnostic Epiphanius? As for the "ikons" of Christ, Paul, Homer and Pythagoras before which Marcellina burned incense in Rome, the Emperor Alexander Severus, who did not pass for a Gnostic, worshipped the same. We can only make conjectures: perhaps some of these sanctuaries resembled one or another of the numerous *mithraea* which have been discovered and in which, as at Doura-Europos, Zoroaster and Ostanes were represented? Indeed, certain elements of the Mithraic décor had precisely the same meaning for the Gnostics: the statues of lion-headed Aion in particular are very close to the figure which the texts attributed to Ialdabaoth. It is true that other cults knew variations of this same figure: the Orphic Phanes of the Modena museum, surrounded by seven coils of a serpent, encircled by the Zodiac; and not forgetting the mysterious figurine of the sanctuary of the "Syrian" gods at the Janicule. But until now we have only been able to connect with Gnosis certain paintings of the subterranean chapel of the Aurelii in the Viale Manzoni in Rome: the sanctuary probably dates from about 220 A.D. The interpretation of its decoration still poses many problems.

But although isolated from the original context and now scattered, a certain number of small objects from antiquity offer us images much closer to the teachings of the sects. They consist, firstly, of numerous carved gem-stones depicting fantastic figures with names and mys-

terious formulas which, until now, have only otherwise been found
in magic formularies and which certain texts from Chenoboskion at
last help us to locate in a precise mythology. On some of these gems
we see lion-headed Ialdabaoth, known also as Ariael; we find Seseg-
genbarpharoggen; some of the mysterious signs on the reverse side
of these stones have scarcely any parallel other than in the schemas
and symbols of the *Books of Ieou*. Even more precise are the figures,
accompanied by formulas, on the Greek magic papyrus 1 of Oslo;
certain details recall entities mentioned in the *Sacred Book* of Eugnostos.
The only problem is to know whether Gnosis, which admits to
borrowings from formularies which did not perhaps originally belong
to it (book of the *Arkhanggelike of Moses; Testament of Solomon;* etc),
artificially introduced such entities into its myths simply to enrich
them and to attract devotees of older magical schools. The same
problem arises with regard to the "Sethian" *tabulae defixionum* which
conjure up, in Seth's name, a turbulent deity, closer no doubt to the
Asiatic god Seth than to the heavenly prophet of Gnosis, albeit certain
features could equally well be appropriate to the latter.

Finally, the object which seems most closely to recall the practices
of the sects is a chased alabaster cup, originating in Syria or Anatolia
and until now usually referred to as "Orphic". Within the bowl appear
sixteen figures lying naked in a circle, their feet towards the centre,
round a coiled serpent. But here again nothing authorizes us to expressly assign this representation to one or another of the sects,
Gnostic or otherwise, who practised this cult of the serpent.

B. *Sacred Places*

It appears that certain sects knew of particularly sacred places: some
of them were probably inaccessible, or even mythical, such as the
mountain of the Treasure Cave of Adam and Seth—although Monne-
ret de Villard has been able to associate the theme of the Magi to the
Kuh-i-Kwaja in Eastern Persia: it would be one of the features of the
"mountain of Seir." We may also mention the mythical mountain of
Seldao (the name of the guardian appointed to it?) and the mountain
of Charax, near the Persian Gulf. The Sethians remembered that
their ancestors lived on Mount Hermon; they attributed to the
Great Seth the mysterious healing powers of the thermal springs of
Sodom and Gomorrha, also mentioned by Josephus (*Ant. Jud.*, XVII,
VI, 5; *Bell. Jud.*, XXXIII, 5). The Kantaeans believed in the presence
of certain holy virgins at Mabboug, Hetra and Harra. The Jordan,

Jerusalem, with the Mount of Olives and also perhaps the traditions which place the tomb of Adam on Golgotha, cannot be separated from the revelations and the baptisms which were instituted there. Moreover the waters of the world were considered either as beneficent if they flowed from north to south, or materialistic and evil if, like the Nile, they flowed towards the north.

C. *Religious Practices*

As with their doctrines and their iconography, their religious practices brought together rites, most of which were borrowed from all sides. If we are to judge by a hymn inserted at the end of the *Sacred Book* ... of Eugnostos, we may suppose the existence of confessions during which the initiate, in order to have access to certain sacraments, himself proclaimed his perfection and his knowledge of the mysteries opening the door of the other world; the tone is rather that of magic, which conjures the powers rather than implores them: the term "repentance" is ill-suited to such an attitude! The essential rites, in any case, were the regenerative baptisms, intended to awaken the spark of light imprisoned in the faithful and to confer on him Gnosis, by means of which he would reascend to his celestial origin. These baptisms seem to have been multiple ones, involving immersions and anointings. The *Pistis-Sophia* describes the fantastic institution of baptisms "of the first oblation", "of Fire" and "of Spirit". However, if we turn to the present practices of the Mandaeans, it would seem rather to be a question of one and the same rite repeated in different circumstances. However that may be, the baptisms that were practised in this lesser world were only a preparation for the baptisms of water or celestial fire which the Perfect would receive after his death when he reached the true springs of living water and their guardians before attaining to anapausis. They also conferred on each other various "seals", intended to protect them from the baser powers and to open the gates of the Mysteries of Light, whether during their earthly life or after death. Some of these "seals" may only have been anointings accompanied by formulas. This was perhaps the case for th "five seals" which, to judge by their number, probably had reference to the five physical senses. Others may have been accompanied by talismans inscribed with figures and diagrams, if we are to judge by the rich catalogue of such signs given in the *Book of Ieou*. With these rites was associated the conferring of mystic surnames, following a practice already attested in mysteries earlier than Gnosticism. The Valentinians and the Marcosians, among others, celebrated "spiritual marriages", which no doubt symbolised the "return" of the initiate to his pristine plenitude, the celestial reunion of his male and female aspects, thus realizing the ideal androgyny already imagined by Plato. The same sectarians administered to the dying a baptism intended to make them invisible and invulnerable during their ascent through the perverse heavens. We can only glean vague allusions to all these rites. We must no doubt imagine them to be rather similar to the austere ceremonies still practised by the Mandaeans.

Certain sects had instituted stranger practices. The worship the Ophites offered to a live reptile around which they placed the loaves which were to be used at their feasts probably goes back to certain Hellenic mysteries: Manilius speaks of the worshippers of the constellation Ophiuchus who used similar practices. Mark the Magus had codified the formulas of strange liturgies during the course of which they made the contents of three cups turn red and overflow, thus symbolizing the blood of the Celestial Mother. The *Pistis-Sophia* recalls rites which claimed to open the planetary heavens whose secrets would then be revealed to the initiates. It is probable that they did indeed try to perform such incantations, for the religion of the Pharaohs already speaks of such alleged visions. In later Gnostic texts these conjurations, complicated in the extreme, appear as so-called liturgies celebrated by the Saviour in the presence of his disciples.

It remains for us to say a word about the licentious practices which have been attributed to certain sects. On this subject we have only the accusations of opponents of the sects who are said to have used them. Mark the Magus, and also others, would seem not to have preserved the symbolic character, apparently accorded it by the Valentinians, of the mystic marriage representing the return to supreme unity. In Egypt, the beautiful women of the sect who tried to attract St. Epiphanius did not only propose to show him their sacred books. The Phibionites—it is claimed—practised rites of sexual union while refusing procreation. Certain of the great "Gnostics" made use of abominable practices. It is true that in the view of the religions of antiquity such rites may have seemed admissible and that it was only with the coming of Christianity that they began to arouse a natural repulsion.

XIII. Origins

If we classify the different elements of the Gnostic systems along with the greater or lesser importance of their rôle, it is possible to recognize what was perhaps the original basis of these doctrines at their beginning, and to realize why something which might have become nothing but a collection of sketchy little religions assumed, quite early, a certain unity under the effect of one or two powerful currents which regrouped the sects, giving them that cohesion which has caused some modern scholars to believe that Gnosis could have been a "world religion".

For the doctrine this basis is the dualism and for the rites it is the institution of purifying baptisms.

The dualism which dominates most of these doctrines was, at its origins, much less a philosophical principle than the popular expression of old myths originating in Sumer and Persia and which suddenly, after centuries of sterility, took on a profound meaning as a response to the pessimism and the need for salvation of an age in which all the great religions seemed full of deception. It told of the descent into this world—an inferior element of a universe, the superior element of which was separated from ours by the abyss of a void till then impassable—of a redeeming entity penetrating to the depths of hell and bringing the revelation of the celestial springs of unfailing purity at which mankind might regain his purity and be delivered from the burden of the flesh which imprisons him in this world. Thus, Gnosticism was to bring about an extraordinary development of the dogmas and practices of the baptist sects of which, even today, the Mandaeans are an eloquent survival. It is noteworthy that it is in almost the very regions where it was born—between Jordan, Mount Hermon, the land of the Medes and Babylonia—that Gnosticism has survived the longest, in independent forms, even in Islamic Persia.

This current was to encounter, farther west, certain exegesises —perhaps themselves already dualist—of the Old Testament and superabundant apocryphal traditions which complete the story of Adam and Seth by embroidering on it (these traditions are already found in *Enoch*, in the writings from the *Apocalypse of Noah* which is connected to it (= *Enoch* LXV-LXIX et passim), and in the Book of *Jubilees*). The traditions were cultivated, it seems, by the baptist sects, Jewish as well as Samaritan, of whose origins we have some indication through the little we know of the Therapeutae, of the community of Qumran, etc. The philosophic ideas evolved by Philo from his allegoric commentary on the O.T., opened the doors to hitherto unheard-of speculations, although Gnostic thought has always had a tendency, it seems, to refashion myths from the abstract entities presented in this way. It is, in any case, the union of these various currents which produces the essential element of the doctrines hostile to the O.T. law of which we are aware through the polemics of the Apostles.

XIV. Evolution of Gnosticism

From this point, the history of Gnosticism was to follow two distinct routes. In the East, the sects were to become stiffened in mythology which only Manichaeism and Mandaeism were to raise to the status of a great religion. In the Roman world, on the other hand, far from their original sources, the Gnostic doctrines, encountering the old mystical teachings of Heraclitus and Parmenides, and of the Orphic doctrines, were to join in the continual evolution of the philosophy in which its rôle was limited to plagiarizing the systems in favour as and when they appeared. This evolution of Gnosticism appears to have been marked, by several clearly-marked stages, which are: 1) quite early, from the most ancient roots of Gnosticism, a pre-Mandaeism was to detach itself which, until the 5th or 6th century, was to complete its evolution by drawing on the sometimes divergent doctrines of other oriental sects; 2) Meanwhile another branch was trying to attract to itself the prestige enjoyed by the revelations apocryphally attributed to the Magi and also (but here our Gnostics were to fail) those of Hermes-Trismegistus. At the same time, these sectarians were to take an active part in the disputes of the Neo-Platonists in the latter part of the 2nd and the first half of the 3rd century. 3) Perhaps at about the same time, recourse to the allegorical commentaries of Homer, sometimes used in the form of commentaries to illustrate their myths, sometimes intimately incorporated into their doctrine in ways which show clearly either the influence of Neo-Pythagorism, or even a fusion with certain Hellenic mysteries. 4) A powerful attempt to adapt to itself Christianity with which the sects had been in rivalry since the apostolic age: Valentinus and Bardesanes deliberately threw a bridge between Gnostic and Christian doctrines: but it was no doubt by accident that Marcion, who wished to have recourse only to Christianity, drew therefrom dualist conclusions. 5) The elaboration, before the end of the 3rd century, of the powerful Manichaean synthesis which reinfused everything it took from the sects with the living breath of the myths which had originally animated the movement; after the triumph of the Church over her persecutors in the Mediterranean world (edicts of 425 against the Manichaeans and the Gnostics in particular), the Gnostics hid under a false cloak of Christianity which was finally to stifle them.

XV. SURVIVALS

What was to be the fate of the Gnoses after this point? As we have said, outside the Byzantine world, in the countries of Asia which have never been Christianized, or but slightly, the sects, dominated by Manichaeism, were to survive the coming of Islam, either in a pure state, as was the case for Mandaeism or the Sabians of Harra, or assimilated to Islam as was the case for certain Persian doctrines. In the Mediterranean world the Bogomils and the Cathars or Albigenses were to represent very vague resurgences either of Manichaeism, which is only conjectural, or of certain doctrines of the sects preserved under the disguise of Christian apocryphas: it appears that, among others, it was the substance of the early work already formerly disguised under the title of the *Secret Book of John* which thus continued a belated career!

For the rest, while Christianity was setting up as a barrier the ever more precise definitions of the Symbols of its faith, and the anathematization of its councils, a certain number of the myths of Gnosticism were nevertheless to be perpetuated by penetrating into the Church, without however doing damage to the doctrine, in the forms which the Gnostic sects had given them; the story of the *Investiture of the Archangel Michael* and the fall of Satan, which had formerly signified the downfall of Ialdabaoth; the heavenly scales for weighing souls; the institution of a day of rest for the damned; and especially the many visions of infernal powers accompanying the soul at its departure from the body and maltreating it in the terrifying circles of hell. To these we may probably add the cycle of the alleged *Revelations of Adam*, preserved especially in Syriac and Armenian translations, the legend of the Cave of the Magi, the story of the Wood of the Cross, picturesque themes which were to penetrate even the Latin cycle of the Grail,

while certain apocryphal traditions about Solomon were in their turn
to be preserved by Islam.

Finally, in a less attenuated fashion, Gnostic themes and even quotations from certain texts were to be preserved in alchemistic literature,
disguised in symbolic formulas, and to survive in this way in the Arab
world as well as in the Latin world.

Did the Gnostic profusion leave behind nothing more positive than
fragments?—Yes, without doubt; for some of the themes it fashioned
were not lacking in value. By brutally posing the question of the
mixture of good and evil represented by this world, a mixture quite
contrary to the optimism of the philosophies most in vogue, the
Gnostics developed perhaps even more than the Christians the idea of
the infinity of the Universe which, for many, had until then been
limited by the visible heavens. They freed the idea of divinity from the
puerile features with which it had been embellished. They outlined a
fuller conception of the elements which, in man, are in opposition to
the flesh and its impulses. Manichaeism owes its loftiests features to
Gnosis: a total respect for the life present, in different degrees, around
us—a feature to which Christianity has not given the same universality.

In spite of that, after some three centuries, Gnosticism failed completely. Its pessimism was, in the final account, irreconcilable with the
idea of divine goodness, an idea which the Gospel had effectively
substituted for the austere justice of the old Law. The fact that Gnosis
attracted some can only be explained at a time when Christianity was
still accessible only incompletely or with difficulty, that is, until the
victory of the Church. The doctrine of the sects, if it touched some
remarkable personalities, does not seem to have held them, differing
greatly in this from Manichaeism, which was able, for some time, to
hold Augustine. It would more easily have spread in the Roman world
among the heirs of Pythagoras, Plato or the Porch, who were faithful
to the early paganism. But, all things considered, it was here that the
Gnostics caused most scandal. No doubt the last adepts of the mysteries and the philosophy did not scorn the oracles, the edifying stories
or the practices of theurgy. But the shameless literary falsifications of
the sects and their parodies of rites made them ridiculous. All things
considered, we see the pagan and Christian polemists casting the
Gnostics at each other's heads like and embarrassing relation. Only the
secrecy which surrounded their mysteries still for a time attracted to
them some of the curious who, if they could have seen the same works
in broad daylight, would have turned aside from them at once.

XVI. Studies of Gnosticism

The study of Gnosticism, because of the scarcity of original documents, took a scientific turn only a hundred years ago. Yet the early works of Mosheim (1739), J. Horn (1805) and Lewald (1818) already suggested that the origin of the early Gnoses was to be sought in Zoroastrian dualism. *L'Histoire critique du Gnosticisme* by Matter (1828) inspired literature—Gérard de Nerval, Flaubert and Barrès—more than it enriched History. The Codex Brucianus and the Codex Askewianus awaited publication from the end of the 18th century until, in 1847, Dulaurier discovered in them the *Pistis-Sophia*; J. H. Petermann and G. A. Schwartze published it in 1851, the year which also saw the first edition of the second part of the *Philosophumena*, which had recently been discovered. It was then necessary to wait until 1884, when Hilgenfeld gave his *Ketzergeschichte*. In 1891 and 1892, one after the other, Amélineau and Schmidt published the Brucianus Codex. 1897 is marked by the work of W. Anz on the problem of the origins of Gnosticism. A year later comes *Der Vorchristliche Gnosis* of Friedländer. In 1896 a coptic gnostic codex is brought from Egypt for the Berlin Museum.

In 1903, Eug. de Faye gives us his *Introduction á l'étude du Gnosticisme*, a preamble to his *Gnostiques et Gnosticisme*, the first edition of which was to appear in 1913. 1904 saw the publication of the *Poimandres* of Reitzenstein which illustrates the connexions between Gnosticism and Hermetism. In 1907 W. Bousset gave his *Hauptprobleme der Gnosis* while C. Schmidt revealed that a section of the Codex Berolinensis corresponds to the work which is analysed in the *Adversus Haereses* of Irenaeus, I, XXIX, and that for the first time, we possess the original of a work mentioned in the 2nd century by a heresiologist.

From 1926 to 1938 the studies of Reitzenstein and Schaeder on the ancient syncretism of Greece and Persia have given rise to, among other things, a study of the Naassene hymn restored by the *Philosophumena*. C. Schmidt re-edited the *Pistis-Sophia*. Charlotte Baynes wrote a commentary on the anonymous treatise of the Codex Brucianus, a commentary which, by its depth and its attention to detail, constitutes a revelation. Hans Jonas published the first volume of *Gnosis und spätantiker Geist*. H. Ch. Puech summed up the state of the problems in his article *Où en est le problème du Gnosticisme*, then, using Syriac writings which had previously been neglected, put forward hypotheses about the lost revelations of *Allogenes*, which were later to be confirmed by the discovery of the original texts. H. LEISEGANG produced the first clear and manageable volume on Gnosis that we possess. Finally, in their *Mages Hellénisés*, J. BIDEZ and FR. CUMONT assembled and commented on the membra disjecta of the pseudo-Zoroaster, of Ostanes and Hystaspes. But this period which, in another connexion, saw the extraordinary discovery of the Coptic Manichaean codices of Medinet-Madi, brought no new original manuscript to the study of Gnosis.

After the second World War renewed research was marked by the publications of P. SAGNARD and G. QUISPEL on Valentinian Gnosis and its texts, and by the penetrating study of ANTONIO ORBE on the Valentinians in face of the anti-Christian Persecutions. Persian Gnosis was explored by H. CORBIN. Doctrines connected with Gnosticism profited from the studies of A. J. FESTUGIÈRE and A. D. NOCK on Hermetism, and H. J. SCHOEPS on Judaeo-Christianity.

However, in 1947, the late TOGO MINA, Director of the Coptic Museum of Cairo laid hands on the first of the 13 Gnostic manuscripts exhumed by chance near the ancient town of Chenoboskion, in the region of Nag-Hammadi in Upper Egypt, and entrusted to us, along with H. CH. PUECH, the task of identifying and studying the lost works which were found there. Shortly afterwards I was able to discover the other manuscripts of the same collection and to identify the forty or so unpublished texts that they gave us. However, the premature death of TOGO MINA in 1949 called a halt to the progress of a critical edition of these texts, which was to be published by the Imprimerie Nationale in Paris. Then, in 1956, came the "Suez Crisis" which held up the work of a new editing committee formed by Dr. PAHOR LABIB, who succeeded TOGO MINA as head of the Coptic museum. In the following years, despite the efforts of Dr. PAHOR LABIB, the publication of the new texts proceeded slowly, in the form of scattered editions, a series not in accordance with the program of publication which the first scholars who worked at the discovery had set up.

The most gratifying result was at any rate the completion of the difficult publication of the texts of the Codex Berolensis, which C. SCHMIDT had left unfinished: with the aid of parallel texts from some of the Chenoboskion writings with which we were able to supply him, W. TILL could start his work and finish it in 1955.

Finally in the spring of 1966 a convention organized under the auspices of the University of Messina thanks to Prof. UGO BIANCHI, brought together a large number of scholars interested in the theme of the origins of Gnosticism.

If research into Gnosticism has proceeded by fits and starts because of the lack of original texts, the position is rather different for Mandaeism which, as the discovery of the parallel texts has shown, can less and less be separated from the study of the other Gnoses.

As early as the 17th century, Mandaean manuscripts had been brought to Europe by various travellers. The first edition of the *Ginza* was published, in a very imperfect form, by NORBERG in 1816. This sacred text was re-edited, properly, by J. H. PETERMANN in 1867. J. H. PETERMANN had in 1854 brought with him from his travels the first accurate description of a Mandaean community. In 1889 W. BRANDT was to publish the first comprehensive work, *Die Mandäische Religion*. While at the beginning of this century the specialists in Gnosis, BOUSSET, REITZENSTEIN and H. H. SCHAEDER were devoting various studies to Mandaeism, M. LIDZBARSKI was publishing the *John-Book* (1905) before giving us a new edition of the *Ginza* (1925). The years 1920-1933 were to see the development of a violent controversy about the possible connexions between Mandaeism and primitive Christianity. This was to be silenced in 1933 although the problem, as H. CH. PUECH could still write in a study dated 1945, "remains open".

Since 1937 the study of Mandaeism has derived considerable benefit from the work of LADY DROWER on the present-day Mandaeans and on the various texts, hitherto unknown, which she has discovered and published. The links between Mandaeism and the ancient religions of Persia and Mesopotamia, Manichaeism and the other Gnoses, have been emphasized and analysed in the penetrating studies of G. WIDENGREN. T. SÄVE-SÖDERBERG, by comparing certain Mandaean writings with Manichaean hymns discovered in the Coptic tongue, has found in them essential facts for the ancient history of Mandaeism. Finally, since 1955, the three large volumes of KURT RUDOLPH, placing the study of Mandaeism, in its context, which is as much Gnostic as Manichaean, show up the considerable significance of all that has been patiently accumulated up to now by scholars in different domains.

SELECTED BIBLIOGRAPHY

G. Bornkamm, *Die Haeresie des Kolosserbriefes*, in *Th.L.Z.*, 1948, p. 17s.

W. Bousset, *Hauptprobleme der Gnosis*, Göttingen, 1907.

R. Bultmann, *Johanneische Schriften und Gnosis*, in *O.L.Z.*, 43, 1940, p. 150s.

——, *Theologie des Neuen Testaments*, Tübingen, 1953.

Colloquium of Messina 13-18 April 1966, The origins of Gnosticism. Texts and Discussions published by Ugo Bianchi, Leiden, 1967.

E. De Faye, *Gnostiques et Gnosticisme*, 2nd édition Paris, 1925.

J. Doresse, *The Secret Books of the Egyptian Gnostics*, The Viking Press, New York, 1960.

——, *Hermès et la Gnose. A propos de l'"Asclepius" copte*. in: *Novum Testamentum*, I, 1956, p. 54-69.

E. S. Drower, *The Mandaeans of Iraq and Iran*, Oxford, 1937.

——, *The secret Adam: A study of Nasoraean Gnosis*, Oxford, 1960.

E. Haenchen, *Gab es eine vorchristliche Gnosis?* in *Zeitschrift für Theologie und Kirche*, 49th year 1952, p. 316-349.

H. Jonas, *The Gnostic Religion. The message of the alien God and the beginnings of Christianity*, Boston, 1958.

H. Leisegang, *Die Gnosis*, 3. Auflage, Leipzig, 1941.

A. Orbe, *Los primeros herejes ante la Persecucion, Estudios Valentinianos V*, = Analecta Gregoriana, vol. LXXXIII, Series Fac. Theol., Roma, 1956.

E. Peterson, *Frühkirche, Judentum und Gnosis*, Wien, 1959.

H. Ch. Puech, *Gnostische Evangelien...*, dans E. Hennecke, *Neutestamentlicher Apokryphen in deutscher Übersetzung*, 3. *völlig neubearb. Auflage, herausg. von W. Schneemelcher, I, Band: Evangelien*, Tübingen, 1959, = chap. VII, p. 158s.

——, *Fragments retrouvés de l'Apocalypse d'Allogène*, in *Mélanges Franz Cumont*, Bruxelles, 1936, p. 935 s.

——, *Le Mandéisme*, dans *Histoire Générale des Religions, sous la direction de M. Gorce et R. Mortier*, Paris, 1945, p. 67-83.

——, *Catharisme médiéval et Bogomilisme*, dans *Convegno di Scienze Morali, Storiche e Filologiche*. 1956, (Accad. Naz. dei Lincei) Roma, 1957, p. 56-84.

——, et A. Vaillant, *Le traité "Contre les Bogomiles" de Cosmas le Prêtre*, traduction and commentary by ..., Paris 1945.

R. Reitzenstein und H. H. Schaeder, *Studien zum antiken Synkretismus aus Iran und Griechenland*, Leipzig-Berlin, 1926.

K. Rudolph, *Die Mandäer*, T. I, *Prolegomena, Die Mandäerproblem*, et T. II, *Der Kult*, Göttingen, 1960-1961.

——, *Theogonie, Kosmogonie und Antropogonie in den mandäischen Schriften*, Göttingen, 1965.

T. Säve-Söderberg, *Studies in the Coptic-Manichaean Psalm-Book*, Uppsala, 1949.

W. Schmithals, *Die Gnosis in Korinth*, 2. neubearb. Auflag. Göttingen, 1965.

H. J. Schoeps, *Urgemeinde—Judenchristentum—Gnosis*, Tübingen, 1955.

——, *Aus frühchristlicher Zeit*, Tübingen, 1950.

G. G. Scholem, *Jewish Gnosticism, Merkabah Mysticism und Talmudic Tradition*, New York, The Jewish Theological Seminary of America, 1960.

G. Widengren, *Der iranische Hintergrund der Gnosis*, in *Z.f.R.G.G.*, IV, 1952-2 p. 97-114.

——, *Iranisch-semitische Kulturbegegnung im parthischer Zeit*, Köln-Opladen, 1960.

Original texts

Ch. A. Baynes, *A coptic gnostic treatise contained in the Codex Brucianus*, Cambridge, 1933.

J. Bidez et F. Cumont, *Les Mages Hellénisés... d'après la tradition grecque*, 2 volumes, Paris, 1938.

A. Böhlig und Pahor Labib, *Die koptisch-gnostische Schrift ohne Titel aus Codex II von Nag-Hammadi*, Berlin, 1960, (= écrit 40, du Codex X, according to our own inventory).

——und——,*Koptisch-gnostische Apokalypsen aus codex von Nag'Hammadi...*, Halle-Wittenberg, 1963. (= codex II according to our inventory).

J. Doresse, *Il Vangelo secondo Tommaso*, Milano, 1960.

——,*"Le Livre Sacré du Grand Esprit Invisible" ou "l'Evangile selon les Egyptiens"*, texte, traduction et commentaire, in *Journal Asiatique*, Paris, 1966, fasc. 4 et 1967, fasc. 3.

M. Malinine, H. Ch. Puech et G. Quispel, *Evangelium Veritatis*, Zürich, 1956.

W. Till, *Die gnostischen Schriften des koptischen Papyrus Berolinensis* 8502, Berlin, 1955

MANICHAEISM

BY

JES P. ASMUSSEN

Copenhagen, Denmark

I. Its Position and Peculiarity in the History of Religion

The religion of redemption which was formed by MANI during the third century A.D. under the Sasanians, considered it one of its duties to teach man about "the two roots," "principles" or "trees" (*duae arbores* in St. *Augustine, Contra Fortunatum* 22) and about "the three periods" (beginning, middle, end; *initium, medium, finis, Contra Felicem* I, 9), i.e. to teach about the Goodness, (the Light) and the Evil (the Darkness), and about the three stages and their relationship to one another, starting from total separation, via the stage when they were mingled, on to the ultimate solution. The mingling brought with it the creation of the world and man and with it the misery and suffering of mankind and its need for a redeemer, "a liberator, to cleanse them (the good souls, *animae bonae*) from erring and to free them from the stage of mingling (*commixtio*) and liberate them from slavery" (*Contra Fort.* 1).

From these two points of doctrine, whose precise application is described in a Chinese handbook for Manichaeans ("Fragment Pelliot," *JA* 1913, 114) as a *conditio sine qua non* for anyone to become a member of the community, it is sufficiently apparent in which spiritual climate Manichaeism is at home. From a religious-historic and religious-phenomenologic point of view Manichaeism is a redemption theory with all the fundamental characteristics of a typical gnostic religion. In the centre of a type-description of the widely branched religious phenomena which are now covered by the collective term "gnosticism," (even though complete uniformity is out of the question), there was what one could call the drama of the soul. With variations in the details, but uniformity in the fundamental characteristics, the gnostic myth relates the fate of the soul, its original home in the pure and unpolluted world of the Light, its imprisonment in the body and in the material world, where the soul is a stranger or a foreigner (*uzdēh* according to an Iranian text) and its ascension through redemption to the place of origin. As part of the heavenly Light the soul itself is divine. However, the soul was delivered to the powers of the darkness by an event, which appeared to be a catastrophy, but which in reality was only the consequence of the intelligent *providentia* of the world of the Light. To those powers, which for a long time had watched with envy the harmonious world of the Light this part of the Light acquired vital significance for them, once they came to know it. On no condition would they be without it again, and this is why their demoniacal play to enwrap the original situation in oblivion became all the greater. This is why man, who *qua* man is part of the violated sum of light, must be lulled to sleep and made dull so that the longing for the Kingdom of Light which his soul may give him is not awakened. But the Light has pity on the suffering human and sends a redeemer from its realm to waken him and through teaching bring forth in him the memory of his lofty origin. On the part of man preparedness of mind is a precondition if the recognition, the understanding, γνῶσι'ς, is to be able to take shape and lead to the work of redemption; for "when one recognises the Father, oblivion is at once destroyed" as it says in the Gnostic Gospel of Truth 18, 10-11. When all the Light which has been damaged is united again the task is fulfilled and the original division between Light and Darkness restored.

Manichaeism must be placed in this kind of religious-historic environment. It has the same basic elements and the same strong emphasis on the necessity of cognition: "understand the religion," it says (*Muséon* 45, 1932, p. 279) for those who "do not understand, do not recognize" (*nē dānēnd*, *BSOAS* XI, p. 58 and 63), are the misled who have no hope. "The great Kingdom of Redemption" is only for "those who perceive, who have gnosis" (*zānēndān*, *BSOAS* XIII, p. 913). However, the ease with which Manichaeism can be interpreted as a typical gnostic religion does not exclude its prominent peculiarity. The speculations, often repeated in other gnostic systems, concerning the Aeons, beings of varying quality, fixed between God and the world, and regarding the demiurge as creator as the lowest of them all, are of no importance to the followers of Mani. Equally, the danger that complete mastery of the gnosis would make all moral laws, superfluous and lead to libertinism is totally unknown to them. On the contrary, the Manichaeans take sin extremely seriously, at least so when the ideals of their teaching are upheld without compromise. Even the Elect possessing complete cognition were permanently aware of the possibility of sin and the fall, the exclusion from absolution, and excommunication. "And you, dear brother, do know that the perfect Hearer (*nywš'k*, *auditor*) is very difficult to find. Forgiveness of sins is granted in the Church only once: at that one time when he turns away from the serious crimes and renounces the tenfold sins and the previous wicked deeds, at that one time he receives absolution and forgiveness" (*M 139, Sogdian, BBB* p. 49). However, should relapses occur, the consequences cannot be estimated. There is no further absolution for the elect (*dēndār*) nor for the hearer "and whatever good deeds he may do (after the fall) will be pulled away in the zodiac heaven (that means by the dark powers); yes, even his previous good deeds will be taken away from his soul" (Ibid. p. 50). The achievement of entire gnosis is not identical with the fact of redemption, but is its precondition and its beginning. For although he who has been redeemed (*liberatus*) by the divine gnosis (*divina cognitio*) will attain eternal life (*Epistola Fundamenti*, quoted by St. AUGUSTINE, *Contra Epistola Fundamenti* XI), this applies only in so far as he lives in accordance with the knowledge which he gained, and in particular does not commit a sin against the "Living Soul," i.e. against the sum of the light which is imprisoned in the world and separated from the Kingdom of Light, for such a sin is so dreadfully blasphemous that it cannot be forgiven: "Even if the entire house were made of gold and pearls and he (the hearer) would give it away for his soul's sake (*rw'n r'd*), he should not be forgiven" (*TII D* 162 I, *Parthian*, W. B. HENNING, "A Grain of Mustard," *Institutio Orientale di Napoli, Annali VI*, 1965, p. 30-31).

In Manichaeism the struggle for the soul is the only true divine worship. Divine worship and soul service are one. According to the Arabic historian CHWĀRAZMĪ (10th century) the Sasanid state administration had a "Ministry for pious foundations" (*ruvānagān dipīrīh*) which took care of what was given "for the soul," *pat ruvān*, that means money, land buildings etc. which the pious gave for the benefit and promotion of their own life on earth, or for the good of a deceased (like a Mass in the Catholic church), a pious deed in man's own interest, a *do-ut-des* relation. In this as in many other cases the Manichaeans took over the Zoroastrian concept. For them, however, this was the basis of the whole religion and therefore the word *ruvānagān* took on a content radically different from its original. The Manichaean soul service was in fact literally everything that aiming at the redemption of the soul, the Living Soul denied a rich life on earth according to the Zorastrian concept. It was a service in the interest of man and—just as much—God!

This is the cardinal point in the teaching of Mani which remained unaltered even when he and his followers relaxed the draconic rules regarding absolution and permitted the remission of sins to a greater extent. For each time a sin is committed against the Living Soul not only the redemption of man but also the total liberation of God or Light is delayed. His condition as a *salvandus*, one to be delivered, is prolonged. Obstacles are placed in the way of that process of reducing the mass of suffering light which is joyfully quoted in a Manichaean hymn, handed down by the Syrian Church Father AFREM:

> From day to day the number of souls becomes small and smaller (in the material world), because they rise upwards purified (A. ADAM, *Texte zum Manichäismus*, 1954, p. 15),

and the gnosis (*scientia*) acquired which otherwise would have enabled the soul washed in the "divine well" and purified from the filth and the imperfection of this world and the body, to return home to the "Kingdom of God" (*regnum Dei*) "from where it originated" (*Contra Fortunatum* 21)—becomes useless because it does not contribute towards making God or Light *salvatus*, i.e. (totally) saved. This gnostic idea of the redeemed redeemer, as formulated by the German scholar Richard REITZENSTEIN, can theoretically be deduced without difficulty from the Manichaean material, although one has to bear in mind that it is formulated from the scripts and the myth and hardly played any part in the practical theology of the Manichaeans.

The fundamental peculiarity of Manichaeism as a *gnosis* religion has, however, not been entirely explored through an exposition of its idea of sin, but was once for all inaugurated through the fundamental guiding lines which Mani himself layed down programmatically for his religion. This religion as HENRI-CHARLES PUECH points out in his fundamental work *Le Manichéisme* in 1949—was *universal, keen on missionary work* and was from the beginning stamped by the clear conviction that it was absolutely necessary to possess genuine sacred *texts*. Furthermore, it was final, as Mani felt that he himself was the seal of the prophets (*xātimu-n-nabīyin*, e.g. in the Arabic writer Ibn AL-MURTADĀ from the Yemen, K. KESSLER, *Mani*, 1889, p. 349, line 13 and p. 355). He called the times in which he lived "this last generation (age)" (*al-qarnu*, BĪRŪNĪ, *Chronologie* 207, 17-18 (Arabic text), *Keph.* 14, 6). This leads to important consequences as regards the analysis of the sources of the religion and its historical development (see II below).

For Mani emphasises that "the religion which I have chosen is in ten points more excellent and better than the other, earlier religions" and at the same time he points out that those religions are spread only "in one country and in one language" while his teachings appeared "in every country and in all languages" (*T II D* 126, *MM II*, p. 295). Also, as he points out that contrary to the earlier religious systems, his own, as a written religion, was safe against falsifications by his successors, he expresses on the one hand a deep mistrust against oral tradition which at his time was taken for granted, and on the other hand he assumes supreme powers about everything which the old religions, however imperfect, had to offer. His attempts to create a canon fixed in written texts were indoubtedly influenced by MARCION, the great Christian heretic of the second century who wanted to have written proofs for his teachings of the loving, strange God, the opponent of God the Creator. Antiquity did not recognise this principle. The general attitude was the same as that expressed by PLATO in the *Phaidros Dialogue* (274c-275a) in SOCRATES' story of the Egyptian King Thamus and the God Theuth. But for Mani a written tradition was simply a precondition for the continued existence of the religion, and he, as the last and perfect apostle, felt entitled to build up his religion in the texts in a deliberately syncretistic way. Apart from the book *Šābbura-gān*, one of his first works, dedicated to the Sasanid King Šāhpuhr I, which was written in Middle Persian and mainly of eschatological contents, Mani wrote all his books in his East Aramaic (Syriac) mother tongue and used a variant of the Palmyrene script. Apart from a few fragments which came to light in Egypt, all the texts in the Syriac original have disappeared. The canon itself was in seven parts but it is not certain whether the *Šābbuhragān* was counted or not.

Together with the *Šābbuhragān* the other six parts are as follows:

1. *The Living (or Great) Gospel*
2. *The Treasure of Life*
3. *Pragmateia*, i.e. "*Treatise, Essay*"
4. *The Book of Mysteries*, which according to the Arab AN-NADĪM comprised 18 or 19 chapters and also contained a refutation of the School of BARDAIṢĀN.
5. *The Book of the Giants* in which the story of the fallen angels (compare Gen. 6) from the *Book of Enoch*, played a prominent part.
6. *The Letters* of which a Coptic translation existed, which unfortunetely appears to be lost now.

However, as the Chinese and Coptic Manichaean leave out the

Šābbuhragān from the tables of contents of the canon, everything supports the view that this book stood quite apart. In that case the 7th part of the canon must have consisted of psalms and prayers. Not one of these books has come down complete, but apart from the *Pragmateia* for whose contents no evidence exists, there are several references to the other books and quotations from them in the genuine Iranian, Uigur, Chinese and Coptic Manichaean material on the one hand, and on the other hand in the anti-Manichaean writers, especially the Arabic historians YA'QŪBĪ (9th century) and MAS'ŪDĪ (about 950 A.D.), the bibliographer an-NADĪM (10th century) and BĪRŪNĪ (died 1048). St. AGUSTINE for example, who was for "about nine years" (*annos fere novem*, De utilitate credendi I, 2) 373-382 A.D. a Manichaean auditor, included in *Contra Felicem* II, 5 and *De natura boni* 44 detailed quotations from the *Treasure of Life* (*Thesaurus*). The non-canonic literature includes among other items the *Kephalaia* and *Homilies* as well as hymn collections (compare 4 below) and the *Ārdhang*, a picture book illustrating the more important aspects of the teaching.

II. HISTORICAL DEVELOPMENT OF MANICHAEISM

According to a quotation from the *Šābbuhragān*, handed down by BĪRŪNĪ, Mani was born in the year 527 after the Seleucid era. Combined with information from other sources the date would be the 14th April 216. The name, which was not unusual among his contemporaries, was adorned by adding the favourite Manichaean adjective, the Syriac *khayyā, vivus* (perhaps best—"participating in life") and became Manikhaios in Greek, generally known like this even in Central Asia. His place of birth and his family are obscure because there is some divergence among the sources. It appears that he was born near Seleucia-Ktesiphon, in any case in the province of Babylon (Sūristān), for in a Parthian text he says about himself: "I am a physician from the land of Babel" (*M* 566, *HR II*, p. 87). This agrees with the Coptic *Homilies* where Mani is "the great ambassador from the land of the great Babylon" (54, 14-15, compare 61, 17). One cannot form any clear idea about his outward appearance. The pictures (in particular murals found in Central Asia) which have been referred to, are quite uncertain, and the details about his person found in the Christian, anti-Manichaean work *Acta Archelai* of the 4th century, attributed to a certain Hegemonius, are somewhat non-descript. According to an Arabic tradition (AN-NADĪM's *Fihrist al-'ulūm*, 10th century) Mani was supposedly lame. But even this information, quite isolated in this case, has been questioned, and undoubtedly rightly so. An-Nadīm who had otherwise genuine Manichaean material at his disposal, relates in the Fihrist that Mani's father came from Hamadān, the old Ecbatana in Media, but settled later in Seleucia-Ktesiphon in Babylonia. According to this and most other sources his name was without doubt Patīg and that of his mother probably Maryam. The information from the Chinese Stein Fragment from Tun-huang (Asia Major N.S. III, 1952, p. 190) that she belonged to the Kamsaragān family seems to confirm the tradition that Mani was of princely (Arsacid) origin. The mere fact that a tradition of that kind could be handed down during the reign of a dynasty which did everything to cover the Arsacids with a veil of oblivion, supports its authenticity. The father was very much involved in religious questions and belonged to a sect of which nothing further is known, and from which he parted when he heard a voice in the "temple of the idols" (baitu'l-aṣnām, Fihrist) which called on him for three days: "Do not eat meat, do not drink wine, and keep away from women." After that he joined a sect, the al-mughtasilah ("those who cleanse, wash temselves") corresponding to the mənaqqədē, "those who cleanse themselves," and the khallē khewārē, "white gowns," mentioned by the Syrian Theodor bar Kōnai in his polemic description (8th century) of Manichaeism (Adam, Texte, p. 75). Mani was introduced into this religious climate by his father, and as these terms clearly indicate a baptist movement, the complex question arises about the relationship between Manichaeism and Mandaeism. The Mandaeans (from mandā, cognition, gnosis) of whom about 5,000 are still living today in southern Iraq and—in very small groups—in Iran, are and were a gnostic baptist sect. They call themselves Nazoraeans (from the Semitic root nṣr "to observe, keep"). The two main parts of the cult are the baptism (maṣbūtā) in flowing water, "Jordan water," a ceremony which did not occur just once but which was repeated by the faithful and was among other things followed by a sacramental taking of bread (pihtā) and water (mambūhā), and a mass for the dead (masiqtā, actually "ascension," i.e. that of the soul to the Kingdom of Light). These sacraments and the cult as a whole are based on the widely developed Mandaean myth complex, whose profusion can only be with difficulty worked together into a complete system, but which after all possesses all the characteristics of a typical gnosis religion with the Great King of the Light, the Lord of Greatness or the Great Mānā(i.e. "vessel") at the head of the divine World of Light; with the creation of the earth (Tibil) and the body of Adam respectively by the demiurge *Ptāhil*, assisted by *Rūhā* (spirit), the wicked world principle, and, by the seven sons of *Rūhā*; with the bestowal of the soul, the Hidden Adam, on the part of the world of light; with the gnosis revelation through the saviour *Mandā dHaiyē* ("Cognition of Life") and through *Hibil-Zīwā* ("Shining Abel"), and with the ascension of the soul through various stages to the Kingdom of Light.

It would be unjustified to deny off-hand any genetic link between the *Mughtasilah* sect and Mandaeism. AN-NADĪM however stresses the demand for asceticism and sexual abstinence, a characteristic which appears to contradict the general Mandaean attitude. But not necessarily; because on the one hand it may be that the information, which stands quite isolated, is based on a misunderstanding on the part of AN-NADĪM, and on the other hand the reference may have been made to a particularly rigorous but otherwise unimportant branch of the baptist community, particularly as the Mandaean literature (especially the *Book of John* and the *Right Ginzā*, the most important sacred texts of Mandaeism) does indeed show clear ascetic tendencies side by side with evidence to the contrary. One can easily imagine that in limited local areas these tendencies may from time to time have been more emphasised than was normally and "officially" the case. In any case Mandaeism did exist in some form before Mani. Sufficient evidence for this is provided by the fact that the Manichaean took over what were obviously Mandaean elements of motif and style in the Coptic *Thomas Psalms* and the Coptic and Parthian death hymns; also the *Haran Gawaitā*, a legendary but in this respect undoubtedly reliable text, mentions a pre-Manichaean Mandaean connection with the Parthian empire (a king Ardbān-Ardavān-Artabanus). It does not, however, follow that Manichaeism should simply be regarded as a variation of Mandaeism or, provided that the religion, expressed in the Mandaean texts late edited, despite everything in its entirety is the final outcome of an inner development over the centuries after Mani, of Proto-Mandaeism. They both have common roots in the Mesopotamian-Iranian-Jewish syncretism which developed in pre-Christian times and which had such essentially gnostic characteristics that these could with the Christianization, which infiltrated later, contribute and lead to the development of the great gnostic systems. The genesis of Mandaeism or of Proto-Mandaeism must undoubtedly be placed in the context of the particularly gnostic-Jewish elaboration of this syncretism among the heretic baptist movements in Jordan and Syria; the genesis of Manichaeism on the other hand in the context of the specifically gnostic-Christian elaboration of that syncretism. Mani discarded his father's heritage but did not free himself completely from its influence. For the last great apostle, who with his universal offer of redemption brought with him what was perfect, was alone capable of separating truth from untruth not only among the baptists but also—and with the same naturally assumed right—among the Christians, Zoroastrians and Buddhists. All in all, the *Mughtasilah* sect was only of secondary importance as a rival to a world religion. The Manichaean texts contain only here and there a polemic attack on the "baptists" (*baptistai*). There were other more important issues on which decisions had to be made. This also applied to the Mandaeans whose later collection of sacred scriptures touches on the tradition of Mani in only one utterly insignificant passage (*Right Ginzā* 228, p. 229 in MARK LIDZBARSKI's translation, 1925).

Mani's break-away from his father's religion was not unmotivated. It goes back to an inspiration from the King of Light, passed on to Mani when he was twelve years old (compare Jesus in the Temple at the age of twelve, Luc. 2, 41 and subsequent) through *at-Taum* (AN-NADĪM), and repeated twelve years later. The messenger *at-Taum* (= twin) is the apostle's heavenly self who reveals himself to his representative on earth. In the Coptic version which mentions only the second visitation "the Living Paraclete came down to me and talked to me" (*Keph.* 14, 32-15, 1). The identity of the twin and therefore that of Mani with the Paraclete (the Holy Ghost) which follows from this, is confirmed e.g. by BĪRŪNĪ, by the Manichaean Felix for whom "Mani himself is the Paraclete—, i.e. the Holy Ghost" (*Contra Felicem* I, 9) and by Evodius, St. AUGUSTINE's friend who mentions "his (i.e. Mani's) twin that is the Holy Ghost" (*De fide* 24). In Eastern Manichaeism this combination which was readily understood by a Christian public (and regarded as objectionable) was replaced by the assimilation to Maitreya, the Messiah figure of Buddhism. For a universal religion leading to perfection there was no *non licet*. The divine inspiration also confirmed the demand for missionary work. It is an obvious assumption that the main principles of the Manichaean missionary work are based in all phases on Mani himself and were examined in practice during his own travels, especially during the period of the death of the Sasanid king Ardašīr I and the succession by his son Šāhpuhr I. Skilful assimilation given a central position contributed very largely to the fact that the outward physiognomy of the religion took on a generally syncretic form which, depending on time and place, emphasised its similarity with the alien religions (Christianity, Zoroastrianism, Buddhism—and to a lesser extent—Taoism) whose followers they tried to win. However, its fundamentally gnostic core with everything pertaining to it ethically and ascetically, and the soul service at the centre, remained by and large unscathed during this process (only the degenerate Chinese elaboration of Manichaeism contains examples to the contrary). In other words, the often surprisingly strong Christian, Zoroastrian or Buddhist elements are due to the application of missionary techniques rather than to religious-historic connotations. As he was the one who fulfilled what had been begun but not completed by Jesus, Zoroaster, Buddha and even Adam, Seth (=Shitil, as with the Mandaeans), Abraham and others, Mani had the right to use such religious material as he found suitable, and he transferred this right to his missionaries. The Manichaean idea of the concept of God (compare III below) and essential aspects of the structure of the great religions had an effect which promoted the assimilation technique in that these aspects were isolated and were used as the starting point for a general *interpretatio manichaica*. In Buddhism one such basis was the negative concept of life which—in conjunction with the use of a clearly eastern terminology (e.g. "Buddhas," "Yakṣas," "Bhikṣu" (in the verb *byxš-*), "Mokṣa," "Parinirvāṇa" etc.) and with existing religious institutions (e.g. monasteries, developments relating to penitence)—could without difficulty serve purely Manichaean interests. The same applied to an even greater extent in the case of Zoroastrianism because of its dualistic form, particularly prominent in the Sasanid period, and of Christianity in so far as its deviations are concerned, based on gnostic developments and exemplified by Marcion and Bardaiṣān both of whom played an important part for Mani as evidence shows, and who were repeatedly mentioned by Christian heresiologists as being spiritually related to him. Mani found already in Christ's parable of the tree (Luc. 6, 43 cont.) an excellent expression of what was his own most ardent concern. How easily Christianity could be subjected to a gnostic interpretation is, for example, evident from the Valentinian Gospel of Philip from Nag-Hamadi whose author considered himself a good Christian! For Mani true Christianity was quite simply *his* understanding of Christ's teachings. His exposition was "just as Christ proclaimed it" (Bīrūnī, Adam, *Texte* p. 26). According to the Christian bishop Theodor Abū Qurra (8th century) the Manichaean were therefore in a position to say: "You must follow the (true) Christians and listen to the word of their gospel. For the true gospel is in our possession,—there is no Christianity apart from us. Nobody understands the interpretation of the gospel except Mani, our Lord." The *interpretatio manichaica* was an *interpretatio definitiva* because Mani was the interpreter of Buddhism, Zoroastrianism and Christianity, "the interpreter of the land of the great Babylon" (Hom. 61, 16-17). This explains why Manichaeism was prepared to take over all sorts of religious ideas and institutions in so far as they were irrelevant to the basic teaching, the soul service. To mention just a few examples among many: Quotations from the New Testament were taken over directly (not however from the Avesta!), also the Christian concept of the Old and New man, the imitation of Buddhist magic (amulet) and the Zoroastrian idea of the *Daēnā* of each human being, that is his religious attitude as the sum total of his good and evil deeds, who will meet him in the next world in the shape of a young girl.

However, these missionary techniques were completely disciplined and guided by them Mani travelled extensively in the very large Sasanid empire. These travels cannot be mapped in detail but he went to India (that ist he eastern part of the empire), Tūrān and Mākrān (in what is Belutchistan today), Persis, Mesene etc., and later to Parthia (Kephalaia) and Adiabene as well as the border districts around the town of Nisibis. The Manichaean fragments, relating the missionary history, of which there are quite a few, place great emphasis on the conversions of rulers which were achieved. Special glamour was attached to the benevolence with which Pērōz, the younger brother of Šāhpuhr I, who had taken over the previous office of the Great-King as Governor of Khorasan, met the new teachings. It was undoubtedly Pērōz who arranged the first meeting between Mani and Šāhpuhr. On this occasion a friendly relationship developed between the two men which—judging by all sources—remained stable throughout the whole of the thirty years of Šāhpuhr's reign. Mani was received "with great honours" and later made his appearance as a royal attendant over a prolonged period (Keph. 15, 31 and subsequent). This appears to be a reference to one of the campaigns against the Roman Empire, most likely under Valerian whose name was mentioned by the anti-Manichaean ALEXANDER OF LYCOPOLIS (about the year 300) in connection with a comment that Mani "fought together with the Persian Sapor (Šāhpuhr)". The reign of Šāhpuhr's son Hormizd I was too short (about 1 year) for Mani to find out exactly what the situation was, but in any case the position of the new religion was tolerable. It

was only after the succession of Šāhpuhr's second son Bahrām I that
conditions changed radically for the worse, leading to the death sentence of Mani. A Middle Persian text (*M* 3), re-edited by W. B. Henning, provides a telling account of the atmosphere of coldness and
reluctance in which he met Bahrām. Bahrām's first words to Mani
were short: "You are not welcome!" After 26 days imprisonment
Mani died in his chains one day during the period 274-277 (Bahrām's
reign), the only witnesses being the teacher Uzzi (Jewish name!) and
2 elects (*T II D* 79 (Parthian) and *M* 454 (Middle Persian), *MM III*,
p. 862 and 892). That Mani died in this way was also mentioned by
bīrūnī and confirmed by the traditions of the Manichaean community
(*Hom.* 60 and subsequent); but even so the pious Manichaean would
talk of crucifixion. This is a deliberate assimilation to the Passion
of Christ, providing another example of the importance which Jesus
had for the Manichaean system. If Christ was the typical bringer of
gnosis and if what was only a semblance of his true body died on the
cross, then Mani, the last great redeemer figure, had to suffer the same
fate. For the whole life story of Jesus was just one great incarnation
of all the essentials of Mani's teachings, the humiliation and uplift of
the soul. The soul, the Light as the imprisoned divine, was Jesus
Patibilis (in North African Manichaeism, identical with *Buddha gotra* in
Central Asia), but once returned to the Kingdom of Light it became
Jesus the brilliant Light (the Splendour)—Jesus *Ziwā*—who comes to
Adam to wake him and bring him the redeeming gnosis. Or in other
words, Jesus comes "unto his own" in order to redeem himself, that is
God. Jesus *Ziwā is* the Jesus of the New Testament, properly understood and interpreted, i.e. interpreted in the Manichaean way. Seen
in isolation Mary's son Jesus, Jesus as represented in the gospels, is a
fake.

Mani's church which called itself "Justice" (*Hom.* 67, 22) was quickly introduced into the whole area of the eastern and central Mediterranean, into Syria, Palestine (e.g. the mission of the Manichaean Julia
in Ghaza, described by Marcus Diaconus in his *Life of Porphyrios*);
into Northern Arabia, and into Egypt where the communities were
at an early date so predominant that the Sasanid king Narsēs, otherwise despised by the Manichaeans, apparently tried to use them politically against Rome, although it is uncertain under what circumstances;
further into North Africa (St. Augustine), Armenia, Asia Minor,
Dalmatia (the tomb inscription of the Lydian Bassa who was *parthenos*,
"virgin" = *electa*) and into Rome (the *Liber Pontificalis* of Pope Miltia-

des, early 4th century). The 4th century became the great Manichaean
century in the west, judging by the almost feverish anti-Manichaean
activities which found expression in polemic writings (the Neoplatonist ALEXANDER OF LYCOPOLIS (about 300), *Acta Archelai* (1st half
of the century), CYRIL OF JERUSALEM (6. *Catechesis*, of the year 350),
SERAPION OF THMUIS (around the middle of the century), TITUS OF
BOSTA in the province Arabia (2nd half of the century), EPIPHANIUS
OF SALAMIS (about 375), DIDYMUS OF ALEXANDRIA (Κατὰ Μανιχαίων,
last half of the century), GAIUS MARIUS VICTORINUS (*Liber ad Justinum
Manichaeum contra duo principia Manichaeorum et de vera carne Christi*, last
half of the century) and in particular AUGUSTINE (end of the century),
and to some extent in edicts—continuing the edict of Diocletian of
297—on the part of the ruling powers constantine the Great (326),
Valentinian (372), Theodosius (381-83)). A considerable part of this
success was due to the corps of missionaries working with the in-
tuition of a genius and whom Mani himself had started off on their
missions. Among the great names in the west are Mār Sīsin who became Mani's successor after a 5 year interregnum (*Hom.* 83) and who
therefore had obviously not been appointed by the apostle himself;
further Mār Gabriab, Innaios (Sīsin's successor), Mār Zakō, Patecius,
Abzakhyā and Addai. But already in the 6th century the decline set in
which gradually reduced Western Manichaeism to a minimum. The
centre was shifted to the eastern regions of the Sasanid empire (Abar-
shahr (apparently "the upper realms" = the (north) east half of the
empire), Marw and the Balkh district). With the introduction of
Parthian as the official language of the Church, Mār Ammō who had
been sent out by Mani established here a solid foundation for further
expansions towards the east. Legend has it that the Central Asian
Manichaeism, called *Dēnāvariyya*, was founded as an institution by
Ammō. Historically, however, it goes back to Mār Shād Ōhrmizd
who died around the year 600. As Sogdian was the main language and
Sogdian merchants became advocates of this Church, it penetrated
further and further east and reached its culmination in prestige and
importance when, for the first and only time in the history of Manichaeism, it was made the state religion by an official act of Bögü Khaghan in 762-63 under the Turkish Uigurs. The motives for this conversion to a religion, whose tendency to renounce life and state is
obvious, are difficult to explain, but strong political motives cannot
be ruled out. Perhaps in a religious-historic context the Manichaeism
of Bögü Khaghan should rather be considered as a somewhat insig-

nificant intermezzo. With the development of the semi-nomadism into urban culture (the Uigur kingdom of Khotsho 850-1250) Buddhism alone seemed to be of decisive influence. In Tibet, towards the south, too, there is literary evidence of Manichaeism (*JA* 1913, p. 314 and subsequent), but nothing further is known regarding its position and expansion. Owing to a correct written tradition which also includes the imperial edicts, the situation in China is much clearer. In 694 and also in 719 a Manichaean priest of high standing was introduced at the imperial court, and already 13 years after the last visit (732) it was considered necessary to reject Manichaeism ("Mo-mo-ni's (Mār Mani) teachings") categorically, but the freedom of the cult was permitted among such foreign peoples in the empire for whom this was their native religion. Later tolerance edicts (768 and 771) were however followed by strict prohibitions resulting immediately in bloody persecutions. Traces of Manichaeism (especially in the province Fu-kien in southern China) continued for several centuries but they seem to reveal a considerable degeneration and in some cases strongly Taoistic elements. The centre of the expansion was shifted somewhat towards the west with the coming of Islam, because Islam, being in favour of written religions (*ahl al-kitāb*), raised hopes for better times to come among many Manichaeans in the Persian empire as well as in Transoxiana. This hope, however, was soon frustrated and the Manichaean renaissance in the west, which had been opened up, came to nothing. There is, however, no doubt that all this was not entirely without importance for Muhammad's religion, but details of this development are not available. How obscure the image of the historical Mani became is evident from New Persian literature where he appears as the painter from China (the Central Asian tradition!), e.g. in Firdausī's Shāhnāme and Gurgānī's *Vis and Rāmin*, not to mention the purely appellative use of the apostle's name ("a Mani"— a great painter!). In the old Sogdiana alone—and this is characteristic —more valuable reminiscences were preserved. The satirical writer Sūzanī from Samarcand (12th century) quotes in a line of verse the important Manichaean terms for "hearer" and "electus" (*niyāšak*, compare sogd. *nywš°k*, and *dīndār, dīnavar*. compare Sogd. *δynδ°r, δyn°βr*).

One condition for the fast Manichaean expansion leading to its culmination in the 8th century was its firm hierarchic structure centering around Mani's successors and their residence which was in Babylon up to the 10th century and after that in Samarcand. The primacy of Mani's successors was uncontested, although the Manichaean church did not escape schismatic shocks altogether, One case, reported by AN-NADĪM (FLÜGEL p. 68 onwards and 98 and subsequent), and placed by him in the 8th century, is confirmed by Manichaean Sogdian letter fragments from Turfan. Below the actual church dignatories was the community, divided into 5 classes with 12 apostles or teachers, 72 bishops, 360 priests (mahistag, presbyter), the elect men and women, and finally the large flock of men and women hearers, the auditors. The number of apostles and bishops undoubtedly followed the Christian practice. AUGUSTINE for example, was aware of this similarity (*De haeresibus* 46) and THEODORET OF CYRUS (5th century) as well as the church historian EUSEBIUS state openly that when Mani chose the number twelve he followed the example (*typos*) of the Church (*Haereticarum fabularum compendium* I, 26). The same can probably also be said of the number of bishops because there was evidence of the same changing numbers between 70 and 72 among the Manichaean as are testified for Christianity in the text groups for Luc. 10, 17.

It seems obvious to ask why Mani's teachings seem to have been so attractive to the people of his time; why this religion, which renounces life in principle and is hostile to the state, even reached a point where it was made the official religion of a nation. The answer must be found in the fact that this religion offered and demonstrated convincingly its monopoly of a redeeming gnosis which here and in the world to come, in theory and practice, satisfied all demands. It is, of course, difficult to imagine the religious everyday life of people in ancient times. They felt surrounded and watched over by forces whose nature remains obscure to us in our present age. When these forces overwhelmed the human being he sought help and Manichaeism claimed that it was capable of offering this help. There is no reason to doubt that the people of that time and many others believed that Mani's teachings could provide an exposition of life and the world that was scientific in the widest sense. Augustine experienced disappointment when he recognized that it was pseudo-scientific, but for large masses of people it was quite sufficient. One of the things which Manichaeism offered is indicated in the Middle Persian text *M* 3, mentioned previously, where Mani declares that he delivered many from "demons and female devils" (*dyw w drwxš*), from disease and from many kinds of cold fever (ed. W. B. HENNING, *BSOAS* X, 1942, p. 950-951) and the quite numerous Manichaean astrological and magical texts contain indications to the same effect. There is further a remark by PROcopius (*Anecdota* XXII, 25) about a certain Barsymēs who was very interested in magicians and felt himself attracted to "the so-called Manichaeans."

III. The Manichaean Concept of God

In the Manichaean myth complex the deity is shown as one unit within the manifold, as the one God within the many Gods. The highest God, the Father of Greatness as Mani himself called him, the good Father, the blessed Father (*Acta Archelai*) the Good one (Titus of Bostra), God Zurvān (in Middle Persian, Sogdian and Uigur texts) etc. delegates to his emanations specific functions in specific situations. But seen in full depth, the Father of Greatness is in fact appearing himself, being identical with his emanations, just as they are identical among themselves. The Father is the Light in all its forms, as they all are "of the same species" (*h'mtwxmg'n* in the Parthian text *M* 737, ed. Mary Boyce, *BSOAS* XIII, 1951, p. 915), "identical in their essence" (*hāmčihrag*, MM III, p. 850), just as in the Kingdom of Darkness everything is Hylē, sin, irrespective of the shape it takes. He, Äzrua (=Zurvān) is "the elder brother (*ǎča = iči*) and elder sister (*apa*) of all gods in the divine heaven," according to an Uigur text. For everything pertaining to Light is derived from the substantia of God, Augustine says in his report on the *Amatorium canticum* (Adam, *Texte*, p. 63), and therefore the individual divine figures and their functions are not clearly defined. Seen in conjunction with the implied sanction of the written tradition and the myths this is what could be called the Manichaean identity principle. It has fundamental and special significance for the entire system and is the actual precondition for the missionary assimilation technique. Now, to illustrate this principle with some examples from the myth (compare IV below) and the changing terminology: When Primal Man advances towards the Kingdom of Darkness to fight Evil he is accompanied by his 5 sons, the 5 Elements of Light who are according to one version "the God of his (i.e. Primal Man's) origin" (*x^uēščihryazd* in the Middle Persian text *MM I*, p. 187). According to an Uigur text this god (also = *viva anima*, the Light in the world) is however put on the Father of Greatness and mingled with him—or in St. Augustine's words—comes from Christ's Father (*a Patre Christi*, *De duabus animabus* III) i.e. from the Father of Greatness, in relation to whom Primal Man is the king's son who carries out the father's will (*M* 10, Parthian, ed. W. Henning, *NGWG* 1933, p. 306 and subsequent). But according to the report of the Syrian THEODOR BAR KŌNAI (8th century) the Father of Greatness says about the expeditions of Primal Man: "I shall go out myself." He sends "his limbs, his substance, that is himself" (*hoc quod ipse est*, AUGUSTINE, *Enarratio in ps. CXL*, 10). In the Parthian and Sogdian tradition Mihr (Mithra) is the *Tertius Legatus*, the Third Envoy, while in the Middle Persian tradition he is the *Spiritus Vivens*, the Second Envoy, whose part is transferred to the Friend of the Lights in AN-NADĪM (FLÜGEL p. 88). *Tertius Legatus*, who is also mentioned by another term in the Persian and Parthian texts, a term which in the Sogdian texts is reserved for *Spiritus Vivens*, is in some versions the real actor of the seduction of the *Archontes* while according to other versions the Virgin of Light or the virtues of the Father (in reality the Father himself, AUGUSTINE, *De natura boni* 44, ADAM, *Texte*, p. 3) take on this task. The bringer of the gnosis, who wakens Adam from his deep sleep is in particular Christ; but also the Great Nous (Vahman), *Tertius Legatus* and—although in only one isolated case (in the Middle Persian text *S* 9, ed. W. HENNING, *NGWG* 1932, p. 221 and subsequent)—even Primal Man can take over this function. In a rather similar manner the "guiding Sage" (AN-NADĪM) (or the Figure of Light, *Keph.* 36) who, accompanied by three angels, sons of God, leads the souls to Paradise, is in most cases Jesus, but also the Great Nous (= Vahman, who holds a corresponding position in Zoroastrianism); the Virgin of Light who (in text *M* 727, Middle Persian) is called "the image of the Father," and Mani himself appear in this function. And in areas where Zurvanism is predominant a term is used according to which the Father of Greatness can appear as the "fourfold God," "the four gods," as an obvious concession to a religion which in its geographical expansion was rather limited. A concept of God clearly fixed by dogmas could hardly have taken such liberties. That is only possible with a concept of God which lacks individuality and is remote from life to such a great extent as the Manichaean concept which is concerned with *something* divine rather than with *God*. No form of Manichaeism which was authoritative in its dogma—if such Manichaeism ever existed—could ever bring God within the grasp of human imagination. As a logical consequence divine figures are nowhere represented in pictures in the otherwise richly documented Manichaean art of Central Asia. A concept of God such as this was undoubtedly insufficient to meet the religious ardour. This explains perhaps the popularity of Christ, because even in the Manichaean Docetic interpretation his effect was, despite everything, far closer to reality than that of the other figures of the system. The question raised in an Uigur text why Christ (*ay täŋri*) precedes the Father of Greatness (*äzrua täŋri*) should probably be seen against this background. Another and equally obvious consequence of the inadequacy of the abstract concept of God for the religious emotions is the adoration of Mani as a God. This is a natural, religious-historic development which has its exact parallel in Buddhism. The hymns to Mani, of which a disproportionately large number are available, are an expression of the emotions—in the same way as they are expressed in the hymns to the great men of the Church—to a much greater extent than the prayers addressed to the actual divine figures which are mostly held in more general terms. In these lyrics Mani is "God," "Father," "compassionate," "redeemer" etc. whose "divine glory" is praised. He has defeated the devil and all demons and Christ is his equal. In any case for the Manichaean layman this is an essential, if not the most essential aspect of his religion, and the most tangible expression of his longing for redemption.

IV. Cult, Myths and Teachings of Manichaeism

In all its aspects the Manichaean community life had only this one cardinal point: to liberate the light, imprisoned in the matter; and everything was judged from this point. A deed which promoted the process was good, a deed which obstructed it, was bad. This was the only yardstick for the cult itself as well as for the ethical foundation. But although a greater capacity and better ability to free the light was equal with greater worthiness, even the most prominent "elect" (*electus*) never achieved a character *indelebilis*, a position which secured in advance permanent freedom from sin. Contrary to the ideas of gnostic systems, the possibility of a lapse was for ever present in Manichaeism. Consequently saints in the real sense of the word were unknown. Man was a tool, more or less effective, in the service of the liberation of the light which was organised as an effective interchanging relationship between the elect, who alone could hold positions in the church, and the hearers who by and large enjoyed ordinary citizens' lives but who at the same time through their soul service, their alms, "the daily offering" (in Sogdian) to the elect enabled the latter to liberate the light more effectively. "The hearer who practices soul service is like a poor man who leads his daughter into the presence of the king. He will receive great honour" a Middle Persian fragment from the "Book of the Giants" says. But this service is also the condition for the hearers' own redemption, for they will be redeemed and purified, "each of them according to his works (depending on) how he offered (gifts) to the church" (*Keph.* 230). In very exceptional cases the hearer may be able to acquire such qualities that his whole conduct is the same as that of the elect, so that he will be redeemed immediately after his death (*Keph.* Chapter XCI). As a rule, however, he is supposed to be purified through the transmigration of the soul which plays such an important part in the Manichaean system, and which Mani himself is supposed to have taken over, according to BĪRŪNĪ (ADAM, *Texte* p. 9), while in India. This assumption is probably though not necessarily true, as the idea is not unknown in gnosticism as a whole; furthermore the Kartīr inscription from Naqš-i Rustam, from the time shortly after Mani's death, proves the existence of Indian religious practices within the boundaries of the Sasanid empire. The elect received the hearers' daily offering at the "table," and it consisted primarily of fruit, in particular cucumbers and melons which were generally believed to possess a great deal of light (God). The meal, probably the only real sacramental element in Manichaeism, was opened by the elect with an "apology to the bread." A question like "Whose flesh and blood is this?" "when receiving the daily gifts from God's table" (*BBB* p. 41) appears to reveal convincingly the influence of the Christian Lord's Supper, even if there can be no question at all of a direct copy. For the Manichaean meal was daily and its intentions were fundamentally different from the Lord's Supper. AUGUSTINE, for example, mentions sarcastically that it was folly to believe one could find God "with the nose and palate" (*De moribus manichaeorum* 39) As in the Manichaean view the meal was a divine act of liberation, it was of vital importance to ensure that those who received the offerings were worthy tools, that is elect, because otherwise one would literally inflict an injury on the Father of the Light himself. This caution and exclusivity provided their opponents with opportunities to accuse the Manichaeans repeatedly of cruelty and brutality (e.g. ἀπανθρωπία in the long Greek abjuration formula, ADAM, *Texte*, p. 100), although similar regulations are also known among Jews and Christians. Apart from the daily meal there were hardly any sacramental acts. Baptism was regarded as a blasphemous act (compare *Keph.* 33, 29 and subsequent); and its terminology was only used for missionary purposes, its meaning being transformed (in the Coptic Psalm book 22, 13 and subsequent and 139, 22). Even the Bēma feast does not give a clear indication of sacramental elements. This feast, the central ceremony of the Manichaean cult, whose liturgy is partially preserved in a Sogdian text (*BBB* p. 45 and subsequent), is an obvious imitation of the Christian celebration of Easter and may as such have been introduced by Mani himself. But it gained its real significance and justification only after his death, his "crucifixion," and the memory and mystic-symbolic presence of the apostle, represented by a picture on a decorated seat (βῆμα), became its central point. AUGUS-TINE says, and undoubtedly rightly so (*Contra Epist. Fundamenti* 8), that it was celebrated on the day "when Mani was killed" and was celebrated "pro Pascha." Following the Uigur confession mirror for auditores (*X^uastvānīft* XIV A) one was supposed to confess to the *Täŋri Burkhan*("the divine prophet" = Mani) one's sins of the whole year and to ask for forgiveness. After that the "seal letter" was read out whose precise contents are not known but which was probably a last message from the jailed Mani. The weekly confession of sins (auditor to an elect, one elect to another elect) took place on Mondays (*X^uāstvānīft* XIII A) with a special liturgy and also with the singing of the so-called "Monday hymns" etc. A peculiar feature of the Manichaean cult was the body-soul rite (*tn gy'n pδk'*) whose contents and aim are, however, still obscure. Only a liturgical instruction and fragments of hymns relating to the celebration which went with this cult have been handed down (compare *BBB* p. 47). Funeral rites in the true sense were unknown in Manichaeism because death, which provided the opportunity to liberate a further part of the light, was regarded as good. Prayers to the dead, confirmed by literature (*Keph.* Chapt. 115) do not weaken this basic aspect. Following the Buddhist example all practices of the eastern Manichaean cult were in particular linked with the monasteries (*mānistānān*), while in the west—judging by the negative attitude of available sources to these institutions—the cult was practiced during meetings in private houses or at a place chosen *ad hoc*. It is, however, immediately evident that the monasteries as settled residences influenced the elect to a high degree in their pursuit of artistic activities, and effectively emphasised their edu-cational value for the religion. Seen against this background it is hardly surprising that Manichaean art developed far more freely and richly in Central Asia than it apparently did in the west, even if its high standard—especially in regard to book illuminations and calli-graphy (compare Mani as the painter par excellence in the later Persian tradition)—was by no means unknown in the regions of its origin. The "writers" (*dbyr'n*) formed a special class among the elect

(*MM* II, p. 325). As every Manichaean, elect as well as hearer, was an instrument for the liberation of the light, he had to have certain ethical qualities. Both categories acquired and improved these qualities through the observance of certain regulations which were laid down for the hearers in 10 commandments and for the elect in 5 commandments, elaborated with extreme rigour, (1) truthfulness, (2) not to injure (the light scattered over the whole world), (3) chastity, (4) purity of the mouth and (5) to live without personal possessions (compare *BBB* p. 14 and subsequent). For the elect the Manichaean ethic was concentrated into the "3 seals," the seal of the mouth, of the hands and of the bosom (signaculum oris, manuum and sinus according to AUGUSTINE, *De mor. man.* 10-18).

Fasting, too, was a natural factor in the life of a Manichaean, but its terminology as well as its practice presents almost impenetrable difficulties. It was probably introduced by Mani himself without any particular guiding lines. It is certain that there was weekly fasting, on Sundays for the hearers and on Mondays for the elect, but Central Asian Manichaica indicate that fasting was also practised at other times and periods. *Keph.* 79 (p. 191 and subsequent) deals with "the fasting of the saints." However, the Manichaean's religious enthusiasm and fervour, as well as his intensive longing for redemption, is nowhere expressed more fully than in his prayers and hymns. There were daily prayers, 7 for the elect and 4 for the hearers; according to AN-NADĪM (FLÜGEL p. 64 and 96) "four or (aw) seven" that is depending on whether one was a hearer or an elect. The Manichaean's religious feeling showed itself here in a much stronger form than one would have expected judging from the abstract concept of God. There is some significance in Fortunatus' question whether Augustine knew something of the Manichaean world of prayers in addition to his theoretical knowledge (*Contra Fortunatum* 1). He would have been equally justified in pointing out the grandiose Manichaean hymn lyrics which also took effect as complete cycles of which parts have been preserved. "Blessed is this day of redemption," "To you, God (*yazd*) we want to pray," "The day of joy, the blessed day, has arrived" and "For salvation, peace and trust" are the beginnings of some of the preserved songs (in a Parthian text, F. W. K. MÜLLER, *APAW* 1912) to which reference is made in a liturgical instruction (*MM* III, p. 870).

The Manichaean myth complex, which has many parallels in Mandaeism as regards ordinary vocabulary and symbolic terminology as well as style, presupposes that in the beginning—before earth and heaven came into existence—there were two principles, Light, the good, and Darkness, the evil; equal in strength, but separated by a dividing line and furthermore without any common ground at all. In the world of light the Father of Light, the Father of Greatness, sits enthroned, with the twelve Light-diadems, surrounded by his twelve sons, the First Born Ones (i.e. born before the attack of the Darkness) or the twelve Aeons. With him, too, are the Aeons of the Aeons, which are in the aër ingenitus. The Father of the Light himself is pater ingenitus and the Kingdom of Light the terra ingenita, the Eternal Paradise. But in the final analysis these tres res ingenitae (also called the "five Greatnesses" together with the twelve sons and the Aeons of the Aeons) are one, the Father, una substantia (*Contra Felicem* I, 18). In the five Greatnesses the Great Spirit blows (in the Coptic *Manichaica*). In the Kingdom of Darkness, consisting of five dwellings (smoke, fire, wind, water (mud), darkness), which correspond to the five membra or dwellings of the Father (sense, reason, thought, deliberation, attitude of mind (expression of the will)) in the Kingdom of Light, the Prince of Darkness, the devil, Ahriman, rules. Ahriman desires the glories of the Kingdom of Light and plans evil. In order to forestall him, the Father of the Light creates the Mother of Life (or of the living), who in turn produces Primal Man (= Ōhrmizd < Ahura Mazdā in the Middle Persian, Parthian and Uigur texts from East Turkistan). Primal Man with his five sons, the five Elements (ether, wind, light, water and fire) as his armour, rushes into battle to destroy Darkness, but meets with (seemingly) total defeat, and light and darkness are mixed. Only this element of the mythus, the defeat of the divine envoy, has no counterpart in the Mandaean myth complex which in its religious-historic aspects is otherwise related to Manichaeism. In the second act of the mythical drama the liberation of Primal Man becomes the central point overshadowing all else. For this purpose the Father of Light creates the Friend of the Lights from whom in turn evolves the great Builder-Master from whom finally comes the "Living Spirit" (*Spiritus vivens*, the demiurge). The *Spiritus vivens* is actually the main actor. With his five sons as helpers (the Holder of Splendour or *Splenditenens*; the King of Honour or *Rex honoris*; *Light Adamas*; the King of Glory or *Rex gloriosus*; and the Supporter or *Atlas*), who constitute a parallel to the five sons of Primal Man, he goes out to the Kingdom of Darkness and calls out with one penetrating call (Iranian *xrōštag*, actually

what was Called) which the Primal Man catches and to which he
sends back his response (Iranian *padvāxtag*, actually what was Re-
sponded). The call as well as the response are then divinified and later
play an important part in the Manichaean theology. Primal Man is
liberated by catching hold of the outstretched right arm of the *Spiritus
vivens*, but he has to leave his armour, the five Elements, behind in the
enemy's power. Eventually, however, these will bring about the ruin
of the power of darkness; they will become a bait for them (δέλεαρ)
which they cannot digest. As the five Elements of Light are still
captives a continuous liberation of the individual parts of the light
(of the Elements) must be ensured, and a decisive blow must be
directed against the powers of darkness. Heaven and earth, a universe
consisting of ten firmaments and eight earths, are created from their
bodies, from "the captivated bodies of the clan of darkness" (*Contra
Faustum* XX, 9). Sun and moon are created from those liberated parts
of the light which are entirely untouched by the darkness; the stars
are made from such parts of the light which are to a slight degree
polluted. In order to liberate the third, apparently hopelessly corrupted mass of light, the world has to be set in motion. Therefore a
third act of calling forth takes effect, and *Tertius Legatus*, the Third
Envoy, "the sign, the self and the aspect" (*p'dgyrb*, W. B. HENNING,
Brahman, *TPS* 1944, p. 212) of the Father, sets the world in motion
after the five sons of Spiritus vivens have been assigned their special
tasks (for example, *Rex gloriosus* is assigned the function of the Three
Wheels, (wheels of the wind, water and fire)). In this way a kind of
permanently functioning light-liberation machine has been set up.
Through a complicated purification process the particles of light can
now be led further and further upwards so that they finally enter
Paradise entirely pure. This process frightens the powers of darkness
out of their senses, and in a desparate attempt to preserve some of the
captured particles of light the first human couple, Adam and Eve, are
created. Through them and their descendents the demons of darkness
hope to secure some of the light for themselves for ever. Man is
created in the image of Tertius Legatus (in the *Acta Archelai* in the
image of Primal Man), and he therefore has his roots in both worlds,
but he is not aware of his lofty origin. He lacks the necessary gnosis.
The work for the redemption must therefore be concentrated on man
(compare V).

There is no doubt that this myth resulted in wild speculations and
in special traditions, locally elaborated, which were not part of the

official teachings even though they appeared to possess systematic stability. Even so, the delight in using rows of numerical figures probably originated with Mani himself. But it was disciplined and served a practical mnemonic purpose. What resulted from it later must not be taken as authoritative dogma. But the question remains what this myth complex meant to the individual Manichaean, and the answer must be that the myth was not a ritual text but represented the theoretical-religious basis of the catechesis, the foundation for the questions "Where does the evil come from?" and "Where does man come from, where is he and whither is he going?" which are typical of the gnostic catechesis (e.g. *De duabus animabus* VIII, Tertullian, *De praescriptione* 7, *The Gospel of Truth* 22, 14-15, Eusebius V, 27, *Keph.*, etc.). These questions must clearly have been of great general human concern, to the extent that even the explicitly antignostic Zoroastrianism seems to have included them in its literature of wisdom, the Handarz literature (for example the lines in the *Dēnkart*, ed. Madan 573, 20-21: "Where have I come from? Why am I here? Whither am I going again?"). Only the right hand of *Spiritus vivens* stretched out, as reported in the myth, appears to have resulted in a symbolic cult gesture, according to which the Manichaeans talked of the "sons ot the right hand" (*MM* II, p. 326) and of the "Right arm of the light" (*Contra Ep. Fund* XI). Furthermore this has an important parallel in Mandaeism.

Even though Faustus, the great opponent of Augustine, simply keeps silent about the myth and ignores it, there is hardly any doubt that in most cases this myth was considered as scientifically valid and that it alone could equip man to understand himself, his environment and also nature both in its regularity and even more in its irregularity (compare the relation between the flooding of the Tigris and the struggle of the original man, *Keph.* 152 and subsequent).

V. The Manichaean Teaching about Man

The Manichaean anthropology establishes unequivocally that man in his external form is the result of the onslaught of satanic forces. Savage cruelty and unrestrained sexuality were the driving forces at his creation, which was effected "though the force (ἐνέργεια) of sin" (*Keph.* 138, 12) as a direct consequence of the seduction of the Archontes which had itself been set in motion by the world of light. The latter fact was maliciously exploited by the opponents of Manichaeism but hardly represented in any cruder way, and their accounts are confirmed by genuine Manichaean texts (especially *MM* I, p. 193 and subsequent). It was carried out by Tertius Legatus (or the Virgin of Light or the twelve Virgins of Lights), who appeared to the female demons in the shape of a man and to the male demons in the shape of a woman, thus inducing them to shed their seeds and by so doing releasing the light which they had swallowed. As a countermove the *Āz̧*, the *Hylē*, the evil itself achieved—with two members of a special class of demons (some-times unnamed, sometimes called *Šaklōn (Saclas,* corresponding to *Šiqlūn* in Mandaean texts and to the demiurge Sacla of the Gospel according to the Egyptians) and *Namraël (Nabroel, Pēsūs)* of opposite sex who were used as instruments, —the creation of man, so that a part "of that light-essence of the Gods - - was imprisoned in his body *(tan)* as his soul*(giyān)*" (*MM* I, p. 196 and 198). As the first woman was created in the same way, AUGUSTINE is right in a sense when he claims that both sexes do not come from God but from the devil (*ex diabolo, De continentia* X, 24). The motive applied in the myth, to defeat an opponent by evoking sexual desire, is one which is by no means unknown in the ancient Orient. Its application in Zoroastrianism can hardly have been without significance for the Manichaean version, especially because Nēryōs-ang (Narsa, Narsē) who was made by Ōhrmizd to walk out naked in order to evoke desire in the women, became the brother in name of *Tertius Legatus* in Middle Persian and Parthian Manichaica.

The Manichaean man qua man possesses therefore elements of the devil as well as of God; a part of God and a part of the *Hylē*, and both are taken equally seriously. The divine part was the precondition for the redemption, while through the devil's part the possibility of cor-ruption was present in the same degree. According to Manichaean thinking the *Hyle* part, the microcosmic *āz̧*, the Greed, was the root of all evil and it spread "as if fire touches dry fire-wood" (*Anhang z̧u den APAW* 1911, p. 17), for this part, too, is alive and possesses actively effective, invisible power, especially as it is manifested in man. But through Jesus the Splendour and Light-Nous, (or Vahman, *Nom qutī*), Adam and mankind after him have been offered the redeeming knowledge. It is therefore left to the individual to recognize and accept the gnosis through an act of free-will (as stated by ĀFREM, the Syrian, and the Muhammedan SHAHRASTĀNĪ (12th century), and by doing so to become the "New Man." As the "New Man" he possesses the "five *membra Dei*" which are the basis of the "five gifts" (love, faith, perfection, patience, wisdom). In the later Manichaean scholasticism everything that constitutes the "New Man" becomes the Great Thought = Call and Response = the ἐνθύμησις of life, the soul's pure will for redemption. If man does not make full use of the possibilities of redemption he remains the "Old Man" with the fatal ἐνθύμησις of death, which is also mentioned by gnostic writings like the Philippus Gospel 108 (Sophia of death) and the *Johannis Apocryphon* (ἐπιθυμία of death). Only the "New Man"—provided sin does not cause a relapse—can redeem completely that inborn divine part in himself, the viva anima, so that he may rise on the Column of Glory, on the Perfect Man" (compare *Ephes.* 4, 13) up to the light-chariot of the moon, and from there further to that of the sun, in order to enter the "New Paradise" built by the Great Master Builder and to remain there until, at the end of the world, this is incorporated into the "Eternal Paradise" of which it is a part (*MM* III, p. 852). Concerning this part of the eschatology there is some uncertainty, because in some versions the soul enters the "Eternal Paradise" directly, and the time of the individual judgment is also not quite definite. With the "Great War" (compare *Hom.* p. 7 and subsequent), the Advent, the Day of Judgement and the destruction of the material world through a fire which is to last 1468 years (compare ADAM. *Texte*, p. 24 which gives an explanation of this otherwise enigmatic number) the work of redemption has been completed, and the original man together with the "Last Statue" (the "last God" ἀνδριάς), i.e. the sum total of the light which was left behind in the world, comes before the Father of Light in Paradise. "Then the whole cosmos will be *frašēgird*" (*MM* I, p. 191) as a term borrowed from Zoroastrianism describes it. But in the Manichaean interpretation this means that everything becomes "healthy, *integrum*" (= *fraša*-) in that the world perishes totally, and not as in Zoroastrianism where the world will only be renewed. In Manichaeism there is only one last reminder of the material world, the great prison lump (*globus*, βῶλος), where the damned and the demons are kept imprisoned. This is the description of the ideal. But in reality the Manichaean concept of sin, taken to its extreme consequences, involves the possibility that the darkness may corrupt that which belongs to the substance of God to such an extent that it perishes, and so that "what of God's own part" (*de ipsa parte Dei*)— to quote AUGUSTINE who drew the logical consequences rigorously— could not be purified, would at the end of the world be tied eternally with chains of punishment" (*Epistola* 236, 2). The average Manichaean would probably shun logical thinking of such blasphemous boldness, but its presence in Manichaean theology is logically related to fundamental aspects of Mani's anthropology.

VI. Historical Effects of Manichaeism

One would have expected a priori that a religion such as Manichaeism, which appealed to mankind to such an extent that it covered the entire civilized world from Central Asia to the Atlantic like an avalanche, would also leave clear traces outside its own circle. There are, however, surprisingly few instances in which a factual historical link can be established and most of these are of a secondary nature and not related to religious dogma. Only the religious basis of the Communist teachings of Mazdak, who made his appearance under the Sasanid king Kavād (488-531), bears indications of elements which are unequivocally Manichaean and which can be historically proved. But Mazdakism was only of a temporary nature, so it excludes the possibility that it helped Manichaeism to spread its own influence further. The Sasanid *Mazdak-nāmak*, the "Book about Mazdak," which is now lost, kept the memory of Mazdak and his deeds alive in the popular literature of the day for a very long time, but apart from the fact that the book was "historical" in its contents rather than theological, it was in any case hardly a useful medium for the Manichaean propaganda, even though Ibnu'l-Muqaffaʿ and al-Lāhiqī, who were thought—and probably not without reason—to have Manichaean tendencies, translated it into Arabic (*Fihrist*, ed. G. Flügel, Leipzig 1871, p. 118, 27 and 163, 10). It is, however, quite likely that such a prolific translator as Ibnu 'l-Muqaffaʿ might have used the popular literature deliberately in order to infiltrate Islam with the Manichaean teachings. For however the teachings of Mani penetrated Islam under the Abbasids, its effects there can be proved historically; although this effect, seen as a whole, was of a decidedly negative character in that it provided in particular a very strong impulse for the development of the Islamic concept of heresy. However, of far greater importance from a religious-historic point of view, is a possible connection between Manichaeism on the one hand and on the other hand the dualistic heresies as represented by the Paulicians (especially in Armenia) and, connected with them, by the Bogomiles (Bulgaria, 10th century) and later by the Catharians or Albigenses (northern Italy, southern France, from the 11th century onwards). But here again, it is not possible to provide convincing and clear historic evidence as a basis for the affiliation which appears to be evident because of the same spiritual climate and the many parallel characteristics, (the rejection of visual images of deities, the circumspection as to whom should receive alms, analogies as regards the hierarchical, structural divisions etc. etc.). The most obvious, but by no means deliberate, result of the activities of the Manichaean missionaries is not of a strictly theological but of a neutral and literary nature, in that the texts used by them to illustrate their religious teachings acquired international importance. The literary achievement which they produced in this way can hardly be overestimated, although it was anonymous and of no consequence for the missionaries' work of spreading the religion, in as much as the literature, spread in this way, was not of a strictly Manichaean content. In Central Asia the Manichaean introduced Aesopian fables ("The Fox and the Monkey," also known through the poet ARCHILOCHOS, W. B. HENNING, *BSOAS* XI, p. 474 and subsequent, and "The Pig the and Sheep," A. VON LE COQ, *APAW* 1922, p. 33) and special material from the west (the story of the PEARL BORER, *BSOAS* XI, p. 465 and subsequent) from the book Kalīla and Dimna, of whose specifically Indian sources, the Pañcatantra collection of stories, they were quite aware. In the west they introduced Buddha legends which they themselves had undoubtedly collected and edited, providing through Arabic and Georgian versions the basic for the very popular, edifying tale of Barlaam and Joasaph, which spread over the whole of Europe and was falsely attributed to the Church Father JOHN DAMASCENUS. It would not come as a surprise if it were proved that the European history of literature owes far more to the Manichaeans than one can already conclude from the examples given.

VII. SURVEY ABOUT THE HISTORY OF RESEARCH

As long as Manichaeism had any meaning in the west, it was the cause of objections or even considered as a dangerous rival that could not be viewed dispassionately, in other words, it could not become the object of unbiased historical research. As Manichaeism was the most prominent and outspoken protagonist of a radically dualistic concept of universe and man, it became at the time the terminus technicus for any form of dualism or even for heresy generally, no matter to what extent Manichaeism could reasonably be held responsible in this respect at all. Even Arius had to witness how his Christology was considered Manichaean. For the Byzantine heresiology, Manichaeism became the heresy par excellence, but in its battle against the dualistic movements of the time, it made use of genuine

Manichaean traditions, so that its anti-dualistic polemics in fact provide valuable sources for the actual Manichaeism. An example is the long Greek formula of abjuration which was directed in particular against the Paulicians. In the context of pure history of research, something similar applies to the Renaissance of "Manichaean" studies, of caused by the Reformation. The opponents of the Reformation considered Luther as well as Melanchton and Calvin to be a *Manichaeus redivivus*, and whatever could be gathered from the old traditions about those heretic teachings was used in support of accusations against the Reformers, and was furthermore used with the same fervour which Luterans showed when, starting from similar premises, they set out to prove the opposite. Research in the true sense, only started with *Gottfried Arnold's "Unparteyische Kirchen- und Ketzerhistorie"* from 1699 while the monumental *"Histoire critique de Manichée et du Manichéisme"* (Amsterdam 1734 and 1739) of the Huguenot ISAAC DE BEAUSOBRE finally brought a real turn of the tide, even though this work is in fact an apology for Protestantism and was not written primarily and exclusively on Manichaeism as such. The fine quality and originality of this work, however, are evident, and the penetrating views of BEAUSOBRE achieved results which have met with general acclamation. One of the points in question is his understanding of the importance which the Enoch literature had for Mani. The reaction of Catholic theologians to BEAUSOBRE's work indicates, however, that they and their contemporaries generally considered his studies purely as anti-Catholic polemics. For this reason, too, his research did not lead to such an extensive revival of Manichaean studies as they deserved. The contributions made after BEAUSOBRE are just part of the ordinary history of heresy, lacking originality. Only the book *"Das manichäische Religionssystem nach den Quellen neu untersucht und entwickelt"* (1831, Göttingen, anastatischer Neudruck 1928) of the theologian FERDINAND CHRISTIAN BAUR of Tübingen brought something entirely new. BAUR's complete command over and deep understanding of the entire ancient Church literature enabled him, despite the fact that his basic approach was wrong (although not quite as wrong as one might have assumed under the conditions at the time—the influence of Buddhism which overshadowed all else- to provide clear and exhaustive answers to many obscure questions (such as the two "animae" or "Gods" within man, vir perfectus, the three seals etc.), to such an extent that even today his research provides an invaluable aid to anyone concerned with Manichaeism. During the years following BAUR's great work ex-

cellent editorial work (by Flügel, E. Sachau, E. Kessler, H. Pog-
non, M.-A. Kugener) added important written Arabic and Syriac
sources to the already known Greek and Latin material of the history
of Manichaeism and prepared the way for a radical, new approach
which resulted in tremendous quantities of genuine texts, brought
back to the museums of Europe by German, English and French expeditions to Central Asia at the beginning of this century. The publication of editions of these texts (in Iranian, Turkish and Chinese by
such scholars as F. W. K. Müller, A. von Le Coq, Carl Salemann,
E. Chavannes, P. Pelliott, W. Radloff, F. C. Andreas, W. Bang,
Annemarie von Gabain, E. Waldschmidt, W. Lentz, W. B. Henning and Mary Boyce) to a wider extent than actual studies of these
texts has then determined research—the more so when the material
was considerably added to by a sensational discovery of *Manichaica*
(the Coptic texts from Egypt, edited by H. J. Polotsky, Charles
R. C. Allberry and A. Böhlig in 1934, 1938, 1940 and 1966). The
material now available inevitably must result in a coherent study of
the teachings of Mani. Such research as has been done, is generally
agreed that Manichaeism is a gnosis religion; but attempts to solve
the problem of its historical background (Christian, Greek or Iranian)
have shown differences in approach. During the past few years L. H.
Grondijs in particular has raised doubts whether the attitude which
considers the entire Manichaean written material as one whole complex without differentiations is justified. In order to understand the
often striking divergencies, he maintains that one should assume, to a
far greater extent than has been done hitherto, that Manichaeism contained a number of relatively independent sects. The complete and
exhaustive understanding of Mani's teachings still lies in the future.

BIBLIOGRAPHY

a) *Texts and translations*

Allberry, Charles R. C., *A Manichaean Psalm-Book*. Stuttgart 1938
Asmussen, Jes P., *Xᵘāstvānīft. Studies in Manichaeism*. Copenhagen 1965
Bang, W., *Türkische Turfan-Texte*. II, *SPAW* 1929, IV, *SPAW* 1930, V, *SPAW*
    1931
Beeson, C. H. ed., *Hegemonius, Acta Archelai*. Leipzig 1906
Boyce, Mary, *The Manichaean Hymn Cycles in Parthian*. Oxford 1954
Chavannes, Ed. et P. Pelliot, *Un traité manichéen retrouvé en Chine. JA* 1911 and
    1913

Coq, A. von Le, *Türkische Manichaica aus Chotscho*, I, *APAW* 1911, II, *APAW* 1919, III, *APAW* 1922
Cumont, Fr. and M.-A. Kugener, *Recherches sur le manichéisme* I-III. Bruxelles 1908
Flügel, G., *Mani, seine Lehre und seine Schriften.* Leipzig 1862
Gabain, Annemarie von und Werner Winter, *Türkische Turfantexte* IX. *ADAW* zu Berlin 1956, Nr. 2, Berlin 1958
Henning, W. B., *Mitteliranische Manichaica aus Chinesisch-Turkestan. Von F. C. Andreas.* Aus dem Nachlass herausgegeben von Dr. W. Henning in Berlin. I, *SPAW* 1932, II, *SPAW* 1933, III, *SPAW* 1934
Henning, W. B., *Ein manichäisches Henochbuch. SPAW* 1934
Henning, W. B., *Ein manichäisches Bet- und Beichtbuch. APAW* 1936
Jolivet, R. et M. Jourjon, *Six traités anti-manichéens.* Bruxelles 1961
Müller, F. W. K., *Handschriften-Reste in Estrangelo-Schrift aus Turfan, Chinesisch-Turkistan. II. Teil. Anhang* zu den *APAW* 1904
Polotsky, H. J., *Manichäische Homilien*, Stuttgart 1934
Polotsky, H. J.-A. Böhlig, *Kephalaia*, Stuttgart 1940. Zweite Hälfte, bearbeitet von Prof. Dr. Dr. A. Böhlig, Stuttgart 1966
Waldschmidt, Ernst und W. Lentz, *Die Stellung Jesu im Manichäismus. APAW* 1926
——, ——, *Manichäische Dogmatik aus chinesischen und iranischen Texten. SPAW* 1933
Zycha, J. ed., *Corpus Scriptorum Ecclesiasticorum Latinorum* Vol. XXV (Sect. VI, Pars I, 1891, Pars II, 1892)

b) *History of research*

Nyberg, H. S., *Forschungen über den Manichäismus. ZNW* 34, 1935
Ries, J., *Introduction aux études manichéennes. Quatre siècles de recherches. Analecta Lovaniensia Biblica et Orientalia*, Serie III, 7 et 11, 1957 & 1959

c) *Selected modern works*

Klíma, Otakar, *Manis Zeit und Leben.* Praha 1963
Polotsky, H. J., *Manichäismus.* Pauly-Wissowa, *Real-encyclopädie der classischen Altertumswissenschaft*, Supplementband VI, Stuttgart 1935, cols. 240-271 (= Abriss des manichäischen Systems)
Puech, Henri-Charles, *Le Manichéisme. Son fondateur—sa doctrine.* Musée Guimet, *Bibliothèque de diffusion.* Tome LVI, Paris 1949
Schaeder, H. H., *Der Manichäismus nach neuen Funden und Forschungen.* Morgenland Heft 28, Leipzig 1936
Widengren, Geo, *Mani und der Manichäismus.* Stuttgart 1961 (English translation revised by the author: *Mani and Manichaeism*, London 1965)

GERMANIC RELIGION

BY

H. R. ELLIS DAVIDSON

Cambridge, England

I. Essence of Religion

The religion of the Germanic peoples was established in Northern Europe by the beginning of the Roman period, and lasted for about a thousand years, since it continued in Scandinavia for some centuries after the conversion of the Anglo-Saxons and the continental Germans.

The people who practised this religion were vigorous, independent folk, living in hard climatic conditions with few comforts and luxuries. They were divided into small tribal groups and later into kingdoms, often at war with one another, and fought in small bands under independent leaders, and sometimes as professional mercenaries. Those at home depended on farming and the sea, and when conditions grew more settled after the period of the migrations many went on trading expeditions. Owing to their capacity for seafaring and adventure, the Germanic peoples came into contact with many other civilizations, but preserved their identity and their own religion to a marked degree. Their culture remained oral until they became Christian, and they possessed a high regard for learning, oratory and traditional law, as well as the gift of poetry and storytelling.

Their religion was in keeping with this heroic background, and emphasised the responsibility of the individual to the family and community, and of fighting men to their leader. A man usually relied on one particular deity for luck and protection, perhaps setting up a local shrine for him, but if things went badly he might well change his allegiance. Communal rites and ceremonies were held in honour of the gods as a whole, led by the king or local leader. Man relied on the gods to bring good fortune in battle, wisdom in the conduct of affairs, inspiration in poetry and art and various skills, favourable weather and good harvests, in return for faithful adherence to the traditional rites. The gods were to protect the community from the anarchy which would overwhelm it if the rule of law broke down. Conditions were precarious during the Migration period and the Viking Age, and the religion shows an acute sense of the constant threat of hostile powers, and of the transitory nature of men's achievements. Communal feasts and sacrifices and traditional lore associated with worship helped to knit the community together.

The Germanic peoples lived close to the earth and sea. The influence of northern mountains, storm-beaten coasts, rain and fog and long dark winter nights are reflected in their mythology. It emphasises the mists and darkness of the underworld, and the constant threat of chained monsters anxious to destroy the inhabited earth. The gods were impressive beings of enormous vitality and authority, robust and sometimes mischievous, but neither savage nor wantonly cruel. Their shrines were in the forests, fens and mountains, on islands and the shores of lakes, and they themselves were personified in the shape of powerful male animals or wild birds of prey. The religion satisfied man's sense of the numinous, and fear of the mysterious implacable forces ruling nature and his own mind. On a lower level there were many ambivalent beings haunting lonely places, such as elves, dwarfs, trolls and giants, and the guardian spirits attached to certain families. Although they could do harm, these were on the whole protective powers, and even the walking dead, the terror of winter nights around the lonely farms, could grant inspiration and wisdom to the living.

There is a marked shamanistic element in the religion of the Viking Age, a belief in the power of the spirit to journey out of the body to other realms. This may owe something to late influences from the East, but belief in divination was part of the Germanic heritage from early times, and the seeking of hidden knowledge by ritual associated with worship of the gods a fundamental part of Germanic religion.

II. HISTORICAL DEVELOPMENT

In the Scandinavian Bronze Age there is evidence for the worship of an all-powerful sky-god, who ruled over nature, war and the life of the community; there may indeed have been twin sky-gods, whose symbols were the setting and the rising sun. There was a goddess of fertility worshipped from the Neolithic period, a chthonic deity associated with the underworld and the dead, and with the fruitfulness of earth. The sacred marriage between god and goddess appears to have been represented in ritual.

After the close of the Bronze Age, about 500 B.C., there is a dearth of evidence for religious cults. By the first century A.D. the Germanic peoples were moving to new areas in the north-west, bringing with them religious ideas from their earlier homelands. A small group of deities now dominated the scene: among them the sky-god Tîwaz, probably the direct descendant of the Bronze Age god, who was equated with Mars by the Romans and associated with battle and law as well as fertility. There was also a thunder-god Donar, with the axe as his symbol, equated with Jupiter, and a third god Wodan, equated with Mercury, who was the god of magic and the dead and the giver of inspiration. He seems gradually to have ousted Tîwaz from his place as god of battle, and to have taken over the spear as his emblem. The same trio of gods was worshipped by the Anglo-Saxons under the names of Tîw, Thunor and Woden. Worship of the fertility goddess continued under many different names.

By the end of the seventh century Christianity was established in England and over a large part of the continental area, but the Danes, Swedes and Norwegians still remained outside the church. The battle cult of the chthonic god of magic, now known in Scandinavia as Odin, flourished in Denmark and Sweden among the aristocratic warriors, and some devoted their whole lives to warfare. The Swedish royal family also worshipped a male fertility god, known as Freyr (Lord) in Sweden, and worshipped elsewhere under different names. He was the twin of the fertility goddess, sometimes called Freyja (Lady). The thunder-god continued to be worshipped in association with the oak, and the wooden pillars supporting the Scandinavian halls were a symbol of his power in a land where oaks were less common than in Germany. As time went on, Thor gained ground in the North, especially among the independent farmers of Norway and Iceland. His cult included the respect for law so strong among the Scandinavian people, and at the close of the Viking Age it seems to have been the dominant one.

Norway was converted in the tenth century, against much opposition, largely owing to the work of two outstanding kings, Olaf Tryggvason and Olaf the Holy. Missionaries worked in Denmark in the ninth century, but not until the mid-tenth was the Danish king Harald Gormsson baptized. Iceland adopted Christianity by general consent in the year 1000, and Sweden finally became Christian in the course of the eleventh century.

Beside the cults of the main deities, there were many holy places where offerings were made to lesser powers, or local variants of the high gods. Many "gods" survive in the literary sources for whose cults no convincing evidence exists, such as Balder, Heimdall and Loki. Such figures may be discarded local deities, personified attributes of the great gods, or purely literary characters inspired by foreign sources, given a fictitious life by antiquarian writers of the post-pagan period. Others from the evidence of place-names must once have been important, but are difficult to identify. Tyr must be the descendant of the once-powerful Tîwaz; Ull and Njord appear to have connections with the fertility deities, while many places are called after the manifold titles of the fertility goddess.

Continual influence from Mediterranean lands, from the Celtic peoples, from pagan regions further East, and from Christian neighbours, must all be taken into account, so that the Germanic religion was never static. There was something of a pagan renaissance in the late Viking Age, when more active opposition was put up to Christianity, together with a renewal of interest in the heroic past. But the infiltration of Christian missionaries, the political importance of the Christian countries of Europe, and a growing lack of confidence in the old gods, meant that this was only a temporary postponement of an inevitable end.

III. CONCEPTION OF DEITY

The idea of a sky-god protecting mankind from the destructive forces constantly threatening him was a powerful one in Germanic religion. Tîwaz appears to have been a god of this type. Odin, who was to lead gods and men in the final battle against the monsters, had some of the sky-god's attributes, although he was primarily a chthonic deity, ruler of the land of the dead. In the Viking Age it was the thunder-god, Thor, who was the defender of Asgard against the giants. The axe was the dominant symbol of the sky-god from very early times, representing the power of the lightning linking earth and heaven, and in Scandinavia this was partially replaced by the hammer. Man could shelter behind this sign to protect him not only from the wrath of the god, but also from danger to the home and perils on the sea or on the battle-field. The conception of an appeal to the gods to establish justice can be seen in the records of Scandinavian law before the conversion.

In contrast to the deity upholding law and preserving order, the Germanic Wodan, later Odin, was a stirrer-up of strife, and sometimes a cunning trickster. His symbol was the spear, possibly taken from

Tiwaz, and he was associated with the wolf, the eagle and the raven. His great gift was escape from self-consciousness into the intoxication of battle, the ecstatic trance, the inspiration of poetry, or strong drink. He was the cunning magician, and in the Viking Age his shamanistic side is emphasised, the power to send his spirit into other worlds to acquire hidden knowledge and to consult the dead, and this aspect is represented by his eight-legged horse on which he could ride through the air and visit the underworld. He was sometimes described as wearing a hood or broad-brimmed hat, and as having only one eye, since the other had been sacrificed in pursuit of knowledge. Like a shaman undergoing initiation, he had hung on the world tree and been pierced by a spear in his pursuit of magic and the runic symbols. From Roman times great sacrifices of war booty, and weapons, men and horses, seem to have been made to him. Towards the end of the heathen period there was a feeling of disillusionment with Odin, however, as a god in whom no lasting trust could be placed. Many tales of kings and heroes were associated with his cult, and some of the pictures carved on memorial stones on the island of Gotland, dating from the Viking Age, show scenes of heroes sacrificed or slain in battle arriving in the realm of the god.

The male fertility god had many names, but the main outline is recognisable over the Scandinavian world of a god of earth and sea, whose gifts to men were rich harvests, good fishing, flourishing flocks and herds and healthy children, as well as peaceful rule. He was symbolised by the powerful male animals, especially the stallion and the boar, and there was a consistent tradition that he came over the sea in a ship as a child to bring the land prosperity. The Swedish kings of Uppland regarded him as the founder of their line, and his cult, linked with mound burial, was practised at Old Uppsala, where the royal burial mounds formed a place of sanctity. The boar and the ship were the chief symbols of Freyr and his sister, said to belong to the family of the Vanir, and elaborate ship-burials in Sweden and Norway from the seventh century onwards appear to be associated with them. The god Njord, said to be the father of the pair, and worshipped along the west coast of Norway, was also associated with ships, and certain local goddesses like Nehalennia, worshipped on the island of Walcheren in the Roman period, were linked with the bringing of plenty and with the ship symbol. The goddess Frigg, the wife of Odin, represents another aspect of the fertility goddess, that of wife and mother; she was connected with the birth of children, the giving of names, and the foretelling of destinies. Other aspects may be represented by the daughters of giants in the underworld, such as Gerd, wooed by Freyr, and Thorgerd *Hǫlgabrúðr*, worshipped by Jarl Hakon of Halogaland in the tenth century. The goddess was indeed an ambivalent figure, associated with dignified and honourable families, but with a more sinister side, involving rites and orgies only hinted at, misrepresented or suppressed by the monks responsible for the written sources.

While the fertility powers were known as the Vanir, the gods collectively were the Aesir, or were sometimes known as the *Tívar*, a word related to the name of Tîwaz. The female fertility spirits, comprising the various aspects of the goddess, and other powers associated with peace and plenty, were known as the *Disar*. The idea of a company of gods must be old; they were invoked in oath formulae, honoured at feasts, mentioned in the poems as holding their own feasts and assemblies, and of banding together to fight the monsters. The conception of a council of twelve gods may be based on analogy with Germanic law, and be pre-Christian in origin. The more rationalised picture of Asgard however, with the deities in their separate halls with wives and children and complex relationships with one another, must be largely due to the efforts of poets and antiquarians of the late heathen period and after.

IV. Worship

1) *Cult* Local cults were at first linked with special holy places, especially in forests and marshland, in the mountains, on islands, and by springs, lakes and waterfalls. Here offerings were made, and wooden figures have survived from the bogs, fenced in or surrounded by stones, which may represent the gods to which men sacrificed; one particularly impressive pair, more than life-size, has been found at Braak in Schleswig. The Scandinavian *hǫrgr* or open-air place of offering, probably developed from this. Small wooden temples are said to have existed in Anglo-Saxon England, but do not appear to have been built in Scandinavia until the late heathen period; one theory is that they developed out of the wooden roof fixed over wooden figures of the gods to shelter them from the weather. The burial mounds of kings and heads of families were also holy places, and ceremonies and law-meetings were conducted from the mounds at Old Uppsala and elsewhere, while this was probably where new kings were crowned. The Tynwald in the Isle of Man, where the Manx parliament still meets, is a relic of the holy mounds of the Viking Age.

Sacrificial feasts in honour of the gods were probably either held in the open or in the halls of landowners and kings, who would be responsible for the service of the gods. Divination ceremonies were held at special festivals, when the comminity was faced with some problem, or when individuals were anxious to know the future.

Magic was associated with the cult of Odin, and also with the Vanir. It was regarded as secret knowledge, to be learned from an expert, and the surviving literature implies a vast field of esoteric poetry, including not only spells and charms but elaborate information about the creation, the underworld, the homes of the gods, and names and titles of supernatural beings. It is difficult, however, to make a clear distinction between magic and the craft of the antiquarian poet, which included a highly technical, specialised language of its own. Runic symbols were part of magic knowledge, although recent discoveries in Bergen have shown that they were also used as a practical means of communication. However verse inscriptions like that on the Eggjum stone from western Norway shows the highly developed use of runes for recording magical inscriptions. Incantations were said to be used at divination ceremonies, to summon helpful spirits. Magical spells were used to protect men in battle, to render them virtually invulnerable to wounds through heightened energy and courage, and to affect the mind of an enemy by driving him into a state of irresolution and panic. Such spells were associated with Tyr and Odin, although the boar of the Vanir and the hammer of Thor were also used to protect warriors. Spells to do with the fertility of the earth and with the movements of animals and fish would come into the province of the Vanir, while those to control the weather would be associated with Thor. However no clear-cut distinction can be made between the magic of different deities; a man turned to his special god, land-spirit or family guardian for help in a tight corner, or good fortune in farming or fighting. Other spells were associated with the cult of the dead and with divination ceremonies. There are some highly complex poems concerned with the journey to the other world, and with the magical knowledge necessary to meet the dangers on the way.

Such evidence as exists for prayer implies that it took the form of special incantations mentioned above, and of poems composed in honour of a god. Some ninth and tenth century poems in praise of Thor survive from Iceland, describing his exploits, and there are accounts of verses composed in honour of a dead hero and recited on his burial mound. Isolated fragments of spells survive from the

Anglo-Saxon period, like the one with an invocation to Mother Earth, and the Merseburg charms from Germany contain reference to the heathen gods. The cutting of runes to protect a grave by invoking the power of Thor, or linked with a divine symbol to give a name to a weapon and make it effective in battle, might be regarded as half-way between prayer and magic. Vows to the gods were also a kind of prayer, and failure to keep them would call down the divine wrath.

There is evidence for sacrifice from both literature and archaeology. Sacrifice to Wodan and Odin included human victims, dispatched by strangling and stabbing, and there is evidence for this form of sacrifice continuing up to the tenth century. The bodies of human and animal victims were said to be hung from trees, and were reputed to have been seen at the sanctuaries of Uppsala and Leire in the late Viking Age. Archaeological evidence exists for vast sacrifices of war booty, from the Roman period till the sixth century, for finds made at Vimose, Nydam, Illerup, Kragehul and Haderslev in Denmark confirm the descriptions by Tacitus and others of sacrifices made in return for victory. The peat bogs also provide evidence for sacrifice to the fertility powers, for pottery, farm implements, food, personal ornaments, and sometimes boats have been found in the bogs. Thorsbjerg, south of the Danish border, is believed to have been the sacrificial place of the Angles for several centuries, while at Karingsjön in Sweden the offerings had been thrown into a lake, by the light of fires burning on the shore, to judge by charred branches found with the objects. Many bodies have also been recovered from the bogs of men and women who died by strangling, throat-cutting, or being beaten to death, and some of these may be sacrificial victims. Some burials of the Viking Age suggest the possibility of a wife or servant killed at the funeral of an important person, and this practice is described in the literary sources, where the picture given is that of a wife or slave-girl dying voluntarily, as by the custom of suttee in India, in order to join the dead man as his wife in the next world; this type of sacrifice is associated with the cult of Odin.

There is plenty of evidence for animal sacrifice. At Skedemose on Öland, large numbers of horses were slain in the Migration period, and some of the bodies had been cut up as if for sacrificial feasts. Horse sacrifice continued until the Viking Age, and seems to have been connected with the cult of the Vanir. In the seventh century ship burials at Vendel and Valsgärde in Sweden, Gokstad and Oseberg in Norway, and Ladby in Denmark, considerable numbers of horses were killed at the funeral, and laid out carefully in or around the ship. Remains of oxen, sheep, pigs and birds (including heron, crane, cocks and one peacock) were also found in the ships. There are many instances of animal bones, animal heads or complete skeletons in graves of the heathen period in Germany, Anglo-Saxon England and Scandinavia. There were also communal "blood-offerings," when horses and cattle were slain and eaten, and the king or leader partook of the blood. The boar seems to have been a regular mid-winter sacrifice to the Vanir, and there are occasional references to the sacrifice of a bull, which may have preceded the horse as the main sacrificial animal of the Early Iron Age.

There is an element of the sacramental discernable in some sacrafices, since certain animals appear to be identified with the deities, and the gods themselves were sometimes described as taking on bird or animal form. The boar helmets possessed by the early kings of Sweden may have been based on the practice of wearing a boar mask to identify the worshippers with their god. The idea behind the blood offering seems to be that the drinking of the blood could inspire the king or priest taking part in divination ceremonies, just as the hero Sigurd the Volsung, according to a long-remembered tradition, was inspired by dragon's blood touching his tongue to understand the secret speech of birds. There was also a tradition of the sacred drink of inspiration, the mead brewed from the blood of the wise giant Kvasir, who could answer all questions. This giant was said to have been formed as the result of a strange ritual, when the companies of the Aesir and the Vanir made a truce together, and all spat in turn into a bowl, from the contents of which Kvasir came into being. Envious dwarfs slew him and made the mead from his blood; this was stolen by giants, and finally won back for gods and men by Odin, by a dangerous journey to the underworld. Myths like this, surviving in a late form, are likely to be based on earlier cult practices, and some of the great ceremonial bowls and drinking horns which survive from the heathen period were probably used for religious ritual.

Certain worshippers of the gods might be regarded as holy persons. There is evidence for special champions among the Germans in the early Roman period, who wore little or no defensive armour because they were under the special protection of the god who inspired them in battle. Some wore metal collars as a mark of this service, which may account for the many splendid collars in gold and silver which survive from Sweden in the Migration period. Later there were similar traditions about the *berserks*, who wore animal skins and despised armour because they were inspired to superhuman strength and fury in battle by the power of Odin. These formed a special band of champions fighting for King Harald Fairhair of Norway in the ninth century, and in the literature they are represented as a privileged class who wandered about the land defying normal laws and conventions, and claiming hospitality at will. Pictures of naked men in horned helmets carrying spears, and of others in animal skins, are found on helmet plates and buckles of the seventh century, and appear to belong to this tradition of special servants and warriors devoted to the battle god.

Other persons with special gifts are the seers and seeresses, represented as men and women who had undergone a training in the use of their mantic powers so that they were able to foretell the future and reveal what was hidden. The seeresses are described as wearing some kind of traditional costume, in particular a hood of animal fur, and carrying a staff, and their ritual included the use of a high platform on which they sat when entering a state of ecstasy, and from which they answered questions put to them by those who attended the ceremony. Their special powers might also be used to affect the minds of others, causing panic, forgetfulness, confusion and temporary blindness, or even death. It is implied that the solitary seeresses described in the sagas were the last descendants of groups and communities who went about the land and visited feasts to perform their rites; there may also have been similar groups of men, for there are traditions of bands of wizards attached to the Norwegian court in the ninth and tenth centuries. Such groups appear to have been associated with the cult of the Vanir, and were inspired and helped by animal spirits. Some of the mythological poems are in the form of replies given by such seeresses, known as *vǫlur* (sing: *vǫlva*), revealing esoteric knowledge about the world of the gods and the future.

These poems suggest the existence of some kind of priesthood or community which preserved traditional lore of this kind and taught it to the next generation. There is little definite evidence however for a professional priesthood. TACITUS knew of a priest serving the fertility goddess Nerthus in Denmark in the first century, and there is some indication of priestesses in the cult of the Vanir, as well as a high priest existing in Northumbria in the seventh century, who was a member of the king's council, tended the shrine of the gods, and was forbidden to carry weapons. The kings in Norway and Sweden appear to have presided at the religious feasts and sometimes to have acted as priests, and later the local landowners in Norway and Iceland performed the same function. The kings were indeed regarded to some extent as holy persons; even after the conversion Olaf Tryggvason of Norway was held to possess special "Luck" which he could pass on to his followers. Some passages imply that a ruler would be put to death if there were bad harvests or ill fortune during his reign; there are stories of early kings who were hanged by their wives, killed by various animals, or burned in their halls, which seem to be rationalised accounts of sacrificial deaths. There was special sanctity also in the remains of a dead king buried in the earth, and the rites held at their graves were in accordance with a belief in the potency of the ruler to give help and blessing to the living community after his death.

2) *Ethics* The strongest ethical conceptions amongst the Germanic peoples from early times were loyalty to the family and the leader, together with a belief in the sanctity and value of traditional law. This continued into the Viking Age, in spite of the opportunism of professional adventurers and the frequent resort to force. Law assemblies were held at religious sanctuaries and beside royal graves. Vows to the god had to be kept at any cost, and oath-breakers were outcasts from the community. Even in late heathen times the ceremonial duel was still regarded as a plea to the gods to decide how victory should fall. The man outlawed from the community for breaking its laws or for anti-social behaviour was supposed to have every man's hand against him, and to have forfeited the protection of gods and land-spirits. Treachery, cowardice and disloyalty were the crimes most condemned. Magic was not a crime, unless used as a dangerous weapon in the community. There was the right to exact vengeance for physical hurt or insult, and the law of wergeld, the payment of a fixed sum as compensation for injury or killing, was of great importance in Germanic law. If this were withheld, then the blood feud which followed was essential to maintain the honour and reputation of the injured family. Linked with the importance of reputation was the great pride in the achievements of ancestors, and the desire to win such fame as would be long remembered after a man's death. The most admired virtues of a leader were courage, reliability and generosity, as well as resourcefulness, practical wisdom and the gift of eloquence to sway men. Ruthlessness was condoned if circumstances demanded it, but there is little delight in cruelty for its own sake to be found in the tales of either the gods or the heroes. Ability to accept reversal of fortune

without complaint, and to go down fighting to the last against over-
whelming odds, was held to constitute true greatness. In such ethical
conceptions women shared to the full, and in training their sons and
urging on their menfolk, they made an essential contribution to the
concept of family pride. They were respected for their position as
guardian of the family traditions as well as for their mantic powers, and
posessed considerable independence. In early times TACITUS stressed
the high standard of marital fidelity among the Germans; in the Viking
Age, concubines were legally recognised, and their rights to some
extent safeguarded, while women as well as men had the right to
divorce, and could claim back their *mundr* or bride-price.

3) *Myth*   Most of the surviving mythological material comes from
Scandinavia and was written down in Christian times, much of it by
the Icelandic poet and scholar SNORRI STURLUSON in the thirteenth
century, and by the Latin historian in Denmark, SAXO GRAMMATICUS,
in the twelfth. Some mythological poems survive, and much skaldic
verse in the form of short poems by Norwegian and Icelandic poets
from the ninth century onwards, whose names and dates are known.
From the tangled web of poems and stories, many confused and obscure, and a few spells and charms from England and Germany,
certain fundamental myths stand out, and some of these are illustrated
by carvings on wood or stone from the pre-Christian period. The most
important can be classified as follows:

a) Creation myths (see below).

b) Myths about the world tree, which formed the centre of the
worlds of gods, men, and giants.

c) Myths about the god of battle and his followers, the Valkyries,
sent down to give victory in battle and to conduct the slain to his
abode. These are connected with the cult of Odin and linked with
many tales of famous heroes.

d) Myths about the acquisition of wisdom by Odin, either by obtaining a drink from the sacred spring under the world tree, or winning
back the mead of inspiration, by sacrificing himself to gain knowledge. He is also represented as seeking wisdom by the consultation
of the dead.

e) Myths about the treasures of the gods and endeavours by the
giants to steal them, examples being the hammer of Thor, the necklace
of Freyja, the apples of eternal youth and the mead of inspiration. In
these Loki, an ambivalent trickster figure, plays a leading part, som-
times committing the theft and sometimes winning back the treasures.

f) Myths about Thor's journeys to the land of the giants, and his battles with giants and monsters. His most famous exploit, the fishing up of the world serpent, is described in several early poems and illustrated in carvings of the tenth century.

g) Myths about a child coming in a boat over the sea to found a kingdom, and returning to the other world when his reign is over.

h) Myths about the wooing of a maiden from the underworld, by a god or a hero.

i) Myths about the death of Balder, the son of Odin, in spite of all that the gods could do to avert it, and unavailing attempts to bring him back from the land of the dead.

j) Myths concerning the binding of the monsters by the gods, and the final crisis at Ragnarök, when the fettered powers break loose, and both sides go down fighting, while the world is overwhelmed by fire and water.

These myths all appear to have formed a part of the religion of the pagan Germanic peoples before the Viking Age.

V. Conception of Man

1) *Creation* Creation myths formed an important part of the religious tradition of the Germanic peoples. They begin with the conception of chaos existing before creation, a great abyss pregnant with potential life. Life came into being by the mingling of intense heat and cold, and a primeval giant, Ymir, took shape from the melting ice. A man and woman came forth from his armpits, and the race of giants was born from his feet. From the body and blood of Ymir, the world and the sea and sky were formed. Another tradition was that of a cow which licked the salty ice-blocks and shaped the figures of the first three gods, who were nourised on her milk. These created the first man and woman from trees on the seashore. The kingdoms of the gods and of mankind were formed around the world tree, which also linked them to the underworld of the giants, and stood at the centre of the universe. The gods built the stronghold of Asgard and defended it against the giants, and the world serpent was curled round the inhabited earth, under the sea.

2) *Nature of Man* Man inhabited the middle kingdom, Midgard, between the gods and the underworld. The gods gave him the gifts of speech, wisdom and understanding, and by the attainment of certain knowledge he might gain entry to the other worlds; there are many traditions of seers and heroes who possessed this power. Man could

hold his own for a while with the gods, if he had the necessary knowledge, and even strike bargains with them, but like them he was
helpless before the omnipotence of fate.

3) *Destiny, Path of Salvation* Destiny was supreme over gods and
men, and beyond it there was no appeal. The Anglo-Saxons called this
power *wyrd*, and the consciousness of it, and of the transitory nature
of men's achievements, was very marked in Germanic literature. Acceptance of destiny was the greatest lesson to be learned, and here the
gods themselves set an example. Prophecies were fulfilled in spite of all
attempts to avert them, and men's destinies might be foretold at birth
by those who had the power to look into the future. Apart from the
conception of certain people who were loyal worshippers of the gods
joining them in their ultimate fight against the forces of evil, there is
little idea of salvation. There is however some indication of faith in
the sky-god as the defender of man in this world and the next.

4) *Personal and General Eschatology* The two enduring realities were
those of the continuity of the family and the race on one hand, and of
lasting fame after death on the other. There are hints of some kind of
survival for privileged groups, such as warriors who died in battle or
by a sacrificial death, who had the right to pass to the realm of Odin.
Champions bound to his service on earth would continue to fight for
him after death, and women choosing to die with their husbands seem
also to have shared a right to survival. Such ideas however probably
applied to a limited aristocratic group only, reaching their height in
the seventh and eighth centuries in Sweden. They are confirmed by
carvings on certain memorial stones, of which a large number survive
in Gotland in the Baltic.

The thunder-god also had the power to protect his followers after
death, and his hammer was placed as a protective sign on gravestones.
The fertility deities of the Vanir had a ship as one of their symbols, and
may have been associated with traditions of a land of the dead across
the sea, possibly in early heathen times the underworld through which
the ship of the sky-god passed when it went beneath the waves. In
the Viking Age there is emphasis on an underground realm under
earth and sea, where the dead might join their ancestors. There is some
indication of beliefs in the dead entering certain mountains and joining
their kinsmen there; and also of life continuing in the gravemound.
Different beliefs were linked with special localities and family traditions, but there seems to have been no official teaching about survival
after death. Allusions to rewards and punishments in a future state

are occasionally found in mythological poems, and may not be wholly due to Christian influence, especially when the sins stressed are oath-breaking and treachery, the outstanding crimes of pre-Christian society.

There is a vigorous tradition in Old Norse literature of the destruction of the present world of gods and men and of a new cycle beginning when the earth rises anew from the sea and life begins once more. Certain chosen survivors among gods and men are sheltered from the final catastrophe to repeople the world. The end of the world comes about by a series of natural phenomena, among them a terrible winter lasting for three years on end, and by the breaking loose of the bound monsters. Certain memorial stones of the tenth century in Scandinavia, the Isle of Man and Northern England show scenes linked with this tradition. Some features in this conception of the world's end suggest that it was partly inspired by new influences coming into Eastern Scandinavia during the Viking Age, but the fundamental idea seems to have been based on early Germanic beliefs.

VI. Subsequent Influence of Religion

The influence of Germanic religion on the teaching of the Christian church in Anglo-Saxon England may be seen in the emphasis on Christ as a warrior leader, and on Christianity as a fighting faith. This is finely expressed in some of the early Christian poems, and especially in that known as *The Dream of the Rood*. Early Christian monuments like the cross of Gosforth in Cumberland show a similar emphasis, when the destruction of the monsters at Ragnarök is used as a symbol of Christ's triumph over evil. The mantic powers of the seers were reflected to some extent in the lives of the early Christian saints. Certain elements in the medieval teaching of the church, such as the bound devil, Judgment Day, and the cross as a tree in the centre of the world, seem to have been brought into greater prominence because they offered continuity with pre-Christian traditions, even though they did not originate in the North. Church festivals, especially St. Joh's Eve at midsummer, All Souls at the beginning of winter, and Christmas, were associated with rites and customs showing continuity with heathen traditions. Ritual connected with fertility and healing, and with the earth and the dead, long survived, sometimes taken over by the church and sometimes condemned by it, and went on in popular seasonal ceremonies, dances and folk drama. Pope Gregory's wise advice in the early seventh century to absorb heathen ceremonies into the church as far as possible was followed to a large extent in the North, and thus some of the most effective symbolism of the heathen religion helped to enrich that of the Christian church. Symbols such as the swastika, the raven and the hammer long outlived the gods with which they were once associated, and retained something of their ancient potency in a secular environment. Traditions of the monsters and the giants, of shape-changing and prophecy, found their way into folktales and popular legends of Germany, England and Scandinavia.

VII. Short History of the Study of Religion

Interest in Germanic religion in England and Germany began with the study of the Anglo-Saxon and Old Norse languages in the seventeenth and eighteenth centuries. Scholars trained in the classics turned to Greek and Latin sources giving information about heathen rites and ceremonies. The formation of the Society of Antiquaries of London in 1717 marks the lively interest in local antiquities among country gentlemen and clergymen about this time. The Royal Commission for the Preservation of Antiquities, founded by King Christian of Denmark in 1807, was an important step leading to the collections of German and Scandinavian antiquities in the great national museums.

Controversies between scholars in England and Germany concerning mythology and folklore in the late nineteenth century led to increased interest in early myths and traditions. The quarrel between Max Muller and Andrew Lang about the sun myth as the foundation of primitive religion went on for years, and was fought out before an audience of European scholars. The collections of laws and early material to do with Germanic beliefs and customs made by Jacob Grimm encouraged the collectors of oral traditions and folklore. In the early twentieth century the new approach of James Frazer in *The Golden Bough* sent scholars back to Anglo-Saxon and Norse sources, searching for evidence to fit into the new pattern of comparative anthropology. Linguistic studies also flourished about the turn of the century, and as more dictionaries were published and texts edited, so the evidence became available to a wider public, and slowly gained a place in University studies. The work of the Chadwicks in Cambridge on the historical development of literature, and the study of early texts combined with that of social history, art and archaeology, threw new light on pre-Christian cultures in North-Western Europe. Meanwhile the study of archaeology proceeded apace, and the wealth of new material from cemeteries, burial mounds, sanctuaries, carved stones, runic inscriptions and symbolism generally added enormously to our knowledge of the pagan Germans and Scandinavians, causing revision of many early theories, but in some cases confirming the evidence of literature to a surprising degree. The scientific study of place-names, particularly in Scandinavia, provided new information about the extent and distribution of early cults. The work of JUNG and his disciples, although sometimes misapplied, gave a new interest and seriousness to the study of the northern myths. Finally the study of the history of religions and the comparative approach of scholars like DUMÉZIL and ELIADE led to the comparison of the general pattern of Germanic religion with that of the other religions of Europe and Asia, and a much fuller understanding of the pagan past of North-Western Europe.

SELECTED BIBLIOGRAPHY

The material in this section has been further developed by H. R. ELLIS DAVID-SON in *Gods and Myths of Northern Europe* (Penguin Books, 1964), and *Pagan Scandinavia* (*Ancient Peoples and Places* series, Thames and Hudson, 1967).

The fullest treatment of the subject as a whole, with a good biography, is J. DE VRIES, *Altgermanische Religionsgeschichte* I and II, (2nd. ed., Berlin, 1956-57).

On the Old Norse written sources:

MacCULLOCH, J., *Eddic Mythology* (*Mythology of All Races*, Boston, 1930)

TURVILLE-PETRE, E. O. G., *Myth and Religion of the North* (London, 1964)

Original Sources:

Edda, die Lieder des Codius Regius, ed. G. Neckel (4th. ed. 1962)

English translation: H. A. BELLOWS, *The Poetic Edda* (1923)

Edda Snorra Sturlusonar, ed. F. JONSSON, 1931

English translation: A. G. BRODEUR, *The Prose Edda* (1920). J. I. YOUNG, *The Prose Edda* (1954): good but incomplete

Danish History of Saxo Grammaticus: ed. A. HOLDER (1886)

English translation: O. ELTON *First Nine books of the Danish History of Saxo Grammaticus* (1894)

Heimskringla. ed. B. Adalbjarnarson (1941-51)

English Translation: E. MONSEN (1931)

The following may also be found useful:

DUMÉZIL, G., *Mitra-Varuna* (1948)

——, *Mythes et Dieux des Germains* (1939)

GRØNBECH, V., *The Culture of the Teutons* I and II, (1931)

CHADWICK, H. M., *The Cult of Othin* (1899)

——, *The Origin of the English Nation* (1924)

PHILIPPSON, E. A., *Germanisches Heidentum bei den Angelsachsen* (1929)

BRØNDSTED, J., *The Vikings* (*Penguin Books*, 1960)

OLSEN, O., *Hørg, Hov og Kirke* (*Aarbøger f. nordisk Oldkyndighed*, 1965)

STRÖMBÄCK, D., *Sejd* (1935)

NECKEL, G., *Walhall, Studien über germanischen Jenseitsglauben* (1931)

DE VRIES, J., 'Ginnungagap', *Acta Philologica Scandinavica*, 1930, 41-46

——, 'The Problem of Loki', *Folklore Fellows Communications* 110, 1933

——, 'Contributions to the Study of Othin...' ibid. 94, 1931

LINDQVIST, S., *Gotlands Bildsteine* I and II, (1941-42)

PAULSEN, P., *Axt und Kreuz in Nord- und Osteuropa* (1956)

THE RELIGION OF THE CELTS

BY

MAARTJE DRAAK

Amsterdam, Holland

I. Method of Investigation

The Pagan Celts left us no religious texts.

They were barbarian tribes beyond the reach (or just on the border) of the great Mediterranean civilizations: "known", but of small importance and definitely "outside". Greeks and Romans took an interest in them mainly for their capacity as enemies—when they looted Rome (about 390 B.C.), when they attacked Delphi (less than a century later), when they opposed Julius Caesar in Gaul.

The third century B.C. was the time of their widest expansion: from the Near East over the valley of the Danube to the Atlantic coasts South of the Rhine, and across the sea to Great Britain and Ireland. But they left no texts.

The Continental Celts gradually merged with different peoples and civilizations, losing their language(s). The Insular Celts—especially in Ireland—stayed themselves much longer and kept their speech; they even took to writing (in "Celtic"), but only after their conversion to Christianity. They transmitted no religious texts from their pagan past.

By harping on the absence of texts I mean to call attention to our greatest dilemma in the study of Celtic Mythology. What are we to accept as evidence? Is all of it "circumstantial"?

There is archaeology—in fact the evidence of the grave-deposits. Nowadays the vicious circle: "Is this a Celtic grave?" (linguistical proof not being available!) has been broken by the great wealth of stylistic data. Nevertheless—even the archaeologists would prefer inscriptions to strengthen their arguments.

Temples seem to have been a phase of Gallo-Roman times, the same as idols, votive offerings, and the like. Places or objects of worship? We know some of these from observations by classical authors, not all of them sympathetic or well-informed.

This brings us to our second kind of testimony: the classical writers—poets, historians, scientists, etc. Where can we accept their information? When do they mix up their "barbarians"? Why must we sometimes fear that they spread inimical propaganda (: the Celts as enemies—see above)? We need a frame of reference.

Is it warrantable to use Insular Celtic texts? Can they throw light on the archaeological and classical data? Then where do we hope to find that knowledge?

The evaluation and interpretation of the Insular texts—specifically the Irish texts—serves as a parting of the ways. For there are two diametrically opposed methods of dealing with the unsatisfactory state of the Celtic sources.

The investigation can start from *The Indo-European Gods* (or *The Gods of the Indo-Europeans*), a useful but "constructed" system (in my opinion as useful and as abstract as *The Indo-European Languages*). It explains roughly about half of the phenomena, and for the other half one has to postulate "additions", "contaminations" and "loss". If one does so in relation to the mythology of the Celts, one takes for granted that the Irish texts have been expurgated of religious detail, that they have been tampered with in their Christian environment. That sounds very plausible but it might not be true.[19]

The other method starts from scratch. It takes into consideration that the oldest cycle of Irish epical texts shows ways of thinking and behaviour more archaic than anything HOMER sung of. (It is a very significant title which KENNETH H. JACKSON chose for his "Rede Lecture, 1964"; he called it "The Oldest Irish Tradition: A Window on the Iron Age".)[21] Therefore it accepts the possibility that the Celts acknowledged "puissances plus anciennes que les Dieux" (the wording is by MARIE-LOUISE SJOESTEDT).

Within the first method one attaches great importance to *names* of "Gods" and "Goddesses" as they are found in the classical writers and in the (late) semi-classical inscriptions. One tries to work out which "God(dess)" must have been equivalent to such and such Greek or Roman divinity, and seeks to explain away the classical contradictions. One expects the worship, the ritual, the sacrifices, etc., to have been somewhat similar to those of the Greeks and Romans. One probes for hints on all this in the Insular texts.

Within the second method one listens to the Irish epic tales and tries to feel alive in a climate of fate and fatality, magic and counter-magic, and in the nearness of supernatural beings who are richer and cleverer than humans, but who are not at all—or only very occasionally—interested in their affairs. Then one works out whether this way of thinking and feeling might not apply to the Continental (classical) data too, and what sort of ritual it might have required.

In the following I shall try to use the second method, according to the lines of investigation shown by A. G. VAN HAMEL (*Aspects of Celtic Mythology*, 1934[4]) and Marie-Louise SJOESTEDT (*Dieux et héros des Celtes*, 1940[6]).

II. How Existence is seen by the Celts

Everything which humans need for their livelihood and shelter comes from (, out of) the earth (, the soil): the trees or bushes that give fruits or wood, the grass that feeds the animals; the plants, the corn, the herbs. The water which animals and humans drink wells out of the earth (running water is better to use than standing (rain-)water).

Everything was there from the oldest times: the earth, the plants, the animals, but the stock is constantly replenished. Probably the animals came out of the earth too—through fissures in the ground, perhaps, or through holes in the mountains.

Quite a lot of things happen in orderly sequence, when circumstances are right (or when the same circumstances occur): the seasons, light and darkness, the building of a shelter, the cooking of a meal, the fighting against an enemy. If you want the same things to happen rightly, you have to arrange the same circumstances. Things have to be done exactly the right way. Nevertheless—outcomes are not always favourable or "the same". A hailstorm destroys the harvest, the well or the river that ought to be full is dry, animals are killed by unknown agencies. There is unnatural death—of humans too.

Why does this happen? First of all there is Fate. Nothing can be done against it in the end. One can try incantations, or the keeping of complicated "taboos", or the avoidance of unlucky times and places to ward it off as long as possible. But *in the end* Fate is stronger.

Then there are presences. They live near wells, or in mountains. They are not human beings, but some people have seen them. Perhaps they withhold the water of the well, perhaps they interfere with the animals: sending wild ones or killing domestic ones. What has happened? Has somebody insulted the presences? Has he gone through a thicket that the presences want for themselves? Has he shouted near a hill? Has he thrown rubbish into the flowing water? Better consult a "druid": he must tell what to avoid.

The presences want to be left alone. They look after their own affairs; the condition of the soil, the growth of living things (, metalcraft and perhaps other accomplishments?), seem to be their concern. There is no relationship with the humans, or only occasionally and for a short time. Some people are said to be their descendants: they have a non-human father or a non-human mother. But the presences do not feel obliged to help the humans, not even their own offspring. Sometimes they help; sometimes they "bargain" and are as hard as nails, keeping to a very literal truth of wording that humans may not understand or understand too late.

Life is not lucky or safe. The best conduct appears to be: live according to your status, keep the customs of your tribe and do not offend the presences.

In the aforesaid I have used the word "presences"—in stead of "gods" or "divinities" as is more usual—because it seems to me uncertain whether the Celts had evolved to real *Gods*. The Irish epic texts do not mention them except in a few formulas, e.g.: "*Tongu do día tongas mo thúath*" ("I swear to the god my tribe swears by") (variants of that: "I swear to the god the men of Ulster swear by", and the like). In this instance the "God" or the presence acts as a witness to (literal) truth. Who listens? Fate perhaps? The spoken word has fatal power.

According to SJOESTEDT[6] the classical authors and the inscriptions mention no less than 374 names for gods of the Continental Celts, of which 305 occur only once. This cannot mean else than that the names belong singly to small areas and have very restricted local importance. It is an endless—and a useless—task to try and fit them into some kind of hierarchy.

In a notorious passage of LUCANUS'[5] *Pharsalia* (which all the handbooks on Celtic Religion quote or mention) we read three names of Celtic Gods who are said to be propitiated by ghastly sacrifices: *Teutates*, *Esus* and *Taranis*. The passage seems clear (and outspoken) enough but the difficulties of interpretation are there, none the less. Many investigators have believed that here at least we find the names of a significant triad of Celtic *high* Gods. However, it is almost impossible to adapt the name *Esus* to a context of Celtic etymology. *Taranis* is easy to understand; it must mean something like *Thunderer* or *He of the Thunder* (*taran* is still the Welsh word for thunder). And *Teutates* is no more than a definition: it means *Tribal-god* and nothing else (compare the Irish "God my tribe swears by", *supra*).

Moreover, they cannot have been universal Gods—their names (or definitions) do not occur often enough, and not much outside LUCANUS' intellectual sphere (in my opinion it is literary influence when LACTANTIUS in the beginning of the fourth century announces: "*Galli Esum atque Teutaten humano cruore placabant*"). Finally it seems rather suspicious that the scholia on LUCANUS disagree about the Roman "equations" (the one equating Teutates = Mercurius, Esus = Mars, Taranis = Dis-pater, the other—"*Item aliter exinde in aliis invenimus*:— Teutates = Mars, Esus = Mercurius, eventually Taranis = Jupiter), and yet know so punctiliously that Teutates is "placated" by drowning a man—pushing his head into a full sitz-bath (*in plenum semicupium*)—, Esus by suspending a man in a tree *usque donec per cruorem membra digesserit*, Taranis by burning several people in a wooden tub (*in alveo ligneo*).

Are we to give credence to those sacrifices?

Though the LUCANUS-scholia may not be over-reliable, the Celts were "barbarians", and there is much about death in their (queerly modern-looking) sculpture. Whosoever has seen the "Tarasque de Noves"[16] in the Annexe of the *Musée Calvet* at Avignon, whoever has looked carefully at the small triangular heads which form a well-known stylistic ornamentation of Celtic objects in bronze, will remember that the heads mostly are tragic, that they suggest people killed. He will recollect that there still are pillars with niches for skulls in several museums of France[16], and that the Irish epics are not reticent at all about headhunting practices of Ulster heroes. In this climate human sacrifice seems plausible.—In addition it must have given just the finishing touch to Roman righteous indignation if and when a reason was needed to attack the "Celts". The Celts sacrificed in earnest, and not symbolically; therefore they were uncivilized.

On the other hand it may well be that in Roman times human sacrifices by Celts were desperate measures under conditions of stress and war—just like "atrocities" in the Congo in our time. And the differentiation of method (drowning, hanging, burning) may be a matter of different tribes, not of different gods. Or—keeping in mind the noteworthy fact that the turbulent Irish epics talk of fate, death, magic and headhunting but *not* of sacrifice—I can venture the opinion that the classical historians may have been misled by the ritual killing of hostages by the Celts under certain circumstances, which procedure derives from a totally different concept.

In fact I consider this aspect of the noticed killings much more to the point—as we lack even the slightest evidence that the Celts ever entered into any durable relationship with a "god", not so much as that of *cliens* and protector. Even when they threw captured weapons into a "sacred" lake, or left other spoils in a sacred grove (*nemeton*) they did not expect a lasting bond with "gods"; everything was "left to" the presences to approve or to spurn, to accept or to overlook.

Within such an intellectual horizon it appears understandable that the Insular names of supernatural beings do not correspond with the Continental ones. The one important exception is that of the "god"(?) *Lug* (whose name we find in several Continental *nomina geographica* and in Irish tales). If he was brought over from the Continent to Ireland he must have been more than a local and purely "earth"-y presence, but how or what?

More differential too is *Epona*, who according to her name (compare *(h)ippos* and *equus*) has to do with horses. In sculptured representations she is shown as a "goddess" with a *cornucopia* sitting on a horse, sometimes with more horses around. (One has to be careful, though. Often we identify a sculpture as an *Epona* because we see a female rider on a horse, with or without a *cornucopia*.) We do not meet the name in the insular tradition; however, I must concede that part of her myth might be concealed in the Britannic traditions about *Rhiannon* (perhaps a "title": *Rigantona* means "great queen"). If this is true she not only rides a horse but represents a mare herself, symbolizing the fertility of the soil (and possibly the domesticated animals).

It is probable that we recognize *Cernunnos* (the Horned One) as a master of the wild animals (: he is sitting on the ground, wearing (a cap with) deer-antlers, holding out a neck-ring to a stag on his right, clasping a snake with his left hand, while other wild animals are near him) on the great "silver" basin of Gundestrup—a very exciting object, even though we are not sure where it was made and when. (The archaeological verdicts range from Northern Gaul to the Danube valley, and from the first-second century B.C. to the third century A.D.) But oh—if it had only the smallest inscription! The scenes depicted on it are certainly of mythological importance but they are very difficult to interpret. In short, we lack the myth. And the same applies to the representations of "the god with the mallet" (small bronzes), the *tarvos trigaranus* [sic!] on the "Altar of Notre-Dame in Paris" (now said to be in *Musée de Cluny*), the "tricephalics", etc., etc.

It is not for want of investigators trying. The same scene on the basin of Gundestrup (which seems to depict a huge person holding a small person head downwards above a vessel) has been "read" as a sacrifice to Teutates (compare p. 633 *supra*), and as a representation of the *peir dadeni* (the "cauldron of Resurrection") as we find it in the Welsh story of Branwen. (It is rather needless to add that the first interpretation rules out the second.) The *tarvos* has been linked with the famous bull(s) in the Irish (epic of the) "Cattle-Raid of Cooley" [2]. But why continue? Such flights of fancy and hypothesis do not help us in the least. They hinder, for they make us forget how much *we do not know*.

If we return to the safer grounds of the local "presences" there appears to be some typological preference for "couples": an important supernatural being with her or his consort (for instance: *Brixia—Luxovius, Sirona—Grannos,* and the like). If we have both names the female partner might be the principal of the two. Yet once again we have to keep in mind that inscriptions and votive tablets are comparatively late and their use influenced by Roman (or Greek) example.

III. CULT AND BEHAVIOUR

There is a most revealing passage from the "Cattle-Raid of Cooley" (in the part known as "Cuchulainn's Boy-Deeds") where the young hero on his first (official) chariot-riding wants to take over the (daily) sentry-duty in an out-laying district from an older fighter. He is told that he is still too young for this, and for the moment he pretends to acquiesce. Shortly after, however, he throws a stone (from his sling) which breaks a shaft of the other's chariot. Asked why he has done so he answers (and now I translate literally :) "To try my hand(s) and the straightness of my throw," said Cuchulainn. "And it is a custom (*bés*; var. *geis*: "taboo") of you Ulstermen that you do not ride over *éclind* (a technical term which means something like "peril", and in my opinion combines and plays upon the words *éc* = death and *glinne* = fixed, secure). Do go back to Emain, daddy Conall, and leave me here watching." "I approve," said Conall. Conall Cernach has not gone beyond that place after that."

Here we have a significant situation in a nutshell. The archaic Irish

law-texts decide cases by precedent; the Irish heroic civilization reck-
ons with inevitable recurrences when the same circumstances
present themselves. Everybody (of any status) is warned by—or has
to take into account—things that have happened to his ancestors, his
family, his tribe, etc. The breaking of the chariot-shaft—in whatever
way it came about—is a bad portent: Conall has to turn back (and go
home). The well-instructed young Cuchulainn knows perfectly which
custom, which "taboo" of the "Ulstermen" he has to violate here to
get his own way. Therefore people must keep customs and taboos,
but malicious enemies—or a mischievous boy—can interfere, using
the knowledge for their own purposes. (The original safe-guarding
has an element of danger: that is why instruction has to be kept very
secret.) And ever afterwards the place where the portent happened is
dangerous for the person it happened to.

Who knows these things, and who instructs the tribe?

Classical authors speak about three sets of "intellectuals" among
the "Celts": the Bards, the Vates, and the Druids (*bardoi te kai ouateis
kai druidai*, according to STRABO[5]); the Irish tradition distinguishes
Bards, *Filid* ("seers") and *Druid*. If we start from the Irish evidence the
Bards probably are not very important; they appear to have practised
poetical arts in a non-magical (or if one prefers: a non-religious) context. The training and the knowledge of the two other groups go
much deeper. Both know and use verbal magic (on that account they
are to be feared), but the *Filid* are the recorders of history-in-the-
widest-sense and as such they have a worldly side also. The *Druid* are
real magicians: they know *how things ought to be done*, they know about
names and omens, lucky and unlucky days, "taboos", hallucinations
against enemies, and the like.

Filid (sg. *fili*) travel with their pupils to different courts and great
houses, tell their tales or recite their poems, and have to know always
(if the audience asks for it) why, how, where and when anything of
great interest happened. The *Druid* (sg. *drui*) belong to a court (and
a region?) and appear to have been—in their official capacity—the
"complement" of the sacral King. In my opinion King and *Drui* in a
religious balance of power protect the tribe and its territory.

Quite a number of anecdotes about the training, the touchiness, the
secret language of the *Filid* have been handed down. It is much more
difficult to gather objective data about the *Druid*, but this is only to be
expected. Their calling does not lend itself to anecdote and their
(daily) ministrations are taken for granted in the epic stories. We hard-

ly ever can observe the *drui* during routine in these texts: he acts or pronounces under abnormal conditions. On the other hand we must never forget his presence. (The view we get of the sacral King is just as lop-sided; usually we meet him in his heroic, worldly function.)

Both *Fili* and *Drui* instruct the tribe; the first before an audience and about general, "paradigmatic" history (verbally recreating what has happened and so can happen again), the second more personal and in secret about measures of safe-guarding and interference.

1) *Druids*

Though the preservation and the reciting of tribal history has a religious aspect, the knowledge of the *Fili* is less magical than that of the *Drui*. The *Drui* is the religious authority *par excellence*, and his (esoteric?) instruction of the (younger) generations is only part of his office. In time of war he "fights" with bewitching spells against the enemy, and in my opinion this has to be counter-balanced by safe-guarding rites and spells during peaceful periods. (Magical action compels reaction.) I even think that the safe-guarding (ritual) had to be repeated daily, as some incantations which have come down to us rather significantly include the word *indiu* (= today[15]). More-over, in a society steeped in the fear of fate and fatal repetition, the *drui* must have been consulted about all public events and—when they took place—he must at least have been ready at hand.

Working backwards from the Irish evidence it seems possible to understand more of the opinions Antiquity held about the Druids on the Continent. Their political importance in Gaul—about which Caesar informs us—appears understandable enough: they take charge of religious matters, "*religiones interpretantur (ad hos magnus adulescentium numerus disciplina causa concurrit*"—just as in Ireland!), they are held in great esteem "*nam fere de omnibus controversiis publicis privatisque constituunt.*" They have the power to outlaw people by banishing them from sacrifices: "*haec poena apud eos est gravissima.*"

Before I can go into the problem of sacrificial practices, I must point out some matters on which CAESAR seems to me not too wel informed. When he writes that the pupils of the Druids have to memorize such a great number of verses that some of them spend twenty years at study, he perhaps is mixed up with the *fili-ouateis*-category; at all events he only acknowledges two classes of Gaulish men as being of any account: "*alterum est druidum, alterum equitum.*"

When he claims that many students flock to the druids to be exempt from military service and taxes, I simply do not believe him. (It sounds too much like "propaganda".) Remains the question of the lofty philosophy of the druids (so eagerly speculated on by romantic writers, and probably inferred by them from): "*Multa praeterea de sideribus atque eorum motu, de mundi ac terrarum magnitudine, de rerum natura, de deorum immortalium vi ac potestate disputant et iuventuti tradunt.*" If ever all this actually formed part of (Continental) Celtic civilization, it has been lost beyond recall.

We now return to the sacrifices—already a point at issue on p. 633 *supra*. Here the whole of caput 16 in CAESAR's *Liber Sextus* is in dispute, especially the statement that the Gauls believe: "*pro vita hominis nisi hominis vita reddatur, non posse deorum immortalium numen placari.*" Once again it is less the cruelty of the measures mentioned which I doubt than the Roman competence to estimate the religious theories or emotions that are involved.

Warring Celts certainly are no nice little boys. They fight to the death: their own or their enemy's. Such a ferocious kind of duel-situation is confirmed by the Irish epic tales, as are the head-hunting trophies and many horrors of the battle-field matter-of-factly told. Human sacrifices on the other hand are not corroborated at all, though the heroic society sketched by the epic stories in Ireland appears more archaic and "barbarian" than anything encountered in Gaul by the Romans.

There then lies the enigma, and therefore I only can offer several hypothetical "solutions".

If the poor wretches who according to CAESAR were burned to death in huge wickerwork cages were "sacrificed", their slaughter belonged to a Continental ritual pattern which was broken when Celtic tribes left the Mainland and "migrated over sea" (and that is why we do not find it in Insular tradition). Or they were not sacrificed, but executed or massacred as unclaimed hostages (if they did not belong to the tribe); perhaps they were even as tribal members punished for alleged witchcraft. (The latter would tie in with measures against "serious diseases" (*gravioribus morbis*).) Or again the whole statement belongs to that kind of slander which in later times provoked progroms.

Whatever the explanation, Druids did not act as "priests"; they mostly supervised the ritual performances of others (this to me seems the correct translation of "*administrisque ad ea sacrificia druidibus utuntur*"

(VI, 16) in correlation with *"Illi"* (i.e. *Druides*) *"sacrificia publica ac privata procurant"* (VI, 13).

There are only a few classical texts from which we get unexpected glimpses of Druids acting ritually. There is the well-known and oft-quoted passage by PLINIUS THE ELDER[5] about Druids in white garments cutting down branches of mistletoe with golden sickles, but only of mistletoe (*viscum*) growing on an oak.

Even we of the twentieth century can appreciate the idea of mistletoe as a symbol of fertility, as a miraculous "sign" of everlasting green leaves and fruitlike berries amidst the winter and death of bare trees. PLINIUS adds that according to the Druids *viscum* taken in drink will give fecundity to barren animals, and that it is a remedy against all poisons.

I think it possible that the Druids had a more esoteric use for the plant also, and that at some occasions they wielded branches of *viscum* as tokens of *bona fides* in their association with the powers of fertility: the same (or a near-related) kind of "golden bough" as the one VERGIL tells of. I find some slight indication for this from Irish story where the detail of the branch with berries, or the branch with flowers and "apples" brought by a supernatural being is a well-known "motif". In Ireland there grew (and grows) no *viscum*, so tradition had to find substitutes. (Sometimes the branch is said to make music: compare the tinkling sound in *"sic leni crepitabat brattea vento"* of VERGIL's bough!)

Another view of Druids in action comes from TACITUS' *Annals* (XIV, 30) where the Roman legionaries against the island of Mona (now Anglesey) had to face "a dense armed mass. Among them were black-robed women with dishevelled hair like Furies, brandishing torches. *Close by stood Druids, raising their hands to heaven and screaming dreadful curses (Druidaeque circum, preces diras sublatis ad caelum manibus fundentes).* This weird spectacle awed the Roman soldiers into a sort of paralysis..." (the translation is by MICHAEL GRANT).

The paralysis was of short duration, but the Druids would have been convinced that they worked it with their spells. Against "barbarians" it would have had a more lasting (psychological) effect.

2) *Cult*

If the Celts think that Nature—peopled with "Presences" or symbolized through them—is a given reality, always there but not created (see p. 644 *infra*), always producing but not without calamities (Who interferes?), always going on without end, unchanging in change (or the other way round), can they have had a "system of religious worship"? Yes, of course: it is just as "logical" to work out a system of religious avoidance, as one of religious approach. The system even becomes one of inevitable complexity.

No calamity can be explained as the Will of God, or The Caprice of A God; it must be the outcome of some un-traditional act by a human being.

Tradition says that the Presences live in such and such a hill—therefore avoid its neighbourhood. If Presences want to meet you they will do so on their own account. (The *Filid* know stories about Kings being invited by Presences. Who are you? No King!) You can show respect: you can leave offerings at a traditional well, at a traditional tree, at a traditional rock. But *leave* them only; avoid prying whether they are accepted or not.

Avoid killing such and such birds—your tribe is not allowed to (there is a story about that). Avoid going on a journey if such and such has happened. Avoid—, avoid. Even doing necessary and usual things can be brought under this negative aspect: avoid doing them in an un-traditional way, and avoid doing them at the wrong time. (The *Druid* know whether a day is *fas* or *nefas*.)

You cannot pray, you cannot be forgiven; you only can make magic as a final way-out. For the mechanistic Unchanging Change often is opposed: you witness that. It must be by magical interference, and you have to counteract.

Here lurks a two-fold danger. The magic can go wrong, and as it is mostly verbal magic, one never knows then what may result. Secondly, any magic (and its effect) becomes a small new part of Tradition, and the complicated system gets an additional turn of the screw. No wonder that CAESAR has written: "*Natio est omnis Gallorum admodum dedita religionibus*" (which the new Penguin-translation not very historically and correctly but rather poignantly renders: "As a nation the Gauls are extremely superstitious").

3) *Ethics*

It is difficult to separate Ethics from Cult and Conduct, as the perception of "right" and "wrong" within the society of (the) pagan Celts does not depend on principles of justice and/or charity, but only on acts which do not endanger the tribe. Therefore the reasoning is not "Act rightly, whatever the outcome", but "You have acted rightly, if the outcome is right and no bad portent occurs".

For instance, the Sacral King as the top of the thoroughly aristocratic hierarchy in Ireland is the *right* King and acts *rightly* if the land is fertile, if the weather is mild, if there is peace[18]. But if the King loses his generosity or gives a wrong verdict, the crops fail or a wall of the royal dwelling falls down. The verdict was wrong *because* the wall fell down.

The ethical code—at least according to the Irish texts—appears to be: act traditionally, consistent with your status in life, keep the tribal customs and your personal *geasa*. Fury, hate and killing are not abhorred, but there is chivalry *avant la lettre*, there is love and friendship. Women have no inferior status because they are female.

Geasa probably are a distinctive Celtic institution. On p. 311 I have used the word in its singular form *geis*, and I have translated it (in the usual way) as "taboo" though the concepts behind the two words are not the same. *Geasa* are (magic) injunctions to do something or nòt to do something, which the *Druid* know about and generally pronounce. (The pronouncement has the power of a magic incantation, as younger folkloristic texts use the term *geasa* with the meaning of spells or curses.) It follows that *geasa* are much more severe and binding than "customs".

The whole system cannot be clearly worked out, though quite a number of tales turn on "the broken geis" for a central motif. For one thing we do not see how many classes of people were involved. It seems logical—Irish heroes being engrossed in the subject of privileges and prerogatives—that the higher a person's rank the higher the sum total of his *geasa*, for in origin they are safety-measures and nòt restrictions. But does that mean that the number works hierarchically downwards to the one personal *geis* of the lowest orders? And what about women? Do *geasa* originally only protect warriors?

If this last supposition is true I think it possible that CAESAR has acquainted us with a Gaulish "warrior-taboo" in his statement "their children are not allowed to go up to their fathers in public until they are old enough for military service" (VI, 18): *"palam ad se adire non patiuntur."* Indeed, the remarkable thing is that just such a kind of prohibition could be a *geis*: part of it somehow understandable for us, but not all. It makes sense (to us) that a hero whose name is Cuchulainn (Hound of Culann) is not allowed by *geis* to eat a hound's flesh; we affix the label "Totemism", and there we are. It makes sense that a King residing at Tara should not be allowed to stay more than eight nights away from it, and that he should not spend the night in a house from which the light of a fire is visible after the setting of the sun and into which one can see from outside. After all: he must not neglect his residence, and it is not safe to be visible as a target for enemies from the outside dark.

But why should he not be allowed to hunt the "bent beasts" of Cernae? Are they a danger to him personally? Or are they dangerous to Kings residing at Tara? Or have they been the destruction of one of his ancestors? (Besides, for even the king does not see what he has hunted till after the chase, who or what are "the bent beasts of Cernae"?)

Why is there a prohibition on the hero Fergus mac Roich to refuse the invitation to ale-feasts? By having him invited to such gatherings at a time when he ought to protect some friends under his guaranty, a tricky king manoeuvres him into a cleft-stick-situation, and a tragedy ensues in which many people die and Fergus loses his honour none the less.

Some intriguing points must be noted about all this. Firstly the manoeuvring procedure is not thought of as un-ethical. Secondly even the keeping of a *geis* cannot always ward off disaster. And lastly one sometimes darkly realizes that—in a vicious circle—Fate warns a hero about his coming destruction by forcing him to violate (all) his *geasa*. That at least is the story-symbolism through which the *Filid* express and teach the inevitability of Fate.

4) *Myth*

Continental myth we do not know (as has already been stated several times). About the Insular texts—especially the Irish ones—we can maintain wholly opposed view-points: either all the epic stories belong to mythology, or none do. Even in modern times historians affirm that "the Irish" interpret their history mythically; that they (can) make myth from any tale, and just as well "history" from "myth".

In the time of the *Filid* certainly there must have existed a religious, mythical aspect of story-telling, because the stories paradigmatically taught about the ways of the (Celtic) world, and because their custody and transmission on that account were linked with the safe-guarding of the tribe(s). Probably people even thought that the story-telling as a ritual had some magic quality, giving protection of itself.

Nineteenth-century scholarship put several Irish texts into a special group of tales belonging to the "Mythological Cycle". The criterion which determined this classification was the important part played in them by supernatural beings, the *áes síde* or "people of the elven-hills". The tales are most interesting, and yet, their grouping together is wrong and misleading. It resulted from the too easy assumption that those tales were the poor remnant of the stories about the old Irish Gods, whereas the Irish themselves did not consider them as a special category (we have two early "lists" of their own groupings!), were used to meet the elven-people in any of their stories, and did as much regard them as Gods as we would superior beings from another planet. There is an un-safe, an un-easy relationship between the Irish humans and the *áes síde*. The *áes síde* are cleverer, richer, longer-lived and more beautiful; they are better magicians, they are to be respected and to be left to their own affairs. *They possessed Ireland first:* some tales make that perfectly clear.

From this point every investigator takes his own bearing. Those beings must be the dead, the ancestors, ancestors turning into gods, they must be the gods of the pagan Irish. I still hold that the "migration over sea"[20] which the (in future Irish) Celts brought to Ireland, gave some twist to their religious thought, broke a part of the pattern, and that therefore the "Presences" in that new island were perceived as more "alien" and more remote even than those on the mainland. In my opinion the small "approved" group of "Mythological tales" has to be weighed and sifted just as critically as all the other Irish stories.

Only one of them—known as "The (second) Battle of Moytura"— could be accepted on an international footing as a definite example of pure myth, because it narrates the fight between two groups of supernatural beings about the possession of Ireland. Nevertheless the "myth" cannot be taken at face-value as the compilated (?) text bears marks of having been worked over at a later period. (For instance the *áes síde* are called here already *Tuatha Dé Danann* ("Tribes of Dé Danann"), a younger appellation which up till now has not been satisfactorily explained but which, by its very mysteriousness, has had an immense vogue. (I think it possible that the name derived from a learned medieval play on words, or a famous slip of the tongue.)

The story as we now have it got caught in the web of the learned historians who composed *Lebor Gabála* ("The Book of Invasions", a fictitious history of Ireland from the earliest times), in an effort to "harmonize and synchronize" the Irish traditions with the framework of events in Universal History (as known by the classical world). As a mythological tale the text of "The Battle of Moytura" badly needs a new examination, though probably after that we may gather less from it about the actual pattern of Irish pagan thought than from the existence (and some of the contents) of the *Dindshenchas* ("Knowledge of Places"), that body of "geographical" lore which must have served the purpose of helping to tame and possess the land by *knowing* about its forts, hills, lakes, cairns, rivers, plains etc., and what happened on or near them.

The two recensions we have of it do not belong to the early stratum of Irish texts, but the principle of the thing comes through in the older stories.

IV. Ideas about Man

In all the accounts we have by and about the (pagan) Celts there is no indication that they ever thought that the world had a beginning and, in consequence, probably would have an end also. There is no creation-myth, and eschatology only crept in with Christianity. It is very pertinent too that the Irish texts use the expression that a certain lake or plain was "found" (after magical interference), as if everything always had been there without people knowing it.

For instance, when one of the *áes síde* is obliged to "buy" the daughter of a king (to be the consort of somebody else), one of the demands (of her father) is that he must "draw out of this territory to the sea twelve important rivers that are in wells and bogs and swamps", and when this has been accomplished (in one night) the text adds: "They had never been seen there until then."

The earth, the soil spreads around "without end" (that is why I imagine that the Celtic tribes were shocked when they migrated over open sea); the seasons, the crops, the animals return in predictable sequence... Then what about the beginning and end of a human being?

The Insular stories begin the life of their heroes (and heroines) with their "conception" (rather than with their birth), and at least one of the two (medieval) Irish tale-catalogues (enumerative alas, not descriptive!) lists the *Compert*-stories as a group.

The hero then makes his career of violence, and at last he dies fighting. And after that? The texts can be very abrupt: "His grave was then dug, his stone fixed, his name written in *ogam*-script; his lamentation was celebrated", but still, it is evident that there were funeral

rites. (The name in *ogam*-script is an anachronism here, but the Irish
—certainly not suffering from an inferiority-complex—were convinced that they had *invented ogam* a long time before it was used.)

During the Hallstatt-La Tène-periods heroes (chieftains, "kings"?)
were sometimes buried on the Continent with important grave-
deposits; the chariot-burials are especially interesting, above all if real
war-chariots have been found. (The distinction two wheels for a war-
chariot against four wheels for an ordinary char(iot) or waggon is not
always made in the older archaeological publications.) I quote from a
note by POWELL[17] on his plates 21, 22: "The chieftain was laid out
on his chariot, the wheels having been let into special holes. He was
equipped with a gold armlet, an iron sword in its scabbard, iron spearheads, and a tall bronze helmet which lay between his feet... Above
the chieftain lay the skeleton of another man armed with an iron
sword. He was presumably the charioteer and personal attendant." (The
double burial is no evidence for a "sacrifice"; the two men could have
been killed in the same fight, and the feeling of mutual respect which
can grow between persons who must so much rely upon each other
is well attested in the Irish stories of the Ulster-cycle.) Such an arrangement can hardly be explained if the (Continental) Celts did not believe
in an after-life. The same applies to the marvellous treasure deposited
in the queen's(?)-grave at Vix which was excavated in 1953 (a Tut-
Ankh-Amon-sensation *in Celticis*!).

However, what kind of after-life? LUCAN's[5] cryptic statement that
the Druids teach "longae vitae mors media est" does not help us
much. If death is a mid-point, I feel inclined to interpret the observation much too arithmetically, and to ask again: "And after that?"
Which brings us to the problem of the metempsychosis the Druids
are said to have taught also.

Decisive evidence from Ireland is wanting. First of all there is, as
far as I am aware, nothing comparable to the discoveries on the Continent in the way of elaborate grave-deposits. Is that because the archaeologists up till now have not been able to locate the Celtic royal
graves? (The great tumuli and other megalithic monuments in Ireland are pre-Celtic.) Or have they all been plundered in later times? No
chariot-burial has been found, and this is the more remarkable because the tales of the Ulster-cycle are full of (war-)chariots, even in
detailed description.

There are "revenants" in Irish stories, a few even in a wholly pagan
context. As to *metempsychosis*: if one seeks diligently there are indeed

indications that the (pagan) Irish thought it possible that the same person was born anew, or had several lives. Still, one has to be wary, as some of the more striking examples could be assigned to the shape-shifting powers of the *áes síde*.

Nevertheless the idea of *metempsychosis* must have seemed a logical potentiality to the more thoughtful individuals of a civilization which regarded the world and "nature" as without beginning and without end, and everything in it subjected to an *"éternel retour"* when circumstances were the same.

V. ENDING AND SALVATION

There could be no destiny for the religion of the Celts; a path of salvation only became visible through Christianity. In the oldest stratum of the Lives of the Irish Saints one can fully appreciate how much the new religion was experienced as a better magic (the Saints overcoming the *Druid* on their own ground), a safer relationship with "divinity" (prayers instead of incantations), and a release from mechanical fatality.

SELECTED BIBLIOGRAPHY

[1] MacCulloch, J. A., *The Religion of the Ancient Celts*, Edinburgh 1911 (famous but antiquated)

[2] Thurneysen, R., *Die irische Helden- und Königsage bis zum siebzehnten Jahrhundert*, Halle 1921 (wealth of story-material)

[3] Kendrick, T. D., *The Druids, A Study in Keltic Prehistory*, London 1927 (matter-of-fact)

[4] van Hamel, A. G., *Aspects of Celtic Mythology*, London 1934 (most stimulating)

[5] Zwicker, J., *Fontes historiae religionis celticae (Fontes historiae religionum ex auctoribus graecis et latinis collectos* edidit C. Clemen, V, 1-3), Berolini-Bonnae 1934-1936 (almost everything one could wish for, though the medieval Insular texts are not chosen too well)

[6] Sjoestedt, Marie-Louise, *Dieux et Héros des Celtes*, Paris 1940 (the best yet)

[7] Clemen, Carl, *Die Religion der Kelten*, in *Archiv f. Religionswissenschaft*, 1941-42, vol. 37, pp. 101-143 (summing-up of 5, posthumously published; "outside information")

[8] van Hamel, A. G., *Mythe en historie in het oude Ierland*, Amsterdam 1942 (specialized)

[9] Lambrechts, P., *Contributions à l'étude des divinités celtiques*, Bruges 1942 (seen from the archaeological side)

[10] O'Rahilly, Th. F., *Early Irish History and Mythology*, Dublin 1946 (wealth of material; unsound in mythological method)

[11] VENDRYÈS, J., *La Religion des Celtes* (*Mana*, Tome 2, III, pp. 239-320), Paris 1948 (sound observations by a non-mythologist)

[12] DILLON, Myles, *Early Irish Literature*, Chicago 1948 (very useful)

[13] SJOESTEDT, Marie-Louise, *Gods and Heroes of the Celts*, London 1949 (Engl. transl. of 6, by Myles DILLON with additions)

[14] DRAAK, Maartje, *Áes Síde*, Amsterdam 1949 inaugural lecture

[15] ——, *Betovering voor een etmaal*, Amsterdam 1955 inaugural lecture

[16] VARAGNAC, A. (and others), *L'Art gaulois*, Zodiaque 1956 (for the illustrations)

[17] POWELL, T. G. E., *The Celts*, London 1958

[18] *The Sacral Kingship, Contributions to the Central Theme of the VIIIth Int. Congr. f. the History of Religions*, 1955, Leiden 1959 (for Ireland pp. 651-663)

[19] DE VRIES, Jan, *Keltische Religion*, Stuttgart 1961 ("outside information" by a good mythologist)

[20] DRAAK, Maartje, *Migration over Sea* (*Numen*, vol. IX, pp. 81-98) 1962

[21] JACKSON, K. H., *The Oldest Irish Tradition: A Window on the Iron Age*, Cambridge 1964

[22] CHADWICK, Nora K., *The Druids*, Cardiff 1966

THE RELIGION OF THE SLAVS

BY

F. VYNCKE

Ghent, Belgium

I. Short Description of the Essence of the Religion

The essence of the Slavic religion cannot easily be fathomed, and the reason lies mainly in the limited number of reliable sources. Archeological data can be utilised to but a slight degree; they only inform us of matters pertaining to the cult of the dead, the funerary ritual and sacrificial sites. The foundations of what were presumably heathen temples discovered at Arkona (the island Rügen) and at Ptuj (Slovenia) are not recognised as such by all archeologists. Nor could the few images which were excavated be ascribed with certainty to the Slavs.

An enormous amount of ethnological material was amassed, which, however, must be used with great circumspection for the direct reconstruction of Slavonic heathendom. Folklore can best be used to confirm or supplement data acquired by other means. The same holds good for linguistic sources, which are mainly comprised of the names of gods and cultic vocabulary.

Hence we must rely principally on written sources. Unfortunately these are considerably limited as regards both time and location; time because practically all the texts date only from the period of the christianisation of the Slavs, and location because they pertain chiefly to only two peoples from the periphery of the Slavonic area of expansion, namely the Russians and the Baltic Slavs.

A certain amount of information about the Russians from the late heathendom of the 10th century is to be found in the *Chronicle of* Nestor. The large majority of the documents (ecclesiastical didactic writings, sermons, confessional questions) describes, however, the post-pagan period from the end of the 10th century onwards, which was characterised by the so-called "double faith," a sort of symbiosis of heathen and Christian elements. A certain amount of heathen customs and conceptions continued to prevail during this period, but as system the Old Slavic religion gradually disintegrated.

The Baltic Slavs lived in the region between the Elbe and the Oder, which later was Germanised. The religious development of these tribes can be followed more or less from the beginning of the eleventh up to the end of the twelfth century, thanks to a series of chronicles and biographies by German and Danish clerics. (*The Chronicle of* THIETMAR OF MERSEBURG; *the Gesta Hammaburgensis ecclesiae* by ADAM OF BREMEN; three biographies of Otto of Bamberg by MONACHUS PRIEFLINGENSIS, Ebbo and Herbord respectively; the *Cronica Slavorum of* HELMOLD; *the Gesta Danorum of* SAXO GRAMMATICUS; *the Icelandic Knytlinga Saga*). They depict the late flowering and the downfall of Slavonic heathendom in the Elbe-Oder region within the framework of the struggle against conversion to Christianity and the German invaders.

Of the other Slav peoples we know little or nothing, Poles, Czechs, all Southern Slavs. Nor have we at our disposal first-hand testimonials from the period preceding the conversion to Christianity. (The earliest document, a short fragment from *De bello Gothico* (III, 14), written about 550 by PROKOPIOS OF CAESAREA, is much contested as source).

Given this considerable limitation of the sources as to time and location, any study aimed at reconstructing the original Slavonic heathendom is beset with very severe handicaps.

Animism and manism almost certainly form the origin and basis of Slavonic heathendom. The texts contain plenty of evidence that all Slav tribes worshipped sources, rivers, trees, woods, thunder, lightning, fire, the sun, etc. They made sacrifices, usually fruit, birds and poultry to all these forms and phenomena of nature. The relationship between the cult of nature and the worship of ancestors is not quite clear. Some make a definite distinction between the two categories (UNBEGAUN); others ascribe priority to one or the other. Archeology has established, however, that the cult of the dead goes very far back in the past, indeed right back to the origin of all human culture (KOSTRZEWSKI, p. 402).

In our opinion the cult of the dead is intimately intertwined with the cult of nature. It should be borne in mind that although the Slavs believed in a realm of the dead, they did not localise it beyond their surrounding nature. In fact, there are certain indications that the deceased were thought to sojourn under the earth. Hence this heathendom—at least in its lower forms—appears to us as a nature-religion which answered the needs of an agrarian people. Within the framework of nature numerous demons and spirits were worshipped.

However, the sources also testify that the Baltic Slavs and the Russians knew higher religious forms—gods, temples, images. On this point the opinions of the experts are even more widely divergent. The discussion revolves around two problems in particular:

1. Are the Slavic gods "evolved demons" or were they borrowed from other peoples.

2. Are they of Common Slavic origin or are they local innovations. According to NIEDERLE, three demons which embodied the essential phenomena of nature or important moments of the agrarian cycle were elevated to the rank of real gods with specialised functions: Perun, god of thunder; Svarog, god of fire; Veles, god of meadows and cattle. This happened already in the Common Slav period, and consequently these three numina were worshipped by all Slav tribes. After the period of expansion both the Baltic Slavs and the Russians developed, under the influence of the higher civilisations with which they came into contact, a local cycle of gods, each with its own cult, hierarchy and sanctuaries.

Other scholars maintain that all the Slav gods are late and local derivations. The supposition is that the heathens deified early Christian saints (Blasius and Vitus) and famous persons (emperor Trajan) or adopted German and Iranian numina (e.g. Perun and Svarog respectively).

JAKOBSON laid special emphasis on Iranian influence. He contends that the Slavs and Iranians experienced a common religious evolution: "The Slavs participated in the Iranian evolution into a clear-cut dualism" (p. 1025) According to him the majority of the numina go back to the Common Slav period and manifest a strong analogy with their Iranian counterparts: "The pantheon of the Slavs offers more Common Slavic than tribal features and partly points to Indo-Iranian, especially Iranian, and perhaps Thraco-Phrygian connections" (p. 1024).

It is our belief that research has thus far taken too little account of the Russian numen Rod-Rožanicy. It is composed of a masculine singular Rod and a feminine plural Rožanicy, who are usually mentioned together in the texts and thus form a pair.

The Russian Church waged a particularly tenacious battle against this pair in didactic works, statutes and confessional questions. Although outwardly Christians, the Russians persisted in holding on the day after Christmas a mortuary feast in honour of this double numen, at which they sang a hymn of praise venerating the Mother of

God. In addition Rod and Rožanicy are often equated with such terms as "fatum, fortune, genealogia" in the texts.

As generic name "rod" has many meanings in Old Russian, all of which, however, are interrelated and can be reduced to one nucleus— the clan. The semantic scope of this word does, indeed, encompass the clan in its full physical range, both spatial (the meanings sib, kin, family, clan, tribe) and temporal (the meanings birth, descent, generation, offspring, posterity). The clan was the basis of the social organisation of the Slavs. It was only during the period of christianisation that they began to form states. It would seem an obvious inference that a godhead whose proper name was *rod* = clan must have been the tutelary numen of the clan. Each clan constituted a social entity and worshipped its own ancestors; hence each probably also had its own patron deity. Consequently Slavonic heathendom was neither monotheistic nor polytheistic. In our opinion it was composed in essence of a series of cognate clan numina.

II. Historical Development

The Old Russian Homily of St. Gregory contains the following lines: "The Slavs likewise began to make sacrifices to Rod and the Rožanicy before they (sacrificed) to Perun, their god; previously, however, they made sacrifices to the Vampires and the Beregyni." This text, which distinguishes three periods in Russian heathendom (the worship of 1) Vampires and Beregyni; 2) Rod-Rožanicy; 3) Perun), provides a good illustration of the line of development of Slavonic heathendom.

The earliest nucleus of the Slav religion lies in the worship of ancestors. As appears from their name, the Beregyni were localised in ravines and on steep shores (Old-Russ. Bereg = ripa; brĕg = cliff, precipice). According to the earliest texts they were comprised of thrice nine or seven sisters. Nothing, however, is imparted about their essence. The Beregyni are no longer known in contemporary Russian folklore, but the (so-called) Rusalki who have only been professed since the 17th century, may be assumed to have taken their place. The people held them to be the souls of children who died unbaptised, or of young maidens who met a premature death. The Beregyni may thus be related to the cult of the dead. For that matter, in the texts they are often linked up with the Vampires, known to all Slav races as the souls of the dead.

This adoration of "shore nymphs" as the earliest religious stratum is also evidenced by the West Slavs. In his *Chronica Boemorum* (I, 4; 11th-12th century), Cosmas Pragensis writes that Tethka, daughter of a legendary tribal chieftain of the Czechs, "stulto et insipienti populo Oreadas, Driadas, Amadriadas adorare et colere... instituit et docuit." When and under which circumstances or influences this primitive manes and nature cult developed into a higher form of religious perception cannot readily be ascertained. Some light is thrown on this point by a remarkable passage in the Old Russian homily of St. Gregory. The compiler writes in connexion with the birth of Osiris: "For when his mother gave birth to him (Osiris), they rendered him a God unto themselves, and the doomed ones brought him great offerings; the Chaldeans learned it from them, they began to make great sacrifices to Rod and Rožanicy after the birth of the accursed god Osiris... hence the Greek learned to make sacrifices to Artemid (sic) and Artemis, that is Rod and Rožanicy, likewise the Egyptians, and so it also came to the Slavs, behold, and the Slavs too began to make sacrifices to Rod and Rožanicy" (Mansikka, p. 163). The compiler identifies Rod-Rožanicy with Osiris-Isis and with what he terms Artemid-Artemis. Through the mediation of the Egyptians, Chaldeans and Greeks, the Slavs are supposed to have learned to worship a numen of the nature of the famous Egyptian pair.

No more details about this religious innovation are to be found in the texts. We may assume, however:

1) that this occurred in the Common Slav period;

2) that as from then each clan worshipped its own tutelary pair of gods;

3) that the latter worship did not attain the full theological development characteristic of the Egyptian pair Osiris-Isis.

During their impressive period of expansion (beginning of the Christian era to the 9th century), the Slavs occupied widespread territories. This must have had an unfavourable influence on the cohesion of the clans. There came into being autonomous families, in the stricter sense of the word, with their own territorial possessions; furthermore communities which united elements from divers clans; and finally a number of towns due to the stimulus of a developing commerce. It is a feasible assumption that these new social units took over the original clan numen, basic concept of the Slav religion, and adapted it to their new needs. The new socially elite groups replaced the designation Rod-Rožanicy, commonly used by the people, with individualising and more striking epithets. This explains why a large number of names are used alongside each other in the texts without any recognisable distinction.

As a result of their migrations, the Slavs penetrated far into western, southern and eastern Europe. Their field of colonisation stretched from the Elbe to the Oka; they crossed the Danube and occupied Bulgaria, Yugoslavia and part of Greece. Thus they were brought into direct contact with Christianity and the big powers of Medieval Christian culture: Byzantium, Rome and the Frankish realm. As a result the Slavs were faced with enormous problems. If they wished to adopt the cultural and technical accomplishments of the Christian world and use them to develop their commercial relationships, then sooner or later they would have to be converted to the new religion. Certain dangers, however, were involved; conversion to Christianity meant an influx of foreign missionaries as well as the institution of an ecclesiastical hierarchy that was largely alien and could therefore lead to political dependence on Byzantium or the Teutonic Kingdom. Nonetheless, the conversion of the majority of the Slav peoples appears to have taken place without giving rise to overmuch friction (Moravians, Poles, Slovenes, Croats, Serbs, Bulgars). At first the Russian princes hesitated. On his ascension to the throne in 980, Grand Duke Vladimir of Kiev instituted a state religion based on paganism. The *Nestor Chronicle* relates: "And Vladimir began to rule alone at Kiev and placed idols on the hill, outside the palace: a wooden Perun, though his head was of silver and his moustaches of gold, and Chors and Dažbog and Stribog and Sěmar'gl and Mokoš' and they made sacrifices to them, and called them gods, and they brought their sons and daughters with them and made sacrifices to the devils and stained the soil with their offerings" (MANSIKKA, p. 38). In all probability Vladimir elevated the tutelary gods of certain princely and prominent families to the status of state gods and thus created a sort of pantheon which had to be worshipped by all subjects of the Russian state.

Perun seems to have been the supreme god, for in the same year Vladimir also had an image of this deity set up at Novgorod. The Russian *summus deus* probably derived from a fusion of Germanic (Thor, god of thunder) and Slavonic elements (the local clan numen). The Russian Grand Dukes were, indeed, of North Germanic descent, whilst in certain Slav languages Perun means "thunder" (Polish: *piorun* = thunder). Very little is known about the other gods of Vladimir's pantheon. In a text Chors is called "thunder angel," together with Perun. Etymologically, the name could be of Iranian origin. Both Dažbog and Stribog mean "give, bestew riches." The former is identified with the sun in a gloss in the Old Russian translation of the Byzantine Chronicle of Malalas. The four above-mentioned gods of Vladimir's pantheon thus manifest common features:

(1) All four appear to be associated with atmospheric phenomena (thunder) or heavenly bodies (sun);

(2) They combine Slavonic with German or Iranian elements. (There are grounds for assuming that the Russian elite was also affected by Scytho-Sarmatic influence).

Only the goddess Mokoš' appears to be a purely indigenous numen. She is often mentioned alongside Rožanicy in the texts and is the only one of Vladimir's gods of whom traces are to be found in Russian popular belief.

Eight years later, however, Vladimir abandoned his desparate endeavour to counter Christianity with a national pagan religion. In 988 he had himself baptised at Korsun', and when he returned to his capital he ordered the destruction or burning of all pagan images. Perun was accorded special treatment, as relates the Chronicle of Nestor: "When he (Vladimir) arrived, he ordered that the idols be cast down, the one to be chopped to pieces, the other to be abandoned to fire; Perun, however, he ordered to be tied to the tail of a horse and dagged along the Boričev to the creek, and he appointed twelve men to beat it with clubs." (MANSIKKA, p. 50).

The course of the evangelisation of the Slavic tribes between the Elbe and the Oder (Baltic Slavs) was more dramatic. Under the first Saxon emperors a powerful campaign was undertaken by the Germans to colonise the regions east of the Elbe. Owing to the narrow relationship between evangelisation and political subjection, the Baltic Slavs strongly resisted conversion to Christianity and made a desperate attempt to expand their own religion and defend it by force. The core of resistance was formed by the powerful tribal league of the Liuticii, who for a century and a half, from the beginning of the tenth to the middle of the twelfth century held out against the German emperors.

In this extremely restless period, the Baltic Slavs developed their original, rather simple nature-cult into a religion with higher cultural forms. In addition to the local demons, penates and clan numina, there were now mighty tribal deities, whose images were placed in wooden temples. Influential priests were in charge of a public and imposing cult. At the beginning of the eleventh century, the most famous temple was located at Rethra, in the region of the Redarii, present-day Mecklenburg-Strelitz. One of the gods worshipped was Zuarasiz, the only name which also occurs in the Old Russian texts (Svarožič) and hence is of Common Slav origin. THIETMAR OF MERSEBURG writesof this sanctuary: *interius autem dii stant manu facti, singulis nominibus insculptis, galeis atque loricis terribiliter vestiti, quorum primus Zuarasici dicitur et pre caeteris a cunctis gentilibus honoratur et colitur* (VI, 23). In the middle of the twelfth century the biographers of Otto of Bamberg recorded information about another influential deity called Triglav, which means *tricephalous*. He was worshipped in the town of Stettin, situated at the foot of three elevations of which the middle and highest one was dedicated to this deity: *Stettin vero amplissima civitas et maior Iulin tres montes ambitu suo conclusos habebat, quorum medius, qui et alcior, summo paganorum deo Trigelawo dicatus, tricapitum habebat simulacrum* (Ebbo III, 1). Apart from these well-known names, a great many other ones occur in the texts. Each social group (clan, tribe, town) worshipped its own particular numen, who was more or less well-known. THIETMAR writes: *Quot regiones sunt in his partibus, tot templa habentur et simulacra demonuma singula ab infidelibus coluntur* (VI, 25). In the town of Wolgast, situated on the Baltic coast opposite the island Usedom, the numen was called Gerovitus, which is Jarovit or "the strong one." In Oldenburg, Wagria, Proven was worshipped (the righteous, cf. Slav *pravo* = right); in the temple of Plön it was Podaga, relating probably to Old Slavonic *podati* = to give. In 1068 the sanctuary of Rethra was destroyed by the Germans, resulting apparently in the Redarii's loss of their leading position in the Liutician league. Arkona, the temple citadel on the island Rügen, then became the stronghold of Slav paganism. There Svantevit (= the mighty) was worshipped. It appears that in the last decades before their fall the Baltic Slavs looked upon him as their most powerful numen. *Inter multiformia autem Slavorum numina prepollet Zuantevith, deus terrae Rugianorum, utpote efficacior in responsis, cuius intuitu ceteros quasi semideos estimabant* (Helmold I, 52). At Garz on the same island, three "private" deities were worshipped as well. Certain prominent families presumably had sanctuaries built in this town to house their tutelary numina. *Insignis hic uicus trium prepollencium fanorum edificiis erat, ingenue artis nitore uisendis. Iis tantum pene ueneracionis privatorum deorum dignitas conciliauerat, quantum apud Arkonenses publici numinis auctoritas possidebat* (Saxo, 577).

Arkona, the last bulwark of paganism, was destroyed by the Danes in 1168. This marked the end of the Baltic Slavs' tenacious struggle to preserve their independence and, at the same time, the end of Slav paganism as an entity.

III. Conception of the Deity

A certain amount of insight into the essence of the clan numen of the Slavs is provided by its identification in the texts with the divine couple of the Egyptians, Osiris-Isis, and of the Greeks, Artemid-Artemis. Rod (masc. sing.) and Rožanicy (fem. plural) form a mythical pair composed of a *paredros* and a *paredra*: linguistically Rožanica is a derivation of Rod. Hence in the history of religion they can be classified with the well-known mythical group "young god-mother-goddess" (cf. Osiris-Isis and Attis-Kybele). Lack of documentary evidence, however, renders it impossible to determine whether the Slav god Rod was the son or the lover of the goddess. The *paredra* Rožanicy was presumably a sort of rudimentary mother-goddess who guaranteed the fertility of the clan and also reigned over the realm of the dead. In the texts she is always referred to in the plural, indicating that she was felt to be a plural being.

The cult of threefold and multifold numina was very widespread among the Slavs. The Russians venerated the Vily and the Beregyni who, according to the texts, were composed of 30 or 3×9 sisters. The divine appelation Trojan (= the threefold), which occurs in a few Old Russian texts, links up with this. Moreover the latter figure has been preserved in popular Serb belief as the three-headed nocturnal horseman. Hence there would seem to be a connexion between the threefold or multiple conception of deity and the polycephalous idols characteristic of the cult of the Baltic Slavs. A similar connexion has been established in the Celtic religion. The fundamental characteristic of the multiple numen is that it operates as a single being, though comprised of several. At Stettin the godhead Triglav (the three-headed) was depicted with three heads, as his name suggests. *Erat autem ibi simulacrum triceps, quod in uno corpore tria capita habens Triglaus vocabatur* (HERBORD, II, 32).

The image of Svantevit at Arkona had four heads, one facing towards each of the cardinal points of the compass. The idols at Garz possessed even more heads or faces. In the largest of the three temples stood the statue of Rugievit, whose head had seven faces converging under a single skull. Seven swords were suspended from his belt, an unsheated eighth sword was grasped in his right hand. In the second sanctuary the object of worship was Porevit, depicted with five heads but unarmed. The image of Porenutius in the third sanctuary had four faces, with a fifth on its bosom.

The purport of these polycephalous representations is difficult to fathom. The simplest interpretation is still that this was the means used by the heathens to express the omnipotence, the irresistible power of their gods (For that matter, the names given to their gods by the Baltic Slavs likewise indicates intensity. Sventovit derives from *svent* = holy, energetic; Jarovit from *jar* = exceptionally powerful; Rugievit from *ruj* = rut).

The *paredros* Rod was probably a young hero, thus explaining the frequent use of diminutives as divine names (Svarožič = little Svarog; Božič = little god). Whether the Slavonic Rod was a sacrifieced hero, like Osiris or Attis, cannot be said. Grounds for assuming he was may be found in the fact that the saints and patrons who were thrust upon the Slavs during the process of conversion to Christianity to replace the local pagan cult were usually martyrs. It seems highly symptomatic that the saint established repeatedly by the church as a patron in the newly converted West Slav countries was Vitus, who died a child-martyr at the age of twelve.

The Slav numina in no way had a functional character. Each deity tended rather to personify for his sphere of influence the principle of the numinous power. Every clan, tribe or town expected its tutelary numen to ensure prosperity, fertility, the blessing of children and the protection of the ancestors. Indeed, all these concepts are encompassed in the semantic scope of the generic name rod.

After the period of expansion the function-cycle of the numen augmented. Prominent families expected as a matter of course that their political and commercial actitives should be safeguarded. The salient feature of the tribal deities of the Baltic Slavs was their militant character. Being involved as they were in a ruthless struggle for their very existence, these tribes hoped for the support of their numina during their military campaigns. THIETMAR reports that the gods in the temple at Rethra wore terrifying helms and armour (VI, 23). HERBORD identifies Jarovit with Mars: *deo suo Gerovito, qui lingua Latina Mars dicitur* (III, 6).

An important function of the Slav numen was that of supreme legislator. In Oldenburg certain oaks were dedicated to Proven, the local godhead, and were enclosed within a wooden fence. Apart from the priest and the sacrifiers, no one was permitted to enter therein.

On the second day of each week the people assembled here with the priest and the prince to render justice (HELMOLD I, 84). The name of the numen also indicates its legislative function (Polish *prawny* = judicial, legal). Zuarasiz, the epithet of the main god of the Redarii points in the same direction. It is derived from the root *svar* = "to bind, unite" (Russian *svariti* = to join in marriage; *svarshtshik* = smith). In the glosses belonging to the Old Russian translation of Malalas' Chronicle, Svarog is equated to Hephaistos, the smith, and his function of legislator receives particular emphasis.

There are indications that the clan numen of the Slavs manifested a highly chthonic character. This is not surprising, since one of its main functions was, after all, the protection of the realm of the dead. Moreover it evolved directly from the manes cult and the worship of nature.

A remarkable Old Russian fragment teaches that the breath of life is instilled by God and that it is not Rod "who, sitting in the air casts mounds on the earth in which children are born." (MANSIKKA, p. 306). This remark appears to refer to a very widespread belief that stones and tumuli promote pregnancy. HELMOND relates that the Slavs upheld the strange custom of circulating a dish at their banquets and drinking-bouts to the accompaniment of solemn addresses to the good and the evil gods. They are said to have attributed all good fortune to a good god and all misfortune to an evil one, and so they called the latter Zcerneboch, the "black god." *Unde etiam malum deum lingua sua Diabol sive Zcerneboch, id est nigrum deum, appellant.* (I, 52).

This testimonial has given rise to numerous misconceptions. Many scholars have deduced from it that the Slavs paid homage to a sort of Iranian dualism, but no trace of this can be found in the sources. HELMOLD was presumably misled by the conception "black," which he confused with the Christian representation of the devil. The swarthy colour characteristic of so many figures in the history of religion seems more typical of the chthonic godhead. The absence of light is characteristic of the realm of the dead, the earth and the underworld. Hence the Slav term Czerneboch (Slav. *čern* = black, *bog* = god) refers not to an evil god but to the chthonic aspect of the clan numen. Various sources confirm that the Slavs pictured their gods as being black. According to the *Liber Miraculorum* of the Cistercian monk HERBERTUS, two travellers chanced upon a sacred wood in which stood an enormous image covered with tar (Text in Palm, p. 44). The three heads of Triglav were silver-plated (MONACHUS PRIEF. II, 12). A deity of Rügen called Tjarnaglofi had a silver moustache (*Knytlinga saga*, 122). The name itself means Black Head (Polish *czarny* = black, głowa = head).

To sum up it may be said that the Slavs conceived of their god as a higher being who allotted to each member of the clan his portion of good fortune and happiness, both regarding the begetting of children and the harvest, livestock and personal enterprises. The semantic parallelism of the two general terms for "deity" in the Slav language, Rod and Bog, fully illustrates this. Both words mean successively: (1) wealth, good fortune; (2) share in that good fortune, prosperity; (3) godhead who metes out wealth and good fortune.

IV. WORSHIP

Among the Russians the cult scarcely progressed beyond a primitive level. The people made sacrifices, mainly fruit, fowl and birds, to sources and rivers, the presumed abode of the numina. Everything indicates that when Vladimir had images erected on the hill beside his palace at Kiev this was an innovation. These idols were carved of wood, the head being ornamented with gold and silver. There is no mention of temples in the texts, though archeological excavations have revealed a few open sacrificial sites. There seems to have been no caste of priests, though often in the texts mention is made of sorcerers, who exercised great influence over the people.

The Baltic Slavs, on the contrary, had by the beginning of the eleventh century evolved a rich cult in emulation of Christendom. Their temples were built on sites difficult of access and were surrounded by fortifications. The sanctuary of the Redarii was located in a vast forest where no one was permitted to enter. A path led to a nearby swamp. At Wollin the temple stood on an island in a river which broadened out at that point. The famous stronghold of Arkona was built at the edge of a rocky promontory washed by the sea on three sides. A few metres from the temple was a source. We see, therefore, that the man-made temples developed out of the cult of nature and constituted a continuation of it. The temple of Arkona was a rectangular construction with wooden walls ornamented with polychromatic wood-carving. Inside curtains depended from four pillars formed an enclosed space which housed the statue of Svantevit. The idols were of wood, often decorated with metal or rich fabrics and provided with diverse attributes, such as armour, helmets, swords, goblets, etc. Some statues were of imposing dimensions; Svantevit was eight and

Rugievit at Garz was three metres high. In the temples was also stored
a large number of sacred objects, such as golden and silver goblets,
huge bulls' horns encrusted with precious stones, gold-plated weapons,
saddles and banners. In each sanctuary was stored a treasure which
was regularly replenished by a percentage of the spoils of war; one-
tenth to Triglav and one third to Svantevit. The latter also had at his
disposal a private following of 300 select horsemen, who donated
their entire booty to the temple.

Such a development of the cult enhanced the prestige and influence
of the priests. HELMOLD relates (I, 36) that the Rugians held their
priests in higher esteem than their king. They solemnly sacrificed to
the gods in the name of the faithful and on festive occasions. The sources stress the fact that human sacrifices were also made. The Redarii
even chopped off the head of a bishop in the temple of Rethra (ADAM,
III, 51).

The main occupation of the priests was, however, divination. Saxo
has left us a lively description of the great annual feast held in honour
of Svantevit at Arkona. After the harvest, the people of the island
gathered in front of the temple. Sacrificial animals were slaughtered,
and then the priest meticulously inspected how much wine was in the
horn held in the hand of Svantevit. This enabled him to foretell
whether next year's harvest would be a prosperous one. Thereafter
he poured the wine out at the foot of the statue as a libation. He refilled
the goblet and drank a toast to the godhead, while beseeching in
solemn words to grant himself good fortune, the people an increase
in prosperity and victory in war. Then he emptied the goblet in one
draught, refilled it with wine and put it back in the right hand of the
statue. A honey-cake the size of a man was then placed before the
priest, who asked the congregation whether he was still visible behind
the cake. If the people answered in the affirmative, he then uttered the
wish that next year the cake would conceal him completely. Then the
priest addressed the Rugians in the name of the godhead, urging them
to remain constant in their belief, in return for which Svantevit would
surely grant them victory on land and sea. To conclude there followed
a ritual meal at which the animals sacrified were eaten by those present,
and excessive eating and drinking was looked upon as a religious
obligation.

The principal medium used for divination was, however, the sacred
horse. Svantevit's horse was white, and no one was permitted to touch
it. Only the priest was allowed to let it graze or to ride on it. The horse

of Triglav at Stettin was black and of impressive stature. When the temple at Rethra was destroyed in 1068, it was Bishop Burchard of Halberstadt himself who mounted the sacred steed of Zuarasiz and triumphantly returned thus to Saxony (Annales Augustani). In three centres approximately the same method was used to divine the oracle of the god through the medium of the horse. At Arkona the priests arranged three rows of spears, grouped in pairs in each row with the spearheads pointing downwards. After uttering a solemn prayer, the priest took the horse by the bridle and led it over the spears. If the horse stepped over them with his right hoof, this was taken as a favourable omen and the projected plans were carried out. If not, no action was taken (SAXO, XIV, 547).

Among the Russians, too, diverse soothsayers and sorcerers had considerable influence over the people, who called them *volchvy*. Long after the conversion to Christianity they continued to play an important part in social and economic life. During times of war or famine they appeared in the villages, stirred the people to insurrection and caused the execution of people whom they held responsible for the catastrophic state of affairs. In certain instances they seemed to act as the defenders of the poor against the propertied groups. The *Nestor Chronicle* relates that in Novgorod in 1071 a sorcerer preached against Christianity and incited the people to assassinate their bishop. Only the prince supported the bishop, and in the end he secured the death of the sorcerer by trickery. In the ordinary matters of daily life the people called on the assistance of the sorcerers, mainly to heal sick children, but also on the occasions of birth, burials and business transactions. In Northern Russia the Finnish shamans were also consulted by the Slav peoples.

V. CONCEPTION OF MAN

Our information on the religious anthropology of the Slavs is scarce and must be inferred exclusively from the cult of the dead. The Slavs believed in life after death, even though in THIETMAR's opinion *cum morte temporali omnia putant finiri*. (I, 14). The German monk, however, held the Christian viewpoint based on the belief in the resurrection and eternal life. The Slav viewpoint, on the contrary, was that the life hereafter was a continuation of this world, possessing the same characteristics and needs. Hence the deceased were buried with great care, and diverse objects were interred along with them. The other world was in no way held to be a pleasant place. The belief was rather that the deceased reluctantly departed from his living kin and even desired to return to this world. The soul was conceived of as a physical shape, which is called "die Körperseele" by MANSIKKA, and "den lebenden Leichnam" by WIENECKE. The essential point is that a narrow bond continued to exist between the living and the dead, as expressed in the belief that the deceased influenced the fertility of the soil. The most salient proof of this was the widespread belief among the Russians, and also other Slavs, that those who died a violent death should not be buried for fear that in revenge they would prevent the revival of nature in the spring. That is why they were not buried until after Easter, when the new spring vegetation had already blossomed forth. Often the corpses of those who died under suspicious circumstances were dug up again, for the people blamed them for drought, spring frost or floods. Right up to the modern era, huge open pits were to be found in the vicinity of most Russian towns, and here were deposited the bodies of those who died by murder, drowning, suicide, etc. These instances demonstrate that essentially the deceased continued to be orientated towards life. Death meant the loss of life, which had to be regained as soon as possible. In our opinion, therefore, the Slavs believed in a cyclic movement of life through death towards renewed life, influenced by the cosmic alternation of the seasons. Just as vegetation blossoms, dies and blossoms once more in an eternal rhythm, the dead spent a certain period in another world and then returned to new life through the wombs of the women of the clan. As a result the Christian expectation of salvation was totally alien to the Slavs, and *vice versa* this cyclic-biological conception must have appeared to the missionaries an unacceptable philosophy of life based on matter. Homilies and polemic writings contain endless references to this antithesis: the pagans worshipped creation instead of the creator. In their ignorance they glorified matter instead of the invisible god. The clan numina constituted the motor of this cosmic rythm, and therefore the faithful took no single action before appeasing his numen and beseeching its approbation. From this fact we can infer that the Slavs entertained no notion of fate in the classical meaning of the word, i.e. of a power predetermining events unalterably from eternity. This explains why the Byzantine PROKOPIOS writes of the Slavs: *fatum minime norunt, nedum illi in mortales aliquam vim attribuant.*

VI. Short History of the Study of the Religion

A. *The period* 1920-1940

About 1920 Slav paganism attracted the renewed and now very profound interest of the Slavists. The most famous scholars of the time participated in that particular field of research (L. Niederle, A. Brückner, V. Jagić). Fundamental work was carried out then in more than one field. As many written sources as possible were collected, sorted out and critically analysed. The complete worthlessness of certain texts and the relative credibility of others were clearly shown. Scepticism was, perhaps, carried too far at times (Brückner, Mansikka), but on the whole this attitude produced salutary results. A number of romantic, traditional views unsupported by a single source were cast overboard. The infra-structure necessary for further scientific research was established by the compilation of a critical catalogue of reliable sources (Mansikka, meyer).

On the other hand there emerged, in spite of polemics and divergent opinions (Niederle, Brückner, Aničkov), a general picture of Slav paganism. Originally dominated by a primitive manism and animism, this religion was believed to have evolved gradually into a polytheistic system composed of deities with anthropomorphic features and more or less distinct functions. A dualism of Iranian origin, which was argued by a couple of "Einzelgänger" was repudiated.

In its final stage, this paganism was believed to have undergone a strong and mainly external development, especially among the Baltic Slavs, marked by an increase in the number of gods, the forming of a priest caste and the expansion of the cult.

Nevertheless a large number of problems remained unsolved, including:

(1) the nature of the evolution from the primitive to higher forms;

(2) the relationship between the Indo-European, the Common Slav and the local numina;

(3) the origin of the gods: evolved demons or derivations;

(4) the intensity of Iranian and Germanic influence.

B. *The period* 1940-1950.

In 1940 E. Wienecke published his comprehensive but contested study on the religion of the West Slavs. The German scholar's judgment proved to be very severe. On the grounds of a renewed and extremely critical analysis of the sources he admitted only the primitive forms. The Slav religion, in his opinion, had been nothing more than a polydemonism bound up with the cult of nature. Common Slav gods were rejected. The numina of the Baltic Slavs were merely local, inflated demons, whilst the temples were only used for hanging up such attributes as weapons, saddles, etc. The polycephalous images clearly evidenced in the texts were said to have existed only in the imagination of the chroniclers.

WIENECKE was hampered in his research by a serious apriorism. He proceeded from the postulation that the cultural level of the Slavs was very low and that even the few cultural forms evolved by them were derived from the Germans. Hence in spite of his merits and his thorough command of the works published on the problem, WIE-NECKE's views can hardly be considered a positive contribution to the knowledge of Slav paganism. It must be admitted, however, that many traditional opinions have been ruled out by WIENECKE's scepticism. He demonstrated that, for the time being at least, a separate treatment of the Baltic and the Russian data was a sounder scientific procedure than an attempt to reconstruct a supposed Common Slav system.

The critical and erudite study of B. O. UNBEGAUN published in 1948 is much more balanced. Though fully aware of WIENECKE's prejudices, UNBEGAUN accepted the critical attitude of the German scholar. His comments on the structure and evolution of the Slav religion are circumspect. Accepting the sources for what they are, namely testimonials of a religion in its final stage, he expressed his preference for a static and synchronic description of that final stage. Hence he did not endeavour to reconstruct a Common Slav pantheon; Russians and Baltic Slavs are subjected to separate treatment. He did not wish to postulate any relationship between the Russian numina. His opinion was, rightly, that the gods of the Baltic Slavs had no specialised functions and that there was not a single hierarchical relationship between them. He repudiated any Iranian influence.

C. *The period from 1950 to the present*

The cautious attitude of UNBEGAUN taught us to distinguish between the certain and the uncertain, but left us somewhat empty-handed. That is something inacceptable to every science: new paths must be tried. Since the fifties attention has been focussed on the problem of Iranian influence. R. JAKOBSON's study of 1950 marked the beginning of this new trend. With the aid of the comparative linguistic method he arrived at the conclusion that the Slav religious vocabulary is remarkably similar to the Iranian. According to him both peoples experienced a common semantic evolution, specifically under the cultural pressure of the Iranians. The establishment of this fact determined JAKOBSON's view of the Slav pantheon: in his view it was largely Common Slav and partly of Indo-European origin, and it manifests a considerable degree of affiliation to the Iranian pantheon. The weaker link in JAKOBSON's reasoning is that it is mainly based on linguistic arguments which are open to criticism, not always supported by the texts and therefore somewhat artificial. JAKOBSON's contribution directed studies in this field back to the concept of the Common Slav supreme god, usually placed in the sign of the sun-god. The basic argument of the majority of summaries published in the last fifteen years is the same: the interrelationship between the Slav and the Iranian mythology proves that the Slavs had one or more supreme gods, whom they inherited from the Indo-Europeans. The numina of the Baltic Slavs are then looked upon as local differentiations of the supreme gods.

In recent years the viewpoint which is gaining ground is that the political and social conditions of the former Slav society on the one hand and the main stages of the historical evolution on the other must be taken into consideration when interpreting its religion. Hence the conclusion is that this religion formed a heterogeneous body of divergent, indeed contradictory strata and elements. DITTRICH , for example, in a study published in 1961 endeavours to determine the stratification of the Slav religion by distinguishing four layers which permeated each other in the course of the historical evolution. The disadvantage of this method of approach is that a number of archeological, ethnological and prehistorical concepts are employed in research which are somewhat hypothetical and in no way borne out by the texts.

In conclusion the rather small share of Soviet Russian scholarship in research in this field must be noted. Naturally any objective interest in religious problems was reduced to a minimum in Russia after the revolution. As a result Soviet scholarship in the field of the history of religion for a long time lagged behind that of the West. In recent years a change has fortunately taken place in this state of affairs. A number of important studies on individual and general problems have been published (IVANOV and TOPOROV). A renewed interest of Russian scholars in Slav paganism may be expected in the future.

SELECTED BIBLIOGRAPHY

1. *Sources*

MANSIKKA, J., *Die Religion der Ostslaven*. I Quellen. Helsinki 1922
MEYER, C. M., *Fontes historiae religionis slavicae*. Berlin, 1931
BRÜCKNER, A., *Die Slaven*. In: A. BERTHOLET, *Religionsgeschichtliches Lesebuch*, 3, 2nd ed. Tübingen, 1926 (anthology of sources in a German translation)

2. *Works*

ANITSHKOV, E. V., *Jazytshestvo i drevnjaja Rus'*. St. Petersburg, 1914
——, *Poslednija raboty po slavjanskim religioznym drevnostjam*. In: *Slavia*, 2, 1923-24
BRÜCKNER, A., *Mitologia slava*. Bologne, 1923
——, *Mythologische Thesen*. In: *Archiv f. slav. Phil.* 40-1926
ČAJKANOVIC', V., *O srpskom vrhovnom bogu*. Belgrad, 1941
DITTRICH, Z. R., *Zur religiösen Ur- und Frühgeschichte der Slawen*. In: *Jahrbücher f. Geschichte Osteuropas*, N.F. 9, Wiesbaden, 1961
HAASE, F., *Volksglaube und Brauchtum der Ostslaven*. Breslau, 1939
IVANOV V. V. and V. N. TOPOROV, *Slavjanskije jazykovyje modelirujushtshije semiotit-shekije sistemy* Moscow, 1965
JAGIĆ, V., *Mythologische Skizzen, I*. In: *Archiv f. slav. Phil.* 4-1880
JAKOBSON, R., *Slavic Mythology*. In: *Standard dictionary of folklore, mythology and legend*, II, New York, 1950
KOSTRZEWSKI, G., *Les origines de la civilisation polonaise*, Paris, 1949
MOSZYŃSKI, K., *Kultura ludowa Słowian*, II *Kultura duchowa*, Cracow, 1934
NIEDERLE, I.., *Víra a náboženství*. In: *Zivot starých Slovanu*, VI, Prague, 1916
——, *Manuel de l'antiquité slave*, II, Paris, 1926
PALM, TH., *Wendische Kultstätten*, Lund, 1937
PASCAL, P., *La religion des Anciens Slaves*. In: M. BRILLANT et R. AIGRAIN: *Histoire des religions*, 5, Paris, 1958
PETTAZZONI, R., *The Slavs*. In: *The all-knowing God*. London 1956
REITER, N., *Mythologie der alten Slaven*. In: *Wörterbuch der Mythologie* I, 6, Stuttgart 1962
ROŽNIECKI, ST., *Perun und Thor*. In: *Arch. f. Slav. Phil.* 23-1901
SCHMAUS, A., *Zur altslavischen Religionsgeschichte*. In: *Saeculum*, 4, 1953
STENDER-PETERSEN, A., *Russian Paganism*. In: *Russian studies*, *Acta Jutlandica*, 28, 2, Copenhagen, 1956
UNBEGAUN, B. O., *La religion des Anciens Slaves*. In: *Mana*, 2, III, Paris, 1948
VYNCKE, F., *Méthode comparative et postulats méthodiques dans l'étude de la religion des Anciens Slaves*. In: *Communications présentées par les slavisants de Belgique au Ve Congrès internat. de Slavistique à Sofia*, Brussels, 1963
——, *La divination chez les Slaves*. In: *La divination*, Paris, 1968
WIENECKE, E., *Untersuchungen zur Religion der Westslaven*, Leipzig, 1940

ANCIENT MEXICAN RELIGION

BY

LAURETTE SÉJOURNÉ

Mexico City, Mexico

I. Essence

Since it treats a profound and complex vision of the world, religion is a spiritual phenomenon for which no simple definition suffices and which only a vigorous symbolic language is capable of translating. Unless they are prepared to condemn themselves to a sterile silence, investigators have to highlight certain aspects at the expense of others and to erect some kind of structure that will be true to its fundamental character. Considered in this perspective, we can define the essence of the prehistoric religion as the sum of the knowledge and practise that permit man to overcome his earthly condition in order to transform himself in a reality that, binding together two opposing terms, rescues them from the finite. In effect, the central core of this religion seems to have been a belief that the creative mobility incarnate in man can redeem the perishable *inertia* not only of matter, which by definition is gross and perishable, but of eternity itself, a spiritual eternity which, unless sustained by the human creature in the brief vital instant of his life, would be condemned to a paralyzing abstraction, to a purity too absolute to be viable. Let us try to place this singular belief in its context.

II. Historical Development

The civilization of the people who once occupied presentday Mexico and Central America is based upon the religious message which it expressed continually, from its beginnings in about the fifth century B.C. down to the European colonization in the sixteenth century A.D. The liturgy, though it remained faithful to the original myths, institutions and iconography, became at times politically orientated; most dangerously so when, fifty years before the Spaniards arrived, symbolic acts were converted into acts of intimidation. Torture and death were then publicly inflicted in the name of a spiritual freedom which the ruling class took good care not to enjoy. The human sacrifices show how strong this religious faith was, even after it had become a mockery. They did, however, contain the seeds of the final destruction of ancient Mexican culture, for the conquerors were able to capture this vast territory precisely by allying themselves with people who had been brutally subdued by the Aztecs.

III. The Idea of the Godhead

The essence of the godhead is its over-riding need to coalesce with matter and to depend upon the world of forms with which it longs to merge. In other words, though originally its essence was quite other and strange, it does nevertheless have to escape from its own solitude in order to fuse with a less pure reality. And it is this lesser reality that it painfully tries to create.

The sacrifice of its purity is described in the myth of the creation of the Four Suns, or Four Ages, each of which is wiped out in a war between two gods. At the moment when the Fourth Sun dies, the universe finds itself in an intensely dramatic situation. Earth and heaven have stopped in their tracks. As in previous cataclysms, the gods are helpless to restore cosmic order although they are dependent on it. "Who shall live now that heaven stands still and the Lord of Earth has stayed his steps?" (*Leyenda de los Soles*, p. 120).

The gods do all they can to give life to humanity. As it wrests from the Beyond that immortality which seems essential to its survival, the creature of the Fifth Age makes a pact with Death. Quetzalcoatl succeeds in reaching the Land of the Dead. Perilously he descends into the bowels of the earth and fights the sombre Lord of the Underworld. He almost loses hope of emerging victorious, but succeeds, in spite of his panic, in rescuing his father's bones which he sprinkles with his own blood.

From the resulting new human species arises the individual whose body, wrapped in flame, becomes the Sun of Movement, saving Nature from outer darkness. The first deliberate act of man transfigured is to demand that the gods be sacrificed. Suddenly motionless in the heavens, he tells the gods—terror-stricken by the threat of a fresh cataclysm—that he will not budge until they are all dead. "Thereupon the gods were massacred - ah - ah in Teotihuacan." (*Leyenda de los Soles*, p. 122). In other versions this heart of man, transformed in solar energy, asks the gods to sacrifice themselves so that he may continue with his redeeming motion.

The disappearance of the deity at the moment when, largely by his own efforts, he achieves his wish, can only mean that he is now united with his substance. His willing acceptance of his fate thus ceases to seem odd. He accepts death because he has completed his task. (Only after his death is this mentioned in the myth). The will of the Fifth Sun demands that his essence be merged into a higher reality.

In stressing the pain and the courage of this creative sacrifice, another version of the myth confirms the importance of the aspiration the godhead has which enables him to go beyond a state which, far from being ideal, appears merely as a step towards a higher realization.

The story tells of a high priest of a great kingdom who seems wrapped for all eternity in a state of pious non-attachment. But everything changes when messengers penetrate his innermost sanctuary and persuade him to go away. The trick they use is to give him a body:

> "He must leave his town and we must live there in his place." And they added: "Let us make *pulque* and give it him to drink so that he will become besotted and stop his penance." Then Tezcatlipoca spoke: "I say we should give him a body." How describe their deliberations to bring this about! First, Tezcatlipoca. He took a double mirror, a hand's breadth, and wrapped it up. And when he came to Quetzalcoatl he told the pages who guarded him, "Go and tell the priest: a youth has come to show you yourself and to give you a body..." Quetzalcoatl said, "Grandfather, let him come." They went and called Tezcatlipoca. He entered, greeted him, and said, "My son, priest Ce Acatl Quetzalcoatl, I greet you and come, Sire, to show you your body." Quetzalcoatl said, "Welcome, grandfather." To which the other replied, "My son, oh priest, I am your vassal. I come from the foothills of Nonohualtepec. Sire, behold your body." Then he handed him the mirror and said, "Look and know yourself, my son, for it is you in this glass." Then Quetzalcoatl saw himself. He was astonished and said, "If my vassals see me, they may run away." (*Annals of Cuauhtitlan*, p. 8).

Bemused with the earthly wine his temptors gave him, Quetzalcoatl experiences carnal desire. After a night of love with the beautiful Quetzalpetatl, he abandons his kingdom, weeping bitterly:

> "At dawn they were very sad, and his heart softened. "Alas for me!" Quetzalcoatl said. And he sang the sad song which he composed in farewell. "I rue the day I left my home. Let those who are far away be made gentle. I took it for a hard and dangerous way. Only he who has an earthly body should be, should sing. I have not grown by affliction and servile labour..." Then they went to Tlillan Tlapallan, the burner...

When he had attired himself he set himself alight and burned himself. It is said that when he burned... they saw his heart rise up. According to their reports he rose to heaven and entered there. The elders say that he became the star that appears at dawn; and they say it appeared when Quetzalcoatl died, and so they call him Lord of Dawn. (*Annals of Cuauhtitlan*, p. 10).

So precise a text cannot be misinterpreted. When he saw a face of flesh, until then unknown to him, Quetzalcoatl was afraid. Spirit and matter had met. It was the moment of transition to a state of intolerable ambiguity. The surprising thing about the way this old theme is dealt with is that, far from implying a fall and degration, the meeting point becomes the very condition needed for the salvation of the spirit. Instead of being paralyzed by the anguish of plunging into multiplicity, Quetzalcoatl acts at once to regain, not his immutable lost unity, but a unity which he must acquire by closing the gap that separates him from the newly-discovered object, and thus by joining with it. Spirit, in other words, far from considering the body as an absolute obstacle, makes of it the very instrument or redemption, a redemption which is also, and strangely, necessary to the divine essence.

IV. THE CULT

The dialectical unity between earth and heaven which the concept of divinity entails is also inherent in the cult. For when the gods are invoked in man's ritual their integrity is dangerously compromised.

The chronicles say that the central object of these rituals was an effigy which received the prayers and offerings; but that instead of being idolized like those of other religions, this one was invariably destroyed. The effigies were made afresh before each ceremony and were of wood, resin, paper or edible flour according to the occasion. They were then either burned or dismembered, the pieces being always distributed among those present. On certain solemn occasions a piece from the image could not be eaten unless the recipient had first spent a year in retreat in a temple.

Although the perishable substances no longer exist, we know from archaeological evidence what the attitude to the god was; for in certain milenary places he is represented only in fresco paintings on the walls of dwellings, and there is not a trace in them of any other kind of image. At the end of each 52-year cycle these dwellings were torn down, and the fragments of wall that held the divine image were used as a banquette for building another room above. The interlocking of these various architectural levels —usually four of them and full of shape and colour—is undoubtedly one of the most remarkable characteristics of the Mexican archaeological seene.

Like the sixteenth-century descriptions, these dwellings dating from the beginning of our era evoke the myth of the first meeting between spirit and matter, which thus becomes the very hub of precolumbian religion. It was a religion so deep-rooted that when it became transformed into a political ideology and interpreted the spiritual dogmas literally, it was able to impose a reign of terror.

1) Fire

Fire was the basic element in the cultural activities, for smoke from burned objects was the most usual offering. Ethnological and archaeological evidence (the latter including countless remains of braziers and incense burners) show that such events as family meals, weddings, funerals, births, coronations or liturgical spectacles were consecrated by a bonfire upon which were heaped the most diverse objects: food, incense, effigies, paper stained with auto-sacrificial blood and so on.

2) Prayer

Prayers, which were a moral supplication, were made by the priests, the wise men, or any person who by age, office, or social rank, held a position of authority in the group. Their words show an extraordinarily high ethic, and their beauty reminds us that the ancient Mexicans regarded discourse as an art.

3) Sacrifice

For initiation into orders of knighthood known as the Eagles and Tigers, which earried enormous prestige, it was necessary to go into long spiritual retirement, and during this time the chief sacrifice was an offering of drops of one's own blood. Again we must repeat that the human sacrifices which Europeans associate with this religion were practised only during the fifty years before the arrival of the Spaniards, and were the result of wars caused by the urgent need to find "living space" due to a demographic explosion which is mentioned in the writings of this time.

4) Sacraments

Communication between the individual and supernatural forces took place through religious acts performed by specialists. These were genuinely sacramental in nature.

Baptism consisted in the sprinkling of water and in a prayer to the appropriate deity (Chalchiuhtlicue). These rites, performed by the god-mother, were intended to eliminate all impurity from the new-born child.

The *eucharist*, in other words the assimilation of a food that has become imbued with the divine essence, was frequently performed. We have already seen how in most liturgical rituals the body of the god was shared among those present. The meaning of this practise is perfectly clear from the acts of purification which took place before-hand, and the ceremonial distribution which the Aztecs made of the spoils of the victims, who were supposed to be incarnations of gods.

Confession was private between the priest and the penitent. It was an inherent part of each man's life, and for every adult it was a moment of great importance. Even in the social sphere forgiveness of sins was respected.

Priesthood. The priest was the only official link between earth and heaven. The priesthood was therefore a sacred order governed by severe demands, especially those of chastity, humility and non-attachment.

Marriage. This was legalized by rites supervised by a godmother and witnessed by fire. The union of man and woman was symbolized by knotting together the robes of the partners to show that it could not be dissolved.

5) *Sacred persons*

The wise man was socially superior to all others. In the texts he is described as the spiritual guide:

> "...a light, a torch, a great torch that does not smoke... Possessor of truth, he never ceases to admonish. He makes the faces of others wise, he causes other men to acquire a face, he causes them to give it shape. He opens ears, illumines..." (BERNARDINO DE SAHAGUN).

6) *Mythology*

The basis of all knowledge was contained in the myths, which were thus the real body of doctrine that ruled over the moral and collective destiny. As with cultural expression generally, the liturgy made full use of this source. The religious festivals that occupied such a large part of the life of the city were simply an illustration of the primordial mysteries contained in the myths.

V. The Concept of Man

1) *His creation*

Man is the result of the god's desire to fuse with matter in order to create a phenomenon that can bring *Movement* into the world. When, after four abortive attempts this wish is realized, the material of man's body is distinguished from the rest of Nature by its ability to assimilate a heavenly substance. (The deity is "the giver of the rain of fire" which allows man to germinate and which is dispensed by *Tlaloc*).

It should be noted that the myths refer to creation only as it concerns humanity, since the ages that are destroyed are distinguished among themselves only by the fate of their inhabitants. Humanity is completely wiped out in the Age *Four Tiger*, but reappears, and is again defeated. At the end of the Age *Four Wind* men are changed into monkeys. In the Age *Four Rain of Fire* a new lot of men are destroyed by a fire that turns them into birds. During the flood that ends the Age *Four Water*, men become fish.

Since each successive regeneration is caused by two gods who cannot rest until the world is lighted by a star sprung from a mortal bosom, we can only suppose that it is precisely such a star the gods are so tirelessly seeking. The nature of their search is underlined by their own confession that they cannot establish the cosmic order without man's help. In fact from among all the creatures raised from the dead by Quetzalcoatl, the gods select one who shall save the universe from the ever-present threat of annihilation: "...they called Nanahuatl and said, "Now you shall keep watch over heaven and earth." " (*Leyenda de los Soles*, p. 121).

Surprisingly, Nanahuatl rejected the privilege. He became very sad, and exclaimed, "What are the gods saying? I am sick and wretched." (*Leyenda de los Soles*, p. 121).

But the gods knew what they were doing. After a long and painful initiation the deformed and pustule-ridden Nanahuatl became the Fifth Sun, most brilliant of the stars. (His rotting flesh seems to have played a positive role, for the myth sets him opposite a handsome and healthy person who nevertheless fails when the other succeeds).

"The name of the Fifth Sun is Naollin (Four-Movement). It belongs to us who are alive today. This is its sign, here, for the Sun fell into the

fire, into the divine furnace of Teotihuacan. That very Sun of Topiltzin
of Tollan, of Quetzalcoatl." (*Idem*, p. 122).

Since victory consists in introducing the universe in the Age
of Movement, the various stages must tell the history of matter's
slow emergence from its original inertia, must tell its salvation from
the nothing by the spirit which finally inhabits it.

2) *His nature*

This bundle of contradictory stuff which is man is fundamental to
precolumbian thought. Every opportunity is taken to emphasize the
various phases of its miraculous appearance in the world. The symbolism is determined not only by the hieroglyphs but even by the
forms, from urban planning and architecture down to the style of
dress. Both it and the mythology show that, far from being the work
of only one protagonist, man's creation is seen as a union of converging desires, as an answer given by the spirit to a call from the object,
from the one to the multiple. It is significant that in SAHAGUN's account the priest from out of his retirement addresses the messenger
with the mirror: "Your arrival is timely, old man, for I have awaited
you these many days..." (*Vol.* I, p. 298). Besides, the drama of matter
is embodied in the plumed serpent who is pounced on by the celestial
bird. There are indications that it is not the spirit alone which is
affected by this event, since the behavior of "the bearer of an earthly
body" is distinguished both by its thirst for knowledge and the in-
tuition that there exists an unforseen reality behind. For if it is true
that the holy priest at first takes no notice of the flesh, so also is the
reptile incapable of knowing what it will discover as a result of its
efforts. Each is moved toward its object by blind desire.

3) *Fate*

The human is conceived of as an effort, a perpetual activity aimed
at transmitting a freedom-giving movement to the whole of nature.
It is a hard task, and if we study the goddesses we shall see what
dangers were necessary, and what suffering was inherent in the enterprise. In the myth of the birth of Huitzilopochtli, for example, the
anguish Matter suffers by her own choice, by her adherence to a
principle which leads her to overstep her boundaries, acquires over-
tones of pathos:

> "...there is a hill named Coatepec (hill of the serpent) close to the town
> of Tulla, where a woman lived who was called Coatlicue, who was the

mother of certain Indians called Centzonhitznahua, who had a sister called Coyolxauhqui. And this Coatlicue did penance each day, sweeping the hill of Coatepec. It happened that once as she was sweeping there descended upon her a little feather ball like a cocoon of thread, and she took it and placed it in her bosom close to her belly and beneath her petticoats. And after she had swept she looked for it and could not find it, for which reason they say she became pregnant. And when the said Centzonhitznahua saw that their mother was pregnant, they waxed wroth and asked, "Who made her pregnant? Who has wronged us and shamed us?" And the aforesaid sister... told them, "Brothers, let us kill our mother for she has shamed us, having secretly become pregnant. And when the said Coatlicue got to hear of this, it weighed heavily upon her and she grew afraid, and her child spoke to her and comforted her, saying "Fear not, for I know what I must do." And when she heard these words the said Coatlicue set her heart at rest and threw off her burdens. And when the aforesaid Centzonhitznahua Indians had made and completed their plans to kill their mother because of the shame and dishonour she had done them... they took weapons and armed themselves for the fight... and one of them called Quauitlicac, who was as a traitor because of what the Indians told him... went to tell Huitzilopochtli who was still in his mother's womb, and told him of it, and he answered and said, "Oh, my uncle, watch what they do, and listen well to what they say, for I know what I must do." (SAHAGUN, *Vol.* I, pp. 286-287).

Then the uncle gave precise information about the plans of the god's enemies, until

"...he answered that they had already arrived upon the hill. Then Huitzilipochtli turned to ask Quauitlicac, "Where are they?" And he replied that they were already close and that Coyolxauhqui was their leader. As the aforesaid Centzonhuitznahua Indians arrived, Huitzilopochtli was born, with a shield... and a spear... He ordered one called Tochancalqui to set light to a snake-coil of torches... and with that Coyolxauhqui was wounded and died dismembered, and his head remained on that hill of Coatepec." (SAHAGUN, *Vol.* I, p. 488).

The brothers were relentlessly pursued and cast out from the hill. Many of them perished. These events, ritually enacted during feasts in honour of Huitzilopochtli, may symbolize the *Movement* which the god engenders in man; while the sister, who represents Nature, lies dismembered forever on the serpent hill (the serpent is the sign of earth).

This tale seems to describe the stages inherent in the difficult human situation, and they constitute as it were the second act of the drama: after the lament of the priest-king in the first act, we witness the desperate struggle of spirit shrouded in earth. For in spite of having passed definitely to the action, its fate depends entirely upon the mother-goddess. If, deaf to the voice within her, she capitulates, the spirit will die imprisoned. Then the risk that weighs on this parcel of rebellious nature that is man is that he may fall into the blind fragmentation, the danger of losing the opportunity of integrating himself with creative time, crumbling into immobility like Huitzilopochtli's beheaded sister.

The death to which the goddess will be victim, in spite of an apparently happy ending (in reality, mother and daughter are inextricably confused in the variants of the myth) marks the stepping beyond one stage. The unity which death brings to the two extremes is symbolically represented by Xochipilli, a creature with a red, flayed body who is associated with flowers, birds and butterflies (three aspects of the souls of the dead) which is the sign of spirit that has finally shaken free from its restrictive sheath. Now Huitzilopochtli is, like Xochipilli, a feather-clad sun-god who is also associated with flowers and butterflies. (During the ceremonies in his honour one whole day is set aside for gathering flowers; and the butterly is the hieroglyph of sun and of flame). Thus these two are really one single image of the awakened essence but on different levels: one represents the escape from the enclosing body, and reminds us of the courage, struggles and dangers that made its birth possible; the other represents its liberation from all materiality and its entry into the world as vibrating, ineffable, spiritual energy.

The hieroglyph representing the dynamic meeting of the above and the below shows two entwined triangles with circles at the points where the apex of one meets the base of the other. I have found from a study of the sculpture and architecture that this meeting takes place in a cavity previously made in the material. This cavity is indirectly suggested in the myth, for the penitent's body is the receptacle for heavenly material. In the architectural treatment it is expressed by an open space at the entrance of each complex. In the language of the sculptural forms the balance of masses make a perfect receptacle for the space (there are even hollow statues whose inner walls are encrusted with wonderful images of gods). We may take it, therefore, that this space wrested from dense matter is an epitome of the existential task.

4) *Eschatology*

Certain indications suggest that the aim of the life of the individual differed in no way from that of the group, since all creatures must take part in the common task. We have seen how, through the intermediary of Xochipilli and through the god who springs armed from his mother's womb, the individual is transmuted into energy. It is not, however, a return to an abstract spirituality, since its utility on earth is immediate. Among other things which support this statement, is the fact the generic name for the great urban centres was Tollan, literally "place of reeds," and the reed, drawn as an arrow, is the sign of Quetzalcoatl transformed into the planet. (It is well to remember that the name of the American prophet is a combination of two words: quetzal, or bird; and coatl, or serpent). Thus the city (a nation of those unnatural beings who are the plumed serpents) was seen as a sheaf of lights projected by men whose hearts, like those of the archetype king, were freed by the flames. Thus, far from serving a merely individual aim, illumination was the basis for collective striving. It is perhaps for this reason that the pieces in the archaeological zones connected with the Doctrine of *Movement* have been found in such quantity (more than a million in one of the buildings we explored) and that Quetzalcoatl's disciples go down in history as *The Great Artificers*.

It should also be mentioned that the place where Nanahuatl is said to have been sacrificed and to have been converted into the Fifth Sun is not a natural but a man-made one, a city so large that only modern industrial complexes can equal it. This fabulous cultural complex bore the double title of Teotihuacan ("where one becomes god") and Tollan. The first of these names is associated with the creation of the Age of Movement, the second with social activity since it figures on some geographical maps. If we add that the event took place on top of a pyramid whose base measures 250 metres, we are convinced of the fact that precolumbian thought is simply expressing the belief that man is responsible for the cosmic order, and that to maintain it he must constantly elaborate his inner light which he manifests in the form of works that beautify and glorify his City.

VI. History of the Study of Prehistoric Religion

The distortions suffered by the religion of this continent makes a study of it not only slow but often painful for it is not always easy to combat the misunderstandings—some of them diliberate—that obscure it.

Nevertheless, thanks to the spell it exercised in spite of the prohibitions surrounding it since the conquest, documents regarding its nature are plentiful. Among these, the most comprehensive and complete is the monumental work of the heroic friar, BERNARDINO DE SAHAGUN, who compiled it with the help of Indian initiates. This tremendous work was redone several times during his long life due to the reprisals which has manuscripts suffered successively because of his impartial judgement towards the conquered people. If it were not for this work, ancient Mexican thought would lack the indispensable basis for its ressurection.

Once this bright point of reference has been established, the other writings ranging from those of the conquerors themselves to the historial resume of JUAN DE TORQUEMADA in the early seventeenth century are useful additions reinforcing and filling out many religious and historical aspects of the subject. There are also dozens of painted books dating either from preconquest or colonial times, the latter based on older models. Some of these codices were deciphered by indigenous scholars, and the glosses they made to the pictures are of incalculable value. They provide us with translations of signs and divine representations which would otherwise be closed to us, and they allow us to throw a bridge between the descriptions of the chronicles on the one hand, and the iconography of the archaeological material on the other. Finally we have the profusion of monuments, frescoes, sculptures and poetry that fill the subsoil like a geological strata.

Valuable as these sources of knowledge may be however, none of them is sufficient by itself. Only by comparative study of them all can we make any coherent sense of the religion that was uprooted four centuries ago.

SELECTED BIBLIOGRAPHY

Fray Bernardino DE SAHAGUN, *Historia de las Cosas de Nueva España*, Editorial Nueva Espana, S.A. México, 1946
——, *Florentine Codex*
——, *General History of the Things of New Spain*, Translated by Charles E. DIBBLE and Arthur J. O. ANDERSON. *The school of american research and the University of Utah*, in thirteen parts. 1963
Fray Diego DURÁN, *Historia de las Indias de Nueva España*, Editora Nacional, México, 1951
DE ALVA IXTLIXOCHITL, Fernando, *Obras históricas*, México, 1891

——, *Anales de Cuauhtitlan* y *Leyenda de los Soles*, Imprenta Universitaria, México 1945

Fray Juan DE TORQUEMADA, *Monarquía Indiana*, Salvador Chavez Hayhoe, México 1943

SELER, Eduard, *Codex Borgia*, Berlin 1904

VAILLANT, Georges C., *Aztecs of Mexico*, Doubleday and Co., New York, 1941

SOUSTELLE, Jacques, *La pensée cosmologique des anciens mexicains*, Hermann, Paris, 1940

CASO, Alfonso, *El pueblo del Sol*, Fondo de Cultura Económica, México, 1953

WESTHEIM, Paul, *Arte antiguo de México*, Fondo de Cultura Económica, México, 1950

LÉON-PORTILLA, Miguel, *La filosofía nahuatl*, Universidad de México, 1959

MORLEY, Sylvanus G., *The ancient maya*, Stanford University Press, 1946

J. Eric S. THOMPSON, *Maya hieroglyphic writing*, Carnegie Institution of Washington, 1950

SÉJOURNÉ, Laurette, *Burning Water*, Thames and Hudson, London, 1957

——, *El universo de Quetzalcoatl*, Fondo de Cultura Economica, México 1963

——, *El lenguage de las formas en Teotihuacan*, México, 1966

——, *Arquitectura y pintura en Teotihuacan*, Siglo XXI Editores, S.A. México 1966

THE RELIGION OF ANCIENT PERU

BY

ANTJE KELM

Berlin, Germany

Peru in the pre-Columbian era until the late Inca period included not only the coastal and mountain regions of the present state of the same name, but also parts of the Ecuadorean Andes, and in the south it stretched across the highlands of Bolivia up to North Chile and Northwest Argentina.

In the course of its more than two thousand year-old history, several so-called pan-Peruvian civilizations, having a far-reaching spiritual sphere of influence, established themselves besides local cultural landmarks within this territory. This may explain, for instance, the presence of a fundamental religious structure, which not only helped the Incas in establishing their state religion but which, we may say, provided the basis for their religion. The belief contained in the Inca religion which can be best deduced from reports by authors of the colonial period, as well as the divergent characteristics of the contemporary Andean religion, may be described as follows:

I. Short Description of the Essence of the Ancient Peruvian Religion

In order to understand the real characteristics of the ancient Peruvian religion, it is necessary to imagine both the geographical surroundings and the means of existence of the people. Not only in the coastal desert, but also in large parts of the Andes regions, considerable efforts were required on the part of the people to change dry lands into agricultural soil and to keep it as such. By constructing ditch and canal systems, fertile river oases of the coast were created. An important part was also played by artificial irrigation and even in the numerous mountain valleys, the bottoms of which were often narrow, people were obliged to terrace the steep slopes in order to obtain sufficient land area for Indian corn (maize) and potatofields. The endeavour to obtain fertile soil and sufficient water, the nursing of the seedlings and the harvesting occupied the people of the pre-Columbian era for over two thousand years and it is in this light that their spiritual world, as well as the real content of their religion, can be best comprehended.

Like numerous other agricultural peoples of the world, the Peruvians closely connected the conception of the cycle of vegetable life with the course of human existence—birth, procreation and death. The idea of the necessary relationship between dying and resurrection as an expression of the anxiety for fertility, is one of the fundamental motives interlacing the myths and the religious practices of the ancient Peruvian; it determines the world creating-activities of the gods as well as the world-conserving acts of man.

One fundamental characteristic of the ancient Peruvian religion must also be seen in the light of the people's conviction of the omnipresence and omnipotence of divine activities. The idea contained in the middle Andean religion that there is a creator god who controls the destiny of the world from a distance recedes in favour of the belief in multiple divine beings who by their actions have directly influenced human life. The Peruvians also attributed supernatural virtues to the deceased who were allotted a kind of intermediary role between men and God. The attitude of the living towards the dead was certainly different in the various civilizations and among the various tribes, but more or less abundant grave gifts and death watches may be considered as typical signs of the ancient Peruvian religion. Embalming, however, was not always practised. An important role in the imaginary world of the people was played by the vast number of spirits which could be present invisibly in any part of the physical world. To ensure the spirits' goodwill or to use the active force which was granted to them for themselves the Peruvians made offerings at certain places in the country and kept and wore amulets.

In this connection the concept *huaca* should be mentioned, which for the ancient Peruvians meant the numinous in itself and which was reserved for all objects of religious worship from the gods down to the stone amulets. In addition *huaca* were all articles which were in some way or another connected with the supernatural, whether they be localities which had become specially well-known by myth, or temples built by man, or even peculiarities in the real physical world, such as the birth of twins or deformed beings, which by their deviation from the usual evoked reverential awe and even terror.

II. Historical Development

Any description of the conditions in ancient Peru must take into consideration the fact that, on the one hand, different civilizations existed simultaneously within this area, and on the other, that a series of cultures followed one another. An attempt shall now be made to explain in brief the fundamental traits of the most important cultures which may have been decisive for the development of religious ideas during the Inca era.

During the Chavín culture (between 1000 and 500 B.C.), the first period of higher civilization of ancient Peru known to us, the worship of a feline deity was dominant. Reliefs, pillars and sculptures from the site of Chavín de Huántar mainly depict reproductions of a feline deity, in connection with which snakes and condors were often portrayed. Decorations depicting a feline being are also present on numerous ceramics found at archaeologic sites of the northern and central coast, which belong to the same period. It is therefore supposed that the cult of a feline deity is one of the first religious movements inherent in various tribes. On ceramics of the older phase of the Paracas culture, the Paracas Cavernas, feline patterns suggestive of Chavín influence have occasionally been found. In the same way as the dead of this period who were buried in large circular chambers in multiple burial mounds, the dead of the younger phase of this culture, Paracas Necropolis, were also buried in a sitting position. They were, however, also mummified. The great importance which the dead, or in other words, the afterworld, possessed at that time, can perhaps be read from the unique, decorated mantles with colourful embroideries in which the mummies were wrapped and which were evidently not used by the living.

The central divine beings of the Mochica culture (around 500 A.D.) are, in addition to a highest creature, astral divinities, especially the sun and the moon as a divine married couple whose connection is closely linked with the fertility of the soil. In addition to this, Mochica ceramic designs portray an immense number of demons and grotesque anthropomorphic creatures as well as evidence of the authority of the priests.—On the south coast, the classical period reached its climax in the Nazca culture (around 500 A.D.). Whereas in Mochica art numerous profane scenes are depicted in addition to the religious themes, the polychromatic ceramics of the Nazca people show a predominant emphasis on the supernatural. The different types of demon figures depicted on the ceramic designs disclose a rich mythical world view. From the many illustrations of demons with characteristic trophy heads as well as other reproductions of heads the skull cult would appear to have been of some importance.—For the topic we are considering here, the Tiahuanaco culture (during the first thousand years after Christ) is of predominant importance because, on its most famous monument, the Gate of the Sun (situated south of Lake Titicaca at Kalasasaya, a place of worship), is the oldest known portrait of a deity, which, according to our present-day knowledge, represents the old Andean creator god Viracocha. Here, too, the puma and the condor appear besides Viracocha, yet their representations differ widely from those of the Chavín style. Contrary to all the cultures described so far, our knowledge of the religion of the Chimú (around 1200 A.D.) is based, in addition to archaeological finds, on a few written sources, amongst which the chronicle of Calancha (4) is the most important. As is the case with the Mochica, the Chimú's religion was centred on the divine couple, sun and moon, who granted fertility. The moon-goddess, however, ranked before the sun-god in this culture. Further aspects of this coastal religion which continued to exist side by side with that of the Incas will be referred to later.

III. Conception of God

Since the acception of a supreme being which was called Viracocha by the highland population and Pachacamac or Cons by the coastal tribes, the numerous deities of the ancient Peruvians were primarily imagined in human shapes and with human characteristics. They could, it is true, alter their outward shape as they were generally seen in close connection with certain natural phenomena such as planets, the elements or prominent geographical features. Occasionally they also appeared as animals. The deities could either be male or female and were related either according to different degrees of kinship or, as was also the case, according to different degrees of hostility. A genuine polytheistic pantheon with individual departmental deities only became known in the late Inca era, mainly following the recognition of the numerous deities of conquered tribes. The same process of acculturation had, however, already led to the fusion of various deities before the influence of the Incas begun to spread. This explains the often ambiguous characters of several gods. Multiple gods, i.e. deities which appeared in three or fivefold forms, appeared quite often.

Whereas the world was created by the uncreated supreme being, the role of culture hero was bestowed upon numerous of the other deities who, often regarded as the sons or successors of the creator himself, perfected the creation through their activities on earth. Some of them were considered as creators of the members of a tribe and were worshipped by them as their "Fathers" or "Mothers". The supreme being, as for instance the Andean Viracocha or Cons of the coastal tribes, combined within himself the characteristics of an uncreated creator of the universe together with those of a culture hero wandering on earth, who would, at times, mix with the people, sometimes even disguised as a beggar. In the state religion of the Incas, a special cult was dedicated to Viracocha; the best known temples consecrated to him were in Cuzco and Cacha.

Also Pachacamac, the supreme being of a tribe living on the central coast, was worshipped in the place of pilgrimage named after him. Originally, this god was called Irma, the name Pachacamac (i.e. world creator) being first bestowed on him by the Incas when they had conquered this coastal strip in the second half of the 15th century.

The real tribal god of the Incas was Inti, the sun, thought of as male, who was considered the mythical ancestor of the dynasty. He was married to the moon goddess Mama Quilla, and the ruling couple on the Inca throne was at the time worshipped as the earthly representatives of the divine couple.

In the pantheon, originally presided over by Inti and later on by Viracocha, the most important figures were, besides those already mentioned, thunder, the weather-god, called Illapa, and Pachamama, the earth-goddess. Although certainly not of Inca origin, the latter two were widely worshipped as they, together with the divine couple Inti and Mama Quilla, played the most important part in the religious belief of a people concerned chiefly with agriculture.

IV. Worship

1. *Cult*

The most frequent occasions at which to perform cultic activities of different kinds were the festivals which took place regularly in the course of human life, namely, in the agricultural year. Of special importance among the festivals held in the Inca state during the course of a year were, besides the two solstices, the sowing and the harvest and the annual reapportionment of the fields. In Cuzco, the Inca capital, all the ceremonies were performed elaborately on the central square *aucay pata*, the present day Plaza de Armas. Here not only a great number of people assembled, but also images of the gods united in the pantheon were brought from the temple of Coricancha and carried along together with the mummies of dead Emperors.

Among the different acts of worship, mention should first be made of the so-called *magic practices*. They could either be performed by an individual or by the cult community. In order to develop the fertility of the fields powerful amulets were buried, chicha was sprinkled and coca was dispersed over the fields. Imminent disaster which could be recognized, for instance, by the occurrence of an eclipse the Peruvians tried to stave off by making a noise. Also little heaps of stones, the so-called *apachita*, were piled up on mountain peaks in order to avoid bad luck. Everybody passing a peak had to add a stone to the already existing pile. Restricted in their action in the Inca empire, but generally widespread in the whole Peruvian culture area from olden times up to the present day were the practitioners of white and black magic who could bring good or bad luck by a variety of charms, using, e.g., the principles of sympathetic and contagious magic.

The custom of *praying* to a deity both individually or in the cult community is a tradition dating back long before the Inca culture. Of special importance were supplications. The assistance of a deity was entreated before accomplishing difficult works or in the case of personal and general disaster such as illness, epidemics or droughts. The people often addressed their prayers to their creator, and no festival passed without a prayer to the founder of the ceremony. The standard gesture of praying consisted in bowing low from the hips having the arms stretched out in front with the hands open and the palms uppermost. Then a kissing noise with the lips was made while the hands were brought to the mouth and the fingertips kissed, a gesture called *muchay*.

Of all the ceremonies practised at the different occasions the *offering* occupied a cardinal place. Although usually performed by a priest at the request of an individual or the cult community, a sacrifice could also be offered personally by an individual as an expiatory or thank offering. In special cases the priests determined the most acceptable sacrifice by divination. But generally the most valuable and most common offering was the llama. In Cuzco, a daily sacrifice was made to the Sungod, using one of these animals some of which were specially reserved for religious purposes. Inti preferred white llamas, while brown ones were sacrificed to Viracocha and particolored llamas to Illapa. Besides the llamas, guinea pigs, chicha and coca were frequently offered to the deities, and the numerous other offerings included llama fat and maize-cake, eyebrow-hairs or eyelashes, but also fine clothing and precious metals or figurines made of these metals. Whereas the llamas were killed by cutting their throats or tearing out their hearts, clothing and coca were burnt and other articles buried.

In ancient Peru, human beings were only sacrificed on special occasions. In the case of pestilence or famine, for instance, or at the coronation of a new emperor, the Incas offered children of about 10 to 15 years of age to the most important divinities. For the ritual of human sacrifice some colonial authors (3,143; 13,229) have handed down the name of "Capac Hucha" or "Capaccocha" (= mortal sin). The sacrifice was killed either by tearing out its heart or by strangulation followed by cutting of its throat, or it was buried alive in holy places.

A practice frequently performed in pre-Columbian Peru (as well as in later times) was *divination* as a means of penetrating things usually concealed to man. The priests sought to ascertain not only the future, but very often the opinion or mood of a deity through the oracle. One favourite method of divination was the inspection of intestines.

When speaking of the ritual practices of the Peruvians mention should also be made of the *night watches* which were held at burials or memorial ceremonies during one or more nights.

2. *Ethics*

One particular characteristic of the ancient Peruvian religion is its morality. It is clearly shown in the work of Francisco de Avila [2] that the complicated legal norms of the Inca empire were deeply rooted in the people's religious consciousness of sin. Thus, for instance, Avila describes both murder and adultery—two of the principal crimes of the Inca empire—as prohibitions decreed by the deity, infringement of which could have bad consequences not only for the culprit but also for the whole family or even the community. In order to prevent such harm, the sinner had to subject himself to certain expiatory measures which were inflicted on him through divine order. Confession, usually before a priest, was a prerequisite for this, and was followed by cultic purification. Sometimes, the purification was limited to ritual washings, but often the penitents were given a penance consisting of fasting, self-castigation, prayers, offerings or exclusion from certain religious ceremonies.

3. *Myth*

To the notes of numerous writers of the colonial period we owe our knowledge of the myths not only of the Incas, but also of quite a few coastal as well as mountain tribes only slightly influenced by the Incas. Among the creation myths the Viracocha Myth (3,82; 15, 110) is of pan-Peruvian importance. The characterization of this deity as the uncreated creator of the universe given to him in this myth can be considered the result of speculations of the Inca priests. For in nearly all pre-incan creation-myths there is, in fact, no mention of the creation of the universe. Only one myth of a coastal tribe mentions the creation of the universe by Cons (6, 493) whereas the majority of the Peruvian tribes were well acquainted with the idea of a world existing from the beginning, but left in darkness, in which time commenced with the creation of light and of man. One central theme of the Viracocha Myth is the incomplete creation of man which is followed by a second real one. Like the mythologem of the incomplete creation, the emergence of man from caves, lakes and hills described in this tradition is a motif not only of pan-Peruvian importance but also known to other Indian peoples. The first Inca, for instance, whose origin belongs to the mythical past, is said to have come into the world, together with his brothers and sisters, from a cave in order to found, in the course of his hero-journey, the Inca empire and its capital Cuzco. In common with the traditions of the highland tribes the creation myth of a coastal people, handed down by CALANCHA (4, 412 f) also has the mythologem of a first human race turned to stone by the deity. In addition, this tradition contains the motif of the emergence of man from three eggs sent by the deity, a golden, a silver, and a copper one, as well as the mythologem of the birth of useful plants from the dismembered and buried limbs of a prehistoric deity.

Corresponding to the various creation myths is a series of different traditions referring to the end of the world. Besides descriptions, according to which the world will come to an end through eclipses or earthquakes, the flood theme is widespread and, among others, forms the subject of two attractive myths (2, 81; 12, 156).

Besides the so-called "true stories," the mythology of the Peruvians comprises numerous myth-like tales among which the most important are the animal tales. The most popular figure, without any doubt, is the fox who is often partnered with the condor. There are also numerous ethiological myths or motifs which explain the occurrence of peculiarities in the environment caused by events which had happened in the mythical past. To mention only a few examples, strangely shaped rocks or single stone blocks are considered beings of the mythical past turned to stone in the course of a certain event, and the tail of the Andean fox is black because, as the Huarochirí believe, he left it hanging into the water during the flood (2, 81).

V. Conception of Man

As is clear from what has already been said, the ancient Peruvian religion lacks a uniform conception of the *creation* of man. The tradition of man's emergence from the *paqarinas*, the places of origin, namely certain places in the environment such as caves or mountain peaks, lakes, springs, or tree-trunks, is widespread. There were also traditions reminiscent of totemistic ideas according to which single groups are descended from certain animals or constellations. The already mentioned belief in the origin of man in eggs would appear to be less widespread. The most frequent belief was the one of the creation of man through a deity. The Peruvians were acquainted with the conception of the modelling of man out of mud or stone as well as the one of his creation through a mere word or even thought. The Viracocha creation myth (3,82)—a relatively young product of Inca priests' reasoning—combines the two most common conceptions whereby Viracocha modelled men out of mud and, then, allowed them to emerge from the *paqarinas* to the light of this world.

The different traditions of the creation of man run parallel with those about his *life after death*. To the same earthbound world view containing the *paqarina* belief belongs the conception of a country of the dead located in the interior of the earth (*upamarca*, 1, 70) in which all men after death indiscriminately continue an existence similar to the earthly one. Of more recent—probably Incan—origin, on the other hand, seems to be the belief in two different realms of the dead, in an upper one to be found in heaven (*hanan pacha*) in which the virtuous enjoyed a joyous existence, and in another situated in the interior of the earth (*ukhu pacha*) for the vicious who had to work hard there enduring hunger and thirst and all imaginable tortures (12, 61). Originally this division, which corresponded to the Inca world (*kai pacha*), was most certainly related to the classes of the Inca empire (17, 145). Later on the emperors of Cuzco may have introduced the ethical interpretation as a means of gaining stricter control over the people.

Both these conceptions of the next world are based on the idea of the living corpse (Lebender Leichnam). Occasionally the spirits of the dead who had to follow a special path leading to the next world could wander the earth for a certain period of time and return invisibly to their relatives who thoughtfully placed food and clothing at their disposal. On the other hand, however, in ancient Peru genuine conceptions of the soul existed. According to one tradition of the Huarochirí (2, 127), the soul which was thought to be in the form of a fly left the body of man on his death to return to its creator. Here appears the idea of the divine soul, yet this belief apparently could not become popular in the religion of the Inca empire which bore the imprint of collectivism.

VI. Subsequent Influences of the Ancient Peruvian Religion

Although the present population living in the area belonging to the ancient Peruvian civilization is officially Roman catholic, quite a few of the pre-Columbian religious forms have survived in the belief held especially by the common people. To mention only a few examples, the Ketschua not only believe in God, Jesus Christ, and the Holy Virgin Mary, but also in Inti, or in the Weather-God, as well as in a number of smaller local deities. The annual Christian festivals still present an opportunity for performing—often in secret—the ancient fertility rites, certain sacrificial or divination ceremonies, for instance. The old ideas are especially alive in the field of magic. Practitioners of white and black magic have a strong influence on the common people, performing not only sacrificial or divination ceremonies but, in addition to various forms of "charms," also healing the sick or determining which power is hidden in an amulet which they have been requested to examine.

VII. SHORT HISTORY OF THE STUDY OF THE ANCIENT
PERUVIAN RELIGION

If we ignore the fact that numerous monographs on ancient Peru offer a more or less extensive description of the religious conceptions and practices we see that this religion has only been properly studied by a few scholars. An invaluable means of reconstructing the pre-Columbian religious world is found in the records of early eyewitnesses. The Jesuit P. JOSE DE ARRIAGA [1] as well as the archbishop of Lima PEDRO DE VILLAGOMES [18] were predominantly concerned with noting down the "idolatries" of the Indians. An especially valuable source of knowledge particularly of non-Inca religious beliefs and practices is the frequently quoted work of FRANCISCO DE AVILA [2] whereas chroniclers such as C. DE MOLINA (de Cuzco) [12] and POLO DE ONDEGARDO [14] mainly refer to the Inca empire.

In our century, REBECCA CARRIÓN [5] and JULIO C. TELLO [16] in Peru and RICARDO E. LATCHAM [10] in Chile were especially concerned with intensive studies of the ancient Peruvian religion. Among the Europeans devoted to the investigation of ancient America we owe valuable studies of the religious world of the Peruvians to RAFAEL KARSTEN [7] and ROBERT LEHMANN-NITSCHE [11]. On the basis of Mochica-ceramics GERDT KUTSCHER [9] was able to reveal the world of ideas of the Chimú, a people living on the northern coast of Peru. The special merit of HERMANN TRIMBORN, to whom we also owe a summary of the religion of ancient Peru [17], is that by his translation from Ketschua into German the work of FRANCISCO DE AVILA has become available to a wide circle of readers. The author of this article has also written a scientific-religious commentary on AVILA's work [8].

SELECTED BIBLIOGRAPHY

[1] ARRIAGA, Pablo Joseph de, *La Extirpación de la Idolatría en el Perú y de los medios para la conversión de ellos. Colección de Libros y Doc. ref. a la Hist. del Perú*, Serie II, Tomo I, Lima 1920

[2] AVILA, Francisco de, *Dämonen und Zauber im Inkareich*. Aus dem Khetschua übersetzt und eingeleitet von Hermann Trimborn. *Quellen und Forschungen zur Geschichte der Geographie und Völkerkunde*, Bd. 4, Leipzig 1939

[3] BETANZOS, Juan de, *Suma y Narración de los Incas. Col. de Lib. y Doc. ref. a la Hist. del Perú*, Serie II, Tomo VIII, S. 73-208, Lima 1924

[4] CALANCHA, Fray Antonio de la, *Coronica Moralizada del Orden de San Agvstin en el Perv, con svcesos egemplares vistos en esta Monarqvia*, Barcelona 1639

[5] CARRIÓN CACHOT DE GIRARD, Rebecca, *La Religión en el Antiguo Perú* (Norte y Centro de la Costa, Período post-clásico), Lima 1959

[6] GUTIERREZ DE SANTA CLARA, Pedro, *Historia de las Guerras Civiles del Perú* (1544-1548) *y de otros sucesos de las Indias*, Tomo III. *Col. de Lib. y Doc. ref. a la Hist. de América*, Tomo IV, Madrid 1905

[7] KARSTEN, Rafael, *Die altperuanische Religion*. In: *Archiv f. Religionswissenschaft*, Bd. 25, Leipzig-Berlin 1927

[8] KELM, Antje, *Mythen und Kulte in Huarochirí*. In: Francisco de Avila, von Hermann Trimborn u. Antje Kelm, Berlin 1967

[9] KUTSCHER, Gerdt, *Chimú, eine altindianische Hochkultur*, Berlin 1950

[10] LATCHAM, Ricardo E., *Las Creencias Religiosas de los Antiguos Peruanos*. In: *Anales de la Universidad de Chile*, 2a Serie, Año VII-VIII, Santiago de Chile 1929-1930

[11] LEHMANN-NITSCHE, Robert, *Coricancha, el Templo del Sol en el Cuzco, y las imágenes de su altar mayor*. In: *Revista del Museo de la Plata*, Tomo 31, La Plata 1928

[12] MOLINA, Cristóbal de ("El Cuzqueño"): *Fabulos y Ritos de los Incas (Año de 1574). Los Pequeños Grandes Libros de Historia Americana*, Serie I, Tomo IV, Lima 1943

[13] PACHACUTI YAMQUI, Juan de Santacruz, *Relación de antigüedades deste reyno del Pirú*. In: *Tres relaciones peruanas*, ed. por M. Jiménez de la Espada (Madrid 1879), Asunción del Paraguay 1950

[14] POLO DE ONDEGARDO, Juan, *Informaciones acerca de la Religión y Gobierno de los Incas* (1571). *Col. de Lib. y Doc. ref. a la Hist. del Perú*, Serie I, Tomo III, Lima 1916

[15] SARMIENTO DE GAMBOA, Pedro de, *Historia de los Incas*. III. edición, Buenos Aires 1942

[16] TELLO, Julio C., *Wira Kocha*. In: *Inca*, Tomo I, Lima 1923

[17] TRIMBORN, Hermann, *Die Religionen der Völkerschaften des südlichen Mittelamerika und des nördlichen und mittleren Andenraumes*. In: *Die Religionen des Alten Amerika (Rel. d. Menschheit Bd. 7)*, Stuttgart 1961

[18] VILLAGOMES, D. Pedro de, *Exortaciones e Instrucción acerca de las Idolatrias de los Indios del Arzobispado de Lima. Col. de Lib. y Doc. ref. a la Hist. del Perú*, Serie I, Tomo XII, Lima 1919